MW00366293

WAR OR PEACE

WAR OR PEACE

The Struggle for World Power

Deepak Lal

OXFORD
UNIVERSITY PRESS

Oxford University Press is a department of the University of Oxford. It furthers the University's objective of excellence in research, scholarship, and education by publishing worldwide. Oxford is a registered trademark of Oxford University Press in the UK and in certain other countries.

Published in India by
Oxford University Press
2/11 Ground Floor, Ansari Road, Daryaganj, New Delhi 110 002, India

First Edition published in 2018

ISBN-13 (print edition): 978-0-19-948212-2
ISBN-10 (print edition): 0-19-948212-8

ISBN-13 (eBook): 978-0-19-909531-5
ISBN-10 (eBook): 0-19-909531-0

Typeset in Bembo Std 11/14.8
by Tranistics Data Technologies, Kolkata 700091
Printed in India by Rakmo Press, New Delhi 110 020

For my grandchildren Ruby, Albert, and Alexander
Hoping they will live in the Long Peace that I have enjoyed

Turning and turning in the widening gyre
The falcon cannot hear the falconer;
Things fall apart; the centre cannot hold;
Mere anarchy is loosed upon the world,
The blood-dimmed tide is loosed, and everywhere
The ceremony of innocence is drowned;
The best lack all conviction, while the worst
Are full of passionate intensity.

from 'The Second Coming' by William Butler Yeats

Contents

Preface

I began this book in 2011 after attending a conference at Fudan University (as described in the Introduction). I was appalled to hear that China wanted to challenge and replace the Pax Americana by its own pax. It saw the US as a declining economic power because of the 2008 global financial crisis and the Great Recession that followed. Its spectacular growth in the past three decades and its successful weathering of these crises led many in China to argue that the country had discovered an alternative and more successful economic model (the so-called Beijing Consensus) to replace the classical liberal economic model (called the Washington Consensus) being promoted by the West. My book was going to challenge this Chinese hubris and to show that it would be foolish to abandon the 'trading state' strategy it had followed to take advantage of the liberal international economic order (LIEO) that the American pax had established. Having argued in my previous foray into foreign policy *In Praise of Empires*[1] that the global order provided by the US Imperium was essential for the LIEO, and that no one had benefitted as a free rider as much as China from this system, it was insane for China to attempt to replace the US hegemon. Given this limited theme, this was to be a short book.

But as I began writing and as international events unfolded over the following years, it became increasingly clear that President Obama was bent on dismantling the US Imperium. This partly reflected the souring mood of the US electorate over the perceived failures of US armed interventions in Iraq and Afghanistan, but also—what became increasingly apparent—Obama's eschewal of using US military might in any international crisis that challenged US hegemony. Having thus disarmed US foreign policy, the US pax began to unravel as various wannabe imperial powers besides China, such as Russia and Iran, began to flex their muscles, with India another aspirant caught in the middle.

The world swiftly moved, particularly in the second Obama administration, from the global order commended in *In Praise of Empires*, to a world of disorder. This was foolishly described as a multipolar rather than an anarchical world. This meant that I needed to expand my horizons from what had seemed a quizzical and hubristic search for hegemony by China to what had become, with the US's implicit retirement from its role as the sole superpower (described by some as resigning as the globo-cop), a new struggle for global dominance. This would be reminiscent of post-Renaissance Europe where, in the anarchical system of nation states that prevailed for nearly three centuries, war among the various states for the mastery of Europe became endemic. That is until Britain, with its victory in the Napoleonic wars and geoeconomic ascendancy as the pioneer of the Industrial Revolution, used its naval supremacy to establish the Pax Britannica.

This has meant that I had to expand my narrow theme of Chinese hubris to geopolitics and geoeconomics to see if another Third World War was likely—and if so, how it could be avoided with an America only willing at best to lead from behind. Though I still believe that even if such a war erupts it is unlikely to breach the nuclear taboo based on the continuing power of the deterrence of MAD (mutually assured destruction), it would, as the continuing proxy wars in West Asia demonstrate, lead to great human misery. Thence the title of this book.

In the first part, on geopolitics, I briefly survey the role of empires in maintaining global order; the role of geography in determining the various strategic options of various powers as well as their culture and domestic politics; and the ideologies—democratic liberalism, nationalism, and religious fundamentalism—that form the 'habits of the heart' of the various powers contending for global supremacy. These provide the emotional grammar of the ideas and beliefs that fuel the hopes and fears of the various contestants for world power.

But as the American diffidence in maintaining its role as superpower is in part based on a perception of declining economic strength and its associated military ascendancy, it also became vital to assess if this perception was justified. The Great Recession and the responses to it are judged by many as the cause of this perception, as well as the belief that the flaws of free market-based capitalism were responsible for the crisis. This makes it important to assess the causes of, and responses to, the Great Recession. Is it necessary to instead adopt the authoritarian state-led capitalism of China and Russia to maintain economic prosperity? These issues are discussed in the second part of the book on geoeconomics.

In this struggle for world power, the liberal democracies are increasingly being faced by a league of dictators. So its outcome is as vital for the cause of liberty—so important for human flourishing—as was the Cold War and that against the Fascist dictators in the 1930s. In this struggle, the ongoing battle for ascendancy between the two largest and growing emerging economies—China and India—is of great importance. In this battle which currently seems to be between the Chinese hare and the Indian tortoise, many see an inevitable victory for China. This will first make China the Asian hegemon, and then having successfully challenged the US, it will rule the world as the book by Martin Jacques[2], the former editor of the now defunct periodical *Marxism Today*, has proclaimed. But I remember similar prognostications about Japan in the 1980s after its equally stunning postwar economic ascent, with a whole shelf of books proclaiming Japan as No.1.[3] This was followed by two decades of Japanese economic underperformance. So I take a cool look at the relative economic prospects of these giant Asian rivals too in the part on geoeconomics.

In the next part of the book I discuss the likelihood of a Third World War. This looks at the continuing economic and military strength of the American Imperium. It outlines how the many missteps by the last two US administrations have led to global disorder. The resulting flashpoints for war are discussed and how a renewal of the American will to maintain its imperial role is essential if the challengers to its pax in Asia, Europe, and the Middle East are to be contained. Only this will extend the long peace the world has seen since the end of the Second World War. It also discusses how India, which is in the vortex of many of these flashpoints, can cope with the global disorder it finds itself in.

At the end of *In Praise of Empires*, I had written 'perhaps, if the United States is unwilling to shoulder the imperial burden of maintaining the global pax, we will have to wait for one or other of the emerging imperial states—China and India—to do so in the future'. This book argues, considering both geopolitics and geoeconomics, that there is a case for hope that it will be India rather than China that will prevail.[4] If, as in the last century, the declining imperial power, the UK, joined the US in passing on the baton of a liberal international order to see off various authoritarian challengers, will the US—with other liberal democracies—join India in seeing that, when and if US power declines (because it is unable or unwilling to maintain its pax), the imperial baton goes to India and not China? That is the central question which animates this book.

As this book is meant for the general reader, much of the scholarly underpinnings have been banished to an extensive set of notes. For the busy reader willing to take my arguments on trust, the final chapter provides my conclusions on the likelihood of a Third World War and how it might be prevented.

Notes

1. D. Lal, *In Praise of Empires* (New York: Palgrave Macmillan, 2004).
2. M. Jacques, *When China Rules the World: The End of the Western World and the Birth of a New Global Order* (London: Penguin, 2009).
3. E. Vogel, *Japan as No. 1* (New York: Charles E. Tuttle, 1987). See also Shintaro Ishihara and Frank Baldwin, *The Japan That Can Say*

No: Why Japan Will Be First Among Equals (New York: Simon and Schuster, 1991).

4. In a Munk Debate on China, Fareed Zakaria made an important point about the role of the different political systems in the two Asian giants likely to determine their future. He said, 'When I compare India and China I think to myself, China has solved all the small problems. They've built the best roads and the best highways and the best high-speed rail, and they have done this so magnificently that it puts India to shame. But India has solved one big problem, which is what it will look like twenty-five years from now politically. It will be the same crazy, chaotic democracy it is today. What will China be twenty-five years from now politically? Will there be a mandarin elite? The Communist Party of China is the most elite political organization in the world today. Everybody looks like David [Li], they all have Ph.Ds and they are engineers, but that's not China. The People they rule are not reflected in the political system. Their views, to a large extent, are filtered through many mechanisms. That strikes me as a huge political challenge for China going forward.' In Niall Ferguson, David Li, Henry Kissinger, and Fareed Zakaria, Does the *21st Century Belong to China?*, The Munk Debate on China (Toronto: Anansi Press, 2011), p. 41.

Acknowledgements

I am extremely grateful for comments by Macgregor Knox of the London School of Economics, David Henderson, my long-time friend and former colleague at University College London, as well as two anonymous readers on behalf of Oxford University Press who have helped to improve the book. Some of the ideas in *War or Peace* were tested on audiences and participants in seminars organized by Intelligence Squared in London and the Hindustan Times in New Delhi. A paper based on the draft of the book was also presented and discussed at a meeting of the Mont Pelerin Society in the Galapagos. I am also grateful to Rajesh Chakravarty for appointing me a Distinguished Fellow at the Bharti Institute for Public Policy of the Indian School of Business, Mohali, when he was its Director. This allowed me to avail of the excellent research assistance provided by Sesha Sairam Meka and Abhishek Das, for which I am most grateful.

Acknowledgements

Introduction

The best way to introduce this book is to relate my travels over the last decade. These have led me to reassess the hopes expressed after the collapse of the Soviet Empire that an all-powerful USA would be able and willing to maintain a global pax, which would ensure global peace and prosperity. Instead, today we see global disorder, whose causes and consequences this book tries to explain.

In September 2008, I was in Shanghai after a meeting of the Mont Pelerin Society (MPS)[1] in Tokyo, where I had been appointed its president. From Shanghai, my old friend and MPS member Steven Cheung took us on a day trip to Suzhou where we saw the fantastic industrial park that the Chinese had built as part of their ascent to becoming the manufacturing hub of the world. I had witnessed—and to some minor extent provided some intellectual input into—this unprecedented economic rise on my frequent visits to China to lecture (mainly at Peking and Fudan universities) and to interact with Chinese policymakers.

My first visit to the country was in 1985 to participate in a conference organized by the Chinese Academy of Social Sciences (CASS).[2] On this first visit, China was still visually very much a Communist state. Beijing's vast boulevards were filled with thousands of bicycles and the odd black limousine carrying some party apparatchiks on their way. Mao suits were ubiquitous, and the famous dilatory and insolent service provided in the country's state-run hotels and shops was the norm. Despite the Stalinist boulevards breaching Beijing's famous ancient city wall[3] and the few grandiose brutalist official buildings, the city still retained many of its beautiful traditional characteristics—not least in the maze of hutongs (narrow alleys lined with residences) that surrounded the Forbidden City.[4]

CASS itself presented an anomaly to a visitor from a US research university. The economists at CASS were either very old and distinguished, many having recently returned from the pig farms they had been sent to during the Cultural Revolution, or very young, having recently graduated from prestigious universities. The intermediate generation was missing, having been denied any worthwhile higher education as they became the Red Guards spearheading Mao's Cultural Revolution.

Shanghai was a rundown and shabby city, with some of its past elegance visible in villas in the French Quarter and in the buildings along the Bund. Pudong was merely a vast area of swampy paddy fields and vegetable patches.

Within a quarter of a century, I saw all this change. With China's economy growing at over 9 per cent p.a. over the period, both Beijing and Shanghai had been visually transformed. Beijing had expanded with three ring roads; most of the hutongs had been replaced by luxury apartment blocks; its streets were clogged with cars rather than bicycles; the ubiquitous Mao suits had been replaced by the latest Western fashions; the dismal state shops had been replaced by gigantic shopping malls with all the iconic symbols of Western consumerism; and ladies' beauty parlours were on every street. The centre of the city now boasted a host of new buildings and stadia designed by a slew of international architects, as Beijing marked its entry into the modern world at the 2008 summer Olympics with the staging of the most expensive, extravagant, and magnificent opening and closing ceremonies, emphasizing its glorious past. These ceremonies also marked China's announcement of its return towards the Great Power status it had held for millennia, before the seaborne Western empires—beginning with the UK's Opium Wars—sliced up the Chinese melon, thereby demonstrating how far the Middle Kingdom had fallen behind a resurgent West, both materially and militarily.

In Shanghai, the small elegant house where the Communist Party had been founded, which when I first visited it in the 1980s had been surrounded by drab socialist apartment blocks, was now at the edge of a gigantic mall. There the young and rich beneficiaries of Deng Xiaoping's 1978 Open Door policy partied and shopped, mocking the Maoist revolutionaries looking down from their Marxist heaven at what had become of their Marxist dreams. The Bund looked almost the same as it had before the Revolution. On an earlier visit, at the famous art deco bar of the Peace Hotel, I had met a young Chinese businessman from Hong Kong who said he was there to buy back the building on the Bund that his family business had owned before they fled as Mao's Red army marched into Shanghai. In fact, looking at a picture of the Bund from the 1930s, most of the buildings with their original neon signs seemed to have returned, including the insurer AIG—which began its life in Shanghai and was to become infamous during the Great Crash of 2008. Looking across the waters of the Huangpu River, Pudong's rice fields had been transformed into a gigantic, futuristic business and financial centre.

Meanwhile, the authorities had created a new Western-trained mandarin class. In the 1980s, China had sent its best and brightest to the top US and UK universities. On their return, they staffed its many new and old think tanks (like CASS), its universities, and its government institutions. Its scientific and technological institutes were now second only to the US in the number (though not necessarily quality) of scientific publications.

So, on the trip to Suzhou, I was not surprised by the industrial park with its impeccable infrastructure and comfortable workers' housing, which were all part of the Chinese economic miracle. But the trip was memorable for another reason. Steve Cheung, with worldwide financial interests, was constantly on his mobile. Halfway to Suzhou, he got a call from someone in New York that Lehman Brothers had gone bankrupt. I did not know then, but the global financial crisis (GFC) had begun. This provides one bookend for the story in this book.

The Great Crash that followed the Lehman bankruptcy reverberated through the global financial system accompanied by a recession in the West that threatened to turn into another Great Depression. Though this was avoided, largely through expansionary US monetary policy, the West has still not fully recovered from the aftermath of the Great Crash. China, by contrast, met the threat of deflation with a massive fiscal stimulus and (along with India) saw only a small fall in its growth rates. But, more recently, the adverse consequences of these fiscal expansions have led to a lowering of China's and India's growth rates.

In early 2009, with the West facing an economic apocalypse, many observers began talking of the end of the globalizing capitalism that had led to unimaginable global prosperity and the largest reduction in structural poverty in human history[5] as China and India joined the US-led liberal international economic order (LIEO).

As president of the MPS, I organized a special meeting to counter these claims. In my address and in subsequent lectures and articles, I emphasized that the GFC was a Hayekian recession with Fisherian consequences. Far from being caused by market failure, it was due to government failure. Chapter 5, which examines the period of the Great Recession and after, is based on these lectures. It explains why the fixation on Keynes'-Hayek's protagonist in the 1930s debates during the Great Depression—fiscal remedies—have not provided the purported quick escape from the Great Recession. The chapter also explains how the rise of universal banks—combining commercial and investment banking—in the 1980s and 1990s led to the crisis and how they might be fixed.

This discussion of policy errors is relevant to another consequence of the GFC and the seeming resilience of the Chinese economy. There is a growing chorus questioning the so-called 'Washington Consensus' in favour of a 'Beijing Consensus' in economic policy, where the former underlies the liberal market capitalism promoted by the US-led LIEO and the latter by the purported dirigiste state-led authoritarian capitalism of China and Russia. These alternative claims for the desirable future economic policy were examined in an article based on a lecture at Fudan University in May 2011,[6] and are partly discussed in Part II of the book, which is focused on geoeconomics. As the future bellicosity of China in global affairs is likely to depend in part on its economic prospects, I examine the basis of its purported economic miracle and likely future prospects in greater detail in that section and also contrast this with those of its Asian competitor, India.

I only became aware of the most important consequence of the GFC when I took part in the Shanghai Forum at Fudan University in May 2011. There was a sense of euphoria about China's economic ascendance and how by 2015 it would overtake the US to become the largest economy in the world. More disturbing were the statements by many Chinese international relations and military experts that, now, the time had come to challenge the US's superpower role with the ongoing military expansion and modernization of the People's Liberation Army (PLA). Many wanted the Chinese armed forces to acquire the means to challenge the US in the Pacific, with the long-term aim of pushing it back to the 'third island chain' of Guam and even Hawaii.

This aim took me aback, as it questioned some important assumptions I had always made about China's rise. I had been much impressed by the argument in my UCLA colleague Richard Rosecrance's book *The Rise of the Trading State.*[7] He argued that the rising costs of war in the twentieth century had made it easier for states to choose the positive-sum game of trade and economic development as the major means of improving their position in world politics, rather than the zero-sum game of using military means to expand their territory. Germany and Japan, as the rising powers in the late nineteenth century, had chosen the traditional military route to challenge the declining British Empire with disastrous consequences for their populace after the two world wars that they provoked. After the Second World War, both had instead adopted the route of the trading state to achieve global prominence.[8] Moreover, Germany had thereby through its economic domination of the European Union (EU) secured its mastery of Europe, which had eluded it since its nineteenth-century rise.

But the old pattern of zero-sum games for territory is alive and well. This is evident from Russia's invasion of eastern Ukraine and annexation of Crimea, despite signing the Budapest Memorandum guaranteeing Ukraine's territorial integrity, and with China claiming the whole of the South China Sea and establishing fortified artificial islands, despite the International Court of Justice rejecting its claims. The threat this poses for a Third World War will be discussed in Part III.

Germany

I first visited Berlin in the late 1960s. West Berlin was a vibrant modern city. By contrast East Berlin across the Wall (which I could visit as I was then travelling on an Indian passport) was a grim, poor city dominated by Stalinist rows of apartments. The next time I visited Berlin was a week after the fall of the Wall to attend a conference sponsored by Deutsche Bank. Sitting on the top floor one could see East Berlin to the left and West Berlin to the right. Listening to a paper presented by an Italian economist, an acolyte of the Marxist Cambridge economist Piero Sraffa, I heard him say that East Germany's economic performance was comparable to the West, and it was only undergoing some minor difficulties. I interjected that all he had to do to see how wrong he was to look through the windows to the left and the right.

On subsequent visits to the united Berlin, now the capital of a united Germany, I once stayed in a hotel overlooking Frederick the Great's parade ground in the East and saw how the old architectural symbols of Prussian and German power that were destroyed in the East were being rebuilt. With the rebuilding of Hitler's Chancery, one could sense how someone sitting there could feel the power of a German Reich. For as the title of A.J.P. Taylor's magisterial book *The Struggle for Mastery in Europe* (1955) suggests, the Germans for the last two hundred years have sought to create a German-led Holy Roman Empire.

The route through two cataclysmic world wars proved a dead end. Since then the German political elites have been creating an indirect 'virtual' European empire through a gradual 'conquest' of the EU. But this is in partnership with the American pax through NATO. Its future will be discussed in Part I.

Japan

Meanwhile, Japan, whose imperial ambitions in Asia also turned to dust after the atomic bombs fell on Hiroshima and Nagasaki, has till recently continued its pacifist trading state strategy under the US nuclear and strategic umbrella. I have been following Japan on numerous visits since I was first posted there by the Indian Foreign Service to learn Japanese at Waseda University in 1965. Japan was in the midst of its remarkable economic resurgence after its post-war devastation. On subsequent visits, I saw this transformation based on 'catch up' growth, much as the Chinese have done by following a variant of the Japanese model. But the inevitable slowing down of this growth and deflation in the 1990s destroyed the hubris it generated.

Yet, with the recent political ascendancy of Shinzo Abe, who is committed to ending deflation and restoring Japan as a military power to contain a revanchist China's threat to the sea lanes through which pass the natural resources on which its economy depends, Japan seems to be returning to its past. This reminds me of a conversation I had with a Japanese diplomatic colleague in 1965 when the Maoist hordes were rampaging across China. On being asked whether he was not worried about this disorder spreading from China, he smiled and replied that the Japanese had always known how to deal with China. This continuance of Japanese traditional attitudes despite appearances of postmodernity was brought home when, on our last visit to Tokyo in 2008, my wife and I were sitting in the outdoor street café of the Hotel New Otani. We saw three Japanese punks with spiky, coloured hair following an old lady. When she stopped to cross the road at a traffic light, we feared that they might rob her and push her in front of an oncoming bus as was likely in the punk haunts of Camden Town in London. Instead, they pressed the stop button and gently walked her across the road.

Russia

Tsarist Russia—the third emerging Great Power in the late nineteenth century after its temporary implosion during the revolution that led to its replacement by the Soviet Union—was on the victorious side of the Second World War. But it chose the military–territorial route to promote its Communist imperium and challenge the new Western imperial power—the US. However, the failure of its economic dirigisme led to its sudden and unexpected demise in 1991.

I have been visiting Russia periodically since Yeltsin's Prime Minister Yegor Gaidar invited me to attend a seminar at the think tank he had set up on leaving the government. At a later seminar organized by the Cato Institute in 2004, Andrei Illaronov—who was Putin's then economic advisor—took us around the Kremlin. The museum had been refurbished with many costumes and carriages from Russia's imperial past. These showed how physically small these czars and czarinas were, including Catherine the Great. I wondered if Putin, who at that time wanted to emulate Peter the Great, found this personally comforting! The speakers at the conference had been asked to wait for an audience with Putin at about 4:00 p.m. As my wife and I had tickets to the Bolshoi for that evening, at 7:00 p.m., I decided to forsake the meeting with Putin and went to the opera instead. From those who did go to meet Putin, I discovered that Putin just sat silently, asking all the others to speak. But he did not make any statements himself. During this period of his second presidency, it seemed that Putin was attempting to create a liberal market economy.

Moscow had been transformed from the sad, impoverished city—with beggars lining the street and sleeping on the air ducts in hotel entrances—that I first visited in the mid-1990s into a thriving modern metropolis. There was a new spring—rising incomes, new buildings, and an élan among a growing and youthful middle class that only rising aspirations accompanied by prosperity can bring. This was symbolized by the massive new shopping arcades in Red Square filled with well-known brands. Outside the gates of these arcades, ladies laden with shopping bags waited in their furs for chauffeur-driven Mercedes and BMWs to pick them up.

My actual (not abortive) meeting with a Russian president was in 2010 with Dmitry Medvedev, when Yevgeny Yasin, the rector of the Higher School of Economics, arranged for the speakers at a conference on culture and development he had organized to meet Medvedev in his dacha.[9] Like Putin, Medvedev was also physically small, and he said all the right things, which gave liberals hope that he would adopt reforms, to wean Russia away from the bane of natural resources and allow a full-fledged market economy—utilizing the country's highly educated workers—to create a high-tech industrial economy. But I had my doubts, as the corruption associated with deploying the rents from natural resources were feathering the nests of Putin's cronies, and they would be loath to see these go to others. At the end of the meeting, as Medvedev went around shaking hands, Yasin had asked me to give him the Russian edition of my *Unintended Consequences.* Little did I realize that Russia was to revert to the 'caesaropapism' I had described as its traditional polity.[10]

This became clear on my last visit to Russia to attend a conference at the Higher School in April 2012. Putin was back as president after a contested election and had been chagrined by a march organized against him by liberals. He now was openly moving to the caesaropapist mode. For the first time since going to Russia in the mid-1990s, I was aware of the growing repression.[11]

This was clear when I heard from the head of the Institute for Dissemination of Information on Social and Economic Sciences (IDISES)[12]—a small publishing house set up by liberal members of the Duma and private businessmen—that the meeting of the academic board (of which I was chairman) had been cancelled. Subsequently, IDISES closed for lack of funding.

I should have been aware of Putin's revanchist turn when Andrei Illarionov resigned as his economic advisor and vociferously denounced his war with Georgia. With Putin's later annexation of Crimea, his proxy war in Ukraine, and most recently with the military intervention in the Syrian civil war, Russia is now clearly challenging the US pax by hoping to resurrect part of its old empire and restore Russia's status as a superpower. It is, thus, a major dramatis persona in my story of the ongoing struggle for world power.

China

What of China? As it had ended its economic stagnation by joining the US-led LIEO after Deng's opening, with immense economic benefits to its people from following the trading state strategy, I had assumed that it would not repeat the late nineteenth century errors of Germany and Japan. It would be content to regain the economic predominance it had enjoyed for millennia within what it considered its historical borders.

I had become aware that there was one issue—Taiwan—on which it might still seek to challenge its major trading partner, the US. I had been taken aback in the mid-1980s when I had asked a Chinese friend and US-trained academic, 'What might bring the Chinese miracle to an end?'. He replied, 'If Taiwan declared independence. For then, China would have to declare war on the US to take Taiwan by force'. He would have no truck with my remonstrations that this seemed highly disproportionate in terms of the relevant costs and benefits of this action. I soon found that all classes of Chinese society shared this sentiment. But, with the peaceful integration of Hong Kong,[13] which was allowed to keep its economic and legal system, the gradual but growing economic integration of Taiwan and China seemed to augur a similar denouement for this longstanding territorial dispute. With the forbearance of Taiwanese politicians in declaring independence, I thought this issue, which could potentially make China change its trading state strategy, had been put on the back burner.

Yet instead, there seemed to be a new, prickly nationalist assertiveness and need to salve hurt lost pride reflected in a desire to become the world hegemon. In a sense this is not surprising. For, as I argue in the Appendix,[14] there is a strong correlation between economic and military strength with the rising economic power also seeking world hegemony. China, as the rising economic power, is, not surprisingly, converting it into military power, seeking to challenge and replace the current world hegemon—the US.

This was also the major theme of my book *In Praise of Empires*. I argue in the book that the international system formed by the anarchic European society of nation states after the fall of Rome was the exception in human history, wherein imperial systems have predominated. With the gradual economic rise of the western tip of Eurasia since the High Middle Ages, and with the slowly unfolding Industrial Revolution, the varying economic strengths of the European nation states was translated into a struggle for the mastery of Europe.

With the development of their sea power and the weakness of the Rest,[15] this struggle among the constituent powers of the West was also translated into a quest for a world empire. Britain won this struggle in the mid-nineteenth century, but was then challenged by the rising economic powers of Germany, Japan, and Russia. This struggle for world hegemony ended with the US—which had taken over the UK's imperial role after the Second World War—seeing off the 'evil empire' with the 1991 collapse of the Soviet Union. This unipolar moment seemingly came to an end with the US's misadventures in Iraq, and Afghanistan. The continuing Syrian imbroglio, leading to a vacuum created by the US reluctance to put any more boots on the ground, has led to the re-emergence of Russia allied with Iran as the power to be reckoned with in the Middle East. Furthermore, the 2008 GFC has been taken by many—not least the Chinese—as the beginning of the end of the US imperium. I will question this assumption in Part II of this book, which is concerned with the geoeconomic fallout of the GFC and the long-term economic prospects of the major contending powers.

But, with the rise of the Rest, the US will now have to compete with many rising powers to maintain its hegemony. For I will argue in Part I on geopolitics that, in many ways, we are reverting to a pre-Renaissance world, with many of the old imperial systems being recreated. Thus, apart from the Chinese and Indians, the Europeans, too, are attempting to create a postmodern Holy Roman Empire. Vladimir Putin, the current de facto tsar of the greatly diminished Russian empire, has lamented the end of the Soviet Empire and is seeking to create another postmodern version modelled on the EU to bring in the near beyond.

Turkey

Turkey, under Recep Tayyip Erdoğan, is another wannabe imperial power but is not as yet challenging the US pax. It might be of interest to relate my experiences of Turkey. I first visited Istanbul in the late 1960s. Like many post-imperial cities it seemed to be suffering a communal melancholy, which the Turks call '*huzun*' and which is brilliantly described in Orhan Pamuk's memoir of the city.[16] It 'stems from poverty, defeat and loss'.[17] This began to change when Kemalist etatism gave way to economic liberalization undertaken by Turgut Özal in 1980. Liberalization opened up the economy and restored some microeconomic sense.[18] This was complemented by the macroeconomic stability established by Kemal Dervis in 2001–02 and maintained by the early moderate Islamic governments of Erdoğan.

These policies have allowed the pious business classes of Anatolia to create a vibrant economy and provided Erdoğan the political muscle to challenge the old Kemalist elites and their main political enforcer—the army. This new-found political and economic vigour was evident in the refurbished physical appearance of Istanbul. But it has also led to the rise of the parvenus—the new economic and political elites—whose seeming vulgarity and crass tastes are derided by the old melancholic and defeated elites they have replaced.

The first and only time I met Erdoğan was when he was mayor of Istanbul, at a conference organized by Leonard Liggio of the Atlas Foundation. I found him a hard-line Islamist and was not surprised when the military banned his AKP party. The next time I visited Istanbul was to attend an MPS meeting in 2011, where many of the papers presented argued that in his latest incarnation, after his massive electoral and economic successes, Erdoğan and his AKP had succeeded in marrying a moderate version of Islamic tradition with the modernity engendered by a globalized market economy. This seemed to me an attractive model, which the Arab countries of the former Ottoman Empire going through their Arab Spring at the time might find appealing. Erdoğan also seemed to hint at times of a virtual neo-Ottoman Empire as he exported the Turkish model.

But the next year, he overreached himself. In 2011, we were staying at the Marmara hotel in Taksim Square near a small park. There had been talk then that Erdoğan wanted to create a monument to himself and the AKP party in the square to compete with that of Mustafa Kemal Ataturk, the secularist father of modern Turkey. Gezi Park was to be incorporated in this hubristic dream. This set off riots by many of the young who used this piece of green to perambulate. Erdoğan crushed the rioters with an iron fist. Soon after, Fethullah Gülen (an influential Muslim preacher living in exile in the US),[19] who had helped Erdoğan to tame the military, fell out with him. Gülenists, who had infiltrated many state institutions including the police, charged Erdoğan and his family with massive corruption as verified by videotapes and recordings of telephonic conversations they circulated. In retaliation, Erdoğan began a massive purge of Gülenists in Turkish institutions and the financial and commercial interests supporting Gülen.

With another massive victory for the presidency, Erdoğan then sought to convert this ceremonial post into an executive one. The referendum this needed requires a two-thirds parliamentary majority, which he failed to get in the June 2015 election or in the rerun in November, though his AKP party restored its parliamentary majority. But with the failed coup purportedly organized by the Gülenists—who had also filled many of the posts in the army after Erdoğan, in alliance with Gülen, had tamed the Turkish army by purging it of its Kemalist brass—Erdoğan has declared an emergency. How this will play out remains to be seen. Will his hope of becoming the sultan of a neo-Ottoman empire be fulfilled?

With the Arab 'Spring' turning to winter and the Syrian civil war it provoked leading to chaos in the Middle East, the rise of the jihadist ISIS state is threatening both Erdoğan's dream and the post-imperial order in the Middle East. This leaves open the question of where and how the monarchical Sunni regimes of Saudi Arabia, the Gulf States, Jordan, and the Jewish outpost Israel will fit in this emerging Middle East.

Yet, with the rise and seeming resilience of the Islamist regime in Iran, there exists the deepened and deepening ancient schism between the Sunni and Shia wings of Islam. Additionally, the Iranians also seem to desire the recreation of their empire as is witnessed by Iran's continuing attempt to acquire the nuclear weapons seen as necessary to acquire status as a Great Power. Their last empire was created by the Safavids—the first native dynasty to rule Persia for more than a millennium. It lasted from the sixteenth to the eighteenth century, when it was destroyed by Afghan tribesmen in 1722 and then conquered and consolidated into another imperial state in 1795 by the Turkic Qajar tribe, who in turn became a pawn in the Great Game between the Russian and British empires in the nineteenth century.

Whether this portending clash of empires might lead to a Third World War is the major theme of Part III of the book. This by its very nature consists of what Donald Rumsfeld inimitably labelled 'unknown unknowns'. For apart from what we can foretell about demographics, relative military and economic strength, and the constraints of geography and natural resources faced by the competitors, their intentions and strategies can only be surmised through a glass darkly. History and geopolitical theories offer some guidelines, as do changing economic and military strengths, and I will be outlining these in Parts I and II.

Moreover, while it is common to look at countries anthropocentrically—that is, as if they were a single person—in practice there are many voices in the polity which will, for good or ill, determine those momentous strategic decisions of war and peace. I will be arguing that there are four major imperial systems which are and will be involved in the new Great Game in Eurasia: the US and its European outpost, the EU; China; Russia; and India. Potentially, Japan could also be involved, as it seeks to alter its post-war pacifist constitution and act, as Britain did for many centuries, as the offshore balancer in the struggle for the mastery of Asia, either as a partner or independent of the US. These players' strategic decisions will determine whether we will see a repeat of the past, with another completely unnecessary world war like the first, or if they will succeed in eschewing this atavism.

There is, however, a greater resonance with the two world wars in the discussion in Part III. This is best brought out by Walter Russell Mead in his important book *God and Gold*.[20] He argues that world politics in the last four hundred years can be best explained by the maritime system created by the Dutch in the seventeenth century and then adopted by the British and subsequently the US to create their imperia. In each version, sea power was used to build up 'global systems of trade and might'. The open, dynamic, and capitalist society this created 'generated innovations in finance, technology, marketing and communication'. The wealth generated provided the basis for military power. Mead states, 'The basic formula of an open society, world trade, and world power was the power secret … and the major driving force in the history of the 400 years'. Of the aspiring superpowers, that is, China and India, and the diminished one, that is, Russia, while all have partially embraced world trade as the route to wealth, only India has embraced the open society element of Russell Mead's 'power secret'. Herein lies the rub; will the current superpower, the US, and the aspirant, India, be willing to accept a world run by an authoritarian, state-capitalist superpower, China? If not, would they be willing to go to war to prevent this outcome? And will the Chinese eschew the trading state route to world power and choose instead to launch a pre-emptive war against the US at a time when it is seen as weak and indecisive? What can be done to prevent this dire outcome? Where will the diminished Russian imperium, a newly revived Japan, the wannabe Turkish and Persian imperia, and the virtual empire of Germany fit into this coming narrative?

The answers to these questions are for me not merely of academic but deep personal interest. For having recently retired from UCLA, I now spend part of the year in the country of my birth—India. Caught as it is in the vortex of this new Great Game, the answers to these questions as well India's response to these new geostrategic challenges will determine whether I spend the last lap of my life in peace or in a repeat of the turmoil my family suffered when the subcontinent was partitioned by the declining British empire. Hence the emphasis of this book on the enfolding geopolitical trends buffeting India and how it can maintain its security and progress economically in a dangerous world. The last chapter of Part III discusses this and provides the second bookend to the book, with a final chapter providing a summary of its arguments.

Notes

1. The MPS is a society of classical liberal academics set up by the Nobel Laureate Friedrich Hayek to counter the dominant dirigisme in economic policy and politics after the Second World War, which he aptly described in his book *The Road to Serfdom* (1944). Many of these ideas were resurrected during the Great Recession, and my discussion in Part II on geoeconomics is a classical liberal response to this contemporary road to serfdom.
2. The paper that arose from this conference was my first contribution to the ongoing debate on Chinese economic reform—see D. Lal, 'The Fable of the Three Envelopes: The Analytics and Political Economy of the Reform of Chinese State Owned Enterprises', *European Economic Review*, 34 (1990), pp. 1213–1. During this meeting, I, along with other foreign speakers, met the Chinese premier Zhao Ziyang who impressed us with his openness to

discussing every issue, except when János Kornai, who was one of the speakers, asked him about the *hukou* (residential permit) system. At this point, Zhao excused himself to go to the bathroom and on his return failed to answer the question! I also wrote a paper comparing China's economic liberalization to that which began in India in 1991. See D. Lal, 'India and China: Contrasts in Economic Liberalization?', *World Development*, 23, no. 9 (1995), pp. 1475–94. My other contributions to the changing debate in China are on the rational deployment of China's burgeoning reserves. See D. Lal, 'A Proposal to Privatize Chinese Enterprises and End Financial Repression', *Cato Journal*, 26, no. 2 (Spring–Summer 2006), pp. 275–86, and most recently taking issue with the much touted 'Beijing consensus'—see D. Lal, 'Is the Washington Consensus Dead?', *Cato Journal*, 32, no. 3 (Fall 2012), pp. 493–512.

3. See Pierre Ryckman's, *Chinese Shadows* (London: Penguin Books, 1978)—an eloquent account of the destruction of these walls by the incoming Communist regime. A Belgian diplomat and later an academic at the Australian National University, Ryckman wrote the account under the nom de plume of Simon Leys.
4. See the young Indian journalist Pallavi Aiyar's *Smoke and Mirrors: An Experience of China* (New Delhi: Fourth Estate, 2008)—an enchanting contemporary account of living in one of the remaining hutongs amid the soullessness of much of the reconstructed modernist Beijing.
5. See D. Lal, *Poverty and Progress: Realities and Myths about Global Poverty* (New Delhi: Oxford University Press, 2013), pp. 21–7.
6. See D. Lal, 'Is the Washington Consensus Dead?'.
7. See Richard Rosecrance, *The Rise of the Trading State: Commerce and Conquest in the Modern World* (New York: Basic Books, 1986).
8. The trading state strategy is a non-zero-sum strategy with mutual gains from trade, unlike war, which is a zero-sum strategy. A neo-mercantilist strategy is a mixed strategy that looks upon trade, too, in some ways like war. In 'Power Versus Plenty as Objectives of Foreign Policy in the Seventeenth and Eighteenth Centuries', *World Politics*, 1, no. 1 (1948)—Jacob Viner's definitive account of mercantilism in the seventeenth and eighteenth centuries—Viner defined this strategy as one between the great powers of the day in which they looked upon their colonies as 'suppliers of raw materials and markets for manufactures of the "mother country" alone, with

foreign interlopers to be excluded by force if necessary'. In *Power and Plenty: Trade, War, and the World Economy in the Second Millennium* (Princeton, N.J.: Princeton University Press, 2007), p. 228, Findlay and O'Rourke postulate that neo-mercantilism, which has been practised by Germany, Japan, and now China in the post–Second World War world, uses an undervalued exchange rate to generate an export surplus converted into foreign exchange reserves, which are seen as a source of power. Though not a pure free-trade strategy as recommended by Adam Smith, it still remains a non-zero-sum strategy.

9. This was the second time I had visited a presidential dacha set in the woods on the outskirts of Moscow. The first was when the Russian edition of my *Unintended Consequences* was launched in what used to be Stalin's dacha. This had its own hospital and all other amenities. Medvedev's dacha was similar and a reminder that not much had changed in the lifestyle of Russia's rulers.
10. See D. Lal, *Unintended Consequences: The Impact of Factor Endowments, Culture, and Politics on Long-Run Economic Performance* (Cambridge, MA: MIT Press, 1998).
11. See D. Lal, 'The Tsar in Winter', *Business Standard* (April 2012). Available online at http://www.business-standard.com/article/opinion/deepak-lal-the-tsar-in-winter-112042100006_1.html (last accessed 16 February 2018).
12. IDISES was set up in 2005 by Valentin Zavadnikov and other academics, politicians, and businessmen to raise the level of intellectual debate in Russia by publishing Russian translations of Western books on economics, political science, sociology, law, history, international relations, and military thought.
13. But this is now in doubt having witnessed the umbrella revolution in Hong Kong in August–September 2014 for greater democratic elections, and the recent whisking away to the mainland of Hong Kong publishers who had published critical books about the personal lives of Chinese leaders.
14. Also see Paul Kennedy, *The Rise and Fall of the Great Powers* (London: Fontana Press, 1989).
15. This refers to what were called 'developing countries' after World War II.
16. See Orhan Pamuk, *Istanbul: Memories and the City* (New York: Vintage, 2006).

17. See Orhan Pamuk, *Istanbul: Memories and the City*, p. i.
18. See Bent Hansen, *The Political Economy of Poverty, Equity, and Growth: Egypt and Turkey* (New York: Oxford University Press, 1991) for a detailed economic history of modern Turkey till the late 1980s. This volume forms part of the country studies for a World Bank comparative studies project Hla Myint and I directed in the 1980s. The synthesis volume is D. Lal and H. Myint, *The Political Economy of Poverty, Equity and Growth: A Comparative Study* (Oxford: Clarendon Press, 1996).
19. He is a preacher 'who has won praise from non-Muslim quarters for his advocacy of science, interfaith dialogue, and multi-party democracy'. The transnational and social movement he has founded referred to as *Hizmet*, 'is active in education with private schools and universities in over 180 countries. Some have praised the movement as a pacifist, modern-oriented version of Islam, and as an alternative to more extreme schools of Islam such as Salafism'. In 1999, Gülen emigrated to Pennsylvania after the Turkish government charged him with an Islamist state in Turkey. (Quotes from 'Gülen movement', *Wikipedia*. https://en.wikipedia.org/wiki/Gülen_movement).
20. See Walter Russell Mead, *God and Gold* (New York: Vintage, 2008).

PART I

Geopolitics

CHAPTER ONE

War and Peace

Changing Human Nature?

This book is about war and peace. A few years ago, in June 2013, sitting in my study in New Delhi reading Steven Pinker's monumental doorstopper of a book *The Better Angels of Our Nature*, I could not help thinking that I was about six minutes' flying time from nuclear missiles from Pakistan to my west and that to the north, the heavily armed Chinese People's Liberation Army (PLA) had just made an illegal incursion twelve miles into Ladakh. Sitting there, it was difficult to believe that Pinker's 'better angels' were about to take over the world. Pinker rightly notes the importance of both the dark and sunny side of human nature as delineated by David Hume: 'There is some benevolence, however small … some particle of the dove kneaded into our frame, along with the elements of the wolf and serpent'.[1] It is heartening to see that mounting neuroscientific and sociobiological evidence, so comprehensively surveyed by Pinker, provides scientific evidence confirming Hume's eighteenth-century conjectures about human nature. Where Pinker has gone wrong in my view is that he believes that the dove has tamed the wolf and the serpent through the various processes he discusses at length, and this has led to (what he terms) the 'Long Peace'.

In my own older book on war and peace, *In Praise of Empires*,[2] I had developed a framework which emphasized the importance of empires (or global hegemons—the equivalent of Hobbes' *Leviathan* in international affairs) in an otherwise anarchical society in maintaining global order and, thereby, peace. I had surveyed the rise and fall of empires since antiquity to show how, in the sphere they controlled, empires provided the order needed to pursue the elementary and universal goals that David Hume maintained any society must pursue if any social life is to exist.[3] These are first, to secure life against violence that leads to death or bodily harm; second, that promises once made are kept; and third, the stabilization of possessions through rules of property.[4] Through their pax, these empires maintained peace and prosperity, and when they declined and collapsed, there was both domestic disorder and a disintegration of the enlarged economic spaces they had created. True, these ancient empires did not seek to end various barbarous, violent practices which were very much part of their 'cosmological beliefs', as I have characterized them in my Ohlin lectures, *Unintended Consequences*,[5] and Pinker is right in the importance of what he calls the 'Civilizing Process' and the 'Humanitarian Revolution', whose evolution I also traced in my book. But nevertheless, given these common failures to tame the instincts of the wolf in all civilizations till recently, the role of empires in maintaining peace and prosperity in their domains cannot be gainsaid.

Thus, despite its abhorrent cultural practices by the standard of contemporary norms, the Roman Empire had through its pax brought unprecedented peace and prosperity to the inhabitants of the Mediterranean littoral for nearly a millennium. When it collapsed, the ensuing disorder and the destruction of the imperial economic space led to a marked fall in the standards of living of the common people inhabiting the fallen empire.[6]

If our concern is with war and peace, the most important variable—completely neglected by Pinker—is the rise and fall of empires. This, in turn, reflects the current sensibilities of American historians and political scientists, as I discovered when promoting my book on empires in the United States (US) that it had fallen between two stools. Empire was a derogatory term in their lexicon. Thus the people who broadly agreed with my argument did not like the US being described as an imperial power, whilst those on the Left who agreed that the US was an empire did not like my praise of empires![7]

Figure 1.1 (which reproduces Pinker's Figure 5.12) purportedly depicts the Long Peace; however, an alternative interpretation shows that it depicts the struggle for mastery of Europe to create another Roman empire (albeit Holy) after the fall of Rome and the success, first of the British in the nineteenth century, and then the US after the Second World War, in creating global empires that mitigated the international anarchy created by competing nation states. Thus, with the consolidation of European nation states during the post-medieval period (from 1500), the religious wars they fought to a stalemate only ended with the Peace of Westphalia in 1648. But, after a brief lull of peace, they resumed their conflicts in wars for the mastery of Europe, until, with its victory in the Napoleonic Wars, Britain established its global imperium in 1820. However, by 1870, Britain's long imperial decline had begun.

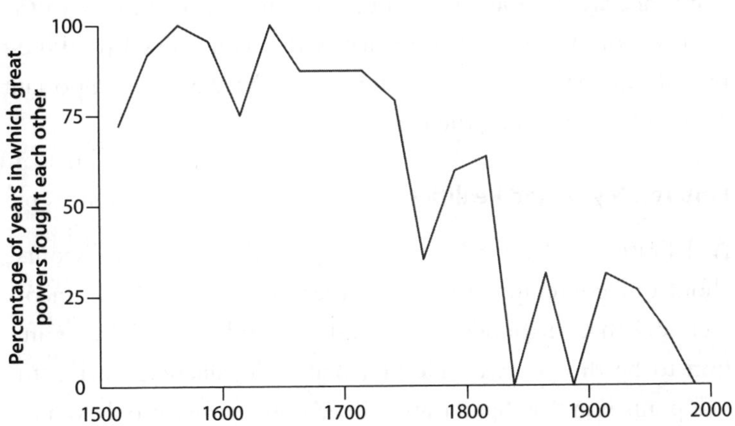

FIGURE 1.1 Percentage of Years in Which Great Powers Fought One Another 1500–2000

Source: From Pinker (2011). Graph adapted from Levy and Thompson, 2011. Data aggregated over 25-year periods.

Challenged with the emerging Great Powers, namely Germany and the US, and temporarily Russia—which imploded in the Revolution—the British were willing but unable to maintain their hegemony. The US, which became a partner rather than a competitor of Britain in the First World War, thereafter turned inwards and was unwilling to take over or share Britain's imperial responsibility for maintaining global order. This led to the global disorder of the interwar years, until after the Second World War, a duopoly of empires—that is, the US and the Soviet Union—succeeded in maintaining some global order, with the mutual assured destruction of nuclear weapons preventing a direct war between the two superpowers and their continuing competition being limited to proxy wars. With the implosion of the Soviet Union, the US became the sole superpower, and the era of warfare depicted in Pinker's figure came to an end. Hence, the Long Peace, I would argue, is the result of the empires established by Britain and the US in the nineteenth and late twentieth centuries respectively. In itself, this does not give any warrant to believe that the dove in our nature has now replaced the wolf as the new norm in international relations.

So, I hope this provides some support for my argument that war and peace are dependent upon the rise and fall of empires. In the next section, I provide a summary of the framework I think best provides an explanation as to why empires have been an important means for maintaining the peace.

Empires: Myths and Realities

A definition of 'empire' is needed, given the confused discourse about our contemporary world order, and the politically incorrect aura that surrounds the term. I still find Thucydides definition to be the clearest.[8] He said that in its alliances during the Peloponnesian War, Sparta was a hegemon because it only wanted to control the foreign policy of its allies, whereas Athens was an empire because it wanted to control both domestic and foreign policy. Thus, empires control both domestic and foreign policy, hegemons only foreign policy.

There are also a variety of empires. They were clearly distinguished by Machiavelli, who noted their control of the domestic domain could take a number of forms. He wrote:

> When those states which have been acquired are accustomed to live at liberty under their own laws, there are three ways of holding them. The first is to despoil them [as Genghis Khan did]; the second is to go and live there in person [as in the direct empires based on colonies]; the third is to allow them to live under their own laws, taking tribute of them, and creating within the country a government composed of a few that will keep friendly to you [as in the indirect empires of Rome and Britain].[9]

Direct and indirect empires are more stable than empires based merely on plunder. Even the Mongols finally had to move to the other two forms of controlling their new domains and in choosing between direct and indirect empire, chose the latter. Wherever imperial power has been exercised, indirect empire has always been preferred because it is less costly for the metropole. But most empires have been a mixture. The Roman and British Empires were mixtures. Because of the genii of self-determination let loose by Woodrow Wilson, direct empire is ruled out today. I would argue that America is an indirect empire that seeks to control both domestic and foreign policy of large parts of the world.

What determines whether international anarchy is replaced by hegemony or empire? What determines whether the empire is ruled directly or indirectly? A theory I developed to explain the rise and fall of empires in India in my *Hindu Equilibrium*,[10] combined with one developed by my late UCLA colleague Jack Hirshliefer,[11] helps to answer these questions.[12] Rather than burden you with the details, which are briefly outlined in the Appendix, I am just going to tell you the answer, which once stated is actually obvious. It is that an anarchical system, which can be stable for some time, breaks down if one of the competing states obtains an asymmetrical improvement in its military technology or the productivity of its economy that it can turn into a decisive military advantage allowing it to overcome its rivals and establish its hegemony or empire. There are two major correlates of power: larger populations can mobilize more warriors and, if they are richer (with a higher per capita income), can translate their relative economic strength into an asymmetric fighting force to protect their own resource base and/or increase it by seizure from others. Relative GDP (population x per capita income) thus provides a crude measure of relative power—though it should be emphasized, given the current debate about the relative power of China vis-à-vis the US, separate measures of population and per capita income are a better metric for gauging relative power. For one can have a very large population of very impoverished people.

In Figure 1.2, I provide estimates of relative GDP of the two imperial states India and China and the states that formed the anarchical system of European states from 1500 to 1998, which have been derived by the economic historian Angus Maddison.[13] The figures are normalized around the data for Russia, so that the figure shows the GDP of the others relative to Russia (taken as 100). From this, it is clear that the great powers in 1500 were India and China. But they went their separate ways and were only

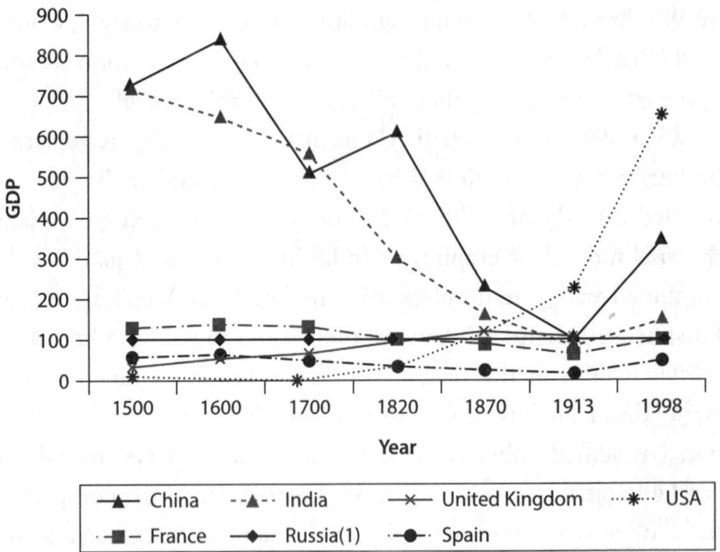

FIGURE 1.2 Index of GDP for Major Countries, 1500–1998 (Russia Equals 100)

Source: Lal (2004). Figure 1.2 derived from Maddison (2001), Table B-18.

tangentially connected with the European states system until they felt the Western impact with the rise of the gunpowder empires.

It is worth noting that China has been an imperial state for millennia, punctuated by periods of warlordism and disorder when the 'Mandate of Heaven' was withdrawn from the existing dynasty. India, by contrast, has seen subcontinental imperial unity for only eight of the twenty-two centuries from 300 BCE to 1900 CE. However, there were numerous regional empires for which the lodestone remained the creation of an All-India empire. Though few, given the difficult logistics, were able to convert their regional into national hegemony. Thus, unlike China, India historically has been marked by political instability.

Among the Europeans there seems to be almost a stalemate, with some empires rising then falling, with no clear dominant economic and military power till the end of the eighteenth century. Any military innovations that were made—such as the adoption and adaptation of artillery for sea warfare or the importance of drill in creating cohesive standing armies—were quickly diffused among the competing European powers. Their overseas empires were merely the extension of this battle for the mastery of Europe. So whenever one of these European powers became stronger, it also acquired an overseas empire, which was then subsequently contested by the next ascendant power.

There are various myths about empires. From Table 1.1, one can see that, far from being ephemeral, most empires have been

TABLE 1.1 Lifespan of Empires

Egypt 2580 BC–30 BC	2,820 years
China 212 BC–1912	2,133 years
Rome 509 BC–AD 476	985 years
Assyria 1356 BC–612 BC	744 years
Byzantine 330 AD–1204 AD	874 years
Venice 687 AD–1799 AD	1,112 years
Caliphate 632 AD–943 AD	312 years
Ottoman c.1350 AD–1918 AD	568 years
Achemenian Persian empire 550–330 BC	220 years
Sassanian Persian empire AD 224–651	427 years
British Empire in India 1757–1947	190 years

Source: Lal (2004). Table 1.1 derived from Finer (1997), vol. 1, pp. 31–2.

long-lived. What is more, they have provided international order, and most importantly, they have provided their pax over a large geographical space, ending the disorder that previously prevailed.

An imperial pax allows previously disparate areas to live together under a common legal order, creating a common economic space, leading to what is today called 'globalization'. This generates the prosperity based on the gains from trade that Adam Smith emphasized. This beneficent economic effect has occurred in most empires of the past. The Greek and Roman empires linked the areas of the Mediterranean; the Abbasids linked the Mediterranean and Indian oceans; the Mongols linked the worlds of China, Central Asia, and the Near East; and the empires in India and China, too, linked their vast subcontinental spaces into one common economic space.

But, in pre-industrial agrarian economies, most economic activity was ultimately limited by the amount of land, which was the basic factor for production and in relatively fixed supply. They all had a period of 'Smithian' intensive growth (with output growing faster than population) when per capita incomes rose because of the gains from trade from the creation of the common imperial economic space. However, this economic impetus soon petered out. Thereafter, the imperial economy merely experienced extensive growth—with output growing at the same rate as population—keeping per capita income constant, though at a higher level than in the constituent pre-imperial subeconomies. Thus, all the ancient empires witnessed a climacteric. In India, it was in about the fifth century BCE under the Mauryas, in Rome about 0 CE under Augustus, and in China about 1100 CE under the Sung.

From the data put together by economic historians (Table 1.2), it appears that in 0 CE, the per capita income of the three major imperial states Rome, India, and China were about the same, with India's being marginally higher. India and Rome had reached their climacteric, but China still awaited its own under the Sung.

Thereafter, the two continuing imperial systems of India and China had extensive growth with output expanding pari passu

Table 1.2 GDP and Population for Ancient Powers, 0 CE

	GDP (In million 1990 $)	POPULATION (million)	GDP per capita
Roman Empire	20,961	55	381
China	26,820	60	450
India	55,146	100	551

Source: Lal (2004), Table 4.

with population, maintaining a constant but relatively high per capita income by historical standards.

(a) Motives

What are the motives for creating empires? They are the same as Hobbes defined as the principal causes of fighting and violence, which are endemic in human nature. These are, 'First, Competition; Secondly, Diffidence; Thirdly, Glory'.[14]

The first motive of gain is common to many founders of empires.[15] But, for Alexander the Great, Romans like Julius Caesar, and Mongols like Genghis Khan, there was also the search for glory—Hobbes' third motive. The second motive of safety was also important for the Chinese, Indians, and late Egyptian and Roman empires, which sought to expand the territorial area of the state to some natural boundaries that would keep the nomadic predators from the steppes to the north and the Arabian Desert to the south—who constantly threatened these sedentary civilizations—at bay. For the Spanish conquistadores, as for the Islamic conquerors, booty and the desire to convert heathens were complementary motives. While for the British and the Dutch, the reluctant extension of empire followed the almost accidental establishment of territorial control over distant countries by their trading companies, whose foreign exploits had been encouraged by their parent countries as part of a long-drawn-out interstate competition in Europe after the Renaissance. The flag, in these cases, followed trade, and the motive of the metropolitan government was as much to maintain a pax to allow trade and commerce to prosper as it was to maximize the direct returns in terms of booty and tribute from their far-flung dominions. Thus, the motives for creating past empires were mixed and cannot be reduced to some simple single motive as theorists of imperialism from Hobson to Lenin to Schumpeter have sought to do.[16]

Empires can also be distinguished by whether they are multicultural or homogenizing. The former included the Roman, Abbasids, the various Indian empires, the Ottoman, Austro-Hungarian, and the British, where little attempt was made to change 'the habits of the heart'[17] of the constituent groups—or if it was, as in the early British Raj, an ensuing backlash led to a reversal of this policy. The homogenizing empires, by contrast, sought to create a national identity out of the multifarious groups in their territory. The best example of these is China, where the ethnic mix was unified as 'Han' through the bureaucratic device of writing their names in Chinese characters in a Chinese form and suppressing any subsequent discontent through the subtle repression of a bureaucratic authoritarian state.[18] In our own time, the American 'melting pot', creating Americans out of a multitude of ethnicities by adherence to a shared civic culture and a common language, has created a similar homogenized imperial state. Similarly, the supposedly ancient nations of Britain and France were created through a state-led homogenizing process.[19] India, by contrast, is another imperial state whose current political unity is a legacy of the British Raj but whose multi-ethnic character is underwritten by an ancient hierarchical structure that accommodates these different groups in a mosaic of different castes.

(b) Mechanics

What have been the instruments (the mechanics) of maintaining an imperial order? Ancient Mesopotamia during Hammurabi's reign provided the essential instruments for maintaining coherent and stable territorially extensive empires. These instruments, according to William H. McNeill, are: 'bureaucracy, law, and market prices'.[20]

Bureaucracy entailed that people in distant parts of the empire had to accept that a stranger who arrived with a document appointing him a governor in the king's name had to be treated as such.[21] Hammurabi's legal code allowed strangers to deal with each other and enforce their property rights. Similarly, effective co-operation amongst strangers was made possible by market prices and the enforcement by courts of law of rules for buying and selling.[22] The wider the territory in which the empire's writ ran, the more predictable human relations became. This creation of an imperial pax, maintained by standing armies with a professional officer corps (devised by the Assyrians) along with the legal and customary definitions of merchant's rights and privileges, facilitated long-distance trade between mutually alien and distrustful populations.[23] The pax thus led to both peace and prosperity.

The Roman, Chinese, and British empires—particularly in India—epitomize these mechanics of empire. The Roman Empire began as a system of indirect rule to protect its inhabitants from the outer barbarians. This required only a slender military framework and a light political structure.[24] But from the reign of Marcus Aurelius (161–80 CE), a centralized, hierarchically organized bureaucracy came to govern the empire and became the unwilling instruments for extracting ruinously heavy taxes from the local notables.[25] In the post-Diocletian period the army and administration were thrown open to any educated Roman citizen. This imperial bureaucracy went to pieces within seven centuries after its inauguration by Augustus.

By contrast, the Chinese mandarinate established by the Han emperor Liu Bang in 196 BCE was recruited on merit by an examination. This provided the Chinese state with the essential administrative spine that continued without interruption till 1911 CE. It is now being recreated in the Communist state since the period of reforms initiated by Deng Xiaoping in the early 1980s.

In India, the predatory servants of the East India Company, the agents of a trading company, were converted into another remarkable civil service.

> A predatory band of harpies was converted in a surprisingly short time into a body of public servants whose incentive was not personal pecuniary gain, and who came to make it a point of

> honour to wield enormous political power without abusing it. This transformation was due to the East India Company's decision to educate their servants for the new political tasks they had undertaken. This training system was superior to that in force for Britain's own civil servants at that time.[26]

With the British Crown replacing the Company after the Mutiny of 1857 (also known in India as the 'First War of Independence'), a system of recruitment based on examinations was instituted that was similar to the Chinese system. The higher reaches in the Indian Civil Service were, however, initially not open to Indians. This failure of the British, unlike the Chinese and Romans, to allow open recruitment to positions in the instruments of imperial control, led—as it did in the other European gunpowder empires—to nationalist 'creole' revolts which eventually destroyed the empire.[27]

In the case of the barbarian empires, most often, the new rulers took over the civil services of their predecessors. But in the case of the Ottomans, the sultans created an administrative class from their personal slave households. With these slaves being recruited from all the ethnicities in the empire and trained in the art of administration, an efficient, multi-ethnic administrative structure was created that, unlike those of the European imperial bureaucracies, was not ethnocentric. In all the empires with bureaucracies open to the talents, a common imperial culture emerged that provided a means of amalgamating the diverse groups in the empire into a cultural and political unity, which reduced the dangers of nationalist revolts.

There were two other public goods that empires created that were essential for their survival. The first was an efficient system of communications. This is an essential instrument for not only maintaining military control over far-flung dominions but also political control through an imperial inspectorate and a secret security police.[28] Both public transportation and an imperial postal service are essential parts of this communications system, which dates back to the Sumero-Akkadian empires. The imperial couriers of their postal system were also spies keeping an eye on the distant satraps (local rulers). Even outside Mesopotamia, from the Chinese to the Incas, empires created vast communications system to control their empires.[29] But, as the Romans and many other imperial rulers discovered, these communication systems, particularly the public transport system of roads and bridges, could be a double-edged sword. For in a world where all roads led to Rome, the same roads could and did convey the barbarian destroyers of their civilizations—a fact which has considerable contemporary relevance with the events of 9/11, where our contemporary barbarians used our modern means of conveyance (the airplane) and the postal service (the internet) for their barbaric mission.

The second public good is a lingua franca with which official business can be conducted, both within the imperial bureaucracy and with its subjects. As most empires were multi-ethnic and multilingual, it was a delicate issue of which local language should become the lingua franca of the empire. As anthropologists tell us, the language group is the most potent identifier of different cultures,[30] and as the latter embody their differing cosmological beliefs, the imposition of the language of one or the other linguistic groups of an empire as its lingua franca could lead to domestic disorder. Empires have, therefore, usually made their mother tongue the official language without granting it a monopoly.[31]

This linguistic flexibility of empires has only been contravened in three instances. The first was in the Islamic Umayyad Caliphate (661–750 CE). But this changed when the Ottomans came to run the Islamic empire, where, in its heyday in the sixteenth and seventeenth centuries, the lingua franca of the Padishah's slave household was Serbo-Croat and Italian was the language of command in the Ottoman navy.[32]

The second was the linguistic monopoly imposed by the Spanish conquistadores of Latin America. But with their eagerness to gather souls for their Christian mission, they had to compromise by allowing the Gospel to be preached in the Andean world in Quechua, the Andean lingua franca of the Incas.

The third, the Chinese, was the most momentous. The Chin emperor Shih Hwang-ti (221–10 BCE) gave exclusive currency to the ideographic language current in his own ancestral state and created a new Han Chinese identity by forcing all the diverse ethnic and linguistic groups in the country to conform to this language by writing their names in these uniform characters in this new Chinese form. This also became the language of the mandarins and imposed a unity on the empire that has lasted to our day.

To see how empires are important to maintain peace consider a counterfactual history of the twentieth century to that depicted in Pinker's figure (Figure 1.1). Suppose in 1905, or thereabouts, the Americans had joined the British in maintaining a joint Anglo-American pax? I think a good case can be made for saying that all the travails and human suffering of the first half of the century might not have happened. The joint industrial and military might of an Anglo-American imperium run, let us say, by the equivalent of a Lord Palmerston could have prevented the Kaiser's gamble to achieve mastery in Europe, and one of the most pointless wars—the First World War—could perhaps have been averted. This, in turn, could have prevented the events that led to the rise of Hitler. Similarly, a joint Anglo-American imperium might have prevented the rise of the Bolsheviks. The rise of the two illiberal creeds—fascism and communism—that have blighted the lives of millions could perhaps have been prevented. Instead, Woodrow Wilson at Versailles destroyed the Age of Empire and, with the US retreating into isolationism, left global disorder and economic disintegration to rule for nearly a century during the Age of Nations.[33]

After the Second World War, eschewing Wilsonian idealism in practice if not in its rhetoric, America has, at first surreptitiously and recently more openly, taken over the task of maintaining an imperial pax. Not merely its relative economic strength but also its ability to transform it into military power leaves it as the only power capable of maintaining the global pax.

Much more importantly, the Americans also have had the revolution in military affairs (RMA), giving them an immense lead in new information based (IT) military technologies, which allow their abundant capital resources to substitute for increasingly scarce and valuable labour. This new military technology, which minimizes the number of body bags in a war, was shown to stunning effect in the recent military operations in Afghanistan and Iraq. The Americans, today, have both a technological and economic preponderance, which is uncontestable for at least the rest of the century (see Chapter 9). Also, unlike much of the rest of Europe, Russia, and Japan, and in the near future China, the USA is forecast to have not a declining but a rising population—largely through immigration.

Thus, today there is again an imperial power that has an economic and military predominance unseen since the fall of Rome. The US is indubitably an empire. It is more than a hegemon, as it seeks control over not only foreign but also aspects of domestic policy in other countries. It is an informal and indirect empire. After its nineteenth-century colonial adventure in the Philippines, it has not sought to acquire territory. Nor is it, like the Spanish and many of the ancient predatory empires, a tribute-seeking empire. It is an empire that has taken over from the British the burden of maintaining a pax to allow free trade and commerce to flourish. This pax brings mutual gains. Given the well-known human tendency to free ride, the US, like the British in the nineteenth century, has borne much of the costs of providing this global public good, not because of altruism, but because the mutual gains from a global, liberal economic order benefit America and foster its economic well-being. It has not yet in this promotion of globalization or global capitalism—as some would derogatively label it—been forced to permanently take direct control over areas which have fallen into the black hole of domestic disorder, as was the case, for instance, with the British takeover of the crumbling Moghul empire in eighteenth-century India.

But, US hegemony is today being challenged by a newly resurgent China, a revanchist Russia, and rival theocracies in the Middle East. The future of war and peace in the rest of the century depends on its outcome, which is the major subject of this book. But before that we need to examine the geopolitical compulsions that are now determining world politics. We seem to be reverting to the period before the ascendancy of Europe led to the Western dominance, which is currently under challenge.

Notes

1. See D. Hume, *An Enquiry Concerning the Principles of Morals* (Oxford: Oxford University Press, 1750), p. 271.
2. See D. Lal, *In Praise of Empires* (New York: Palgrave Macmillan, 2004), pp. 4–7.
3. D. Hume, *A Treatise of Human Nature* (Oxford: Oxford University Press, 1740), p. 578.
4. The late Hedley Bull, who wrote to my mind the best book on international relations *The Anarchical Society*, also noted the importance of these goals for international order. See H. Bull, *The Anarchical Society*, Second edition (New York: Columbia University Press, 1995), p. 4.
5. See D. Lal, *Unintended Consequences: The Impact of Factor Endowments, Culture, and Politics on Long-Run Economic Performance* (Cambridge, MA: MIT Press, 1998), pp. 7–8
6. This is how the late Samuel Finer, the distinguished Oxford historian of government, has described the economic consequences of the end of the Roman Empire: 'If a peasant family in Gaul, or Spain, or northern Italy had been able to foresee the misery and exploitation that was to befall his grandchildren and their grandchildren on and on and on for the next five hundred years, he would have been singularly spiritless—and witless too—if he had not rushed to the aid of the empire. And even then the kingdoms that did finally emerge after the year 1000 were poverty stricken dung heaps compared with Rome. Not till the full Renaissance in the 16th century did the Europeans begin to think of themselves as in any ways comparable to Rome, and not till the Augustan age of the 18th century did they regard their civilization as its equal.' See S. Finer, *The History of Government from the Earliest Times* (Oxford: Oxford University Press, Vols. 1, 2, 1997), Vol. 1., p. 34.
7. By contrast, the Oxford historian John Darwin has no problem with viewing the US as an empire. See his excellent book, *After Tamerlane: The Global History of Empire* (London: Penguin, 2007), pp. 458–71.
8. As quoted in M. Doyle, *Empires* (Ithaca: Cornell University Press, 1986), p. 40.

9. See N. Machiavelli, *The Prince* (New York: Modern Library, 1513/1950), p. 18.
10. See D. Lal, *The Hindu Equilibrium: India c. 1500 B.C.–2000 A.D.*, Abridged and Revised Edition (Oxford and New York: Oxford University Press, 2005 [1988]), pp. 364–79.
11. See J. Hirshleifer, 'Anarchy and Its Breakdown', *Journal of Political Economy,* 103 (1995): 26–52. Reprinted in his *The Dark Side of the Force: Economic Foundations of Conflict Theory* (Cambridge: Cambridge University Press, 2001), 364–79.
12. See D. Lal, *The Hindu Equilibrium: India c. 1500 B.C.–2000 A.D.*, Abridged and Revised Edition. (Oxford and New York: Oxford University Press, 2005 [1988]), ch. 13.2. The tax-cum-public goods equilibrium that can be derived from the model also allows a classification of what I have termed autonomous states (as opposed to factional ones) into predatory, Platonic guardian, and bureaucrat-maximizing states. (See D. Lal and H. Myint, *The Political Economy of Poverty, Equity and Growth,* pp. 264–7.) These differ in the objectives they seek to subserve. The predatory state is only concerned with maximizing its net revenue; the Platonic guardian state, with maximizing social welfare; and the bureaucrat-maximizing state, with the number of bureaucrats. It can be shown that the Platonic guardian state provides the optimal level of public goods with the lowest tax rate. The bureaucrat and predatory states' tax rate is determined by the entries to barriers to rivals, but they differ in the level of public goods provided, with the bureaucrat-maximizing state providing more than the predatory state, and perhaps even overproviding them beyond the optimal level.
13. See A. Maddison, *The World Economy: A Millennial Perspective* (Paris: OECD, 2001), Table B-18.
14. T. Hobbes, *Leviathan* (Cambridge: Cambridge University Press, 1996 [1651]), pp. 88–9.
15. It is the net revenue-maximizing objective of my predatory state model. See D. Lal, 'Nationalism, Socialism and Planning: Influential Ideas in the South', *World Development*, 13 (6) (1985): 749–59.
16. The Marxist theories of imperialism, which look upon it as a reflection of finance or monopoly capitalism, reached their most popular form with Lenin (1916). But even Marxists acknowledge these theories are seriously flawed. See, for instance, J. Brewer, *The Sinews of Power: War, Money and the English State, 1688–1783*

(Cambridge MA: Harvard University Press, 1990). See also J. Schumpeter, *Imperialism* (1955) and J. A. Hobson, *Imperialism: A Study*, Revised Edition (London: Allen and Unwin, London, 1948 [1902]). Both emphasized the link between capitalism and formal imperialism (see Cain and Hopkins, *British Imperialism 1688–2000*, Second Edition (Harlow: Longman, 2002), pp. 31–3) and shared 'the naive idea that it was possible to find a form of capitalism that would bring peace and prosperity to all' (Cain and Hopkins, p. 33). Neo-Marxists like Wallerstein (*The Modern World System*, 3 vols., [New York: Academic Press, 1980]) and Gunder Frank (*Reorient: Global Economy in the Asian Age* [Berkeley: University of California Press, 1998]) consider industrialization as having precipitated imperialism. But Cain and Hopkins show that this view is unfounded. Also see Charles Tilly, *Coercion, Capital and European States AD 992–1992* New York: Wiley-Blackwell (1990).

17. See D. Lal, *In Praise of Empires*, p.160.
18. See Jenner (1983).
19. See L. Colley, *Britons: Forging the Nation 1707–1837*, Revised Edition. (New Haven: Yale University Press, 1992).
20. W. McNeill, *A World History*, Third Edition (New York: Oxford University Press, 1979), p. 36.
21. McNeill, *A World History*, 3rd edtn, p. 36.
22. McNeill, *A World History*, 3rd edtn, p. 36.
23. McNeill, *A World History*, 3rd edtn, p. 63.
24. See A. Toynbee, *A Study of History*, Abridged Edition (New York: Barnes and Noble Books, 1995), p. 278.
25. Toynbee, *A Study of History*, abridged edition . p. 278.
26. Toynbee, *A Study of History*, abridged edition pp. 313–14.
27. See B. Anderson, *Imagined Communities* (London: Verso, 1991).
28. See A. Toynbee, *A Study of History*, Abridged Edition (1995 [1972]), p. 288.
29. A. Toynbee, *A Study of History*, Abridged Edition (1995 [1972]), p. 288., notes: 'The Incas were builders of roads and fortresses; and like the Roman conquerors of Italy, they used these instruments to consolidate each gain of ground in preparation for the next advance in their systematic movement of conquest northward' (p. 289).
30. See C. Hallpike, *The Principles of Social Evolution* (Oxford: Clarendon Press 1986). Lal, *Unintended Consequences*.
31. Lal, *Unintended Consequences*, p. 296.

32. Lal, *Unintended Consequences,* p. 297.
33. In a speech in 1964, the doyen of this post–Second World War foreign policy Dean Acheson noted that this high-sounding principle of national self-determination 'has a doubtful moral history. After the Second World War the doctrine was invoked against our friends in the dissolution of their colonial connections ... On the one occasion when the right of self-determination—then called secession—was invoked against our own government by the Confederate States of America, it was rejected with a good deal of bloodshed and moral force. Probably you will agree it was rightly rejected'. See D. Acheson, 'Ethics in International Relations Today' in D.L. Larson, *The Puritan Ethic in United States Foreign Policy* (Princeton, N.J.: Van Norstrand, 1996), pp. 134–5. But as MacGregor Knox has rightly pointed out to me, before the Great Powers met in Versailles, enraged nationalists had torn Eurasia's four great empires to shreds.

CHAPTER TWO

Geography

In an anarchical Hobbesian society of states, it is not moral arguments and exhortations which count but, as Robert Kaplan—echoing Lenin—puts it, 'What can do what to whom?'[1] The relevant units are states into which current human populations are grouped. This implies that geography—or the spatial divisions of men as represented by maps that show the political boundaries and also the physical terrain, and hence natural barriers, between them—becomes crucial in answering this central realist question.

Geography is also important to two other determinants of what unites and divides humankind-cultural and physical borders. Of these, the most important is cultural traits, which I have called 'cosmological beliefs' in my Ohlin lectures (*Unintended Consequences*).[2] They are beliefs about, in Plato's words, 'how one should live', as distinguished from the other component of cultural beliefs, the *material* ones about 'how to make a living'. I cited the considerable ethnographic evidence that whereas material beliefs were fairly malleable—changing and adapting to a changing environment—there was more hysteresis in cosmological beliefs that were dependent upon both the geographical features of where a particular civilization emerged and the languages that evolved in the region.

There are, then, two types of frontiers, natural and linguistic. Whether these are of importance in political affairs differs from region to region and over time, as we shall see.

Among cosmological beliefs, the most important for our purposes are the political habits that have provided the legitimacy for the different types of polities that have been supported in different civilizations. Here again, as I have argued in *Unintended Consequences*, it is the geographical features under which these civilizations developed that underline these differing political habits, be it the centralized, authoritarian, bureaucratic state of China; the decentralized polities of Hinduism, Islam, and Christendom, politically disunited but culturally united; the democratic republics of ancient Greece and the Aryan republics in the Himalayan foothills; or the democratic egalitarian republicanism of the United States.

Geopolitical Theories

The Bear vs the Whale

Geographers have propounded various theories of geopolitics. Raymond Aron has defined this field as combining 'a geographical schematization of diplomatic-strategic relations with a geographic-economic analysis of resources'. Thus for geopolitics, the conduct of foreign affairs is instrumental. Resources are mobilized for security or expansion by states, and the lines of expansion as well as threats to security are indicated in advance by a world map which shows what Aron calls 'the natural data on which the prosperity and power of nations depends'.[3]

The foremost proponent of geopolitics was the British geographer Sir Halford Mackinder. He divided the world map by two concepts 'the World Island' and the 'Heartland'. Oceans cover nine-twelfths of the globe. Three continents—Asia, Europe, and Africa—cover two-twelfths. Small islands, North and South America, and Australia are the last twelfth. The Americas, in this world map of the World Island, are like the British Isles in relation to Europe. Aron describes the Heartland as thus:

> [It] covers both the northern part and the interior of the Eurasian land mass. It extends from the Arctic Coast to the deserts of Central Asia.... It constitutes the largest flat area on the surfaces of the globe: the plain of Asia, the steppes of European Russia which extend across Germany and the Low Countries through the Ile-de-France and Paris, heart of the West. Several of the world's greatest rivers flow through it either to the Arctic Sea or to inland seas (the Caspian, the Aral). Lastly, it is a grassland favorable to the mobility of populations and warriors, whether on camels or horses. The Heartland, at least in its eastern section, has been closed to the intervention of naval power. It opened a way to the incursions of horsemen riding westward.[4]

To get a better understanding, see the Map of Eurasia (Figure 2.1). From this map, Mackinder derived his three famous propositions: (1) Anyone controlling Eastern Europe controls the Heartland; (2) Anyone controlling the Heartland controls the World Island; and (3) Anyone controlling the World Island controls the world.

Mackinder was, of course, concerned with the future of his island state, which depended upon its seafaring prowess. The prophet of the importance of sea power was the US Admiral A.T. Mahan.[5] Mahan argued that sea power was more important in the fight for dominance than land power. Unlike Mackinder who thought the Heartland of Eurasia was the geographical pivot of empires, Mahan saw the Indian and Pacific oceans as constituting the hinges of geopolitical destiny.[6] Whereas Mackinder feared the strength of Russia with its control of the Heartland, Mahan emphasized Russian vulnerability without access to the warm waters of the Indian Ocean. In fact, the Great Game in the nineteenth century was between Britain and Russia, with the seafaring British imperial power preventing the Russian imperial land power from gaining this access. Mahan called the area of conflict in this Great Game, the 'debatable ground', which the Yale international relations expert Nicholas Spykman was to later, more evocatively, call 'the Rimland'.[7] This comprised China, Afghanistan, Iran, Turkey, and India. These remain of pivotal geopolitical significance today. China extends from the Eurasian Heartland to the warm waters

FIGURE 2.1 Map of Eurasia

of the Pacific. India, Mahan noted, was of particular importance for naval strategy. As Kaplan notes, 'Located in the center of the Indian Ocean littoral, its rear flanks protected by the Himalayan mountain system, [India] is critical for the seaward penetration of both the Middle East and China. Sea power, it emerges, provides the Mahanian means by which a distant United States can influence Eurasia in a Macinderesque "closed system"'.[8]

As Aron emphasizes, this contest between the 'Bear' (land power) and the 'Whale' (sea power) has been fundamental throughout history. The two elements—land and sea—represent two ways of life.

> The land belongs to someone, to the *landlord*, individual or collective; the sea belongs to all because it belongs to no one. The empire of continental powers is inspired by the spirit of possession; the empire of maritime powers is inspired by the spirit of commerce.... If land and water represent the two elements of conflict on the global stage, it is because international relations are in Clausewitz's formula, exchange and communication. Wars create relations between individuals and collectivities, but in a manner different from those of commerce. Nomads, of both land and water, horsemen and sailors, are the builders of the two types of empires, the professionals of the two kinds of combat.[9]

The Indian historian and geopolitician K.M. Panikkar rightly noted that 'history may well be conceived as the pressure of the nomad—both of the land and the sea—against civilization. Those countries which stand directly in the way of these nomads are destroyed and broken up from time to time. Those that are protected by geography receive a backwash and after turmoil settle down again'.[10] China and India—the most important constituents of the Rimland as compared with the countries and civilizations of the Heartland—provide important examples of these trends through their clashes with the land nomads from the steppes of Eurasia.

Thus, India experienced one of the earliest movements of such land nomads, with the eruption of the Aryans from the Central Asian steppes, who occupied Iran and overran and settled Europe. When they reached India, they had to divert their course first to the Hindu Kush and, thus, lose a great deal of momentum. This made the Aryan invasion of India a trickle. It left abiding marks on India, but had to compromise with the local population and establish a new society.[11] A similar story can be told of a China constantly threatened by the nomads from its adjoining northern steppes and the Mongolian plateau. Genghis Khan's Mongol hordes, having destroyed the Mesopotamian civilizations, conquered the plains of Russia, which they ruled for over 250 years. By the time Genghis' descendants conquered China and ruled it for two centuries, Panikkar says, 'the momentum of the movement had been lost, and it was not the barbarian Mongol but the very civilized Kublai who ascended the Dragon Throne'.[12] This acculturation of the barbarians by a dominant civilization was also true of the Roman Empire. It was only the whirlwind conquest by the southern land nomads—the Arabs—of the classical world that was able to create an alternative Islamic civilization to rival that of classical Greece and Rome.

By contrast, until the end of the fifteenth century, the sea nomads were confined to nearby regions. The most famous of these were the Vikings, who plundered, destroyed, and looted every area of Europe open to the sea. It was only with the knowledge of oceanic geography and the development and the technical advances in shipbuilding in the fifteenth, sixteenth, and seventeenth centuries that 'the sea nomads enter the world stage to loot, plunder and conquer areas that lay exposed to attacks from the sea'.[13]

However, it was the rise of the Western maritime powers (the new sea nomadic states) deploying these new found means of controlling the sea—first with the rise of Portugal, then the Dutch, and finally the British—which led to the conquest of distant areas non-conjoined to the metropole in the interest, initially, of trade and commerce. But faced with disunited land powers, their flags soon followed trade. So unlike land power (the Bear) where proximity is necessary, distance does not affect the expansion of sea power (the Whale).

Moreover, as Panikkar emphasized, there is a difference in conquest by a land power than by a sea power. Thus, even though foreigners often conquered large portions of north India, India was never ruled by a monarch who did not have his capital in India until the arrival of the naval power of the British. Panikkar says, 'The indivisibility of the sea and the ubiquitousness of naval power were responsible for the long domination of India from London'.[14] The carving up of the Chinese melon after the Opium Wars, though maintaining the nominal unity of China, meant that the Western naval powers controlling their respective treaty ports, in effect, controlled the hinterland. When their collective interests were threatened, they joined forces to fight the Chinese suzerain and to loot and plunder—as in the destruction of the Manchu emperor's Summer Palace in Beijing.

British naval supremacy underwrote its global imperial dominion. But when challenged by the prospects of a Europe united under a German hegemon, the British were forced to rely on the naval (and material) might of the emerging nomadic sea power of the US to defeat this challenge. This led—after the Second World War with Britain's diminished material means and the nationalist revolts—to the dismantling of Britain's empire, beginning with India, the 'Jewel in the Crown', and its replacement by the US as the imperial sea nomadic state.

There are two points that Mackinder made about the competition between the Bear and the Whale that are still relevant and which Aron summarizes in his work. First, in the struggle between maritime power and continental power, 'a maritime power will not survive, despite the qualities of its fleet and sailors, if it is confronted by a rival possessing material and human resources which are superior to its own'. The second lesson is that 'a maritime power can be conquered on land as well as at sea'. As Aron notes, 'The British Empire risks destruction, Mackinder concludes, if a continental state accumulates overwhelming resources or if the network of British bases established on islands and peninsulas around the Eurasian land mass is destroyed or occupied from the land'.[15] This remains relevant, as we shall see in the confrontation between the maritime power of the US and the continental power of the resurgent Chinese Communist state today.

Air and Fire

The twentieth-century advances in developing airpower—from bombers to intercontinental ballistic missiles—has led to the conquest of distance and space, while developments in munitions and the development of thermonuclear weapons has led to a destructive force in war unimaginable to our ancestors. Aron writes:

> In terms of myth, we might say that earth and water are henceforth subsumed to the law of air and fire. The same spirit is imposed upon law and sea forces: that of science.... Because of the aerial weapon, the sea is no longer the province of adventure. Because of fire, the bases are losing their military importance or, at least, the bases no longer have a fixed site.

Retaliatory forces to prevent surprise attacks are no longer

> protected by distance in relation to the enemy than by ubiquity. Atomic submarines, armed with Polaris rockets are everywhere and nowhere, they are somewhere on or under the sea, invulnerable and pacifying. History has decided between the theory of *res nullius* and *res omnium*: the sea belongs to all. The air too, starting from a certain height, will belong to all *because of satellites.*[16]

With these satellites and the development of the digital computer and their deployment in guiding missiles, cyberspace has also become a new frontier of warfare. Armed, unmanned aerial drones, controlled via satellites by computers sitting in the US Heartland, can fire missiles at enemies thousands of miles away in the Eurasian Heartland or the Rimland. Virtual war is no longer science fiction but a deadly reality.[17] Cyberspace is making a mockery of distance and thence of geography. But geography is not dead. For as Panikkar puts it, even in the age of air and fire, air control still 'requires fuelling bases, repair centers, etc., in the same way as ships do at sea'.[18]

The New Great Game

Contending Powers

We consider the military balance given these old and new elements of warfare—earth and land, air and fire—in the struggle for the mastery of Eurasia in greater detail in Part III. But before that, we need to delineate the powers in contention. Here, we need to distinguish between superpowers and great powers.

Superpowers, as the late Hedley Bull reminds us in his magisterial *The Anarchical Society*, are what were called great powers during the period when the balance of power characterized the international states system. Great powers were 'two or more powers that are comparable in status'.[19] The term 'superpowers' was first applied to Britain, the US, and the Soviet Union by W.T.R. Fox in 1944 in his book *The Super-Powers*. He recognized a new class of power that was superior to the traditional European great powers and alone capable of undertaking the central managerial role in international politics that they had played in the past. With the decline of Britain during the Cold War, the US and the Soviet Union were the twin superpowers in the bipolar world.

For a brief moment after the Second World War, when the US was seen to have overtaken the USSR in every correlate of power, US analysts, such as George Liska,[20] argued that the US with no other rivals was not a mere great or superpower, but like Rome was the sole dominant (imperial) power in international politics. With the collapse of the Soviet Union, the US became the sole dominant imperial power in the world. In fact, I prefer to call superpowers imperial powers. Thus, when Fox devised the term, the superpowers he identified were in fact the custodians of two imperial systems, the Anglo-American one (taken over by the Americans with the post-war decline of Britain) and the Soviet. The bipolar world of the Cold War is thus better seen as the clash and accommodation between two imperial systems. This is similar to the ancient world when there were a number of imperial systems coterminous with Rome but which did not clash (till the later stages of the Roman empire when it was challenged by the new Arab empire) because of geographical distance.

Today, with just one indubitable superpower—the US—who are the other powers in Eurasia contending or in alliance with the US to manage or dominate international relations in Eurasia? As Bull emphasized, there were traditionally three criteria to judge a state as a great power. The first was their standing in the international society of states, given 'by the degree of attention paid to them by other states in their foreign and military policies'.[21] The second is being a front-ranked military power. The third criterion is that great powers 'are recognized by others to have, and conceived by their own leaders and peoples to have, certain special rights and duties'.[22] These are by and large former imperial states (or part of one) created to secure the borders against the land and sea nomads who posed a perpetual threat to their relatively prosperous civilizations.

The two main contenders are the Heartland power of Russia and the Rimland power of China. India and Japan as Rimland powers are also major players in the emerging conflict between the US and the two former Communist states, which were the major antagonists of the US in the post–Second World War period until Deng's opening of China and the Soviet Union's implosion in 1989. In addition Iran, as the successor state of the Safavid Empire (which itself was a late imperial successor of the ancient Persian empire of Darius), has become the new pivot of Mackinder's Heartland rather than the steppes of Central Asia.[23] Apart from the Iranian plateau, the Arabian Peninsula and the Anatolian land bridge are the major geographical features of the Middle East, which remains, as it has since classical times, a cauldron of volatile politics and competing territorial and religious claims. Within the Middle East, Saudi Arabia, controlling the Arabian Peninsula, and Turkey, controlling Anatolia and the Bosporus, are two major powers. Along with Israel and Egypt, they provide the modern version of the bewildering flux of warfare and politics in the Greater Middle East since antiquity.[24]

Finally, there are the two defeated wannabe superpowers of the twentieth century. After the two-century-old conflict for the mastery of Europe, Germany has achieved hegemony in its postmodern virtual empire of the EU. And there is the other belligerent great power of the twentieth century—Japan. Like Germany, it has been able to remain as a pacifist state under the US military shield of the US–Japan security treaty. They remain great powers in their regions but because of the US shield are able to pursue a trading state strategy to gain greatness as major economic powers. But with China and, increasingly, Russia contesting US military and geopolitical dominance, and with the credibility of the US deterrent against both revanchist powers coming into question under Obama and now Trump, there is a likelihood that Japan and, perhaps, Germany too will seek to become independent military players in the Eurasian Great Game. This could mean that both these countries, whose imperial dreams were shattered by Anglo-American imperial might, could feel that economic prowess, and US words alone no longer credibly provide security in a dangerous world.

There could be a return to their acquiring the military prowess of a great power—of which there are visible sign's in Abe's Japan. For though rich as compared to when they sought to establish mastery over the western and eastern parts of Eurasia through force of arms, they may no longer be willing to be spectators of the great conflicts of history, particularly as they see themselves challenged by the revanchist powers—Russia and China. The citizens of both imperial Japan and Nazi Germany, though poorer than their contemporary descendants, notes Aron, 'participated in [the] glory of a great power. [Today they are] spectator[s] of the great conflicts of history. In other words, the imperial attempts were perhaps not irrational if their goal was collective power, the capacity to affect the course of history'.[25] The same imperial impulse of seeking glory—explicitly in the case of Putin's Russia and implicitly, until his recent explicit embrace, by Xi's China—motivates Russia and China's challenges to the US. Will a German-led EU and a rearmed Japan become independent actors like them, even if, as is the case today, they are in alliance with the US?

Geography is also of importance as a determinant of the political habits (which are part of a civilization's cosmological beliefs) that have arisen in these great powers. We next discuss these cultural roots of the government forms to be found in the major contending powers and civilizations.

During the process of post-war decolonization, Sir Ivor Jennings went around parts of the former British Empire writing model democratic constitutions for the successor states. These were soon torn up or modified to kill their liberal spirit by many of the succeeding autocrats. For, as Antony de Jasay has quipped, a constitution is like a chastity belt whose key is left within reach, whereupon nature will take its course.[26] By contrast, India, one of the largest and poorest countries, has succeeded in maintaining a liberal democracy for seventy years since its independence. This success needs an explanation. It is to be found in the political habits of different cultures, which have been formed more by the geography of the territory where the relevant culture exists than by any ideology.[27]

China

Thus China, in its origins in the relatively compact Yellow River valley, constantly threatened by the nomadic barbarians from the steppes to its north, developed a tightly controlled bureaucratic authoritarianism as its distinctive polity. This has continued for millennia to our day.

But it has also led to a distinctly Chinese attitude to foreign policy, succinctly anatomized by Edward Luttwak.[28] He notes, that as the sole great power bordered by 'sparsely populated high-altitude plateaus, deserts, semi-deserts, frigid steppes, and tropical jungles', in which there were no comparable states for habitual interaction, the Chinese never needed to develop the political habits of inter-state interaction between states, which presume a formal equality, as in the states system in Europe. Instead, the Chinese developed the Sinocentric tributary system of foreign relations, premised on the formal inequality of states: with the Chinese emperor at the centre, receiving deference through the tribute paid by lesser nations.

To deal with the periodic military threats from the northern steppes, Luttwak identifies three tools of 'barbarian handling'[29] that have echoes today. The first is 'induced economic dependence'. This was developed after 140 years of protracted warfare with the Xiongnu, the formidable mounted nomad warriors, by the Western Han (206 BCE–9 CE). The self-sufficient Xiongnu were made economically dependent on Han-produced goods, which were first supplied free 'as unrequited tribute' but, when the Han became stronger, were turned into 'exchange for services rendered' as de facto vassals. This continues till today in Chinese foreign economic policy.

The second was indoctrination.[30] The conflict with the Xiongnu, which led from the equal treaty of 198 BCE to the vassalage treaty of 51 BCE, has provided the template for Han dealings with powerful and violent states. This is how the US is seen today by the Chinese Communist Party (CCP). This leads to sequential rules of conduct:

(1) First, 'initially, concede all that must be conceded to the superior power to avoid damage, and obtain whatever benefits or at least forbearance that can be had from it'.
(2) Second, 'entangle the ruler and ruling class of the superior power in webs of material dependence that reduce its original vitality and strength, while proffering equality in a privileged bipolarity, that excludes every other power'. Hence, China's current demand for a 'G-2', and its co-opting of influential US academics, politicians and business to its purposes.
(3) 'Finally, when the formerly superior power has been weakened enough, withdraw all tokens of equality and impose subordination.'[31]

The third tool, for managing 'barbarians', was bilateralism. 'There can only be two protagonists: the tamed barbarian bearing tribute, and the benevolent emperor ready to reward his homage with valuable gifts.... The one thing rigidly prohibited was any ganging-up, [so] the emperor would not receive them as a group; tributary rituals are inherently bilateral'.[32] This, of course, has contemporary echoes in China's dealings with the other claimants in the maritime disputes in the South China Sea and its preference for dealing with the riparian states of the two major rivers flowing from Tibet (the Brahmaputra and the Mekong) bilaterally.[33]

Luttwak also questions the stubborn faith of the Chinese in Sun Tzu's *The Art of War*, given the strategic incompetence they have shown over the millennia—being regularly defeated by less numerous and advanced enemies from the steppes. The Tang, Liao, the Jin, and the Yuan dynasties were established by conquerors from the steppes, with the Han ruling for only a third of the last millennium. The last imperial dynasty (the Manchu) preserved its separate ethnic identity, own language, and script, and was not assimilated by the Han, as Chinese nationalists claim.[34] The Manchus were responsible for establishing Chin's contemporary borders. But China was a conquered land, with Manchu garrisons distributed in every Chinese province as occupation troops. Luttwak notes, 'Yet today the Han routinely manifest proprietary feelings over non-Han lands conquered by the Manchu—by the same token, Indians could claim Sri Lanka because both were ruled by the British'.[35]

Also relying on Sun Tzu, Chinese officials believe that long-unresolved disputes with foreign countries can be resolved, 'by deliberately provoking crises, to force negotiations that will settle the dispute'.[36] As witness, the latest incursions into Ladakh and the denial of a visa to an Indian IAS official from Arunachal Pradesh on the grounds he was from 'South Tibet', provoking vast public protests against China in India. Their recent military provocation in the South China Sea has only succeeded in creating a potential coalition against China by its neighbours.

The Han, also from their tributary past, 'attribute superior cunning to themselves as compared to the non-Han world,' writes Luttwak, considering Americans, though strong and violent, 'as especially naïve, but easily manipulated'. This for the Chinese has been triumphantly confirmed over the years, 'as the Chinese watched with increasing incredulity the absence of any American attempt to impede [its] rise', instead contributing to its rapid economic growth, 'without demanding anything resembling full reciprocity'.[37] This might be about to change under newly elected President Trump.

India

By contrast, Hindu civilization developed in the vast Indo-Gangetic plain, protected to a greater extent than China by the Himalayas from the predation of barbarians to the north. As I argued in *The Hindu Equilibrium*, this geographical feature (together with the need to tie down the then scarce labour to land) accounts for the traditional Indian polity, which was notable for its endemic political instability among numerous feuding monarchies and its distinctive social system embodied in the institution of caste. The latter, by making war the trade of professionals, saved the mass of the population from being inducted into the deadly disputes of its changing rulers, while the tradition of paying a certain customary share of the village output as revenue to the current overlord meant that any victor had little incentive to disturb the daily business of its newly acquired subjects. The democratic practices gradually introduced by the British have fit these ancient habits like a glove. The ballot box has replaced the battlefield for the hurly-burly of continuing aristocratic conflict, while the populace accepts with a weary resignation that its rulers will, through various forms of rent-seeking, take a certain share of output to feather their own nests.

But the Himalayan shield, which protected the Indo-Gangetic plain, the Heartland of Northern India, also led to an insular attitude. As Panikkar says, 'For the Hindus the world ended with the Himalayas … Politically India was isolated from the rest of the continent and became introspective in its attitude. There was no appreciation of the point of view of other nations who, to the Hindus, virtually did not exist or were known only by distant rumor'.[38] This introversion had deleterious effects on its political habits. 'In the first place, it gave the Hindus and Indians in general, a sense of contempt for the foreigner.' Secondly, it led to a 'Maginot-line' mentality. 'They were surprised when an invasion took place, as they never looked beyond their mountain barriers'.[39] Thus all the decisive battles took place in the interior of the Indo-Gangetic plain, at Panipat. Finally, notes Panikkar, 'India never developed a proper system of international relations'. Her closest neighbour Afghanistan, except for brief periods, was not organized as a single state, while 'the interest in Persia was limited and China was altogether inaccessible'. So unlike China, which had to deal with the frontier states that continually challenged its security, or Persia, which had to deal continuously with Greece, Rome, and Byzantium, India never developed a continental tradition of being one among a number of other states of varying power. The only doctrine Indian rulers adhered to was that of the *chakravartin*, or great emperor, who brought the whole of India under one control. Once this was achieved and the unity of India reasserted, they never entered into permanent relationships with states outside India.[40]

It was only with the British Raj that India became aware of the importance of international relations and frontiers. Lord Curzon was the chief architect of the Raj's system for protecting its Indian empire. A central concern of every imperial system is to define and protect its frontiers. In his 1907 Romanes Lecture, Lord Curzon discussed the nature of frontiers. For as he wrote, 'frontiers are indeed the razor's edge on which hang suspended the modern issues of war or peace, of life or death to nations'.[41]

Curzon distinguished between natural and artificial frontiers. The former were defined by geographical features, which in order of their degree of impassability were the sea, deserts, mountains, and rivers. Among the artificial barriers, he discusses the modern idea of a 'deliberately neutralized territory, or state or zone … to keep apart two Powers whose contact might provoke collision', as in the guarantee by Britain and Russia 'to the independence and integrity of Persia, creating a buffer state between their two dominions'.[42]

But, for the Indian empire, the modern expedient was a policy of protectorates reminiscent of the Roman empire. Curzon created buffer states to separate the spheres of other great powers. As Curzon says, 'The result in the case of the Indian Empire is probably without precedent, for it gives to Great Britain not a single or double but a three–fold Frontier, (1) the administrative border of British India, (2) the Durand Line, or Frontier of active protection, (3) the Afghan border, which is the outer or advanced strategical Frontier'.[43] Furthermore, 'to the east and north the chain of protectorates is continued in Nepal, Sikkim, and Bhutan'.[44] He did not need to mention India's maritime frontier as this had been breached to acquire India and thereafter secured by Britain's global naval supremacy.

This frontier heritage of the Raj was progressively dismantled with the end of the British empire, and India is still living with the consequences. The first was the Partition, which led to the dismantling of Curzon's three-fold frontier preventing the usual route of invasions from the West. There is now a nuclear-armed irredentist power on the traditional invasion route to the north Indian heartland. Nehru, conscious of the geopolitical requisites of Indian security, even as he agreed to the Partition, believed that the needs of a common defence might lead gradually back to a reintegration of India. 'I have no doubt whatever,' he wrote to K.P.S. Menon in April 1947 'that sooner or later India will have to function as a unified country. Perhaps the best way to reach that stage is to go through some kind of partition now'.[45] As an IFS probationer listening to one of his last speeches in the Lok Sabha in April 1964, I heard him say that 'he continued to cherish the hope that India and Pakistan would be able to come together, much closer, "even constitutionally closer"'. For as he had told the *Washington Post* correspondent in December 1962 '"confederation remains our ultimate goal. Look at Europe, at the Common Market. This is the urge everywhere. There are no two peoples anywhere nearer than those of India and Pakistan, though if we say it, they are alarmed and think we want to swallow them"'.[46] But after sixty years, this hope is still belied. Just as the fall of the Roman empire, with the dismantling of its frontiers, led to centuries of bloody warfare among its successor states—including two world wars—for the mastery of Europe, till Germany by promoting the EU found a peaceful path to establish its dominance, will so too Nehru's hope fructify only after such a bloody denouement?

The second consequence was Tibet. In his little gem on Indian geopolitics, K.M. Panikkar (1959) noted that, it was not the Himalayas themselves with a width of 150 miles, but the Tibetan plateau behind it that provided India's northern shield. With 'an elevation of about 15,000 feet and ... guarded on all four sides by high mountains.... the vast barren upland behind the Himalayas provides India with the most magnificent defense in depth imaginable'.[47] The reason the Himalayan passes opening out to the Indian plains were not penetrated for an attack 'was because the Tibetan plateau was never in the past organized as a great military state.' But he feared that the Chinese Communists might be able to do so. Today, this has come to pass because of Nehru's naiveté in misreading Chinese intentions.[48]

Nehru's appeasement of China began soon after a Chinese attack to liberate Tibet became imminent in the autumn of 1950, never having 'taken seriously suggestions, made even by Panikkar during the civil war in China, of establishing an independent Tibet.'[49] Reluctant to ask for military help from the US or Britain, given India's own military weakness and his policy of non-alignment, Nehru only expressed India's interest in maintaining Tibetan autonomy 'whilst recognizing China's suzerainty over Tibet'. But even this stance was undermined by the official Indian statement in which 'by an oversight the word "sovereignty" had been used instead of "suzerainty" and, though it was later decided to correct this error, the Chinese were never formally informed of this correction', misleading 'the Chinese about India's understanding of the status of Tibet'.[50]

With the Chinese invasion of 1962, the shades finally dropped from Nehru's eyes. He asked for Western military aid and 'sought to strengthen political ties [with the US] even though his hands were tied to some extent by the need to maintain a *public posture* of non-alignment' (emphasis added).[51] But non-alignment was in effect dead, with facilities granted to U-2 planes to land and refuel in India on their way into Tibetan airspace and permission to the

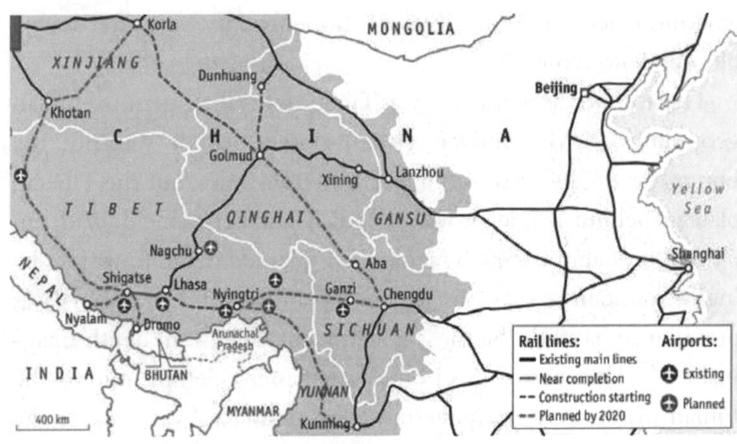

FIGURE 2.2 Chinese Infrastructure in Tibet
Source: 'Taming the West', *Economist*, 21 June 2014.

US to attempt the installation of a remote sensing device operated by a nuclear battery near the peak of Nanda Devi for securing information about the Chinese missile development.

With the breaching of its imperial frontiers and the strategic alliance between the two hostile powers on its western and northern frontiers, an understanding of Chinese intentions, which Nehru had so fatally misjudged, becomes of vital importance for Indian security. No clearer indication of these intentions is provided than by the Chinese infrastructure build-up in Tibet as shown in Figure 2.2.

The Chinese have claimed that the Indian state of Arunachal Pradesh is part of Tibet. Their lightning 1962 attack in this region showed their intentions. Now, the Chinese have six airports on the Tibetan plateau, four of them opened or expanded since 2010, and two more are planned.[52] At the same time, Tibet has been connected to China by various railroads, and more are planned. Two of these from Shigatse (Tibet's second city) 'to the Nepalese and Indian borders, at Nyalam and Dromo, are also planned, to the alarm of the Indian government, which [on 14 June 2014] announced plans to fortify 54 new border posts in Arunachal Pradesh'.[53]

Apart from the seeming strategic advantage it gives China in any future military confrontation with India, this Tibetan infrastructure development is also a part of China's plans to access Tibet's immense natural resources. These are valued 'at 600 billion yuan ($96 billion). One mine in Shethongmon county, near Shigatse, is expected to produce 116m pounds (53m kg) of copper, 190,000 ounces of gold, and 2.4m ounces of silver annually. Mining could make up a third of the region's GDP'.[54] This will allow China to replace the subsidies it currently provides to buy off Tibetan dissent.

But it is doubtful if these policies will succeed in integrating Tibet into mainland China. In 2008, unrest spread across the Tibetan plateau. Through religious control, the erosion of the Tibetan language, intense surveillance, and policies of patriotic education, China has sought to suppress traditional beliefs and customs. More than 130 Tibetans have set fire to themselves in protest between 2009 and 2014. It has become impossible for ordinary Tibetans to travel abroad, and border security has been tightened. A 2014 article in *The Economist* states, 'Before 2008 the number of Tibetans escaping into Nepal each year was as high a 3,000. Last year [2014] only 300 made it out'.[55]

But with the exiled and aging Dalai Lama having relinquished his political role to a civilian government in exile in Dharamshala, India, China's hope that his demise would end the extraterritorial threat to its plans for ending Tibetan resistance to the extinction of their culture and autonomy maybe belied. This, of course, also means that Tibet and the massive Chinese military build-up on its plateau will remain a potential flashpoint for military conflict between the two Asian giants. For India, this historic amnesia about threats across its purportedly impenetrable Himalayan shield has now resulted, as Panikkar feared and Curzon sought to prevent, in a resurgent China creating a military encampment on the Tibetan plateau, which presents a serious and unprecedented security threat from the north.

The Americas

Both North and Latin America shared similar resource endowments, with an abundance of land and scarcity of labour.[56] But very different polities and societies developed in part because of the differing ecologies and religious cosmologies of the two sets of Europeans who colonized the continent—the English Puritans in the north and the Catholic Iberians in the south.

In the subcontinental US (except for the South), grains were the most suitable crops for cultivation. As there are no economies of scale in their production, the small family farm is suitable for their cultivation. It was the gradual westward spread of the family farm that tamed the land-abundant US subcontinent. With no landlord class to support and protected by two vast oceans from the need for a warrior class to fend off nomadic predators from its borders, a unique egalitarian and democratic polity could develop.

By contrast, in the tropical areas of the Americas (including the southern states of the US), the ecology favoured the development of plantation crops like sugar and cotton, which have increasing returns to scale. The same is true, to a lesser extent, of tobacco and coffee.[57] Where climatic conditions in the Americas were suitable for cultivating tropical crops, the use of coerced labour had enormous cost advantages over free labour, which led to great social and economic differentiation in society with large inequalities of income and wealth.

That these factor endowments (including the climate), rather than the cultural differences between the Protestant North and Catholic South, were responsible for the development of these different types of societies in the Americas is illustrated by the case of the Puritan colony of Providence Island, which developed the Caribbean and Latin American pattern of land ownership and settlement rather than the North American one of its co-religionists.[58]

Cultural differences were, however, vital in the different polities that were established in the areas of Iberian and Anglo-Saxon colonization. R.M. Morse, in his essay 'The Heritage of Latin America' (1964), argues that Spain after the re-conquest (from the Moors) was a patrimonial state in which feudalism never developed fully. It was a centralizing state without the decentralization of rights of the manorial system.

The patrimonial rather than feudal states that Latin America inherited were further distinguished by their Catholic lineage. In the Protestant colonies—as Luther succinctly expressed in his 'Open Letter to the Christian Nobility'—the duty of Christians who found themselves in a land populated by pagans was not to convert the pagans but to elect their own religious leaders and to tame or exterminate the American Indians. There was no notion of saving one's neighbour in the Calvinist ethic, as for them only divine grace, not human action, can save man. So they felt no evangelizing mission.[59]

By contrast, evangelism was the public justification given for the Conquest and for the Spanish and Portuguese domination of Latin America. New Spain, even more than its parent state, adopted the neo-Thomism developed by Suarez and his disciples as part of the Catholic Church's revitalization during the Counter-Reformation.[60] Its economic correlate was corporatism.

This political and economic system was an 'enterprise association' in Oakeshott's sense.[61] By contrast, the Protestant colonies were relatively indifferent to religious orthodoxy. In the previously cited work, Luther maintained that in the colonies, if a group of Christians had no priest or bishop among them they should elect one of themselves as a priest, and this election would not only legitimize their authority but also consecrate it. As Paz notes, 'Nothing similar exists in all of Catholic tradition'.[62]

Thus in the Protestant North a pluralist society developed, with the view that 'the world is composed ... of a multitude of unrelated societies, each of them a congregation of similar persons which in finite time and place are ordered by the declarative terms of a compact rather than by common symbolic observances'.[63] This allowed the notion of the state as a 'civil association', in Oakeshott's terms,[64] to develop, with the state as the umpire between many competing interests. This difference in cosmological beliefs explains the observation by political scientists that 'politically, North Americans confine their feuds primarily to selecting officials and debating public policies, but in Latin America feuds are more fundamental ... democrats, authoritarians, and communists ... all insist they know what is best for themselves and their neighbors'.[65] This 'universalism' of the neo-Thomist tradition was further strengthened by the attempt of the Jesuits in Latin America (and in other parts of the world) to promote a religious syncretism which would lead to a 'unification of diverse civilizations and cultures.... under the sign of Rome'.[66,67]

This fundamentalist universalism also provides, in my view, an explanation for the continent-wide swings in political and economic fashions over the last two hundred years.[68] This penchant for universalist ideological beliefs has also meant that there is a continuing dissonance between the Latin American social reality of extreme inequalities, which are the result of its ecological and political heritage, and its Christian cosmological beliefs emphasizing equality—which it, of course, shares with the North. There is no such northern dissonance as, both for ecological and political reasons, a uniquely egalitarian social and political society developed there. Thus, as many Latin American commentators[69] have noted, the historic and continuing inequalities of Latin America make democracy insecure largely, I would argue, because of the dissonance between 'society' and 'cosmology' noted previously.

Russia

The major geographical space that became the Russian empire after the Mongolian Yoke had been removed was the open, flat plain which provided an immense area that was richly endowed with natural resources, and so its relatively small population could survive natural disasters that would have engulfed a more modestly provided polity. As both Napoleon and Hitler found to the cost of their imperial ambitions, 'they could retreat almost endlessly, bide their time almost indefinitely and probe the weaknesses of their adversaries without being destroyed by their own'.[70]

But Russia also suffered from grave geographical disadvantage. It could be attacked from outside. It was remote from the seas and major trade routes. Its land was relatively infertile, situated in an agriculturally marginal area, sometimes extremely cold, and its internal communications were cumbersome. This made mobilizing resources and people difficult, particularly as people with different languages, customs, laws, and religions inhabited this vast territory.[71] The answer to ruling this vast territory became an alliance between a patrimonial monarchy and the Greek Orthodox Church, which had embraced caesaropapism. Unlike its Latin cousin, which came to embrace Augustine's doctrine in the *City of God* that the things which were both God's and Caesar's should be rendered unto God, the Orthodox Church came to accept that both the things which were Caesar's and God's should be rendered unto Caesar.

It was during the rule of Vladimir, who ruled the Kievian state—the precursor of the future Russian empire—from 980 to 1015, that Orthodox Christianity was adopted as the Russian state religion and it has underwritten the autocratic Russian state ever since. With the fall of Constantinople in 1453, Ivan III laid claim to the inheritance of the Kievian state with the assumption of the title of Sovereign of Russia. Having declared its independence from the Mongol's Golden Horde, Moscow became the Third Rome, taking over from Byzantium the centre of Greek Orthodox civilization. This meant that Russia remained outside the Latin Church and Western Christendom, leaving it in relative isolation from the rest of Europe. Thus Russia was separated culturally, religiously, politically, and ideologically from the centre of innovation in Western Europe. It perceived Western Europe—which reciprocated—as something alien and foreign. This led to narrowing cultural exchange and more suspicion and isolationism.[72]

The Mongol invasion of the thirteenth century and the proximity of the great steppes also led Russia and Western Europe to follow different development paths.[73] The major difference was in the form and nature of taxation. By the late fifteenth century, particularly in northwest Europe, safeguarding of private property was being entrenched. Russia, by contrast, had adopted the Mongol tax system based on the mutual responsibilities of communities, which did not represent the interests of taxpayers.[74] Thus by the fifteenth century, Russia was a traditional centralized state, with an omnipotent ruler, subjects with no rights, absence of democratic institutions, weak protection of private property, and absence of independent cities and local self-government.[75]

The invention of gunpowder and the accompanying revolution in military technology led the Russian state to create its own 'gunpowder empire'. It tamed the steppe nomads who had long threatened it by expanding the imperial domain to the south and east. So while during Europe's 'great age of expansion' Western Europeans were creating their ultimately doomed maritime empires, the Russians created one of the largest and longest-lived land-based extra-European empires in Siberia.[76]

This imperial expansion by bringing new fertile lands into Russian control, also led to a further imbalance between land and labour resources. This relative scarcity of labour relative to land was aggravated by the growing military needs of Moscow as it confronted various enemies—the Swedes and Poland–Lithuania in the north and west and the Tatars in the south—from the second half of the fifteenth century. By the middle of the seventeenth century the peasants had been enserfed.

The institution of serfdom tied the peasants down to the land, allowing the state to garner part of the agricultural surplus for its own ends. For as Evesy Domar has argued,[77] free labour, free land, and a non-working upper class cannot coexist, of these any two, but not all three, can coexist. In Russia, with the centralized state and its functionaries and the military to be financed and fed, serfdom was the only answer. Thereafter, the wealth of the landowners was not measured by the number of acres they owned but by the number of 'souls' cultivating their estates.

But this Eastern feudalism was different from its Western cousin, where contractual ties between vassals and their sovereign developed. Russia remained a 'tribute collecting hierarchy' where the noble landowners had total authority over their peasant serfs and the tsar had unchallenged and complete authority over the nobles. Tsar Alexander II finally abolished this system with the emancipation of the serfs in 1861.

This provided the second attempt by Russia, after its divorce from Latin Christendom, to catch up with the cosmologies and technology of the rising West. The first period of catch up was during the reign of Peter the Great. The third was under Stalin in the 1930s. The first two 'pushes' sought to emulate the fruits of the 'individualism' that had led to the growing ascendancy of the West. The third was also based on a Western import: the collectivist body of Marxist thought that had arisen in the late nineteenth century.

The forced industrialization under Stalin was in part an attempt to catch up with the economic ascendancy of the West, but as Yegor Gaidar emphasizes, 'the main feature of socialist industrialization was its militarism: it was not implemented for the sake of improving the lives of the people, as one might assume, but in order to prepare for the war that Stalin considered inevitable'. But it did feed the long-standing Russian imperial dream and desire for great power status. By the late 1960s and early 1970s, the Soviet Union had the largest army in the world and parity of nuclear weapons with the United States.[78] The world was now controlled by a duopoly of superpowers, both seeking global dominance.

The Soviet nemesis came when the easier stage of transforming an agrarian economy to an industrial one had been completed. The shift of rural workers to industry, giving high rates of industrial growth, lasted no more than forty years. From the early 1970s, the economic growth rates in the socialist countries united in the Soviet empire went down.[79] This was in large part because of the economic inefficiencies built into the non-market, centrally planned, autarkic model of development that the Soviet Union had adopted. This finally led to the internal collapse of the Soviet Union in 1991.

In his brilliant book *Collapse of an Empire*,[80] Gaidar provided a detailed account of the political economy leading to the collapse of the Soviet Union and warned against two major dangers facing Russia. The first is post-imperial nostalgia combined with nationalism, which is reminiscent of the German Weimar Republic. The second is what Hla Myint and I have called the 'precious bane' of natural resources.[81] The importance of the latter in explaining the Soviet Union's last two decades is graphically illustrated in the diagram below, which compares how the precious bane led to the similar collapses of both the Soviet and earlier Spanish empire—whose precious bane was the inflow of gold from its colonies in New Spain.[82]

Gaidar's central thesis is that the recent economic history of the Soviet Union can only be understood by the interplay of domestic grain supplies and their prices and those of natural resource intensive exports.

Russia's grain problem goes back to the outcome of the famous 'scissors debate' in 1928–9 which Bukharin and Rykov lost to Stalin.[83] The former argued for what became Deng Xiaoping's reform strategy for China in 1979, preserving peasant farms, financial stability, and market mechanisms under the political control of the CCP. Stalin, instead, chose the path of collectivization and forced industrialization, coercing the kulaks to disgorge grain for the towns, which while working in the short run, condemned Soviet agriculture to stagnation for decades and its industry to endemic inefficiency.

With population growth, the demand for grain outstripped stagnant domestic supplies. By the late 1960s, the Soviet Union had become the world's largest importer of grain and agricultural products. Manufactured exports, being uncompetitive, could not finance these imports. Fortunately, the growing output of oil from Western Siberia and the rise in oil prices in 1973 provided sufficient oil revenues to finance an adequate food supply to the cities. The subsequent economic and political fortunes of the Soviet Union came to depend on the price of oil.

Rising oil revenues in the 1970s allowed adequate grain imports as well as finance for the investments in arms, which led to the military adventure in Afghanistan. But, just as in seventeenth-century Spain, argues Gaidar, the unstable profits from natural resources meant that when these revenues declined, the imperial power had to cede control over its 'colonies' even though it had not suffered any military defeat (see Figure 2.3). By 1990, without the means to pay for the grain imports needed to maintain the

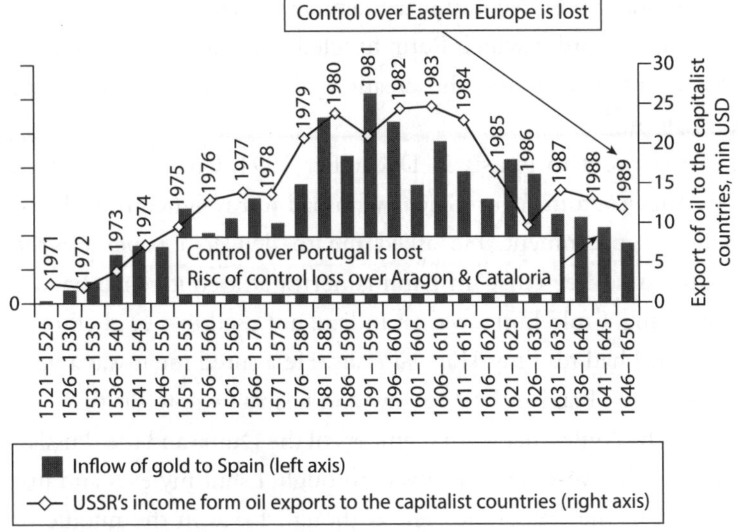

FIGURE 2.3 The Precious Bane and Collapse of Spanish and Soviet Empires
Source: Gaidar (n.d.).

domestic food supply and avoid food riots, the only alternative was to seek loans from the West, which made it clear these were only available if force was not used to maintain the empire. In 1990, when Lithuania declared independence and the Soviets threatened military force to regain control, Gaidar notes, the West sent 'an unambiguous signal: "Do what you will. Please do not bother asking for hundred billion [dollars] of politically motivated loans"'.[84] Thus began the disintegration of the Soviet empire.

On assuming power, Yeltsin was faced with the same problem of feeding the towns that faced the tsarist regime in late 1917, the Provisional Government, and the Bolsheviks. But, unlike his predecessors, he realized that grain from the peasantry could not be taken by force, while, with the deterioration of the oil industry, there was not enough foreign exchange for imports. He opted for price liberalization, enabling farmers to sell their produce at an acceptable price. These necessary but unpopular measures—which formed the big bang economic reforms taken to deal with the revolutionary situation Yeltsin inherited with the collapse of the Soviet state and empire—meant that his popularity slumped.

The ensuing post-revolutionary democratic chaos led to popular demands for order, which Putin fulfilled, leading to his continuing soaring popularity and the creation of a form of authoritarian capitalism.[85]

I first went to Russia in December 1994. I received a call in Los Angeles from Yegor Gaidar who had just resigned from Boris Yeltsin's government. He asked me to deliver a paper on the 'natural resource curse' in Latin America at a conference he was organizing. I told him I was an Indian, not used to a cold climate, and that I had read my *War and Peace.* He assured me it was a very mild winter. I arrived in Moscow and nearly froze to death.

But the conference with members of the Duma and the Russian elite was an eye-opener. Halfway through, I shut my eyes and just listened to the translator. I felt as though I was in the middle of a Chekov or Turgenev play, replete with the nineteenth-century anguished literary and philosophical discussions between modernizers and traditionalists—the keepers of the Russian soul! On my subsequent visits to Russia, I have felt that it has still not resolved this existential dilemma.

There are two questions that have been hotly debated not only in Russia but also by foreign observers.[86] The first is political: can Russia become a liberal democracy? The second is economic: is the Russian economic miracle sustainable? I briefly outline my answers in the light of the arguments in my *Reviving the Invisible Hand* and in my earlier book, *Unintended Consequences.*

The two opposing views on Russia's political future, as seen by Russian observers, were further expounded in Gaidar's recent book[87] and in Dimitri Trenin's study *Getting Russia Right.*[88]

Gaidar rightly argued that the rise in oil prices in the late 1990s had led to solid economic gains. The economic reforms undertaken after the 1998 debt default—to provide a more stable and transparent taxation system (based on the flat tax) and a Stabilization Fund to smooth natural resource rents—had made the economy more resilient to external shocks. But the accompanying order created by Putin's turn towards authoritarianism (which is highly popular) has put demands for political freedom on the back burner. However, Gaidar believed that, with its level of GDP and education, these political demands will arise in the future as they did during the authoritarian Kuomintang regime's tenure in Taiwan.

By contrast, Trenin argued that because of its cosmological beliefs (in my terms), Russia is likely to continue to be ruled by a tsar—the only question being whether he turns out to be a good or bad tsar. Yet, Trenin also felt that the change in Russian material beliefs (in my terms) with the embrace of capitalism is likely to be irreversible because of the undeniable prosperity it has already brought and the increases in popular opulence it promises. I take up the question of Russia's economic prospects in Part III.

Meanwhile, the Russian Orthodox Church has resumed its promotion of caesaropapism ('render unto Caesar not only what are Caesar's but also God's'). Not only did the Patriarch of Moscow urge his flock to vote for Putin, calling his rule a 'miracle of God', but he was caught in a Photoshopping scandal when he tried to doctor a published photograph showing him wearing a $30,000 Breguet watch, purportedly a gift from Putin.

What then of civil society and the middle-class protests after the Duma elections, which so rattled Putin? They are part of a two-hundred-year tradition in which Russia's intellectuals and literary figures come out of their cafes and salons onto the streets to fight an oppressive state apparatus and then, at the first whiff of grapeshot, rush back. The anti-Putin protests followed the same pattern. But, why did they rattle the then president-elect?

In a recent biography, *The Man without a Face: The Unlikely Rise of Vladimir Putin* (2012), Masha Gessen delves into whatever is known about Putin's past and his motives. She describes him growing up in a shabby flat, fierce and vengeful in street fights, and dreaming of joining the KGB. After coming home ten years after his dream was fulfilled, he unexpectedly found himself the de facto tsar of Russia. He used the art of secrecy learnt from his time in the KGB to control personal information to create his own myth. Putin, argues Gessen, wants to turn the country into a supersize model of the KGB, without room for dissent or independent actors.[89]

In a remarkable article in the *Moscow Times* (4 April 2012), Yulia Lataniya, a radio talk show host, reported on Putin's plan after the street disturbances to create a 400,000 men personal National Guard; an institution adopted by dictators in the Middle East and South America, where lower-class men's best option was to join the presidential praetorian guard, which was unconnected to the army or the police. The Haitian President 'Papa Doc' Duvalier's infamous Tonton Macoutes is the most sinister example of this.

Clearly, Russia will have to wait for its spring.

Meanwhile, in his actions against the Ukraine, Putin has clearly overreached himself. With the resulting Western financial sanctions and the slumping oil price, he is facing the familiar problems that Russia's Communist tsars faced with the precious bane. But his geopolitical aim of restoring Russia's great power status is now being compromised by his foolish attempt to look westwards when his putative empire is being nibbled away from the east. Russia faces no threat from its west. Its strategic challenges lie to the south and east.

To the south, the brutal suppression of the rapidly growing Muslim population aspiring to greater autonomy could yet pose a threat to Russian control. These threats will divert scarce resources from other tasks. But it is to the east that there is a growing power vacuum, which is being gradually filled by China. With the growing Chinese population involved in agriculture and trade on the Russian side of the Amur River, it will increasingly look to Beijing for protection. Some analysts have speculated that a few power-hungry local leaders under the sway of Chinese money as well as tactical interventions by the Red Army to protect Chinese citizens could lead to 'The People's Republic of Eastern Siberia' being born.

Instead of recognizing this potent geopolitical challenge, given his obsession with the 'near abroad' in the West and desire to contest US hegemony, Putin has responded to Western sanctions by signing a natural gas export deal on extremely favourable terms with China. If Putin 'continues down this path, Russia will not only slide bit by bit down the dragon's throat, but will have missed one of the great geopolitical opportunities of the last one hundred years'.[90] For if it gave up its obsession with seeing the West as the enemy, Russia has a historic opportunity to not only preserve its sovereignty over natural resource riches but also to contain a revanchist and expansionist China, which is Russia's real long-term security threat.

If Putin were truly a grand strategist, he would see the value of a broad framework agreement with Japan. This deal would provide the financial resources, technology, and expertise for the economic development of Eastern Siberia and the Russian Far East. For Japan, apart from the economic benefits from such a deal, it would also serve its geostrategic interests in containing Chinese ambitions in the South China Sea and, thereafter, the whole of the Pacific.

Is Putin likely to follow this course?[91]

Peninsular Europe and Germany's Virtual Empire

After the collapse of the Roman empire in the fifth century, Peninsular Europe[92] was in its Dark Ages. Covered by ephemeral German kingships, its Scandinavian north was still pagan and tribalized, as were its eastern borders beyond the Elbe. Not till the eleventh century did durable feudal polities arise.[93] By the fifteenth century, with the fall of Constantinople in 1453, powerful kingdoms were formed in Poland, Bohemia, and Hungary. In the middle zone of Europe, from the Baltic to the Mediterranean (part of Mackinder's Heartland), there were no consolidated territorial states but only principalities and city states, among which Venice was supreme in power and empire. In Western and Northern Europe, feudal polities were being converted into national states.[94] In the succeeding contest for the mastery of Europe, the disunited Holy Roman empire of the German principalities, which comprised the German nation, would remain at the centre.

In his masterly history of European geopolitics since the fall of Constantinople,[95] Brendan Simms shows how 'the Holy Roman Empire and its successor states lay at the heart of the European balance of power and the global system it spawned. It was here that the strategic concerns of the great powers intersected. In friendly hands, the area could serve as a decisive force multiplier, in hostile hands it would be a mortal threat'.[96]

Also, Simms notes, the title of 'Holy Roman Emperor' has been sought by all those who wanted political legitimacy to speak for 'Europe' from Henry VIII to Suleiman the Magnificent. Simms writes:

> The echoes in Hitler's 'Third Reich' could not be clearer, and the European Union originated from the same area and in the same spirit, though with a very different content. In short, it has been the unshakeable conviction of European leaders over the past 550 years, even those who had no imperial ambitions themselves, that the struggle for mastery would be decided by or in the Empire and its German successor states.[97]

Following Mackinder, 'whoever controlled Central Europe for any length of time controlled Europe, and whoever controlled all of Europe would ultimately dominate the world'. In the modern era, Simms says,

> Bismarck knew it; the Allied high command in the First World War knew it; Franklin Delano Roosevelt knew it; Stalin knew it; Gorbachev knew it; the Russians who fiercely resisted the eastward expansion of NATO after the fall of the wall know it; and the elites trying to keep the European Union together today for fear of allowing Germany to slip its moorings know it.[98]

A.J.P. Taylor in his *The Course of German History* argued that certain geographical features have influenced German history. 'The Germans are the peoples of the north European plain, the people without a defined natural frontier'. This meant that, 'there is no determined geographic point for German expansion, equally none for German contraction ... Every German frontier is artificial, therefore impermanent; that is the impermanence of German geography'.[99]

The second permanent feature of Germany, says Taylor, is its ethnographical position as people of the middle. 'Always they have had two neighbours and have shown two faces. To their west was the Roman Empire and its heir, French civilization; to their east, the Slavs, new barbarians pressing on the Germans as the Germans pressed on Rome'. To the West, they have shown their benign cultured face (of Mozart, Beethoven, and Goethe), that of the most 'civilized of barbarians, eager to learn, anxious to imitate.' To the East, they have shown a less benign face to the Slavs. 'Ostensibly the defenders of civilization, they have defended it as barbarians'. Hence, argues Taylor, that 'no one can understand the Germans who does not appreciate their anxiety to learn from, and imitate, the West; but equally no one can understand Germans who does not appreciate their determination to exterminate the East'.[100]

Writing just after the Second World War, Taylor commended the fortuitous partition of Germany between the West and the East, which 'reverted by accident to the old device of a divided Germany which saved Europe trouble over many centuries'. Though unlikely to be permanent, he saw it at least partially settling one side of the twofold German problem—'how can the peoples of Europe be secured against repeated bouts of German aggression?' The second side was: 'how can the Germans discover a settled, peaceful form of political existence?'[101] Democracy was the answer, but Taylor was not sanguine about the success of educating the Germans in democracy. However, he held out greater hope that with West German post-war prosperity helped by economic reconstruction with the Marshall Plan and the general prosperity engendered by the post-war economic boom in the West, 'maybe the Germans will forget their imperialist dreams so long as they remain prosperous'.[102] After the Second World War and its disastrous attempts to attain European supremacy in two world wars, West Germany switched to what has been labelled (and what I have previously mentioned as) a 'trading state strategy',[103] to acquire wealth and influence. East Germany as part of the Soviet empire followed its dirigiste economic policies and soon fell back economically from its western capitalist twin.

In the ensuing Cold War, the allies took the risk of establishing a democracy in Western Germany. It was a federal state, and it was disarmed. To prevent the Soviet Union from absorbing the new state by stealth, 'the Basic Law enshrined the right to private property, which effectively excluded any move to a planned economy, and included a strong defense of basic individual rights'. And West Germany's accession to the General Agreement on Tariffs and Trade (GATT), 'ensured that West Germany would not succumb to economic protectionism, but remain integrated into the global economic system'.[104]

Two essential geopolitical questions facing the allies remained. The first was how to thwart Stalin's ambition of incorporating West Germany in his Soviet Empire? The second, how to prevent German revanchism? NATO and the EU were the answers. Though primarily directed against the Soviet Union, NATO was also aimed against German revanchism. Simm says, 'As the British General "Pug" Ismay, the first Secretary General, famously quipped, NATO was designed to keep the Americans in, the Russians out and the Germans down'.[105] But it also marked 'a peacetime geopolitical revolution in Europe: not only was the US (and Canada) now a guarantor of the post-1945 territorial order, but the long-existing community of fate between Europe and North America had been given international legal expression'.[106]

The EU was also born out of the US's desire during the Korean War to harness the growing economic might of Germany to deter the Soviet Union along the Rhine and the Elbe. This raised the question, 'should there be a strong Germany to deter the Soviet Union, with all the potential dangers to her neighbours, or should German strength be diluted through some form of supra-national European political integration in which Germans gave up their sovereignty along with everyone else?' The American preference was for a politically and militarily united Europe 'to stop Stalin, and relieve the burdens on the Americans'.[107]

The first step was the European Coal and Steel Community (ECSC) promoted by the Schumann Plan for the joint administration of German and French coal and steel resources. It was a device to bring the war-making potential of Germany under multilateral control. In effect, Paris wanted to Europeanize Germany, before it Germanized Europe.[108] Thereafter economic integration—but not the political or military integration that the Americans had hoped for—continued as the European Economic Community (EEC) morphed into the EU.

But the collapse of the Soviet Union and the other countries 'of really existing socialism' led to the reunification of Germany in 1990 despite the protests and fears of Gorbachev, Mitterrand, and Margaret Thatcher because of American insistence. Gorbachev acquiesced as 'private assurances were given that NATO would not expand any further eastwards'.[109] Mitterrand thought he had tied down German economic power when he got Chancellor Kohl to agree to the European Exchange Rate Mechanism, the precursor to the Euro. The fears of a united Germany throwing its weight around proved unfounded. As Simms puts it, 'The whole country was afraid of power and indeed of military conflict. "War—that is something we leave to the Americans" was the prevailing view for most of the decade to come'.[110]

The collapse of the Soviet Empire, soon led to the expansion of the EU eastwards, beginning with the Czech Republic, Hungary, Poland, Slovenia, and Slovakia in 1994, after they had satisfied the required political and economic conditions. A year later Austria, Sweden, and Finland joined the EU. Simms says, 'Germany appeared well on the way to surrounding herself with friendly democratic states while simultaneously diluting her national power through ever greater pooling of sovereignty.'[111] The US welcomed this, and President Clinton was determined to complement this integration of the former Warsaw pact with the enlargement of NATO. Membership or prospective membership of the NATO alliance had a powerful stabilizing effect on fragile new democracies in Eastern Europe as did the prospect of joining 'Europe'. Peninsular Europe through this enlargement of the EU and NATO had created a virtual empire with Germany at its core.

By the end of 2010, two flaws in the structure of this virtual empire were threatening its survival and once again raising the German question. The first was the monetary union and the creation of the Euro. In 1999, I gave a lecture at Politeia (a UK think tank)[112], emphasizing this was a misguided project as the Eurozone was not a natural 'optimum currency area' and that without a fiscal-*cum*-political union, a monetary union was unsustainable—a judgment being increasingly borne out by the current travails of the Euro. I had argued that its future depended on a contest between the 'dinosaurs', who saw the Euro as a means to maintain the unreformed labour markets, and generous welfare states of the 'social market economy' and the 'modernizers', who saw the need to create flexible labour markets and to curb the excesses of their burgeoning welfare states. Germany turned out, par excellence, to be a modernizer; the Club Med countries continued to be dinosaurs.

With the worldwide boom and its reformed labour markets, Germany's real wage fell relative to those in the Club Med countries. Tied to the Euro, the traditional route of devaluation to regain competiveness was unavailable. The Club Med countries (and Ireland) ran trade deficits financed by the growing trade surpluses of Germany. This inflow of capital, in turn, fuelled a boom in non-traded services—particularly housing and banking (as their *real* exchange rates rose)[113]—and allowed 'entitlement economies' to flourish. With the global financial crisis of 2008, the unsustainability of the public and private debt (which was foolishly converted into public debt, as in Ireland) accumulated during the earlier boom became manifest. The Club Med countries have an actual or incipient sovereign debt crisis. There is little hope that they can grow themselves out of the crisis even if the private and public holders of their debt take sufficient 'haircuts', as without a devaluation they cannot attain competiveness. The alternative they have been forced to accept is an *internal* devaluation through massive and prolonged deflation to lower their real wages below those of their Northern European peers, particularly Germany. This seems politically unviable in the long run, unless the Germans and the other Northern Europeans are willing to continually subsidise their southern neighbours—an unlikely prospect.

The second lacuna in the creation of the EU's virtual empire was the democracy deficit, which is now also threatening its survival. In a profound irony, while the democratic and economic requirements for entry into the EU were a major attraction to the new entrants as the virtual empire expanded eastwards, one major complaint against the running of the EU by the planners of the European Commission is the democracy deficit. This has come to the fore in the rise of Euroscepticism in many of the constituent nation states of the EU. With the recent success of Brexit, this threatens the European dream of creating an ever closer union till a United States of Europe is established. Tony Judt, in his powerful essay on Europe—*A Grand Illusion?*—traced how this dream was turning into a nightmare.

Judt argues that there were four factors after the end of the war that led to a history of continuing attempts to form an ever closer union.[114] The first was that 'everywhere the organization of society for war paved the way for a presumption that in peacetime there would be comparably high levels of state involvement in everything from social welfare to economic planning'.[115] Furthermore, the Europeans given their common memory of the war

> became collectively, 'defeatist'—not only unwilling to fight one another but wary of any commitment to fighting at all.... They showed a common reluctance to express any confidence in their own state's military capacity, little support for high military expenditure, and no sustained inclination to treat military prowess as measure of national greatness ... The two outstanding exceptions to this pattern are Great Britain and Finland—the only two West European states to have emerged from the Second World War with a creditable military record of which to boast.[116]

This was accentuated by another common experience arising from this defeatist attitude. It was 'the memory of things best forgotten' (except for the British and the Finns). Despite the overblown myths of collective resistance in France, Italy, and Holland, Hitler and his collaborators 'made it impossible henceforth to dwell with comfort upon the past'.[117]

The Cold War was the second factor that facilitated the construction of Europe. The US commitment to Europe, in the form of an increased US military presence and direct economic aid via the Marshall Plan, helped Western Europeans to square the circle; the Cold War forced them into a greater measure of unity and collaboration while sparing them attendant military expenses.[118]

The third factor facilitating the construction of 'Europe' was the post-war economic boom. This was 'catch up' growth, with Western Europe catching up not just to 1939, 1929, or even 1918, but to 1913. West German recovery was particularly rapid. By the last quarter of 1949, the western sectors of Germany had regained their 1936 output level only to see it rise 30 per cent more a year later.[119]

The fourth factor was that this economic boom was accompanied by social and economic reforms postponed for a generation or more. These included the creation of welfare states.

These were singular, unrepeatable transformations. Till 1989, they allowed the continuing incorporation of the relatively wealthier countries of Western Europe into the union. This luck, however, led the European Community and its successor entities to claim that the benefits to the existing members could 'best be ensured by extending to others their own rules and benefits. *This* is the foundation myth of modern Europe—that the European Community was and remains the kernel of a greater, pan-European prospect'.[120]

It was the dissolution of the Soviet empire that opened up the structural faults in the European project. The Eastern Europeans were keen to join the EU, and most were rapidly absorbed in waves into the EU. But this brought the old geographic and religious differences to the fore. It also raised the old cultural distinction between 'the countries west of the Elbe and Leitha rivers [which] have for a long time *been* Europe, whereas the lands to their east are always somehow in the implied process of *becoming*'.[121]

With the slowing down of economic growth in the EU (then the European Communities) from the 1970s, the fiscal burden of the entitlements created by their post-war welfare states had been rising. With its expansion to the poorer East, it would be entitled to the transfers paid for by the richer West. It became clear the bringing of the new members *on the same terms as present ones* was unaffordable.[122] Thus immigration from the poorer parts of Europe and access to the welfare states of the richer countries have become divisive political issues in many Western European countries.[123]

These woes have been worsened by Chancellor Merkel's decision to open German borders to refugees fleeing the wars in the greater Middle East. Absorbing and integrating these migrants is proving to be difficult. It is leading to rescinding the free movement within the EU promised by the Schengen agreement.[124]

All these woes affecting the dream of a United States of Europe have been aggravated by the 2008 Great Crash and the long Great Recession. This has hit the debt-ridden Club Med countries particularly hard. The internal devaluations and fiscal consolidations required for internal and external balance in the counties of the Eurozone has led to massive deflations and the accompanying unbearable rise in unemployment and reductions in GDP. As Germany is at the heart of these woes and (along with the ECB and the IMF) at the heart of imposing these policies of 'austerity' on these countries, old fears of German domination are being openly expressed, as in Greece where there are posters of the German Chancellor Angela Merkel in a Nazi uniform. With Grexit a possibility and Brexit a reality, the myth of 'Europe' is beginning to explode.

Brexit

The UK's decision at the end of June 2016 to exit the EU is merely the capstone of the disintegration of Europe, which, as I mentioned previously, had begun with the ill-fated decision to create the Euro and to insist on open borders within Europe after the incorporation of the former eastern vassals of the Soviet Empire into the EU. But there was a deeper emotional reason that led a slim majority to vote 'Leave' in the UK referendum. This majority said they 'wanted their country back'. This shows the serious deficiency in the European project. Believing that nationalism had caused the internecine wars that had torn Europe apart in two world wars, the European project was to be guided by technocrats in the European Commission who were immune to any stirrings of nationalist passions in the countries comprising the EU. But as we shall see, nationalism remains an important emotion in nearly every country. As Reva Goujon (2016) has rightly noted, when people feel that

> leaving domestic decisions to foreign leaders with completely different priorities, customs, and interests is unfair; that national culture is being eroded by outsiders; that the will of the ordinary should prevail over that of a privileged elite—these are all valid, deep-seated 'emotions' that easily transcend demographic divides. Emotion, in other words, becomes synonymous with nationalism, and some level of nationalism resides in every one of us.[125]

But there was another reason in the sequential construction of the EU that has proved fatal. I along with many of my peers, who in 1975 had voted in a referendum to join the European Common Market, came to see that we had been lied to by the Europhile political elites. While selling us a free trading area they were in fact surreptitiously co-opting us in the creation of a political union, a United States of Europe, a state run by unelected technocrats.

In an important article, Charles Moore, Lady Thatcher's biographer, shows the linguistic sleight of hand that allowed the Eurocrats to change the Common Market that Britain had joined into a Single Market. As Moore notes, while both apply to a free trade area, '"Common" means shared. "Single" means uniform.' Markets allow people to buy and sell freely. When the Eurocrats combined the two words in the 'single market' by the Single European Act signed by Margaret Thatcher, 'it did not create a market: it created a single control of that market' by imposing a single regulatory regime for trading standards on all its members. This Single Regulated Market's 'bosses were—and are—the European Commission, under the European Court of Justice [ECJ].'[126]

With the Maastricht and Lisbon Treaties, the political project of creating a technocratic federal state not subject to democratic control had become clear. The most momentous aspect was the sweeping new powers given to the ECJ by the Lisbon Treaty—not only over commercial disputes but also over defence, foreign affairs, immigration, and home affairs. The EU's charter of fundamental rights was made legally binding at Lisbon, the perfect tool for the ECJ's ambition to advance the cause of European integration. The British government's claim that it had an 'opt out' from this charter was soon brushed aside by the ECJ as having no legal force. Thus a thousand years of the development and application of Britain's Common Law was now to be set aside by the superior powers granted to a court following an alien continental Napoleonic legal code based on 'rights'. It is this central issue of sovereignty—who makes and enforces the laws of the land—which was, for me and for many others, I believe, the central question.

With its exit from the EU, the UK also has the economic opportunity to complete the Thatcher government's supply-side reforms. Nigel Lawson, then Chancellor of the Exchequer, has recently written that judicious deregulation was a critically important part of these reforms. He writes:

> But it was only indigenous UK regulation that we could repeal or reform. And increasingly we are bound by a growing corpus of EU regulation which, so long as we remain in the bloc, we cannot touch. Brexit gives us the opportunity to address this; to make the UK the most dynamic and freest country in the whole of Europe; in a word to finish the job that Margaret Thatcher started.[127]

With no similar regulatory reform on offer in the EU, and tied to the albatross of the Euro, the economic prospects for Europe look bleak.

One other consequence for the UK after Brexit is worth noting. After it joined the European Common Market, it had broken its trading and migration links with the Commonwealth much to the chagrin of the old Commonwealth countries—Australia, Canada, South Africa, and New Zealand. These can now be restored. Australia, Canada, and New Zealand have already offered their trade negotiators to help Britain with Brexit, as its own Board of Trade had been disbanded when the EU took control of all its trade relations through the European Commission. The revival of its Commonwealth links would also be a reaffirmation of a fact I noted in my *In Praise of Empires*—that compared with the first millennium the most important event of the last millennium, which was 'the ascent of the English-speaking peoples to predominance in the world'.[128] A refurbished and recommitted Commonwealth, with some of the fastest growing economies in the world promoting the values of an LIEO, would be the best international organization to partner the US in the emerging confrontation with today's League of Dictators. Perhaps this might also persuade the prodigal son to return to the Commonwealth. This association would be a better replacement for the sclerotic and dysfunctional EU, which the UK is now leaving.

It is difficult to see which way the rump EU will turn. Will it try to complete its political project of 'ever closer union' or will it implode into its constituent nation states? It is difficult to tell. But as long as all the EU countries remain and fulfil their obligations in NATO, there should not be any damage to their security.

What of the geopolitical consequences of the implosion of the EU? The growing fragmentation of 'Europe' is recreating old geopolitical divides. As George Freidman has noted 'the Continent's primordial issue is the relationship between the largely unified but poorer mainland, dominated by Russia, and the wealthier but much more fragmented peninsula. Between Russia and the peninsula lies a borderland that at times has been under the control of Russia or a peninsular power, or more often divided'.[129] This borderland has two tiers: the first and furthest east is the tier comprising Belarus, Ukraine, and parts of the Baltics; the second consists of Poland, the Czech Republic, Slovakia, Hungary, Romania, and Bulgaria.

With the collapse of the Soviet Union, this second tier was absorbed into the EU, providing an attractive option for newly sovereign states in the borderland. This posed a strategic threat to Russia as the Baltics were incorporated in the second tier, and the dividing line and buffer between the peninsula and Russia became Belarus and the Ukraine. Though the Europeans looked upon this integration as benign, the Russians 'saw something they had never seen before: integrated institutions, with ambitions amongst some members to become a federation of nation states that might go well beyond economics.... Without buffers a united Europe with a shifted intent might well pose an existential threat to Russia'.[130] This explains Putin's revanchism.[131]

The fragmentation of the EU after the 2008 Great Recession, with the divergent interests of Germany, Southern Europe, France, and Central and Eastern Europe coming to the fore, has given Russia some geopolitical relief. With the further fragmentation of the EU with Brexit and the rise in the relative power of Russia, the US will once again be drawn into the European fray.

Japan—Its Rise, Fall, and Rise

Japan, is part of the East Asian archipelago: a string of islands and peninsulas stretching from the Aleutians to the Malay Peninsula–Java interface.[132] It is the most important eastern Rimland of Eurasia. It was unique during the nineteenth century Age of Empires in realizing the military threat presented to its sovereignty when Commodore Perry's black ships appeared off its coasts and learning within a few decades to imitate the West to modernize without losing its soul. Its near continental neighbour, by contrast, remained helpless to the Western powers 'carving up the Chinese melon'[133] after the weakness of the Chinese state had been exposed with the mid-nineteenth-century Opium Wars.

The secret of this success and the explanation of Japan's international behaviour since the Meiji Restoration lies in its unique political culture. This was shaped by its geographical isolation in pre-modern times, which created a distinctive culture with a keen sense of uniqueness and independence.[134]

The differences in the Japanese and Chinese polities[135] go back to the Taika reforms and the enactment of the Seventeen Article Constitution in 604 CE. This, in effect, created a constitutional monarchy where the emperor was only the de facto ruler for a brief period. For most of the historical era in Japan, there was dual and, at times, triple government, when political power lay with military chiefs (shoguns), or prime ministers, or chief advisers backed by military power.[136] This system of dual government is in marked contrast to the unified bureaucratic imperial state that has governed China for much of its history. Also, whereas in China established dynasties that had unified the mainland seldom lasted for more than two hundred years, Japan maintained 'a long line of Emperors unbroken for ages eternal' through the political neutralization of the emperor while making him sacred and inviolable.[137] This unbroken, divine imperial house provided the focus for Japanese loyalties and nationalism, which continues to our day.

Despite its geographic isolation, Japan always feared strategic threats from Korea, which was part of the Sinocentric system of vassalage. For Korea has till today been a 'dagger pointed at the heart of Japan'.[138] In the seventh century, an internally disunited Japan feared the expansive Chinese Tang empire's alliance with Japan's old enemy the Korean kingdom of Silla, which had destroyed the other two Korean kingdoms. When in 672 Silla moved to break its ties with the Tang and were moving to seize the entire Korean peninsula, the Japanese felt threatened by the possibility of a unified and hostile Korea. This led the Emperor Tempu to strengthen the state through adoption of Chinese institutions.[139] But this borrowing of a Chinese-style bureaucratic state to increase the power of the government did not lead to the Japanese deferring to Chinese political claims. 'With rare exception, Japanese leaders refused to accept a subordinate position in the Chinese world order centered on the theory of the universal preeminence of the Chinese emperor.'[140]

Given its isolation, pre-modern Japan was mostly a closed society that from the twelfth century developed its own form of feudalism. Till the Tokugawa shogunate (from 1600–1868) imposed its pax, Japan had a weak central authority and political anarchy with competing feudal states. The dynamics of Japan's political system, with feudal states competing for both political and economic power, was similar to the modern state system. In this struggle between fiefs, only the fittest survived. Thus, the six centuries of feudalism in Japan left a legacy of an overriding concern with the maximization of military power as a condition of survival.[141]

Even after the Tokugawa pax was established, the feudal structure was maintained. The continuing competition among the semi-autonomous feudal states[142] was increasingly to maximize their relative economic strength through mercantilist trade policies, 'a zero-sum affair akin to warfare'.[143] This mercantilism was a precursor of the post–Second World War policies that initiated the Japanese 'economic miracle'.

But this did not mean that the military traditions died out. They were preserved and persisted in the outlying domains that overthrew the Tokugawa.[144] Also, M. Morishima has argued[145] that the difference in responses of China and Japan to the appearance of the 'foreign devils' was due to the differences in their respective Confucian elites. The Chinese bureaucracy was learned in the Chinese classics and skilled at poetry and literature. By contrast, Japan's warrior bureaucracy was interested in weaponry and thence science and technology. Unlike the Chinese mandarins who were stolidly opposed to Western science, Japan's leaders—from the Tokugawa shogunate to the Meiji reformers—were enthusiastic about acquiring Western science and the development of modern weapons that it enabled.

Nothing shows the difference between the Confucian Chinese and Japanese to military power more than the mutations in Confucian doctrine in the 'Imperial Rescript to Soldiers and Sailors' in 1882. Morishima argues that,

> in this document five of the Confucian virtues were emphasized—loyalty, ceremony, bravery, faith and frugality…. [By contrast in] Chiang Kai-shek's army the major elements required for a soldiery spirit were wisdom, faith, benevolence, bravery and strictness: in the ancient Silla dynasty of Korea the qualities stipulated of soldiers … were loyalty, filial piety, faith, benevolence and bravery. Only faith and bravery are virtues common to all three countries. Benevolence is common to both China and Korea, but there is no mention of it in the case of Japan. Loyalty is common to both Japan and Korea but does not appear on China's list of virtues…. In Japan it was loyalty rather than benevolence which came to be considered the most important virtue … [loyalty] in conjunction

> with filial piety and duty to one's seniors, formed a trinity of values which regulated within society the hierarchic relationships based on authority, blood ties and age respectively.[146]

Thus whereas 'Chinese Confucianism is … humanistic, Japanese Confucianism is remarkably nationalistic'.[147] As was the case, mutatis mutandis, of non-French Continental Europe,[148] it was in part a reaction against the cultural and, for long periods, military superiority of China vis-à-vis Japan. This defensive Japanese nationalism marked the Japanese response to the West.

Kenneth Pyle[149] has argued that, as with its response to the threat of the resurgent Chinese Tang empire in the seventh century, Japan since the arrival of Commodore Perry's black ships has repeatedly changed its domestic order sweepingly to new configurations of the international order. He identifies five fundamental changes to the international order:

1. The collapse of the Sinocentric system and the establishment of the Western imperialist order in the mid-nineteenth century;
2. The end of the imperialist system after World War I and the beginning of a new American-inspired system worked out through several treaties negotiated at the Washington Conference in 1921–22;
3. The disintegration of this American-led system and the anarchical situation of the 1930s that prompted Japan to create its own East Asian order;
4. Destruction of Japan's new order and the establishment of a new American-dominated liberal order after 1945 and the beginning of the cold war;
5. The end of this cold war bipolar system with the collapse of the Soviet Union in 1989.

Of these, the Japanese reaction to the first of these international orders—the imperialist system—which was the longest lasting from the Treaty of Nanjing in 1842 (which ended the Opium Wars) to the end of World War I, was the most radical in the form of the Meiji Restoration. It created a modern elite from the younger samurai who sought to acquire all the accoutrements of power to overthrow the unequal treaties that Japan had to sign on its opening by the Western powers. They embraced all the institutions of the great powers of the day: western law, banking systems, military organizations, scientific knowledge—all aspects of the imperial powers' civilization became models for the rapid transformation of Japan. Playing by the rules of the game, within the space of a generation, Japan became itself an active participant in the system.[150]

By 1894, these reforms bore fruit when, recognizing the effectiveness of the Japanese legal reforms, the Western powers ended the extraterritorial privileges of the unequal treaties Japan had been forced to sign. Within two weeks of the revision of these unequal treaties, Japan declared war on China, 'its first great foreign adventure in three centuries. The Sino-Japanese War of 1894–95 worked fundamental changes in the imperialist system, bringing Japan fully into the system as a new imperial power'.[151] With its subsequent victory in the Russo-Japanese War of 1904–5, 'Japan had achieved major power status with its own expanding empire'.[152,153]

The Meiji reforming oligarchs through their marriage of Confucianism and Shintoism created a constitutional-monarchic but bureaucratically run state. They also aimed to inoculate curious Japanese minds against potentially subversive foreign ideas such as individualism, liberalism, and democracy. A 'national identity' was invented that allowed power to be explained and justified in new ways and enabled new methods of control to be introduced.[154] The ideology of the 'family state', set out in the 'Imperial Rescript of Soldiers and Sailors' of 1882, was spread through military conscription and indoctrination in the national educational system.

At the same time, the Meiji oligarchs created a political system in which there was no single focus of effective political power. This reflected their reluctance to write a constitution in which power could be concentrated in the hands of a leader legitimized by the emperor, inasmuch as this would have threatened the positions of some of them, and the oligarchy would have disintegrated.[155] Thus 'an uncertain sharing of responsibility was preferred, so that no one person could be pointed out as bearing the ultimate responsibility for decisions. It is obvious that it had the danger of developing into a colossal system of irresponsibility',[156] as was shown by the events leading to the Second World War.

The Meiji oligarchs' propaganda that all politicians were unpatriotic, moved by narrow party and personal self-interest, meant that they could not be trusted to exercise power, and another group had to be found to manage the country. This was the meritocratic bureaucracy created in the early days of the Meiji Restoration. One of the oligarchs, Yamagata Aritomo, made it immune to political meddling by obtaining a 'a personal communication from the emperor—as distinct from a formal Imperial edict—[which] could never be overruled', and which made the Privy Council the guardian of edicts drafted by 'Aritomo relating to examinations, appointments, discipline, dismissal and rankings of the bureaucracy.'[157] Since then, bureaucrats, largely recruited from the Law Department of Tokyo University (Todai), have in effect governed Japan.

This did not lead to the creation of an 'administrative state' as in France.[158] For, reflecting the relationship between insiders and outsiders, the bureaucracy was riven with internal strife, essentially with each intra- or inter-ministerial bureau trying to preserve or expand its turf. With no political overlord to settle or adjudicate these bureaucratic disputes, decisions could only be made by 'consensus', which in many cases was just a polite word for paralysis.

Throughout modern Japanese history, this conservative elite has governed Japan and has never been displaced, even with the US Occupation after the Second World War. It has had an insatiable appetite for power. It has been inclined to side with the powerful. As Pyle notes, 'As a matter of self-interest, Japan has repeatedly allied itself with the dominant ascendant power: with Great Britain from 1902 to 1922, with Germany from 1936 to 1945, and with the United States since 1952.'[159]

Japan has never subscribed to the transcendental abstract universal principles of internationalism, which legitimize the international order in which it has had to live. But after its industrialization, it was dependent on the security of its sea lanes for supplies of energy and raw materials. It could not take a stand on principle. As an island economy dependent on trade, it was left with a feeling of insecurity that engendered a persistently opportunistic foreign policy. 'Resource poor and a late arrival in the modern world, Japan was uniquely vulnerable to shifts in the international system'.[160]

Japan has sought to read the trend of the times. It did not try to change them but to move with them to the nation's advantage. In this, argues Pyle,[161] Japan's actions resemble the advice given by Machiavelli in *The Prince* about dealing with Fortuna: an impersonal external force which rulers cannot manage but against which a far-sighted ruler can make provision, like dykes and banks against the unpredictable force of an impetuous river.[162] Thus having adjusted and accommodated to the imperialist system after the Meiji Restoration, Japan was faced with Woodrow Wilson's new anti-imperialist order after World War I. In the Far East, says Pyle, this consisted of the Washington Treaty system 'with its opposition to balance-of-power principles and its commitment to universal ideals of self-determination and the Open Door. With their characteristic realism, the Japanese leaders accepted the new order in East Asia, even though one of its principal objectives was the containment of Japan'.[163]

In the chaos of the interwar years, as the liberal international economic order imploded, Japan saw other powers forming closed regional spheres. The international system was collapsing, and fascism seemed to be the wave of the future. Pyle says, 'They did not want to miss the bus.' This led to their fateful decision 'to gamble their nation's future by going to war with a country eight or ten times more powerful.'[164] This decision, Japan's leaders claimed, was impelled by the great impersonal forces of Fortuna.

The decision was also characteristic of Japan's concern with rank and honour. Throughout Japanese modern history, it has sought to be recognized as a great power. Dependent for its economic survival on raw materials, particularly oil, it was faced with the choice of facing a US embargo on importing these unless it withdrew from its Chinese incursions. Pyle notes, 'Prime Minister Tojo declared that compliance would render Japan a third-rate power'. This reflected the honorific culture of the samurais in feudal Japan,[165] whose lower reaches were the leaders of the Meiji Restoration. They revitalized this honorific culture, 'but now with a focus on the nation itself, prompting samurai activists to confront the challenge of Western imperialism ... [with] a distinctive "honorific nationalism"'.[166]

With the disastrous end of the campaign to create a Japanese order in 1945, the emperor in his surrender edict referred to Fortuna. He said the surrender was necessary because 'the war situation has developed not necessarily to our advantage, while the trends of the world have all turned against our interest.... It is according to the dictate of time and fate that we have resolved to pave the way for a grand peace'. He enjoined his subjects to 'work with resolution to not fall behind the progress of the world.'[167]

After the Japanese surrender, the US imposed far-reaching reforms to establish democratic government, free trade, collective security, and the rule of law. These had been planned during the war to establish a new worldwide liberal democratic order. But with the failure of the Yalta agreement—which had promised US–Soviet co-operation in establishing such an order—and the beginning of the Cold War, the US had to build a security system in Asia. It reoriented its policy towards Japan's. Instead of demilitarization and reform, it now sought to rebuild Japan as its principal Pacific ally in the Cold War.

While in the immediate aftermath of Japan's surrender its status as one of the traditional great powers had come to an end, the Cold War allowed it an unexpected opportunity to restore its status as a great power within three decades. Japan again showed its skill in adapting to the international system. It adapted to both the liberal democratic order and the Cold War system and focused its efforts single-mindedly on economic growth. It rose now as a trading state within the US-led free trade regime of the liberal democratic order, while being protected by the US security guarantee under the Cold War order.

This Cold War foreign policy pioneered by the post-war Prime Minister Yoshida Shigeru, and referred to as the 'Yoshida Doctrine', is 'best characterized as "mercantile realism"'.[168] The economic nationalism that underlay it was tolerated by the US, which given its Cold War confrontation with the Communist bloc, was keen to see Japanese economic recovery and progress. Also the Occupation authorities, while seeking to ensure that 'the Japanese state would not be motivated by its traditional pursuit of national power' in their wide-ranging revolution of the political structure, made two omissions. They left the pre-war bureaucracy intact, and 'chose to retain the imperial institution and absolve the emperor of any war responsibility'.[169] This allowed the old political system to be resurrected, albeit in a democratic system with popular sovereignty. This meant that unlike the post-war transformation of Germany where the political and emotional links to the Nazi regime were erased, in Japan there has remained the sense that the post-war trials of those held responsible for the war represented victor's justice, and Japan's apologies for its atrocities in the war are viewed by both the sufferers and the perpetrators as at best being half-hearted. This has continued to poison relations with China and Korea.

One of the provisions of the MacArthur constitution, Article 9, renounced rearmament and the right to use force in foreign affairs. This rebounded on the US when—with the Cold War and the Korean War that followed—it was keen to get Japan to participate actively in its alliance system. With the signing of the Mutual Security Act (MSA) in 1951, the US 'pressed Japan to accept military aid for a threefold expansion of its forces from the 110,000 man National Security Force to an army of 350,000'.[170] Yoshida succeeded in gaining the economic aid for Japan's reconstruction while avoiding the strategic obligations in the MSA agreement signed between Japan and the US in March 1954. The Defense Agency was established with a total of 150,000 men responsible for ground, maritime, and air self-defence forces. Using the elite bureaucratic agency—the Cabinet Legislation Bureau—to interpret Article 9 as permitting a military with only 'the minimum necessary' for self-defence if Japan was invaded, the Self-Defense Forces 'could not be sent abroad or participate in any collective defense'.[171] This narrow interpretation of Article 9 of the Yoshida doctrine held for nearly four decades.

Furthermore, with the Chinese nuclear test of October 1964, conservatives in the Liberal Democratic Party (LDP) believed that the Japanese should also have nuclear weapons, as 'exclusion from the "nuclear club" would relegate Japan permanently to second-class status as a power'. But, as a secret study commissioned by Premier Sato in 1966 concluded, Japan's civil nuclear programme gave Japan 'the option of pursuing nuclear weapons, but that it ought not to be exercised in light of both public and international opinion'.[172] The position stated in 1969 in an internal Foreign Ministry document was that 'for the time being, we will maintain the policy of not possessing nuclear weapons. However regardless of joining the NPT or not, we will keep the economic and technical potential for the production of nuclear weapons, while seeing to it that Japan will not be interfered in this regard'. And so it has remained till today, as Japan remains a potential threshold nuclear state.

The centrepiece of the Yoshida Doctrine was to maximize power through the creation of a trading state rather than an armed state.[173] This 'economic realist' strategy was immensely successful. By the 1970s, Japan was a major economic power. In 1972, it overtook he UK and soon after Germany to become the world's second largest economy. By 1990, 'a US government study ... warned that Japan led the United States in five of twelve emerging technologies and was gaining rapidly in five others'.[174] In 1979, a Harvard sociologist wrote a book titled *Japan as Number One*. But then in the late 1980s, with the bursting of a financial bubble, the Japanese economy went into a recession and deflation and has been in an economic coma for nearly two decades. I take up the explanations for this spectacular rise and fall of the Japanese economy in the next part, which also examines its possible resurrection with Abenomics.

This implosion of the Japanese economy coincided with that of the Soviet Union and the end of the Cold War. This cast Japanese foreign and economic policy adrift, particularly with the meteoric rise of China, which in the second decade of the twenty-first century overtook Japan as the second largest economy in the world. This also led to China's military expansion and a growing assertiveness in enforcing its self-proclaimed rights in the East and South China Seas. The rising nationalism in China, Korea, and Southeast Asia posed problems for Japan. The young nationalists in these countries—particularly China and Korea—used Japan's wartime colonial record to fuel their antipathy to Japan. Emotional issues like that of the Korean 'comfort women', the wartime 'rape of Nanking' by Japanese soldiers, and the visits of Japanese leaders to Yaskuni Jinja—the shrine to Japan's war dead—became issues of foreign policy.[175]

As the US–China relationship ebbed and flowed after the Tiananmen Square massacre, the Japanese feared 'both entrapment and abandonment in their relationship with the United States'. But 'in the long run, the alliance is a hedge against an aggressive China dominating the region. The United States and Japan are status quo powers'. It is Beijing that wishes to change the East Asian and ultimately the world order to replace the US as the world hegemon. Japan recognizing the Chinese challenge has, since the end of the Cold War, quietly strengthened its military despite Article 9 of the constitution.

The sabre rattling by the North Koreans by firing a missile in December 2012 allowed Japan to show the formidable conventional capabilities it had developed since the end of the Cold War, when North Korea became the dubious adversary to replace the Soviet Union. It deployed its '$12 billion missile defense system, including land-based Patriot Advanced Capability-3 interceptors and SM-3 equipped-Aegis destroyers, to mainland Japan, Okinawa and locations in the East China Sea and Japan Sea'. These technological advances have led Japan into the US air defence network and associated collective security system. North Korea's nuclear proliferation programme had led to a more proactive defence posture in Japan in 2004. The Defense Agency became a ministry in 2007. This marked the end of post-war Japanese pacifism.[176]

Shinzo Abe succeeded in July 2015 in getting Japan's lower house of parliament to pass new laws which amend Article 9 of the constitution to allow Japanese troops to fight overseas for the first time since the Second World War. Its recent defence white paper, issued five days after the change to Article 9, for the first time explicitly criticizes China's aggressive stance in its maritime disputes in the East and South China Seas. It states that 'China has attempted to change the status quo by force based on its own assertion which is incompatible with the existing order of international law'. Without having any claims of its own in the South China Sea, it objects to China's land reclamation efforts around the Spratly Islands (with pictures which confirm that China is creating infrastructure suitable for military use), which would increase Beijing's influence over the sea lanes handling trillions of dollars of trade every year.[177] How a rearming Japan, increasingly free from the shackles of its pacifist constitution, will confront these unilateral aggressive Chinese maritime moves remains to be seen.

This gradual movement of Japan towards becoming a 'normal' country is being aided by the so-called Heisei generation, which was born in the 1960s and 1970s. They have no living memory of the war or Occupation, and feel no 'guilt or remorse for Japan's imperial past; nor are they defensive about Japan's traditional political values.'[178] The politicians of this generation 'are impatient with the slow pace of change in economic restructuring, in developing a more assertive foreign policy, and in rethinking the constitution.' But they are still elitist, as they are the second or third generation of political dynasties.[179] Shinzo Abe is representative of this generation; Abeconomics and his recent constitutional changes to Article 9 are symptomatic of the changes that are likely. But this Heisei generation, despite its seeming attraction to internationalism, shows no signs of wanting to reverse its deeply embedded insularity. Japan continues to resist foreign direct investment, refugees, and foreign residents.[180] And therein lies the rub.

For Japan faces a demographic challenge if it is to maintain and enhance its economic and military power. It has a rapidly aging and declining population. The elderly population nearly doubled between 1970 and 1990. At the same time the fertility rate among the generation born between 1971 and 1974 saw a dramatic fall. The Japan Statistics Bureau estimates Japan's population

> peaked at 128 million in 2004, and is projected to sink to 115 million in 2030 and to 95 million by 2050. Meanwhile between 2010 and 2050, children under 14 years of age will fall from 13 per cent of the population to less than 9 per cent, while adults over the age of 65 will rise from 23 per cent to 40 per cent. The working age group will fall from 64 per cent to 50 per cent of the population. With the Japanese people vanishing and growing gray, Japan faces the evisceration of its economic, political, and military capabilities.[181]

How Japan copes with its demographic challenges will determine if Japan's potential Phoenix-like rise will occur and be maintained so that it continues to be a great power at least in Asia.

Muslim Societies[182]

The Middle East is sandwiched between the world's two great domains of pastoral nomadism, which has coloured the nature of its polity. Despotism and a disjunction between state and society have been characteristic features of Muslim society since its meteoric rise when it smashed the classical world of antiquity. The reasons for this go back to the origins of Islam.

The first problem arose after Mohammed's death in 632 CE. It concerned political legitimacy; an issue which has subsequently haunted Muslim society and states. The Prophet's decisions while he was alive could be assumed to reflect the will of Allah; so disobedience was tantamount to impiety. But without the Prophet's link with God, how could divine guidance of the community be maintained?[183] This led to the split with the Shias, who claimed that the Ummayad caliphate, which succeeded Mohammed, had usurped power by armed force and perpetuated a hereditary principle supported neither by piety nor tribal custom.[184] The Shias favoured the descendants of Ali, Mohammed's son-in-law. The majority Sunnis came to accept a compromise devised in the

Abbasid caliphate that had replaced the Ummayads, again through bloodshed. This too, in the eyes of true believers, was a usurpation. However, through the Abbasid compromise, the ulama (a body of legal experts) became the true heirs of the Prophet, by expounding the Sacred Law and applying it to particular cases.[185]

It might have been expected that the outcome of these constitutional crises in the early years of the Islamic empire would be a rejection of absolute rule for some form of consultative government.[186] But this was unlikely because of the scale of the Arab conquests. They could not have been held together without an imperial polity. The polity that emerged was, moreover, one in which the unruly tribal conquerors had to be constantly repressed to maintain order. While being dependent for their income upon state handouts,[187] the tribal nobility was unlikely to have much leverage over the caliph. The distribution of public revenues among those entitled to a share became the locus of disputes, not the allocation of the tax burden among those obliged to pay.[188] The leverage exercised by medieval barons against the impoverished sovereigns of Western Europe, which eventually led to these monarchs ceding fiscal and later legislative control to various forms of popular assemblies, was not available to the Arab nobility. Thus despotism would seem to have been unavoidable in the new Islamic polity, however much it went against the religion Mohammed had founded.

The unique aspect of Islamic polities, which allowed long periods of political stability in the millennium since its birth, was the induction of slaves as instruments of government. These *mamlukes* came to form an essential part of the conquest society that Arab arms had created. It was a conquest society where the conquerors clung to their tribal past. Physically separated from their subjects in the equivalent of modern-day military cantonments, the initial Arab conquerors were faced with the problem of administering and maintaining their new-found empire. The caliphs and sultans who ruled the Islamic state were unable to rely on their tribal clansmen, both because of their limited numbers as well as their lack of aptitude for civilian pursuits. From the beginning of the

Arab empire, Islamic rulers turned to an alternative solution to provide themselves with a loyal and trustworthy military and administrative apparatus. It consisted of slaves.

Islam had household slaves but, except for the plantation economy in the marshes of Southern Iraq created under the Abbasids, it had no tradition of slave labour in production. From its earliest conquests, Islam had acquired slaves by capture. Many of them were converted, manumitted, and placed in military and administrative positions. This had a number of benefits for the rulers. These manumitted slaves were normally aliens who were completely dependent on their master. The ruler would bring up his foreign slaves as his children, and they existed in the Muslim polity only through him.[189]

Unlike the feudal soldiers of Europe, who were not aliens but members of their own polity, home-born mamlukes who could have acquired a political commitment to Islam were excluded from the army. This mamluke institution spread throughout the Islamic world. The crack troops of settled rulers from the mid-ninth century into modern times consisted of slaves.

But these servile armies needed to be controlled, as an uncontrolled mamluke army could lead to the total disintegration of the state.[190] This happened frequently in Islamic history. The Ottomans, who in the Islamic tradition relied on the *dervishme*[191] for their administration and armies, broke this trend. The Ottoman sultans managed to maintain control of the state for a considerable period because of their personal qualities, which were tested in fratricidal wars for succession to be master of the Porte and which were in the nature of a Darwinian contest for the survival of the fittest. When this system was replaced for humanitarian reasons by the *kafe*, or system of 'the cage',[192] the quality of the sultans deteriorated and was partly responsible for the Ottoman decline.

Ibn Khaldun[193] praised the mamluke institution as God's gift to save Islam as he saw them as institutionalized tribal conquerors. For him, the medieval polity consisted of a settled non-political society and a tribal state, either imported or imposed by conquest.

Whereas the Chinese in their cyclical view of history looked upon settled rule as the norm and the change of dynasties as resulting from the loss of virtue of an old tired dynasty, the Islamic polity never accepted the notion of settled rule,[194] which Ibn Khaldun considered effeminate. This has been the 'black hole' of the Islamic polity from its inception. It has retained the lineaments of a conquest society.[195]

The only Muslim society that has been able to escape from this despotic heritage is Turkey. But even there, the democracy that was instituted was till recently supervised by the army, which—until it was defanged by Erdoğan's AKP—had vetoed popular Islamist initiatives. In Pakistan, democratic regimes have been toppled by the military, which has proved to be less corrupt than the democrats it replaced.

Ibn Khaldun is also of help in understanding the current turmoil in the Middle East, particularly the latest form that the jihadist threat is taking in the Middle East. His macrohistory of the Islamic polity saw history as punctuated by dynastic cycles linked to tribal conquest. His is a world of dynamic interaction between the barbarian nomadic pastoralists and the sedentary civilizations of the cities. *Asabiyah* (a spirit of solidarity) every now and then throws up a tribe with enough warriors to conquer the cities of the towns of the sedentary civilizations and found a dynasty. But, in time, the luxurious temptations of civilization sap the moral fibres and the asabiyah of the dynasty. With its growing appetite for the fruits of the city, the tribal dynasty bears down harder on the sedentary civilization by raising the burden of taxation and, as its members lose their initial fighting vigour, dependent outsiders are introduced to shore up the dynasty. They or some other tribal group eventually take over, making use of the discontent that the increased burden of taxation has caused among the sedentary population. This pattern was established by the Arab conquests of the seventh century. The conquests of the Seljuk and Ottoman Turks and those of the Saffavids in Iran and the Mughals in India also followed this pattern. And so did the conquests of Ibn Saud, in the mid-nineteenth century, which created Saudi Arabia. Ironically, it itself is now in deadly battle with ISIS and other jihadis who see the house of Saud succumbing to the temptations of 'the city'. The battle between them is repeating the Ibn Khaldun pattern.

The Ottoman Empire had kept a lid on this cycle and provided six hundred years of stability to the region under the Ottoman state, and its various offshoots. But with the collapse of the Ottoman Empire, at the peace imposed at Versailles, as the young Field Marshall Wavell observed, 'after "the war to end all war" they seem to have been pretty successful in Paris in making a "peace to end all peace"'. The post World War I settlement consisted of League of Nations mandates enforcing the Sykes–Picot agreement, which gave the French a mandate covering Syria and Lebanon; and a British mandate over a truncated Palestine incorporating the flawed Balfour Declaration, and British-controlled states created for the Hashemite princes of Iraq and Transjordan. The Kurds, who had been promised their own country by President Wilson, never got their Kurdistan, which was carved up into the successor states of Turkey, Syria, Iraq, and Iran. The subsequent history of the unravelling of this new order need not concern us (but see the excellent history of the creation of the modern Middle East by David Fromkin: *A Peace to End All Peace*), except to note that with the Ba'thist coups in Syria and Iraq and Gaddafi's in Libya, these new authoritarian rulers had succeeded in keeping a lid on the potential challenges from the tribal warriors in their regions.

The Iraq war and its flawed denouement till the 'surge' in 2007 also reopened an ancient fault line in Islam going back to the Battle of Karbala in 683 CE, which created the schism in Islam between the Sunnis and the Shias. With the Sunnis subsequently controlling much of the Arab Middle East and the Shias Iran, the downfall of Saddam led to the empowerment of the Shias in a major Arab state. The Sunni insurgency was put down by US arms, and a new democratic Iraqi state with power sharing among the Shias, Sunnis, and the Kurds was created. But with President Obama's decision to remove US forces from Iraq in 2011 and the installation of the sectarian al-Maliki as the head of the Iraqi government, this post-invasion Iraq is also unravelling.

In Syria, the sectarian civil war between the Alawite Shia Assad regime and various Sunni factions has led to its implosion, with ISIS gaining the upper hand and effectively detaching large parts of eastern Syria for its new caliphate. They have now spilled over into the Sunni regions of Iraq, echoing Ibn Khaldun's nomadic tribal attacks on sedentary civilizations. Meanwhile, the Kurds have grabbed Kirkuk and, in effect, created an autonomous Kurdistan in Iraq. With the Kurds in Syria also having broken away, if those in Turkey can come to some sort of arrangement with Erdoğan, the Kurds could get the state denied them at Versailles. Though, given Erdoğan's actions since the recent attempted recoup, this appears to be unlikely in the immediate future. In Libya, the deposition of Gaddafi and the failure of the successor government to establish its authority over their nominal state has reignited the old Ibn Khaldun cycle with tribal warriors spilling over not only into Libya but also into northern Nigeria and Mali.

Closer to my retirement home in India, the tribal warriors of the badlands of the North-West Frontier Province (NWFP) are now threatening the integrity of Pakistan. This is deeply ironical, for Pakistan as a successor state of the British Raj had, until the Inter-Services Intelligence (ISI) decided to use them as asymmetric proxy warriors, followed the policy established by Lord Curzon when he was the Viceroy of India. He had withdrawn British Indian troops from the fortifications on the Durand line and replaced them by tribal levies to police their own territory and 'after the roads and passes which it is necessary for us to keep open, to pay him and humor him when he behaves, but to lay him out when he does not'.[196] But, the ISI turned the Pathan warriors into the Taliban to fight the Soviet Union in Afghanistan, which has now mutated into the Pakistani Taliban seeking to overthrow the Pakistani state.[197]

All this disorder flows from a number of flawed decisions taken by the previous US president. It was a mistake once Iraq had been pacified by General Petraeus's surge to remove all US troops from Iraq. As an imperial power, the US could have maintained order in the Middle East by its hard fought for military presence, for which—as the preceding British imperial rulers had demonstrated—only a small force with recognized overwhelming military power would have sufficed. Similarly, by announcing a pre-determined date for a withdrawal of US troops from Afghanistan (since suspended), it has opened up the grave danger of disorder in the AfPak region. For in the geopolitical game—much like poker—one never shows one's hand, and, even worse, if one draws 'red lines', he does not show they are written on sand. With Obama's disastrous renunciation of the use of the US's military muscle, the world is faced with the prospect of serious disorder.

Geopolitics of the Contemporary Middle East

There are four major local powers engaged in today's turmoil in the old Mesopotamia—Turkey, Iran, Saudi Arabia, and Israel and the putative Palestinian state. The non-state jihadists of ISIS, having conquered wide swaths of Iraq and Syria and aspiring to be a pan-Islamic State, are adding to the turmoil. It is worth considering the geopolitics of the state actors in turn.

Two of these states are the successors of ancient Mesopotamian empires, Turkey as the successor state of the Ottoman and Byzantine empires, and Iran of the ancient and medieval Sassanid empires. The other states are the creation of the 1918 treaties.

Turkey

The core of the Ottoman Empire—like the Byzantine—was the Sea of Marmara and its two choke points in the Dardanelles and the Bosporus, which make Marmara virtually an inland lake. It links the Aegean and Mediterranean Seas with the Black Sea, granting Turkey full command of any trans-sea trading and providing it with natural, nearby opportunities for expansion.[198] To secure these, it has to secure the mountainous Anatolian peninsula, which today forms a major part of geographical Turkey.

Having secured their rear, the Ottomans expanded along the Danube till they were stopped at Vienna. This move into Eastern Europe provided Turkey with productive land roughly five times the size of that around the Sea of Marmara. But what to do with the peoples they had to conquer during their expansion? They could not be dispossessed and replaced with Turks from Marmara as there were too few. Rather than exploiting these conquered people, the Ottomans integrated them into a multi-ethnic, multi-faith empire. As a *Stratfor* article states, they forged a state that 'granted its conquered people solid reasons to live in, work with, profit by, and even die for the empire'.[199]

With the collapse of the Ottoman Empire, Turkey was left only with its core Marmara region and Anatolia. With further expansion blocked with the establishment of nation states in its former empire, the only avenue left was to develop Anatolia using the capital riches of Marmara to invest in infrastructure, education, and urbanization. As Anatolia developed, it created its own merchant class. It also expanded its presence in Turkey's bureaucracy, police forces, and military. By the 2000s, combined Anatolian cultural and economic strength had matured sufficiently to challenge the heretofore unassailable hold of the Sea of Marmara region on Turkey's political, cultural, economic, and military life.[200] The Marmara region was the cosmopolitan heart of the Ottoman Empire and also of the secular regime imposed by Mustafa Kemal Ataturk; Anatolia remained religious. The disputes between the secular and religious factions represented this geographical divide.

With the victory of Erdoğan's neo-Islamist AKP and its association with the Gülenists, the Islamic faction succeeded in purging the military of the secularists. They were replaced by Gülenists, who had also infiltrated large sections of the police, bureaucracy, and educational institutions. But with Erdoğan's falling out with Gülen—who went into exile in Pennsylvania—and the recent failed coup against Erdoğan purportedly organized by the Gülenists, the two Islamist partners have split irrevocably. Erdoğan is currently in the process of a massive purge of Gülenists from the military, bureaucracy, and educational institutions. How this plays out in maintaining Turkey's military strength and civil institutions still remains to be seen.

Furthermore, while the Turks, under the Ottomans, needed the active local participation of non-Turks in the Danube to develop the land, there was little useful land in Anatolia. This meant that unlike in the Danube, there was little incentive for the Ottomans to grant political or economic concessions to the non-Turkish populations of the region, mainly Kurds and Armenians. So modern Turkey is no longer the multi-ethnic polity it once was. As stated in the *Stratfor* article, 'The Turkish political demographic has shifted, from a proactively multicultural governing system to that of a dominating Turkish supermajority, that attempts to smother minority groups out of public life'.[201]

There is also the deep divide between the secular faction of the Sea of Marmara, which sees the country's future in association with Europe, and the religious faction of Anatolia—currently represented by Erdoğan's AKP—which wants to pursue relations with the Islamic world. But with the EU and NATO blocking the traditional routes for imperial expansion of the secular Marmara group, its power base is confined only to Marmara, which 'was not enough for the Ottomans, and alone it will not be enough for the secularists'.[202]

Meanwhile, with its rising population, the 'religious' Anatolian faction also hope to extend their influence throughout the Islamic world, remembering that the Ottomans also held the caliphate. But, there is little economic gain to be had—despite attempts to forge economic links—as 'the entire Middle East from Morocco to Iran, boasts an economy that is but three-quarters of the size of Spain spread over a region larger than all of Europe'.[203] This region does not provide any hope of fuelling a return to Turkey's past greatness.

Iran

The most important geopolitical fact about Iran is that it is a mountain fortress. To the west, the Zagros Mountains run along Turkey and Iraq's borders, ending nearly at the Straits of Hormuz. At its southern end, there is a marshy plain with the Shatt-Al

Arab dividing Iran from Iraq. This is where most Iranian oilfields are. To the north, are the Elburz Mountains, running along the Caspian to Afghanistan and in whose foothills the capital Tehran is located. These mountains are high enough for skiing near Tehran for many months in the year. The centre of Iran consists of two desert plateaus, which are uninhabited and uninhabitable, with the northern desert consisting of salt plains in which it is easy to break through the salt layer and drown in the mud. This mountain fortress has been impregnable to invasion. Only Alexander and the Mongols have briefly succeeded in breaching it. The 1980–8 Iran–Iraq war showed that an assault from Mesopotamia against the Zagros Mountains will fail (albeit at an enormous cost to the defender).

Iran's seventy-eight million people mostly live in the mountains, though its total area is bigger than France, Germany, and the UK combined, which support two hundred million. Despite its oil, Iran's per capita GDP in purchasing power parity ranks it as the seventy-first country in the world, on par with Panama and Belarus. This is because heavily populated mountain regions are generally poor because of the costs of transportation. This has meant that for its prosperity ever since the first Persian Empire (550–330 BCE), the Iranians have sought to expand westwards into historical Mesopotamia and Babylon—modern-day Iraq. The fertile lands watered by the Tigris and the Euphrates, combined with its own population, were the foundation of Persian power.

As with the Ottoman expansion northwards along the Danube, the Persians needed the co-operation of the conquered people. They allowed them a great deal of autonomy, respected their culture, and made certain that these nations benefitted from the Persian imperial system. Despite this, because they needed this wealth at minimal cost and could not afford to pacify the empire, there has been a limit to Persian and Iranian power as recreating relationships with the inhabitants of modern Iraq has historically been very difficult. For most of its history, domination of the plains by Iran has been impossible. Other imperial powers—Alexandrian

Greece, Rome, the Byzantines, the Ottomans, the British, and the Americans—have either seized the plains or used them as a neutral buffer against the Persians.

The Iranians have also had an internal problem. Mountains allow various distinct ethnic groups to protect themselves against assimilation. Thus though a Muslim state, with a population that is 55 to 60 per cent ethnically Persian, Iran is divided into a large number of ethnic groups. It is also divided between the vastly dominant Shia and the minority Sunnis, who are clustered in three areas of the country—the northeast, the northwest, and the southeast. The greatest threat to Iran has been not a direct assault by a foreign power, but it manipulating the ethnic divisions within Iran. The British based in Iraq were able to do so, as did the Soviets to the point that Iran virtually lost its national sovereignty during World War II. This still resonates. During the current Syrian civil war, witness the testy withdrawal of the permission granted to the Russians to bomb Syria from an Iranian base after this became public.

With the US invasions of Iraq and Afghanistan, the Iranians met with the same problem they faced with the British in the early twentieth century. It is not the threat of a direct invasion, as can be witnessed by the catch phrase of the US military at the time of the Second Gulf War when, after entering and conquering Iraq from the south they could have taken a right turn to invade Iran, but said 'We do deserts, not mountains'.[204] Iran feared that the US would use these platforms to foment ethnic trouble in Iran, and there was some evidence that they did try to do this in the southeast in Baluchistan and among the Arabs in Khuzestan. But with the US withdrawal of its forces from Iraq and imminently from Afghanistan, this threat has gone. Moreover with President Obama's implicit acceptance of Iran as a threshold nuclear power in the deal he signed—and with their Shia beachheads among the Alawites in Syria, Hezbollah in Lebanon, Hamas in Gaza, and with Southern Iraq a virtual Shia protectorate—Iran is on the path of achieving partial regional hegemony.

Various Arab tribes had helped the British against the Ottomans in the First World War, and Britain had promised both the Hashemite Sheriff of Mecca and Ibn Saud's tribe control of the Arabian Peninsula. As both were at daggers drawn, and when Lord Kitchener—misunderstanding the nature of Islam—offered the caliphate to the Hashemite leader, Ibn Saud could not let this happen. For it would mean that he as the leader of the fiercely puritanical Wahhabi sect would have to recognize the spiritual authority of the Sunni ruler of Mecca. He instead conquered the Hejaz and the holy cities of Mecca and Medina in 1924 and drove Hussein bin Ali into exile. The British then created two states for Hussein's sons as a consolation prize, Jordan and Iraq.

Saudi Arabia is bigger than Iran but most of it is desert—the Empty Quarter. Most of the population of twenty-eight million live on the peripheries. Once oil was discovered on its eastern shore by Aramco, Saudi Arabia has become immensely rich. But as the population of its oil region is primarily Shia, the Saudis face a permanent internal threat of subversion by the growing regional Shia power of Iran.

The deal signed by President Franklin Roosevelt with King Ibn Saud in 1945, aboard the US navy ship the *Quincy*, promised US security to the kingdom in exchange for a steady flow of oil to match the Soviet's reserves during the Cold War. But there was always a tension at the heart of the arrangement. On the *Quincy*, Ibn Saud said that he could not compromise on his opposition to a future state for the Jews in the Muslim land of Palestine. The US dilemma ever since has been to reconcile its backing of Israel with its protection of Saudi Arabia.[205]

This Faustian pact began to come unstuck after the 9/11 attack on New York's twin towers. Most of the jihadis turned out to be Saudis. The Saudis have balanced their alliance with the infidels, and the untold riches thereby provided to the dynasty, by maintaining what is the most virulent and medieval form of Islam in their own country and used it to propagate it by financing mosques and Wahhabi preachers around the world. The madrasas in Pakistan that turned out the Taliban are all run by Wahhabis. The charitable donations all believers are required to make, have often—perhaps innocently—ended up in charities that funded al-Qaeda. The Saudis have directly and indirectly funded the mosques and madrasas that preach hatred against the infidels—Jews, Christians, and Hindus—to young minds, who learn little if anything about the modern world. But for the Saudis to eschew or put a stop to this funding would undoubtedly create a Wahhabi backlash in Saudi Arabia and end the dynasty. Osama bin Laden, the scion of a wealthy Saudi family involved in construction contracts for the royal family, also turned his ire against Riyadh after the Saudis allowed US troops to be stationed in the kingdom during the First Gulf War. ISIS, the successor to al-Qaeda, has also announced their desire to march on Mecca as they believe that the Saudi royal family are not true Wahhabis. Disaffected Saudi youth are reported to be flocking to the ISIS banner.

Combined with all these woes is the US shale gas and oil revolution, with the US surpassing Saudi Arabia as the world's biggest oil producer. The US once imported about half its petroleum, much of it from the Persian Gulf. Now only about a quarter comes from abroad, with Canada far outpacing Saudi Arabia as the leading supplier. If the US could do without Saudi oil how credible is unconditional US support?[206]

Then there is the US nuclear deal with Iran. Together with Obama's unwillingness to intervene against the Iranian-backed Assad regime and the US–Iranian joint support for Iraq's Shia-led government, the US seemed to be turning against the Sunni monarchies. This had created an existential crisis for the new aging and ill King Salman. His answer has been to nominate his young son Muhammad bin Salman (known as MBS) as the crown prince and his successor.

MBS has promptly shaken up the Saudi establishment. He has imprisoned most of his rivals in Riyadh's Ritz-Carlton hotel, and concentrated both economic and security policy in his own hands. He has launched a sweeping agenda to wean the kingdom of oil, modernize the economy, and attract foreign investment. He hopes to sell a part of ARAMCO, the state oil company. He has also challenged the Wahabbi establishment by proclaiming his desire to loosen its stifling moral code, and issued a royal decree to allow women to drive.[207]

He is also fighting Iran's proxies in the Yemen and Lebanon and trying to organize a joint alliance against the Saudi's traditional enemy Iran, and even cosying up to Saudi's proclaimed arch enemy Israel. It is early days to know how all this will play out, and whether the impetuous Saudi crown prince will succeed in his ambition. But it appears that events are gearing up for a replay of the battle of Karbala between the Sunnis and Shia's of the Middle East.

Israel and Palestine

In an article on the geopolitics of Israel, George Friedman's global geopolitical intelligence and forecasting company Stratfor[208] provides a fascinating discussion of the common principles of Israeli foreign policy over three thousand years, encompassing the three manifestations of Hebrew and Jewish entities that have existed in the Levant. The first was the invasion led by Joshua in 1200 BCE, which ended with the Babylonian conquest and deportation to Babylon in the early sixth century BCE. The second manifestation began with the defeat of the Babylonians by the Persians in 540 BCE. The nature of this manifestation changed when Greece overran the Persian Empire and Israel in the fourth century BCE and again when the Romans conquered the region in the first century BCE. The third manifestation began with the creation of Israel in 1948 as part of British imperial policy.

Geographically, Israel has consisted of three regions, the northern hill regions from the foothills of Mount Hebron south to Jerusalem, which it has always held; some of the coastal plain from Tel Aviv to Haifa; and the area between Jerusalem and the Jordan River—the West Bank. At times, it has controlled parts of the Negev and the coastal region between the Sinai and Tel Aviv.

Its geography has protected it from most directions, except from Syria in the northeast. The Sinai desert protects it from Egypt unless the Egyptians can move rapidly north through the Sinai to the coastal plain, which is unlikely unless Israel is internally weak or Egypt is acting with an external imperial power. To the south-east of Eilat–Aqaba, the deserts are also impassable. To the east, 20–30 miles east of the Jordan River, is also desert, and the tribes east of the river have not been large enough to penetrate west of the Jordan River. As long as the West Bank is under Israeli control, the East Bank of Jordan has been under the political or military control of Israel. To the direct north, there are no natural buffers between Israel and Lebanon. But this coastal area, heavily dependent on commerce, is not a serious threat and is more concerned with trade by sea to the west in the Mediterranean basin than with its south.

The only geographic threat to Israel is from whoever controls Damascus in the northeast. For Syria, when it is internally secure and does not face a threat from the mountainous region to its north or the unlikely threat from the desert to its east stretching to the Euphrates, will seek access to the sea. This primarily means westwards through Lebanon but could also be south-westwards toward the Levantine coast controlled by Israel. But to do this, Syria has to move through a narrow gap between Mount Hebron and Galilee, which would be difficult given the extended Syrian supply lines involved.

Thus, if internally united, though seemingly lacking strategic depth, Israel can easily defend itself against its neighbours. Its danger lies from external great powers. For its location in the Levant means no Mediterranean power or an Eastern power in Mesopotamia could leave the Levant unoccupied. Israel therefore occupies what might be called the 'convergence zone of the Eastern Hemisphere'. A European power trying to dominate the Mediterranean or expand eastward; an eastern power trying to dominate the space between the Hindu Kush and the Mediterranean; a North African power moving toward the east; or a northern power moving south—all must converge on the eastern coast of the Mediterranean and therefore on Israel. 'Of these,' the *Stratfor* article states, 'the European power and the eastern power must be the most concerned with Israel. For either, there is no choice but to secure it as an anchor'.[209]

Israel is conquered when external powers form empires. Babylon, Persia, Macedonia, Rome, Turkey, and Britain all controlled Israel. After its formation in 1948, modern-day Israel became subject to the Cold War between the US and Soviet Union. From its founding till the Camp David Accords, which re-established the Sinai as the buffer with Egypt, Israel had needed arms to deal with the Egyptian threat from the Sinai. The two Cold War contestants sought to align Israel to their interest by giving it arms. Israel's first patrons were the Soviet Union and then France. The US became an ally in 1967. In its competition with the Soviet Union, it was imperative to help Turkey—controlling the Bosporus—to keep the Russian navy out of the Mediterranean. With the Soviets having armed and gained Syria and Iraq as allies in the late 1950s, Turkey's positon was precarious, with the Soviets pushing from the south and the Syrians and Iraqis from the north. The US used Iran to divert Iraq, Israel, and Syria, thus securing Turkey.

By allying itself with a great power, Israel lost some of its external autonomy but remained autonomous internally. Following the Camp David Accords, modern-day Israel looked very much like traditional Israel. Its real danger remains a great power seeking to dominate the Mediterranean Basin or to occupy the region between Afghanistan and the Mediterranean. After the collapse of the Soviet Union and with Israel allied to the only remaining superpower, this seemed unlikely. But with President Obama's withdrawal from Iraq and Afghanistan and the impetus given to Iran's regional ambitions by the phased withdrawal of the economic sanctions and the implicit recognition of it as a threshold nuclear state from his nuclear accord, there is the sceptre of a possible Iranian empire emerging from the ongoing battle between the Sunnis and Shias in Mesopotamia. No wonder Prime Minister Netanyahu is so distressed by the accord. On the Sunni side, the possibility of ISIS winning this territory is equally unappealing though unlikely. The Saudis are unlikely to have the manpower to maintain their supremacy if they win as part of the Sunni coalition in the next battle of Karbala. The most likely Sunni winner is likely to be Turkey, which will once again—as the Ottomans did—pose a threat to Israel as it seeks to secure an anchor in the eastern Mediterranean for its sea-based neo-Ottoman empire. But all these outcomes will only come into play if the US decides to retire as a superpower.

What of the Palestinians? The tragedy of the Palestinians, as Tim Marshall puts it, is that 'to this day Egypt, Syria, and Jordan are suspicious of Palestinian independence, and if Israel vanished and was replaced by Palestine, all three might make claims to parts of the territory'.[210] This again goes back to the collapse of the Ottoman empire. The Ottomans had considered the area west of the Jordan River bordering the Mediterranean as part of the region of their province of Syria, which they called Filistin. This area became Palestine under the British mandate after the First World War. After the Second World War, when the region was divided up into nation states, Syrians saw Palestine (like the Ottomans) as an integral part of Syria, and 'those we call Palestinians today were simply Syrians. The Syrians have always been uncomfortable with the concept of Palestinian statehood ... and actually invaded Lebanon in the 1970s to destroy the Palestine Liberation Organization (PLO) and Fatah'.[211]

After the 1948 partition of British-administered Palestine, the Jordanians took control of the West Bank and East Jerusalem. They could have, if they wanted, granted the Palestinians an independent state between 1948 and 1967. But they were deeply suspicious of the Palestinians and, in September 1970, fought a bloody war against them forcing the PLO out of Jordan into Lebanon. The Hashemite monarchy of Jordan has seen the Israelis as a guarantor of Jordanian security against the Palestinians.

For the Egyptians, when in the 1948 war they drove into Gaza, they saw it and the Negev as an extension of Sinai and Egypt, not a separate state. Nasser with his vision of a secular, socialist United Arab Republic did not see Palestine as an independent state. This pan-Arab nationalism did see the liberation of Palestine from Israel as a central aim, but not as an independent Palestinian republic. Nasser's pan-Arab nationalism was also aimed at overthrowing the conservative monarchies of the Arabian Peninsula. They then 'saw Arafat, the PLO and the Palestinian movement as a direct threat'.[212]

Palestinian nationalism was thus not only directed against Israel, it also represented a challenge to the Arab world, 'to Syrian nationalism, Jordanian nationalism, to Nasser's vision of a United Arab Republic, to Saudi Arabia's sense of security. If Arafat was the father of Palestinian nationalism, then his enemies were not only the Israelis, but also the Syrians, the Jordanians, the Saudis and—in the end—the Egyptians as well'.[213]

During the 1967 Six Day War, Israel won control of the whole of Jerusalem, the West Bank, and Gaza. It left Gaza in 2005, but large numbers of Israeli settlements remain in the West Bank, which is nominally under the control of the Palestinian authority based in Ramallah. These two parts—Gaza and the West Bank—are the putative Palestine, with its capital in East Jerusalem. The two parts are physically separated by a powerful hostile state—like Pakistan was from 1947 to 1971—and it is unlikely that they can be united, particularly as they have very different economic environments. Gaza is a densely populated city state, incapable today of supporting itself and dependent on foreign aid. The West Bank is largely self-sufficient. In an independent united Palestine, there would be a massive outflow of population from Gaza to the West Bank, which it could not absorb, leading to a buckling of its economy. The only alternative would be mass emigration of Palestinians to seek work in neighbouring economies. Egypt, Syria, and Jordan would be unwilling and unable to absorb these economic migrants—particularly given the current turmoil in Mesopotamia. The only economy that could absorb this surplus Palestinian labour is Israel. 'Security concerns apart, while the Israeli economy might be able to metabolize this labor, it would turn an independent Palestine state into an Israeli economic dependency'.[214]

Thus, 'Palestine cannot survive in a two-state solution. It must therefore seek a more radical outcome—the elimination of

Israel—that it cannot achieve by itself'.[215] It cannot expect any help from Egypt and Jordan, whose interests are in opposition to this Palestinian requirement. Nor, despite its rhetoric, is a risk-averse Saudi Arabia likely to help. Given the ongoing civil wars in Syria and Iraq, these Arab nations cannot be counted on to achieve the Palestinian aims. Nor would the Arab world welcome Iran or Turkey to destroy Israel by deploying forces in their heartland. There would also have to be a global shift that would create a global power that is able to challenge the United States and is motivated to arm the new regimes. It is the divergence of interests between the Palestinians and the existing risk-averse Arab states that has been the Achilles heel of Palestinian nationalism. The Palestinians must defeat Israel to have a state, and to achieve that they must have other Arab states willing to undertake the primary burden of defeating Israel. As this is as unlikely as any Arab victory against a militarily powerful Israel, they are stranded, as they 'can neither live with a two-state solution, nor achieve the destruction of Israel … They are trapped, as Palestinians seemingly destined not to have a Palestine'.[216,217]

Notes

1. Robert D. Kaplan, *The Revenge of Geography: What the Map Tells Us About Coming Conflicts and the Battle Against Fate* (New York: Random House, 2012), p. 26.
2. D. Lal, *Unintended Consequences: The Impact of Factor Endowments, Culture, and Politics on Long Run Economic Performance* (Cambridge Mass: The Ohlin Lectures, MIT Press, 1998), pp. 6–12.
3. Raymond Aron, *Peace and War: A Theory of International Relations* (London: Weidenfeld and Nicolson, 1966), p. 191.
4. Aron, *Peace and War*, p. 192.
5. A.T. Mahan, *The Influence of Sea Power upon History 1660–1783* (New York: Dover Publications, 1987 [1894]).
6. Kaplan, *The Revenge of Geography*, p. 103.
7. Nicholas J. Spykman, *America's Strategy in World Politics: The United States and the Balance of Power* (New Jersey: Transactions Publishers, New Brunswick, 2007 [1942]), p. xvi.

8. Kaplan, *The Revenge of Geography*, p. 104, citing A.T. Mahan, *The Problem of Asia: And Its Effect upon International Policies* (London: Sampson Low, Marston, 1900).
9. Aron, *Peace and War*, p. 193.
10. K.M. Panikkar, *Geographical Factors in Indian History* (Bombay: Bhartiya Vidya Bhavan, 1959), p. 18.
11. Ibid. Also see Lal, *The Hindu Equilibrium: India c 1500 B.C.–2000 A.D.*, Abridged and Revised Edition (Oxford and New York: Oxford University Press, 2005), pp. 22–55.
12. Panikkar, *Geographical Factors in Indian History*, p. 19.
13. Panikkar, *Geographical Factors in Indian History*, pp. 20–1.
14. Panikkar, *Geographical Factors in Indian History*, p. 89.
15. Aron, *Peace and War*, pp. 193–4.
16. Aron, *Peace and War*, p. 208.
17. For details, see the magisterial study by Max Boot, *War Made New: Technology, Warfare, and the Course of History, 1500 to Today* (New York: Gotham Books, 2006), parts IV and V.
18. Panikkar, *Geographical Factors in Indian History*, p. 29.
19. H. Bull, *The Anarchical Society*, Second Edition (New York: Columbia University Press, 1995).
20. G. Liska, *Imperial America: The International Politics of Primacy* (Baltimore: Johns Hopkins Press, 1967).
21. Bull, *The Anarchical Society*, p. 197.
22. Bull, *The Anarchical Society*, p. 196.
23. Kaplan, *The Revenge of Geography*, notes, 'Iran is the Middle East's very own universal joint. Mackinder's pivot, rather than in the Central Asian steppe-land, should be moved to the Iranian plateau just to the south', p. 269.
24. J.K. Fairbank and M. Goodman, *China: A New History* (Cambridge, MA: Harvard University Press), pp. 40–1, cited in Kaplan, *The Revenge of Geography*, p. 258.
25. Aron, *Peace and War*, p. 201.
26. Anthony de Jasay, *The State* (Indianapolis: Liberty Fund, 1985), p. 193.
27. See Lal, *Unintended Consequences: The Impact of Factor Endowments, Culture, and Politics on Long-Run Economic Performance* (Cambridge MA: MIT Press, 1998), p. 15.
28. E. Luttwak, *The Rise of China vs. the Logic of Strategy* (Cambridge, MA: Belknap Press, Harvard University, 2012), p. 24.

29. Luttwak, *The Rise of China vs. the Logic of Strategy*, pp. 26–8.
30. Luttwak, *The Rise of China vs. the Logic of Strategy*, p. 27.
31. Luttwak, *The Rise of China vs. the Logic of Strategy*, p. 28.
32. Luttwak, *The Rise of China vs. the Logic of Strategy*, p. 34.
33. Luttwak, *The Rise of China vs. the Logic of Strategy*, p. 159.
34. See Pamela Crossley, *The Wobbling Pivot: China since 1800* (W. Sussex: Wiley-Blackwell, Chichester, 2010), pp. xii–xiv.
35. Luttwak, *The Rise of China vs. the Logic of Strategy*, p. 91.
36. Luttwak, *The Rise of China vs. the Logic of Strategy*, p. 78.
37. Luttwak, *The Rise of China vs. the Logic of Strategy*, p. 87.
38. Panikkar, *Geographical Factors in Indian History*, p. 68.
39. Pannikar, *Geographical Factors in Indian History*, p. 68.
40. Pannikar, *Geographical Factors in Indian History*, p. 69.
41. George N. Curzon, *Frontiers* (Oxford: Clarendon Press. Facsimile Edition, Elibron Classics, 1907), p. 7.
42. Curzon, *Frontiers*, p. 31.
43. Curzon, *Frontiers*, p. 41.
44. Curzon, *Frontiers*, p. 40.
45. S. Gopal, *Jawaharlal Nehru*, Vol. 1-3 (New Delhi: Oxford University Press, 1975, 1979, 1984), vol. 1, p. 343.
46. Gopal, *Jawaharlal Nehru*, Vol. 3, pp. 261–2.
47. K.M. Panikkar. *Geographical Factors in Indian History* (Bombay, Bhartiya Vidya Bhavan, 1959), p. 70.
48. See the excellent history of Tibet by Lezlee Brown Halper and Stefan Halper, *Tibet: An Unfinished Story* (Gurgaon: Hachette India, 2014), and the recent account of the Sino-Indian war in Bruce Riedel, *JFK's Forgotten Crisis: Tibet, the CIA, and the Sino-Indian War* (Washington D.C.: Brookings, 2015).
49. Gopal, *Jawaharlal Nehru*, Vol. 2, p. 105.
50. Gopal, *Jawaharlal Nehru*, Vol. 2, p. 106.
51. Gopal, *Jawaharlal Nehru*, Vol. 3, p. 254.
52. *The Economist*, 'Taming the West', 21 June 2014, pp. 65–6.
53. *The Economist*, 'Taming the West', p. 65.
54. *The Economist*, 'Taming the West', p. 66.
55. *The Economist*, 'Taming the West', p. 65.
56. Whereas much of development economics is concerned with the development of labour-surplus economies of relevance for Asia, it is the economics of land-abundant, labour-scarce economies that is relevant for the New World. A seminal essay by E. Domar, 'The

Causes of Slavery or Serfdom: A Hypothesis', *Journal of Economic History*, 30 (1) (March 1970): 18–32, provides the necessary theoretical framework. He cogently argues that in a land-abundant economy, free labour, free land, and a non-working upper class cannot coexist. Any two can but not all three. This is because with free land, there are no diminishing returns to labour, whose marginal and average product are the same. If employers seek to hire labour, they will have to pay a wage equal to this common marginal and average product of labour, leaving no surplus rents from land for the employer. Hence the agrarian form that will emerge is family-labour-based farms, as any form of hired labour or tenancy will be unprofitable and landlords—who have to depend on one or the other—cannot exist. Next, suppose the government wants to create an independent class of landowners and grants the chosen few sole rights of ownership to land. In order to provide the landlords with a surplus some means will have to be found to restrict or abolish the peasant's freedom to move. Various forms of tying labour down to land—serfdom, slavery, and the caste-system—emerged in the great agrarian civilizations. Finally, as the labour force expands from natural increase and/or migration and land becomes scarce relative to labour, diminishing returns to labour appear, with labour's marginal product being less than its average. This allows landlords to obtain the rents from land and an assured labour supply to work it through hired labour paid its marginal product, or else through various forms of tenancy.

57. See Stanley Engerman and Ken Sokoloff, 'Factor Endowments, Institutions and Differential Paths of Growth Among the New World Economies: A View from Economic Historians of the United States', NBER Working Paper, Historical Paper No. 66, Cambridge, MA (1994); Barbara l. Solow, 'Slavery and Colonization' in Solow (ed.), *Slavery and the Rise of the Atlantic Economies* (Cambridge: Cambridge University Press, 1991). For evidence on the substantial economies in producing certain crops on large slave plantations see Fogel, *Without Consent or Contract* (New York: Norton, 1989); Engerman, 'Contract Labor, Sugar, and Technology in the 19th Century', *Journal of Economic History*, 43 (1983); and Deer, *The History of Sugar* (London: Chapman and Hall, 1949).
58. See Kupperman, *Providence Island, 1630–1641: The Other Puritan Colony* (Cambridge: Cambridge University Press, 1993).
59. Paz, *Sor Juana* (Cambridge, MA: Harvard University Press, 1988), p. 27.

60. This provided an ideological justification for the patrimonial state. 'Religious orthodoxy was the foundation of the political system.' Paz, *Sor Juana*, p. 30.
61. Michael Oakeshott, *Morality and Politics in Modern Europe* (New Haven: Yale, 1993). p. 92. Also see M. Oakeshott, *On Human Conduct* (New York: Oxford University Press, 1991), pp. 272–4.
62. Paz, *Sor Juana*, p. 27.
63. R.M. Morse, 'The Heritage of Latin America' in L. Hartz (ed.), *The Founding of New Societies* (New York: Harcourt, Brace and World, 1964), p. 152.
64. Oakeshott, *On Human Conduct*, p. 243, and Oakeshott, *Morality and Politics in Modern Europe*, p. 49.
65. G. Wynia, *The Politics of Latin American Development*, Second Edition (Cambridge: Cambridge University Press, 1990 [1984]), p. 3.
66. Paz, *Sor Juana*, p. 39.
67. But there was also a more positive aspect of the common Catholic culture of Latin America. As compared with North America, the Latins succeeded 'socially' where the US 'failed'. This was in part due to the common Catholic culture, which left their personal and social mores closer to the 'communalist' ones of the other great ancient civilizations than those based on the new-fangled 'individualism' of their Protestant brethren.
68. Claudio Veliz, *The New World of the Gothic Fox* (Berkeley: University of California Press, 1994), contrasts this universalism of Latin America with the greater tolerance of diversity in beliefs in North America as between the Baroque hedgehogs of the South and the Gothic foxes of the North in the New World, reflecting Archilochus's maxim, 'the fox knows many things, but the hedgehog knows only one thing', quoted in Isiah Berlin, *Russian Thinkers* (London, 1978).
69. See for instance J.G. Castaneda, *The Mexican Shock* (New York: New Press, 1995).
70. Geoffrey Hosking, 'Power and People in Russia', in K. Almqvist and A. Linklater (eds), *On Russia* (Stockholm: Axel and Margaret Ax:son Johnson Foundation, 2009), p. 79.
71. Hosking, 'Power and People in Russia', p. 79.
72. Yegor Gaidar, *Russia: A Long View* (Cambridge, MA: MIT Press, 2012), p. 148.
73. Gaidar, *Russia*, p. 148.
74. Gaidar, *Russia*, pp. 149–50.

75. Gaidar, *Russia*, p. 151.
76. F. Fernando-Armesto, *Millennium: A History of the Last Thousand Years* (New York: Scribner, 1995), p. 94.
77. Domar, 'The Causes of Slavery or Serfdom'. Also see Lal, *Unintended Consequences*, Appendix 4, pp. 191–5.
78. Gaidar, *Russia: A Long View*, pp. 179–80.
79. Gaidar, *Russia–a Long View*, p. 181.
80. Gaidar, *Collapse of an Empire: Lessons for Modern Russia* (Washington D.C.: Brookings, 2007). Also see, Gaidar (n.d.), 'Public Expectations and Trust towards the Government: Post-Revolution Stabilization and Its Discontents', available at www.iet.ru/files/persona/gaidar/un_en.htm, accessed on 2 October 2017.
81. Lal and Myint, *The Political Economy of Poverty, Equity, and Growth: A Comparative Study* (Oxford: Clarendon Press, 1964), p. 394.
82. This is from the earlier paper by Gaidar (n.d.), 'Public Expectations and Trust towards the Government'.
83. See A. Erlich, *The Soviet Industrialization Debate, 1924–1928* (Cambridge, MA: Harvard, 1967).
84. Gaidar, 'Public Expectations and Trust towards the Government', p. 7.
85. There is an ongoing debate, not least in China, whether the Soviet Union could have followed the example of the CCP, with gradualist economic liberalization, and avoided the economic and social dislocations of the big bang economic reforms that Yeltsin and Gaidar undertook. As I noted in Lal, *Unintended Consequences* (p. 168), unlike China, most of the labour force in the Soviet Union was in state-owned industrial enterprises. The rural big bang, which allowed China to convert the majority of state employees into private owner-operators, was not feasible in the Soviet Union. The only route was to dismantle the state-owned industrial enterprises in an industrial big bang.
86. These were the central questions discussed by a galaxy of scholars and politicians from Russia and Europe at the 2008 Engelsburg seminar 'On Russia' organized by the Swedish Axel and Margaret Ax:son Johnson Foundation.
87. Gaidar, *Collapse of an Empire.*
88. D.V. Trenin, *Getting Russia Right* (Washington: Carnegie Endowment, 2007).
89. See Amy Knight, 'Getting Away with Murder', *Times Literary Supplement* (5 August 2016): 12–13. In the article, Knight reviews

a book on the poisoning in London in 2006 of the former FSB officer Alexander Litvinenko and the subsequent report of a UK High Court judge, Sir Robert Owen, providing overwhelming evidence of the Kremlin's complicity. Luke Harding, whose book (*A Very Expensive Poison*, London: Guardian Faber) Knight is reviewing, argues that a report by Litvinenko for a British consulting firm on Viktor Ivanov, a close Putin ally, was the motive for his murder. But Knight argues though this dossier was explosive, 'it was probably not what triggered the decision to kill Litvinenko.' Citing information provided by Marina Litvinenko, she writes, Litvinenko, 'waged a public campaign to discredit Putin,' and his allegations that Putin was a pedophile hit a raw spot.

90. William A. Nitze, 'Putin's Failure as a Grand Strategist', *The Globalist*, 9 July 2014, available at www.theglobalist.com/putins-failure-as-a-grand-strategist, accessed on 28 September 2017.
91. In a recent article *The Economist* ('Enter Tsar Vladimir', 28 October 2017, pp. 21–7) argues that Putin has emerged as a 21st century tsar. Like the tsars, he has monopolized politics and the commanding heights of the economy 'by evoking the symbols of tsarist rule and appealing to cultural stereotypes'. Thus, 'the beginning of his second term in 2004 was marked by an inauguration which closely resembled a coronation'. Like with the tsars, 'economic and political resources are made available not by the rule of law but by privileges granted from above'. Politically this is a tsarist system where the boyars (clients) are beholden to their patron (the tsar). This patron-client system 'cannot be imposed on a society, but requires its consent, which in turn depends on the popularity of the chief patron'. Putin has achieved this by appearing 'both as a defender of his people against a greedy and predatory elite, and the defender of the elite against a popular uprising'. This makes the succession to Tsar Putin crucial. With no bloodline to depend upon, it is more likely that his rule will 'be followed by chaos, weakness and conflict'. Few people in Russia's elite, including Putin's ideologue Alexander Dugin 'expect the succession to happen constitutionally or peacefully'.
92. This is the term used by George Friedman. It denotes 'the region that lies to the west of a line drawn from St. Petersburg to Rostov-on-Don, becoming increasingly narrow until it reaches Iberia and the Atlantic Ocean. France, Germany and Italy are on the peninsula, with its river systems of the Danube and the Rhine. To the line's east

is Russia. Whereas the peninsula is intimately connected with the oceans and is therefore engaged in global trade, Russia is landlocked. It is very much land constrained, with its distant ports on the Pacific, the Turkish straits its only outlet to the Mediterranean, and its Baltic and Arctic access hampered by ice and weather. On the peninsula, particularly as you move west, no one is more than a few hundred miles from the sea. Russia, reliant upon land transportation, which is more difficult and expensive than maritime trade, tends to be substantially poorer than the peninsula'. See 'A Net Assessment of Europe', *Geopolitical Weekly*, Stratfor.com, 26 May 2015.

93. Finer, *The History of Government* (Oxford: Oxford University Press, 1997), Vol. 2, p. 620.
94. Finer, *The History of Government*, p. 621.
95. Brendan Simms, *Europe: The Struggle for Supremacy 1453 to the Present* (London: Allen Lane, 2013).
96. Simms, *Europe*, p. 4.
97. Simms, *Europe*, p. 5.
98. Simms, *Europe*, p. 5.
99. A.J.P. Taylor, *The Course of German History* (London: Routledge Classics, 2001 [1945]), p. 2.
100. Taylor, *The Course of German History*, pp. 2–3.
101. Taylor, *The Course of German History* p. xix.
102. Taylor, *The Course of German History*, p. xx.
103. See Rosecrance, *The Rise of the Trading State: Commerce and Conquest in the Modern World* (New York: Basic Books, 1986).
104. Simms, *Europe*, p. 402.
105. Simms, *Europe*, p. 402.
106. Simms, *Europe*, p. 402.
107. Simms, *Europe*, p. 410.
108. Simms, *Europe*, p. 411.
109. Simms, *Europe*, p. 488.
110. Simms, *Europe*, p. 490.
111. Simms, *Europe*, p. 495.
112. Lal, 'EMU and Globalization', Policy Series No. 17, *Politeia*, London (1999), reprinted as Ch. 4 in my *Lost Causes: The Retreat from Classical Liberalism* (London: Biteback Publishing, 2012).
113. The real exchange rate is the relative price of non-traded to traded goods. With a fixed exchange rate, the price of traded goods is fixed, and any adjustment required to bring the balance of payments

into equilibrium can only come about through a change in the price of non-traded goods. Devaluation (which raises the nominal exchange rate) by raising the price of traded goods reduces the real exchange rate. With a fixed exchange rate, as in the Euro zone, the required fall in the real exchange rate to cure a balance of payments deficit can only be brought about through a fall in the price of non-traded goods, which, if labour markets are rigid, can only be brought about by deflation, which lowers real wages (as labour costs predominate in the price of nontraded goods). For an accessible explication of this modern theory of balance of payments adjustment see Lal, *Reviving the Invisible Hand: The Case for Classical Liberalism in the Twenty-First Century* (Princeton, N.J.: Princeton University Press, 2006), Ch. 4.

114. Tony Judt argues that the history of the formation of ever closer union 'has followed a consistent pattern: the real or apparent logic of mutual economic advantage not sufficing to account for the complexity of its formal arrangements, there has been involved a sort of ontological ethic of political community; projected backward, the latter is then adduced to account for the gains made thus far and to justify further unificatory efforts. It is hard to resist recalling George Santayana's definition of fanaticism: redoubling your efforts when you have forgotten your aim'. Judt, *A Grand Illusion? An Essay on Europe* (New York: New York University Press, 2011), pp. 23–4.
115. Judt, *A Grand Illusion?,* p. 25.
116. Judt, *A Grand Illusion?,* p. 26.
117. Judt, *A Grand Illusion?,* p. 27.
118. Judt, *A Grand Illusion?,* pp. 28–9.
119. Judt, *A Grand Illusion?,* p. 31.
120. Judt, *A Grand Illusion?,* p. 41.
121. Judt, *A Grand Illusion?,* p. 60.
122. Judt, *A Grand Illusion?,* p. 92.
123. Judt, *A Grand Illusion?,* p. 121.
124. See D. Lal, 'The Migrant Crisis and "Europe"', *Business Standard* (January 2016).
125. Reva Goujon, 'The Global Order After the Brexit', *Stratfor Worldview,* (28 June 2016), available at https://www.stratfor.com/weekly/global-order-after-brexit?newer=1477472433&topics=284, accessed on 2 Oct 2017.

126. Charles Moore, 'David Cameron's Beloved Single Market is a Ploy Designed to Subjugate British Rights', *The Telegraph*, 10 June 2016, available at www.telegraph.co.uk/news/2016/06/10/david-cameron-is-offering-voters-a-false-choice-in-the-eu-refere, accessed on 28 September 2017.
127. Nigel Lawson, 'Thanks to Brexit We Can Finish the Thatcher Revolution', *FT* (3–4 September 2016).
128. D. Lal, *In Praise of Empires* (New York: Palgrave Macmillan, 2004), p. 45.
129. George Friedman, 'A Net Assessment of Europe', Geopolitical Weekly, *Stratfor Worldview* (26 May 2015), available at https://worldview.stratfor.com/weekly/net-assessment-europe, accessed on 2 October 2017.
130. George Friedman, 'A Net Assessment of Europe'.
131. George Friedman, 'A Net Assessment of Europe', also notes that 'the single institution that historically has held Russia together was the secret police. In a poor country with minimal communications and transportation, the ability of the center to control the periphery is limited. The institution of an efficient security system would be indispensable if Russia were to avoid fragmentation. From the Czars onward, this is what held Russia together. It followed that when the first shock of collapse passed, the security apparatus would reassert itself and stabilize Russia. It was not the personality of Vladimir Putin that mattered; if not for him, another leader would have emerged and halted the disintegration of the Russian economy and polity'.
132. George Friedman, 'A Net Assessment of East Asia', Geopolitical Weekly, *Stratfor Worldview* (16 June 2015a), available at https://worldview.stratfor.com/article/net-assessment-east-asia, accessed on 2 October 2017.
133. This is the evocative phrase used by Harold Vinacke, *A History of the Far East in Modern Times* (London: Allen and Unwin, London, 1950) to label his Chapter VII concerning the battle of Chinese concessions among the Western powers. This was the textbook for the course in Far Eastern history I took for my BA honours degree at St. Stephen's College, Delhi, in the late 1950s.
134. Kenneth B. Pyle, *Japan Rising: The Resurgence of Japanese Power and Purpose* (New York: Public Affairs, 2007), notes that 'Japan is separated from the Eurasian continent by more than 100 miles, five times the distance that separated England across the Straits of Dover from the

Continent. This distance across the Korean Straits is surpassed by the 450 miles of open seas that lie between Japan and China'.

135. The discussion of these cultural differences is based on my Lal, *Unintended Consequences*, Ch. 8.
136. M. Morishima, *Why Has Japan 'Succeeded'?* (Cambridge: Cambridge University Press, 1982), p. 9.
137. Morishima, *Why Has Japan 'Succeeded'?*, p. 35.
138. Vinacke, *A History of the Far East in Modern Times,* p. 137.
139. Pyle, *Japan Rising*, p. 36.
140. Pyle, *Japan Rising*, p. 36.
141. Pyle, *Japan Rising*, p. 39.
142. This has led to what I described in *Unintended Consequences* (p. 148) as the cultural difference between US-type individualism and Japanese communalism. The latter consists of 'loyalties' to concentric in-groups from the family to the firm to the nation. Behaviour within in-groups is based on status differentials and the proper deference that is entailed. Shame is the emotion evinced by the social maladroitness of 'losing face'. But the distinction made between in-groups and out-groups leads to competition between in-groups, which can be fierce and quite brutal. They are only tempered if there is a possibility of future harmonious relationships. Hence the apocryphal story of how someone pushing a fellow passenger to get into a subway stopped dead in his tracks when he turned and looked at this attacker and said, 'I know you'.
143. Pyle, *Japan Rising*, p. 40.
144. Pyle, *Japan Rising*, p. 40.
145. Morishima, *Why Has Japan 'Succeeded'?*, p. 16.
146. Morishima, *Why Has Japan 'Succeeded'?*, p. 9.
147. Morishima, *Why Has Japan 'Succeeded'?*, p. 9.
148. See Lal, *The Repressed Economy* (Aldershot: Edward Elgar, 1993).
149. Pyle, *Japan Rising*, p. 28.
150. Pyle, *Japan Rising*, p. 30.
151. Pyle, *Japan Rising*, p. 87.
152. Pyle, *Japan Rising*, p. 30.
153. The following few paragraphs are based on Lal, *Unintended Consequences*, pp. 146–7.
154. For this creation of Japan's modern myths see C. Gluck, *Japan's Modern Myths: Ideology in the Late Meiji period* (Princeton, N.J.: Princeton University Press, 1985).

155. See Karel van Wolferen, *The Enigma of Japanese Power* (London: Macmillan, 1989), p. 302.
156. Maruyama Masao, 'Japanese Thought', *Journal of Social and Political Ideas in Japan* (7 April 1964): 44. Cited in van Wolferen, *The Enigma of Japanese Power*, p. 302.
157. van Wolferen, *The Enigma of Japanese Power*, p. 307.
158. As Van Wolferen, *The Enigma of Japanese Power,* notes, pp. 155–7.
159. Pyle, *Japan Rising*, p. 44.
160. Pyle, *Japan Rising*, p. 49.
161. Pyle, *Japan Rising*, p. 51.
162. Niccolo Machiavelli, *The Prince* (New York: Modern Library, 1950 [1530]), Ch. 25.
163. Pyle, *Japan Rising*, p. 54.
164. Pyle, *Japan Rising*, p. 54.
165. Pyle, *Japan Rising*, p. 63. Their codes of conduct 'exalted fighting and were based on physical strength, martial skills, valor power, and self-discipline. Individual warriors were attentive, even obsessed, with preserving their reputation, self-esteem and personal dignity. This concern for reputation was ritually embodied in *seppuku*, or disembowelment in self-willed death.'
166. Pyle, *Japan Rising*, p. 64. He also quotes Togo Shigenori, the Japanese foreign minister in 1941, who wrote in his autobiography, 'Entirely aside from the question whether Japan had or had not been engaged in aggression, had or had not invaded foreign rights and interests, it has to be remembered that she was struggling to maintain her status as a Great Power' (p. 65).
167. Pyle, *Japan Rising*, pp. 54–5.
168. Pyle, *Japan Rising*, p. 212.
169. Pyle, *Japan Rising*, p. 220. In a biography of emperor Hirohito based on recent research, *Hirohito and the Making of Modern Japan* (New York: Harper Collins Perennial, 2001), Herbert P. Bix shows that far from being a mere figurehead 'Hirohito and his key advisers participated, directly and decisively, as an independent force in policy making.... From the very outset Hirohito was a dynamic emperor, but paradoxically also one who projected the defensive image of a passive monarch ... The history of the Showa monarchy and its justifying ideologies up to 1945 is inextricably bound up with the history of Japanese militarism and fascism; after that date it is connected to efforts by ruling elites to roll back occupation

reforms, check Japanese pacifism, and regain the attributes of a great-power state', pp. 11–13.

170. Pyle, *Japan Rising*, p. 234.
171. Pyle, *Japan Rising*, p. 236.
172. Pyle, *Japan Rising*, p. 251.
173. Pyle, *Japan Rising*, p. 256.
174. Pyle, *Japan Rising*, p. 262.
175. See the excellent discussion of these historical disputes, and their veracity, which continue to poison relations between Japan, China, and Korea in Bill Emmott, *Rivals: How the Power Struggle between China, India and Japan Will Shape the Next Decade* (London: Penguin Books, 2009), Ch. 7. Also see Rana Mitter, *China's War with Japan 1937–1945* (London: Penguin Books, 2014).
176. *Stratfor Worldview*, 'The Geopolitics of Japan: An Island Power Adrift', Analysis (18 March 2012), available at https://worldview.stratfor.com/article/geopolitics-japan-island-power-adrift, accessed on 2 October 2017.
177. Leo Lewis, 'Tokyo Steps Up Warnings over Beijing's Maritime Ambitions', *Financial Times* (22 July 2015).
178. Pyle, *Japan Rising*, p. 358.
179. Pyle, *Japan Rising*, p. 360.
180. Pyle, *Japan Rising*, p. 361.
181. *Stratfor Worldview*, 'The Driving Forces Behind Japan's Remilitarization', Analysis (17 December 2012b), available at https://worldview.stratfor.com/article/driving-forces-behind-japans-remilitarization, accessed on 2 October 2017.
182. This section is based on Lal, *Unintended Consequences*, Ch. 4.
183. Patricia Crone and Michael Cook, *Hagarism: The Making of the Islamic World* (Cambridge: Cambridge University Press, 1977), p. 77.
184. W.H. McNeill, *The Rise of the West* (Chicago: Chicago University Press, 1963), p. 431.
185. McNeill, *The Rise of the West*, p. 434.
186. As Crone and Hinds, *God's Caliph: Religious Authority in the First Centuries of Islam* (Cambridge: Cambridge University Press, 1986), note, 'the widespread insistence that the caliphate be elective (al-amr shura), the endless demands for observance of "kitab" and "sunna", good practice and past models, the constant objections to Ummayad fiscal policy, and the general readiness to take up arms against what was perceived to be oppressive rule, all these features

indicative of so stubborn a determination to keep government under control that one might have credited it with a good chance of success' (p. 106).

187. 'The caliph Umar created a system of stipends for those who had fought in the cause of Islam, regulated according to priority of conversion and service, and this reinforced the cohesion of the ruling elite, or at least their separation from those they ruled', Albert Hourani, *A History of the Arab Peoples* (Cambridge, MA: Harvard University Press, 1991), p. 24. In today's Saudi Arabia, the practice continues in modern form, where, besides the vast army of princes living off their stipends as members of the family of Saud, much of the military hardware that has been acquired is to provide honorific posts to the favoured (with stipends attached), rather than to serve any useful military purpose. See S. Schwartz, *The Two Faces of Islam* (New York: Doubleday, 2002).
188. Hourani, 'Taxing Times Loom for Offshore Rules', *Financial Times* (13 June 2014), p. 107.
189. 'It was this extinction of the soldier's autonomy which made the mamluke such a superb instrument of his master's will when it was coupled with personal obedience.... Mamlukes were not supposed to think, but to ride horses, they were designed not to be a military elite, but military automata', Crone, *Slaves on Horses: The Evolution of the Islamic Polity* (Cambridge: Cambridge University Press, 1980), p. 79.
190. Crone, *Slaves on Horses*, p. 84.
191. These were Christian children obtained as a 'tax' on Christian subjects in the Balkans, who were then enslaved, converted, and manumitted and who rose to high office under the Ottomans.
192. With the end of parricide, unelevated princes from among a sultan's children were confined in gilded 'cages' in the harem. 'Here pillow talk was of politics, and women and eunuchs conspired to secure the succession for a potential patron from among the sultan's brood ... For much of the 17th century the effective chief executives of the state were queen-mothers who knew nothing first hand of the world beyond the harem walls', Fernando-Armesto, *Millennium*, p. 239.
193. Ibn Khaldun, *The Muqaddimah: An Introduction to History* (Princeton, N.J.: Princeton University Press, 1967 [1379]).
194. See Crone and Hinds, *God's Caliph*; F. Rahman, *Islam* (Chicago: University of Chicago Press, 1979).

195. The 'handing over of power to slaves ... to the more or less complete exclusion of the free males of the community bespeaks a moral gap of such dimensions that within the great civilizations it has been found only in one'. Crone, *Slaves on Horses*, p. 81.
196. David Gilmour, *Curzon: Imperial Statesman* (New York: Farrar, Strauss and Giroux, 1994), p. 196.
197. In this context, it may be useful to outline the policy first laid down by Lord Curzon for pacifying the turbulent and anarchic tribes in the NWFP of imperial India. This has been described by Akbar Ahmad, an anthropologist and former political officer in this region and currently a Professor in American University, as the 'Waziristan model', Akbar Ahmed, *The Thistle and the Drone: How America's War On Terror Became a Global War on Tribal Islam* (Washington D.C.: Brookings, 2013).

This model is based on three distinct but overlapping, mutually interdependent, though often opposed, sources of authority: (1) the tribal elder; (2) the religious leader; and (3) the political agent (PA) representing the central government, who was the key to Britain's tribal administration. The PAs came from an elite within the prestigious ICS (Indian Civil Service), the Indian Political Service. As Ahmed writes 'If India was the jewel in the crown, this elite cadre was the sparkle in the jewel'. (*The Thistle and the Drone*, p. 60) For in Curzon's vision, the first line of defence of the northwest frontier were not British regiments but British political officers.

Another point Ahmed makes is the betrayal of these tribal societies by the British—and later the Americans—with the resulting disorder spilling over into widespread Middle East. The tribes—who are fiercely resistant to modernization—have taken to terror as an instrument of defiance against the modernizing 'centre', whether national or international. Ten of the nineteen hijackers who perpetrated the 9/11 atrocities were from the Asir tribes of Yemen; as was Osama bin Laden. Their actions, argues Ahmed, resulted from a breakdown and mutation of tribal and Islamic systems. They justified their terrorist acts by 'combining the notion of revenge from their tribal background with Islamic concepts [like jihad] applied carelessly and with abandon' (*The Thistle and the Drone*, pp. 106–7).

Curzon, who had a deep understanding of tribal cultures, understood the constant threat that the tribes of the NWFP posed for the Indian government. He is reported to have said 'no patchwork scheme will settle the Waziristan problem. Not until the military steam-roller has passed over the country from end to end, will there be peace. But I do not want to be the person to start that machine' (cited by Ahmed, *The Thistle and the Drone*, p. 59).

198. *Stratfor Worldview*, 'The Geopolitics of Turkey: Searching for More', Analysis (3 August 2010), available at https://worldview.stratfor.com/article/geopolitics-turkey-searching-more, accessed on 2 October 2017.
199. *Stratfor Worldview*, 'The Geopolitics of Turkey'.
200. *Stratfor Worldview*, 'The Geopolitics of Turkey'.
201. *Stratfor Worldview*, 'The Geopolitics of Turkey'.
202. *Stratfor Worldview*, 'The Geopolitics of Turkey'.
203. *Stratfor Worldview*, 'The Geopolitics of Turkey'.
204. Tim Marshall, *Prisoners of Geography* (London: Elliot and Thompson, 2015).
205. G. Kepel, 'The Jihad in Search of a Cause', *Financial Times* (2 September 2002).
206. Hugh Eakin, 'Shifting Sands in Saudi', *The Spectator* (6 June 2015), p. 19.
207. See *The Economist,* 'All the Crown Prince's Men', 11 September 2017, pp. 42–3.
208. *Stratfor Worldview*, 'The Geopolitics of Israel: Biblical and Modern', Analysis (14 May 2011).
209. *Stratfor Worldview*, 'The Geopolitics of Israel'
210. Marshall, *Prisoners of Geography*, p. 142.
211. *Stratfor Worldview*, 'The Geopolitics of the Palestinians', Analysis (15 May 2011a), available at https://worldview.stratfor.com/article/geopolitics-palestinians-0, accessed on 2 October 2017.
212. *Stratfor Worldview*, 'The Geopolitics of the Palestinians.'
213. *Stratfor Worldview*, 'The Geopolitics of the Palestinians'.
214. *Stratfor Worldview*, 'The Geopolitics of the Palestinians'.
215. *Stratfor Worldview*, 'The Geopolitics of the Palestinians'.
216. *Stratfor Worldview*, 'The Geopolitics of the Palestinians'.
217. I had believed, until a trip to Jerusalem in October 2014, that a two-state solution was the only solution to the Arab-Israeli conflict. My doubts after this trip are outlined in Lal, 'The Future of Palestine', *Business Standard*, (19 December 2014), available at http://www.business-standard.com/article/opinion/deepak-lal-the-future-of-palestine-114121901411_1.html, accessed on 2 October 2017.

CHAPTER THREE

Ideologies

There are three competing intellectual traditions in international relations. Hedley Bull defines these as 'the Hobbesian or realist tradition, which views international politics as a state of war; the Kantian or universalist tradition, which sees at work in international politics a potential community of mankind; and the Grotian or internationalist tradition, which views international politics as taking place within an international society'.[1] In my *In Praise of Empires*, I had explained at length that I found the Kantian idealist position unpersuasive. The book largely accepted the Hobbesian or realist position. But there is something to be said about considering Grotius's view, which allows us to examine the distinction between an international system and an international society, whose members (unlike a neutral mechanistic system) do have shared common beliefs—which can be described as a common ideology.[2]

After Fukuyama's declaration of 'the end of history' with the implosion of the Soviet Union and its satellites, it also seemed possible to declare the end of ideology with the global victory of the market over the plan. This would lead in time, through the prosperity engendered by participating in a US-led global liberal economic order, to even those states recalcitrant to the charms of liberal democracy—like China and Russia—eventually embracing the ideology of the West. So, there would in effect be a global international society of common values. But it has not turned out this way. The two former Communist giants—China and Russia—who were the ideological foes of the West during the Cold War have now adopted variants of a nationalistic authoritarian ideology in opposition to the US-led liberal political and economic order. What will the consequences for international order be?

Bull discusses the evolution of the notion of international society from its European religious origins to the post–French Revolution view of a global or world society. This divided humankind into civilized humanity, barbarous humanity, and savage humanity. According to Bull:

> Civilized humanity comprised the nations of Europe and the Americas, which were entitled to full recognition as members of international society. Barbarous humanity comprised the independent states of Asia—Turkey, Persia, Siam, China and Japan—which were entitled to partial recognition. And savage humanity was the rest of mankind, which stood beyond the pale of the society of states, although it was entitled to 'natural or human recognition'.[3]

With decolonization, and non-European states in a majority in the United Nations, this Eurocentric view of international society representing a particular culture or civilization is unacceptable. But in the ensuing confused babble about the 'international community', there does remain the reality of an international society in some sense.[4]

Today, even if hypocritical, states do try and justify their reasons for going to war. The latest example is Putin's annexation of Crimea. Bull says, 'The state which alleges a just cause, even one it does not itself believe in, is at least acknowledging that it owes other states an explanation, in terms of rules they accept.'[5] While the 'element of international society is real … the elements of a [Hobbesian] state of war and transnational loyalties and divisions are also real, and to reify the first element, or to speak as if it annulled the second and third, is an illusion.'[6]

On Grotius's view of an international society of states, there is neither a complete conflict of interest among states, as on the Hobbesian view, nor a complete identity of interest, as on the Kantian view. Instead, it resembles a game that is partly distributive but also partly productive. The particular international activity on Grotius's view is best typified not by war between states, but trade or, more generally, economic and social intercourse between one country and another.[7]

But, in the unipolar post–Cold War period, when the US had achieved a global ascendancy comparable to Rome, it also sought to convert the global system of states it dominated into a global society conforming to its own habits of the heart. In my *In Praise of Empires*, I had warned against this form of hubris, as the values enshrined in the US Constitution were not universally accepted, and attempts to enforce them through military means would evoke nationalist resistance, which would threaten the US ascendancy.[8] To see this, it is best to examine the potentially most globally acceptable of these values, summarized in the shorthand 'democracy', and then go on to examine the idea of 'nationalism' which seems robustly alive despite repeated predictions of its demise. This leads on to another divide, which many had come to believe was dead. It is the divide created by various forms of religious fundamentalisms, leading to various forms of disorder in the world. This belies the hope that the Enlightenment value of secularism embodied in the US-led LIEO would also be globalized.

Democracy

The late Oxford political scientist Samuel Finer in his magisterial three-volume *The History of Government* underlined the two great revolutions that had created the modern state.

The first was the American Revolution, which introduced six inventions in the theory of government:

> The notion of a Constitutional Assembly to frame a constitution; the written constitution; the Bill of Rights which this constitution embodies; the use of courts of law … to signal breaches of the

> constitution and exercise powers to obstruct or cancel them; the so-called Separation of Powers on different lines from the 'mixed' constitutions of the past; and finally, true Federalism.[9]

Of these, the separation of powers was in a sense pre-eminent in maintaining liberty. For, as James Madison said in *The Federalist Papers (no. 4)*:

> The great security against a gradual concentration of the several powers in the same department consists in giving those in each department the necessary means and personal motives to resist encroachments of the others. Ambition must be made to counteract ambition.... It may be a reflection on human nature that such devices should be necessary to control the abuses of government. But what is government itself but the greatest of all reflections on human nature?[10]

Finer sums up the legacy of the American Revolution as having 'shown how political power may be bridled; and it has stood for two centuries as the ultimate exercise in law-boundedness. This is a formidable achievement'.[11]

The French Revolution is Finer's second great revolution, creating the lineaments of the modern state. I take up its legacy in the next section on nationalism.

By the late nineteenth century, the slowly rolling Industrial Revolution affected the social structure and thereby the nature of Western democracies. With the extension of the franchise, the 'notables' were replaced by organized mass parties based on the new agenda of politics: that of capital versus labour. Voters came to belong to their parties, and the act of voting became an expression of identity and commitment rather than a mere choice between competing alternatives. In this golden age of mass democracy, the constitutional principles that ensured government *for* the people were conjoined with mass electoral representation, which also ensured government *by* the people.

In its unipolar moment, the proclaimed aim of US foreign policy became to promote democracy around the world. This was based on the belief that democracy's spread through the exercise of American power would lead to the Kantian democratic peace envisaged by many liberals. In examining whether this is feasible and not merely desirable, we need to make a crucial distinction between political, civil, and economic liberty (freedom). It is now a commonplace that economic liberty as embodied in the market is a necessary condition for development.[12] Similarly, civil liberty as embodied in the Common Law, with its impartial enforcement of contracts, is also required for development. These two 'freedoms' are better described—as John Stuart Mill did in *On Liberty*—as the general liberty to undertake any *feasible* action that does not harm others or break any obligations. But is political liberty, as entailed by democracy, also necessary to promote and sustain economic and civil liberties?[13]

Democracy and Liberty

The constitutional liberalism that arose in Britain and was adopted by America sought above all to protect civil and religious liberties. Representative democracy arose along with the growth of constitutional liberalism. This meant that not only were there free and fair elections in these countries but also the rule of law and the protection of the liberties of free speech, assembly, religion, and property. But while this liberalism (which was the end) and representative democracy (a particular means) were conjoined in the rise of the West, they need not be.

For, even if there are free and fair elections—which is the sine qua non of democracy—the result may turn out to be *illiberal democracy*,[14] where the majority instead of upholding these liberal civil and economic liberties suppresses them. In many Muslim countries the autocrats are more liberal than the mass of the people, and if the majority had their way, they would undoubtedly suppress even the liberties currently granted by the autocrats. This has been demonstrated by the outcomes of the Arab Spring. Wordsworth extolled the French Revolution, saying, 'Bliss was it in that dawn to be alive/But to be young was very heaven!' A sentiment widely echoed around the world in the aftermath of the revolutionary victory in Egypt's Tahrir Square in 2011. But the 'natural history of revolutions' should have warned us that if the

Egyptian revolution follows the course of many of its predecessors, this euphoria might soon turn to ashes—as it has.

On Revolutions

Glued to the television as the revolution in Egypt unfolded, I was reminded once again about an old book by Crane Brinton: *The Anatomy of Revolution*,[15] which I had to read before I went up to Oxford to read Politics, Philosophy, and Economics (PPE) in 1960. Having surveyed the pattern of events in the English Revolution of 1640, the American Revolution of 1776, the French Revolution of 1789, and the Russian Revolution of 1917, Brinton produced what has been called, as I mentioned earlier, 'the natural history of revolutions'.[16] It still remains the best guide to the pattern of events that unfold in a revolution. It has been added to by other social scientists to explain why revolutions arise. Can these analyses help us explain the Egyptian revolution and its possible outcomes?

It is a common myth to assume that it is the wretched of the earth who resort to revolutions. I was in China in May 1991 while visiting Peking University, which was plastered with hoardings and signs by the students who were in the vanguard of the democracy movement in Tiananmen Square. Their main grievance was, in part, the heavy-handed surveillance of their personal lives by the authorities and, more seriously, the system of job assignment by the state. They did not want democracy as understood in the West but the civil and personal liberties associated with it. Seeing the similar young, educated middle-class protestors in Tahrir Square on my TV screen, I could not help have a sense of déjà vu. In both cases, the revolutions arose not at a time of economic stagnation but during a period in which the economy had been doing well. However, the economic gains—particularly high-income employment—were widely perceived to be going to the 'well connected' in corrupt regimes. But in both cases, it was rising food prices hurting a much larger swathe of the population, which fuelled support for the young urban revolutionaries.

The pattern of revolutionary outcomes depends crucially upon whether the ancien régime has the will to assert its authority. This depends on its control of the military. In 1991, the Chinese had to deploy a unit stationed on its borders to fire on the demonstrators, as the units around Beijing were not willing to kill them. In Tahrir Square, the military was, again, unwilling to fire on the people from whom its soldiers were recruited. In China, where the government did not blink, the revolution ended in a bloody massacre. In Egypt, with the army maintaining the peace between anti- and pro-Mubarak groups, the revolutionaries succeeded in toppling Mubarak. But, with the military still calling the shots, it was difficult to predict whether the constitutional democracy they promised would be delivered.

In fact, the pattern identified by Brinton repeated itself as it had when the Shah was toppled in Khomeini's Iran in 1979. Brinton argued that having toppled the ancien régime, the internal conflicts among the hitherto united revolutionaries emerge: conservatives seeking to minimize change (like the military council which ran Egypt); radicals seeking widespread change (like the Muslim Brotherhood and Gama'a Islamiyya); and moderates (like most of the young demonstrators) seeking a middle course.

Moderate reformers are the first group to seize power, like Bazargan in Iran. Meanwhile, the radicals attempt to compete with the moderates through mass-mobilization, for example, the Jacobins competing with the moderate Girondin assembly in France, or the moderate executive in Iran competing with the mass-mobilizing mullahs led by Khomeini. The next stage, which is not inevitable, comes when the radicals supplant the moderates: the Jacobins in France, the mullahs in Iran, and the Muslim Brotherhood in Egypt. Typically, moderates have a better chance of staying in power if the revolution is against a colonial power but less so when their enemy is an internal ancien régime. Both the American Revolution of 1776 and the Glorious English Revolution of 1688 bucked this trend.

The next stage is 'Thermidor', or the imposition of order by terror: Robespierre's rule by guillotine; Stalin's Gulag; Mao's

Cultural Revolution; the summary executions of opponents under Khomeini; and the attempt by Morsi on winning the election to take control of the organs of the state, which threatened the moderates in Egypt. The struggle between moderates and radicals, often exacerbated by external threats, sees the rise of a Napoleonic figure. Iran seemed close to this stage with the Revolutionary Guards being the power behind Ahmadinejad and Khamenei's throne. In Egypt, General Sisi's coup against the Muslim Brotherhood's President Morsi in 2013 fits the pattern. In the final phase, the radicals are defeated or dead, and the moderates return to power, seeking economic progress rather than political change—as with the fall of Robespierre, in Khrushchev's denunciation of Stalin, and Deng's of Mao's Gang of Four. Iran has still not reached this stage, but Egypt under Sisi, with the Brotherhood decimated by imprisonment and being outlawed, may now be in this stage.

Given the time it takes for a successful revolution to run its course and the serious danger of contagion facing the other authoritarian Arab regimes, the Middle East is going to be a volatile, disorderly, and dangerous place for some time to come. Yemen, Jordan, Syria, and Saudi Arabia are particularly at risk. The first stage in Brinton's natural history of revolutions is already in place. The regimes have lost the support of their intellectuals, with the educated young demanding reform. Faced with the risk of revolution, the rulers have offered some reforms—the second stage in Brinton's natural history. But these are likely to be too little, too late.

With their burgeoning youthful populations, the roots of the crisis facing the Arab dictators is their failure to generate economic growth through creating open market economies by adopting liberal economic reforms. Predatory elites have garnered the fruits of the limited reforms that have been undertaken.

There is, however, a deeper reason why democracy has turned out to be the enemy of liberty in the Arab world. In an important book based on personal interviews with many of the dramatis personae and the periodic public opinion polls carried out by the

Pew Foundation, Shadi Hamid has documented that in democratic elections political Islam has a dominant resonance.[17] The failure of Islam to separate the public from the private sphere—as liberal democracies do in line with J.S. Mill's prescriptions in his essay *On Liberty*—means the devout, who are the main foot soldiers of political Islam, inevitably want to enforce sharia laws, which are a gross infringement of personal liberties.[18] As Hamid shows, this is the major raison d'être for each of the parties of political Islam. But, given the opposition of the autocrats (and the substantial minority of liberals), who are more attuned to the cause of liberties in the private sphere, proponents of political Islam moderate these demands in the hope of persuading their autocratic rulers (and the outside world) that they have changed their spots and would abide by liberal norms in the personal sphere if elections were held.

Hamid also shows that, as seen in case after case in the Arab world, increasing repression leads to greater moderation by the Islamists. When elections are allowed, they are then torn between the demands of their devout electorate to enforce sharia and the minority of liberals and moderates who demand their ouster for this very reason, if necessary by military means, as happened in Egypt. So, ironically, elections lead to *illiberal* democracies in these countries, and the supporters of liberal democracy both in the country and outside are left with a Hobson's choice of supporting either illiberal democracy or a form of liberal authoritarianism.[19]

Conclusion

The attraction of democracy is supposedly that it prevents the corruption of absolute power in autocracies, which was decried by Lord Acton. But, as attested to by the example of the innumerable autocrats who have been elected in many Third World countries and the successor states to the 'evil empire', this hope may not be fulfilled. Though the elections through which they gained power were not always as free and fair as in the West, by and large they still represented the popular will. Ever since the rise of Hitler and Mussolini through the ballot box, theorists of democracy have been haunted by the fear that demagogues playing to the 'irrational' impulses of the masses may exploit popular participation.[20] Thus democracy and liberty are not coterminus.[21] While for classical liberals, civil and economic liberties are the ultimate moral good, comprising the content of good governance, they are not necessarily served by one form of government—representative democracy. The fathers of the Scottish Enlightenment and the American Founders were well aware of this possible conflict between liberty and democracy.[22]

Democracy and Peace

What of the claim that democracy is needed to maintain the peace? Statistical evidence is purported to show that modern democracies never fight each other. This does not, however, show that democracies are more pacific. In fact, they have gone to war more often and with greater ferocity than other states. This is contrary to the belief of Immanuel Kant—the original proponent of the democratic peace theory. He argued that because in democracies the public who pay for wars also make the decisions of going to war, they would be cautious and more pacific than non-democratic states. They clearly are not. Furthermore, the purported statistical evidence is questionable. There have been only a small number of both democracies and wars over the last two hundred years, so one can have little confidence in the correlation. As Fareed Zakaria has pointed out, 'no member of his family has ever won the lottery, yet few offer explanations for this impressive correlation'.[23]

Popular rule in the past was widely associated with aggressiveness (by Thucydides) or imperial success (by Machiavelli). Zakaria, quoting Doyle, says, 'The decisive preference of [the] median voter might well include "ethnic cleansing" against other democratic polities'.[24] Note, for example, Gaza's democratically elected Hamas government's stand on the existence of Israel.

The statistical evidence, for what it is worth, shows that while mature democracies do not fight each other, previous autocracies that are democratizing are more prone to go to war.[25] This is because, from both the historical and contemporary record, nationalism and democratization tend to go together, and the inflaming of nationalist passions usually leads to war and ethnic cleansing. Examples include France under Napoleon III; Wilhelmine Germany; Taisho Japan; and, more recently, Chechnya, Armenia, Azerbaijan, and the former Yugoslavia.

I, therefore, do not find the claim that democracy is needed to maintain the peace—oft-cited by international relations theorists—persuasive.

Democracy and Prosperity[26]

Nor is there any necessary connection between democracy and prosperity. The historical evidence does not support any necessary connection between a particular form of government and the promotion of prosperity. In the post-war period, one only has to consider the Far Eastern Gang of Four or the more successful economies in Latin America—Chile, Mexico, and, until the 1980s, Brazil—to realize, as Lee Kuan Yew has been proclaiming from rooftops, that there is no causal relationship between democracy and development.[27] Even in the rocky transition from the plan to the market, as the contrasting experiences of Russia and China show, glasnost may not help perestroika! This does not mean that authoritarianism or military autocracies are necessarily good for development either. The essential point is that various types of government, as long as they maintain the essentials of a market order, can promote development.

Statistical Evidence

However, a number of cross-sectional statistical studies claim to have found a relationship between democracy and development.[28] But the statistical proxies used for the political variables in these studies do not inspire much confidence, which are further plagued by the econometric problem of identification. In our book[29] *The Political Economy of Poverty, Equity and Growth*, Myint and I found no relationship between the form of government and economic performance during the thirty-year economic histories of the twenty-five developing countries that we studied. Rather than the type of polity, the initial resource endowment, in particular the availability or lack of natural resources, was a major determinant of policies that impinged on the efficiency of investment and thereby the rate of growth. This was basically due to the inevitable politicization of the rents that natural resources yield, with concomitant damage to growth performance. By contrast, natural-resource-poor countries, irrespective of the nature of their government, were forced to develop their only resource—their human subjects. Thus, the economic performance of natural-resource-poor countries like the Far Eastern Gang of Four tended to be much better on average than that of those with abundant natural resources like Brazil and Mexico. Countries like India and China, whose factor endowments fall in between these extremes, swerved between following the policies of their resource-abundant and resource-poor cousins, with a resultant indifferent intermediate economic performance. The difference in performance was further explained by the other major determinant of growth—the volume of investment. Thus while the efficiency of investment in India and China during both their dirigiste and more economically liberal periods was about the same, China's investment rate has been about twice India's, resulting in its growth rate also being twice as high. This might be taken as providing some support for the view that democracies will tend to have shorter-term horizons and hence discount the future more heavily (thereby saving less) than autocracies. But considering dictators like Mobutu of Zaire or Marcos of the Philippines, it would be difficult to sustain this view.

Despite these reasons for doubting whether democracy necessarily serves the ends of either liberty or prosperity, there is one virtue it does possess above other forms of government. It does allow the people to evict the incumbents. But even if desirable, is it feasible?

Liberal democracy is likely to be a fragile flower in much of the world, as it is unlikely to fit the political habits of many cultures. But does this also apply to what can be called economic freedom? Unlike political freedom, whose value is likely to be determined by the cosmological beliefs of different cultures, the value of economic freedom depends on the material beliefs of a civilization. With the gradual spread of globalization around the world and the increasing recognition that economic freedom brings prosperity, many politically illiberal societies are nevertheless gradually changing their material beliefs and introducing economic liberty, most notably China. Thus the Fraser Institute's Economic Freedom Index shows that since 1980, economic freedom has been rising around the world and has accelerated since the 1990s.[30] Many of the countries/regions where economic freedom is secure are not those that have political freedom. Thus Hong Kong, which tops the list, has economic but not political freedom.

Similarly, in the Islamic world, even though democracy is unlikely to flourish, there is no reason why Muslim countries should not be able to establish economic liberty. Thus, even though it is an autocracy, the UAE has an economic freedom index that places it at number 16 in the national rankings, above Belgium, Germany, Japan, and Sweden.[31] Therefore, the US, through its imperium, should be promoting globalization, which will lead to economic freedom. The promotion of the Wilsonian ideals of national self-determination and democracy will not necessarily aid this spread of the liberties that really matter. For it could lead to a backlash as cultural nationalists come to identify globalization with an attack on their cosmological beliefs and erroneously come to believe that modernizing is going to lead them to lose their souls.

But the ultimate case for liberal democracy must rest on its protection of individual liberties from a state that must be given the monopoly of coercion to prevent the disorder of the anarchical Hobbesian state of nature. The Rule of Law, as established in the ancient English Common Law and adapted for our own day in the US Constitution's separation of powers, is the essential bulwark for ensuring that democracy leads to liberalism and not illiberalism.

Nationalism

The French Revolution is Finer's second great revolution creating the lineaments of the modern state. For, as he states:

> It bequeathed to us the universalistic 'Rights of Man and the Citizen' which is the charter of all would be nation-states … the ideology, the new secular religion of nationalism; citizen armies and the *levee en masse*; and military interventions and the Palace/Forum type of polity—the regime of populist autocracy. Moreover, all four of these are still alive, working like a leaven throughout the globe. In that sense the revolution is a Permanent Revolution. Nothing was ever like it before and nothing foreseeable will turn this Revolution back.[32]

In his 2002 book *The Ideas That Conquered the World*, Michael Mandelbaum saw the three Wilsonian triads as being: peace, democracy, and free markets. There has, however, been increasing doubt since he wrote about this conquest; even at the turn of the last millennium there was a missing guest at Mandelbaum's feast of world conquering ideas—nationalism. For, as the historian of ideas Isaiah Berlin has observed:

> There was one movement which dominated much of the nineteenth century in Europe and was so pervasive, so familiar, that it is only by a conscious effort of the imagination that one can conceive a world in which it played no part ... but, oddly enough, no significant thinkers known to me predicted for it a future in which it would play an even more dominant role. Yet it would, perhaps, be no overstatement to say that it is one of the most powerful, in some regions the most powerful, single movement at work in the world today.... This movement is nationalism.[33]

Nationalism is a European idea of the last two hundred years. How did it arise?

Nationalism arose as a political doctrine in Europe at the beginning of the nineteenth century.[34] The doctrine holds that humanity is naturally divided into nations defined by distinctive cultures, and the only type of government that is legitimate is national self-government.[35]

Nationalism is different from both patriotism and xenophobia.[36] Nationalism divides humanity into different primordial entities—nations. Language, race, culture, and religion constitute their different aspects. It demands from people loyalty to 'their own nation by sinking their own persons in the greater whole of the nation'.[37] This is different from a loyalty to particular political institutions, as say in Britain and the US.[38] Nor is nationalism a form of tribalism.[39]

There have been four waves of political nationalism identified by Benedict Anderson in his *Imagined Communities.*[40] The first were the 'creole' wars of liberation in North and South America, which were prompted by the policy of the European powers of barring the entry of the creole elite to higher official and political office in the metropole, even as the *peninsulares* (or the Spanish-born) had access to high positions in both the colonies and the metropole. The accident of birth in the Americas seemed to condemn the creole to an inferior status, even though in every other respect—language, descent, customs, religion, and manners—he was indistinguishable from the peninsular. The nation-serving demos, which has been a defining characteristic of the modern age, was born.

The second wave of nationalism was the result of the spread of a 'vernacular' nationalism. The world of Christendom had a common language—Latin—but this was the lingua franca of administration, diplomacy, theology, and scholarship. In the localities, there was a multiplicity of tongues. The vernacular languages became important with the spread of the printing press. Some of these vernacular languages—for example, French and early English—had become competitors of Latin as languages of power by the sixteenth century. The emergence of a commercial bourgeoisie also expanded the demand for the products of the vernacular presses.

The threat that this vernacular nationalism posed to the dynasts of Europe led to 'official' nationalism, the third wave of nationalism, whereby the dynasts sought to identify themselves with the new-found vernacular nation. The spread of this official nationalism was in turn to lead to the scramble for empire and the First World War.

The final phase of nationalism was in areas where, directly or indirectly, the spread of Western imperialism had damaged the amour propre of indigenous high-status groups, as in India. The Treaty of Versailles at the end of the First World War buried the dynastic age, and the nation state became the international norm.

However, it is important to note that Woodrow Wilson's notion of self-determination, which launched the Age of Nations, was based on a misconception of the difference between what Lord Acton in his essay 'Nationality'[41] called the 'Continental' and 'Whig' notions of nationality. The Whig notion, which goes back to Locke and which the Americans inherited, looks to representative government as the best guarantee of freedom. However, John Stuart Mill muddied the waters by his statement in *Representative Government* that, 'It is, in general, a necessary condition of free institutions that the boundaries of government should coincide with those of nationalities'.[42] But by nationality, Mill, and the Whig tradition he represented, did not mean the 'nation' as defined by nationalists.[43] The Whig tradition was primarily concerned with individual liberty.[44] This is a very different notion of nationality from the Continental one based on that of a primordial nation defined by race or culture.

When Wilson—versed in this Anglo-American Whig tradition of nationality—came to Versailles, he thought that the various claimants to statehood believed in the same things as his revolutionary forefathers. But they did not. Instead, as E. Kedouri states:

> The Englishmen and Americans were saying, People who are self-governing are likely to be governed well, therefore we are in favor of self-determination; whereas their interlocutors were saying, People who live in their own national states are the only free people, therefore we claim self-determination. The distinction is a fine one, but its implications are far-reaching.... [I]n the

> confusion of the Peace Conference liberty was mistaken for the twin of nationality.[45]

Thus was the virus of nationalism spread, which gave predatory nationalist elites the power to unleash the disorder caused by their self-aggrandizement in many parts of the Third World with the end of the Age of Empire.

The ex-colonial, new nation states of Africa and Asia did not, however, follow the practice of vernacular nationalists in basing their nationhood on a particular vernacular nation. This was in large part, because these Third World nationalists inherited states that had been created by imperial powers whose territorial borders were determined as much by realpolitik and the fortunes of war as by any coherence in terms of ethnic or linguistic homogeneity. These artificial boundaries were deemed to be sacrosanct by the succeeding nationalist elites, who then faced the problem the Austro-Hungarian empire faced during its period of official nationalism—what official language should it adopt? If the language of any group in a multilingual state is adopted as the official language that immediately puts its speakers at an advantage and will be fiercely resisted by other groups. To allay these discords, like the Austro-Hungarians, the colonial nationalists have kept the old imperial lingua franca as the official language.

But, this then leaves them with the problem of forging a sense of nationhood out of their multilingual polyglot inheritance—similar to that faced by the absolute rulers of Renaissance Europe.[46] Like these European predecessors, Third World nationalist elites also adopted nationalism and dirigisme to modernize. This has proved to be a double-edged sword. For unlike the German, Italian and, to some extent, Slav nationalists whose task was to create a state for a pre-existing cultural and political nation, most African and some Asian nationalists inherited and cherished states created by colonialists, within which they have since sought to create a modern nation.

The process of economic development, which all the Third World elites seek to foster, involves profound changes over time in existing patterns of income distribution and thence in the status hierarchy. This is to be thought of not merely in the statistical sense, but in terms of what happens to the incomes (and status) of particular households over time. Even without any marked change in the statistical measure of this distribution, economic growth is likely to lead to a considerable and often rapid shuffling of the relative economic position and prospects of particular individuals and households. In a genuine nation state, the ensuing resentment of the losers maybe mitigated by the solace they may find in the accompanying national gains. The resentment is, therefore, unlikely to turn into the deadly conflicts to be found in the pseudo-nation states of the South, with their ancient and still pervasive cleavages of race, religion, or tribe, where the shuffling can be so easily identified as the humiliation of one sub-nationality by another. The newly independent South Sudan—torn between the ancient tribal rivalries between the Nuer and the Dinka—is the latest example of this. The nationalist rhetoric of the political elite can then rebound (as it has done quite often in the recent past) into demands to dismember the territorial state, whose preservation was the prime end for which nationalism was conjured up in the first place.[47]

Not surprisingly, therefore, it is in the relatively culturally homogenous polities of East Asia that nationalism has performed the integrative emotional and economic function it did in the West. In the more fragile and pluralistic polities of South East Asia, South Asia, and Africa, by contrast, nationalist rhetoric to gain independence from colonialism has created as many problems of national integration as it was hoped it would solve.

After the post–Second World War wave of decolonization, these new nation states of the Third World found themselves caught in the vortex of the Cold War, in which two empires—one embodying the Whale, the US, and the other the Bear, USSR—and their allies sought to woo or suborn these newborn states into their vortex. Many resisted by forming the grouping of non-aligned states, which successfully played off the two behemoths for favours.

With the collapse of the Soviet empire, its inhabitants suffered the same fate as those at the demise of earlier empires. The lid that empires successfully place on ethnic and cultural divisions was lifted, with ensuing disorder in the name of various local nationalisms. The two remaining major land-based imperial states are China and India. Their imperialism is of the direct kind, with China's being of the homogenizing kind and India's of the multi-ethnic variety, as discussed in Chapter 2. Both face threats of sub-national nationalisms threatening the territorial integrity of their states. But their robust response has ensured that at least for the foreseeable future their empires will remain intact.

What of the new American imperium? Can indirect imperialism maintain a lid on the various divisions that still threaten disorder in so many failing, failed, and rogue states, or will resort have to be made to direct imperialism? From the recent outcomes in Afghanistan and Iraq, it appears that a 'coalition of the willing' led by the US has failed to maintain even indirect control over these areas because the domestic bases of support of the members of the coalition has eroded, not allowing even a residual indirect imperial presence in these countries. This has already led to growing sectarian violence and disorder in Iraq, and which will in all likelihood continue in Afghanistan even as Obama's stated desire to remove all US troops from Afghanistan by the time he left office in 2016, has now been postponed by his successor. The continuing denial that the US is an empire, along with the moral resonance of the Wilsonian case against empires and in favour of nation states, is likely to erode the domestic bases of support over time.

Globalization and the Rise of Cosmopolitanism

Marx and other socialist thinkers thought nationalism would be undermined by the powerful cosmopolitan forces unleashed by the first period of globalization under Pax Britannica. But this was not to be, in part because of the nationalist passions unleashed by the two world wars and the global economic disorder of the first half of the twentieth century. It is only with the second period of globalization from 1980 that cosmopolitanism has begun to contest the nationalist impulse.

The globalization associated with the post–World War II US-led LIEO has created a global cosmopolitan class whose associations, residences, and businesses are not tied to particular national boundaries. They have often gone to one of the same group of elite universities (still mainly in the US and Europe), joined public international organizations or private multinationals and global financial institutions with transnational interests and loyalties, and they are increasingly intermarried. Today's cosmopolitan elite has evolved from the commercial bourgeoisie of the nineteenth century whose national community was not based on personal relations but on an imagined community visualized through the medium of the vernacular presses.

By contrast, Benedict Anderson argues, there was a pan-European aristocratic ruling class with a feeling of solidarity as part of a community with a common identity, which was linked fairly closely, despite differences in their vernacular languages and cultures, by—as he puts it—'the personalization of political relations implied by sexual intercourse and inheritance'.[48] Theirs was no *imagined* community. On the other hand, as by the nineteenth century, the vernacular languages had replaced the common European lingua franca as the print language for more than two centuries, the imagined community of the rising bourgeoisie could not extend beyond the vernacular boundaries, like the political community in the Age of Aristocracy. For, as Anderson puts it 'one can sleep with anyone, but one can only read some people's words'.[49]

But in this second age of globalization this, too, has changed. With the spread of literacy around the developing world and the emergence of English as the new lingua franca, all aspirants to join the new cosmopolitan elites speak English (at least as a second language), as witnessed by the demand for English-language schooling in primary schools in both China and India. So, like the aristocrats of yore, the new cosmopolitan bourgeoisie not only sleeps with one another but also can read each other's words!

This has had the paradoxical effect of creating a tension between the cosmopolitan openness demanded by globalization and the sense of a loss of national identity with the transnational flow of labour, capital, and goods and services removing former economic and social national niches. The international mobility of both capital and skilled labour induced by globalization makes it difficult to tax both by national fiscs to the extent that was possible in much of the pre-globalization era before, say, 1980. This has meant that the central issue that led to political mobilization by mass political parties—the conflicting interests of labour and capital—has lost its resonance. With the resulting erosion of the national tax base, the ameliorative measures taken to mitigate this conflict through the creation of welfare states based on progressive taxation have also become unsustainable. This has led to the formation of a union of national predatory states led by the US and organized by the Organisation for Economic Co-operation and Development (OECD) to prevent tax competition among national fiscs, which the cosmopolitan bourgeoisie and associated institutions (such as multinationals) had used to legally limit their tax liabilities in high-tax regions.[50] Whether this will succeed remains doubtful and, certainly, undesirable from the viewpoint of classical liberalism.

One important effect of the creation of a cosmopolitan bourgeoisie is that its members can, if they are in the political arena, mitigate the nationalist and illiberal impulses of their countrymen. Thus, it is reported that many of the 'princelings' in China who have been educated at Ivy League universities have lobbied with their elders to reduce the sentence of the democracy advocate and Nobel laureate Liu Xiaobo-but to no avail. But this has, in turn, created a tension between nationalism and cosmopolitanism. Tony Blair, UK's former prime minister, had argued soon after leaving office that the central ideological axis was no longer 'left versus right' but 'open versus closed'. This has created a problem for Janus-faced political parties like the Conservatives in the UK who—as in the nineteenth-century Age of Reform with the abolition of the protectionist Corn Laws—are seeing a conflict between 'market liberals who cherish Britain's openness and national conservatives who resent the disruption it brings'.[51] The success of populist parties in recent European elections shows that this is a trend that has become common in Western democracies since the Great Recession. In the US, the growing concern about the rise in inequality with a stagnation of middle-class incomes and phenomenal rise in the incomes of the top 0.1 per cent of the population has also led to protectionist pressures, a backlash against easing immigration laws, and also a questioning of the US global role bordering on isolationism. This is the agenda on which Donald Trump won the recent US presidential election. Thus, despite the global benefits that globalization has brought, there is a danger, as in the 1930s, of its reversal with the rise of economic nationalism.

Religious Fundamentalism

One of the more surprising survivals of the premodern age is the continuing cleavage along religious lines, despite the seeming victory of the Enlightenment value of secularism, separating the public sphere from the private sphere where individual beliefs—including religious—can thrive. In the late 1980s, the American Academy of Arts and Sciences (AAAS) sponsored the Fundamentalism Project to assess the fundamentalist religious movements, which seemed to have become a major source of domestic and international disorder.[52] These encompassed the rise of political Islam in the Middle East and South Asia; Hindu fundamentalists in India; Buddhist fundamentalists in Sri Lanka, Thailand, and Myanmar; Christian fundamentalists in the US; and Jewish fundamentalists in Israel. In their conclusions in the final volume of the series, *Fundamentalisms and the State*, Martin Marty and Scott Appleby, the editors and sponsors of the project, noted that religious fundamentalism arose in the twentieth century as many developing countries saw the rapid modernization of their traditional societies resulting in 'profound personal and social dislocations' without 'mediating institutions capable of meeting the human needs created by these dislocations'.[53]

Religious fundamentalists reject distinctions between the 'public' and 'private' spheres. They want the 'observances of a religious community to permeate the whole of life, an organic unity that the agents of secular modernity have wrongly segmented and compartmentalized. The boundaries that matter are not between the "private" and "public" but between the believer and the infidel'.[54]

These religious fundamentalisms are a form of cultural nationalism and reflect the Romantic revolt against the Enlightenment and its 'disenchantment of the world'. For them, too, like the Romantics, globalization and the modernization it brings is, as Charles Taylor puts it, a 'desert in which everything has been leveled, and all beauty stamped out to create a mundane serviceable world of use objects'.[55]

As Benedict Anderson has noted, there is a similarity between the imagined communities of nationalism and the imagined communities of religious fundamentalists. Both reflect a deep human desire for cosmological beliefs, which not only give meaning and purpose to their lives and their relationships to others but, most important of all, which also help them explain and come to terms with death: Man's inescapable mortality. The rationalist secularism of the Enlightenment brought with it its own modern darkness. Anderson says, 'Disintegration of paradise: nothing makes fatality more arbitrary. Absurdity of salvation: nothing makes another style of continuity more necessary. What was then required was a secular transformation of fatality into continuity, a contingency into meaning'.[56] The nation was the answer.

But, religious fundamentalisms hark back to older imagined communities, which formed part of the great sacral cultures.[57] Thus while the nations are concerned with defined territorial boundaries, religious communities are often imagined as transnational, for example the umma (or community) of Islam. As Marty and Appleby state, 'Both the nation and the fundamentalist community are conceived of as deep horizontal comradeships, "sacred" fraternities for which people may die or kill other people. Like nationalisms, fundamentalisms possess hegemonic political ambitions and demand colossal sacrifices from their devotees'.[58]

The majority of these fundamentalisms are to be found in the monotheistic Semitic religions that destroyed the classical world of antiquity. The seventh century was the turning point in the Middle East.[59] In about 600 CE, two long established great empires dominated western Eurasia—the truncated Christian Roman empire centred on Constantinople, and the neo-Zoroastrian Persian empire reconstituted by the Sassanian dynasty in the third century. Both could mobilize vast resources for war. The Romans could mobilize those of North Africa and much of Italy, the Balkans, and the near Middle East—most importantly Egypt, which along with parts of North Africa were the granaries of the empire. The Persians were an equally well-organized and well resource-endowed state with the fertile lands of Mesopotamia and highland Iran. Their territories abutted, and they competed for influence over the peoples of the north Caucasus and the Bedouin tribes of Arabia. Both had established patron–client relationships with particular Bedouin tribes to guard their respective desert frontiers. They were commercial rivals, competing for the lucrative overland trade from China and the seaborne trade across the Indian Ocean from India and South East Asia.

By the second quarter of the eighth century, the Persian Sassanian empire had been extinguished. The Roman empire had shrunk to Byzantium, controlling Asia Minor, the islands of the Aegean, and the southern extremities of the Balkans. It was now in a mortal struggle with the new imperial power of the Bedouin Arabs. In a short space of time, since their eruption from the marginal lands beyond the zone of direct confrontation between the two existing imperial powers, the Arabs had defeated the imperial field armies in open battle and soon controlled three of the four power-centres of the Middle East—Egypt, Mesopotamia, and highland Iran. The binary world order of late antiquity was replaced by the new unitary Arab power in the seventh century.

How had this astonishing new world order been established? Howard-Johnston argues that of the two contending explanations—circumstances like the Roman–Persian war lasting from 603–28, and the ideological changes brought about in Arabia by the Prophet Muhammad—it is the latter which accounts for the extraordinary rise of the Arab Muslim Empire.

Howard-Johnston says:

> His [Muhammad's] God was a remote and awesome divinity. There was nothing human about him. He was susceptible to none of the emotions of the Old Testament God. There was no question of empathy with mankind, let alone suffering for the salvation of his human creatures.... The monotheism of Islam was gaunt, austere, stripped of all those saints and deities, with local shrines, which provided human beings in most societies with access to the divine. Paradoxically, the greatest appeal of Muhammad's monotheist message lay in its bleakness, in its clear-eyed view of a universe governed by a single divine autocrat.... The traditional passive fatalism of the Bedouin, conducting life according to a tribal code of man's creation, was transformed by faith, which required complete submission to Allah.... This engendered an *active fatalism* in genuine converts, a commitment to serve God with their persons and worldly goods together with indifference to the personal cost. It may be termed a *whole faith*, one which permeated the whole being of the believer. This in turn endowed Muslim troops with extraordinary élan. They were committed unto death. The armies which invaded the Roman and Persian empires were in essence ordered arrays of suicide fighters, endowed with extraordinary courage and daring.[60]

There were two other political innovations that transformed Islam's prospects after the Prophet's flight to Medina. The first was to change Muslims direction of prayer

> from what it had been (almost certainly Jerusalem, the holiest place on earth for both the previous monotheist religions) to the Ka'ba, the premier pagan sanctuary of Arabia.... The incorporation of the Ka'ba and its associated rites into Islam, forced though it was on the prophet, was a political act, which transformed the fortunes of the *umma* in the short run ... but enabled it in due course (once Mecca had formally submitted in 630) to draw on the developed institutional endowment, diplomatic expertise, and mercantile ingenuity of a well-established trading city.[61]

Secondly, It was this Meccan statecraft that allowed the early Muslim caliphs to devise and implement a grand strategy, in which they husbanded the military resources of Arabia, directed operations at a distance, established priorities, and deployed the requisite resources at the right place to achieve their objectives.[62]

And its success was phenomenal. 'By the 16th century, when Christendom was taking to the oceans, Islam was in firm control of the whole Middle East and had cast its net over all but the western, eastern and southern extremities of the Eurasian continent.'[63]

Monotheism and Polytheism

But as Sam Finer in his *History of Government* argues, this whole period between classical antiquity and modernity, described as the 'Middle Ages' in European history, also applies to the historical periodization of China and India, but the dates would be different from the European ones of 450–1450 CE. For, globally these Middle Ages saw three developments in the civilizations of Eurasia: the emergence of the 'historic' religions; the destruction of the old established state structures and the creation, after a time of troubles, of completely novel ones; and, finally, the interruption of this same process of state and community building by wild incursions of uncivilized hordes from the Eurasian 'Heartland'.[64]

There was a major difference between the historic religions (which by and large were monotheistic) and the polytheism of the classical pagan world of antiquity, which they replaced. They shared the view that they and they alone worshipped the 'true' god and/or professed the 'true way'. They were *exclusive*, and in Europe and the Middle East, as far as the Jaxartes and north India, rulers enforced them on their subjects under more or less severe sanctions for the first time in history.[65]

They were also congregational with the individuals professing common beliefs forming 'what the Jews called the *kabal*, Christians the *ecclesia*, Muslims the *umma*, and ... Buddhists the *sangha*.'[66] These monotheistic religions, particularly the Semitic ones, unlike those of the pagans, claimed to be universal. They worshiped the only true god. Christianity and Islam—though not Judaism—sought to convert heathens, if necessary by the sword.

This has led to incessant strife, not only between the votaries of these religions and the Rest but even between different sects within these religions, who all claim to have the ultimate truth. Finer says that states with their rulers following one of these religions, began 'for the first time in history to deprive, or humiliate, or mulc, or mutilate, stab, and burn to death not only those of their subjects who rebelled against them, and not only those who did not outwardly conform to their rituals, but even those who simply held different religious opinions from their own.' This was based on the belief that worldly life was merely a transient probation for the real—and eternal—life to come, and 'to their unshakable conviction that only right thinking, not just good conduct, could the human soul be saved from eternal torment hereafter'.[67]

After the split in Christendom with the Reformation, the whole of Europe was plunged into the Thirty Years' War between Protestants and Catholics, which only ended with the Treaty of Westphalia. The Scottish and French Enlightenment then tamed the religious passions of Christian states by their promotion of secular values and the acceptance by most European states and their offshoots of the important distinction between the private and public sphere. This was best emphasized by Queen Elizabeth I of England. On seeing her kingdom torn by religious strife and on hearing the demands to eliminate all heretical thinking, she demurred saying that she 'did not want to make windows into men's souls'.

The most virulent form of monotheism today is Wahhabism. The Saudis have used their considerable oil wealth to spread Wahhabism around the world. As David Gardner rightly notes, 'Saudi Arabia not only exports oil but tanker-loads of quasi-totalitarian religious dogma and pipelines of jihadi volunteers, even as it struggles to insulate itself from the blowback'.[68]

Much worse, the Saudis are contributing to the 'closing of the Muslim mind',[69] which has been the major reason for the decaying of the glorious Islamic civilization built under the earliest caliphs of the Abbasid dynasty. They do this through direct and indirect financing of Wahhabi mosques and madrasas in the Balkans and south, central, and southeast Asia, which preach hatred against the infidels—Jews, Christians, and above all Hindus—to young minds, who learn little if anything about the modern world. As I noted in my *In Praise of Empires*, this poison being spread by Wahhabi evangelism is becoming intolerable. To see how pernicious it is, imagine if German schools only had lessons in anti-Semitism and American schools just taught the young to hate blacks. But this ethnic and religious hatred is being taught in the large number of madrasas around the world being funded by Saudi petrodollars. It also makes the Enlightenment, which Islam desperately needs, more difficult to achieve.

The taming of similar religious passions in Islam's close monotheistic religion—Christianity—is instructive, Monotheistic religions like most others have a 'natural religion', which is presumed to be based on reason, and a 'revealed religion', based on faith and the special rituals associated with the particular religion which allow God to reveal himself and perform miracles for the faithful. David Hume was devastating in both his *Dialogues* and *Natural History of Religion* about both aspects of Christianity. As he noted about the belief in an omnipotent, omniscient, and benevolent deity ruling the world—how could one, then, explain evil in such a world? 'Epicurus's old questions are yet unanswered. Is he [God] willing to prevent evil, but not able? Then he is impotent. Is he able, but not willing? Then he is malevolent. Is he both able and willing? Whence then is evil?'[70]

On the revelatory part of religion, Hume argues that there is no essential difference between polytheism and monotheism. Polytheism, which is the original religion of mankind, 'arose not from a contemplation of the works of nature, but from a concern with regard to the events of life, and from the incessant hopes and fears that activate the human mind'.[71] Monotheism by contrast believes in a supreme deity, the author of nature, the omnipotent creator.

Comparing the two—polytheism and monotheism—Hume notes:

> The greatest and most observable differences between a *traditional, mythological* religion, and a *systematical, scholastic* one are two: The former is often more reasonable, as consisting only of a multitude of stories, which, however groundless, imply no express absurdity and demonstrative contradiction; and sits also so easy and light on men's minds that, though it may be as universally received, it happily makes no such deep impression on the affections and understanding.[72]

But he also noted in his *Natural History*, discussing the relative merits of polytheism with monotheism, 'idolatry is attended with this evident advantage, that, by limiting the powers and functions of its deities, it naturally admits the gods of other sects and nations to a share of divinity, and renders all the various deities, as well as rites, ceremonies, or traditions, compatible with each other.'[73] He cites Pliny's *Natural History* as affirming

> that it was usual for the Romans, before they had laid siege to any town, to invocate the tutelar deity of the place, and by promising him greater honours than those he at present enjoyed, bribe him to betray his old friends and votaries. The name of the tutelar deity of Rome was for this reason kept a most religious mystery; lest the enemies of the republic should be able, in the same manner, to draw him over to their service.[74]

All this leads him to conclude, 'The intolerance of almost all religions, which have maintained the unity of God, is as remarkable as the contrary principle of polytheists. And if among Christians, the English and Dutch have embraced the principles of tolerance, this singularity has proceeded from the steady resolution of the civil magistrate, in opposition to the continued efforts of priests and bigots'.[75]

This inability of Islam, to date, to embrace tolerance through the 'steady resolution of civil magistrates' is due to a unique feature of its cosmological beliefs, its inability to separate church and state. As Bernard Lewis has noted 'for Muslims, the state was God's state, the army God's army, and of course the enemy was God's enemy.... The question of separating Church and state did not arise, since there was no church as an autonomous institution, to be separated. Church and state were the one and the same'.[76] It is only in the twentieth century that the question of privatizing religion became an issue, and then only in Turkey, the only Muslim nation to legally formalize the separation of church and state. But which, too, under its current moderate Islamic government seems to be backsliding. Clearly, it is Islam itself that is at the root of the problems of the Muslim world in coming to terms with modernity.

It is worth looking back historically at the roots of the problem.[77] The Muslim civilization that Muhammad and his successors created was the dominant world civilization at the end of the first millennium. Their poets described it as providing 'tastes of paradise'. This paradise was shattered by the rise of the West. Though, it was not till the Ottomans were turned back after the siege of Vienna in 1683 that this Islamic world went into relative decline.

Most of the ancient civilizations traumatized by the rise of the West have had three major responses. The first is that of the oyster, which closes its shell. The other was to modernize, to try to master the foreign technology and way of life and to fight the alien culture with its own weapons, as the Japanese did when Commodore Perry's black ships appeared off the coast at Yokohama. Some Islamic countries—in particular Ataturk's Turkey and Mehmed Ali's Egypt—also took the second route, but only partially. The third remedy was socialism, which claimed to be able to combine modernity with tradition, through a combination of principles derived from both the Enlightenment and the Romantic Reaction.

This third remedy, which was the common response of many other traumatized ex-colonial elites, was also tried by the Muslim nationalist elites who came to power after the withdrawal of the West, as epitomized by Nasser in Egypt. Nasser, like many other nationalist socialist leaders in the Middle East, realized that to avoid social unrest, leaders had to come to terms with the low

Islam of the common people.[78] This low Islam was often syncretic and much influenced by the mystical form of Islam preached by the Sufis and their cult of saints. By contrast the high Islam of the scholars (ulama), from which the Islamists arose, was seen as a threat to the nationalist's modernizing ambitions and was ruthlessly suppressed. But the popular low Islam had little influence on the growing mass of educated youth in the cities. An attempt was then made to co-opt high Islam. In Egypt, Nasser in effect nationalized Al-Azhar, the Islamic seminary that had instructed the ulama for a thousand years, and sought to get its teachers and pupils to argue for the compatibility of Islam with Nasserist socialism. But this attempt backfired, as the ulama came to be looked upon as stooges of the state and could no longer fulfil their traditional function of mediating between the state and society.

It was the shattering Arab defeat in the 1967 Arab–Israeli War (also known as the Six-Day War) that destroyed any hope that socialist nationalism offered a solution to the Muslim predicament. This military defeat was compounded by the failure of Arab socialism to increase the economic pie sufficiently fast enough to allow the lower middle classes and the rural and urban proletariat to share in the material gains that had been promised to all at independence but were garnered mainly by the traditional elites.

The Islamic intelligentsia, financed by Wahhabi Saudi money, then turned to the other common remedy—that of the oyster. They turned away from nationalists and toward Islamism and the creation of an Islamic state as the answer to Muslim woes. This response—in which Muslims sought to purify Islam from all the corruptions that had crept over the centuries into Muslim lives and thereby to regain Allah's favour—has had much greater resonance in the Muslim world than the other Eurasian civilizations. While other civilizations have come to realize that modernization does not entail Westernization, and hence ancient cosmological beliefs can be maintained even when material beliefs have to change to modernize, it was (as William McNeill notes) Islam's misfortune that, despite many voices (e.g., Sir Syed Ahmed in nineteenth-century India) stating that Islam could be reconciled with modernity, the two remedies of the oyster and the modernizer 'seemed always diametrically opposed to one another. Reformers' efforts therefore tended to cancel out, leaving the mass of Muslim society more confused and frustrated than ever'.[79]

Much worse, unlike the other Eurasian civilizations that came in time to recognize that modernity and tradition could be reconciled—not least because of the growth of a Western-educated elite which has imbibed some of the messages of the Enlightenment—in Muslim countries, Western education and other trappings of modernity, instead of creating modern rational societies, have in part led to the Islamist backlash. The hijackers who flew into the World Trade Center were not poor, illiterate peasants, but the children of well-off middle-class parents who had been given a technical education. The important study of fundamentalism by the AAAS[80] found that in the Arab world, and in Muslim states from Iran to Pakistan, there is a consistent pattern in the educational and socio-economic status of Islamic militants. Fundamentalists are mainly students and university graduates in the physical sciences with rural or traditionally religious backgrounds. They are the recent beneficiaries of the expanded university systems, were raised in a traditional family, and have had to make recent adjustments to a modern cultural and intellectual environment. Moreover, in a study[81] of the educational profiles of the Marxist and Islamic guerrilla movements that overthrew the Shah of Iran, researchers found that the Islamists were mainly students of natural sciences, the Marxists of the humanities and the social sciences.

Malise Ruthven has provided persuasive reasons why the students from rural and traditionally religious lower middle-class families are turning into Islamists in the Muslim world. It is caused, argues Ruthven, by the failure to integrate 'the dual identity of the village Muslim and the applied scientist … The religious mind inherited from the village or suburb is conditioned to believe that knowledge is "Islamic", that all truth is known and comes from Allah. The scientist operates in a field of epistemological doubt'.[82] One way out of the dilemma would be for the villager-turned-scientist to pretend that the truths of science are already contained in his/her religion. But this escape is not possible for those trained in the natural sciences. They could just accept this dual identity, but it is not possible for many. Moreover, for the devout Muslim, the real scandal is that knowledge acquired through doubt has proved more powerful in creating material prosperity than the revealed knowledge of their religion. During the initial phase of Islam's expansion, its stupendous conquests, which provided booty for the material prosperity of the umma, were seen as proof of God's approval. The success of the post-Enlightenment West then becomes unbearable.[83]

And, paradoxically, it is in this cognitive dissonance of educated Muslim youth that the hope for a prospective Muslim Enlightenment lies. If this were to occur, it would be able—as Hume said of the England and Holland of his time—to embrace the principles of toleration 'in opposition to the continued efforts of priests and bigots'. For, it should be remembered that Hume and his contemporaries of the Scottish Enlightenment were changing minds in the Western world only a few decades after the iron grip of the Calvinist kirk seemed to have closed all Scottish minds.

In 1696, Arthur Herman, the historian of the Scottish Enlightenment, informs us that Thomas Aikenhead, a 19-year-old theology student, was hung for blasphemy at the instigation of the Scottish Presbyterian Church. This Calvinist church established by John Knox, and of which young Aikenhead became a victim, is described by Herman as follows, 'The kirk wiped out all traditional forms of collective fun … Fornication brought punishment and exile; adultery meant death. The church courts, or kirk-sessions, enforced the law with scourges, pillories, branks, ducking-stools, banishment, and, in the case of witches or those possessed by the devil, burning at the stake'.[84] This sounds eerily similar to what we read in our newspapers about Shiite Iran, Wahhabi Saudi Arabia, and the Afghan Taliban.

By 1725, Frances Hutcheson (a clergyman and a teacher) and Lord Kames (a lawyer and judge) had launched the Scottish Enlightenment. Could not a similar change occur in Muslim societies? It would take me too far afield to speculate on this likelihood. But, with a number of liberal voices appearing in Muslim societies and realizing that as in Christendom it was only after its sectarian religious wars had burnt out the rival religious passions that Enlightenment could be achieved, perhaps the end of the coming war between the Shias and Sunnis in the Middle East will finally lead to that Muslim Enlightenment which can only come from within Islam.[85]

Conclusion

After the seeming triumph of the West with the disintegration of the countries of 'really existing socialism' in 1991, it seemed capitalism was the only economic and democracy the only political form that was universally viable. Yet, with China abjuring democracy but embracing its own form of capitalism; many of the 'new' democracies and, most importantly, Russia slipping into the palace/forum type of polity adumbrated by Finer, or into various forms of kleptocracy as in the Ukraine; and with the democratic dawn heralded by the Arab Spring turning again to darkness, the global future of democracy seems less secure.[86]

Similarly, nationalism and religious fundamentalism—which, it was hoped, would have been undermined by the march of Enlightenment values—have also been belied. They are the ideologies that have growing resonance in the world.

With the world descending into disorder reminiscent of the post-Renaissance world, how will the resulting contest for Eurasia play out among the contending powers? Relative economic strength will be a major determinant. Hence we turn in the next part to geoeconomics, beginning with the causes of the Great Recession, which has been taken as a sign that the US imperium is on the decline.

Notes

1. H. Bull, *The Anarchical Society*, Second Edition (New York: Columbia University Press, 1995), p. 23.

2. In his little gem of a book *Politics: A Very Short Introduction* (Oxford: Oxford University Press, 1995), Kenneth Minogue outlines the origins of the term 'ideology' from its invention by the French philosopher Destutt de Tracy in 1797 as part of the project of the philosophers to create a science of politics. But it was with *The German Ideology*, Marx and Engels' 1846 work, that the word took off. It now embodied 'two quite opposite ideas: that of truth and that of falsity. Ideology meant (for the ideologues themselves) a philosophical hygiene revealing truth, and (for Marx) the very falsity which needed to be cleansed'. The term was then taken up by American political scientists to encompass the whole miscellany of political beliefs. The concept remains useful, because 'ideologies, by contrast with political doctrines, claim exclusive truth. They explain not only the world, but how to abolish politics and establish the perfect society'. Minogue also notes that, though there is a difference between ideologies and political doctrines, 'enthusiasm may infect *any* political doctrine with the belief that its principles alone can save the world from evil', and turn it into an ideology (pp. 104–7). It should be noted that the three 'ideologies'—democracy, nationalism and religious fundamentalism—considered in this chapter fit this description.
3. Bull, *The Anarchical Society*, pp. 36–7. Bull also notes tartly that this distinction is also made by contemporary social scientists between 'modern societies, traditional societies and primitive societies'.
4. For a useful discussion of the various senses in which the term use is used, see Tod Lindberg, 'Making Sense of the "International Community"', Working Paper, International Institutions and Global Governance Program, Council on Foreign Relations, New York (2014).
5. Bull, *The Anarchical Society*, p. 43.
6. Bull, *The Anarchical Society*, p. 49.
7. Bull, *The Anarchical Society*, p. 25.
8. D. Lal, *In Praise of Empires* (New York: Palgrave Macmillan, 2004), pp. 59–171.
9. S. Finer, *The History of Government from the Earliest Times*, Vol. 3 (Oxford: Oxford University Press, 1999), p. 1502.
10. Finer, *The History of Government*, vol. 3, p. 1502.
11. Finer, *The History of Government*, vol. 3, p. 1516.
12. See for instance S.H. Hanke and S.J.K. Walters, 'Economic Freedom, Prosperity, and Equality: A Survey', *Cato Journal*, 17(2) (1997):

117–46, for those persuaded by the statistical cross-section type of evidence that has proliferated in this field over the last decade. I prefer the more qualitative and historical evidence based on case studies as in D. Lal and H. Myint, *The Political Economy of Poverty, Equity and Growth: A Comparative Study* (Oxford: Clarendon Press, 1996).

13. It should be noted that the formal conditions for democracy—like periodic elections—may be met by many states that do not uphold political liberty. Fareed Zakaria has labelled these as 'Illiberal Democracies' (see following note). I am concerned mainly with true, that is, liberal, democracies.
14. Fareed Zakaria, *The Future of Freedom: Illiberal Democracies at Home and Abroad*, Revised Edition (New York: W.W. Norton, 2003 [1997]).
15. C. Brinton, *The Anatomy of Revolution* (New York: Vintage, 1938).
16. Jack Goldstone (ed.), *Revolutions: Theoretical, Comparative, and Historical Studies*, Third Edition (Belmont CA: Thomson Wadsworth, 2003), pp. 1–21.
17. Shadi Hamid, *Temptations of Power: Islamists and Illiberal Democracy in a New Middle East* (New York: Oxford University Press, 2014).
18. Hamid writes about Egypt, 'A striking result from a Pew survey conducted after the rise of the Brotherhood and Salafis had provoked fears of Islamist overreach: Egyptians said they preferred the "model of religion in government" of Saudi Arabia over that of Turkey (61 to 17 per cent)' (p. 173).
19. Hamid, *Temptations of Power*, concludes, 'Liberalism cannot hold within it Islamism. One possible resolution to this is the Turkish model, where Islamists, over time, gradually give up on their larger project and make peace with secular democracy' (p. 188). But with Erdoğan's recent turn to authoritarianism, the continuing support he receives from the pious Muslims of Anatolia, and his stated desire for an elected presidency to change Ataturk's secularist constitution, this peace may soon be in doubt.
20. See S.M. Lipset, *Political Man: The Social Bases of Politics* (London: Heinemann, 1959).
21. In fact, even in the US, the supposed paradigm of liberal democracy, many observers see its gradual move from a representative to participatory democracy. See Zakaria, *The Future of Freedom*.

22. Thus D. Hume, in his essay 'Of the Independence of Parliament' (David Hume, *Essays, Moral, Political, and Literary* [Indianapolis: Liberty Classics, 1777/1989] Part 1, Essay 6, p. 42), noted:

    Political writers have established it as a maxim that, in contriving any system of government and fixing the several checks and controls of the constitution, every man ought to be supposed a knave and to have no other end, in all his actions, than private interest. By this interest we must govern him and, by means of it, make him, notwithstanding his insatiable avarice and ambition, co-operate to public good. Without this, say they, we shall in vain boast of the advantages of any constitution and shall find in the end that we have no security for our liberties or possessions except the goodwill of our rulers; that is we shall have no security at all.

23. Zakaria, *The Future of Freedom*, p. 115.
24. M. Doyle, *Ways of War and Peace: Realism, Liberalism, and Socialism* (New York: W.W. Norton, 1997), cited in Zakaria, *The Future of Freedom*, p. 116.
25. E.D. Mansfield and J. Snyder, 'Democratization and War', *Foreign Affairs*, 74, no. 3 (1995), pp. 79–97.
26. This is based on D. Lal, 'Is Democracy Necessary for Development?', in S. Ramaswamy and J.W. Casson (eds), *Development and Democracy* (Lebanon, NH: University Press of New England, 2003).
27. See P.A. Gourevitch, 'Democracy and Economic Policy: Elective Affinities and Circumstantial Conjectures', *World Development*, 21, no. 8 (August 1993), pp. 1271–80, for a further elaboration of the tenuous link between forms of government and their promotion of markets.
28. See Adam Przeworski and Fernando Limongi, 'Political Rights and Economic Growth', *Journal of Economic Perspectives*, 7, no. 3 (1997), pp. 51–69 for a survey. The most cogent critique of the econometrics involved by A. Deaton and R. Miller, 'International Commodity Prices, Macroeconomic Performance, and Politics in Sub-Saharan Africa', *Princeton Essays in International Finance*, 79, Princeton N.J (1995).
29. Lal and Myint, *The Political Economy of Poverty, Equity and Growth*.
30. J. Gwartney and R. Lawson, *Economic Freedom of the World: 2003 Annual Report* (Vancouver: Fraser Institute, 2003).

31. Gwartney and Lawson, *Economic Freedom of the World*, Exhibit 2, p. 11.
32. Finer, *The History of Government*, Vol. 3, p. 1566.
33. Berlin, *Against the Current* (London: Pimlico, 1979 [1972]), p. 337.
34. The hinge for both the rise of demos and nationalism is the Reformation. This shattered the ideological unity of Western Christendom. Until then both rulers and ruled were bound by the Common Law of Christendom, and by being god's law there could be no question of disobedience (J.S. McClelland, *A History of Western Political Thought* [London: Routledge, 1996], p. 171). But after the Reformation who represented god's law—the Catholics or the Protestants?—and whose law should you obey if you were a Catholic in a Protestant kingdom or vice versa? The notion of the social contract was born. In the seventeenth century, the distinction between state and society was propounded by social contract theorists distinguishing between the beginning of society and the construction of a state.

    Further associations were subsequently abstracted from the state. First, the economy, whose relationships seemed to be governed—as Adam Smith was the first to show—by abstract laws, resembling the laws of nature. Second, with the Romantic revolt against the Enlightenment, the separation of culture from society led to nationalism. Thus, modernity in the West came to distinguish between different forms of human associations. The polity, the economy, and the culture came to be seen in Western thought as equally important but differing forms of association between human beings. These 'self-conscious associations set the scene for the dramas of modern political conflict' (K. Minogue, *Politics*, p. 49).

    Furthermore, if as the Protestant claimed the traditional interpreters of god's will appointed by the pope were sinful where were the true interpreters of his word to be found? 'If not the Church, then only the congregations' (Minogue, *Politics*, p. 175). These became self-governing, choosing and dismissing their pastors. But if the Church is to be governed by its members, why not the state? Thus were the seeds for the rise of demos sown.
35. See E. Kedourie, *Nationalism* (Oxford: Blackwells, 1993 [1960]), p. 1. Also Berlin, *Against the Current*; J. Plamenatz, 'Two Types of Nationalism', in E. Kamenka (ed.), *Nationalism: The Nature and Evolution of an Idea* (London: Arnold, 1973). This part is based on D. Lal, 'Nationalism, Socialism and Planning: Influential Ideas in

the South', *World Development*, 13, no. 6 (1993 [1985]), pp. 749–59, reprinted in D. Lal, *The Repressed Economy* (Aldershot: Edward Elgar, 1993).

36. 'Patriotism, affection for one's country, or one's group, loyalty to its institutions, and zeal for its defense, is a sentiment known among all kinds of men; so is xenophobia, which is dislike of the stranger, the outsider, and reluctance to admit him into one's own group. Neither sentiment depends on a particular anthropology and neither asserts a particular doctrine of the state or of the individual's relation to it. Nationalism does both; it is a comprehensive doctrine which leads to a distinct type of politics' (Kedourie, *Nationalism*, p. 68).
37. Kedourie, *Nationalism*, p. 67.
38. For 'a British or American nationalist would have to define the British or American nation in terms of language, race, or religion, to require that all those who conform to the definition should belong to the British or American state, that all those who do not, should cease to belong, and to demand that all British and American citizens should merge their will in the will of the community' (Kedourie, *Nationalism*, p. 68).
39. For, 'a tribesman's relation to his tribe is regulated in minute detail by custom which is followed unquestioningly and considered part of the natural or divine order. The tribesman is such by virtue of his birth, not by virtue of self-determination' (Kedourie, *Nationalism*, p. 69).
40. Benedict Anderson, *Imagined Communities: Reflections on the Origin and Spread of Nationalism* (London: Verso, 1991).
41. Lord Acton, *Essays on Freedom and Power* (Boston: Beacon Press, 1985 [1862]), pp. 166–95.
42. J.S. Mill, *Representative Government* (London: Everyman Library, 1910), p. 362.
43. For he goes on to say, 'Whatever really tends to the admixture of nationalities, and the blending of their attributes and peculiarities in a common union, is a benefit to the human race' (Mill, *Representative Government*, p. 164).
44. As Acton, *Essays on Freedom and Power* wrote, 'If we take, the establishment of liberty for the realization of moral duties to be the end of civil society, we must conclude that those states are the most perfect which, like the British and American Empires, include various distinct nationalities without oppressing them ... A state, which is incompetent to satisfy different races condemns itself' (p. 432).

45. Kedourie, *Nationalism*, p. 129.
46. This is based on Lal and Myint, *Political Economy of Poverty Equity and Growth*, Ch. 8.
47. Ernest Gellner, *Nations and Nationalism*, Second Edition (Ithaca: Cornell University Press, 1983), has argued that industrialization requires mobility, literacy, and cultural standardization, which are supplied by nationalism. But, Kedourie rightly argues against these and other sociological theories of nationalism. 'To narrate the spread, influence and operation of nationalism in various polities is to write a history of events, rather than of ideas' (Kedourie, *Nationalism*, p. 139).
48. Anderson, *Imagined Communities*, p. 77.
49. Anderson, *Imagined Communities*, p. 79.
50. Thus it has been reported that US pharmaceutical and Internet companies like Oracle, Google, Pfizer, Merck, and Apple have pushed more of their profits offshore and pushed their effective tax rates down up to 24 per cent. See Vanessa Houlder, 'Taxing Time Ahead As Offshore Rules Come Under More Scrutiny', *Financial Times*, (13 June 2014). Available at https://www.ft.com/content/2b4c7be8-f233-11e3-ac7a-00144feabdc0 (last accessed 19 February 2018).
51. Janan Ganesh, 'UKIP has Exposed the Conflict in the Tory Soul', *Financial Times* (3 June 2014), p. 13.
52. I was associated with this project and wrote a paper on 'The Economic Impact of Hindu Revivalism', published in the third volume of the project *Fundamentalisms and the State* discussed in the text (see the next note).
53. Martin E. Marty and R. Scott Appleby (eds), *Fundamentalisms and the State: Remaking Polities, Economies, and Militance* (Chicago: University of Chicago Press, 1993), p. 620.
54. Marty and Appleby, *Fundamentalisms and the State*, p. 621.
55. C. Taylor, 'Socialism and Weltanschung', in L. Kolakowski and S. Hampshire (eds), *The Socialist Idea: A Reappraisal* (London: Weidenfeld and Nicholson, 1974), p. 49.
56. Anderson, *Imagined Communities*, p. 11.
57. Anderson, *Imagined Communities*, p. 13.
58. Marty and Appleby, *Fundamentalisms and the State*, p. 623.
59. The history of this pivotal century has been contested by three sets of historians. As this century saw the astonishing rise of Islam, one of the major sets of historians are those who accept the picture

painted by Muslim sources and largely accepted by Western scholars, for example, the French scholar of the Middle East Ernest Renan in 1883 and, more recently, by Maxime Rodinson, *Muhammad* (London: Pelican Books, 1973). These sources (mainly the Koran and the Hadith), which date some two centuries after the events they describe, have been questioned, by and large, by contemporary American historians. For example, John Wansbrough, *The Sectarian Milieu: Content and Composition of Islamic Salvation History* (Oxford: Oxford University Press, 1978), uses the method of textual analysis developed by biblical scholars to determine the authenticity of these classical sources and to provide a different timeline and location for the events they describe. A popular and highly readable and controversial account of this revisionist story of the rise of Islam and the end of antiquity is provided in Tom Holland's *In the Shadow of the Sword* (London: Little, Brown, 2012). The third account is by my old friend (since we were young lecturers together at Christ Church, Oxford) James Howard-Johnston, the Oxford scholar of Byzantium. In his important book *Witnesses to a World Crisis: Historians and Histories of the Middle East in the Seventh Century* (Oxford: Oxford University Press, 2010), he builds on the pioneering work of the Princeton historians Patricia Crone and Michael Cook and their students, *Hagarism: The Making of the Islamic World* (Cambridge: Cambridge University Press, 1977), by a scholarly and persuasive vetting of the Muslim and non-Muslim historians and histories of the seventh century. Briefly the story he tells is related in the text.

60. Howard-Johnston, *Witnesses to a World Crisis*, pp. 450–1.
61. Howard-Johnston, *Witnesses to a World Crisis*, p. 528.
62. Howard-Johnston, *Witnesses to a World Crisis*, p. 527.
63. Howard-Johnston, *Witnesses to a World Crisis*, p. 516.
64. S. Finer, *The History of Government*, vol. 2 (Oxford: Oxford University Press, 1997), p. 613.
65. Finer, *The History of Government*, vol. 2, p. 615.
66. Finer, *The History of Government*, vol. 2, p. 614.
67. Finer, *The History of Government*, vol. 2, p. 615.
68. D. Gardner, 'Look Beyond Saudi Arabia for Sunni Leadership', *Financial Times* (8 August 2014).
69. See D. Lal, *Unintended Consequences: The Impact of Factor Endowments, Culture, and Politics on Long-Run Economic Performance* (Cambridge, MA: MIT Press, 1998), pp. 63–65.

70. David Hume, *Dialogues and Natural History of Religion*, Oxford World's Classics (Oxford: Oxford University Press, 1757; 1993 [1779]), p. 100.
71. Hume, *Dialogues and Natural History of Religion*, p. 139.
72. Hume, *Dialogues and Natural History of Religion*, p. 176.
73. Hume, *Dialogues and Natural History of Religion*, p. 160.
74. Hume, *Dialogues and Natural History of Religion*, p. 187.
75. Hume, *Dialogues and Natural History of Religion*, p. 162.
76. B. Lewis, 'Muslims, Christians, and Jews: The Dream of Coexistence', *New York Review of Books*, 39, no. 6 (1992).
77. See Lal, *Unintended Consequences*, Ch. 4, and Lal, *In Praise of Empires*, pp. 85–102, for fuller accounts of this and other aspects of the Islamic predicament.
78. This distinction between high and low Islam was made by the great Arab historian Ibn Khaldun and was picked up in his analysis of Muslim society by Ernest Gellner, *Muslim Society* (Cambridge: Cambridge University Press, 1981).
79. W. McNeill, *The Pursuit of Power* (Chicago: University of Chicago Press, 1979), p. 390.
80. Marty and Appleby, *Fundamentalisms and the State*, which summarizes and presents some of the AAAS studies, including mine, on Hindu fundamentalism. In this, I had reported my interview with L.K. Advani, the leader of the Hindu nationalist party, the Bharatiya Janata Party (BJP). He rightly noted that given the polytheism of Hinduism there cannot be Hindu fundamentalists. He said his promotion of Hindu nationalism was a purely political ploy as it helped to garner votes form the large anti-Muslim minority of voters who resented Muslim proselytizing and the fact that they had ruled the Hindus as conquerors for over five hundred years. Its more recent stance against Christian missionaries seeking to convert tribals in India is based on similar motives.
81. V. J. Hoffman, 'Muslim Fundamentalists: Psychosocial Profiles', in Marty and Appleby, *Fundamentalisms Comprehended*, p. 206.
82. M. Ruthven, *A Fury for God: The Islamist Attack on America* (London: Granta Books, 2002), p. 124.
83. Ruthven, *A Fury for God*, p. 132.
84. A. Herman, *How the Scots Invented the Modern World* (New York: Three Rivers Press, 2001), p. 16.

85. Here it is worth noting an important difference between Sunni and Shia jurisprudence. See Vali Nasr, *The Shia Revival: How Conflicts within Islam Will Shape the Future* (New York: W. W. Norton, 2007), and the relevant entries in Gerhard Bowering (ed.), *The Princeton Encyclopedia of Islamic Political Thought* (Princeton, N.J.: Princeton University Press, 2013). It concerns the role the ulama play in the two sects. The major difference is that unlike the Sunnis, the Shia community relies on its clerics 'not only to interpret religion but to make new rulings to respond to new challenges and push the boundaries of Shia law in new directions.... Shia ulama are first and foremost lawyers—they interpret and expand on religious law, first codified in the eighth century' (Nasr, p. 69). They are educated at seminaries in Najaf in Iraq and Qom in Iran, studying through tutorials and lectures under a senior ulama. On graduating they 'become a full member of the ulama, someone who can practice *itjihad* (independent reasoning to give a new ruling)–a *mujtahid*— collect religious taxes, and serve as the guardian of a flock' (p. 70). The senior clergy's stature is determined by 'the religious taxes and donations that believers give him for charitable purposes and to help educate seminary students. The bigger a senior cleric's purse, the wider a patronage network he can build in the clerical ranks below him. Because the Shia hierarchy depends not only on knowledge but on money, its desire to maintain strong ties to the bazaars has always been among its major priorities' (p. 71).

Once the Safavids came to rule as a Shia dynasty in Iran, 'the Shia ulama, many of whom had become part of the Safavid aristocracy as landowners and courtiers, crafted a new theory of government.... Shia ulama would not recognize the Safavid monarchy as truly legitimate but would bless it as the most desirable form of government during the period of waiting' for the coming of the Twelfth imam (p. 74).

This 'Safavid contract' survived for five hundred years until the Iranian revolution of 1979 and Khomeini's overthrow of the monarchy. Khomeini erased this Shia distinction between church and state underwritten by the Safavid contract with his theory of *velayat-e faqih* (guardianship of the jurist) and creating a populist theocracy in Iran. But the other Shia ulama did not accept Khomeini's doctrine, most importantly Grand Ayatollah al-Khoei, the mentor of

Ayatollah Sistani in Iraq. Khomeini's notion of velayat-e faqih was a neo-Platonic notion 'of a specially educated "guardian" class led by the "philosopher-king"' (p. 126).

Khomeini's influence and his deviant theory has now lost influence even in Iran, where the quietest traditional view of a less politicized faith, as represented by the Iraqi Ayatollah al-Khoei and his disciple Sistani, are gaining influence (p. 219). It is this victory of the old quietest Shia Islam—with its opening to alternative interpretations through itjihad, and its implicit acceptance of the separation of church and state—over Khomeini's political Shia Islam which offers the best hope of a Muslim Enlightenment.

86. However, recently the *Economist* ('The New Arab cosmopolitanism', Nov. 4, 2017) reports that according to the pollster Arab Barometer many of those who backed the Islamists during the Arab Spring in 2011 have changed their minds about enforcing sharia law. 'In Egypt support for enforcing sharia fell from 84% in 2011 to 34% in 2016' (p. 56). Also from Saudi Arabia, where Crown Prince Muhammad bin Salman has 'curbed the religious police, sacked thousands of imams and launched a new Centre for Moderation to censor "fake and extremist texts", and started the process of enforcing gender equality by allowing women to drive and enter sports stadiums' (p. 55), to the UAE where Crown Prince Muhammad bin Zayed has financed Western universities, and allowed women into the military, a crop of young new Arab leaders are relaxing religious and social restrictions and leading a regional campaign against Islamist movements. They are imitating Kemal Ataturk in Turkey who 'abolished the caliphate and sharia, and banned traditional garb, all the while consolidating his power' (p. 56). But, in 'Algeria, Jordan and Palestine, polls show that support for Islamist movements is high and growing' (p. 56). So though the tide of political Islam seems to be turning, it is too soon to proclaim that all of West Asia has embraced modernity and the disorder that still prevails in the region will come to an end.

PART II

Geoeconomics

CHAPTER FOUR

The Great Recession and After

It is the global financial crisis of 2008 (GFC), which began with the collapse of Lehman Brothers, and its aftermath that has led many of the wannabe imperial powers to believe that it marked the beginning of the end of the American imperium. Many also saw it as signalling that the liberal market-based capitalist system was deeply flawed and that a dirigiste system needed to replace it. There has also been a continuing debate about the causes of the Great Recession as well as whether the best means were used to deal with it, in which a crude Keynesianism has resurfaced. Finally, the GFC and its denouement, where the financial Masters of the Universe who caused it are not seen to have paid for their mistakes and were allowed to take their money and run, has caused widespread popular discontent as reflected in the various Occupy movements in Western capitals and in the electoral successes in the primaries of right- and left-wing political insurgents Donald Trump and Bernie Sanders in the race for the White House. This popular discontent has now put the improbable Donald Trump in the White House with unknown consequences for US economic and foreign policy. This chapter examines all these economic controversies.

Financial crises have been ubiquitous throughout human history. They have usually been associated with the debts of sovereigns. For sovereigns have always been short of money: to fight wars, to pay retainers, build palaces, keep mistresses, and sundry other expenses. As sovereigns are needed to end the 'war of all against all' in what would otherwise be a Hobbesian state of anarchy, they have to be given a monopoly of force to provide the basic public goods of law and order and national defence. To pay for this, they have to be given the sole power to tax. Given this access to revenue—both current and prospective—they have been able to borrow by promising to pay their debt and its servicing from their future earnings. But given the uncertainty of these future revenues as well as expenditures, they have often found themselves unable to pay back their debts. They have resorted to various methods to balance their books, the most common being debasement of their currency, raising tax rates, cutting inessential expenditure, or resorting to further borrowing; if all this fails, they have defaulted on their debt, thereby ruining their creditors. Edward III of England defaulted on his debt to Italian lenders in 1340 to overcome his fiscal problems after a failed invasion of France set off the Hundred Years' War. Henry VIII debased the currency and expropriated the Catholic Church's large estates and monasteries. The French abrogated their foreign debt eight times between 1500 and 1800 and, for good measure, also executed their domestic creditors while they were ruining their foreign bankers. Spain defaulted on its foreign debt six times between the sixteenth and eighteenth centuries and seven times in the nineteenth century.

Carmen Reinhart and Kenneth Rogoff in their monumental study of eight centuries of financial crises—*This Time Is Different*—have charted the occurrence of these financial crises.[1] Figure 4.1 (a) and (b) show the percentage of all independent countries in default or debt restructuring on their external debt from 1800 to 2006. They attest not only to the large number of countries that have defaulted on their external sovereign debt but also that since 1800, there have been periods of what could be called a global

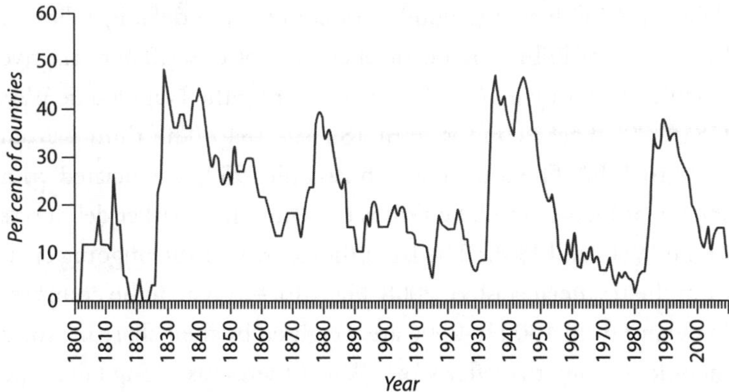

FIGURE 4.1(A) Sovereign External Debt: 1800–2006 Per cent of Countries in Default or Restructuring

Source: Reinhart and Rogoff (2008): *This Time Is Different*, Fig. 1.[2]

Notes: Sample size includes all countries, out of a total of sixty-six, that were independent states in the given year.

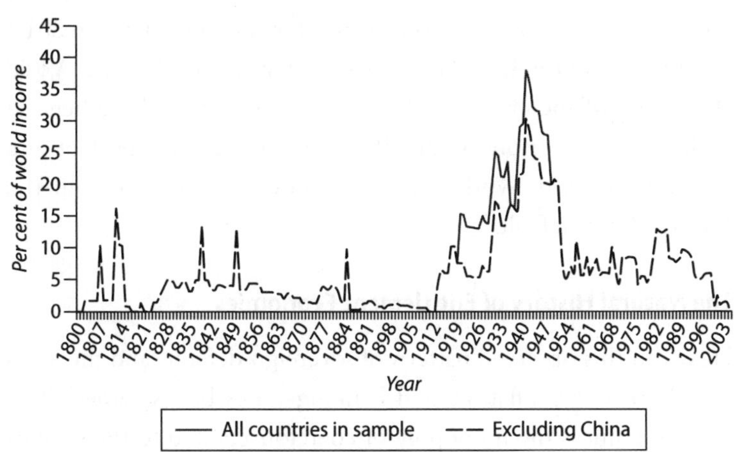

FIGURE 4.1(B) Sovereign External Debt: 1800–2006 Countries in Default Weighted by Their Share of World Income

Source: Reinhart and Rogoff (2008): *This Time Is Different*, Fig. 2.

Notes: Sample size includes all countries, out of a total of sixty-six that were independent states in the given year. Three sets of GDP weights are used: 1913 weights for the period 1800–1913, 1990 weights for the period 1914–90, and finally 2003 weights for the period 1991–2006. Derived from same sources as in Fig. 4.1(a).

debt crisis (with a large number of countries in default) followed by periods of lull in the occurrence of debt crises. There are five default cycles in Fig 1(a).[3] The first is during the Napoleonic Wars (1810–20). The second is from 1820 to 1840. The third is from 1870 to 1890. The fourth, which lasts till 1950, is associated with the Great Depression. The fifth is the emerging market debt crisis of the 1980s and 1990s. The latest (not shown) is the ongoing crisis from the financial crash of 2008. Fig. 1(b)—in which the countries in default from 1800 to 2006 are weighted by their share in world income—shows that after World War II there was a long lull in the default cycle, matching that in the two decades before World War I—the heyday of the Gold Standard. The only post–World War II spike (till the recent GFC) was with the emerging markets debt crisis in the 1980s and 1990s. This had a similar peak to those in the early 1800s.

These sovereign external debt crises have been accompanied by defaults on domestic debt, banking and currency crises, and stock market crashes. Reinhart and Rogoff have developed a composite index of these joint crises for the period 1900–2010, charted in Figure 4.2.[4] This shows that since the Second World War, none of the crises till the latest crash of 2008 have been as widespread or serious as the 1907 banking panic, the debt and inflation crises of World War I, the Great Depression, and the World War II defaults.

The Natural History of Entitlement Economies

How can this observed pattern of sovereign defaults and the associated currency, inflation, and banking crises be explained? The starting point is the monopoly of coercion granted to the state to prevent anarchy. This monopoly of coercion includes the power to tax (or take), to finance the classical public goods of maintaining law and order and protection against internal and external aggression. But, except for the benevolent Platonic guardian state of our economic textbooks, most states will in effect be predatory, engaged in what can best be described as a Mafiosi protection racket. They will tax their prey—to the extent allowed by

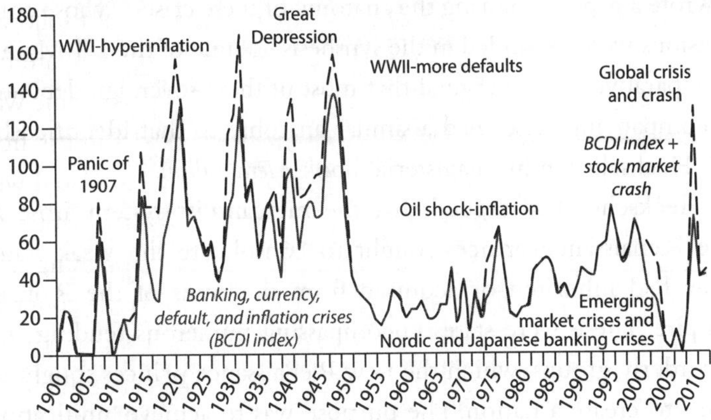

FIGURE 4.2 Varieties of Crises: World Aggregate, 1900–2010. A Composite Index of Banking, Currency, Sovereign Default, and Inflation Crises and Stock Market Crashes (Weighted by Their Share of World Income).
Source: Reinhart and Rogoff (2008): *This Time Is Different*, Fig. 3.
Notes: The banking, currency, default (domestic and external), and inflation composite (BCDI index) can take a value between 0 and 5 (for any country in any given year), depending on the varieties of crises taking place on a particular year. For instance, in 1998 the index took on a value of 5 for Russia, as there was a currency crash, a banking and inflation crisis, and a sovereign default on both domestic and foreign debt obligations. This index is then weighted by the country's share in world income. This index is calculated annually for the sixty-six countries in the sample for 1800–2010 (shown above for 1900 onwards). They have added, for the borderline banking cases identified in Laeven and Valencia (2010)[5] for the period 2007–10. In addition, they use the Barro and Ursua (2009)[6] definition of a stock market crash for the twenty-five countries in their sample (a subset of the sixty-six country sample—except for Switzerland) for the period 1864–2006; we update their crash definition through June 2010 to compile our BCDI+ index. For the United States, for example, the index posts a reading of 2 (banking crisis and stock market crash) in 2008; for Australia and Mexico it also posts a reading of 2 (currency and stock market crash).

competition from prospective internal or external competitors to their natural monopoly in coercion—to maximize their net revenue. This net revenue can be used for their own purposes in absolutist monarchies of yore, or to expand the bureaucracies in bureaucratic authoritarian states like China or the Soviet Union, or to buy the votes of the 'median voter' in democracies

In the 1980s, working as the research administrator at the World Bank, I observed the emerging market debt crisis first hand.

I wrote a paper exploring the anatomy of these crises[7] whose conclusions were expanded in the synthesis volume of the Lal-Myint[8] comparative study. I argued that most of these sovereign debt and accompanying crises had a similar anatomy to that identified by Eli Heckscher in his magisterial book *Mercantilism*.[9]

Heckscher had argued that the mercantilist system arose as the Renaissance princes sought to consolidate the weak states they had inherited or acquired from the ruins of the Roman empire. These were states encompassing numerous feuding and disorderly groups, which the new Renaissance princes sought to curb to create a nation. The purpose was to achieve 'unification and power', making the 'State's purposes decisive in a uniform economic sphere and to make all economic activity subservient to considerations corresponding to the requirements of the State'. The mercantilist policies—with their industrial regulations, state-created monopolies, import and export restrictions, and price controls—were partly motivated by the objective of granting royal favours in exchange for revenue to meet the chronic fiscal crisis of the state. Another objective was to extend the span of government control over the economy to facilitate its integration.

The nineteenth-century Age of Reform was motivated less by the writings of Adam Smith than by the desire of governments to regain their fiscal bases, which had been destroyed by the unintended consequences of the dirigisme promoted by mercantilism. The results were spectacular. As Heckscher noted, the new-found economic liberalism achieved the goal sought by mercantilism. 'Great power for the state, the perpetual and fruitless goal of mercantilist endeavour, was translated into fact in the 19th century. In many respects this was the work of laissez-faire, even though the conscious effort of the latter tended in an entirely different direction'.[10]

An uncannily similar process accounts for the contemporary move from mercantilist controls to economic liberalization in the Third and Second Worlds. In Lal and Myint,[11] we documented how many of the twenty-five countries in the comparative study had set up dirigiste neo-mercantilist regimes after the Second World War but switched policies in the 1970s and 1980s in the face of fiscal-cum-balance-of-payments crises. A major consequence of dirigisme is that it creates politically determined current and future income streams for various favoured groups (infant, declining, or sick industries; industrial labour; regional interests; the deserving and undeserving poor; and old age pensioners, to name just a few). They can all be labelled 'entitlements'.

As these entitlements are implicit or explicit subsidies to particular groups, they have to be paid for by explicit or implicit taxation of other groups in the economy. In fact, all government interventions—including regulation—are equivalent to a set of implicit or explicit taxes or subsidies. However justified on grounds of purported social welfare, the gradual expansion of this transfer state entailed by burgeoning entitlements leads to some surprising dynamic consequences. They are similar to those adumbrated by Heckscher for the European seventeenth and eighteenth centuries.

The gradual expansion of politically determined entitlements creates specific property rights. The accompanying tax burden to finance them leads, at some stage, to generalized tax resistance—promoting tax avoidance and evasion—and to the gradual but inevitable growth of the parallel or underground economy. With inelastic or declining revenues and burgeoning expenditure commitments, incipient or actual fiscal deficits become chronic. There are only three ways to finance them: domestic borrowing, external borrowing, or the levying of the inflation tax.

Many countries at different times and places have tried all three with dire consequences. Domestic borrowing to close the fiscal gap crowds out private investment, damaging future growth and, thereby, future tax revenues. The fiscal deficit may be financed by foreign borrowing for a time, but this form of financing is inherently unstable. The debt-service ratio can become unviable if the interest costs of foreign borrowing increase and the ability of the economy to generate the requisite fiscal surpluses to service the higher interest costs of publically guaranteed debt is limited. Thereupon, foreign lending can abruptly cease, leading to the kind of debt crisis that plagued emerging markets in the 1980s and 1990s and that plagues the Club Med countries today. The third way of financing the deficit, through the use of the inflation tax, is also unviable over the medium run, for it promotes a further growth of the parallel economy and a substitution of some indirect or direct form of foreign-currency-based assets for domestic money as a store of value. The tax base for levying the inflation tax thus shrinks rapidly as the economy veers into hyperinflation.

With taxes being evaded, domestic and foreign credit virtually at an end, and private agents having adjusted to inflation to avoid the inflation tax, the government finds its fiscal control of the economy vanishing. It may not even be able to garner enough resources to pay the functionaries required to perform the classical state functions of providing law and order, defence, and essential infrastructure. This dynamic process, whereby the expansion of the transfer state leads to the unexpected and very un-Marxian withering away of the state, has rarely reached its full denouement, although in the 1980s in some countries—Peru, Ghana, Tanzania—it came close.

The usual response is to regain a degree of fiscal control through some liberalization of controls, some tax reform, and monetary correction. Their aim is to raise the economy's growth rate as well as the yield from whatever taxes are being paid and to improve the debt-service ratio, in the hope that this will lead to a resumption of voluntary lending. But unless the underlying fiscal problem (which is that of unsustainable public expenditure commitments, that is, entitlements) has been tackled, these liberalization attempts have been usually aborted.

It is only when the near-complete breakdown of the society and economy poses the danger of an even greater loss of future income streams than that resulting from the rescinding of the existing political entitlements created by past dirigisme—which are the source of the problem—that the bitter pill of a complete change in policy regime is swallowed. Many countries in

Latin America, Africa, Asia, and the countries of 'really existing socialism' did finally swallow the pill in the 1980s and early 1990s, ushering in another Age of Reform. The most notable were China, India, and Russia's movement from the plan to the market. But, as in the nineteenth century, in this latest period, too, the classical liberal policies of Gladstonian finance, sound money, and open economies—which as before delivered unimagined world prosperity—were soon threatened by a new dirigisme in the old votaries of classical liberal economics, the developed countries. It is this creeping Western dirigisme and the entitlements it has created that lie at the root of the continuing GFC. These entitlements cover not only the usual explicit entitlements of the welfare state, but the even larger implicit ones created for the Masters of the Universe of the financial system, as I argue in the next two sections.

On this natural history of entitlements, the crisis will ultimately have to be resolved through rescinding most of these unsustainable entitlements. But, as the experience of developing countries like Ghana showed, there is a lot of ruin left in countries when the entitlement crisis hits. This is even more so in the much richer countries of the West. It would be a brave soul who would predict when the reform phase of the cycle will begin in earnest. From the political gridlock in the US and the slow dance of death of the eurozone, it could still be a long time coming and could, as it has in the past, be accompanied with nasty political upheavals.

The Great Recession[12]

It has now been more than nine years since the Great Crash of September–October 2008. An immense amount has been written about its causes, and the consequences are still being worked out, not least by policy makers divided by fears of future deflation or inflation. The crisis has brought all kinds of dirigiste panaceas to the fore, and there seems to have been a revival of crude Keynesianism amongst the commentariat and policymakers. Some have seen the crisis as the sign of the collapse of capitalism.

This section begins by examining the major reason purported for this crisis based on so-called 'global imbalances', which I argue is mistaken, before going on to describe a major structural change in the US financial system (still disputed), and then to list the commonly agreed policy errors which led to the crisis. I then discuss the theoretical framework, which in my view provides the best diagnosis of the crisis, and the errors of omission and commission of the monetary authorities that led to the crisis as well as assessing their response in its aftermath. This leads on to the basic underlying cause of the crisis, which is similar to that found in many other past crises as discussed in the last section—the creation of unsustainable entitlement economies. But this must be supplemented by what Milton Friedman called 'monetary mischief'—also the title of his last book. I end with what a classical liberal response would be to prevent or mitigate such crises in the future.

Global Imbalances

The ongoing concern with global imbalances (seen as a cause of the crisis, as well as the 1980s Third World debt crisis) expressed by a host of commentators[13] and officials[14] gives me a tremendous sense of déjà vu. In my 1990 Wincott lecture,[15] I had examined the case for international co-ordination to deal with the purported global imbalances of the 1980s and found it wanting. Though no doubt the purported problems leading to these imbalances (the low consumption share in China and its undervalued exchange rate, the inflexible labour markets in Europe and dysfunctional welfare states, Japanese reluctance to allow immigration and foreign investment, etc.) may be of concern to the citizens of the respective countries being lectured to, should they be of concern to the rest of the world? The discussion of global imbalances implicitly assumes they are because of the supposed spillover effects of these various domestic policies on the global economy. But what are these spillover effects and should internationally co-ordinated public policy or international moral suasion be used to counter them?

To answer this question, it is useful to look upon the global economy as an integrated economy, where governments, central banks, households, and firms in each nation are all distinct economic agents acting in their own perceived self-interest, with their own objectives. The international markets for goods and assets will co-ordinate these myriad decisions into changing relative prices, which at the national level will be reflected in changing macroeconomic variables like interest rates, real exchange rates, and savings rates. With both public and private agents maximizing their own perceived interests, this decentralized international system is exactly like a market system.

The changes in prices and outputs that arise as a result of the different actions of these agents are exactly like the increase in demand, say, for shoes within a national economy, which, ceteris paribus, raises the price of leather and hence affects the financial circumstances of the purchaser of handbags. The macroeconomic international spillovers are exactly like those affecting the handbag buyer, which (in the economist's jargon) are 'pecuniary' externalities mediated through the price mechanism and of no significance for the efficiency of the economy. They are synonymous with market interdependence and the price system and irrelevant for public policy.[16]

Changing Financial Structures

As I mentioned earlier, in the early 1980s, I was working as the research administrator at the World Bank while the Third World was engulfed by a debt crisis. The current GFC has eerie similarities, but different outcomes. Why?

First, both the crises arose because there was a surplus of savings in a number of countries—the oil producers in the 1970s, the Asian economies and commodity exporters today—which was recycled through the international banking system. Second, highly liquid banks imprudently funnelled cheap credit to non-creditworthy borrowers: the fiscally challenged and inflation prone countries of Latin America and Africa in the 1970s, and the *ninja* (those with no income, no jobs, no assets) subprime mortgagees of the current crisis. Third, there was a rise in commodity prices and a worsening of the terms of trade of the OECD, posing the stagflation dilemma for their central banks, which had aided and abetted the earlier asset boom. Fourth, the imprudent banks sought bailouts from taxpayers, claiming their demise would fatally damage the world's financial system.

But, the outcomes have been different. The 1980s crisis was finally solved, after a prolonged game of cat and mouse, when the banks accepted substantial write downs of their Third World debt, sacked their imprudent mangers, and shareholders suffered large losses. But no systemic threat to the world's financial system (or the global economy) emerged.

What then explains this difference in outcomes in the current GFC from the Third World debt crises of the 1980s and 1990s? It cannot be purported global imbalances, even if they were, as is claimed, the origins of both crises. It is the differences in financial structures within which these temporally separated but largely similar crises occurred. In the 1970s, the recycling of the global surpluses was undertaken by the *offshore* branches of Western money centre banks, which were neither supervised nor had access to the *lender of last resort* (LLR) facilities of their parent country's central bank. Hence, when their Third World euro/dollar loans went into default, there was no direct threat to the Western banking system.

The present crisis emerged in a radically different financial structure: the rise of universal banks from the UK's Big Bang financial liberalization in the 1980s and the Clinton-era abolition of the Glass–Steagall Act, which had kept a firewall between the *commercial* and *investment* banking parts of the financial system since the 1930s. The former had implicit deposit insurance and access to the central banks' LLR facilities. The latter did not. It is worth explaining why this matters.

This distinction between what were previously non-bank financial intermediaries (NBFIs) and banks is important because it is only clearing banks which can add to (or reduce) the stock of money. A clearing bank holds deposits in cash (legal tender base money) from non-banks, repaying deposits in notes and making payments for depositors by settlements in cash through an account in the central bank. When a clearing bank extends a loan, it adds to its assets and simultaneously creates deposit liabilities against itself, increasing the broad money supply at the stroke of a pen. This ability to create money out of thin air is limited by the bank's capital and cash. As cash can be borrowed from the central bank, the ultimate constraint on its ability to create money is its capital. But it is only because banks take in cash deposits—Keynes' 'widow's cruse'—that they can create money.

By contrast, an NBFI, say a mortgage lender, when it takes deposits or makes a mortgage loan has to 'clear' these through deposits held at the clearing banks. Thus when someone deposits 'cash' at an S&L, this comes out of the depositor's bank account with a clearing bank. Similarly, when the S&L makes a loan to a mortgagee, this comes from the S&L's bank account with a clearing bank. Thus, the essential difference between NBFIs and clearing banks is that they cannot create the bank deposit component of broad money (M2 or M4).

When the Federal Deposit Insurance Corporation (FDIC) was created as part of Roosevelt's New Deal, to prevent the bank runs which the earlier universal banks' gambling had engendered, Marriner Eccles—who redesigned the Federal Reserve system for FDR in the Great Depression—insisted that with deposit insurance, the banking industry must be split in half: the public utility part of the financial system, which constitutes the payments system, *must* be kept separate from the gambling investment banking part, which still remains an essential part of a dynamic economy. For these gambles impart the dynamic efficiency through the cleansing processes of creative destruction. But if these gambles are protected against losses by taxpayers, as the payment system activities have to be because of deposit insurance, the gamblers will always win, keeping their gains when their gambles are correct and passing their losses onto taxpayers when their gambles turn sour. Hence, the Glass–Steagall Act.

Given this 'moral hazard', many classical liberals have favoured free banking. Banks combining the payment and investment functions and issuing their own notes should be *monitored by their depositors*, who would stand to lose if their banks undertook imprudent lending. But with the near universality of deposits as a means of payment, there is little likelihood of this monitoring function being effectively exercised. Simultaneously, the rise of demos precludes any government being able to resist pressures to bail out imprudent banks to protect their depositors. This makes deposit insurance inevitable, and to prevent investment banks from gambling with the taxpayer-insured deposit base, something akin to Glass–Steagall remains essential.[17,18]

Policy Errors

The recent emergence of universal banking was followed by a number of public policy mistakes on the path to the current crisis. The *first* was the bail out of Long-Term Capital Management (LTCM) in 1998. Its failure posed no obvious systemic threat.[19] Its public salvation changed expectations of market participants that NBFIs could also hope for bailouts. *Next*, the infamous 'Greenspan put', which put a floor to the unwinding of the dot-com stock market bubble, promoted excessive risk taking.[20] *Third,* the promotion of affordable housing for the poor by the Clinton administration, through the unreformed and failed Freddie mortgage twins, led to the development of subprime mortgages. *Fourth*, the Basel II capital adequacy requirements led banks to put their risky assets into opaque, off-balance-sheet structured investment vehicles—or SIVs. *Fifth*, when the housing bubble burst and the credit crunch began, with the gambles taken during it turning sour, the Fed chose to bail out Bear Sterns, sending the signal that the Fed's balance sheet was open to non-deposit taking 'banks' as signalled by the earlier LTCM bailout. *Sixth,* and most heinously, given all that had gone before, the US authorities then chose *not* to bail out Lehman—like a fallen woman suddenly finding virtue. This dashing of the bailout expectations, which the authorities had endorsed only in the spring, led to the intensification of the credit crunch. *Seventh*, as the authorities finally seemed to tackle the toxic subprime infected financial assets—which caused the crisis—through the Troubled Asset Relief Program (TARP), it calmed the markets. When TARP was changed to be used only to recapitalize banks, markets went into free fall. The essential steps of forcing banks to come clean on their balance sheets and then removing the toxic assets they revealed into a newly created institutional cordon sanitaire were not taken. Worse, instead of recreating a firewall between the payment part and the gambling part of the banking system, even the pure investment banks, such as Goldman Sachs, were pushed into becoming universal banks with access to the Fed's balance sheet and thence taxpayer's money.

Given these public shortcomings, the near universal calls for greater regulation and state intervention are astounding. Public agents, not private ones—who reacted rationally to the implicit or explicit 'rules of the game' promoted—are to blame for the crisis. It would be foolish to blame the puppets for the failings of the puppeteer.[21]

Remedies

What of the remedies? Because of the association of Keynes' name with the Great Depression, the crisis and its cures are being seen through 'crass Keynesian' lenses. Is this appropriate?

Here, a personal note is in order. When I got my first academic job as a lecturer at Christ Church, Oxford, my senior colleague was Sir Roy Harrod—Keynes' first biographer and keeper of his flame. On having to provide a reading list for my tutorials on economic fluctuations and growth, I asked him what I should ask my pupils to read. I expected him to say Keynes, and his own work on trade cycles and growth. But, after some reflection, he said, Wicksell. So before I prescribed this to my pupils, I immersed myself in *Interest and Prices* and *Lectures on Political Economy*. Since then I have been pleasantly surprised that most of the macroeconomic perspectives on offer really hark back to Wicksell.[22]

Wicksell asked how the price level could be anchored in a pure credit economy. Bagehot had observed in *Lombard Street* that the whole of the Bank of England's note issue depended on a slender and declining gold ratio. Wicksell asked: What if this ratio went to zero? His answer was that if the bank rate were set at the *natural* rate of interest, which balances productivity with thrift, the price level could be kept constant. This is, of course, the theory underlying inflation targeting, as embodied in the Taylor rule.[23] As John Taylor has noted, it was the failure of the Greenspan Fed to follow this rule that led to the credit bubble after the dotcom bust.[24]

The reasons for this failure are provided by Hayek's refurbished Austrian theory of the trade cycle. Hayek saw divergences between the Wicksellian natural and market rates of interest as causing booms and slumps. If increased bank credit leads to market interest rates below the natural rate, businesses will undertake relatively more capital-intensive projects with relatively low rates of return. There will also be an unsustainable boom, with more projects undertaken than can be completed, leading to resource scarcities that end the boom. The financial crash which follows will lead to the liquidation of these 'maladjustments', followed by an economic recovery with resources being reallocated in line with inter-temporal consumer preferences and resource availabilities. While broadly accepting the quantity theory of money, Hayek argues that it assumed the absence of 'injection' effects, which even with prices stable could lead to false signals in the pattern of inter-temporal prices and thence to maladjusted investments. The recent US housing boom, with a stable general price level, provides an example of these maladjustments.[25]

Though Hayek provides the best diagnosis of the cause of the crisis, neither he nor Keynes provide an adequate explanation of the financial aspects of business cycles, assuming these are endogenous to the fluctuations in the real economy. It is Irving Fisher who provided the correct diagnosis of the nature and cures for the current crisis. Fisher saw a 'balance sheet recession' as an essential element in the Great Depression. He argued that, while there were many cyclical factors behind trade cycles, for severe economic depressions the two dominant factors are '*over-indebtedness* to start with and *deflation* following soon after'.[26] Like Hayek and other Austrians he saw over-indebtedness as caused by 'easy money'.[27] This provides a succinct explanation of the crisis and pointers to its cure. The Great Recession was a Hayekian recession with Fisherian consequences.[28] I turn to examine the various means to deal with the crisis.

Central Banks and Monetary Policy

The first means is monetary policy.

The Bank of England, the oldest central bank, evolved over the centuries. With its notes becoming legal tender, it had two functions as the central banker: to maintain the purchasing power of its notes (monetary stability) and to ensure that the commercial deposit-taking banks' deposit liabilities are always convertible into the legal tender at par (financial stability).[29] Inflation targeting by a central bank independent of political influence from the government (which has an incentive in democracies to use monetary policy to generate political business cycles) is now recognized as essential to maintain monetary stability. The Taylor rule provides a rough and ready guide to central banks to achieve this aim.[30] It was the Greenspan put, which neglected this rule, that led to the excessive growth in the US money supply[31] and was a proximate cause of the crisis.[32]

The second part of the central bank's task to maintain financial stability is fulfilled in a crisis by following the rules Bagehot laid down in the nineteenth century in *Lombard Street* for dealing with a financial panic. The central bank should act as an LLR to the commercial banks by lending unlimited cash to a *solvent* but *illiquid* bank at a penalty rate against good collateral. The Bank of England successfully followed these principles without any bank runs till the bank run on Northern Rock in September 2007. Its failure was in part due to the tripartite system introduced by Gordon Brown. As per this system, the Bank of England was independent and had sole responsibility for maintaining monetary stability, and an independent Financial Services Authority along with the Treasury was charged with maintaining financial stability. When the Northern Rock run started, the central bank with no knowledge of its balance sheet could not perform its traditional LLR function. Instead, the bank was in effect nationalized—with all the deposits protected, but with most of the shareholders wiped out. It turns out that the bank was illiquid and not insolvent.[33] The return of responsibility for financial stability to the bank by the Conservative-Lib Dem government was a move in the right direction and should be able to avert similar panics in the future.

The US Federal Reserve, as Allan Meltzer's magisterial history shows, has by contrast

> in nearly a century of experience with financial failures … never developed and announced a lender of last resort policy. Sometimes it lets the institution fail: sometimes it lends to keep it solvent. Failure to announce and follow an explicit strategy increases uncertainty and encourages troubled institutions to press for bail-outs at taxpayer's expense. The credit crisis after 2007 is the latest example.[34]

This, despite the fact that the Federal Reserve has recognized 'that it is the lender of last resort to the entire financial system'.[35]

Accepting the LLR role to provide liquidity to solvent banks or to all financial institutions (as in the US) would avoid financial panics. But what should be done about the insolvent banks and, for the US (given the Federal Reserve's extended LLR role), insolvent financial institutions? They need to be closed down in an orderly bankruptcy procedure. The 1991 Federal Deposit Insurance Corporation Improvement Act (FDICIA) extended the FDIC's authority to cover even solvent banks whose capital had been reduced (by losses) below regulatory limits and allowed them to be merged or sold. A simple measure to maintain the financial stability mandate would be to extend the FDICIA to *all* financial institutions.

But, despite fulfilling the LLR function, how can the central bank avoid the deflationary Fisherian consequences of a financial crisis when—after the Hayekian boom—deleveraging is required by most agents in the economy? It has been claimed (most stridently by Paul Krugman in his *New York Times* columns) that once the central bank cuts interest rates to close to zero, it will face the fabled Keynesian liquidity trap, and so the only recourse is to keep aggregate demand up through massive fiscal spending. Japan is cited as the prime example of a country that has been in such a trap with deflation and a stagnant economy since its asset price bubble burst in the early 1990s. But is this argument valid?[36]

Meltzer has emphasized that there can be no Keynesian liquidity trap, which eliminates the effect of monetary expansion on the real economy. On the Keynesian view, he says:

> Once the interest rate reaches a minimum value, monetary policy becomes impotent; changes in the stock of money are absorbed by money holders at an unchanged interest rate. But this implication is wrong in monetarist analysis. Market interest rates are only one of the relative prices affected by monetary impulses. An increase in the monetary base would not lower the interest rate but asset prices would increase. Relative price changes and their effects on spending would not be eliminated by a liquidity trap for interest rates.[37]

In the 1970s, these monetarist arguments came to be accepted and many countries, including the US and UK, began setting broad money growth targets. But, financial innovations (the end of ceilings on the interest rates commercial banks could pay on deposits in the US; the UK Big Bang; and new ways of making payments along with new close substitutes for money) in the 1980s led to predictions of growth outcomes on the basis of the money growth targets being undermined by the changes in the velocity of circulation the innovations induced. Instead of being the stable and predictable constant that Friedman and Schwartz had found from their empirical historical studies, it was now found to 'vary in the long run, as institutions, technology, and regulations evolved'.[38]

But this should not have led to the abandonment of the link between growth in nominal broad money and national income. In fact, in his empirical study of money and income, Alan Walters, one of the leading monetarists in the UK, had found[39] sub-periods when the link had broken down. Yet, that did not persuade him that monetary policy was not potent. He felt that even if the statistical estimates of the link between money and income were weaker in the 1980s than the 1960s, there was still a powerful influence on the economy from a lower to a higher money growth path.[40]

Fiscal Policy

For countries with a low or no structural deficit, it makes sense to raise aggregate demand when facing a severe financial crisis by running a temporary budget deficit.

The US had an arguably unmanageable structural deficit. Moreover, the stimulus package it adopted in 2009 was a dog's breakfast and failed to achieve its objectives. It failed to adopt the obvious means to restore household and firm balance sheets—by a massive across-the-board tax cut accompanied by an equivalent fiscal deficit. It is argued that most of this extra income will be saved not spent. But this is to be bewitched by the wholly inappropriate Keynesian income–expenditure analysis, which fails to deal with balance sheets. If this Fisherian aftermath of a Hayekian recession is caused by attempts to reduce unsustainable debt, the 'savings' generated by the tax cut (that is, reducing liabilities to the government)[41] will allow the necessary deleveraging without a downward spiral in income and increased bankruptcies. By facilitating households to pay off their mortgage and credit card debts, it will prevent further impairment of bank assets. As the *Financial Times*[42] reported, the parts of the Obama stimulus package that worked were the 'fast acting tax breaks and transfer payments [which] largely explain why disposable income rose 2.9 per cent from January to May 2009, even as earned income fell 0.7 per cent, allowing the savings rate to rise without a collapse in spending'. If the whole of the $787 billion stimulus package had consisted of an across-the-board tax cut, there would have been a large deleveraging of the economy with an increase in private savings without an equivalent cut in private spending. The increased private savings being matched by public dis-savings would have been reflected in the increased budget deficit. Also the tax cut could be reversed once the economy recovered, providing an easy 'exit strategy' from the fiscal stimulus.[43]

This inept fiscal stimulus was then accompanied by the misguided healthcare reforms, which have added significantly to the US structural deficit. This has made any further fiscal stimulus politically difficult. In the UK, with a large structural deficit fuelled by increased welfare spending by the Labour government, there was little space for any further fiscal expansion. The new coalition government was therefore right to create more fiscal space by a sharp cutback in public spending through rolling back the unsustainable welfare state. The spending cuts were followed by the Bank of England loosening its monetary policy through quantitative easing.

Similarly, in the eurozone, the European Central Bank (ECB) rightly undertook quantitative easing during the crisis while urging reduction of fiscal deficits. The success of Germany in following this advice, by reversing the stalling in its GDP, points to the success of this policy. The eurozone problems now concern financial stability related to the Greek debt crisis. As many of the banks in the non–Club Med members of the zone are exposed to Greek sovereign debt, a Greek debt default would lead to a serious eurozone banking crisis. To avoid this, the ECB and IMF have imposed an IMF-type stabilization programme on Greece. But unlike similar stabilization programmes in developing countries, two essential elements are missing: a large devaluation and a restructuring of the country's debt. The former is precluded by the fixed exchange rate of the euro, the latter by the external holdings of Greek sovereign debt by European banks. But the alternative imposed on Greece is a large *internal devaluation* to engineer a large fall in domestic wages and prices through a massive deflation. It is difficult to believe that Greek politics will allow the country to follow this path, particularly when even at its end, Greece is likely to be left with a debt-GDP ratio of 150 per cent. A Greek default and exit from the euro seems the most likely eventual outcome. The other Club Med countries should, however, be able to politically manage the fiscal retrenchment required in their less indebted economies.

The Great Recession also led to the advocacy by numerous academics and commentators of what I had believed was the defunct crude Keynesianism.[44] In arguing against George Osborne's 'austerity budgets', there is a repeat of the opprobrium hurled at the fiscal consolidation undertaken by the first Thatcher government; 364 economists wrote a letter to *The Times* denouncing it, claiming that it would lead to a slump. I refused to sign this letter. Similarly, during the current crisis, many of the Keynesian critics of George Osborne's fiscal consolidation have condemned it for again prolonging the slump, while in the US, the debate about the so-called 'fiscal cliff' has led to howls that the fiscal tightening would aggravate the crisis. The IMF, which has changed its previous robust defence of classical liberal policies in favour of crude Keynesianism, has decried these so-called policies of 'austerity' for damaging growth.

But, Congdon has recently argued that based on US and UK experience, the Keynesian claim that fiscal contractions necessarily depress demand and output is dubious. He examines the change in the cyclically adjusted public sector borrowing requirement (PSBR), with a reduction representing fiscal tightening, and sees if it is accompanied by below trend growth and a reduction in the 'output gap' with more spare capacity and higher unemployment. If the Keynesian view is valid, one should see an inverse relationship between changes in the cyclically adjusted budget balance and changes in the output gap.

For the US, he finds in the early 1980s the fiscal structural balance was negative for five years because of the Regan tax cuts, and there was a strong recovery from the deep recession of 1980. This was a Keynesian policy on the lines I have advocated previously for dealing with the balance sheet Great Recession. Thereafter, during the Clinton presidency, deep cuts in defence and welfare spending and the conversion of the large budget deficit (at the beginning of the presidency) into a large surplus (by its end) led to an economic boom, contrary to Keynesian fiscalism. The increases in the structural deficit in 2007–9 during the Great Recession were accompanied by a large fall in the output gap. But reductions in the structural deficit since 2010 (including the 2012 fiscal cliff) were associated with somewhat above trend growth.

For the UK, he finds there are five phases from 1980. During the first, 1981–8, the Thatcher government's fiscal policy was contractionary, but the government structural balance improved, refuting the claims of the 364 economists who had signed the letter to *The Times*. From 1989 to 1993, fiscal policy was expansionary to counter the downturn associated with the membership of the European Exchange Rate Mechanism (ERM), leading to a fall in the structural surplus. From 1994 to 2000, which includes the last years of the Conservative and early years of the Labour government, fiscal policy was contractionary with, again, a strong surplus delivered in 2000. Thereafter, from 2001 to 2009, Gordon Brown's large fiscal expansion led to the 2000 structural surplus being replaced by a structural deficit of over 10 per cent of GDP in 2009. Under George Osborne during the Conservative–Lib Dem coalition, fiscal policy was again tightened, and contrary to the academic and media commentariat's Jeremiahs, there has been a rise in the structural surplus. The IMF, which under its French chief economist Olivier Blanchard had railed against Osborne's fiscal austerity on traditional Keynesian grounds, had to eat its words when the UK economy was the fastest growing European economy in 2014.

Conclusions

Three conclusions follow. First, the professional consensus on macroeconomic policy[45] till about 2000 was correct. Keynesian countercyclical fiscal policies do not work.[46] Fiscal policy should be concerned with the microeconomy and the financing of public goods. It should aim to balance the budget over the business cycle. Second, during a balance sheet recession to avoid Fisherian deflation, temporary tax cuts to help private agents to maintain their spending and hence aggregate demand may be required, as in the US during its 1981–4 recession. Third, monetary policy based on the classical monetarism of rules rather than discretion (say the Taylor rule) should be the preferred way to deal with macroeconomic instability.

The Global Financial Crisis

The Great Recession was triggered by a global financial crisis with Lehman's collapse.

The story of financial engineering—which created more and more complex debt instruments in which tail risk was ignored and was induced by the low interest rates during the Great Moderation and exacerbated by the Greenspan put—is by now well known,[47] and I will not labour it here. Two lessons, however, are important. First, it was the policy of the US government, ever since the Great Depression, to promote housing by giving implicit subsidies to homeowners through the financial system, which led to the subprime mortgage crisis. Second, it was the moral hazard begun with the LTCM bailout, and the subsequent bailouts of financial firms which were not commercial banks and whose bankruptcy did not threaten the deposit base, which led to the mispricing of risk—with financial intermediaries coming to believe that if their increasingly risky bets were successful, they stood to make immense financial gains, and if they turned sour, the authorities would get taxpayers to bail them out.

These distortions in the US financial system were then internationalized by the asset-backed securities (ABSs) that increasingly came to be held by banks around the world. Packaging a host of different securities, including subprime mortgages, into increasingly opaque securities—in the belief that this diversification of the assets in each security basket would lower the risk of holding the security—made these securities even more insecure. It was like packaging different types of meat into pies and selling them around the world. When then it turned out that there was an infected piece of meat that had been baked into many of the pies in the form of subprime mortgages that turned sour with the downturn in the US housing market, none of the holders of the pies around the world knew if their pies contained the infected meat. All interbank lending based on these opaque ABSs ceased, triggering a global financial crisis.

The immediate official response to the crisis, in which the insurer AIG was bailed out, which then led it to fully repay its counterparties like Goldman Sachs, bailing them out in turn, only justified the beliefs of those who had undertaken the imprudent lending that any losses would be borne by taxpayers. Moral hazard increased even further. It was further accentuated with the classification of institutions as being 'too big to fail', giving an incentive for the creation of even larger universal banks that were too big to fail. With the authorities egging on the conversion of previous investment banks into bank holding companies, the US financial structure has become even more oligopolistic.

Much worse, the recently passed Dodd–Frank Wall Street Reform and Consumer Protection Act now formalizes the Federal Reserve's role in being the supervisor and LLR of the whole US banking system, which flies in the face of the classical liberal view that, once investment and commercial banking are kept separate (as it is politically impossible to end deposit insurance), the central bank should have nothing to do with the investment banking part. Investment banking can follow whatever innovations and risk-taking it chooses in competitive markets, but it must be made to bear the full costs of any mistakes.

By contrast, as Peter Wallison of the American Enterprise Institute has argued:

> [All] financial firms will, under this new structure, inevitably be subordinated to the supervisory judgments about what the firms can safely be allowed to do.... Where financial firms once focused

> on beating their competitors, they will now focus on currying favor with their regulator, which will have the power to control their every move. What may ultimately emerge is a partnership between the largest financial firms and the Federal Reserve—a partnership in which the Fed protects them from failure and excessive competition and they in turn curb their competitive instincts to carry out the government's policies and directions.[48]

In short, it is likely to substitute a sclerotic corporatist economic model, replacing the highly competitive and innovative model that, despite its flaws, has brought untold prosperity around the world.

Systemic Problems

There is, however, a more systematic problem with the Western banking system as it has evolved over the last two centuries. Banks have come to take on too much risk, whose costs have been socialized, while the returns have accrued to bank shareholders and managers.[49] This is largely because with the abolition of Glass–Steagall and the Big Bang in the UK, the global investment banks, which had continued to be private partnerships with unlimited liability, became limited liability companies, and the financial safety net created with deposit insurance was extended to virtually the whole of the Western banking system.

Remedies

How can this gross distortion in the functioning of a market economy be ended? Haldane (the chief economist at the Bank of England) suggests ways to reduce the incentives for excessive risk taking in banking. The first would be to remove the tax deductibility of debt and permit firms to deduct an allowance for corporate equity from profits. This would switch the incentives for banks to finance themselves through equity rather than debt. This would make the minimum equity capital ratios being recommended by the various versions of the Basel rules redundant.[50]

The second is to remove the asymmetric payoffs caused by the switch to limited from unlimited liability in banking. Contingent convertible securities (CoCos), which are debt in good times and convert to equity in bad, could combine the risk incentives of debt and equity. Equity prices would provide an automatic non-discriminatory trigger for the conversion. 'Equity prices called the crisis early and differentiated the sick from the sound. Market discipline worked'.[51]

The third would be to replace the return on equity (ROE) as the basis for managerial remuneration by the return on assets (ROA). Covering the whole balance sheet, ROA is not improved by leverage and hence is better adjusting for risk. Haldane estimates that if from 1989, the remuneration of the CEOs of the seven largest US banks had indexed ROA rather than ROE, their remuneration would have risen from $2.8 million to $3.4 million by 2007. Instead of rising to five hundred times the median household income, it would have fallen to around sixty-eight times. An even more 'incentive-compatible' method would be to remunerate CEOs in neither cash nor equity but in CoCos, giving them a potent incentive to prevent equity from conversion if their equity price signalled their bank was in distress.[52]

But will the political system allow these necessary reforms? In an important book, Luigi Zingales[53] has described how the US financial system has become an Italian form of crony capitalism, where government and big business are co-partners.

Competing Perspectives

What I have outlined above is the Friedmanite monetarist perspective. The stagflation of the 1970s was cured by Paul Volcker's application of the monetarist rules in the 1980s. Their continuation under Greenspan, until about 2000, led to the Great Moderation and to an academic and policy consensus that aggregate demand and changes in the price level were best managed through monetary policy. Moreover, given the uncertainty attached to the various outcomes from monetary policy instruments, it was best to follow a monetary rule. This allowed expectations about the monetary policy actions to be anchored, thereby reducing one source of uncertainty during the business cycle. Fiscal policy was to be used to mainly affect the structure of the economy and not aggregate demand. Underlying this consensus was an implicit judgement that despite the fluctuations during the business cycle, a market economy based on free enterprise and without publicly created monetary disorder would be stable.

This consensus disappeared in the recent Great Recession. Economist Robert Hetzel in his book *The Great Recession* describes how there was a revival of the view 'dominant in the 19th and early part of the 20th century that the business cycle derives from excessive swings in risk taking by investors … These fluctuations in investor sentiment between optimism and pessimism ["animal spirits" as Keynes called them] overwhelm the price system and, especially, the real interest rate to maintain full employment'.[54]

In his detailed event-based study of US monetary and business cycle history during the last century, Hetzel shows convincingly how the 2008–9 recession fits in with the 'monetary disorder' view, which focuses on the monetary instability created by central banks, rather than the 'market disorder' view which focuses on the boom–bust cycle in financial markets.[55] We need to get back to the monetarist perspective—which since the 1980s, by reversing the stop-gap policies of the 1960s and 1970s based on the market disorder view, served the West so well till the GFC of 2008–9.

Conclusions

In their monumental study of past financial and banking crises, Reinhart and Rogoff have estimated that it takes about seven years for the overhang of unsustainable public and private debt which leads to a Hayekian recession to be unwound. The debt overhang of the public sector has seldom been reduced by robust economic growth. It has instead required fiscal austerity and debt defaults (often concealed as debt restructuring). While this deleveraging is taking place to deal with the Fisherian balance sheet consequences of the recession, on monetarist prescriptions, aggregate demand can still be maintained by following the Friedmanite rules.

My conclusions can be brief. First, to avoid future crises, the entitlement economies (including the substantial implicit entitlements to bankers), which currently dominate advanced economies, need to be tamed if not dismantled. Second, with the continuance of deposit insurance, a separation between commercial banks, which can create deposits, and investment banks, which can gamble with these deposits in a 'universal' bank at taxpayer's expense, must be created.[56] Third, the investment banks should be free to take whatever risks they want without any possible bailout by the authorities. This would require them to revert to partnerships with unlimited liability. In the US, the orderly closure of failed and failing institutions should be done by the FDIC. Fourth, for the commercial banking part of the financial system, the Bagehot rules for the LLR function of central banks should be formally established and publicized. Fifth, for the monetary stability part of their mandate, central banks should monitor and control the broad money supply to mitigate booms and slumps. In essence, this is the classical liberal perspective on dealing with financial crises, which will always recur.

Notes

1. C.M. Reinhart and K.S. Rogoff, *This Time Is Different: Eight Centuries of Financial Folly* (Princeton, NJ: Princeton University Press, 2009).
2. This figure was derived from Peter H. Lindert and Peter J. Morton 'How Sovereign Debt Has Worked' in *Developing Country Debt and Economic Performance*, vol. 1, ed. J. Sachs (Chicago: University of Chicago Press, 1989), pp. 39–106; James Macdonald, *A Sovereign Nation Deep in Debt: The Financial Roots of Democracy* (New York: Farrar, Strauss and Giroux, 2006); Angus Maddison, *Historical Statistics for the World Economy, 1–2003 AD* (Paris: OECD, 2004); John Purcell and Jeffrey Kaufman, *The Risks of Sovereign Lending: Lessons from History* (New York: Salmon Brothers, 1993); Carmen Reinhart, Kenneth Rogoff, and Miguel Savastano, 'Debt Intolerance', Brookings Papers on Economic Activity, 1 (Spring 2003), pp. 1–74; Christian Suter,

Debt Cycles in the World Economy: Foreign Loans, Financial Crises and Debt Settlements, 1820–1990 (Boulder, Colo: Westview, 1992); and Standard and Poor's (various years).

3. C.M. Reinhart and K.S. Rogoff, 'This Time Is Different: A Panoramic View of Eight Centuries of Financial Crises', NBER Working Paper, No. 13882 (2008).
4. From C.M. Reinhart, 'A Series of Unfortunate Events: Common Sequencing Patterns in Financial Crises', NBER Working Paper, No. 17941 (2012).
5. Luc Laeven and Fabian Valencia, 'Resolution of Banking Crises: The Good, the Bad, and the Ugly', IMF Working Paper, No. WP/10/146.
6. Robert Barro and Josef Ursua, 'Stock Market Crashes and Depressions', NBER Working Paper, No. 14760, February 2009.
7. D. Lal, 'The Political Economy of Economic Liberalization', *World Bank Economic Review*, 1, no. 2 (1987), pp. 273–99.
8. D. Lal and H. Myint, *The Political Economy of Poverty Equity and Growth* (Oxford: Clarendon Press, 1996).
9. E. Heckscher, *Mercantilism*, Two Volumes (London: Allen and Unwin, 1955).
10. Heckscher, *Mercantilism*, p. 325.
11. Lal and Myint, *The Political Economy of Poverty, Equity and Growth.*
12. There are two recent major analytical economic histories available of the Great Recession that also compare it with the Great Depression. Robert Hetzel, *The Great Recession: Market Failure or Policy Failure?* (New York: Cambridge University Press, 2012), and Barry Eichengreen, *Hall of Mirrors: The Great Depression, the Great Recession, and the Uses—and Misuses—of History* (New York: Oxford University Press, 2015). Whilst Hetzel takes an explicitly monetarist view, Eichengreen is more eclectic and also more global in his analysis. But, by and large, Eichengreen takes what Hetzel characterizes as the 'market-disorder' view about the reasons for macroeconomic instability, whilst Hetzel takes the 'monetary disorder' view of Friedman, which I find more persuasive. Hetzel succinctly characterizes these two contrasting explanations of the business cycle: 'one highlights the market disorder resulting from swings in the psychology of financial markets from excessive risk taking to excessive risk aversion; the other highlights monetary disorder based on central bank interference with the operations of the price system' (p. 1).

13. Like the *Financial Times* star economics commentator Martin Wolf.
14. Like the former chairman of the US Federal Reserve, Ben Bernanke.
15. D. Lal, 'The Limits of International Cooperation', 20th Annual Wincott Lecture, Occasional Paper 83 (190) (London: Institute of Economic Affairs, 1989).
16. Also see R. Cooper, 'Living with Global Imbalances', Brookings Papers on Economic Activity, 2 (2007): 91–107, and W.M. Corden, 'Those Current Account Imbalances: A Sceptical View', *The World Economy*, 30 (2007), which also support this view expressed in my February 2006 Business Standard article 'Global Imbalances?' But see M. Obstfield, 'Does the Current Account Still Matter?', *American Economic Review*, 102: 3 (2012), for a contrary view, although he does not establish whether the imbalances were the cause rather than the symptom of macroeconomic stresses in the 1990s.
17. The recent emergence of universal banking has, however, been lauded by many on the classical liberal side, and the repeal of the Glass–Steagall Act is seen as a sensible measure of deregulating the financial system. See C.W. Calomiris, *US Bank Deregulation in Historical Perspective* (Cambridge: Cambridge University Press, 2000), and A.H. Meltzer, *A History of the Federal Reserve*, 3 vols (Chicago: University of Chicago Press, 2003–2009), p. 1245. Much of their argument is based on assessing whether the Glass–Steagall Act was necessary or an immoderate response to the Great Depression. But Calomiris also notes that another concern behind the Glass–Steagall Act 'was largely that of economists who correctly worried about the abuse of deposit insurance and the discount window—the possibility of government subsidization of risk in new activities' (p. xiv). This is the worry, which has not gone, particularly as he notes that deposit insurance is the only part of the 1933 Banking Act that now remains 'and it is difficult to imagine circumstances that will lead to its repeal' (p. xviii). This is the nub. It is deposit insurance alone that provides a reason for public regulation of any aspect of banking. If the Glass–Steagall firewall between commercial and investment banking is maintained, there is no reason why the investment banks should not be set completely free.
18. It has also been rightly noted, for instance by the Chicago University finance professor Luigi Zingales, that the financial institutions which were at the heart of the crisis—Bear Sterns and Lehman brothers—were investment banks not universal banks, and Bear Sterns was

'bailed out because the Federal Reserve deemed it too interconnected to fail. So why did it matter whether a commercial bank and an investment bank were jointly owned' (L. Zingales, *A Capitalism for the People: Recapturing the Lost Genius of American Prosperity* [New York: Basic Books, 2012], pp. 204). But Zingales changed his mind after attempting to read the 2,319-page Dodd–Frank financial reform bill passed in 2010, to 'fix' the financial system, and gave up. That is why the simplicity of the Glass–Steagall Act of 1933, which was just thirty-seven pages long, retains its growing popular support. As Zingales concludes, 'while Glass–Steagall may not be the most efficient form of regulation, it worked for more than sixty years.'

19. Hetzel, *The Great Recession*, rightly points out that these policy errors were based on the gradual extension of the financial safety net initially covering only deposit insurance (pp. 152–3). Thus, the crisis caused by excessive risk taking by financial institutions did not come from Wall Street's excessive greed but 'from a government created system that subsidizes the use of leverage to make risky bets' (p. 186).
20. There is an ongoing dispute on whether easy money in the US in 2003–4 following the dotcom boom contributed to the crisis. Hetzel, *The Great Recession*, argues that it did not. By contrast John Taylor argues using his Taylor rule that monetary policy was stimulative in 2002–3, whilst Ben Bernanke defends the Fed by showing that even within the Taylor framework it was not. See John B. Taylor, 'Housing and Monetary Policy', NBER Working Paper, No. 13682 (2007), and Ben Bernanke, 'Monetary Policy and the Housing Bubble', speech at annual meeting of the American Economic Association (3 January 2010), available online at http://www.federalreserve.gov/newsevents/speech/bernanke20100103a.htm. The dispute is about rules versus discretion in the conduct of monetary policy, with Hetzel and Taylor supporting a rule-based (though with different rules) and Bernanke a 'constrained discretionary' monetary policy. I, by and large, take the side of those advocating rules rather than discretion.
21. Hetzel's 'monetary disorder' explanation for the Great Recession, discounts 'any role for expansionary monetary policy in 2003–4 and instead points to contractionary monetary policy in 2008' (Hetzel, *The Great Recession*, pp. 204–5).

22. The following section has benefitted from a paper by my UCLA colleague Axel Leijonhufvud, 'Wicksell, Hayek, Keynes, Friedman: Whom Should We Follow?', paper presented at the Special Meeting of the MPS on 'The End of Globalizing Capitalism? Classical Liberal Responses to the Global Financial Crisis', New York City (5–7 March 2009).
23. See later note on Taylor rules.
24. J.B.Taylor, *Getting Off Track: How Government Actions and Interventions Caused, Prolonged, and Worsened the Financial Crisis* (Stanford, CA: Hoover Institution Press, 2009).
25. But Hayek's prescription that the slump should be allowed to run its course came to be disowned even by his LSE circle led by Robbins in the 1930s. As Gottfried Haberler, a close friend and member of Hayek's Austrian circle, noted in his astute appraisal of Hayek's business cycle theory, 'Keynes, Robbins, and many others were correct: if a cyclical decline has been allowed to degenerate into a severe slump with mass unemployment, falling prices, and deflationary expectations, government deficit spending to inject money directly into the income stream is necessary. Moreover, Hayek himself has changed his mind on this point' ('Reflections on Hayek's Business Cycle Theory', *Cato Journal* 6, no. 2 (1986), p. 422).
26. I. Fisher, 'The Debt-Deflation Theory of Great Depressions,' *Econometrica*, 1 (4) (October 1933), p. 341.
27. Fisher, 'The Debt-Deflation Theory of Great Depressions', p. 348.
28. This was also my diagnosis of the Japanese slump in Lal, 'The Japanese Slump', in R. Pethig and M. Rauscher (eds), *Challenges to the World Economy* (Berlin: Springer, 2003), pp. 281–90.
29. Tim Congdon, *Central Banking in a Free Society* (London: Institute of Economic Affairs, 2009) provides a succinct account of the evolution of central banking.
30. See later note for an explanation and discussion of this rule as an adaptation of the monetarist policy.
31. See Taylor, *Getting Off Track*.
32. But Hetzel, *The Great Recession*, argues that 'Taylor rules provide no uniform message about the appropriateness of monetary policy in the post-2002 period ... because different plausible ways of estimating Taylor rules provide very different implications for the optimal funds-target rate' (pp. 198–9).

33. See Congdon, *Central Banking in a Free Society*.
34. Meltzer, *A History of the Federal Reserve* (2009), p. 1233.
35. Meltzer, *A History of the Federal Reserve* (2009), p. 1234.
36. Central to answering this question is the transmission mechanism of monetary policy, whether monetary impulses work principally through changes in interest rates or through changes in broad money through the real balance effect, which changes relative prices and net wealth. On the traditional 'monetarist' case, fluctuations in output reflected changes in the quantity of money, and monetary policy was the main stabilization instrument. This monetary policy was to be operated 'through a combination of two blades of a scissors, the one blade being what in the USA is called the "discount rate" and in Britain is called "Bank rate", the other blade being open-market operations, the purchase and sale of government securities' Milton Friedman: 'The Counter-Revolution in Monetary Theory', Inaugural Wincott Memorial Lecture, Occasional Paper 33 (London: Institute of Economic Affairs, 1970), p. 6. This doctrine was widely accepted, including by Keynes in his *A Tract on Monetary Reform* (New York: Harcourt Bruce, 1924).

    There have been constant complaints that, the 'money to spending' transmission mechanism of Friedman's monetarism is a 'black box'. But papers by Karl Brunner and Allan Meltzer in the 1960s and 1970s and, above all, Meltzer's recent magisterial three-volume history of the US Fed should put these doubts to rest. See, e.g., K. Brunner and A. Meltzer, 'Liquidity Traps for Money, Bank Credit and Interest Rates', *Journal of Political Economy*, 76 (January-February 1968), pp. 1–37; K. Brunner and A. Meltzer, 'The Uses of Money: Money in the Theory of an Exchange Economy', *American Economic Review*, 61 (December 1971), pp. 784–805; Meltzer, *A History of the Federal Reserve* (2003, 2009).

    This complaint has, nevertheless, led within the monetarist camp to a deviant version, named by one of its progenitors, Ben Bernanke, as 'creditism' to contrast with traditional 'monetarism'. See B. Bernanke and M. Getler, 'Inside the Black Box: The Credit Channel of Monetary Policy Transmission', *Journal of Economic Perspectives*, 9, no. 4 (1995), pp. 27–48. He has argued that the relevant channel for monetary policy transmission was the credit channel, that is, bank lending to the private sector. A.H. Meltzer, 'Monetary, Credit (and Other) Transmission Processes: A Monetarist Perspective', *Journal of Economic Perspectives*, 9, no. 4 (1995), pp. 49–72, provides a monetarist reply to the creditism (or as he calls it the 'lending view'). He argues cogently that money and credit are different, and it is money that matters for the economy.

37. Meltzer, 'Monetary, Credit (and Other) Transmission Processes', p. 56. The confusion about a 'liquidity trap' and thence the impotence of monetary policy when interest rates have fallen to zero arises as in the Keynesian model, apart from money there is only one asset, short term Treasury bills.
38. Congdon, *Central Banking in a Free Society*, p. 316.
39. Alan A. Walters, 'Money in Boom and Slump: An Empirical Inquiry into British Experience since the 1880s', Hobart Paper 44, Third Edition (London: Institute of Economic Affairs, 1971).
40. See Congdon, *Central Banking in a Free Society*, Ch. 14, for a cogent critique of the UK critics of monetarism in the 1980s and 1990s. He provides an account of the institutional changes in the 1980s—which led to the 'equilibrium ratio of money to income to rise substantially' (n. 26, p. 453). Moreover, the statistical demand for money function for the personal household sector, which has been the largest money holder in the non-bank, non-public sector since the 1960s, remained stable, as shown in a Bank of England study by R. Thomas, 'The Demand for M4: A Sectoral Analysis. Part 1–The Personal Sector', Bank of England Working Paper, no. 61 (1997).
41. Unlike in the 1930s, more recently, governments in developed countries have much more leeway to do this as the share of general government revenue (their tax cut) as a share of GDP had increased from about 20 per cent in the United States and Great Britain to about 32 per cent in the United States and 38 per cent in Britain in 1997 See V. Tanzi and L. Schuknecht, *Public Spending in the Twentieth Century* (Cambridge: Cambridge University Press, 2000), p. 52.
42. K. Guha, 'White House Hit in Skirmishes Over Spending', *Financial Times*, 9 July 2009.
43. The theoretical worry that temporary tax cuts will be saved rather than raising consumption and aggregate demand is irrelevant to this case, as the purpose of the temporary tax cuts is to allow economic agents to raise their savings without reducing their previous consumption.

44. See D. Lal, *Reviving the Invisible Hand: The Case for Classical Liberalism in the Twenty-First Century* (Princeton, N.J.: Princeton University Press, 2006), p. 107. The main academics are Paul Krugman, Larry Summers, and Joseph Stiglitz in the US and Keynes's biographer Robert Skidelsky in the UK. One of the major and most influential commentators has been Martin Wolf in the *Financial Times*. See his 2013 Wincott lecture, M. Wolf, 'How the Financial Crisis Changed the World', *Economic Affairs*, 34, no. 3 (2014), pp. 286–303.
45. For a summary of this consensus, see Lal, *Reviving the Invisible Hand*, p. 107.
46. This supports the views of what have been pejoratively labelled 'Bocconi Boys' (to make them comparable to the 'Chicago Boys', the purported godfathers of the Chilean economic miracle) by M. Blyth, *Austerity: The History of a Dangerous Idea* (New York: Oxford University Press, 2013). They are economists at Bocconi University in Italy, who identified, what they describe by the malapropism, 'expansionary fiscal contractions'. F. Giavazzi and M. Pagano, 'Can Severe Fiscal Contractions Be Expansionary? Tales of Two Small European Countries', in O.J. Blanchard and S. Fischer (eds), *NBER Macroeconomics Annual 1990* (Cambridge, MA: MIT Press, 1990). This idea was taken over by Alberto Alesina, who wrote a number of papers with Bocconi economists. See A. Alesina and S. Ardagna, 'Large Changes in Fiscal Policy: Taxes Versus Spending' NBER Working Paper, no. 15438 (2009). Their view challenges the standard Keynesian view that 'fiscal contraction' depresses demand and output. IMF, *Reassesing the Role and Modalities of Fiscal Policy in Advanced Economies* (Washington, DC: IMF, 2013) provides a review, which has a distinctly Keynesian bias.

    Friedman, 'The Counter-revolution in Monetary Theory', had emphasized that budget deficits caused by increased public expenditures would lead to a 'crowding out' of private expenditures. The Bocconi school, by contrast, emphasizes the effects on private sector confidence of a credible programme of fiscal consolidation, which reduces the size of government and hence future taxes, which then leads to a rise in private spending.
47. See J. Authers, *The Fearful Rise of Markets: Global Bubbles, Synchronized Meltdowns, and How to Prevent Them in the Future* (Upper Saddle River, NJ: FT Press, 2010); Raghuram Rajan, *Fault Lines: How Hidden*

Fractures Still Threaten the World Economy (Princeton, NJ: Princeton University Press, 2010); and Gillian Tett, *Fools Gold* (London: Little Brown 2009) for incisive accounts.

48. Peter J. Wallison, 'The Dodd-Frank Act: Creative Destruction, Destroyed', *Financial Services Outlook* (American Enterprise Institute, 30 August 2010). Available online at http://www.aei.org/publication/the-dodd-frank-act-creative-destruction-destroyed/ (last accessed 20 February 2018).
49. In his brilliant 2011 Wincott lecture, Andrew Haldane (the executive director for financial stability at the Bank of England, at the time) has documented this evolution and its consequences for British and *mutatis mutandis* for US banking. It is a terrifying story. See A.G. Haldane, 'Control Rights (And Wrongs)'. Wincott Annual Memorial Lecture, (London, 24 October 2011), p. 11. Available online at https://www.bis.org/review/r111026a.pdf (last accessed 20 February 2018).

    He shows that until the mid-1800s, British banking consisted of five hundred unlimited partnership banks and seven hundred mutually owned building societies. This was converted in stages from separating ownership and control in the 1930s, into the recent system where ownership and control of banks has been reunited. But they now rest with short-term traders in equity and with managers, neither of who have an interest in the long-run health of their banks or the economy. But, this has been largely due to the extension of the financial safety net (a polite term for bailouts) to virtually the whole of the Western banking system. It is no intrinsic feature of capitalism, but public policy that has led to the socialization of the costs and privatization of the gains from excessive risk-taking in banking that is being currently decried.
50. On the Basel framework see Haldane's paper for the 2012 Jackson Hole meeting of the Kansas Fed: 'The Dog and the Frisbee', paper for Federal Reserve Bank of Kansas City's 36th economic policy symposium, 'The Changing Policy Landscape', Jackson Hole, Wyoming, 31 August 2012. Available at https://www.bankofengland.co.uk/-/media/boe/files/news/2012/august/the-dog-and-the-frisbee-paper-by-andy-haldane.pdf (accessed 5 February 2018). His major conclusion is that when the environment is complex and uncertain (with no basis for assigning actuarial type probabilities to

alternative outcomes, which themselves maybe unknown), simple rules are better than complex ones. So instead of the regulatory route based on pricing risk followed by Basel, simple regulatory commandments like '"thou shalt not" … are likely to be less fallible than: "thou shalt provided the internal model is correct". That is one reason why Glass–Steagall lasted for 60 years longer than Basel II' (p. 23).

51. Haldane, 'Control Rights (And Wrongs)', p. 11.
52. Haldane, 'Control Rights (And Wrongs)', p. 13.
53. Zingales, *A Capitalism for the People.*
54. R.L. Hetzel, *The Great Recession: Market Failure or Policy Failure?* (New York: Cambridge University Press, 2012), p xiii.
55. Hetzel, *The Great Recession*, pp. 115–6, notes that the most fundamental and still seemingly unsettled issue in macroeconomics is 'How well do the self-equilibrating powers of the price system work to maintain output at potential?' The monetary disorder view works well enough with monetary shocks, which 'interfere with determination by market forces of real variables, especially the real interest rate'. The central bank should follow a rule providing a stable nominal anchor and let the price system determine real variables. While on the market-disorder view, the central bank should intervene to control real variables like the unemployment rate, superseding the price mechanism to maintain output at potential. As he shows, by comparing periods when one or the other view has governed policy, the money disorder view trumps the market disorder view, including the current Great Recession.
56. This remains controversial even amongst American conservative economists. See Calomiris, US Bank Deregulation in Historical Perspective, and Meltzer, *A History of the Federal Reserve* (2009), p. 1245.

CHAPTER FIVE

Growth and Global Structural Change

Though, as we saw in the last chapter, the short-term future of the Western economies remains clouded, what of the long-term future and the future of the other major future geopolitical actors: China, Russia, India, and Japan? Numbers of studies have tried to answer this question. But inevitably, given the uncertainties involved, they are all looking through a glass darkly. The two studies I find most persuasive are by my late friend Angus Maddison,[1] which also puts his prognostications about the evolution of the global economy till 2030 in historical perspective, and the other, a recent study by Johansson et al., for the OECD,[2] which provides estimates of global growth till 2060.

Growth Projections

Both studies use what has been called the 'growth accounting' framework based on the aggregative neoclassical growth model named after its progenitors Robert Solow and Trevor Swan. Within this framework, growth of output was to be explained by increases in the basic inputs of capital and quality-adjusted labour and an unexplained residual identified as technical progress.[3]

Maddison's basic building blocks were the population projections made for individual countries by the US Bureau of the Census for 2030 and on assumptions made for per capita GDP for major regions and countries with the biggest shares of world GDP. As he says, 'They were not the result of an econometric exercise, but are based on an analysis of changes in the momentum of growth [in 1990–2003] in different parts of the world economy, and my assessment of the likelihood of their continuation or change'.[4] His estimates of the historical dimensions and future prospects for the major countries from 1500 to 2030 are charted in Figure 5.1.

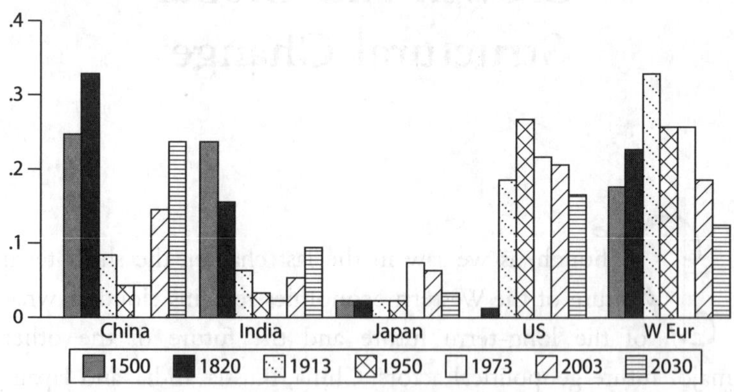

FIGURE 5.1 Ratio of Country to World GDP (By Country; 1990; USD)
Source: Maddison (2007).

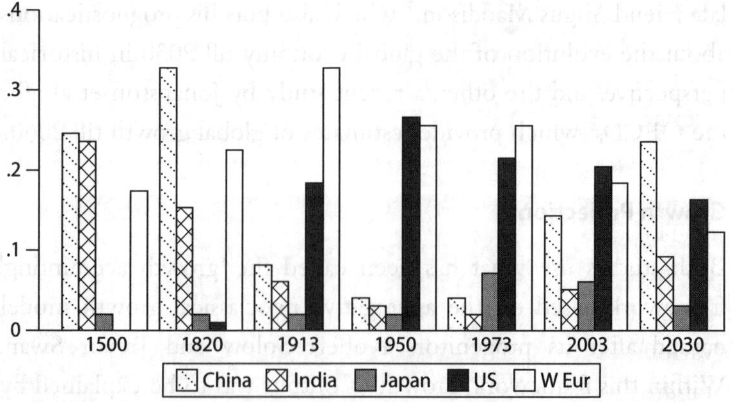

FIGURE 5.1A Ratio of Country to World GDP (By Date; 1990; USD)
Source: Maddison (2007).

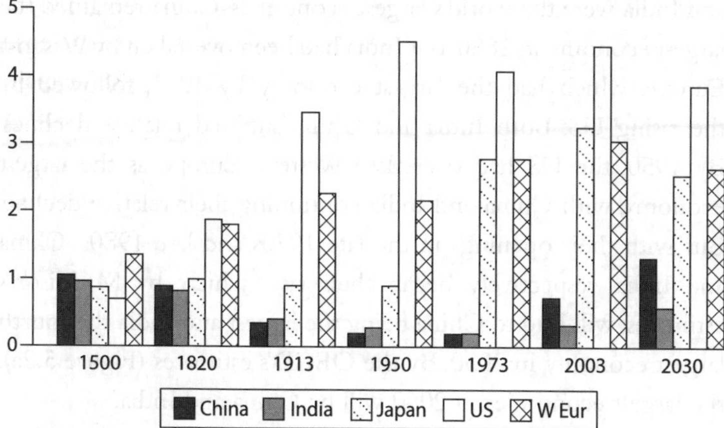

FIGURE 5.1B Ratio of Country to World Per Capita GDP (By Date; 1990; USD)
Source: Maddison (2007).

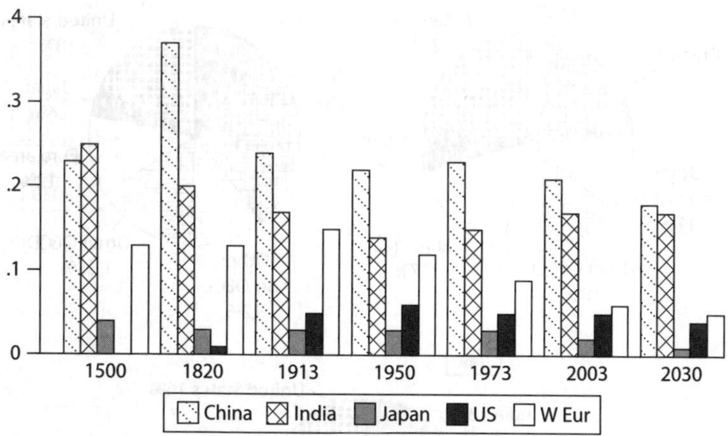

FIGURE 5.1C Ratio of Country to World Population
Source: Figures 5.1–5.1c: Maddison (2007).[5]

The OECD, by contrast, makes it projections on the basis of the neoclassical growth model with so-called 'conditional convergence' of GDP to that of the US. The resulting estimates for the various dimensions of growth from 2011 to 2060 are graphed in Figure 5.2 (a) and (b).

There are a number of important points about the evolution of the world economy shown by Figure 5.1. First, in 1500, China and India were the world's largest economies. China remained the largest economy in 1820, but India had been overtaken by Western Europe, which had the largest economy by 1913, followed by the rising US. Both India and China suffered relative declines. By 1950, the US had overtaken Western Europe as the largest economy, with China and India continuing their relative decline. But with their openings in the late 1970s and late 1980s, China and India, respectively, began their rise, which, by Maddison's estimates, will lead to China being the largest and India the fourth largest economy in 2030. By the OECD's estimates (Figure 5.2a), the largest economies in 2060 will be China and India.

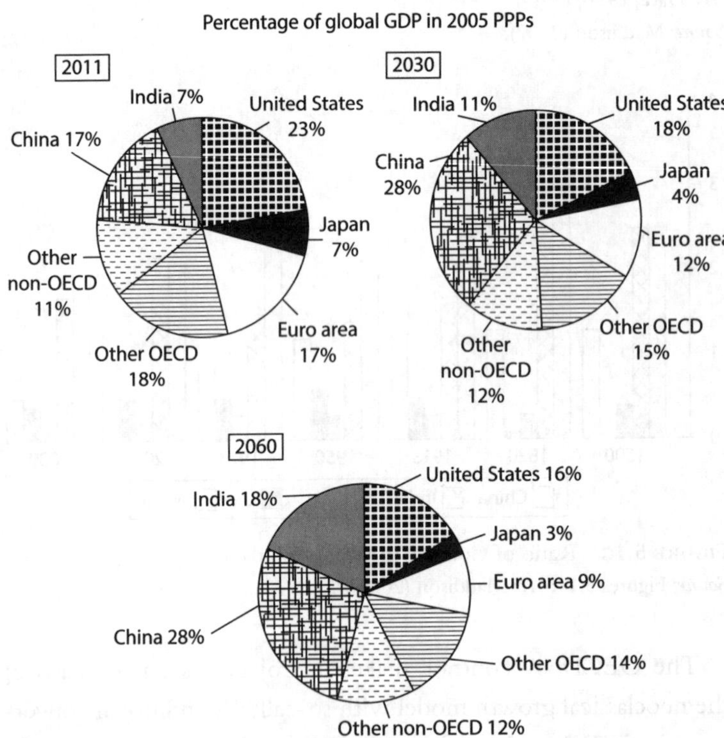

Figure 5.2a There Will Be Major Changes in the Composition of Global GDP

Source: OECD.[6]

Note: Global GDP is taken as sum of GDP for 34 OECD and 8 non-OECD G20 countries.

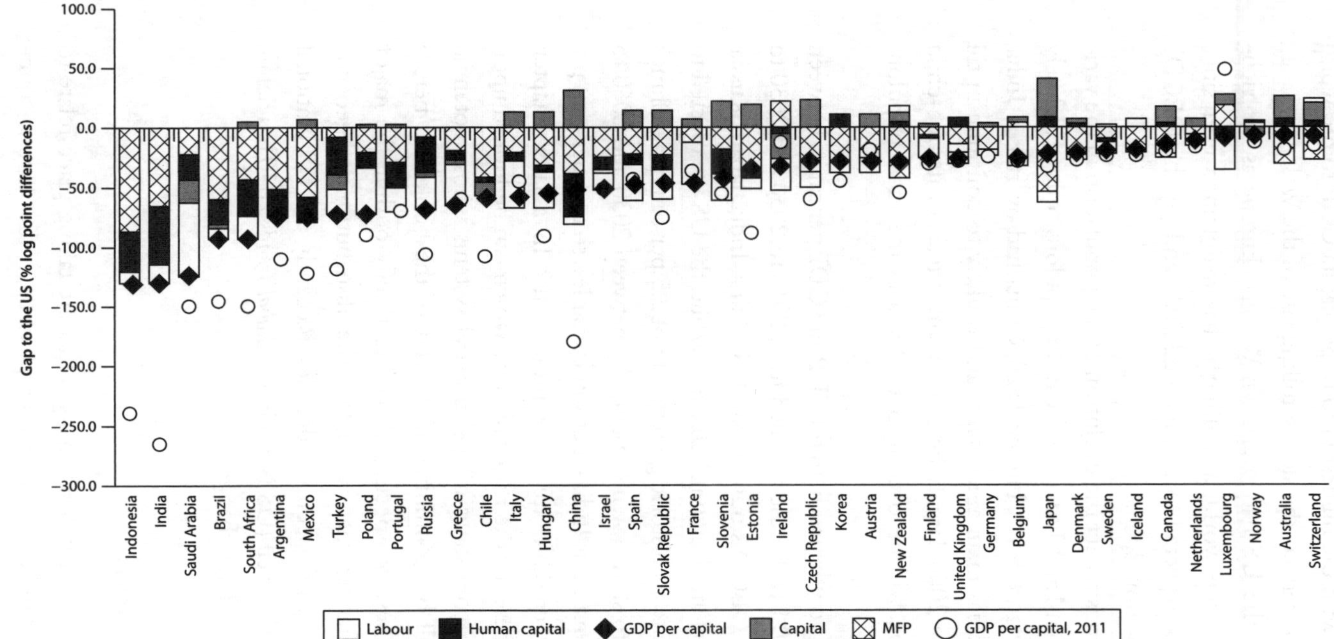

FIGURE 5.2B Despite Substantial Gains by Emerging Countries, Differences in GDP Per Capita Still Remain in 2060 Contribution of Production Factors to Differences in GDP Per Capita Relative to the United States (Constant 2005 PPPs)

Source: OECD.[7]

Note: To ensure that the percentage gap in the components of GDP add up to GDP per capita, the decomposition is done in log point differences, since the decomposition is multiplicative. GDP per capita is equal to the product of the components MFP, human capital, (physical capital/GDP)$\alpha/(1-\alpha)$ and employment/population, where α is the labour share.

Secondly, as seen in Figure 5.2b, in 1500, Western Europe was the richest (with the highest ratio of per capita GDP to the world average). This reflects the slowly rolling rise of the West.

By 1820, the US had overtaken Western Europe as the richest region in the world, a ranking it has maintained ever since and which is expected to continue till 2030 and (by the OECD's estimates) even in 2060.

These trends reflect the evolution of the population in the various regions. In 1500, India was the most populous, followed closely by China (Figure 5.1c); but, by 1820, China had overtaken India, a position it has maintained since and is likely to continue in till 2030. But by 2060, largely because of the effects of its one-child policy, China will be overtaken by India as the most populous country.

The past growth rates in trend GDP and GDP per capita between 1995 and 2011 and those assumed from 2011 to 2030 and 2030 to 2060 in the OECD study for the US, China, India, Japan, Russia, and Germany are shown in Table 5.1. While, the US is expected to remain close to its historic growth rate of 2.5 per cent p.a., China's is expected to slow down substantially between 2030 and 2060 to 2.3 per cent p.a., as is India's, but somewhat less so to 4 per cent p.a.

But how credible are these projections? In a later chapter, I examine these for the major regions, which can be looked upon as being the core states of the imperial systems whose potential clash we will be examining in the rest of the book. But before examining these prospects, we need to briefly outline the major structural changes that will affect the distribution of geoeconomic power in the coming decades. Recently, the US National Intelligence Council (US NIC) in its *Global Trends 2030* has delineated some of these changes.

Structural Changes

The three major structural changes that are taking place relate to energy, the changing demographic patterns in the various countries/regions, and the pace of urbanization. I deal with each in turn.

TABLE 5.1 Average Growth Rate in Trend GDP and Trend GDP Per Capita in USD 2005 PPPs

	Average Growth in GDP in USD 2005 PPPs				Average Growth in GDP per Capita in USD 2005 PPPs			
	1995–2011[1]	2011–2030	2030–2060	2011–2060	1995–2011[1]	2011–2030	2030–2060	2011–2060
Australia	3.3	3.1	2.2	2.6	1.9	2.0	1.7	1.8
Austria	2.0	1.5	1.4	1.4	1.7	1.2	1.4	1.3
Belgium	1.8	2.1	2.0	2.0	1.3	1.5	1.7	1.6
Canada	2.6	2.1	2.3	2.2	1.6	1.3	1.8	1.6
Switzerland	1.7	2.2	2.0	2.1	1.0	1.5	1.8	1.7
Chile	3.9	4.0	2.0	2.8	2.8	3.4	2.0	2.5
Czech Republic	3.2	2.7	1.8	2.1	3.1	2.6	1.9	2.2
Germany	1.4	1.3	1.0	1.1	1.4	1.5	1.5	1.5
Denmark	1.5	1.3	2.1	1.8	1.1	1.0	2.0	1.6
Spain	2.9	2.0	1.4	1.7	1.9	1.6	1.3	1.4
Estonia	3.6	2.8	2.0	2.4	3.8	3.1	2.3	2.6
Finland	2.5	2.1	1.6	1.8	2.2	1.8	1.5	1.6
France	1.7	2.0	1.4	1.6	1.1	1.6	1.2	1.3
United Kingdom	2.3	1.9	2.2	2.1	1.9	1.3	1.8	1.6
Greece	2.4	1.8	1.2	1.4	1.9	1.7	1.3	1.4
Hungary	2.4	2.5	1.7	2.0	2.6	2.7	2.0	2.3
Ireland	4.7	2.1	1.7	1.9	3.2	1.3	0.9	1.1
Iceland	3.0	2.2	2.4	2.3	1.8	1.2	1.9	1.6

(*Cont'd*)

TABLE 5.1 (*Cont'd*)

	Average Growth in GDP in USD 2005 PPPs				Average Growth in GDP per Capita in USD 2005 PPPs			
	1995–2011[1]	2011–2030	2030–2060	2011–2060	1995–2011[1]	2011–2030	2030–2060	2011–2060
Israel	3.7	2.7	2.6	2.6	1.5	1.3	1.6	1.5
Italy	1.0	1.3	1.5	1.4	0.6	0.9	1.5	1.3
Japan	0.9	1.2	1.4	1.3	0.8	1.4	1.9	1.7
Korea	4.6	2.7	1.0	1.6	4.0	2.5	1.4	1.8
Luxembourg	3.8	1.8	0.6	1.1	2.3	0.7	0.1	0.3
Mexico	2.6	3.4	2.7	3.0	1.2	2.5	2.6	2.5
Netherlands	2.2	1.8	1.6	1.7	1.7	1.5	1.7	1.6
Norway	3.0	2.9	1.9	2.3	2.2	2.0	1.4	1.6
New Zealand	2.7	2.7	2.6	2.6	1.6	1.8	2.2	2.0
Poland	4.3	2.6	1.0	1.6	4.4	2.6	1.4	1.9
Portugal	1.7	1.4	1.4	1.4	1.3	1.4	1.6	1.5
Slovak Republic	4.5	2.9	1.4	2.0	4.4	2.8	1.7	2.1
Slovenia	2.6	2.0	1.6	1.8	2.2	1.7	1.8	1.8
Sweden	2.5	2.4	1.8	2.0	2.1	1.7	1.5	1.6
Turkey	4.2	4.5	1.9	2.9	2.8	3.6	1.8	2.5
United States	2.5	2.3	2.0	2.1	1.5	1.5	1.5	1.5
Argentina	3.6	3.6	2.2	2.7	2.6	2.9	1.9	2.3
Brazil	3.3	4.1	2.0	2.8	2.1	3.4	2.1	2.6

China	10.0	6.6	2.3	4.0	9.3	6.4	2.8	4.2
Indonesia	4.4	5.3	3.4	4.1	3.1	4.5	3.3	3.8
India	7.5	6.7	4.0	5.1	5.8	5.6	3.6	4.4
Russia	5.1	3.0	1.3	1.9	5.4	3.2	1.7	2.3
Saudi Arabia	4.4	4.2	2.4	3.1	1.3	2.5	1.7	2.0
South Africa	3.4	3.9	2.5	3.0	2.1	3.4	2.3	2.7
World unweighted average[2]	3.1	2.8	1.9	2.2	2.3	2.2	3.1	2.0
World weighted average[2]	3.5	3.7	2.3	2.9	2.5	1.8	2.3	2.6
OECD unweighted[2]	2.8	2.3	1.7	2.0	2.1	1.8	1.6	1.7
Non-OECD unweighted	2.5	4.3	4.7	3.3	3.1	4.0	2.4	3.0
OECD weighted[2]	2.2	2.2	1.8	2.0	1.5	1.7	1.7	1.7
Non-OECD weighted[2]	2.8	6.7	5.9	3.9	2.7	3.7	5.6	5.2

Source: OECD.[8]

Notes:

1. 1995 or first year available.

2. Aggregate calculations start in 1996; for a few countries, where trend GDP is not available at the beginning of the sample period, actual GDP is used in place of trend GDP.

3. World GDP is taken as sum of GDP for thirty-four OECD and eight non-OECD countries.

Energy

Modern economic growth began when humankind learnt to harness the energy contained in fossil fuels—first coal, then oil and natural gas. Until then, most energy was provided by products of the land, for example, charcoal from wood. These competed with the other uses of land required to provide basic necessities like food, clothing, and housing. With population expanding to the land frontiers, diminishing returns set in with the more intensive uses of land. Hence, despite short periods of intensive growth (with output expanding faster than population and thereby raising per capita incomes), growth would fall back as diminishing returns set in. Most past growth was therefore mainly extensive (with output expanding pari passu with population).

But with the invention of the steam engine, humankind began to learn how to use the bounty it had inherited from nature in the form of fossil fuels. This removed the land and accompanying energy constraint. Extensive growth based on a potentially unbounded source of energy became a possibility, first in the West and now in the Rest. The Malthusian Trap, under which humankind had lived for millennia, was finally sprung. Poverty, which had been humankind's fate for millennia, could at last be eliminated, first in the West and now the Rest, as unending intensive growth based on the inherited endowment of fossil fuels became globalized.

There have, however, always been Jeremiahs who have doubted how long this natural bounty would last. Others see this as the rape of nature, which could destroy the Earth. I deal briefly with both.

Peak Oil

The first fear is that as most parts of the world use fossil fuels, their available stock—particularly oil—would gradually be used up. The world would have to rely increasingly on more expensive or unreliable renewable sources of energy based on sun, wind, nuclear, and land (biofuels).

Figure 5.3a shows the total energy consumption in the world from 1965 to 2010 by different energy sources, and Figure 5.3b, the total energy consumption by major countries/regions for the same period. From Figure 5.3a, it is evident that oil, and since the 1980s oil and natural gas, have been the main sources of energy in the world.While Figure 5.3b shows the dramatic rise in the energy consumption based on coal of China, which has overtaken the

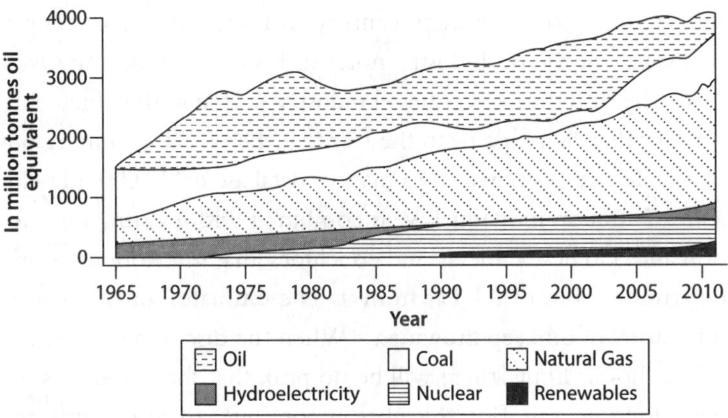

FIGURE 5.3A World Energy Consumption
Source: BP Statistical Report of World Energy, 2012.

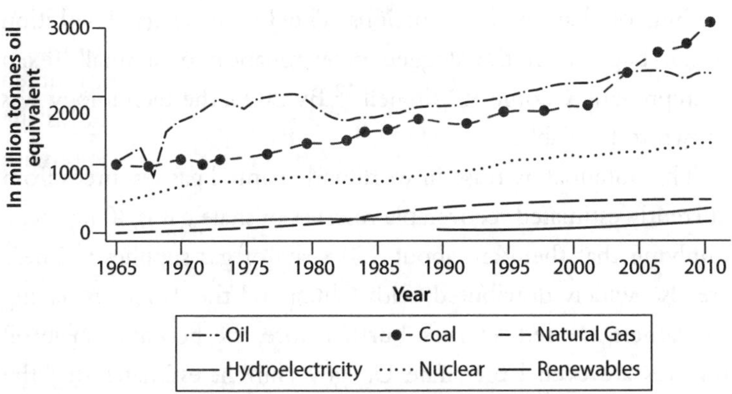

FIGURE 5.3B Total Energy Consumption by US, EU, China, India, and Japan
Source: BP Statistical Report of World Energy, 2012.

US and EU as the largest consumer of world energy. But whereas most of the developed countries have used oil as their main energy source, for China and India, coal remains their primary energy source.

Even though there has been a dramatic fall in the oil price since US shale oil came on the market and Saudi Arabia increased its production to maintain its market share, there was a scare when the oil price spiked in 2010 that the world may soon be running out of oil.[9] This so called 'peak oil' theory has been pervasive since the beginning of the present century. As Daniel Yergin, the doyen of analysts of the oil industry, notes in his latest book *The Quest*, this is the fifth time since the oil industry started in the nineteenth century that there has been the fear that the world is running out of oil. He cites a study using a massive database of '70,000 oil fields and 4.7 million individual wells combined with existing production and 350 new projects' and concludes 'that the world is clearly not running out of oil. Far from it. The estimates for the world's total stock of oil keep growing'.[10] When the discoverable stock of oil reaches its limits, there will be no peak that the world falls off, but a long plateau. But 'this plateau continues to recede into the horizon'.[11] This is likely to recede even further with the recent shale gas revolution.

This revolution is based on hydraulic fracking, and horizontal drilling of shale rock formations. The US shale gas revolution began because of the dogged determination of a small Texan entrepreneur, George P. Mitchell.[12] By 2003, the technology was shown to be viable.

The potential increase in worldwide natural gas resources from currently estimated recoverable reserves of shale gas is 40 per cent, implying that there are about 250 years of gas supplies.[13] These are also widely distributed, with China and the Americas having the largest assessed reserves. Furthermore, the potential shale oil reserves are even larger. The US government estimates that the Green River Formation in the Western US contains three trillion barrels of shale oil—three times larger than total global oil consumption over the past hundred years.[14]

This increase in cheap natural gas will allow the replacement of coal-fired power stations—which account for 46 per cent of the electricity produced globally—by gas-fired ones, reducing CO_2 emissions by half. Moreover, this will happen through normal market processes without any need for the mandates and taxes currently in place to decarbonize the world. Because of the shale revolution, the US has cut its carbon footprint by 5 per cent, well ahead of those hankering after a new Kyoto protocol on climate change.

But, for the next decade or two, this imminent energy revolution will be confined to the US because of the robustness of American entrepreneurship, its system of property rights, and the depth of its financial markets. The technology of fracking was developed by small companies experimenting in the 1980s and 1990s, was supported by venture capital from Wall Street, and took off in 2005 when the Barnett Shale in Texas was shown to be commercially viable. Other shale formations were then rapidly developed. These small companies were aided by the unique US system of property rights, whereby owners of land also own rights to subsurface minerals, which in much of the rest of the world belong to the state. The exploration and production companies have to negotiate with these private property owners for the right to drill in return for negotiated royalties. This provides an incentive for the locals to allow fracking, unlike the Nimbyism prevalent in much of the world. The shale gas and oil revolution thus attests to the robustness of US capitalism despite its current woes.

The fall in the price of natural gas in the US, from $16 to $3.30 per mBtu, has meant that the US is reindustrializing as petrochemical and energy intensive industries shift from Europe, the Persian Gulf, and China back to the US. All the predictions of US relative economic decline are soon to be overturned. The renaissance in US manufacturing, particularly in petrochemicals, has been estimated to increase US manufacturing employment by one million by 2025. This increase in high-paying jobs should help to mitigate the stagnation of US wages and the attendant rise in its inequality indices. Just as the proponents of 'Japan as No. 1' had written off the US in the 1980s with the stagnation of US productivity, all those rushing to anoint 'China as No. 1' are likely to be nonplussed by the coming resurgence of the US economy.

Other parts of the world with large shale gas reserves are also unlikely to realize their potential. Argentina, with large reserves, has become a pariah for the direct foreign investment needed after its nationalization of the oil firm YFP. Meanwhile China, with shale reserves greater than the US, has a shortage of the water needed for fracking. Given the continuing 'green' uproar over mining and nuclear energy, India's polity also seems unlikely to be able to exploit this bounty. This might change with the Modi government's more sceptical attitude towards 'greenery'.

The Geopolitics of Oil and the Dollar[15]

It is the geopolitical consequences of this US economic renaissance and energy independence that are likely to be momentous, allowing greater freedom of manoeuver in its foreign policy—most importantly in its relationship with the Middle East. Ever since President Roosevelt struck the deal with the Saudi King Ibn Saud on the *Quincy* in 1945, the US has been unable to counter the fundamentalist Wahhabi poisoning of the Muslim mind.

Ever since Saudi Arabia unleashed the 'oil weapon' after the 1973 Yom Kippur war and seriously damaged the US economy, I have wondered why it did not use military force to take over the Saudi oil fields? A recent financial newsletter provides the answer.

Its editor, Jim Rickards,[16] discloses that in February 1974, he was asked by Professor Robert Tucker, the head of the American Foreign Policy Institute, to join him and four other foreign policy experts for a meeting with Kissinger's deputy on the National Security Council, Dr Helmut Sonnenfeldt, to discuss a possible invasion of Saudi Arabia. This would secure the oilfields and produce enough oil for Western and Japanese needs—priced at a level that would not be inflationary—to avoid worsening US stagflation and prevent any further erosion in the dollar's value.

Meanwhile, William Simon, the deputy secretary of the Treasury, along with Kissinger and Sonnenfeldt had another plan to deal with the Saudis: the creation of the petrodollar. The Saudis would continue pricing oil in dollars, reinvesting the proceeds in US Treasuries and Eurodollar deposits. The US would stabilize the dollar so that its weakening did not erode the value of Saudi Arabia's dollar investments. The US would also sell advanced weapons to the Saudis.

The Saudi's dithered. In August 1974, Nixon resigned because of the Watergate scandal. To hasten the stalled negotiations, Kissinger got Robert Tucker to write an article that set out the invasion plan he and the others had discussed earlier.[17]

Tucker argued on grounds of realpolitik that, until quite recently, the oil crisis attacking vital US interests would 'never have arisen because of the prevailing expectation that it would have led to armed intervention'. He then disposed of arguments against intervention based on political inexpediency and morality. On the danger of the Saudi's following a scorched earth policy on their oil fields, he argued it would take only take three to four months to restore production and recommended a Western strategic oil reserve to store oil for this period of possible disruption of oil supplies. Tucker's article led the Saudi's to swiftly accept the petrodollar deal—with a proviso that the Saudi holdings of US Treasuries would remain secret.

By 1978, continuing high inflation in the US led the dollar to fall by 13 per cent from its 1975 high. The Saudi's retaliated by doubling oil prices between 1979 and 1980. The appointment of Paul Volcker as the chairman of the Federal Reserve to tame US inflation by tight money led to a rise in the value of the dollar to its level when the petrodollar deal was signed. Thereafter, all the US administrations intoned the 'strong dollar' mantra. The petrodollar deal stayed intact till 2010, and the dollar's role as the main reserve currency was strengthened.

The Great Recession upturned the petrodollar deal. To deal with the need to increase US jobs and growth, the US gave up the 'strong dollar' policy it had followed for thirty-five years. The cheapening dollar hit oil-dependent Russia and US Treasuries-rich China. Their response was to buy gold. In the last seven years, Russia has bought more than a thousand tons of gold, and China more than three thousand tons. Together, they now hold more than 10 per cent of the world's gold. Though not subject to the risk of confiscation like their holdings of US Treasuries and other investments in the West, they are faced by the volatility of the gold price and its likely collapse from a large-scale conversion of these gold reserves into foreign currencies.

With the IMF's inclusion of the yuan in the basket of currencies constituting the Special Drawing Rights (SDR), China is hoping that these will provide a safer reserve asset than the dollar. Rickards claims that China has 'acquired billions of SDRs in secret secondary market transactions brokered by the IMF'. But the IMF's hope that the SDR would replace the dollar as the main global reserve asset has been belied.

The main loser from the 'cheap dollar' policy is Saudi Arabia. The deal that President Roosevelt struck with King Ibn Saud aboard the *Quincy* in 1945 is now dead. For with its shale oil revolution, the US has the highest oil reserves in the world. It is no longer dependent on Saudi oil. Moreover, owing to the flexibility with which shale oil drilling rigs can be taken in and out of production, the oil price is now bounded by a 'shale band' of \$40 to \$60.[18] At this price band, the Saudi's cannot close their fiscal deficit, which is being financed by sales of their dollar assets and a proposed divestment of their crown jewel ARAMCO.

President Obama's signing of the Iran nuclear deal signalled that Iran is the leading regional power. The release of US data on the previously secret Saudi holdings of US Treasuries and top-secret sections of the 9/11 Commission report—which reveals links between the Saudi royal family, 9/11 hijackers, and Al Qaeda—shows that the US is no longer willing to allow the Saudis to use their oil wealth to finance the jihadists and the madrasas, with Wahhabi clerics fomenting religious hatred against all non-Wahhabis throughout the world.

Unlike Rickards, I do not think Obama's weakening of the dollar will mean the end of its primacy as a reserve currency. Instead, through the shale band and the end of the petrodollar, the US is on the way to hit the enemies of its values and imperium where it hurts most—in their pockets.

With its ending of reliance on Middle Eastern oil, the US could cut back on its implicit protection of the Wahhabi state and its policing functions in the Straits of Hormuz. It needs only to act as an off-shore balancer in the coming internecine war amongst the Shias and Sunnis in the region. It will be the Chinese, Indians, and, above all, the Europeans who will no longer be able to remain as 'free riders' relying on US arms to secure their oil supplies from the continuing turbulence in the Middle East.

Moreover, the prospective global abundance of oil and gas could spike the Russian threat to world order, which is based on deploying the rents from these natural resources. This could eventually lead Russia to move from its authoritarian crony capitalism to the advanced liberal market economy, which it needs for its future prosperity. Equally important, allowing a shift of US military resources from the Middle East to the Pacific might give the other authoritarian capitalist state—China—cause to pause in its recent aggressive attempts to challenge the US pax in Asia. I take up all these themes in the next part of this book.

Global Warming[19]

Since 1990, when I gave the Wincott lecture titled 'The Limits of International Co-operation' and unwittingly stumbled into the increasingly heated debate on global warming, I have been arguing that it is humankind's use of the mineral energy stored in nature's gift of fossil fuels that allowed the ascent from structural poverty, the scourge of humankind for millennia. To put a limit on the use of these fossil fuels is to condemn to perpetual structural poverty a Third World in the process of converting its traditional land-based organic economies into modern mineral-energy-using economies. Rather than going into the history of the debate since then, I refer the reader to chapter 10 of my last book *Poverty and Progress*, which summarizes this debate.

The essential point is that, despite claims to the contrary, the science of climate change is still unsettled. There is no dispute that global warming is occurring, although the stalling of the warming trend and the cooling observed over the last decade should give one pause. The question is: what is the cause of the rise?

Sun and Stars versus CO_2

The International Panel on Climate Change (IPCC) has espoused the current orthodoxy that greenhouse gases, particularly the mushrooming CO_2 emissions since the Industrial Revolution, are in large part responsible for the rise. The evidence usually cited is the apparent correlation between temperature and CO_2 emissions as revealed by the Vostock ice-core data for millions of years. But correlation does not imply causation. When a correct lagged regression is done for this and other ice-core data, 'on long timescales, variations in Vostock's CO_2 record *lag behind* those of its air temperature record'.[20] So CO_2 cannot be the cause of temperature changes. It is changes in temperature that seem to cause changes in atmospheric CO_2. But how?

The answer lies in the oceans, which are both the primary sink for as well as emitters of CO_2. By comparison, the human contribution to global carbon emissions is negligible. When the oceans cool, they absorb CO_2; when they warm, they emit CO_2. Given the vastness of oceans, it takes a long time for the warming of the atmosphere to heat the oceans (and vice versa). This explains the lag between the rise in global temperature and a rise in CO_2, as shown by the millennial ice-core evidence.

What then causes global temperatures to wax and wane, as they have done for millennia? The alternative to the CO_2 theory is that changes in solar radiation have caused changes in the global climate. This alternative theory labelled 'cosmoclimatology'[21] argues that the climate is controlled by low cloud cover, which when widespread has a cooling effect by reflecting solar energy back into space. When there is no cloud cover, solar energy warms the climate.

These low clouds are formed when subatomic particles called cosmic rays, which are emitted by exploding stars in our galaxy, combine with water vapour rising from the oceans. The constant bombardment of the planet by cosmic rays, however, is modulated by a solar wind, which prevents the cosmic rays from reaching the earth and creating the low clouds. Varying sunspot activity causes the solar wind. When the sun is overactive with lots of sunspots and the solar wind is blowing intensely, fewer cosmic rays get through to form the low clouds, and the planet experiences global warming, as it is doing in the current transition from the Little Ice Age of the seventeenth and eighteenth centuries. Thus, according to this alternative theory, global temperature would be correlated with the intensity of the sun. When it is shining more brightly, global temperatures will rise, and when it is not, global temperatures will fall.

However, there is still a missing piece in the cosmoclimatology theory. It depends upon the untested hypothesis that cosmic rays influence the formation of clouds. Researchers conducting a recent experiment at CERN called CLOUD found a 'significant' cosmic ray cloud effect.[22] More recent research by Svensmark and his colleagues has shown how cosmic rays lead to low cloud formation. This confirms the cosmoclimatology theory. The sun and stars control our climate rather than puny human CO_2 emissions.

Air Pollution and Fossil Fuels

There are still environmental problems requiring public action. The most important for citizen's welfare is local pollution. Anyone who has choked in the foul air of Beijing or Delhi will know their importance. These are in part caused by coal-fired thermal power stations and the use of diesel in cars. But there are available remedies. When I first came to London in 1960 it was covered in dense smog. In less than a decade, it disappeared as thermal power stations adopted coal-scrubbing technology. The use of diesel in cars has been encouraged by subsidies to its use, as it was purported to emit less CO_2 than petrol. However, it emitted more of the small P25 particles, which get embedded in the lungs and in the blood stream causing serious respiratory diseases. Recognizing this danger, the Indian government is reducing and hopefully eliminating diesel subsidies. With the substitution of natural gas for coal in power stations, some of the air pollution will hopefully be reduced.

Demographic Structure

Aging

One major change is going to be *the aging of the population* in China and in currently developed countries. In its *Global Trends 2030*, the US NIC notes that 'today more than 80 countries have populations with a median age of 25 years or less. As a group, these countries have an oversized impact on world affairs—since the 1970s, roughly 80 per cent of all armed civil and ethnic conflicts (with 25 or more battle-related deaths per year) have originated in countries with youthful populations'[23]. This resulting 'demographic arc of instability' will contract due to fertility declines to about 50 countries by 2030, mainly in the equatorial belt of Sub-Saharan Africa; the West Bank, Gaza, Jordan, and Yemen in the Middle East; Bolivia, Guatemala, and Haiti in the Americas; and East Timor, Papua New Guinea, and the Solomon Islands in the Pacific Rim. In South Asia, only Afghanistan is projected to remain youthful by 2030, while the tribal belt in Pakistan and the northern states of Uttar Pradesh and Bihar in India will continue to have youthful populations. In the absence of employment opportunities, this could contribute to instability.

It has been argued that as the US population will age less than other powers contesting its dominance, it will have more resources available for providing military power than others, who will have to spend more on social security for their proportionately larger aging populations. This will be a powerful means to maintain the US's power domination.[24]

While the greying of the population in Northeast Asia requiring substantial increase in social security spending might limit the regional arms race, 'by 2030, Japan, South Korea, and China will become too old for military rivalry'.[25]

Sex Ratios

Set against this trend for a geriatric peace is the second important demographic feature, *the worsening sex ratio* (males per 100 females) in China, northern India, and parts of the Middle East. In their book *Bare Branches*,[26] Valerie Hudson and Andrea den Boer provide a historical and strategic analysis of skewed sex ratios. These are defined as sex ratios at birth that are greater than 105 to 107 males born per 100 females, and for the whole population (of all ages), which is expected to be close to 100 males per 100 females.[27] But for our purposes, to see the strategic consequences of distorted sex ratios, the sex ratio for those under 15 is most relevant as it provides the relevant population of young males in the next two decades. It also highlights the future problem posed by what the Chinese call 'bare branches': males who cannot find spouses because of high sex ratios. According to the *CIA World Factbook 2012*, this ratio was 117 for China and 113 in India.

The most skewed sex ratios are in northern India and parts of China (which have been exacerbated by its one-child policy). In the northern Indian states of Punjab and Haryana, the sex ratios for 0–6 years population in 2011 were 118 and 120, respectively, and 115 in Delhi NCT as compared with an All India ratio of 109.

What are likely to be the consequences of these distorted Indian and Chinese sex ratios? Hudson and den Boer show that, historically, when the sex ratio of the 15–34 age group is close to 120 males for 100 females, and if there is resource scarcity and a lack of productive jobs, there is likely to be 'chronic violence and persistent social disorder and corruption'.[28] They estimate that by 2020, there will be twenty-eight to thirty-two million 'surplus' males in the 15–34 age group in India[29] and between twenty-nine and thirty-three million in this age group in China.

How will these countries cope with these huge numbers of often low-status, testosterone-fuelled, and, most often, economically challenged males in the prime of their youth? The history of how societies have coped with such gender imbalances is not encouraging for the maintenance of internal and external order and hence for our major theme of war and peace.

Since anthropologist Napoleon Chagnon's 1968[30] study of a Stone Age Brazilian tribe (entitled *Yanomamo: The Fierce People)*, it has been known that much primitive warfare was not (as on the standard anthropological view) about material possessions—as an exasperated shaman he was interrogating on the subject expostulated, 'Don't ask such stupid questions! Women! Women! Women! Women! Women!' The sex ratio for the below-15 age group among the Yanomamo was 128.6. The resulting bare branches are augmented by the polygamous monopolization of the available women by successful high-status warriors.

In nineteenth-century Rajasthan and Oudh, female infanticide was common. For Rajput clans, kidnapping was often the only way to get wives for their sons.[31] In Oudh, where the juvenile sex ratio in 1875 was reported to be 118.6, W.H. Sleeman, the scourge of the Thuggees (immortalized in John Masters' novel *The Deceivers*), reported how bands of bare branches rebelled openly against the government. One particularly bloody mutiny by these robber-barons led to the British annexation of Oudh.[32]

Nineteenth-century China was also plagued by armed revolts by bands of bare branches. The most serious was the Nien rebellion in 1851, when an organized group of bandits from the poor northeastern province of Huai-pei combined with the Taiping rebels in the south to form an army of over one hundred thousand bare branches, which nearly overthrew the Qing dynasty. The sex ratio in nineteenth-century Huai-pei has been estimated to have been 129.[33]

Bare branches share many characteristics in high sex ratio societies. They are in the lowest socio-economic class; they are more likely to be underemployed or unemployed; they are usually landless with few other resources that would improve their chances of marrying; they are largely transients with few ties to communities where they seek work; they live and socialize with other bare branches, creating distinctive bachelor subcultures. Often treated as social outcasts, they are prone to vice and violence. This is linked to the higher testosterone levels of unmarried men as compared with married men.[34] Unemployment and lack of good jobs exacerbate these tendencies.[35]

It is in this context that India's failure to reform its colonial-era labour laws,[36] with their restrictions on exit and the concomitant monopolization of good formal sector jobs by 'insiders' creating a virtual aristocracy of labour, has prevented India (unlike China) from making full use of its most abundant resource for labour-intensive industrialization.[37] The increased informalization of Indian labour markets will worsen the dangers from India's bare branches. Labour market reform remains imperative, not only to raise India's growth rate but also to tame the impending social disorder from its bare branches.

In India and China, we can also expect to see the other social and political consequences found in high sex ratio societies: increased prostitution, homosexuality, the growth of monastic orders and polyandry, as well as the capture and trafficking of women. In India, because of the large regional differences in sex ratios, marriage migration of women from the south and northeast is already happening and is likely to increase. This will alleviate the problem of bare branches in India. In China, because of its relatively homogenous Han culture, there is resistance to taking alien brides. The reported trafficking of girls from South East Asia is more likely to be for prostitution.

But, it is the political consequences that are most disturbing. Hudson and den Boer conclude that, historically, there have been two ways by which governments have sought to quell the disorder flowing from a large number of bare branches. The first is to organize them to be exported abroad through colonization or war, while suppressing disorder at home through authoritarian means. This is most likely to be China's route, with its massive increase in spending on defence and internal security. The second, in culturally diverse societies, is to direct bare-branch violence towards various minorities. This, Hudson and den Boer conjecture, is the most likely outcome for India. But there is a third possibility, with both China and India mobilizing their bare branches in an arms race, whose denouement of mutual male slaughter culls their 'surplus' males. Welcome to the Dangerous New World of emergent Asia!

Urbanization

In 1950, the world was largely rural, with just 30 per cent of the world population of 2.5 billion estimated to live in urban areas. Today, roughly half of the world population of 7.1 billion live in urban areas. By 2030 nearly 60 per cent of the world population of 8.3 billion (4.9 billion) will be urban. The largest increase in numbers will be in China and India, 276 and 218 million respectively.[38] But unlike China, which will be a mix of urban and rural, India is likely to remain mainly rural.

Most of India's urban growth is expected to be outside the current twenty-seven megacities with populations of over ten million. They will be stifled by land constraints, vehicular congestion, deteriorating sanitation, health problems, and 'entrenched criminal networks and political gridlock'.[39] The major growth will be in 'peri-urban' or 'rurban' areas, with metropolitan regions spilling over into mega-regions with multiple jurisdictions. It is expected that by '2030, there will be forty large bi-national and tri-national metro regions'.[40]

Urbanization will be accompanied by an unprecedented growth of the middle class, particularly in India and China. Estimates of the global middle class (those with a per capita household consumption of PPP $10–$50 per day) range from the current 1 billion to 2–3 billion by 2030. The living standards of the top end of this new emerging market middle class will be similar to those of the Western middle class; those at the lower end, even though enjoying middle-class status, would be considered 'poor' in the West. This 'new' upper middle class will rise from 330 million to 679 million by 2030.[41] This will lead to pressures for individual empowerment, and rising expectations, which, if thwarted, could—as in the past—lead to political turmoil.

Urbanization will also put pressure on food and water resources. The US NIC expects food demand to be met with existing supplies, particularly if the diversion of agricultural land to biofuels is reversed, as the world comes to recognize the 'global warming scam'. But, water is set to become a more significant source of intra-state and inter-state contention till 2030.

The NIC also charts the high water-stress belt in different water basins around the globe by 2030. Many of these—particularly in South and East Asia—are shared by many countries and could lead to inter-state conflict. The Indus Waters Treaty negotiated by the World Bank in 1960 provides a co-operative solution (though currently being contested), which has held between India and Pakistan despite their continuing conflict, including three wars. The most serious potential conflict concerns the water basins in the rivers arising in the Tibetan plateau in China.

For, China is increasingly looking upon the massive water resources of the Tibetan plateau to meet its impending water shortage in northern China and its ever growing need for hydroelectricity.[42] It has created a series of dams for hydroelectricity in the various river systems of South and South East Asia that originate in Tibet. It also has long developed plans to divert the waters of the Brahmaputra to the Yellow River, which are on hold but are likely to be activated as the water stress in northern China worsens. Its exploitation of the upper riparian stretches of the Brahmaputra, Mekong, and Salween could devastate the economies of eastern India, Bangladesh, and most South East Asian countries. As we discuss in the next part, as in the South China Sea, Chinese exploitation of Tibet's natural resources could provide a flashpoint for conflict between China and India, drawing in many of the countries of South East Asia with their water basins dependent on the immense hydro-resources of the Tibetan plateau.

How are these structural features likely to play out on the relative economic strengths of the current superpower (the US), the wannabes (China and India), and the other geoeconomic heavy weights (Russia and Japan) in the future? I examine these in succeeding chapters of this part.

Notes

1. A. Maddison, *Contours of the World Economy, 1–2030 AD: Essays in Macro-Economic History* (Oxford: Oxford University Press, 2007), Part III.
2. Åsa Johansson, Yvan Guillemette, Fabrice Murtin, David Turner, Giuseppe Nicoletti, Christine de la Maisonneuve, Phillip Bagnoli, Guillaume Bousquet, and Francesca Spinelli, 'Long-Term Growth Scenarios', *OECD Economics Department Working Paper*, no. 1000, Paris (2012).
3. For when this framework was applied to the US and other advanced economies in so-called 'growth-accounting', it appeared that these economic inputs accounted for just over half of the observed output growth. The remainder or the 'residual' of the unexplained part came to be attributed to exogenous technical progress.
4. A. Maddison, *Contours of the World Economy 1–2030 A.D.*, p. 338.
5. A. Maddison, *Contours of the World Economy, 1–2030 AD*, Part III.
6. OECD, 'Looking to 2060: Long-Term Global Growth Prospects', OECD Economic Policy Papers, No. 03, A Going for Growth Report (Paris: OECD Publishing, 2012), Figure 10.
7. OECD, 'Looking to 2060', Figure 11.
8. OECD, 'Looking to 2060', Table A.1.
9. Martin King Hubbert, the godfather of the recent scare on peak oil, predicted 'in 1978 that children born in 1965 would see all the world's oil used up in their lifetimes. Humanity, he said, was about to embark upon "a period of non-growth"' (Daniel Yergin, *The Quest: Energy, Security, and the Remaking of the Modern World* [New York: Allen Lane, 2011], p. 235).
10. Yergin, *The Quest*, p. 239.
11. Yergin, *The Quest*, p. 240. While discussing the theories of the US geologist Marion King Hubbert, the progenitor of the most recent version of the peak oil theory, Yergin points out that he assumed that the typical history of an oil field followed a bell shaped curve with 'the decline side [after the peak, being] a mirror image of the ascending side'. But most oil fields do not follow this symmetrical pattern. 'They eventually do reach a physical peak of production and then often plateau and more gradually decline, rather than falling sharply in output … Based on current knowledge, it is a more appropriate image for what is ahead than the peak. And the world is

still, it would seem, many years away from ascending to that plateau.' (Yergin, *The Quest*, pp. 238–9).

12. See Yergin, *The Quest*, pp. 325–32 for the evolution of this revolution. Also Matt Ridley, 'The Shale Gas Shock', GWPF Report 2, London: Global Warming Policy Foundation (2011) and US Energy Information Administration (EIA), *World Shale Gas Resources* (2011).
13. US EIA, *World Shale Gas Resources*.
14. See the website for The Global Warming Policy Foundation, available at www.thegwpf.org (last accessed 30 October 2017).
15. This is based on D. Lal, 'Geopolitics of Oil and the Dollar', *Business Standard* (31 August 2016).
16. J. Rickards, 'R.I.P. the Petrodollar', *Strategic Intelligence* (2016).
17. Robert Tucker, 'Oil: The Issue of an American Intervention', *Commentary* (1 January 1975). Available online at https://www.commentarymagazine.com/articles/oil-the-issue-of-american-intervention (last accessed 30 October 2017).
18. Neanda Salvaterra, 'Oil at $50 Tests Shale-Band Theory', *Wall Street Journal* (23 August 2016).
19. This is based on D. Lal, *Poverty and Progress: Realities and Myths about Global Poverty* (Washington, DC: The Cato Institute) pp. 181–4.
20. M. Mudelsee, 'The Phase Relations Among Atmospheric CO_2 Content, Temperature and Global Ice Volume Over the Past 420ka', *Quaternary Science Reviews*, 20, no. 4, (2001), pp. 583–9, p. 587 (emphasis mine).
21. H. Svensmark, 'Cosmoclimatology', *Astronomy and Geography*, 48, no. 1 (2007): 1.18–1.24; H. Svensmark and N. Calder, *The Chilling Stars: A New Theory of Climate Change* (London: Icon Books, 2007); Nir Shaviv and Jan Vezier, 'Celestial Driver of Phanerozic Climate?', *Geological Society of America Today*, 13, no. 7 (2003), pp. 4–10.
22. Jasper Kirkby et.al, 'Role of Sulphuric Acid, Ammonia and Galactic Cosmic Rays in Atmospheric Aerosol Nucleation', *Nature*, 476, no. 7361 (2011), pp. 429–33. Also see D. Lal, 'Climate Change Redux', *Business Standard*, 31 January 2018, for the latest research confirming the comoclimatology theory.
23. US National Intelligence Council (NIC), *Global Trends 2030: Alternative Worlds* (Washington, DC: US NIC, 2012), p. 22. Available online at https://www.dni.gov/files/documents/GlobalTrends_2030.pdf (last accessed 30 October 2017).

24. Mark L. Haas, 'A Geriatric Peace? The Future of U.S. Power in a World of Aging Populations', *International Security*, 32, no. 1 (2007), pp. 112–47.
25. Seongho Sheen, 'Northeast Asia's Aging Population and Regional Security: "Demographic Peace?"', *Asian Survey*, 53, no. 2 (2013) pp. 292–318.
26. Valerie Hudson and Andrea den Boer, *Bare Branches: The Security Implications of Asia's Surplus Male Population* (Cambridge, MA: MIT Press, 2005).
27. As women have longer life expectancies than men, America and Europe—which have large elderly populations—will have higher female to male sex ratios. This will also be true of countries which have had large numbers of men killed in war, as was true of Europe (and Japan) during the two world wars of the twentieth century.
28. Hudson and den Boer, *Bare Branches*, p. 261.
29. Hudson and den Boer, *Bare Branches*, p. 124.
30. N. Chagnon, *Yanomamo: The Fierce People* (New York: Simon and Schuster, 1968).
31. Hudson and den Boer, *Bare Branches*, p. 214.
32. See D. Lal: *The Hindu Equilibrium: India c. 1500* B.C.*–2000* A.D., Abridged and Revised Edition (Oxford and New York: Oxford University Press, 2005), pp. 235–7.
33. Hudson and den Boer, *Bare Branches*, p. 208.
34. Hudson and den Boer, *Bare Branches*, p. 196.
35. Hudosn and den Boer, *Bare Branches*, p. 197.
36. See Lal, *The Hindu Equilibrium*.
37. This was outlined in Chapter 2, written by Professor Raghuram Rajan, in India's *Economic Survey 2012–13*.
38. US NIC, *Global Trends 2030*, p. 26.
39. US NIC, *Global Trends 2030*, p. 28.
40. US NIC, *Global Trends 2030*, p. 28.
41. US NIC, *Global Trends 2030*, pp. 8–9.
42. For details, see Brahma Chellaney, *Water: Asia's New Battleground* (Washington, DC: Georgetown University Press, 2011), Ch. 3.

CHAPTER SIX

The United States

Recently, there has been a deepening pessimism about US's growth prospects unrelated to the short-run adjustments needed to deal with its fiscal and debt problems. I begin by examining these prospects.

Technology and Growth

Two widely cited works by Robert Gordon[1] and Tyler Cowen[2] suggest that US economic growth is over. There are few innovations in the offing, and those of the current third industrial revolution—based on IT, genomics, and biotech—are less important than those at the end of the nineteenth and early parts of the twentieth century. They are unlikely to match the increases in labour productivity of the first industrial revolution, which was based on the steam engine and the railroad. Nor can they match the levels reached in the second industrial revolution, which was based on electricity, indoor sanitation, the automobile, chemicals, petroleum, and the airplane. Gordon's main evidence for his pessimistic view about future US growth is that US labour productivity (and with it per capita income) grew much more slowly after 1970 than from 1890 to 1970 (see Figure 6.1).

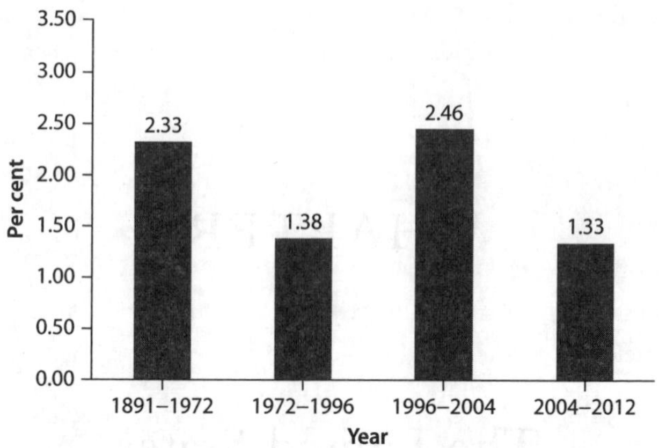

Figure 6.1 Average Growth Rate of US Labour Productivity Over Selected Intervals, 1891–2012
Source: Gordon (2012).[3]

He argues that as during most of history there was virtually no growth in world per capita income until the first industrial revolution, perhaps we are reverting to this norm with the three industrial revolutions being the exception. The classical economist's 'stationary state' will once again be with us. As Cowen argues, America has 'eaten all the low hanging fruit' from its past inventiveness.

I find these views profoundly mistaken. The trouble lies in the vision of the growth process that economists have, which is based on the aggregative neoclassical growth model, the Solow–Swan model—named after its progenitors, Robert Solow and Trevor Swan—and as discussed at the beginning of Chapter 5. In this model, in the 'steady state', only demography and technical progress matter for growth.

This technological determinism underlies Gordon and Cowen's currently fashionable growth pessimism.

Troubled by the implication that the rate of investment cannot affect the steady-state rate of growth, theorists have developed so-called 'endogenous' growth models. They assume that there are externalities to investment in physical and human capital that influence the pace of technical progress and thence the steady-state rate of growth. But, there has been no convincing empirical evidence for these externalities.

A different vision of the growth process has been provided by two of my mentors: my UCLA colleague Arnold Harberger and my late Oxford tutor Maurice Scott.[4] Both came to their alternative visions through the development and application of cost-benefit analysis to investment projects in developing countries. Both see the growth process through the eyes of the firms that make up the economy. They also were both influenced by the firm-level studies of investment and invention by Jacob Schmookler[5] and Edwin Mansfield[6], who argued that 'the *prospective profitability* of an invention was the main determinant, in most cases, of its birth and survival'.[7] This does not undermine the importance of the growth of basic scientific knowledge. But that in itself does not determine which profitable inventions will arise. This depends upon a whole host of economic factors.

The best way to see this alternative 'bottom up' view of the growth process is to follow Harberger's model rather than Scott's more elaborate model. Harberger defines the 'residual' or 'total factor productivity' (TFP) as 'real cost reductions' (RCR)—or in the case of negative TFP, 'real cost increases' (RCI)—which occur at the level of the firm, but which can be readily aggregated to the industry or economy level. In studies done by his UCLA students, what emerges at the firm and industry level from this RCR accounting is similar to what appears in the stock market pages of newspapers: 'There are winners and losers every day, every month, and every year. The gains and losses come for all sorts of [economic] causes.' The picture is analogous to Joseph Schumpeter's vision of 'creative destruction', which, in Harberger's words, says, 'yes, it's a jungle out there, but the processes of that jungle are at the core of the dynamics of a market-oriented economy. They are what got us to where we are, and they hold the best promise for further progress in the future'.[8]

The Next Hundred Million: America in 2050, a book by Joel Kotkin,[9] provides a necessary corrective in outlining how the process of creative destruction is still alive and well in the US and how some of its structural advantages in terms of demography, natural resources, technological inventiveness, and adaptive culture are likely to keep it as the dominant economic power for the foreseeable future.

Unlike Europe, Japan, Russia, and (after 2025) China, the US will keep adding to its population. By 2050, there will be one hundred million more people living in the US, giving a total population of four hundred million. This is due to a higher fertility rate than other advanced countries. It is '50 percent higher than Russia, Germany, or Japan and well above that of China, Italy, Singapore, Korea, and virtually all of Eastern Europe'.[10] Added to this is continued large-scale immigration from around the world. Thus, most of the 'developed countries in both Europe and East Asia will become veritable old-age homes: a third or more of their populations will be over 65, compared with only a fifth in America.'[11] Even though the US will have lower population growth and an ageing population, relatively 'it will maintain a youthful, dynamic demographic'. This is important for our geopolitical theme in the next part. For despite the fear created by environmentalists and rabid Greens, 'throughout history low fertility and socioeconomic decline have been inextricably linked, creating a vicious circle that affected such once-vibrant civilizations as ancient Rome and 17th-century Venice and that now affects contemporary Europe, South Korea, and Japan'. As a British commentator noted about the increasingly childless Scotland, 'This looks like a society which has lost the will to live'.[12]

America also, unlike other industrial and developing countries, has the largest expanse of arable land and natural resources. Kotkin notes, 'On a per capita basis, its endowment is far richer than that of its prime competitors, including the European Community, India, China, or Japan'.[13] Additionally, with the shale gas and oil revolution, the US will have abundant supplies of the basic fuel that has powered modern economic growth.

Immigration

This, of course, reflects the continuing technological inventiveness of the US. Kotkin states, 'The US still produces far more engineers per capita than either India or China'.[14] The openness to immigration—particularly of the world's best and brightest, lured from around the world by its outstanding and still unchallenged research universities—will allow the US to retain its technological lead. Kotkin notes, 'The US has more than twice as many foreign students as any other country; Asia is the source of nearly two out of three'. America also continues to retain its skilled immigrants.[15]

Openness to migration also provides a constant spur to entrepreneurship. As I have argued elsewhere,[16] there is apparently a genetic determinant of those who choose to become migrants. Those of our ancestors who walked to the ends of the earth from the African savannahs have a variant of a gene that is a determinant of risk-taking, an essential feature for entrepreneurship. As the US is constantly replenished by fresh waves of migrants from around the world, it is virtually collecting the self-selected risk-takers and, hence, entrepreneurs of the world. By contrast, the culturally homogenous societies of East Asia—Japan, China, and Korea—are resistant to immigration, while in Europe, there seems to be growing reluctance to open their borders because of perceived difficulties in integrating immigrants, particularly Muslims. Though, with the recent opening of its borders to refugees from Syria and Iraq by Germany's Chancellor Merkel, this might change. But, witness the continuing reluctance to admit Turkey into the EU, even as the entrepreneurial Turks, particularly from Anatolia, are making their own country into a new economic tiger.

With its deep capital markets and venture capital funds that are willing and able to financially back any new idea, the US has provided a seedbed for entrepreneurs with no other collateral than their promised inventiveness.[17] The role of immigrant entrepreneurs, particularly from India and China, in the new IT industry in Silicon Valley is notable. According to Kotkin, 'Between 1990 and 2005 immigrants, mostly from the Chinese diaspora and India, started one of every four US venture-backed public companies. In California, they account for a majority of such firms, particularly in technology'.[18]

Other Asian immigrant groups, just like previous immigrant groups—for example the Jews and Italians—have found business niches. Thus, the large numbers of Indians who immigrated in the 1970s have specialized in motels and hotels; Koreans in groceries in Los Angeles and New York; Vietnamese in nail parlours; and Cambodians in doughnut stores. Kotkin notes that 'overall Asian enterprises expanded by roughly twice the national average through the first years of the new century'.[19]

As a nation of immigrants, the US has over time created a unique civilization where ethnic and, increasingly, racial differences are subsumed into a common US identity based on the Constitution and its classical liberal vision in which anyone, irrespective of their background, can pursue the American Dream. That this melting pot, with its inbuilt dynamism, is still the most attractive pole for the world's aspiring individuals is borne out by the recent Gallup survey based on interviews with 501,366 adults, which found that despite the Great Recession and the US's current fiscal woes, of the 630 million adults around the world who want to migrate, 138 million want to move to the US, which is three times the numbers who want to migrate to the UK. Of these, nineteen million are from China, ten million from India, and six million from Brazil—the BRIC countries purported to be the current engines of growth. They are among the top five countries from where most migrants to the US are likely to come, followed by Nigeria and Bangladesh.[20]

With the increasing ethnic and racial diversity of America, the non-white population is likely to reach 50 per cent by 2050, compared with 30 per cent today. This growth will be largely due to the higher birth rates amongst the current Asian and Latino immigrants. Kotkin says, 'The multiracial society now emerging in a few places—such as Southern California—will become ever more commonplace in the rest of the country'.[21] A hybrid culture is developing,

This is being aided by major shifts in attitude concerning racial miscegenation. Kotkin reports, 'In 1987 slightly less than half of Americans approved of dating between black and whites. By 2007, according to the Pew Center, 83 percent approved. Such changes are most evident among the millennial generation, the very people who will make up the majority of adults in 2050; 94 percent of them approve of such matches'.[22]

By 2050, one in five Americans will have a 'mixed race' heritage, continuing a trend which began with the 2000 Census documentation of respondents identifying themselves as of two or more races—7.3 million Americans, or 3 per cent of the population, claimed they were mixed race. Kotkin notes, 'Over two-fifths of mixed race Americans are under eighteen years of age'. Even among blacks, where interracial marriages with whites were rare, interracial marriages 'increased seven times as rapidly as marriages overall'[23] in the 1990s.

Inequality

Against this rosy picture, there is an alternative narrative propounded by many academic and popular writers on the Left and embraced by President Obama that the American economy has developed a fatal flaw—inequality. This, it is argued, will hold back growth, impoverish the poor and middle class, and threaten American democracy as economic elites capture the machinery of government and ensure national decline. As Obama put it in his second inaugural address: 'Our country cannot succeed when a shrinking few do very well and a growing many barely make it.'

In a forensic examination of this 'declinist' literature, Scott Winship of the Brookings Institution makes a number of points.[24] The first concerns an old debate in development economics of whether growth accompanied by a worsening income distribution will still 'trickle down' to the poor.[25]

Winship graphs the income growth of the bottom fifth, middle fifth, and the top 5 per cent of the US income distribution for subperiods from 1948 to 2007 (which were both business cycle peaks) into six roughly ten-year periods (each starting and ending with a peak)—see Figure 6.2 for a graphical representation. The inequality between the poor and the middle class in all

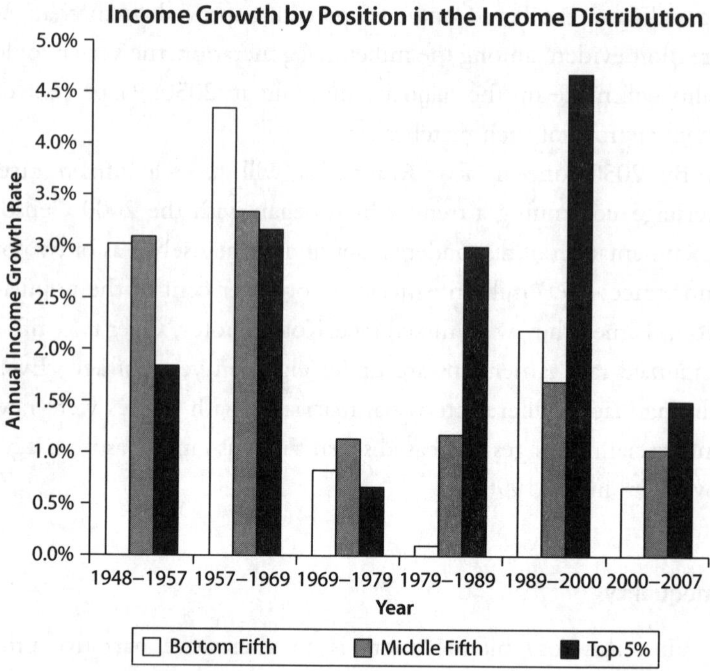

Figure 6.2 US Inequality
Source: Winship (2013).[26]

these periods, except the 1980s, 'grew only modestly or declined. Indeed, the decline in inequality between the poor and the middle class during the 1990s was so great that, despite a partial reversal in in subsequent years, inequality between these groups in 2007 was no higher than it was in 1989'.[27] Between 1969 and 2007, the incomes of the bottom fifth rose by 46 per cent compared with an increase of 63 per cent for the middle fifth.

There has however been a dramatic increase in high-end inequality since 1979—comparing the poor and middle fifth with the top 5 per cent. This contrasts with the previous thirty years when the poor and middle classes saw bigger rises than the rich. But this does not mean that the incomes of most Americans have stagnated while those of the rich have soared. The middle fifth 'was actually more than one-third richer in 2007 than it was in 1979'.[28] Moreover, 'the median family today has nearly twice the purchasing power of its counterpart in 1960'.[29] Winship also states, 'Such growth could be called "stagnation" only in relation to the golden age of the post-war boom, when the incomes of the middle fifth of Americans doubled over 20 years.'[30]

It has been claimed that the current status quo is unfair as workers' pay has not kept up with productivity increases, so that the income gains for the top 5 per cent were stolen from the middle classes, in contrast with the golden age when workers' pay rose faster than productivity. Winship provides a simple explanation: 'Compensation outpaced productivity growth during the mid-20th century (in the peak years of unionism) and recent decades have seen a correction in which productivity levels have had to catch up to pay'.[31] There is no case to decry the ending of the monopoly rents earned by unionized workers, just as there are none (as we have argued) for those earned by bankers who exploited the moral hazard created by deposit insurance to feather their own nests.

Does increasing inequality damage growth? Much of the evidence cited is based on cross-country regressions of developing countries. But these econometric studies are plagued by the problem of 'identification', which is required to determine causality. Does inequality cause lower growth rates? There are no robust econometric answers that these cross-country econometric studies can provide.[32]

Moreover, it is doubtful whether these studies of developing countries are relevant for the US. Citing recent research, Winship notes that 'over the course of the 20th century, within the United States and across developed countries, there was no relationship between changes in inequality and economic growth. In fact, between 1960 and 2000, rising inequality coincided with *higher* growth across these countries'.[33]

What of the claim that rising inequality inhibits social mobility? In a speech on inequality, Alan Krueger, a past chairman of Obama's Council of Economic Advisors, drew the Great Gatsby Curve, which plotted the levels of inequality and a measure of intergenerational mobility (the relationship between the incomes of fathers and their sons) for several developed countries.

This showed that higher inequality corresponded with lower intergenerational mobility. But this, like the cross-country econometric studies of inequality and growth, does not establish causality. Most devastatingly, as Winship reports, 'Manhattan Institute scholar Jim Manzi found that the Great Gatsby Curve[34] was just as evident when countries' inequality levels were replaced with the sizes of their populations'![35]

More serious for the validity of The Great Gatsby curve is the important and robust study by Chetty et al.[36] of trends in intergenerational social mobility in the US. Their findings question the growing public perception that a child's chance of moving up in the income distribution relative to their parents is declining in the US. They find that despite the rise in inequality in incomes, 'children entering the labor market today have the same chances of moving up in the income distribution (relative to their parents) as children born in the 1970s'.[37] Thus they find that 'the probability of reaching the top quintile conditional on coming from the bottom quintile of parental income is 8.4 percent in 1971 and 9 percent in 1986'.[38] However, they find that there are substantial differences in mobility across regions in the US. Thus, in the 1980–5 cohorts, the authors show 'the probability that a child rises from the bottom to the top quintile is 4 percent in some parts of the Southeast but over 12 percent in other regions such as the Mountain [and Pacific] states ... with New England in the middle'.[39]

Given the increased income inequality, but stability in the rank-based measures of intergenerational income mobility, the consequences of the '"birth lottery"—the parents to whom a child is born—are larger today than in the past'. This can be visualized by thinking of 'income distribution as a ladder, with each percentile representing a different rung. The rungs of the ladder have grown further apart (inequality had increased), but children's chances of climbing from lower to higher rungs have not changed (rank-based mobility has remained stable)'.[40] This picture provides a powerful visual demonstration of why classical liberals have maintained that intergenerational income mobility is more important than the distribution of income in assessing economic performance. The US is still the land of opportunity.

A reason Chetty et al. cite for the falsification of Krueger's Great Gatsby predictions is that much of the increase in the income inequality in the US has been driven by the rise in the relative income of the extreme upper tail (the top 1 per cent income shares).[41] In an accompanying paper,[42] they show that 'there is little correlation between mobility and extreme upper tail inequality both across countries and across areas within the United States'.

Yet, Thomas Piketty has written a massive tome, called *Capital in the Twenty-First Century*, echoing his Marxist master and purporting to derive new laws of capitalism from the rise in inequality due to this recent rise in the income share of the top 1 per cent. These portend an even worsening income distribution in the future for advanced economies with the capitalists—assumed to be the to 1 per cent—increasing and passing on their higher income to their progeny through assortative mating, creating plutocratic class-based societies. I deal with this dystopic view in an extended footnote below.[43]

I read Pikettys' book while drifting down the Mekong in a luxury boat from Siem Reap (where we had visited the ancient Hindu temples of Angkor Wat) to Saigon (Ho Chi Minh city) and visiting the remains of the socialist nightmare that had been Pol Pot's Cambodia. There was one striking feature about the Cambodians who could speak English: they were about the same age as my daughter born in 1980. I had seen a similar phenomenon when I first visited China in 1985 as a guest of the Chinese Academy of Social Sciences—the age distribution of the Chinese academics was bipolar. They were either the very young (just out of graduate school) or else the very old who had returned from the pig farms they had been sent to during the Cultural Revolution. The intermediate generation had all become uneducated Red Guards.

On the trip, we visited the chilling museums of the Golgotha of skulls left by the Khmer Rouge and the notorious secret prison and extermination centre at the Tuol Sleng Museum of Genocide, where the archives of the torture and murder of about fourteen thousand educated Cambodians are graphically presented. Ben Kiernan[44] details how Pol Pot's regime emptied the cities, abolished money, put everyone to work in the fields, separated families, fed the workers gruel in communal halls to meet unrealistic targets of exporting rice, smashed the skulls of educated professionals and intellectuals (to equalize human capital or 'status inequalities'—see below), and forced mass marriages with the disabled and 'ugly' (a la Amartya Sen's 'capabilities approach' to equality). This was the ultimate socialist Utopia—an indentured agrarian state where all inequalities, including those inherited, had been abolished. The regime could rightly claim in a secret document in 1975 that 'compared with the revolutions in China, Korea, and Vietnam, we are thirty years ahead of them'.[45]

Reading Thomas Piketty's neo-Marxist tome gave me a tremendous sense of déjà vu. For in the mid- and late 1970s, when there had been a great surge of interest in questions of income and wealth distribution, I wrote two review articles: 'Distribution and Development'[46], which surveyed a plethora of books concerning developing and developed countries, including the World Bank volume *Redistribution with Growth*, and a review of John Roemer's *A General Theory of Exploitation and Class* in 1986.[47]

In the first, I had argued that this new interest in distributional questions was the result of the mid-1960s to early 1970s crisis of American politics and economics. Since the rise of the Soviet Union, Western liberal democracies have been haunted by the possible irreconcilability of the two Enlightenment ideals of liberty and equality. In the post–Second World War boom, it seemed America had established the Good Society, where residual problems of class and group conflict could be easily resolved. But with the failure of traditional attempts to solve the problems of poverty and race, the questioning of whether equal access to education could reduce the inequalities of opportunity, and the sharpening of domestic conflicts during the Vietnam War, the views of the previous decade about the end of ideology and conflict in America seem complacent. Dealing with the problems of equity seemed urgent.

This was reinforced by the inflationary pressures in most OECD countries, seen as a 'constant war of all against all' for a larger share of the national income. But with the resurgence of monetarism, Thatcher's and Reagan's partial adoption of classical liberal economic policies, and the dissolution of the countries of 'really existing socialism', these fears were belied. Instead, the following Goldilocks decades were seen as being 'the end of history'.

But history has a way of biting back. The Great Crash of 2008—and the obscene incomes derived from rent-seeking by bankers it exposed, and which were not punished—brought questions of equity again to the fore.

In my second review article, I had delineated Roemer's distinction between feudal, capitalist, and socialist exploitation. The first ceases when rural producers are paid their marginal product. Capitalist exploitation ceases when there are no differential endowments of produced goods, but there would still be socialist exploitation. This was because of 'producers' different endowments of inalienable assets', like skills (Roemer, pp. 20–1). Roemer argued that even with the ending of feudalism and capitalism, 'if skills and needs are truly inalienable, then those forms of property cannot be socialized or eliminated' (p. 282). The Pol Pot regime belied this by chillingly showing how the ultimate socialist Utopia could be reached, with all human beings turned into institutional inmates—with an albeit benevolent guardian dictating who does what and gets what.

Piketty does not advocate such a radical transformation of capitalism. But, it is the emphasis on inequalities of *wealth* and their likely perpetuation that is the new wrinkle added in Piketty's book. He is particularly against inherited wealth, which he argues is unmerited, and argues for a confiscatory global wealth tax. This, he claims, is needed to provide equality of opportunity.

Here Friedrich Hayek's discussion in his *The Constitution of Liberty* is pertinent. As he shows, the essential equality needed for a free society is equality before the law. This recognizes that individuals are very different, but 'the demand for equality before the law means that people should be treated alike in spite of the fact that they are different'.[48] It rules out any end-patterned distribution of income or wealth enforced by the State. On inheritance, Hayek argues that there is no

> greater injustice involved in some people being born to wealthy parents than there is in others being born to kind or intelligent parents. The fact is that it is no less of an advantage to the community if at least some children can start with the advantages which at any given time only wealthy homes can offer than if some children inherit great intelligence or are taught better morals at home[49]

Even Janet Yellen, the past chairperson of the United States Federal Reserve, who is also concerned with rising inequalities of wealth (and incomes) in the US, has noted that based on the Federal Reserve's Survey of Consumer Finances, 'inheritances are also common among households below the top of the wealth distribution and sizeable enough that they may well play a role in helping these families economically … I think the effects of inheritances for the sizeable minority below the top that receive one are likely a significant source of economic opportunity.'[50]

Piketty's tract is ultimately based on envy. However, as Hayek noted, this human failing is not one a free society can eliminate, but 'it is probably one of the essential conditions for the preservation of such a society that we do not countenance envy, not sanction its demands by camouflaging it as social justice, but treat it, in the words of John Stuart Mill, as "the most anti-social and evil of all passions"'.[51]

One of the claims of the current 'inequality warriors' is that the concentration of wealth documented by Piketty also threatens democracy. A cross-country regression econometric study by Daron Acemoglu and James Robinson argues that inequality results in the rich buying elected representatives to create extractive political institutions that redistribute income towards the rich.[52] This study is flawed by the problem of identification and the ensuing failure to establish the hypothesized causal relationship.[53] There is, however, no consensus on this issue amongst political scientists. As Winship notes, 'In 2004, the American Political

Science Association Task force on inequality and American Democracy concluded, "We know little about the connection between changing economic inequality and changes in political behavior, governing institutions, and public policy." The past eight years have not seen new research that ought to alter that conclusion.[54]

Class

While these purported economic effects of rising inequality may be unsubstantiated, the rise of a class society in the US would mitigate against one of the basic features of the common culture that Americans have built and celebrated over the years. An important book by Charles Murray, *Coming Apart*,[55] delineates and outlines the causes of this changed cultural landscape.

To control for race and ethnicity, he examines the social trends for the non-Latino white population of prime-age adults from ages 30 to 49 (to control for changes in ages of marriage or retirement). He divides this population into two groups: a broad new upper class (who have at least a bachelor's degree and are in professional or creative jobs), who he labels Belmont (after an archetypal Boston neighbourhood), and a new lower class (who have no more than a high-school diploma and are in blue-collar or low-skill service and white-collar jobs), who he labels Fishtown (after a working class neighbourhood in Philadelphia). About 20 per cent of the white population aged 30–49 in the US is in Belmont, and 30 per cent in Fishtown.

Since the 1960s, striking differences have emerged in the cultural norms of the two groups relating to marriage, single parenthood, industriousness, crime, and religiosity. In 1960, marriage was the norm in both groups, with 94 per cent married in Belmont and 84 per cent in Fishtown. There was a similar decline in these percentages in both groups in the 1970s, but in the 1980s, a great divergence emerged. Marriages stabilized in Belmont, with 83 per cent in Belmont married in 2010, whereas they continued to decline to a mere 48 per cent in Fishtown.

Similarly, non-marital births in Belmont rose marginally from 1 per cent in 1970 to 6 per cent, in 2008, but in Fishtown they exploded from 6 per cent to 44 per cent over the next near-half century. All the available evidence shows that controlling for income and education of parents 'on any measure of development you can think of, children who are born to unmarried women fare worse than the children of divorce and far worse than children raised in intact families'.[56]

These trends have little to do with the labour market and the purported disappearance of the family wage, which allowed working-class men to support a family in the 1960s. In 1960, the mean annual earnings of males in Fishtown were $33,302 (in 2010 dollars). In 2010, they were $36,966 (using the identical definitions of working-class occupations).[57]

There has also been an erosion in the famed US work ethic, whereby every able-bodied male is available for work. This norm survives in Belmont, with only 3 per cent out of the labour force. In Fishtown, however, the percentage out of the labour force rose from 3 per cent in 1968 to 12 per cent in 2008. This had little to do with the state of the economy, as in Fishtown the non-participation rate in the labour force, in good times and bad, has steadily risen. As Murray explained in his earlier book *Losing Ground*,[58] the reason for this trend is the perverse incentives created by a growing welfare state.

The rise in crime from the mid 1960s through the 1980s mainly affected Fishtown. The violent crime rate remained flat in Belmont but more than sextupled in Fishtown, and despite the fall in the national violent crime rate since the mid 1990s, it is still 4.7 times the rate in 1960.

Religiosity, which Alexis de Tocqueville, in his monumental study of *Democracy in America*,[59] saw as a defining feature of American culture has also declined in both groups, but much more in Fishtown. The numbers of irreligious (defined as those who either profess no religion or attend a place of worship only once a year) increased from 29 per cent in 1970 to 40 per cent in 2006–10 in Belmont, and from 38 per cent to 59 per cent in Fishtown.

This divergence in cultural norms between the two groups is accentuated by their different lifestyles. Moreover, through assortative mating—with children of the elite increasingly intermarrying—and with the importance of brains rather than brawn in determining incomes, there is a tendency for the upper middle class to perpetuate itself, with many third generations being brought up with the values and tastes of their grandparents, along with their higher incomes in professional jobs. Murray argues that there is little that public policy can now do to reverse these trends and that the only way to restore the civic culture that was 'the American way of life' is for the upper classes not to condone the behaviour of the underclass but hold them to the same standards and values concerning 'marriage, honesty, hard work, and religiosity'[60] that they apply to their own.

The second measure Murray recommends is to end the spatial segregation in which the 'members of the elite have increasingly sorted themselves into hyper-wealthy and hyper-elite ZIP codes' that he calls the 'super-ZIPs'. These were also present in the 1960s, but these were not uniformly wealthy or affluent. In 1960, across 14 fourteen of these 1960 super-ZIPs, codes the median family income was only $84,000 (in 2012 dollars), and only 26 per cent of their inhabitants had college degrees. By 2000, their median family income had doubled to $163,000 and 67 per cent had college degrees. Murray recommends that, members of this elite should relocate, recognizing that, 'America outside the enclaves of the new upper class is still a wonderful place, filled with smart, interesting, entertaining people'. Isolating themselves from this part of America denies them from participating in the unique American way of life, whose cultural equality Alexis de Tocqueville characterized as follows—: 'The more opulent citizens take great care not to stand aloof from the people. On the contrary, they constantly keep on easy terms with the lower classes: they listen to them, they speak to them every day.'

This class divide is already having political consequences. Donald Tump's ascendancy to the presidency was fuelled by the rage of Fishtown. How President Trump deals with it in office will affect both future US domestic and foreign policy.

In a more optimistic reading of emerging social and spatial trends in America, Kotkin recognizes the residential polarization that has occurred. But, he argues that a new model of urbanization pioneered by the sprawl of Los Angeles is now spreading. This is in contrast with the old urbanization model of a city, with a concentration of cultural activities in a downtown centre where the upper middle classes lived, surrounded by areas of the middle and working classes, employed in small-scale manufacturing and personal services for the relatively rich. New York and Chicago epitomize these previously aspirational cities, which were beacons of opportunity for the world's immigrants.

But they have now become 'cultured' historic cities where the new upper class live and work in high-end white-collar professions like banking, finance, design, and the media. New York Mayor Michael Bloomberg has dubbed these superstar cities as 'luxury cities'. The well-educated, wealthy, and nomadic denizens[61] of these super cities do not need the public institutions that provided services in the past. Their wealth allows them to 'purchase critical amenities—such as child care and open space—on the private market, without dependence on grassroots social networks.'[62]

But, with their high cost of living,[63] these luxury cities no longer provide the upward mobility and a home for the middle class, who have moved further out to the periphery. In Manhattan, peopled by a large semi-permanent upper class, surrounded by poorer people living in the surrounding suburbs, 'the elite group is supplemented by a constantly rotating, nomadic population of younger, often highly educated people who come to the city for school or for the early part of their careers, then they leave as they reach middle age'.[64]

They are moving, along with many of the aspiring new immigrants, to the growing number of sprawling cities in the Sun Belt and the Rust Belt, epitomized by Los Angeles and Phoenix. These have no prominent metropolitan centre as represented by the downtowns of the aspiring cities of the past. They are multipolar—a disbursed collection of suburban villages with more than one job centre and a multiplicity of occupations. The links between them are being provided by the car and the Internet, which allows people to work increasingly from home. They provide what the American Dream has been about: 'A good job, a decent school, proximity to relatives, a safe neighbourhood', and the features of suburbia—trees and open spaces a 'low-key shopping street, a place for a spacious apartment, a townhome, or even a single-family residence'.[65] They are likely to maintain the American civic culture, which Murray feels is under threat.

My conclusions can be brief. Despite the current fiscal impasse, the need to fix the unsustainable entitlements and the banking system, America remains by and large a country of classical liberal values enshrined in its Constitution. As in the past, the processes of 'creative destruction', which are vital for economic regeneration and growth, continue to function. America continues to be a magnet for the world's best and the brightest and is creating a hybrid multiracial and multiethnic culture, where the new urban model represented by the sprawling cities of Los Angeles and Phoenix provides the new environment for the American Dream to be pursued. With its relatively youthful and entrepreneurial population, there is little reason to believe that, despite the Jeremiahs, it will not continue to maintain its economic predominance in the world for the foreseeable future.

Notes

1. Robert Gordon, 'Is US Economic Growth Over? Faltering Innovation Confronts the Six Headwinds', NBER Working Paper, no. 18315 (2012).
2. Tyler Cowen, *The Great Stagnation* (New York: Dutton, 2011).
3. Robert Gordon, 'Is US Economic Growth Over?', Figure 4.
4. See Arnold Harberger, 'A Vision of the Growth Process', *American Economic Review*, 88, no. 1 (March 1998), pp. 1–32; and M.F. Scott, *A New View of Economic Growth* (Oxford: Clarendon Press, 1989).
5. J. Schmookler, *Invention and Economic Growth* (Cambridge, MA: Harvard University Press, 1966).

6. Edwin Mansfield, *The Economics of Technical Change* (London: Longmans, 1968).
7. Scott, *A New View of Economic Growth,* p. 138.
8. Arnold Harberger, 'A Vision of the Growth Process', *American Economic Review*, 88, no. 1 (March 1998), pp. 16–17.
9. J. Kotkin, *The Next Hundred Million: America in 2050* (New York: Penguin Books, 2010).
10. Kotkin, *The Next Hundred Million*, p. 4.
11. Kotkin, *The Next Hundred Million*, p. 6.
12. Kotkin, *The Next Hundred Million*, p. 7.
13. Kotkin, *The Next Hundred Million*, p. 109.
14. Kotkin, *The Next Hundred Million*, p. 13.
15. Kotkin, *The Next Hundred Million*, p. 242.
16. See D. Lal, *Reviving the Invisible Hand: The Case for Classical Liberalism in the Twenty-First Century* (Princeton, N.J.: Princeton University Press, 2006), pp. 3–4.
17. See R. Rajan and L. Zingales, *Saving Capitalism from the Capitalists* (New York: Crown Business, 2004).
18. Kotkin, *The Next Hundred Million*, p. 156.
19. Kotkin, *The Next Hundred Million*, p. 156.
20. 'America Still Remains the Promised Land for Most Migrants, Says Survey', *Business Standard* (23 March 2013). Available at http://www.business-standard.com/article/economy-policy/america-still-remains-the-promised-land-for-most-migrants-says-survey-113032200582_1.html (last accessed 7 November 2017).
21. Kotkin, *The Next Hundred Million*, p. 22.
22. Kotkin, *The Next Hundred Million*, p. 167.
23. Kotkin, *The Next Hundred Million*, p. 167.
24. S. Winship, 'Overstating the Costs of Inequality', *National Affairs,* 15 (Spring 2013).
25. This debate was concerned with the so-called Kuznets curve, and it was claimed that growth accompanied by a worsening income distribution might not alleviate poverty. All the evidence has been against this claim. For a discussion and references, see D. Lal and H. Myint, *The Political Economy of Poverty, Equity and Growth: A Comparative Study* (Oxford: Clarendon Press, 1998), pp. 39–44.
26. Winship, 'Overstating the Costs of Inequality'.
27. Winship, 'Overstating the Costs of Inequality', p. 37.
28. Winship, 'Overstating the Costs of Inequality', p. 38.

29. Winship, 'Overstating the Costs of Inequality', p. 36.
30. Winship, 'Overstating the Costs of Inequality', p. 39.
31. Winship, 'Overstating the Costs of Inequality', p. 39.
32. See Angus Deaton, 'Instruments of Development: Randomization in the Tropics, and the Search for the Elusive Keys to Economic Development', NBER Working Paper, mo. 1469 (2009); D. Lal, *Poverty and Progress: Realities and Myths about Global Poverty* (Washington, DC: Cato Institute, 2013).
33. Winship, 'Overstating the Costs of Inequality', p. 42.
34. Named after the rags to riches hero of F. Scott Fitzgerald's novel of the same name.
35. Winship, 'Overstating the Costs of Inequality', p. 42.
36. Raj Chetty, Nathaniel Hendren, Patrick Kline, Emmanuel Saez, and Nicholas Turner, 'Is the United States Still a Land of Opportunity? Recent Trends in Intergenerational Mobility', *American Economic Review*, 104, no. 5 (2014), pp. 141–7.
37. Chetty et al, 'Is the United States Still a Land of Opportunity', p. 141.
38. Chetty et al, 'Is the United States Still a Land of Opportunity', p. 145.
39. Chetty et al, 'Is the United States Still a Land of Opportunity', p. 145.
40. Chetty et al, 'Is the United States Still a Land of Opportunity', p. 141.
41. Thomas Piketty and Emmanuel Saez, 'Income Inequality in the United States, 1913–1998', *Quarterly Journal of Economics*, 118, no. 1 (2003), pp. 1–39.
42. Chetty et al, 'Is the United States Still a Land of Opportunity', p. 145.
43. As Lawrence E. Blume and Steven N. Durlauf, 'Capital in the Twenty-First Century: A Review Essay', *Journal of Political Economy*, 123, no. 4 (2015), pp. 749–77, note, Piketty's book should be called 'Wealth in the Twenty first Century', as it conflates capital as an input in the production function with wealth, so that 'the rate of return on capital as a productive input is conflated with the rate of return from its ownership, which includes any capital gains and losses' (p. 752). Secondly, he ignores human capital, pensions, and social security entitlements. Ignoring this conflation of capital with wealth, Piketty claims that one of the fundamental laws of capitalism, which he derives as 'the central contradiction of capitalism'—Thomas Piketty, *Capital in the Twenty-First Century* (Cambridge, MA: Belknap Press, 2014), p. 571—is given by the relationship $r>g$, where r is the rate of return on private capital and g is the economy's growth rate. He argues that with $r>g$, the wealth of the capitalist class will grow faster

than the incomes of workers, leading to an 'endless inegalitarian spiral' (p. 572).

Daron Acemoglu and James A. Robinson, 'The Rise and Decline of General Laws of Capitalism', *Journal of Economic Perspectives*, 29, no. 1 (2015), pp. 3–28, in their Appendix provide a simple model based on Nicholas Kaldor's work—'Alternative Theories of Distribution', *Review of Economic Studies*, 23, no. 2 (1955), pp. 83–100—to derive Piketty's Laws and show transparently the dubious assumptions that have to be made. Ironically, I had used the same Kaldorian distribution model to calibrate the effects of rapid growth in India leading to a rising savings rate through changes in aggregate savings dependent on distributional effects, and thence to still higher growth—a virtuous circle. See D. Lal and I. Natarajan, 'The Virtuous Circle: Savings, Distribution and Growth Interactions in India', in D. Lal and R.H. Snape (eds) *Trade, Development and Political Economy* (Basingstoke: Palgrave, 2001), Ch.12, pp. 213–28.

For other critiques of the theory and concepts underlying Piketty book, see Per Krusell and Anthony A. Smith Jr., 'Is Piketty's "Second Law of Capitalism" Fundamental?', *Journal of Political Economy*, 123, no. 4 (2015), pp. 725–48; David N. Weil, 'Capital and Wealth in the Twenty-First Century', *American Economic Review*, 105, no. 5 (2015), pp. 34–7; N. Gregory Mankiw, 'Yes, r>g. So What?' *American Economic Review*, 105, no. 5 (2015), pp. 43–7.

From his dubious theory, Piketty argues for a global capital tax to address the patrimonial capitalism he deplores. But he rightly sees this as utopian. His other policy proposals have been ably criticized by Blume and Durlaf, 'Capital in the Twenty-First Century'. The most cogent and succinct critique is by Kevin Murphy in a seminar at the Becker Friedman Institute of the University of Chicago at which Piketty was present—see Becker Friedman Institute, 'Explaining Inequality' (2015), available at https://bfi.uchicago.edu/feature-story/explaining-inequality (Last accessed 7 November 2017). Murphy argued that the best and simplest explanation for inequality was in terms of supply and demand for human capital in labour markets.

44. Ben Kiernan, *The Pol Pot Regime: Race, Power, and Genocide in Cambodia under the Khmer Rouge, 1975–79*, Third Edition (New Haven, CT: Yale University Press, 2008).

45. 'Examine the Control and Implementation of the Political Line to Save the Economy and Prepare to Build the Country in Every Field', trans. Chanthou Boua, CPK Center Document No. 3 (19 September 1975), p. 2, cited in Ben Kiernan, *The Pol Pot Regime: Race, Power, and Genocide in Cambodia under the Khmer Rouge, 1975–79,* (New Haven, CT: Yale University Press), p. 97.
46. D. Lal, 'Distribution and Development', *World Development*, 4, no. 9, (1976), pp. 725–38.
47. H. Chenery, M.S. Ahluwalia, C.L.G. Bell, J.H. Duloy, and R. Jolly, *Redistribution with Growth* (New York: Oxford University Press, 1974); and D. Lal, 'Review of John E. Roemer, *A General Theory of Exploitation and Class*, Harvard, 1982', *Journal of Economic Behavior and Organization*, 7 (1986), pp. 101–14.
48. Fredriech Hayek, *The Constitution of Liberty* (London: Routledge and Kegan Paul, 1960), p. 86.
49. Hayek, *The Constitution of Liberty*, p. 90.
50. Janet Yellen, 'Perspectives on Inequality and Opportunity from the Survey on Consumer Finances', Speech delivered at the Conference on Economic Opportunity and Inequality, Federal Reserve Bank of Boston, Boston, MA (17 October 2014). Available at https://www.federalreserve.gov/newsevents/speech/yellen20141017a.htm (last accessed 7 November 2017).
51. Hayek, *The Constitution of Liberty*, p. 93.
52. Daron Acemoglu, Simon Johnson, and James A. Robinson, 'Reversal of Fortune: Geography and Institutions in the Making of the Modern World Income Distribution', *Quarterly Journal of Economics*, 117, no. 4 (2002), pp. 1231–94.
53. For a fuller discussion, see Deaton, 'Instruments of Development' and Lal, *Poverty and Progress*.
54. Winship, 'Overstating the Costs of Inequality', p. 48.
55. Charles Murray, *Coming Apart: The State of White America, 1960–2010* (New York: Crown Forum, 2012).
56. Charles Murray, 'The New American Divide', The Saturday Essay, *Wall Street Journal* (21 January 2012).
57. Charles Murray, 'Why Economics Can't Explain Our National Divide', *Wall Street Journal* (18 March 2012).
58. Charles Murray, *Losing Ground: American Social Policy, 1950–1980* (New York: Basic Books, 1984).

59. A. De Tocqueville, *Democracy in America* (New York: Vintage Books, 1990).
60. Murray, 'The New American Divide'.
61. 'In 2007 nonresidents made up to 10 percent of all Manhattan apartment purchases, up from 5 percent eight years ago … In some newer buildings, nonresidents are more than half of new buyers. "Living in a superstar city," a Wharton study concludes, "is like owning a scarce luxury good."' (Kotkin, *The Next Hundred Million*, p. 55).
62. Kotkin, *The Next Hundred Million*, p. 54.
63. 'An individual from Houston who earns $50,000 would have to make $115,769 in Manhattan and $81,695 in Queens to live at the same level of comfort, according to the Council for Community and Economic Research's Cost of Living Calculator. Similarly, earning $50,000 in Atlanta is the equivalent of earning $106,198 in Manhattan and $74,941 in Queens. Over the past few decades even educated workers, particularly when they enter their thirties, have tended in increasing numbers to leave more expensive cities for less expensive ones like Phoenix, Dallas, Atlanta, and Raleigh-Durham' (Kotkin, *The Next Hundred Million*, p. 56).
64. Kotkin, *The Next Hundred Million*, p. 57.
65. Kotkin, *The Next Hundred Million*, pp. 62–3.

CHAPTER SEVEN

China and India

As we have seen in Chapter 5, China and India are likely to be among the largest economies by 2060. How likely are these projections to be realized, and would that imply that the US's economic predominance is likely to end?

Similarities

In discussing the economic prospects of the two Asian giants, the first point to be noted is their similarity in their periods of economic repression and liberalization. Both countries lost their economic predominance with the rise of the West after the Industrial Revolution. This Western economic rise was accompanied by the expansion of their gunpowder empires. Both China and India were subject to Western domination: in China, after the Opium Wars in the 1820s and in India, since the British victory in the Battle of Plassey in 1757. These led to the wounding of these ancient Eurasian civilizations.

On their independence and creation of nation states—in China after the victory of Mao-Tse Tung's CCP over Chiang's KMT in 1949, and in India, with the British withdrawal and partition of the Indian subcontinent in 1947—both countries were faced by a common dilemma: how to modernize without losing their souls? Modernization was needed to provide the means to counter any future danger of submission by superior arms. Their ancient traditions, which were part of their cosmological beliefs, were threatened by the westernization assumed to accompany modernization.

As we saw in Chapter 3, three ways have been adopted to deal with this cognitive dissonance. The first way is that of the oyster, neither modernizing nor westernizing; the second is to imitate Japan by modernizing but not westernizing; the third is to find a 'middle way' through socialism. Both China and India chose this route.

This was undertaken in two markedly different political systems, reflecting their ancient political habits. These were determined by their geographical compulsions when these ancient civilizations were created, as discussed in Chapter 2.

Despite these differences in their polities, the economic policies followed by the Asian giants since their independence have greater similarities than differences. They both adopted central planning with state control of industry and the adoption of an inward-looking, capital-intensive, heavy-industry-biased programme of forced industrialization. In these labour surplus, capital scarce economies, this strategy required financial repression to lower the relative price of capital to labour. As this strategy was against their comparative advantage, it led to grave economic inefficiencies. It also led to distortions in the markets for land and labour.

Both attempted to collectivize their hitherto private agriculture—first by various forms of land redistribution, and then, in India, through Nehru's attempts at introducing co-operatives and various forms of price controls and regional restrictions on movement of foodgrains and (much more drastically) in China, through Mao's creation of communes. Both led to agrarian crises and reform. This happened much sooner in India, given its democratic polity, than in the authoritarian polity of China, dominated by Mao and his ideological predilections. This led to one of the largest famines in human history in China with over thirty million excess deaths. In India, the quiet crisis in agriculture was diffused in the late

1960s and early 70s through the adoption of Green Revolution technology, which led to a shifting of the agricultural production function and spectacular increases in output and incomes in the regions whose ecology permitted its adoption. In China, it was not until 1978, after Mao's death and Deng Xiaoping's ascendancy, that the communes were replaced by the household responsibility system. This de facto privatized land through implicit long leases, restoring Chinese agriculture's health. Agricultural output, which had grown at about 3 per cent p.a. between 1952 and 1978, grew at 7.6 per cent p.a. between 1978 and 1984.

The distortions in the labour markets were more extreme in China than in India. With rural-urban migration controlled by the hukou system; the extinction of any agrarian labour mobility in the communes; and all urban workers assigned to state enterprises for life, with tied entitlements to housing, food, health, and retirement benefits, there was virtually no labour market in Maoist China.

In India, the distortions in the labour market were confined to the industrial sector, where the colonial labour laws, based on rights granted to UK workers after its Industrial Revolution, were introduced to hobble India's nascent industries, particularly textiles—which had, in a few years, turned the tables on Lancashire. These labour market distortions were continued and extended by Nehru's daughter Indira Gandhi during her rule. They created an artificial dual labour market, where the implicit wage in the so-called formal sector was well above the supply price of labour in India's labour abundant economy. India's industrial enterprises became increasingly capital intensive. As soon as small- and medium-scale industrial enterprises (SMEs) employed more than one hundred workers, they became subject to these stringent labour laws. These did not allow the firing of workers or the exit of bankrupt firms. Besides preventing the growth of the labour intensive SMEs, these labour laws led to an industrial caste system and India's failure to generate labour-intensive industrialization.

With the foreign exchange crises in the mid-1960s, due to the stringent import controls which were an implicit tax on exports, industrial growth slowed, and India was mired in what came to be called the Hindu rate of growth of 3.5 per cent p.a. In 1991, a balance of payments-cum-fiscal-cum-inflation crisis led to a process of liberalization where many of the controls on imports, industrial production, and prices were removed; the exchange rate was devalued and fiscal policy was tightened. Financial repression was gradually reduced, and India became increasingly integrated (but less so than China) in the global economy. This movement from the plan to the market allowed what seemed to be an economic miracle with growth accelerating for a time after 1998 to 8 per cent p.a. and a large reduction in structural poverty. But the reform process (as we shall see) has stalled, and India's economic future remains clouded.

After the chaos caused by China's Cultural Revolution and the agrarian crisis, Deng's opening of the Chinese economy began the process of moving it from the plan to the market. This led to what has been called the Chinese miracle, with growth of over 7 per cent p.a. for nearly three decades as China industrialized rapidly, becoming the 'workshop of the world'. This rapid and sustained growth led to a massive reduction in structural poverty.

We examine these trends and current economic problems in greater detail in the next two parts of this chapter to form a judgement on whether, in the competition between these two Asian giants, the Indian tortoise will overtake the Chinese hare in the near future.

The Chinese Economic 'Miracle'

Aggregate Performance

In the following sections we examine how China has generated its miracle economy with the rise of Deng Tsiao Ping, and how more recently its growth performance has stalled.

Growth and Productivity

Noting the deficiencies of Chinese official statistics, the late Angus Maddison had produced the most careful analysis and

Table 7.1 China GDP Growth Rates 1952–2012 (Per cent Per Annum)

Years	Official Data	Adjusted Data
1952–57	6.7	6.0
1957–65	2.4	3.2
1965–71	5.3	5.2
1971–77	4.0	3.4
1952–77	4.3	4.3
1977–84	9.2	7.8
1984–91	8.6	4.9
1991–01	10.4	7.0
2001–07	11.3	10.3
2007–12	9.3	6.5
2010–15*	7.8	5.5
1978–12	9.8	7.2

Source: Wu (2014), Table 13.

Note: *Paul Roderick Gregory's Conference Board estimate from *Forbes*, 15 August 2016.

reworking of Chinese statistics.[1] His collaborator, Harry Wu, has revised and updated these.[2] Table 7.1 shows the official and his adjusted data for Chinese GDP growth from 1952 to 2012, which includes the planning period of 1952–77 and the subsequent reform period.

The periodization in the Table corresponds to shifts in policy regime and external shocks to the economy. The first period, 1952–7, corresponds to that of the adoption of Soviet-style central planning. The Maoist Great Leap Forward and its aftermath are in the 1956–65 period. The early chaos in the Cultural Revolution is in the period 1966–71, while the rest of this period until the fall of the Gang of Four is in the 1972–7 period. The reform period begins with agricultural reform in 1978–84. The next period, 1985–91, saw the beginning of industrial reform, with a double-track price system. From 1992 to 2001, there is the adoption of the 'socialist market economy' and the reforms of the state-owned enterprises. The 2002–7 period marks the years after China's accession to the World Trade Organization (WTO), while the 2007–12 period covers the GFC and its aftermath. From 2010 to 2015, growth has slowed to 5.5 per cent on the Conference

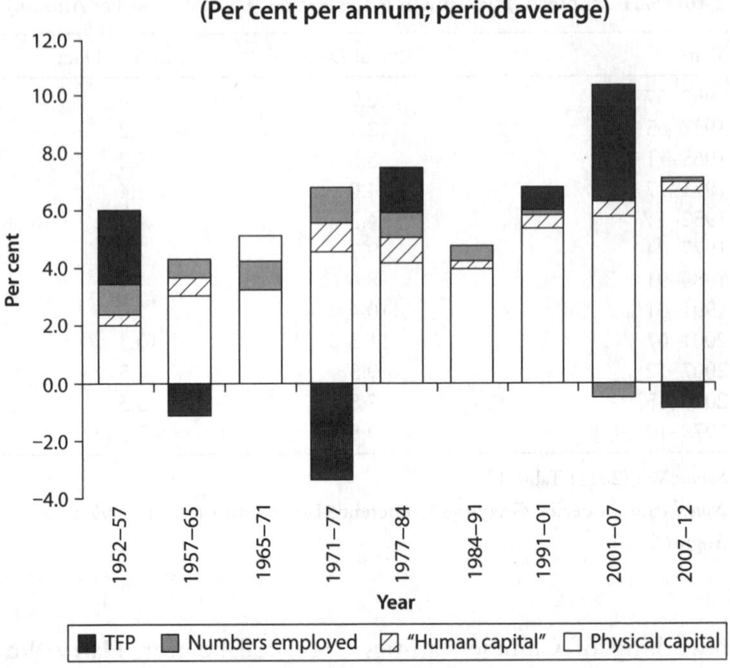

FIGURE 7.1 Sources of Growth in the Chinese Economy
Source: Wu, 'China's Growth and Productivity Performance Revisited', Figure 9.

Board figures, compared with the official figure of 7.8 per cent (Paul Roderick Gregory, 2016).

Figure 7.1 shows the sources of China's growth in each of these periods.

During much of the planning period, except for the first 1952–7 period, TFP was negative. The efficiency gains in the 1952–7 period can be attributed to it being the first peaceful period since the late 1930s. From the late 1950s, the planning period was, in general, a graveyard for productivity. Apart from a recovery gain in TFP in 1965–71, after the failure of the Great Leap Forward and its aftermath, most of the 1970s (up to 1978 when reforms began) saw a huge loss in TFP, wiping out half of the gain by increased factor inputs.[3]

The early reform period, 1978–84, saw a TFP increase because of the one-off incentive gains from the institutional changes in agriculture, but this was not sustained. The early industrial reforms in 1984–91 did not promote TFP growth, partly because of the political shock of the Tiananmen massacre, resulting in a zero TFP growth in 1984–91. In the following 1992–2001 period, 'the fastest ever physical investment only achieved a slightly improved TFP performance'.[4]

It was in the following period, 2001–7, after China joined the WTO and before it was hit by the GFC, that China saw significant and sustained TFP growth. China had built up a huge production capacity in the previous decade that was significantly underutilized, resulting in persistent deflation from 1998 to 2002. The opening to world markets allowed China to utilize this capacity in labour-intensive manufacturing, in line with its comparative advantage. China's WTO entry was thus greatly productivity enhancing as it allowed China to benefit more not only from its comparative advantage but also by speeding up the process of China's 'learning by doing' process through a deeper and wider exposure to international markets and the further institutional reforms this prompted.[5]

The massive investment drive in 2007–12 did not see any rise in productivity. The growth generated was entirely due to a massive increase in physical capital through a rise in the investment to output ratio. This had the effect of raising both the capital–output ratio and reducing the returns to capital as rapidly diminishing returns set in, as can be seen from Figure 7.2. From 2010 to 2015, TFP growth declined by 2.1 per cent.

So, in the whole reform period, while the official TFP figures based on the official growth rates yield productivity growth five times higher than the Conference Board series, both series show falling TFP after 2001. By 2012–15, both series yield either near zero or negative TFP growth. Thus, on the more robust Conference Board figures, capital and labour inputs expanded faster than output for negative productivity growth (Gregory 2016).

China has by and large followed the economic model pioneered by Japan and followed by other East Asian countries. They have all experienced rapid economic growth during their 'catch-up' periods. Comparing these countries' performance with China's

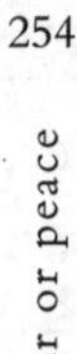

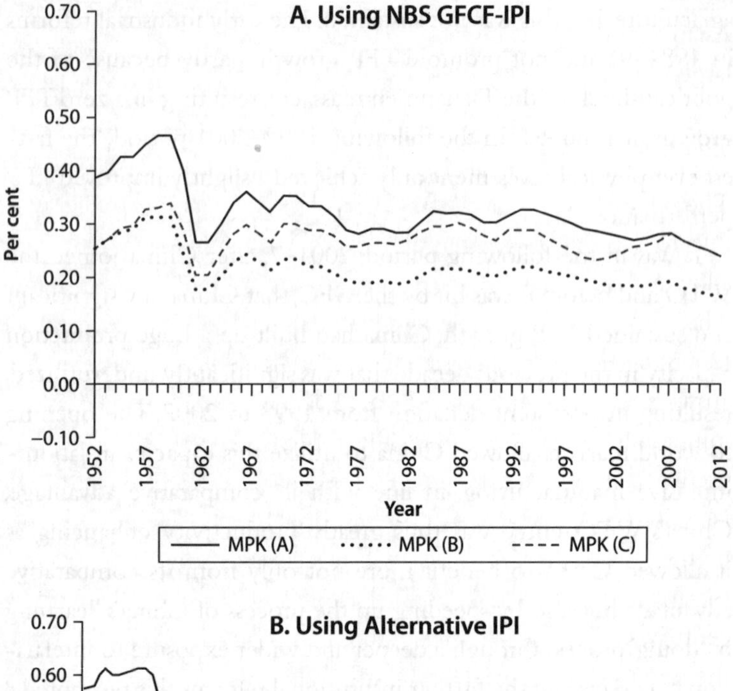

A. Using NBS GFCF-IPI

Per cent: 0.70, 0.60, 0.50, 0.40, 0.30, 0.20, 0.10, 0.00, −0.10

Year: 1952, 1957, 1962, 1967, 1972, 1977, 1982, 1987, 1992, 1997, 2002, 2007, 2012

MPK (A) MPK (B) MPK (C)

B. Using Alternative IPI

Per cent: 0.70, 0.60, 0.50, 0.40, 0.30, 0.20, 0.10, 0.00

Year: 1952, 1956, 1960, 1964, 1968, 1972, 1976, 1980, 1984, 1988, 1992, 1996, 2000, 2004, 2008, 2012

MPK (A) MPK (B) MPK (C)

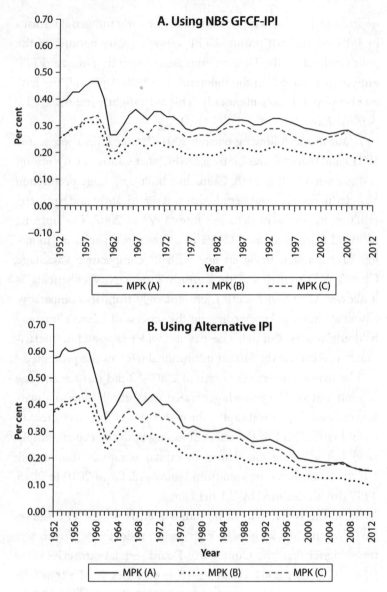

FIGURE 7.2 Returns on Capital of the Chinese Economy
Source: Wu, 'China's Growth and Productivity Performance Revisited', Figure 8.

(from 1994 to 2015), when their per capita PPP income rose from $2,000 to $8,000 (Japan 1950–68, South Korea 1969–89, and Taiwan 1966–87), Wu finds that the pace of China's growth is similar to or even slightly slower, rather than faster, than the East

Asian economies.[6] The Chinese economic miracle is, thus, by and large similar, but less spectacular, to that of the other Asian tigers.

State Capitalism vs Market Economy

There has been much discussion about whether this miracle was due to wise state intervention rather than China inadvertently allowing capitalism to emerge in its attempts to save socialism. Three important books by Yasheng Huang (2008), Steven Cheung (2008), and Ronald Coase and Ning Wang (2012)[7] provide the answers. They argue that the unintended consequence of Deng's injunction of 'seeking truth from the facts', in contrast with Mao's predilection for basing policies on an overarching ideological Marxist model, turned China into a capitalist market economy by the end of the century, even as the aim of the CCP remained to save socialism. However, in the following decades of the new century, China has partially restored the control of the state over the economy in a new form of authoritarian state-led capitalism while still keeping the façade of a market economy. This has fooled many observers into believing that China is now like any other capitalist economy, albeit—in the Party's characterization—'with Chinese characteristics'.

At the centre of the dispute about whether, in the first decades of reforms in the 1980s, China was progressing towards a market economy or had invented a new form of state capitalism is the role of the household responsibility system introduced in Deng's reforms to replace the commune system in 1978. Both Huang's and Coase and Wang's books emphasize two separate periods of reform: one till the Tiananmen student uprising in 1989 and the other from then till China joined the WTO in 2001.

Coase and Wang distinguish two types of reforms in China. The first was state led and its purpose was to revitalize the state sector and save socialism. The other consisted of what they call 'marginal revolutions', which were based on grass-roots initiatives. These made China turn capitalist and fuelled its miraculous growth. Four of the revolutions that transformed the Chinese economy in the 1980s were private farming, township and village enterprises

(TVEs), privatization of services in the towns, and the Special Economic Zones (SEZs).

Deng's state-led reforms were fathered by Chen Yun. He was the architect of China's first Five-Year Plan and a believer in central planning. But given his Shanghai origins, he also saw a critical but limited role for the private sector and the market under socialism. He was purged during Mao's Cultural Revolution. On Deng's return to power he became the economic tsar of the state-led reforms. He sought to dilute the heavy industry bias of Chinese industrialization by channelling more investment into consumer goods and agricultural production. The purchasing prices for agricultural products were raised by more than 20 per cent in 1979, and grain imports were increased. Foreign trade was decentralized and gradually opened, and provinces were given more fiscal autonomy. But the major thrust of Chen Yun's plans was to reform the state enterprises, which he saw as socialism's economic foundation. It began with devolving some rights—like retaining profits—to the enterprises. This attempt to provide incentives to increase the efficiency of state enterprises continued throughout the 1980s.

The 1980s' Capitalist 'Marginal Revolutions'

But the real story of China's economic rise was taking place outside the ken of the state in Coase and Wang's marginal revolutions. The first was private farming. After Mao's death, and the disaster his collectivization of agriculture had wrought, the peasants began to return to private farming, which had existed in China for millennia, even though the state was still promoting the communes.[8] Giving into the inevitable, the ban on private farming was lifted in 1980, and it was officially recognized in January 1982.[9] It was not top-down state direction but bottom-up clandestine private initiatives that led to decollectivized Chinese agriculture. The state merely acquiesced in what had become spreading grass-roots practice.

The second 'marginal revolution' arose with the TVEs. These were the most dynamic sector in the 1980s and were the base from which Chinese labour-intensive industry took off. As these were classified as collective enterprises, a whole academic industry has grown up that described the Chinese growth model as being based on a unique form of collective enterprise in which the TVEs provided an efficient substitute in a weak institutional environment. This challenges standard economic claims that private ownership rights motivate entrepreneurs to invest and take risks. But as so many theoretical curiosa spawned by development economists, this too is built on empirical sand.

For, as Huang has shown, the identification of TVEs as 'collective enterprises' is based on a statistical misunderstanding. The term used by the official Chinese statisticians includes 'both TVEs controlled by townships and villages and TVEs controlled by private entrepreneurs'. Disaggregating these data by ownership type, Huang found that 'private TVEs absolutely dominated the total pool of TVEs'.[10] As they operated outside the state system, they were handicapped compared with the state-owned enterprises (SOEs), by having to get raw materials on the black market; by not receiving subsidized credit; and by not having access to the state distribution system. They had to operate as normal business enterprises, albeit in a distorted environment stacked against them. Yet, they outperformed the state enterprises.

The third marginal revolution took place when the twenty million high-school urban students—fifteen to eighteen years old—who had been sent to the countryside during Mao's Cultural Revolution returned to the cities with Deng's return to power. They had no job prospects and formed a young, jobless, restless group, often taking to the streets and threatening civil disorder. In the face of this pressure, the state allowed self-employment in the service sector. This ended the state monopoly in the urban economy.

The fourth marginal revolution was through the creation of the SEZs. The first in Shenzen was created in a marginal area near Hong Kong where socialism did not exist and others in areas where socialism had failed. It avoided the potential resistance to reform from the state-sector and minimized the risk of a failed reform.[11] The idea of setting up these zones came from the local government in Guangdong, which faced the problem of dealing with illegal immigration across the border to Hong Kong. This was dealt with by inviting Hong Kong businessmen to set up factories employing local labour in Guangdong.[12] The other SEZs and industrial parks sought to 'create a confined environment to try out a highly uncertain and politically risky experiment outside the socialist economy. Socialism could thus be preserved while capitalism was allowed a chance in the periphery'[13].

Post-Tiananmen

These marginal revolutions of the 1980s created a growing private economy even as the inefficient state sector became increasingly insolvent and struggled to survive. It was the capitalism of these marginal revolutions by non-state actors, not the state, which created the Chinese miracle.

This set the stage for the second stage of reforms, which the CCP felt it had to undertake if it was not be buried as the Soviet Communist party had been by the 1991 implosion of its economic system. The brutally suppressed Tiananmen student uprising was however seen as an awful portent and blamed in part on the economic liberalism of Hu Yaobong and Zhao Ziyang—the general secretaries of the CCP in the 1980s. The planners under Li Peng, seeking a return to the Maoist agenda, seemed in the ascendant until Deng's summer tour in 1992 put economic reform, under Jiang Zemin and Zhu Rongji, back on the agenda. The 14th National Congress of the CCP officially recognized for the first time that the market economy was the ultimate goal of China's economic reforms.

Market Promoting Reforms

The first crucial market promoting reforms were the abolition of price controls and various barriers impeding a national market for goods. The second was significant trade liberalization with a significant reduction in import tariffs for over 3,000 items. The third was the 1993 tax reforms, which introduced a uniform value-added tax (VAT) on all manufacturing firms and a tax sharing scheme. This assigned to local governments an urban land-use tax,

VAT on land, property tax, and business tax not covered by the VAT and 25 per cent of the national VAT.

These market-promoting reforms unleashed the competition between local governments, which Steven Cheung has emphasized lies at the heart of the dynamic industrial capitalism China has created. It fuelled the continuation after Tiananmen of China's phenomenal economic growth.[14]

The competition between municipalities *(xians)* was based on the incentives provided to local bureaucrats by granting 'user rights' to urban and industrial land to the xians. They could act like landlords, selecting and granting sharecropping contracts to investors. The economic power of the xians lay in their sole right to decide and allocate the use of land. The right did not belong to villages, towns, cities, provinces, or even Beijing. The xians are part of seven geographically determined layers: country, provinces, cities, xians, towns, villages, and households. These layers are vertically linked by responsibility contracts (which, from their Chinese name, imply 'guarantee what I want and you can do what you want'). But horizontally, there are no contractual links and they are free to compete.

The pecuniary basis of the set of bureaucratic incentives at the level of the xian was the uniform national VAT of 17 per cent paid by investors in a xian. The xian could keep a quarter of this VAT, which allowed the bureaucrats to receive various perks like houses. It gave them the incentive to compete for maximizing the takings from VAT in their area. So the xians are like landlords whose investors are the sharecroppers, and they themselves are sharecroppers with the upper geographical units.[15] In his earlier work, Cheung had shown that if the landlord could vary the share of output given by his tenants, he could obtain the efficient outcome that maximized the productive use of land and his share, with the tenants putting in the optimum effort to maximize production.[16]

But how could the xian 'landlord' ensure this efficient outcome if he could not vary the 'share' that is determined by the nationally uniform VAT? Cheung's answer is that if the landlord is also providing 'capital', then through its variation, he can obtain the efficient outcome even if his share is fixed. The capital the xians can offer are the price of land they charge investors and the costs of the infrastructure they provide, as well as offering rebates on the VAT to be paid. This is how the xians have competed for highly productive industrial investments in their areas. A trip in September 2008 to the showpiece industrial park in Suzhou near Shanghai (which we took with the Cheungs) provided a visible demonstration of this fierce local competition by the xians. By using the capital at their disposal to lure the high value-added, labour-intensive export industries (set up by most of the Fortune 500 companies), they have made China the workshop of the world.

SOE Reform

This virtual local auction of user rights to land led to a marked rise in the value of industrial land. One unintended consequence was that it permitted the reform of the Maoist era's inefficient loss-making state enterprises. They had hung like an albatross around the neck of the Chinese economy, despite repeated attempts to reform them in the 1980s.

The Chinese state enterprises suffered from what Justin Lin[17] has described as a dual policy burden. They had been set up under the old heavy-industry-biased, capital-intensive strategy, which defied comparative advantage. With price and trade reforms, they had become uncompetitive. This was the 'strategic' burden they faced. They also carried the 'social' burden of overstaffing, as the state wanted to maintain full employment in the urban sector. By 1988, 10.9 per cent of state enterprises were insolvent—a proportion that rose to 40 per cent by 1995.[18] In 1992, faced with financing these losses, the local government in Zhucheng in Shandong began to sell its local state enterprises to their employees.

Zhu Rongji, who oversaw the second wave of state-led economic reforms from 1993–2003, adopted this model, and it was pioneered by Shanghai, which had put all its myriad, scattered state enterprises into a State Assets Management company. With privatization being officially recognized in 1997, the state gave up its sole ownership of these enterprises, becoming a minority shareholder, with outside investors and employees becoming the majority shareholders. The employees who were redundant were paid a cash settlement in exchange for their right to the 'iron bowl' of lifetime social entitlements.

The final piece of the jigsaw to resolve the policy burden was to follow the Shanghai model nationally, with all local assets of state enterprises put into a common pool. As the major asset of these enterprises was land, whose price had risen because of the rapid economic growth in the previous decade, the compensation received by state employees could be equalized (including those in insolvent enterprises). This removed any resistance to privatization.

The Rise of State-led Authoritarian Capitalism

In the following years, almost all small and medium SOEs had been privatized. Of the large state enterprises, those deemed to be of strategic importance were given monopolistic or oligopolistic rights in the market and became profitable. The others continue to depend upon government protection and subsidies. This marked the beginnings of the creation of the dual system—a private non-state market economy and an increasingly state-led authoritarian capitalism in which these strategic industries controlled the commanding heights of the economy.

Continuing Financial Repression

The continuing implicit and explicit subsidies to the SOEs have made it difficult to end the financial repression that was the hallmark of the planned economy. China had inherited the financial system common to most Communist countries, with all the surpluses of the national economy collected and allocated—including to the SOEs—by the Ministry of Finance. There was only one bank, the People's Bank of China (PBOC), where the unspent balances of the allocations of the SOEs and any household savings had to be deposited. Four state-owned commercial banks were opened at the start of the reforms in 1979, with the hope that with the end of central planning they would be able to evaluate and monitor investment projects. But these hopes were belied as financial repression, which took the form of giving depositors low administratively determined interest rates well below the market interest rate, had to be maintained if the government had to continue bailing out the loss-making SOEs.

Creating the Façade of Market-based State Banks and Enterprises

With the privatization of most of the SOEs, Zhu Rongji sought to convert the state-owned banks into normal commercial banks. He converted them into stock-holding banks and liberalized the interest rate, so that the stop-go cycles that had characterized Chinese financial policy could be ended. Instead, as shown in *Red Capitalism*, a detailed study of Chinese financial reforms by Carl Walter and Fraser Howie—two China-based Western financiers—an opaque system, which has the trappings of a market system but not the substance, has been created.[19]

These trappings include a stock exchange, a bond market, and purportedly commercial banks, like Western ones, which have been listed on world stock markets. This complex system gathered the massive savings of thrifty Chinese households to be used for the purposes determined by the interests of the princelings, who increasingly control the party. Walter and Howie say: 'Zhu Rongji's effort to push the banks towards an international model has been stopped and the banks have reverted to their traditional role [of acting like public utilities]. Without question they are again huge deposit-taking institutions, extending loans as directed by their party leaders'.[20]

Role of Wall Street

But how did China manage to create the façade of a market-based financial system, with some of the largest banks and effectively state-controlled companies listed on Western banks, which are now entering the Fortune 500 list of companies? The opening step was Zhu Rongji's decision in early 1993, at the suggestion of the chief executive of Hong Kong's stock exchange, to allow selected SOEs to list on Hong Kong's stock exchange. He realized that this would require the restructuring of SOEs to conform to international legal, accounting, and financial requirements. Zhu Rongji hoped that foreign regulatory oversight would improve their management.

Enter Wall Street bankers and lawyers. Investment banks led by Goldman Sachs and legal firms like Linklaters and Paine were 'the creators of the New China of the twenty first century … just as surely as the Cultural Revolution flowed from Chairman Mao's Little Red Book'.[21] The model was provided by the creation of China Mobile in 1997 by Goldman Sachs out of a poorly managed assortment of provincial post and telecoms entities. They sold the resulting package to international fund managers as a national telecommunications giant. Even with the Asian financial crisis raging, China Mobile completed a dual listing on New York's and Hong Kong's stock exchanges, raising $4.2 billion. There was no looking back. China's oil companies, banks, and insurance companies sold billions of US dollars of shares in initial public offerings (IPOs) 'that went off like strings of fire crackers in the global capital markets. All of these companies were imagined up, created, and listed by American investment bankers'.[22] The government's target was to have as many Chinese companies as possible listed on the Fortune Global 500 list. With the willing help of international investment banks, lawyers, and accounting firms, China soon achieved this goal. Forty-four of its firms in the National Team were on the Fortune list in 2009.[23]

As a result, if the stock exchanges of Shanghai and Shenzhen are combined with Hong Kong's (48 per cent of whose market capitalization is due to Chinese companies), China has the second largest equity capital in the world after New York. It dwarfs those of Japan and India. In fact, 'from 1993, when IPOs began, to early 2010, Chinese SOEs have raised US$389 billion on domestic exchanges and a further US$262 billion on international markets, adding a total of US$651 billion in capital to the US$ 818 billion contributed by foreign direct investment'.[24]

These two sources of capital have had two effects. The foreign direct investment (FDI) flows created the non-state economy of the non-state private sector, with the transfer of technology and management techniques to Chinese entrepreneurs who created new domestic industries. By contrast, the capital raised on domestic and international stock exchanges created and strengthened the companies 'inside the system.... The market capitalization in Hong Kong, Shanghai, and elsewhere belongs to companies controlled outright by China's Communist Party: only minority stakes have been sold'.[25]

Privatization of State Assets to Nomenklatura

The party itself has increasingly become an oligarchy of the revolutionary families (the princelings) who are the political elite. China is a family-run business. 'The oligopolies dominating the national landscape are called "National Champions" and the "pillars" of China's "socialist market" economy, but they are controlled by these same families'.[26] Greed is the driving force behind the protectionist walls of the 'state-owned' economy 'inside the system', and money is the language. 'A clear view over this wall is obscured by a political ideology that disguised the privatization of state assets behind continuing state ownership'.[27]

But while China's state sector has assumed the guise of Western corporations, this hides their true nature: that they are a patronage system centred on the CCP's nomenklatura. They are not autonomous corporations. 'Their senior management and, indeed, the fate of the corporation itself, are completely dependent on their political patrons'.[28]

The creation of these new SOEs out of the dross of the old SOEs is the work of Wall Street bankers, who have provided the 'lipstick, the mascara, the pedicure, the hair weave' so they closely resemble Western corporations, and built their image 'so that minority stakes in these companies could be sold at high prices, with the Party and its friends profiting handsomely'.[29] And the Wall Street investment banks, too, have profited handsomely. As Shankar Sharma of FIRST Global wrote in his review of Walter and Howie's book in India's *Business Standard*:

> Ever wonder why Morgan Stanley's Stephen Roach and Goldman Sachs's Jim O'Neill remain resolutely hyper-bullish on China, despite the country's huge, and to my mind, insurmountable debt problem ($22 trillion by 2016)? Also, ever wonder why these very gentlemen remain so resolutely bearish on India? Go take a look

at the fees that India pays these investment banks to raise capital through divestment deals—these wouldn't fund even a day's supply of coffee. On the other hand, in just one Chinese bank IPO, the government paid these banks $220 million as fees. Research reports by Wall Street banks have always been up for sale to the highest bidder, and nobody knows this better than the Chinese.[30]

China Development Bank (CDB) and China's Post-2008 Hubris

The second pillar of the state economy 'inside the system' was created by an explicitly state-owned vehicle: China Development Bank (CDB). Chen Yuan, the princeling son of Chen Yun, converted CDB over time from the main instrument for channelling China's massive infrastructure spending into a major instrument of Chinese economic foreign policy so as to create a unique form of state capitalism meant to transform China into a major economic power around the world. *China's Superbank*, an important book by Henry Sanderson and Michael Forsythe, two Bloomberg journalists who have been based in China, dissects the story of how this was done.[31]

Chen Yuan began by converting the zombie bank he came to head in 1998 into the major financial conduit for China's massive expenditure on infrastructure. He used the same financial instruments created in the local competition of the xians (which had promoted the FDI-based non-state sector in the first decades of China's economic rise) to turn his zombie bank into a global bank. The instrument he copied was the monetization of the rising value of land, which had provided the means to get rid of the social burden of state enterprises inherited by the xians.

Financing Infrastructure

Chen Yuan realized that the infrastructure being built as part of China's urbanization was raising the price of land, which would continue to rise with urbanization. The local authorities who owned the land could collateralize these land revenues. Moreover, these revenues were extra budgetary and so had no oversight over their use. As China's infrastructure spending started increasing with the onset of the Asian financial crisis in 1996–7, rising nearly three times by 2002, 'China and local officials became addicted to investment. What was better than an ever-rising state-owed asset that could be used as collateral?'[32] Chen Yuan devised a system 'to leverage the future value of land into large up-front loans, such as one it gave the port city of Tianjin in 2003'.[33]

Local Government Finance Vehicles (LGFVs)

But how were these loans financed? Unlike commercial banks, as a policy bank, CDB did not have direct access to China's burgeoning household savings as it could not take deposits—nor after Zhu Rongji's tax reforms could the local government. They were forbidden from running deficits or issuing bonds. So, Chen Yuan created the following system: The country's commercial banks used people's savings to buy bonds sold by CDB on the nation's bond markets. CDB would then help local governments to set up companies to borrow (local government financial vehicles [LGFVs]) and give them initial long-term loans from the proceeds of the CDB bonds it had sold to commercial banks. As Sanderson and Forsythe[34] observe:

> Thus dressed up and empowered, the LGFVs were free to go on a further borrowing spree seeking short-term loans from the commercial banks or selling bonds themselves on the bond market to banks and securities companies. If the central government wanted to stimulate the economy, it could send money flowing down this cash waterfall. The risk in the end came back to their front door.

Post 1997–8, these LGFVs became the force that created China's economic growth. They were used to fund China's huge stimulus on infrastructure with the onset of the 2008 GFC. Other commercial banks followed suit. This credit had little oversight. Projects that had been proposed over the last thirty years and mothballed or rejected were approved. With a guaranteed spread between fixed lending and deposit rates, 'the commercial banks didn't need to worry about making a profit from good projects and felt they were following orders to stimulate the economy'.[35] Total bank lending to LGFVs rose 'from 1.7 trillion yuan of outstanding loans at the beginning of 2008 to nearly 5 trillion yuan just two years later.... In two years, 2009 and 2010, China increased its total government debt at the same speed that America did in the five years before the housing market bust in 2007'.[36] China's local government debt has risen fivefold since 1995, with more than 80 per cent going to infrastructure. 'Like subprime debt in the United States, these off-balance-sheet vehicles have infected the balance sheets of all China's major banks'.[37]

The first cracks in the system appeared when land prices began to fall in 2011, and the LGFVs could not pay back the principal or even the interest on their borrowings. Banks were ordered by China's Banking Regulatory Commission to roll over their LGFV bank debt, which had short-term maturities. The LGFV loans by the banks became essentially illiquid. The market created by the CDB failed to value risk and capital correctly. It was like the credit default swap products the United States had invented to insure against losses in subprime debt. 'The risk has been passed from the local governments to the banks and then back to the central government'.[38]

The collateralizing of land requires local governments to acquire land cheaply and sell it at a profit. They have done this by expropriating farmers and expanding cities into rural areas. This has led to widespread protests and rural unrest, with 'a total of 60 per cent of all large-scale protests in China ... due to land grabs and compensation disputes'.[39]

With Chen Yuan's firm belief that urbanization and the infrastructure it needs is the key to development, China has taken a huge gamble that the infrastructure created by his CDB model will raise growth, which will raise incomes, which will pay for the debt on which this infrastructure has been financed. With the negative real interest rates paid to savers by commercial banks, which they use to buy CDB bonds, 'if the infrastructure build-out is not efficient, it wouldn't be a stretch to say China's savers have been robbed'.[40]

But Chen Yuan had wider ambitions. With the collapse of the Western banking system in 2008, he decided to extend his collateralized land-based model—which had funded all the grandiose projects from the Three Gorges Dam to the Olympic stadia, to metros and highways within China—to developing countries. The CDB would give large loans to the state enterprises owning natural resources in Africa and Latin America. These loans would be collateralized by revenues from the sale of these natural resources to Chinese state-owned natural resource companies, like Sinopec. In just three days in February 2009, as Western banks were tottering on the brink of collapse and global oil demand had dropped, China signed CDB-backed oil-for-loan deals with Brazil, Russia, and Venezuela. The total sum made available was some 600,000 barrels a day, equal to 17 per cent of China's 2008 imports. Sanderson and Forsythe noted, 'CDB loans are a crucial part of these deals, locking the countries into supply contracts that make them increasingly dependent on China's purchasing power and the revenue sources the commodity sales bring their treasuries'.[41]

Part of the loans is tied to the development of infrastructure. These proceeds are used 'to buy Chinese goods and service from Huawei phones to CITIC-built railroads. China wins twice, and CDB helps foster another Chinese goal, pushing its top companies to "go out" and become globally competitive multinationals'. Most of 'these companies are state-owned, and almost all are long-term clients of CDB'.[42]

This CDB lending has been enormous. Sanderson and Forsythe observe[43]:

> [Beginning] from almost nothing prior to 2008 … in 2010, its loan commitments were more than those of the World Bank, Inter-American Development Bank and the US Export-Import Bank combined.… The model is also used around the globe, from Russia, to Ghana, to Turkmenistan, as a means for China to secure energy supplies and for its state-owned infrastructure companies to win contracts. China's money is secured by winning business for Chinese companies, rather than setting policy conditions on the borrowing country.

Though China through the CDB is attempting to use its growing economic strength as an instrument of its foreign policy,

> the problem, like that of the rows of empty skyscrapers now dotting the Tianjin skyline, is one of hubris. In the case of local government debt, CDB might be guilty of ignoring basic laws of supply and demand. In Venezuela, it may be ignoring history.... Does China, with the CDB as its executor, really believe it is immune from two centuries of Venezuelan debt defaults?[44]

Fragilities

The nemesis of this CDB-fuelled Chinese hubris could come in many forms. With a turn in the political wheel, developing country governments might appeal to the emerging internationally accepted norm of 'odious debt'. These are debts given to despotic regimes that are not for the common good but to strengthen the state and repress opposition. The point of promoting the concept of odious debts in international law is to make lenders pay more attention to the character of the regimes they are lending to and free new governments from the burden of paying off the illegitimate debts of past despots. After the fall of Saddam Hussein, the new Iraqi government won forgiveness of much of the debt incurred by the despot on this argument.

Equally worrying for the Chinese government is that this CDB model is increasingly facing a backlash, particularly in Africa, for being a new form of neo-colonialism.[45] Will the Chinese be willing and able to use 'gunships and Gurkhas' to protect these investments like the imperial powers of yore?

Nor do these oil-for-loan deals promote China's energy security. For instance, China does not have the refining capacity to process heavy Venezuelan oil, but the US does. So, the Chinese oil companies have sold much of their Venezuelan heavy oil in the North American market, taking delivery of the same amount of crude oil from other sources closer to home. The brute fact is that geography guarantees that as long as oil is an essential economic input, China, like its German predecessor, will never have a blockade-proof supply.

Thus, the 'CDB's assets and lending are a large black hole in global finance'.[46] The money lent by the CDB to Africa and Latin America, without any political conditions attached to the loans, faces the same problems that faced the World Bank and IMF in the past. As these 'loans are no different from the money Africa has taken in the past.... It has conditions and requirements and it is not free money. The same problem that confronted the International Monetary Fund and World Bank will haunt China, Without government reforms, effective institutions, and civil services, the money will not be paid back'.[47]

Thus, the CDB is an extension of the Chinese state and the CCP, which through financial repression has garnered all of China's household savings. They will ultimately have to pay the price, as Japanese savers did in the implosion of the Japanese economy because of the wasteful deployment of their savings by its own 'National Team' of firms.[48] For, both the CDB's gamble on domestic infrastructure spending through its LGFV vehicles and the gambles it has taken on the political stability of the many odious regimes it has financed through loans for natural resources in the Third World may not pay off. Any default on these loans would ultimately land on the balance sheet of the central bank, the PBOC.

China might think that its massive foreign exchange reserves provide the wealth to deal with the financial consequences if these gambles fail. But these foreign exchange reserves give a false appearance of wealth. When the PBOC acquires these foreign currencies, it has already created renminbi (RMB). Using these reserves again *domestically* would create even larger monetary pressure. As Walter and Howie state: 'The reserves are simply assets parked in low yielding foreign bonds, and Beijing's ability to use them is very limited'.[49] If the CDB's Third World loans fail that will also be a net drain on these foreign exchange reserves.

Worst of all,

> China's state-owned companies have over-benefitted from the country's controlled interest rates that have enabled the state banking system to make an easy profit out of depositors' money

> without considering the returns of projects, hindering many of the desirable functions of a market economy. While [the CDB-backed LGFVs] have been able to raise money for highways and stadiums, private companies have had to turn to unregulated underground banks.[50]

Repressing Finance for Private Entrepreneurs

In his detailed comparison of the rural economy in the 1980s and late 1990s—which was the hotbed period for the entrepreneurship that launched the first of Coase and Wang's marginal revolutions—Yasheng Huang argues that there was a Great Reversal.[51] At the core of the system to meet the financial needs of these rural entrepreneurs were the rural credit cooperatives (RCCs), which were established in 1951 as genuinely private institutions.[52] But in the Maoist turmoil of the 1960s and 1970s, they were placed under the control of the Agricultural Bank of China (ABC) and local governments. One of the first reforms, after Deng's opening in 1978, was to move back to the 1950s' system of management of RCCs. 'In 1985, RCCs accounted for 76.8 percent of all agricultural loans and 47.8 percent of all loans extended to TVEs'.[53]

Furthermore, in both the 1980s and 1990s, informal finance was important in providing credit to rural entrepreneurs and households. But whereas in the 1980s, informal finance was encouraged, in the 1990s, there was a protracted, costly, and ultimately futile effort to stamp out informal finance on the one hand and to intervene and micromanage the operations of the formal financial institutions on the other. The combination of these two led to substantial credit constraints in rural China in the 1990s. This attack on the credit channels, which had fuelled private entrepreneurship in the 1980s, was meant to eliminate the competition for state-owned financial institutions and thus prevent the diversion of financial resources from the states' industrial policy programmes.

Privatization of the smaller SOEs following the policy of 'grasping the large and letting go of the small' did proceed in the 1990s, as an estimated 30–40 million workers were laid off. But grasping the large led to the industrial policy state. In 1990, the

State Council had guaranteed 234 SOEs access to bank loans and materials. In 1994, it was decreed that four industries in which the SOE were dominant—electronics, petroleum, chemicals, and construction—,were to be the four 'pillar industries' of the economy. In 1997, 120 large enterprises that were to be given preferential treatment with tax and debt relief, import licenses, greater access to domestic and foreign listing facilities, and substantially increased operating powers—such as powers to purchase and sell assets and to transfer assets across geographical and bureaucratic jurisdictions—were also SOEs.[54]

Huang contrasts the state capitalist model epitomized by Shanghai to the private-sector-led development of neighbouring Wenzhou. 'The essence of the Shanghai model is to restrict the opportunities for Shanghai residents to become capitalists but to create an efficient and attractive platform for foreign capitalists to set up production facilities'.[55] As the wages paid by MNCs are higher than those that can be paid by indigenous entrepreneurs, 'the average Shanghainese are the richest proletariat in the country but among the poorest capitalists in the country'.[56]

Shanghai was politically favoured by the Shanghai leaders Jiang Zemin and Zhu Rongji, who ran China for most of the 1990s. Crony capitalism became rampant in the state-led Shanghai development. Its extent and ramifications were revealed in the 2006 arrest of Shanghai's party secretary Chen Liangyu for corruption. In its maturity in the late 1990s, the Shanghai model represented an extreme urban bias with massive implicit transfers from the rural and the small-scale and labour-intensive entrepreneurial sectors. The Pudong project, which converted an area of paddy fields into the giant skyscrapers, malls, and hotels that now awe visitors, was emblematic. It was built on a massive taking of land from rural incumbents. Chongqing is the most recent example of this model as revealed in the recent Bo Xilai affair.

Nemesis?

China might however may soon be seeing the nemesis of its hubris. Some signs of this are discussed next.

The widespread official corruption and the confiscation of property have led to mounting social protests. Martin King Whyte, a Harvard sociologist, reports that 'according to confidential but widely circulated Chinese police estimates, there are now about 180,000 mass protest incidents each year, roughly 20 times more than there were in the mid 1990s.' Though, as he says, given the regime's sensitivity about any systematic surveys about procedural injustices in reviewing the recent mass protests,

> the most common grievances are confiscation of farmland and urban homes without sufficient consultation and compensation, failures to protect the public from toxic chemical spills and adulterated food products, coercive enforcement of family planning rules, deaths that could have been avoided with proper enforcement of building codes, diversions of public resources for official enrichment, illegal incarcerations, and deaths in detention of individuals who try to seek redress for official mistreatment.[57]

Xi Jinping, the new Chinese leader, and his colleagues have expressed alarm at these increasing protests and believe they are caused by rising inequality. China's Gini coefficient 'has increased sharply from .28 in the early 1980s to .49 in 2007. By this measure, China is more unequal than Japan (.31), India (.34), the United States (.36), and Russia (.44)'. But from his surveys in China, Whyte finds that the Chinese are not worried about these income inequalities and are more optimistic about their own chances about getting ahead. When asked whether talent determines who gets rich, '73 percent of Chinese interviewed in 2009 said it is an important factor, compared with only 48 percent of Russians (1996), 52 percent of East Germans (2006), and 60 percent of Americans (1991)'.[58]

China, like America and India, is an aspiring and not an egalitarian society. The Chinese are generally less inclined than citizens elsewhere to limit top incomes or redistribute from the rich to the poor. As China's spectacular growth has trickled down to the poor (particularly in the 1980s), well over 60 per cent of those interviewed in each China survey said that their families were doing better than they were five years earlier. Similar percentages predicted that they would be doing even better in the future. In turn, they see wealth that others have achieved as more a goal to aim for than something to be resented.[59] That is why the CCP remains worried about any slowing down in China's economic growth, as this could dash these expectations and the implicit public acquiescence in its rule.

Procedural Injustice and Rule of Law

Currently, it is the procedural injustices and massive official corruption, not a worsening Gini coefficient, which are fuelling public anger and the mushrooming mass protests. The CCP probably understands this, but most measures which would address procedural injustices 'such as greater judicial independence, press freedom, and genuine guarantees of freedom of association and peaceable assembly—not to mention allowing electoral challenges to those in authority—would strike at the heart of the CCP's Leninist principles.'[60]

This is the nub of the problem China faces. It does not have the rule of law embodied in Western legal traditions, which involves the substantive separation of the judicial and executive functions of government. This means that even governmental executive decisions are contestable in civil courts. It implies, as Cohn (1987) says: 'equality in the eyes of the law, judicial ignorance of complainants, the ideal that economic relations are based on contract not status, the goal of settling the case at hand and only in that case, and the necessity of a clear-cut decision rather than compromise' (p. 105). It above all means that even if a judicial decision goes against the government, it will abide by it. Hong Kong provides such a legal system. India does too, having adopted it in the nineteenth century. As we shall see, it is this difference with a China ruled by the CCP that is the major reason that despite similar current travails, India's long-term economic prospects remain brighter than China's.

But, it is the continuing financial repression, as outlined previously, that poses the greatest danger to China's medium-term economic prospects. The gamble that China has taken on using its massive household savings on an infrastructural binge and investment by SOEs already seems to be turning sour. A recent paper by Atif Ansar et al. found that on seventy-four road and twenty-one railway projects built from 1984 to 2008 across China, worth $65 billion in 2015 prices, the benefit cost ratio (BCR) of 55 per cent of these projects had an ex-post BCR of less than one, implying they were unviable from the outset and were destroying economic value. They conclude, 'generalizing from our sample, evidence suggests that over half of the infrastructure investments in China made in the last three decades have been NPV [net present value] negative. Far from being an engine of economic growth, a typical infrastructure investment has destroyed economic value in China'.[61]

Another sign of the failure of this gamble is that since the big surge in public spending of US$640 billion after the Great Crash, industrial producer prices have been falling since the end of 2011. This deflation in the industrial sector is partly due to the fall in global commodity prices, which are in turn due to China's partial slowdown but also due to overcapacity in a number of major Chinese industries, including steel, coal, glass, aluminium, solar panels, and cement.[62] The avenue of dumping these surpluses abroad through exports is being increasingly undermined by the growing realization in the world that seemingly autonomous Chinese companies are merely instruments of the CCP, as witness the EU's recent proposal to slap anti-dumping duties on imports of Chinese solar panels and the growing recognition, as in the US and Australia, that the Chinese telecom major Huawei, though clothed in private market form, is an instrument of the Chinese state in cyber espionage and possibly cyber warfare.

Chinese citizens (including the princelings) are increasingly seeking the exit route from a dysfunctional polity and economy by moving their capital overseas. A recent purported surge in Chinese exports turns out to be mainly to Hong Kong. It is part of the process whereby Chinese households and private enterprises are circumventing Chinese capital controls through over-invoicing exports or under-invoicing imports.[63]

Declining Returns to Debt-Fuelled Growth Model

A second sign of Chinese economic dysfunction is that the bang for the buck from China's credit-fuelled growth model is declining. From various estimates made by different observers, it seems that now for every RMB1 of nominal GDP growth, RMB3.3 of new credit is required.[64] With the rate of credit creation outpacing the rate of economic growth there is a growing danger of an eventual debt crisis. With the recent surge in credit to counter the slowdown in growth to about 7.7 per cent in 2011,[65] there has been a further accumulation of debt in the formal and shadow banking systems. CLSA has estimated that China's 'new debt added over 2009–12 was about 110% of GDP … most of which came from shadow banking and bonds'. They estimate 'total China debt (consumer, government and corporate) at Rmb 107tn or 205% of GDP, at the end of 2012'. Since then, in the first quarter of 2013, credit has grown by 58 per cent.[66]

But, as Walter and Howie have emphasized, China has created a financial system which 'is an empire set apart from the world'. It cannot have a traditional debt crisis like the Mexican crisis in 1994, Argentinian crisis in 1999, and the post-2008 crises in Iceland and Ireland or the current Greek, Spanish, and Cypriot debt crises. Walter and Howie claim:

> Aside from trade finance, China does not borrow money overseas and, because of the non-convertibility of the RMB, offshore investors are overwhelmingly excluded from the domestic capital markets.... There is simply no way that offshore speculators, investors, hedge funds, or others can get at China's domestic debt obligations and challenge the Party's valuation of these obligations. In short, the closed nature of China's financial markets suggests a deliberate government strategy based on a particular understanding of past international debt crises.[67]

But, this does not imply that there are no costs to this accumulation of debt. Much of the debt incurred in the last three years, as Xiao Gang of the Bank of China has said, consists of Ponzi schemes. The extent of the non-performing loans (NPL) in the system remains unclear. It has been argued by bulls on China[68] that it resolved its banking crisis through Zhu Rongji's clean-up of the banking system in the 1990s—when the share of NPLs was estimated to be from 20 per cent to 40 per cent of total loans. Zhu Rongji recapitalized banks—directly by injecting capital and indirectly by purchasing bad loans at very high prices—and matched very rapid growth with even more rapid loan growth. China could do the same again and the cost would be minimal.

But, as Michael Pettis of Peking University rightly notes, this view is mistaken, as the costs of resolving the last banking crisis were very high. They depended, as in the resolution of all banking crises, on a direct or indirect transfer of wealth from the household sector to clean up the banks. In China, the financial repression involved in the 'wide spread between deposit and lending rates … [of] 3.0–3.5 percentage points', is an implicit tax on household savings, which are transferred to the banking system. In addition, China has kept these lending and deposit rates about 4–6 percentage points below the Wicksellian natural rate of interest, which balances savings and investment. This means that the 'borrower is effectively granted debt forgiveness equal to the difference between the two'. The combination of these two means of financial repression were, in effect, 'a large hidden tax on household income, and it is this transfer that cleaned up the last banking crises'. This explains the systematic divergence between the high GDP growth and the substantially lower growth of household income in the post-Tiananmen period. It has meant that the share of household consumption, which was already low at 45 per cent in 2000, reached a low of 36 per cent in 2010.[69] This is the only method through which China's current incipient debt crisis will ultimately be resolved. But despite its rising wages, with its already too-low household consumption, it will be very risky to force households to clean up yet another surge in NPLs.

As Chinese leaders have said repeatedly, China's current growth model is unbalanced and unsustainable. The most important source of the imbalances is the continuing financial repression. Ending it through reducing the spread between deposit and lending rates and by raising interest rates to the natural rate, would not only eliminate the current high tax on household savings, but also allow an end to the massive misallocation of capital. The former would lead to the rise in the consumption share, which alone can make domestic consumption—not trade surpluses and infrastructure investments—the main source of growth. The latter would lead to productive investments, instead of the current pattern where debt-financed investment is rising much faster than the growth in debt-servicing capacity. This is leading to 'the same problem that has historically afflicted other countries with similar investment-driven growth models [e.g., Japan—the pioneer of the so-called "Asian model"]: a long, painful period of very low growth, as the economy grinds away at excess debt and rebuilds national balance sheets.'[70]

Unlikely Reforms

But are these reforms likely?[71] The rise in interest rates required to end financial repression will cause extreme economic pain to large manufacturers, many local and provincial governments, and even the central bank itself, who are addicted to low rates and have built up great, debt-laden balance sheets around them. It would also mean a reversal of the process by which, over the last three decades and especially the last decade, economic growth has disproportionately benefitted the state sector at the expense of Chinese households and the private agents of Coase and Wang's first marginal revolution of the 1980s. Moreover, will the oligarchy of princelings—who increasingly control the CCP and have benefitted handsomely from the state-led authoritarian capitalist model developed in the late 1990s and fully embraced in the mid-2000s—accept these needed economic reforms? Or will they continue with the same credit-fuelled investment led model as they did with the slowdown in 2011, despite proclaiming the need to switch to a more balanced model? Chinese medium- term growth prospects will depend upon their answer. It is as likely that they will continue on the same path and deal with any rising discontent with the continuing squeeze on household consumption it entails by playing the nationalist card. There are already signs, fuelled by their current hubris on being the second largest economy in the world, of their growing military and territorial assertiveness.[72] These are questions we take up in the next part of the book.

An Indian Economic Miracle?

Until 2009–10, there were many, including me, who thought that India was on a high growth path and would follow China's path with a lag (as its reforms started in 1991 compared with China's in 1980), and we would soon see an Indian economic miracle.[73] But this has not happened. Instead, since 2011, India seemed to be slipping back towards what has been termed the 'Hindu rate of growth'. But with the resounding victory of Narendra Modi's Bhartiya Janta Party (BJP) in the 2014 general election, the economy is slowly recovering.

In this part, I begin by putting the change in India's economic fortunes after the 1991 economic reforms in historical perspective. Next, I explain the sources of the growth acceleration, leading on to examine the reasons why this has faltered. Finally, I conclude with the prospects of India getting back to the high growth path after the recent general election.

Repression, Crisis, and Reform

Like many other developing countries, India after its independence in 1947 followed a dirigiste, inward-looking, heavy-industry-biased industrialization strategy. This was in part a reaction to the laissez-faire and free trade policies followed by the British Raj in the nineteenth century, which were erroneously thought to have led to India's continuing stagnation.[74] Though contemporary research has questioned the validity of this nationalist and often Marxist perspective, it still colours the minds of Indian elites. Like elites in many other developing countries, they have been haunted by their helplessness against the Western assault in the Age of Imperialism. They have sought (like the Chinese) a middle way between the modernity promised by Western globalizing capitalism and their own ancient traditions. There were two alternative Indian responses. The first— represented by Gandhi—was to hold on to tradition and to reject modernity. The second—represented by Nehru—was to reconcile modernity with tradition by adopting a form of Fabian socialism.[75]

At Independence in 1947, with Gandhi dead soon thereafter at the hands of an assassin, it were Nehru's ideas that determined India's economic policies. They entailed massive dirigiste interventions in the form of centralized planning and a draconian set of economic controls on foreign trade, capital flows, and prices. They, however, yielded a higher growth rate than that experienced under the Raj (see Figure 7.3).[76]

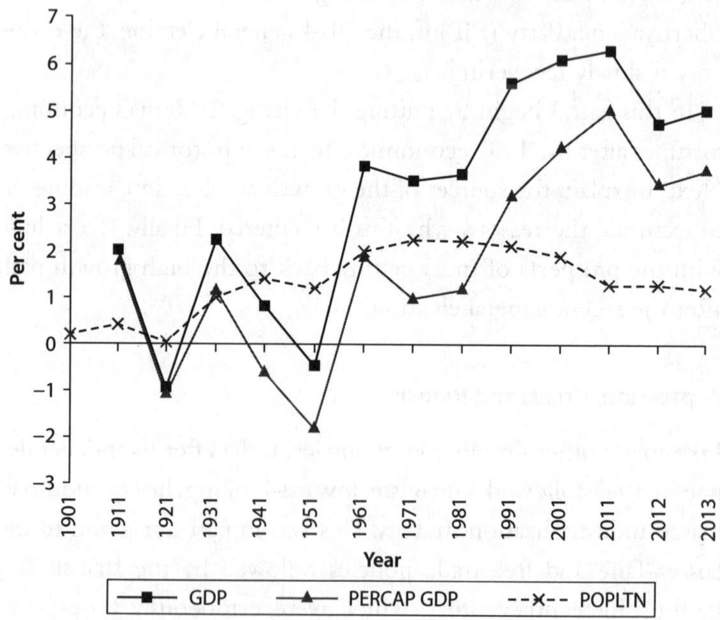

FIGURE 7.3 Annual Growth Rates in India (1901–2013)
Source: Lal (2016b).[77]

This acceleration of growth was based on three factors.

The first was a rise in public social overhead investment, particularly on irrigation and, from the late 1960s, on R&D in agriculture. The British Raj had been hamstrung in raising public investment, as it was always wary of a nationalist revolt that might be provoked by any rise in taxes for its finance. With no such constraint faced by independent India, public investment, which had averaged about 2.2 per cent in the interwar period, rose to nearly 7 per cent of GDP by 1960–1.

The second was a rise in the rate of savings and capital formation in the economy compared with the century of alien rule. Gross domestic savings, which were about 8 per cent of GDP at Independence, rose to 11.6 per cent by 1960–1 and have continued to rise, particularly after the 1991 economic liberalization (see below), reaching 37 per cent of GDP by 2007–8, and then declining to 31 per cent in 2011–12.

The third was the rise in population from 1921, induced by a declining death rate, which led to a rising labour force in agriculture. It had grown by 12.6 per cent between 1901 and 1940, but rose by 25.4 per cent between 1950 and 1970. This growth spurt, on Boserupian lines,[78] led to an intensification of agriculture, in terms of an increase both in the labour and capital input per unit of land, and a rise in the annual growth rate in agriculture from 0.44 per cent between 1900 and 1947 to 3.3 per cent between 1950 and 1965.[769]

The economic repression under the Nehruvian settlement, however, had led by the mid-1960s to a 'quiet crisis' in India,[80] with the Hindu rate of growth of 3.5 per cent and population growing at 2.2 per cent until the early 1980s yielding meagre annual rises in per capita income of just over 1.3 per cent. This performance failed to make any marked dent on India's ancient poverty.

The first signs of crisis appeared in agriculture, as the Boserupian process, with an unchanged agricultural technology, soon faced diminishing returns. The food crisis of the 1960s forced the government to reverse its previous neglect of agriculture, based on the faulty prescriptions of the Arthur Lewis and Feldman-Mahalanobis models, which stated that the route to growth in a labour surplus economy was through massive industrialization, with agriculture being left alone until the surplus labour had been worked off.

India then adopted the new technology embodied in high-yielding seeds and large inputs of fertilizers and water that led to the Green Revolution. The average annual agricultural growth rate had slowed to only 1.8 per cent from 1960 to 1973. The Green Revolution of the 1970s, which was by and large a wheat revolution, raised the growth rate of agriculture to about 2.9 per cent from 1973 to 1999. Thereafter, after first slowing, the area under high-yielding varieties reached its limits; the potential irrigable area was declining. However, the introduction of GM crops[81] (particularly Bt cotton in Gujarat), crop diversification, the catch-up by many of the low agricultural productivity states, and the emergence of contract farming and rural business/service hubs have led to continuing robust agricultural growth rates. After the drought induced negative growth rate in 2002–3, the average agricultural growth rate has been 4.1 per cent between 2007 and 2008 and between 2011 and 2012. The share of agriculture has declined to 18 per cent of total GDP in 2013–14. While still accounting for 54.6 per cent of total employment, the number of cultivators has declined from 127 million in 2001 to 119 million in 2011. This implies a shift from farm to non-farm employment, causing real farm wages to rise by over 7 per cent annually in recent years.[82]

Industrial growth, which had been 6.8 per cent between 1950 and 1965, slowed to 4.3 per cent between 1976 and 1980, as the limits of import substitution were reached. There was a foreign exchange crisis in the mid-1960s that led some Indian economists (including the author) to question the dirigiste, inward-looking path India had taken. This reaction was strengthened by the neoclassical resurgence in the 1970s, which questioned the intellectual basis of post-war development economics.[83] But it was the switch made by Deng Xiaoping from the plan to the market in China in 1978 that probably most concentrated official Indian minds.

With its tradition of Gladstonian public finance, India had avoided the chronic macroeconomic imbalances associated with dirigisme. However, the creation of a rent-seeking society, through the microeconomic distortions introduced by public policy in the planning era, gradually led to a fiscal crisis.[84]

The internal pubic debt rose from 42 per cent of GDP in the early 1980s to nearly 58 per cent in 1991, as the government tried to meet its fiscal bind through promoting large inflows of short-term capital from the Indian diaspora after 1985.[85] When they took fright at the deteriorating fiscal and inflation position and moved their money out of India, a Latin-American-style crisis was finally triggered (see Figure 7.4).

In the dash for growth, a half-hearted liberalization effort began with Rajiv Gandhi's election after his mother's assassination in 1984. It raised the growth rate, but this liberalizing impetus soon petered out as his government was caught in a web of corruption scandals. The dash for growth did generate an unsustainable boom, with

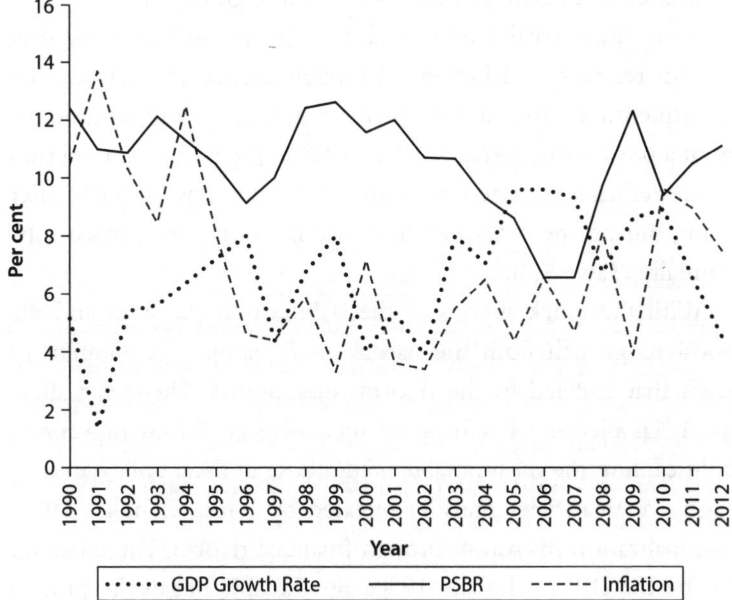

FIGURE 7.4 PSBR, Inflation Rate, and Growth Rate (1990–2012)
Source: Lal (2016b).

GDP growing at 7 per cent in 1989. A weak coalition came to power in 1989 and was unable to deal with the impending crisis. When it collapsed and a minority Congress government, led by Narasimha Rao with Dr Manmohan Singh as the finance minister, came to power in 1991, the country was essentially bankrupt, with foreign exchange reserves barely sufficient to finance ten days of imports, galloping inflation (by Indian standards) of 14 per cent, a PSBR of nearly 12 per cent, and an impending growth collapse.

The new finance minister began the reversal of nearly a century's creeping—and under Mrs Gandhi, galloping—dirigisme. The PSBR was squeezed by about 2 per cent of GDP with little pain. The permit raj began to be dismantled with the virtual ending of industrial licensing and with the removal of import controls (except on consumer goods, which were only removed in 2001 when they were declared illegal by the WTO). The import-weighted tariff was cut from an average of 87 per cent in 1991 to 27 per cent in 1996. The rupee was devalued initially by about 20 per cent. Direct foreign investment was once again welcomed, though it was still controlled and restricted to 51 per cent foreign ownership.

Even these partial reforms lifted the growth rate, exports, foreign reserves, and inflows of foreign capital. The savings and investment rates rose and the incremental capital–output ratio fell from a pre-reform average of 4.5 to 3.8 in the post-reform period as the reforms increased economic efficiency. Poverty rates, after rising during the short period of stabilization, came down substantially (Table 7.2).

With the quick success of the stabilization measures and the boost to growth from the partial liberalization, the element of crisis that had led to the reforms disappeared. Thereafter, there has been piecemeal reform by successive coalitions of varying political hue, the most notable being those in fiscal policy and the easing of financial repression (created by Indira Gandhi's 1970s nationalization of banks) through financial reform. The coalition led by the BJP in the late 1990s also notably began the process of privatizing the inefficient public sector. But this process was stalled with the veto imposed by the following Congress Party

TABLE 7.2 Large Reduction in Poverty Rates

Growth and Poverty Reduction in India, 1999/00–2011/12			
Method	NSS Large Sample Survey		
	1999/00	2009/10	2011/12
Preferred Method			
Monthly per capita expenditure, Rs	613	782.6	903.1
per cent growth in expenditure (%)		27.7	15.4
Poverty, Head Count Ratio, HCR (% of population)	39.6	21.7	**12.3**
Change in HCR (%)		−17.9	−9.4
Poverty reduction for 1 percentage point of growth percent growth		−0.65	−0.61
Mixed Method			
Monthly per capita expenditure, Rs	592	715	827
per cent growth in expenditure (%)		20.8	15.7
Poverty, Head Count Ratio, HCR (% of population)	43.2	29.9	**18.6**
Change in HCR (%)		−13.3	−11.3
Poverty reduction for 1 percentage point of growth percent growth		−0.64	−0.72
Uniform Method			
Monthly per capita expenditure, Rs		693	814
per cent growth in expenditure (%)			17.5
Poverty, Head Count Ratio, HCR (% of population)		34.3	**22**
Change in HCR (%)			−12.3
Poverty reduction for 1 percentage point of growth percent growth			−0.70

Source: Bhalla (2013).

Notes: 1. Monthly per capita expenditure is in real 2004/5 rural prices.

2. Poverty calculations based on Tendulkar poverty line and household level information on per capita expenditures.

3. The Tendulkar poverty line has been extended to 2011/12 using state level CPIAL data for rural areas and CPIIW data for urban areas.

government's Communist coalition partners. They also prevented the dismantling of the labour laws imposed by the British Raj in the late nineteenth century (at the behest of protectionist Lancashire Textiles manufacturers), which have raised the price of using Indian's most abundant resource for industrialization and led to a century of a growing capital-intensive bias in Indian industry.

Figure 7.3 shows the growth rates of GDP, population, and per capita GDP for the twentieth century. It shows the rise in the GDP and per capita growth rates from 1951 until the 1960s, compared with the pre-Independence period. One can also see the stagnation in the 1960s and 1970s, with the trend rate of growth until the early 1980s being a meagre 3.5 per cent per year—dubbed by Raj Krishna as the 'Hindu rate of growth' (as previously mentioned). In the 1980s, with partial economic liberalization under Rajiv Gandhi and with the abandonment of many aspects of the permit raj and industrial planning, growth accelerated to 5.6 per cent, and from 1991 to 2000, growth increased to 6.6 per cent per year. Since that time, there has been a further acceleration of economic growth to nearly 9 per cent per year from 2003 to 2007, but since 2011 it has stalled to 5 per cent p.a. in 2012–13.

Sources of Growth

Bosworth, Collins, and Virmani[86] (hereafter BCV) have produced a growth account for the Indian economy from 1960 to 2004. Their estimates for the aggregate economy are presented in Table 7.3.

This shows that the acceleration in growth from the mid-1980s was due less to an increase in factor inputs and more to an increase in TFP, unlike the period until 1983, when most of the growth was due to increased factor inputs. However, improvements in the quality of the labour force from education have contributed modestly to growth performance.[87]

The rise in the growth of industrial employment from 1999 to 2004 and the acceleration of industrial growth from 6.4 per cent to 8.4 per cent and to 10.8 per cent in 2006–7 suggests that the economic effects of the ending of the permit raj in 1991 and India's growing integration with the world economy are now at last bearing fruit. This enhanced performance is consistent with the experience of supply-side reforms in other countries. For example, Thatcher's reforms of the 1980s did not begin to bear fruit until the mid-1990s. But with the stalling of the economy since 2011, recent trends do not augur well for the future growth of the industrial sector.[88]

TABLE 7.3 Sources of Economic Growth, Total Economy, 1960–2005 (Annual Percentage Rate of Change)

Period	Output	Employment	Output per Worker	Contribution of:			
				Physical Capital	Land	Education	Factor Productivity
1960-04	4.7	2.0	2.6	1.2	−0.1	0.3	1.2
1960-80	3.4	2.2	1.3	1.0	−0.2	0.2	0.2
1980-04	5.8	1.9	3.8	1.4	0.0	0.4	2.0
1960-73	3.3	2.0	1.3	1.1	−0.2	0.1	0.2
1973-83	4.2	2.4	1.8	0.9	−0.2	0.3	0.6
1983-93	5.0	2.1	2.9	0.9	−0.1	0.3	1.7
1993-99	7.0	1.2	5.8	2.4	−0.1	0.4	2.8
1999-04	6.0	2.4	3.6	1.2	0.1	0.4	2.0

Source: Bosworth, Collins, and Virmani (2006).

Summing up, agricultural growth based on the Green Revolution has been a major source of India's acceleration of growth from its pre-Independence levels. Agriculture has also absorbed much of the increase in the labour force, even as its share in output has shrunk. Even with diminishing returns setting in on the Green Revolution, agricultural production function, the shift in agriculture from farm to non-farm work, the introduction of the new GM technology, and the adoption of rural business/service hubs should still allow some employment growth in the rural-urban sector. Industrial and manufacturing growth rates have risen, most markedly in 2004–8. But industrial employment growth has been anaemic. Increased factor inputs, rather than dramatic increases in TFP, account for most of the growth in the industrial and manufacturing sectors. The fastest growth rate has been in services, which accounts for a large part of the recent growth acceleration. This has been due to both increased factor inputs and high rates of TFP growth, which is not only confined to the modern services of business, finance, and communications but also has occurred in the traditional services. This is an internationally atypical pattern of growth. But, statistical problems in underestimating the price of services and, hence, an exaggeration of the real growth rate of the sector may explain this anomaly.[89]

The Growth Slowdown

Post Liberalization Rent-Seeking

There is a new form of rent-seeking that has arisen in India, China, and Russia, after their various degrees of movement from the plan to the market. Their economic liberalizations would have been expected to see a decline in rent-seeking. Yet, the daily revelations of various scams suggest rent-seeking is alive in India. In fact, one of the puzzles about its economic liberalization was how it could occur in a country that for nearly four decades had created an equilibrium of rent-seeking interests and mired the economy in the dismal Hindu rate of growth. Many observers saw little hope of a seemingly dysfunctional Indian democracy being able to deliver economic liberalization. In an important book, *Democratic Politics and Economic Reform in India*, Rob Jenkins[90] showed how the political players, particularly at the Centre, used both a rearrangement of the previous spoils system and the various conflicts of interest within the numerous rent-seekers to both institute and consolidate economic reforms. In terms of my predatory state model,[91] the improved productivity of the economy resulting from economic liberalization provided larger rents to the predators. They got an unchanged share of a larger pie. It is these new forms of rent-seeking that are the source of all these scams. But this raises its own puzzle, whereas the earlier pre-1991 form of rent-seeking had led to growth rates well below potential, the new forms of rent-seeking have been accompanied by phenomenal growth rates. What explains these differences in outcomes and is this new corruption likely to damage growth like the old?[92]

The basic reason is that the new rent-seeking is based on acquiring the rents from land and natural resources. These are like lump sum taxes, which do not affect the efficiency of the economy. By contrast, the earlier rent-seeking was based on monopolies created by governments in commodity markets, which affected the marginal decisions of consumers and producers and damaged efficiency. These monopoly rents were like distortionary taxes-cum-subsidies, unlike the lump sum taxes on land and natural resources in the new forms of rent-seeking.[93]

Economic liberalization in former highly controlled economies like India (but also China and Russia) reduces or eliminates these monopoly rents. With the boost given to economy-wide productivity by the liberalization, the value of 'economic' and 'composite quasi-rents' will rise. This allows the polity to substitute an even more highly valued source of rents to compensate the losers from the abolition of monopoly rents, but without any damage to the productive efficiency of the economy. This explains the paradox that post-liberalization rent-seeking has been accompanied by high growth rates and an increase in the rents garnered in these predatory states, while the pre-liberalization rent-seeking had led to growth rates well below their potential.

There is, however, one continuing major source of monopoly rents. These are the colonial labour laws creating monopoly rents for the small aristocracy of organized labour. By limiting entry and exit and artificially raising the price of India's most abundant resource, they have damaged labour-intensive industrialization in India. This situation will be made worse by the minimum wage and other purported labour rights being implemented in the unorganized sector. Much worse, the proposal to introduce minimum wages in the Rural Employment Guarantee Scheme will remove the main reason for the efficiency of this poverty-redressing policy: self-targeting.[94] Though the immorality of rent-seeking associated with pure economic and composite quasi-rents maybe reprehensible, it is less damaging to growth than the continuing monopoly rents generated in the labour market.

Stalled Projects and Falling Project Starts

One baleful reaction to these scams has been that they have paralyzed the government, particularly as they have led its various executive decisions to be questioned by the Supreme Court.[95] Their decisions have also been used by environmental and other activists (in the National Advisory Council [NAC]—see later) to create another environmental and land acquisition permit raj, which has stalled mining (so that existing power stations are short of coal) and put the spokes in many planned and approved infrastructure projects. The new Modi government, fortunately, seems ready to change course. But without a majority in the Rajya Sabha (the upper house of Parliament), it is hamstrung in the necessary amendments and changes in existing environmental and land acquisition laws that are needed.

The 2014 *Economic Survey*[96] presented data on the number and volume of investment projects where implementation has stalled since 2009. Of these, 80 per cent are in electricity, roads, telecommunications, steel, real estate, and mining—all part of the essential infrastructure needed to maintain and raise the growth rate. In addition, new investment projects, both in the private and public sectors, have dried up.[97]

Moreover, this stalling of projects has led to overleveraged firms unable to service their debts, and corresponding banks have over-lent for infrastructure and are finding it difficult to recover their debt. They have lent $153 billion from 2007 to 2013. Of this, $22 billion has already been restructured, and another $8.5 billion accounts for 20 per cent of the banking systems NPLs.[98] So India has a banking crisis similar to China's based on the bad debt generated by its infrastructure spending, with the difference that China did get its infrastructure but India did not!

This paralysis in governance has meant that the resulting stalled investment in infrastructure has led to a sharp rise in the incremental capital–output ratio (ICOR) since 2011 (see Figure 7.5). This declining productivity of capital has contributed to the latest slowdown in growth.[99]

Populist Responses to GFC

India's recent growth collapse is reminiscent of many of those I charted with Hla Myint in our comparative study *The Political Economy of Poverty Equity and Growth*.[100] While the proximate causes were severe macroeconomic imbalances, the deeper causes were numerous microeconomic distortions and unsustainable

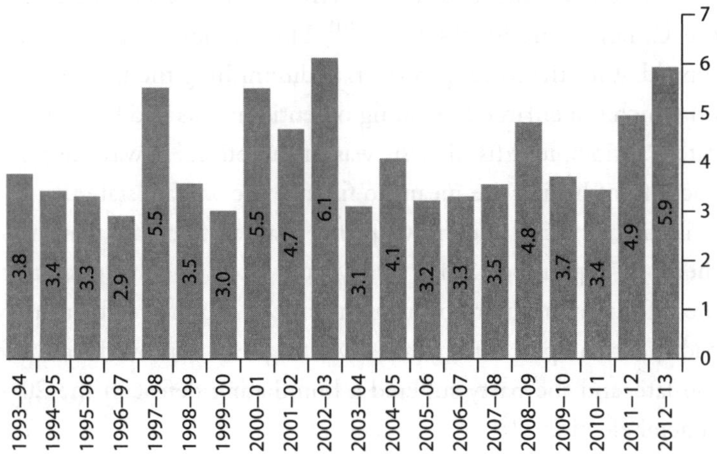

FIGURE 7.5 Incremental Capital–Output Ratio for India
Source: Gokarn (2014).

fiscal expenditures on politically determined income streams. Bad policy has been the basic reason for these collapses. But, the Indian growth collapse poses a puzzle: why have the economic reformers who initiated the economic liberalization of 1991, and were in charge from 2004 to 2014, allowed such bad policies to undermine their liberalization legacy?

The answer lies in the baleful effects of the political sway of the Nehruvian dynasty over most of India's independent history and its basic misunderstanding of Indian society. It is notable that the two bursts of economic liberalization in 1991 and 2000–4 occurred under two non-dynasty prime ministers, Narasimha Rao and Atal Bihari Vajpayee. While Rao, as the head of a Congress Party-led government, had to defend the Manmohan Singh reforms as a continuation rather than repudiation of Nehruvian policies, Vajpayee had no such inhibitions, and under his watch, major economic reforms were undertaken which put the Indian economy on an 8 per cent p.a. growth path.

It was with the subsequent diarchy—where the dynastic matriarch Sonia Gandhi held the power and the reforming 1991 finance minister Manmohan Singh, as prime minister, the responsibility—that there was a massive enlargement of entitlements and the thwarting of the economic reformers in the government by the coterie of NGO activists constituted into the Congress president's NAC.[101] The economy's growth rate slipped. With the lower growth rate diminishing the tax revenues on which the enlarged spending on entitlements had been predicated, an incipient fiscal crisis was in the offing. It was the prospect of not having the means to finance the welfare state that the dynastic matriarch and crown prince wanted to create that made them, in September 2013, finally come out openly to support the reformers in their government for the minimal reforms they had spent the past three years thwarting. But it proved too little too late, and the party suffered a humiliating defeat in the 2014 general election.[102]

This in turn reflects a distinction in the beliefs of two wings of what I have termed Macaulay's children.[103] They were the inheritors of Macaulay's famous nineteenth century 'Minute on Education' seeking to create an English-speaking middle class. The Nehruvian wing embraced English as their first language; the Gandhian wing saw English as an instrumental second language. As the primary language of a group determines the cosmological beliefs, that is, world view, of the speakers,[104] the Nehruvian wing came to mirror those of their European cousins, which was infected with various forms of 'noblesse oblige' disguised as egalitarianism. By contrast, the Gandhian wing, still wedded to their native tongues, subscribed to tradition. This, as the sociologist Louis Dumont has emphasized in his *Homo Hierarchicus*,[105] was based on hierarchy, in which given the Hindu belief in reincarnation, promoting equality of outcomes (as opposed to opportunity) in this life, would reverse the just deserts which one had earned from one's actions in one's past life. The Hindu majority has thus always formed an aspiring and not an egalitarian society.

With the Gandhian wing having accepted that tradition can coexist with the modernization on which India's future depends, it is much more in tune with the aspiring classes, which comprise the majority of the Indian electorate. In the 2014 election, the sons of the soil from small district towns and villages, who are part of this reformed Gandhian wing, overthrew the westernized Nehruvian wing. Modi claimed that he could implement the 'Gujarat model' to India as a whole, which would lead to the economic revival that its youthful supporters so earnestly seek. They are part of the growing urban middle class, which Minna Saavala[106] argues is being replenished by a 'neo-middle class' of Other Backward Castes (OBCs) migrating from the villages. They are an aspiring class whose caste identity has been eroded. They want growth, which offers them a brighter economic future. They are also intensely religious, adhering to Hindu rituals in a form of Sanskritization.[107] But, like their upper caste compatriots, they want a meritocracy and are against reservations.[108] They are part of the Modi wave. They are attracted by Modi's slogan of 'development not doles'.

But whether Modi will be able to deliver on his promises still remains an open question, though the final passage of the

Goods and Services Tax (GST) law establishing a national system of value-added taxation to create a nearly subcontinental internal market augurs well for the future. The devolution of over half of national revenues to the states by the latest Finance Commission is also a sign of progress. Competition among states—reminiscent of that between the Chinese xians—is likely to promote the reforms of distortions in labour and land markets (which constitutionally are within the joint domain of the Centre and states), which are needed to accelerate Indian growth.

Prospects

Liberal Economic Reforms?

At a recent panel discussion entitled 'The Economic Agenda of the Next Government: Is an Economic Regime Change Necessary and Possible' at the Indian School of Business in Mohali, I answered that it was necessary but not likely. Why?

The 1991 reforms ended the Nehruvian license permit raj, removing major policy-induced distortions in commodity markets but not in the markets for labour and land. Most of these distortions go back to Indira Gandhi's leftward turn after she won her '*Garibi Hatao*' (remove poverty) election in 1971. She nationalized the banks and coal. She attempted to nationalize the wholesale grain trade and the tightened the Industrial Disputes Act to apply to any establishment employing over one hundred workers. These and other dirigiste measures still cripple the Indian economy. Rajiv Gandhi, her son, loosened the Nehruvian permit raj, but Sonia Gandhi, his widow, by promoting various 'rights-based' subsidies in her decade-long reign, has saddled India with a premature European-style welfare state. My suggestion at the panel that it would be best for India's future economic performance if the incoming government rescinded all the economic Acts passed during the Indira and Sonia reigns got loud cheers from the assembled students! My answer to the second question was that such a change was unlikely, as the intellectual hegemony of Nehruvian socialism was still in place, though the coming crisis of the demographic dividend turning into a demographic bomb might at last induce a change.[109]

What of the new BJP government? Do its election slogans—'development not doles', 'minimum government, maximum governance'—constantly reiterated by its prime minister, mean that he and his party are shorn of the Nehruvian social democratic mindset? During the previous Congress-led UPA government's ten-year reign, the BJP (including many in the current cabinet) did not vote against various rights-based entitlements enacted at the behest of Sonia Gandhi's *jhollawalas*[110] in the NAC. Moreover, in the 1980s, the BJP was burning effigies of Arthur Dunkel—the former head of GATT. Though its tune changed in the 1990s, the continuing hold of 'Gandhian socialism', as Vajpayee called it, is still evident in the party's support for 'swadeshi',[111] its backsliding on FDI in retail, and its purported support for public sector undertakings/enterprises (PSUs), instead of their privatization as in Thatcher's flagship UK programme. Maybe this will change with a Thatcherite Damascene conversion of Modi and his party. With the government having recently liberalized FDI rules and having accepted the need to privatize the loss-making national airline, Air India, there is some hope

For me, a full conversion would be signalled if Modi does battle with the 'insiders' of the industrial labour aristocracy, who have kept the massive number of semi-skilled workers willing to work for much lower wages as 'outsiders' in the manufacturing sector. There seems to be widespread acceptance of the industrial caste system India has created, with its segmentation through distortions of the industrial labour market. As the experience of China and the other Asian tigers has shown, it is impossible to jump the labour-intensive industrialization phase, and move into a post- industrial service economy. It is not top-down skill development that India needs, but removing all the colonial labour market restrictions preventing freedom to hire and fire labour, as China—an ostensibly socialist economy—has done. This requires rescinding the colonial-era labour laws[112] and the 1947 Industrial Disputes Act.

Modi has recognized India's failure to promote labour-intensive industrialization. With the political difficulty in passing national legislation to rescind these archaic laws, the new government used a constitutional provision that allows states (with permission from the national government) to change these laws. Rajasthan, a BJP-governed state, has done this, but surprisingly other BJP-ruled states have not been prodded to do the same. If this were done, a free market corridor could be created from Gurgaon (near Delhi) to Mumbai.

The other aspect hampering Modi's 'Make in India' campaign is India's failure to wholeheartedly follow China's example of complete trade liberalization, so that with many industrial inputs subject to various tariffs with none on the final outputs, many manufactured products face negative effective protection. Instead of dealing with this by unifying Indian tariffs to a low uniform rate, the 2016 Budget proposed a complex fiddling with the tariff structure.

The same continuing discretionary dirigiste mindset is discernible in the draconian law promising to incarcerate Indians holding foreign bank accounts and assets, which are purportedly based on tax evasion. This will just raise the dowries new entrants to the revenue services will demand because of the new avenues for corruption opened up with the draconian discretion this bill will provide!

Without fully embracing economic liberalism, India's demographic dividend will turn into a demographic nightmare as the millions of unemployed, semi-skilled, sex-starved youth[113] increasingly disturb social order. Perhaps only then will India's continuing dirigiste intellectual mindset change.

The Prize Available

If the new government does have a Damascene conversion to economic liberalism, there is a very rich economic prize awaiting. For if the wholly unjustified subsidies to power, fertilizers, and petroleum products, and the new ones to food (and the attendant public distribution system) and rural employment in the name of the poor, which Surjit Bhalla[114] has rightly characterized as crony socialism, are eliminated and replaced by a simple targeted cash subsidy through the new digital Aadhar cards to the poor, not only could poverty be eliminated but the fisc would be restored to health (see Table 7.4). This would also help to bring down inflation with the reduction in the PSBR, which in turn would allow a reduction in interest rates, thereby boosting investment.

TABLE 7.4 Deconstruction of Crony Socialism, 1999/00–2013/14

	1999/00	2004/05	2009/10	2011/12	2013/14
Population (in mil)	1009	1097	1179	1212	1244
Percentage poor (Tendulkar line)	43	38	30	22	19
Poor Population (in mil)	437	414	353	269	236
Poverty line (Rs. Per Year)	5196	5820	8796	10328	12492
Mean consumption of poor (Rs. Per Year)	3876	4368	6720	8503	10475
Percent poor gap (% deviation of poor consumption and poverty line)	25.4	24.9	23.6	17.7	16.1
Cost of removal of poverty with perfect targeting (in 000 cr)	58	60	73	49	48
Nominal GDP (in 000 cr)	1852	2971	6088	8356	11000
Perfect targeting (% of GDP)	3.1	2.0	1.2	0.6	0.44
Transfer Subsidies (% of GDP)	1.1	1.6	2.7	2.9	2.8

Source: Bhalla (2014).

Notes:

1. All data for 2013/14 are estimates.
2. Transfer Subsidies consist of: Subsidy on Fertilizers, Food, Fuel (Kerosene, LPG and Diesel) and Employment Guarantee Schemes.
3. Perfect targeting means that each poor person gets just enough extra income to make her consumption to be equal to the poverty line.

For, the basic economic fundamentals and, thus, the long-term prospects of the economy remain bright. As India has just begun its demographic transition, it can be expected to have a private savings bonanza until the population stabilizes by 2045, when the United Nations estimates it will be 1.6 billion, and thereafter begins to age. The proportion of the population in the 15–64 working-age group is expected to increase from 62.9 per cent in 2006 to 68.1 per cent in 2026. With the total fertility rate reaching the replacement rate of 2.1 by 2010, total population will continue to increase until 2045. During these three decades of the demographic transition, India's savings rate should rise. Private savings rates could well rise to over 30 per cent by 2030. If the public sector does not dissave and corporate savings remain at the current level of 8 per cent, India's gross domestic savings rate could well be 38–40 per cent over the next two decades. So, clearly India does not face any savings constraint in the near future.

Foreign capital inflows into India before the 1991 economic reforms were mainly in the form of FDI, and only 0.2 per cent of GDP on average until 1992–3. Since the reforms, they increased to 1.6 per cent of GDP in 1996–7 and about 2 per cent of GDP since 2003.[115] In the years since 2003, most of the foreign investment in India has been portfolio rather than direct investment, in the form of foreign institutional investment (FII). Thus, in 2004–5, of the total of $12 billion of foreign inflows, FDI flows were only 3.2 billion, the rest being FII, while in the year before the slowdown, 2010–11, of the total foreign inflow of $42 billion, portfolio investment was $31 billion and FDI $11 billion.[116] Bhalla[117] has estimated that because China's inflows are mainly in the form of FDI, reflecting the limited financial reforms it has undertaken, the share of both FDI and FII in GDP in the two countries since 2003–4 have been about the same at 3–5 per cent of GDP (as China has a higher GDP than India's). This trend continues.

Gross domestic investment had risen to 31.5 per cent of GDP in 2004–5 and 36.8 per cent in 2010–11, and then slumped due to the slowdown discussed before. If the domestic savings rate increases to 35 per cent and the foreign savings rate to 5 per cent, gross domestic investment could increase to 40 per cent. With an ICOR of about 4, this would yield a 10 per cent growth rate in the foreseeable future,[118] assuming the causes of the current problem of stagflation are dealt with speedily.[119]

India's infrastructure is likely to expand with its accelerated growth rate. Despite protestations to the contrary, the Indian state has by and large failed to aid economic development. Under the Nehruvian settlement, despite large increases in public investment, the Indian state abysmally failed to efficiently provide the requisite quality and quantity of non-traded goods—like power, transport, clean water, and sanitation—as well as the merit goods of health and education. Since the 1991 reforms and the ensuing acceleration of per capita income, many of the old avenues for rent-seeking have been closed. With the fiscal burden of large, unjustified public subsidies to power and irrigation continuing and with the limits of overt taxation having been reached, the government remains in a fiscal bind and has had to rely on public-private partnerships for the provision of these non-traded goods. But these have not performed well, largely because of the misallocation of risks, with the private sector taking on all the risk that should have been taken by the government or vice versa.[120]

Finally, and most important of all, by greatly diminishing the area in which the dead hand of the state now operates, the 1991 reforms have created much more space for private agents to act. Unlike China, India has had a flourishing civil society for over one hundred years (some would say for millennia). It is increasingly taking over in areas where the state has failed to provide the necessary services.[121]

The greatest prize offered by economic liberalization is in the changed perceptions of the young. One of the baleful effects of the Nehruvian settlement was that the economic policies supported by the English-speaking castes damaged the prospects of their progeny—except for those agile enough to become rent-seekers. They, as well as others among the political classes, then sought and succeeded in placing their progeny in jobs abroad—thereby demonstrating by their private actions the bankruptcy of the public policies they supported. From international experience, I have come to see the ability of a country to retain its 'best and brightest' as an important sign it is on the road to economic prosperity. With economic liberalization, the perceptions of the young about the possibilities of a fruitful life in India have changed. There is a vitality and élan among the best and the brightest in India, with a growing belief that even when based in their homeland, the world is now their oyster. But this optimism could change with the previous government's desire to extend caste-based reservations of places in government-aided educational institutions and public employment, hitherto confined to the scheduled castes and tribes to the more numerous OBCs. These would amount to 50 per cent of the available places. It is even proposed to extend these reservations to employees in the private sector, which has not been repudiated by the new government.

If all these proposals of basing economic outcomes on birth not merit are enacted, we can say goodbye to the knowledge-based 'Incredible India' being touted by politicians. It would be a re-enactment on an Indian canvas and with Indian characteristics based on caste of the Chinese Cultural Revolution, which had implemented class-based reservations for employment and education and in the process lost a whole generation of well-educated youth. Deng reversed this policy and oversaw the creation of a highly educated, technocratic class of meritocratic mandarins, and increasingly a meritocratic society.[122]

There had been fears that as a member of the Rashtriya Swayamsevak Sangh (RSS), the ideological movement to which the BJP is affiliated, Modi would follow its Hindutva social policies. Though many of the hard line Hindutva supporters have indulged in using the Hindu veneration of the cow to indulge in violence—including murder—on those killing and eating cows, Modi's recent firm repudiation of them and their actions should allay the fears that the BJP would worsen communal relations.

Despite these prospective woes and the ever-present danger that a dysfunctional political system might still shoot the economy in the foot, I believe that, given the space available since the 1991 liberalization for private action combined with the flexibility private agents in civil society have shown in getting around state failure, issues of governance are now less likely to damage India's economic future. This is also likely to be aided by the Modi government's acceptance of the latest Finance Commission's recommendation for transferring about 60 per cent of the taxes collected by the Centre to the states. The resulting competitive federalism through tax devolution should allow states to compete in creating the growth-promoting environment that national governments in the past, and it seems even today, are unable or unwilling to create.

To see the prize on offer to India and to judge how its failure to renounce its Nehruvian mindset has hurt, comparisons of Chinese and Indian growth rates since they began their economic liberalizations, (Figure 7.6) and the dramatic effects of the sustained surge in Chinese growth by comparing the respective GDPs of the two countries since 1980 (Figure 7.7) are instructive.

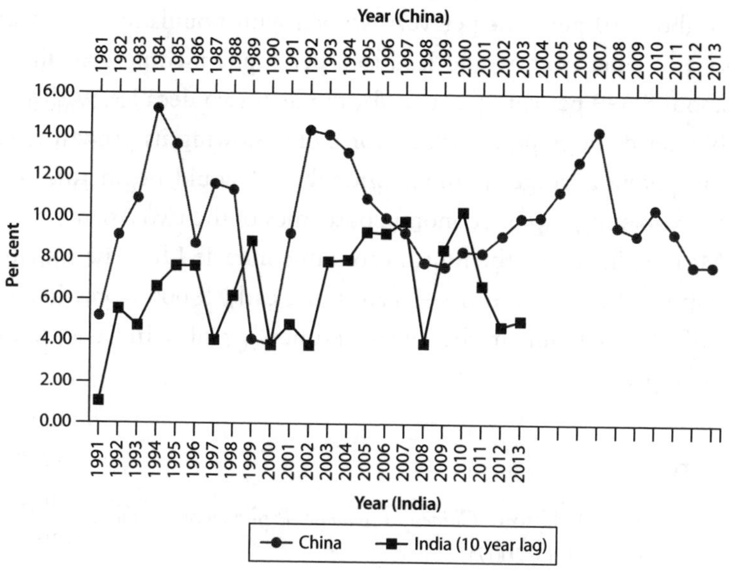

FIGURE 7.6 India and China, GDP Growth Rates
Source: Lal (2016b).

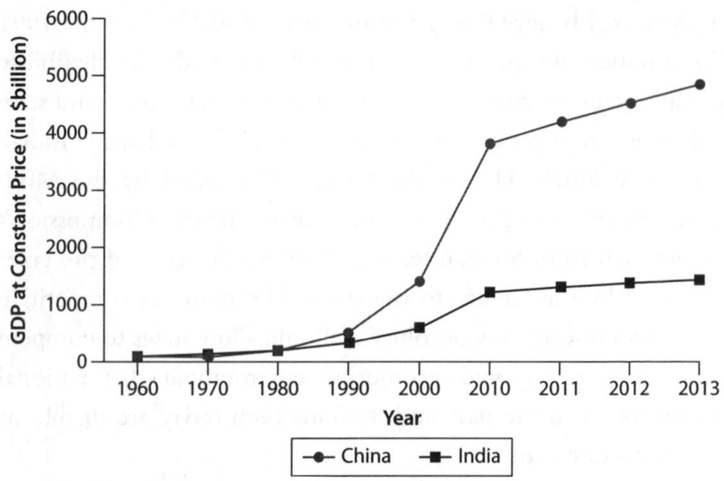

Figure 7.7 India and China, GDP at Constant Prices
Source: Lal (2016b).

It is in the 2000s that there was a dramatic divergence in their economic fortunes.

But, given its economic fundamentals, it seems highly probable that with improved policies, India would be able to grow at about 10 per cent per year, which, with population growing at 1.5–1 per cent, would lead to a per capita income growth of about 8.5–9 per cent per year for the next two decades. With the bleaker demographic outlook for China slowing its growth rate, the potential surge in India's growth rate could begin to close the widening gap in economic outcomes of the two Asian giants. Meanwhile, at last, the fourth economic miracle I have personally witnessed in my lifetime—Japan in the early 1960s, Korea in the early 1970s, China in the 1990s, and now possibly India—would be in place.

Notes

1. Angus Maddison, *Chinese Economic Performance in the Long Run* (Paris: OECD, 2007).
2. See Harry Wu, 'China's Growth and Productivity Performance Revisited—Accounting for China's Sources of Growth with a

New Data Set', *Conference Board*, EPWP #14–01 (2014). Available at https://www.conference-board.org/pdf_free/workingpapers/EPWP1401.pdf (last accessed 13 November 2017).

3. Wu, 'China's Growth and Productivity Performance Revisited', p. 65.
4. Wu, 'China's Growth and Productivity Performance Revisited', p. 65.
5. Wu, 'China's Growth and Productivity Performance Revisited', p. 66.
6. Wu, 'China's Growth and Productivity Performance Revisited', p. 70.
7. See Yasheng Huang, *Capitalism with Chinese Characteristics: Entrepreneurship and the State* (Cambridge: Cambridge University Press, 2008); Steven Cheung, *The Economic System of China* (Hong Kong: Arcadia Press, 2008); and Ronald Coase and N. Wang, *How China Became Capitalist* (New York: Palgrave-Macmillan, 2012).
8. Coase and Wang, *How China Became Capitalist*, describe how 'the first known incidence of private farming in post-Mao China occurred in Pengxi county of Sichuan province. Aware of the political risk, [the Party secretary of the commune and his cadres] decided to allocate only marginal land to households in two production teams, while keeping collective farming intact elsewhere. That year, the output of the marginal but privately cultivated land was three times higher than that of the collectively cultivated fertile land ... By 1978, before the Third Plenum was held in Beijing, private farming was practiced across the whole commune, but was kept secret from the local authorities' (pp. 46–7) Despite the continuing ban on private farming, with the *People's Daily* 'castigating private farming for eroding socialism in rural China ... private farming continued to develop in many disguised forms' (p. 48).
9. Coase and Wang, *How China Became Capitalist*, p. 49.
10. Page 18 in Yasheng Huang, 'Rethinking the Beijing Consensus', *Asia Policy*, 11 (January 2011), pp. 1–26.
11. Coase and Wang, p. 65.
12. Coase and Wang, p. 160.
13. Coase and Wang, p. 160.
14. Cheung, *The Economic System of China*.
15. This is reminiscent of the system of sub-infeudation through the zamindari system in Mughal and British India. See D. Lal, *The Hindu Equilibrium: India c. 1500 B.C.–2000 A.D.*, Abridged and Revised Edition (Oxford and New York: Oxford University Press, 2005), pp. 177–82.

16. Steven Cheung, *The Theory of Share Tenancy* (Chicago: Chicago University Press, 1969).
17. Justin Lin, *Demystifying the Chinese Economy* (Cambridge: Cambridge University Press, 2012), p. 199.
18. Coase and Wang, *How China Became Capitalist*, p. 130.
19. C.E. Walter and F.J.T. Howie, *Red Capitalism: The Fragile Financial Foundation of China's Extraordinary Rise* (Singapore: John Wiley & Sons, 2011).
20. Walter and Howie, *Red Capitalism*, p. 78.
21. Walter and Howie, *Red Capitalism*, p. 159.
22. Walter and Howie, *Red Capitalism*, p. 10–11.
23. Walter and Howie, *Red Capitalism*, p. 11.
24. Walter and Howie, *Red Capitalism*, p. 13–14.
25. Walter and Howie, *Red Capitalism*, p. 14.
26. Walter and Howie, *Red Capitalism*, p. 22.
27. Walter and Howie, *Red Capitalism*, p. 23.
28. Walter and Howie, *Red Capitalism*, p. 31.
29. Walter and Howie, *Red Capitalism*, p. 159.
30. Shankar Sharma, Review of Walter and Howie, *Red Capitalism*, *Business Standard*, 4 May 2012.
31. H. Sanderson and M. Forsythe, *China's Superbank: Debt Oil and Influence—How China Development Bank Is Rewriting the Rules of Finance* (Singapore: John Wiley & Sons, 2013).
32. Sanderson and Forsythe, *China's Superbank*, p. 7.
33. Sanderson and Forsythe, *China's Superbank*, p. 7.
34. Sanderson and Forsythe, *China's Superbank*, p. 6.
35. Sanderson and Forsythe, *China's Superbank*, p. 32.
36. Sanderson and Forsythe, *China's Superbank*, p. 13.
37. Sanderson and Forsythe, *China's Superbank*, p. 14.
38. Sanderson and Forsythe, *China's Superbank*, p. 31.
39. Sanderson and Forsythe, *China's Superbank*, p. 20.
40. Sanderson and Forsythe, *China's Superbank*, p. 34.
41. Sanderson and Forsythe, *China's Superbank*, p. 125.
42. Sanderson and Forsythe, *China's Superbank*, p. 137.
43. Sanderson and Forsythe, *China's Superbank*, p. 139.
44. Sanderson and Forsythe, *China's Superbank*, p. 143.
45. D. Lal, *Poverty and Progress: Realities and Myths about Global Poverty* (New Delhi: Oxford University Press, 2015), pp. 174–8.
46. Sanderson and Forsythe, *China's Superbank*, p. 178.

47. Sanderson and Forsythe, *China's Superbank*, p. 179.
48. See D. Lal, 'The Japanese Slump', in R. Pethig and M. Rauscher (eds), *Challenges to the World Economy* (Berlin: Springer, 2003), pp. 281–90, which describes Ando's estimate.
49. Walter and Howie, *Red Capitalism*, p. 73.
50. Sanderson and Forsythe, *China's Superbank*, p. 180.
51. Huang, *Capitalism with Chinese Characteristics*.
52. Huang, *Capitalism with Chinese Characteristics*, p. 146.
53. Huang, *Capitalism with Chinese Characteristics*, p. 146.
54. Huang, *Capitalism with Chinese Characteristics*, pp. 169–70.
55. Huang, *Capitalism with Chinese Characteristics*, p. 209.
56. Huang, *Capitalism with Chinese Characteristics*, p. 209.
57. Martin King Whyte, 'China Needs Justice, Not Equality: How to Calm the Middle Kingdom', *Foreign Affairs* (5 May 2013). Available at https://www.foreignaffairs.com/articles/china/2013-05-05/china-needs-justice-not-equality (last accessed 13 November 2017).
58. Whyte, 'China Needs Justice, Not Equality'.
59. Whyte, 'China Needs Justice, Not Equality'.
60. Whyte, 'China Needs Justice, Not Equality'.
61. Page 377 in Atif Ansar et al., 'Does Infrastructure Investment Lead to Economic Growth or Economic Fragility? Evidence from China', *Oxford Review of Economic Policy*, 32, no. 3 (2016), pp. 360–90.
62. Bob Davis and Richard Silk, 'China's Producers Struggle to Absorb Free Fall in Prices', *Wall Street Journal* (9 May 2013). Available at https://www.wsj.com/articles/SB10001424127887324059704578472412943132102 (last accessed 13 November 2017).
63. See 'China's Fiddled Figures', *Wall Street Journal* (9 May 2013).
64. Kate Mackenzie, 'China Is Having a Credit-Fuelled Non-Recovery', *Financial Times* (15 April 2013). Available at https://ftalphaville.ft.com/2013/04/15/1459132/china-is-having-a-credit-fuelled-non-recovery (last accessed 13 November 2017).
65. See James Gruber, 'Why a China Crash May Be Imminent', *Forbes* (23 February 2013). Available at https://www.forbes.com/sites/jamesgruber/2013/02/23/a-china-crash-may-be-imminent/#40d89eb42f7e (last accessed 13 November 2017).
66. 'China Addicted to Debt, Now at 205% of GDP: CLSA', *ValueWalk* (8 May 2013). Available at http://www.valuewalk.com/2013/05/china-addicted-to-debt/ (last accessed 13 November 2017).
67. Walter and Howie, *Red Capitalism*, p. 229.

68. The most notable has been the CLSA analyst Andy Rothman, 'Misunderstanding China: Popular Western Illusions Debunked', Special Report, *CLSA Asia-Pacific Markets* (May 2012). But see also the post by two Peking University graduate students questioning his arguments: Wang Chen and Chen Long, 'Debunking Misconceptions on China?', *Institute for New Economic Thinking* (28 June 2012), www.ineteconomics.org/blog/china-seminar.
69. Michael Pettis, 'The Last Chinese Banking Crisis Actually WAS Painful, and the Next Will Be Worse', Op-Ed, *Business* Insider (21 January 2011). Available at http://www.businessinsider.com/china-non-performing-loans-2011-1 (last accessed 13 November 2017).
70. Michael Pettis, 'Hello 2013: Chinese Banking and Economic Reform', beyondbrics blog, *Financial Times* (8 January 2013).
71. For evidence that the Chinese leadership is aware of the reforms needed as well as the political obstacles they face, see the joint report by the Wen Jiabao-controlled Development Research Centre of the State Council and the World Bank, *China 2030: Building a Modern, Harmonious and Creative High Income Society*. (Washington, DC: World Bank, 2012).
72. The PLA is part of the princeling party, and though it was forced by Wen Jiabao to divest itself of many of its industrial and economic assets, it still is part of the web of high-level institutional corruption engulfing China, see John Garnaut, 'Rotting from Within'. Available at http://foreignpolicy.com/2012/04/16/rotting-from-within/ (last accessed 30 January. 2018).
73. D. Lal, 'An Indian Economic Miracle?', *Cato Journal*, 28, no.1 (2008), pp. 11–34.
74. See my socio-economic history of India, Lal, *The Hindu Equilibrium*.
75. See D. Lal, *Reviving the Invisible Hand: The Case for Classical Liberalism in the Twenty-First Century* (Princeton, NJ: Princeton University Press, 2006).
76. The most recent GDP data, with a new 2012 base, produced by the Central Statistical Office (CSO) has raised the GDP growth rates for 2013–14 to 6.3 per cent with a further acceleration to 7.5 per cent in 2014–15, which most observers, including official ones like the Reserve Bank of India and the Finance Ministry's own *Economic Survey 2014–15*, find dubious. Therefore, in this section we end our growth series with the old base of 2004–5 for 2013. For doubts about the new series, which also does not provide numbers

for earlier years, see S. Acharya, 'How Fast Is India Growing?' *Business Standard* (8 April 2015). Available at http://www.business-standard.com/article/opinion/shankar-acharya-how-fast-is-india-growing-115040801305_1.html (last accessed 13 November 2017). For a defence of the new series, see S.S. Bhalla, 'No Proof Required: New GDP Is for Real', *Indian Express* (18 April 2015). Available at http://indianexpress.com/article/opinion/columns/no-proof-required-new-gdp-is-for-real (last accessed 13 November 2017); and Central Statistics Office, 'No Room for Doubt on New GDP Numbers', *Economic and Political Weekly*, 50, no. 6 (April 2015). A new committee has been appointed to review and revise the GDP series, and until that is done, current, past, and prospective growth rates will remain in doubt.

77. D. Lal, 'The Indian Economy: From Growth to Stagflation to Liberal Reform', *World Economics*, 17, no. 1 (2016), pp. 63–104.
78. E. Boserup, *The Conditions of Agricultural Growth: The Economics of Agrarian Change under Population Pressure* (London: Allen & Unwin, 1965), and D. Lal, 'Nationalism, Socialism and Planning: Influential Ideas in the South', *World Development*, 13, no. 6 (1985), pp. 749–59.
79. The elasticity of agricultural output with respect to rural labor remained constant at about 2.5 in both the pre-Independence period (1900–40) and the post-Independence period (1950–70), while that of capital to labour rose from about 1 to 2.54, as predicted by the Boserupian model (Lal, *The Hindu Equilibrium*, Table 7.4).
80. See J.P. Lewis, *Quiet Crisis in India: Economic Development and American Policy* (Washington, DC: Brookings Institution, 1962).
81. A. Gulati, 'Emerging Trends in Indian Agriculture: What Can We Learn from These?', *Agricultural Economics Research Review*, 22 (July–Dec 2009): 171–84, notes that this GM revolution, particularly in Bt cotton since 2002, has been due to private companies, unlike the earlier Green Revolution technology for wheat and rice, which was developed and spread largely by the government. But, many activists and opponents of private enterprise have pointed to the number of farmer suicides in areas where Bt cotton has been adopted to cast doubt on the viability of a private-enterprise-based GM technological revolution. Gulati cites an International Food Policy Research Institute (IFPRI) study that found that 'Bt cotton seeds per se cannot be blamed for these unfortunate suicides' (p. 174). For the needed reforms in agriculture for it to continue growing at

4 per cent p.a., also see A. Gulati, 'Accelerating Agriculture Growth', in S. Acharya and R. Mohan (eds), *India's Economic Performance* (New Delhi: Oxford University Press, 2010); A. Gulati, 'Reforming Agriculture', *Seminar*, 629 (January 2012); and A. Gulati, 'Economic Survey 2015: Growth in Agriculture Remains a Worry', *Economic Times* (28 February 2015). Available at https://economictimes.indiatimes.com/news/economy/agriculture/economic-survey-2015-growth-in-agriculture-remains-a-worry-says-ashok-gulati/articleshow/46402798.cms (last accessed 13 November 2017).

82. Government of India, *Economic Survey 2013–14* (New Delhi: Ministry of Finance, 2013), p. 137.
83. See D. Lal, 'Nationalism, Socialism and Planning', *World Development*, 13, no. 6 (1985), pp. 749–59 and I.M.D. Little, *Economic Development: Theory, Policy, and International Relations* (New York: Basic Books, 1982).
84. See D. Lal, 'The Political Economy of Economic Liberalization', *World Bank Economic Review*, 1, no. 2 (1987), pp. 273–99, reprinted in Lal (1993). The first sign was the growth of the underground economy, variously estimated to be 18 to 45 per cent of GDP. Second, government revenue, which had risen from about 11 per cent of GDP in 1960 to about 20 per cent in 1986, stagnated thereafter. Public expenditures rose from about 19 per cent of GDP in 1960 to more than 32 per cent by 1986. Thus, the PSBR rose from about 8 per cent of GDP in the 1960s and 1970s to more than 11.5 per cent in 1990, the year preceding the crisis and reform (Lal, *The Hindu Equilibrium*, Table 12.1). Third, the growing fiscal crisis was met by internal and external borrowing and, finally, by levying the inflation tax. Inflation, which had hovered around 4–5 per cent, except for years of drought, rose steadily from 1988 to reach a peak of nearly 14 per cent in 1991, a year with a bumper harvest.
85. Lal, *The Hindu Equilibrium*, Table 12.1b.
86. B. Bosworth, S.M. Collins, and A. Virmani, 'Sources of Growth in the Indian Economy', in S. Bery, B. Bosworth, and A. Panagariya (eds) *India Policy Forum 2006–07*, Volume 3 (Washington, DC: Brookings Institute; New Delhi: NCAER; and New Delhi: Sage, 2006).
87. The increase in TFP shows the effects of improved efficiency that followed the movements from the plan to the market and the gradual easing of the economic repression of the Indian economy. Those efficiency gains from economic liberalization, which have become

most marked since the 1991 Manmohan Singh reforms, were—as BCV show—due to reallocation effects. Usually, these reallocation effects are due to shifts in employment from low productivity uses in agriculture to higher productivity uses in industry. But in India, while the share of agriculture in total output has declined, it has only decreased marginally as a share of employment.

88. The most surprising feature of the BCV sectoral Indian growth accounts is that services have been the main growth agent since the 1980s. The data imply that the bulk of TFP growth in services is accounted for by traditional services. But this goes against all international experience. BCV's hypothesis is that the prices of services in the Indian national accounts are being underestimated, leading to an overestimate of their real rate of growth.
89. Swaminathan Aiyar, in a private communication, has questioned this scepticism, arguing that imports and exports and internal trade have been rising much faster than nominal GDP. Hence trade, transport, and storage have been rising faster than GDP and from a higher base than IT. Also with the rise of private banks and non-bank housing and transport companies, there has been an explosive growth of financial services, which have been growing faster than nominal GDP.
90. R. Jenkins, *Democratic Politics and Economic Reform in India* (Cambridge: Cambridge University Press, 1999).
91. Lal, *The Hindu Equilibrium*, Ch. 13.2.
92. See D. Lal, 'The Indian Economy: From Growth to Stagflation to Liberal Reform', *World Economics*, 17, no. 1 (2016): 63–104, for an explication of the distinction between economic rent, composite quasi-rent, and monopoly rent and why while most scams involved economic or composite quasi-rents they did not affect the efficiency of the economy and only had distributive effects.
93. See also D. Lal, 'India's Post-Liberalization Blues', *World Economics*, 12, no. 4 (2011) for an explanation of the differences between economy rent, composite quasi-rent, and monopoly rent.
94. This is an extension of a scheme first introduced in Maharashtra to provide poor, unemployed labourers with work on public works at a wage just below the market wage.
95. These justices, unlike many who have gone through the excellent law and economics courses set up by Henry Manne at George Mason in the US, are without economic reasoning.

96. Government of India, *Economic Survey 2014–15* (New Delhi: Ministry of Finance, 2014).
97. The survey cites a Centre for Monitoring Indian Economy (CMIE) study that found that in 2011–12, 70 per cent of the total cost of shelved projects was accounted for by twenty projects, and the cause of their problems included 'difficulties in land acquisition, coal linkages and mining bans'. For projects like telecoms, issues concerning the allocation of spectrum have been responsible. This rise in stalled projects has also led to the drying up of new investment, as these infructuous investments 'reduce the ability of firms to start new ones', Government of India, *Economic Survey 2014–15*, Box 1.1, p. 8.
98. Amy Kazmin, 'India Struggles to Build Up Infrastructure Dream', *Financial Times* (28 July 2014). Available at https://www.ft.com/content/a4152f94-1627-11e4-93ec-00144feabdc0 (last accessed 13 November 2017).
99. Subir Gokarn has said that whereas in the previous pre-crisis period when the ICOR spiked (2000-3) it was due to business cycle effects, the recent spike since 2011 was different. He argues this was due not only to business cycle effects but also to declining capital productivity because of what he labels the 'portfolio effect' in infrastructure, like the large capacity of thermal power stations being left idle because of lack of investment in coal mines, in part because of environmental clearances and judicial responses to various mining scams. See S. Gokarn, 'Bang for the Buck', *Business Standard* (24 March 2014). Available at http://www.business-standard.com/article/opinion/subir-gokarn-bang-for-the-buck-114032300691_1.html (last accessed 13 November 2017).
100. D. Lal and H. Myint, *The Political Economy of Poverty, Equity and Growth: A Comparative Study* (Oxford: Clarendon Press, 1996).
101. See Sanjaya Baru, *The Accidental Prime Minister: The Making and Unmaking of Manmohan Singh* (New Delhi: Viking-Penguin, 2014).
102. The basic problem is that the dynasty and its acolytes have never come out openly to develop a public consensus for the classical liberal economy that is needed to replace the defunct Nehruvian model. The expansion of unsustainable entitlements lies in the failure of the Nehruvians to distinguish between two kinds of populism. The first, embraced by the Congress, is redistributive with an

extension of state largesse. It views the majority of its citizens as being dependent children who need the state to provide for them. The other kind of populism strives to empower the people who are fully capable, autonomous beings held back by various impediments created by dirigisme and the state's failure to provide the basic public goods of law and order and the merit goods of health and education. In the recent election, the Congress crown prince campaigned on the first form of populist programme, while his opponent, BJP's Narendra Modi, campaigned on the second form of populism and trounced him.

103. D. Lal, 'The Great Crash of 2008: Causes and Consequences', *Cato Journal*, 30, no. 2 (2010), pp. 265–77.
104. See D. Lal, *Unintended Consequences: The Impact of Factor Endowments, Culture, and Politics on Long-Run Economic Performance* (Cambridge, MA: MIT Press, 1998).
105. L. Dumont, *Homo Hierarchicus: The Caste System and Its Implications* (London: Weidenfeld and Nicholson, 1970).
106. Minna Saavala, *Middle-Class Moralities: Everyday Struggle over Belonging and Prestige in India* (New Delhi: Orient Blackswan, 2012).
107. This is a form of social mobility identified by the eminent Indian sociologist M.N. Srinivas. It is a process by which lower castes aspiring to raise their social status emulate the lifestyles of superior castes. The new Indian urban middle class seeks to raise their status by adopting the rituals of the upper Hindu castes, but as they do not wish to emulate the westernized castes who they think are deracinated, they are immune to Nehruvian blandishments as the Gandhi family has found out to its electoral cost.
108. The Indian form of reservations for the lower castes harms the economic prospects of this urban neo- middle class, and they are against them.
109. In Lal, 'The Indian Economy: From Growth to Stagflation to Liberal Reform', I present a little personal history to explain these answers.
110. The NGO activists typically carry a coarse cotton bag called a *jholla*, hence this colloquial name to describe them as unworldly dreamers!
111. That is, indigenous economic activities including industry.
112. See Lal, *Hindu Equilibrium*, Ch. 9.

113. Given India's abysmal and worsening sex ratio, see my, 'A Demographic Time Bomb', *Business Standard* (16 March 2013). Available at http://www.business-standard.com/article/opinion/a-demographic-time-bomb-113031500651_1.html (last accessed 13 November 2017).
114. S.S. Bhalla, 'Billionaires and Crony Socialism', *Indian Express* (7 February 2014). Available at http://indianexpress.com/article/opinion/columns/billionaires-and-crony-socialism (last accessed 13 November 2017).
115. Government of India, *Economic Survey 2006–07* (New Delhi: Ministry of Finance, 2006–7), p. 127.
116. Government of India, *Economic Survey 2014*, Table 6.2.
117. S.S. Bhalla, *Second among Equals: The Middle-Class Kingdoms of India and China* (Washington, DC: Peterson Institute for International Economics, 2007).
118. Bhalla, *Second among Equals*, maintains 'that projections based on econometric analysis of investment spending, non-food credit, bank credit to industry, real interest rates, etc., give a minimum estimate of investment spending as a share of GDP of 41 per cent in 2006–07.' If this is correct it would yield a growth rate of 10 per cent in 2006–7. Given the doubts about recent official national income statistics expressed in note 473, we will have to wait and see if this is true.
119. India has a wealth of private entrepreneurial talent. The recent rush of India's big business houses to go global by purchasing foreign companies (of which Tata's acquisition of Corus and Jaguar Land Rover are examples) also demonstrates Indian industry's newfound confidence in taking on the world. This global thrust by private Indian entrepreneurs is different from the state-led one being organized by China to convert some of its state and state-fronted large enterprises into global champions. See D. Lal, 'A Proposal to Privatize Chinese Enterprises and End Financial Repression', *Cato Journal*, 26(2) (Spring/Summer 2006b): 275–86.

    The Indian corporate sector is also beginning to extend its reach into the rural sector by organizing contract farming as part of a seamless supply chain from the farm to local urban supermarkets. This is going to lead to the next stage of agricultural development (the Green Revolution having reached its limits) with the move to more high-valued crops like fruits and vegetables. The Indian corporate sector, envisaging a supply chain from the farm to the towns and then to export markets, is also increasingly investing in the infrastructure that will be required. But the recent political backlash against the growth of retail supermarkets, which it is feared will kill the traditional 'mom and pop' stores that have dominated retail trade in India, may delay these developments.

120. Thus the implementation risks associated with the new license permit raj concerning land acquisition and environmental clearances should have been borne by the government. Given the past failures of the badly designed public-private partnership infrastructure projects, the recent budget rightly increased public investments in infrastructure, particularly in the railways. The alternative route of foreign financing is still being poisoned by the past Congress government's bill to allow retrospective taxation of foreign investors to overcome the Supreme Court's judgement against the tax authorities. The 2015 budget failed to rescind this bill.

However, the proposed introduction of a bankruptcy bill will hopefully allow a cleaning up of the many 'sick' units in the industrial, infrastructure and banking sectors. There is a lukewarm embrace of the alternative of financing infrastructure through the proceeds from privatizations of the large number of public enterprises, many of which are loss making. Its recent decision to privatize the massively inefficient and loss-making national airline (Air India) is not yet a sign that it is going to adopt Thatcherite privatization policies.

121. A few examples will suffice:

- The failure of the state to provide primary education for all the people has led to the growth of private schools used by even the poorest. See James Tooley, *The Beautiful Tree: A Personal Journey into How the World's Poorest People Are Educating Themselves* (Washington, DC: Cato Institute, 2013).
- In agriculture, the private provision through tubewells to meet failures of state provision and the corrupt state-controlled allocation of irrigation water has created a massive problem of 'the commons', as the unregulated growth in ground water irrigation leads to over-exploitation of the subcontinental aquifer. See A. Vaidyanathan, 'Agrarian Crisis: Nature, Causes, and Remedies', *The Hindu* (8 November 2006). The government has at last woken up to this problem.

- The failure of the state to provide a reliable power supply has led to the development of an informal parallel grid in many urban areas.
- The granting of private licenses to mobile phone companies in the 1990s has created a virtual telecommunications revolution that has reached even remote villages. This is in stark contrast to the old regime monopolized by state telephone companies, which are now gradually going to the wall.

122. India's past policy of reservations has already seriously affected governance by damaging the functioning of the public sector—see A. Shourie, *Falling over Backwards: An Essay on Reservations and Judicial Populism* (New Delhi: ASA Publications, 2006). Moreover, as the eminent Indian sociologist, the late M.N. Srinivas, *Village, Caste, Gender and Method: Essays in Indian Social Anthropology* (New Delhi: Oxford University Press, 1996) noted, existing reservations led the 'forward' castes to evolve a strategy for survival—namely, emigration. It would be retrograde and greatly damage India's economic future if the current rush to reservations were to lead India's best and brightest to once again look abroad for their future. As many Indian observers have noted, the best way to deal with the problems faced by the economically and socially disadvantaged is to provide them the means to compete in a meritocratic society. This is happening with the rise of a Dalit (untouchable) capitalist class. See Devesh Kapur, 'Western Anti-Capitalists Take Too Much for Granted', *Financial Times* (23 July 2014), who shows how India's untouchables are being emancipated by economic growth. This, above all, requires access to primary and secondary schools. The Indian state's abysmal failure to provide the merit goods of education and health to its populace has increasingly led even the poorest to rely on private provision.

CHAPTER EIGHT

Japan and Russia

The two other major powers competing in the struggle for Eurasia are Japan and Russia. We examine their geoeconomics in turn.

The Japanese 'Economic Miracle' and After

As we have seen in Part I, Chapter 2, after its disastrous defeat in the Second World War, Japan switched to a 'trading state' strategy to resurrect its status as a major power. This policy of 'mercantile realism' was spectacularly successful. But we also saw that—because of some omissions in the Occupation reforms under Macarthur—Japan reconstructed its old political system, which it had established during the Meiji Restoration. Its effective lack of a political centre to adjudicate disputes continues to haunt Japan. How, then, did this political black hole deliver the Japanese miracle?[1]

It clearly could not have been—as so many Western commentators have suggested—because of the enlightened dirigisme of a developmental state. In fact, as the detailed comparative growth experience of the OECD countries by Maurice Scott[2] shows, there was no miracle. The 9.2 per cent p.a. growth rate from 1960–73 during these 'miracle' years (as the growth rate fell to

3.8 per cent p.a. from 1973–85) can be explained entirely by the investment rate, the growth in the quality adjusted labour force, and a catch-up variable.

This is also shown in the magisterial Brookings study edited by Hugh Patrick and Henry Rosovsky[3] for the supposedly miraculous period till 1973. Bill Emmott[4] also emphasizes that the laws of economics have not been abrogated in Japan. It could not and did not succeed by getting the prices wrong! As other recent surveys of the evidence show,[5] Japan's success is in spite rather than because of the Ministry of International Trade and Industry (MITI), which was purported to have channelled the large savings of Japanese households in the state-controlled postal system to 'industrial winners'. The fierce competition between the keiretsu—the reconstituted conglomerate successors of the pre-war zaibatsu abolished by the Occupation—and the continuing battle for export markets have determined the efficiency of the considerable savings the Japanese have been able to make.

In the 1990s, the Japanese economy crashed after the popping of a spectacular stock market and property bubble. This bubble was caused by loose credit in the 1980s. This, in turn, was due to the continuing trade frictions with the US after Japan opened its capital account. Since President Nixon closed the gold window and the world entered a system of floating exchange rates, the US has tried to tackle its chronic trade deficit with Japan by pressuring it to appreciate the yen. The threatened and actual actions against Japanese exports forced Japan to comply. The Bank of Japan (BOJ) delivered the requisite appreciation through tight domestic monetary policy. With the opening of the Japanese capital account in the early 1980s, Japanese interest rates were tied to those in the US but were lower by the expected rate of yen appreciation. These lower domestic interest rates allowed some moderation of the effects of the high yen on domestic output, but by inducing more capital–intensive investment, they also initiated the Hayekian process of 'mal-investment' identified in Chapter 4.

The Plaza and Louvre accords of the 1980s committed Japan to a massive appreciation of the yen, leading to a recession and a lowering of Japanese nominal interest rates to close to zero.[6] This meant that even with the worsened prospects of the tradeable sector because of the high yen, the capitalized value of future income streams from investments in fixed capital and, particularly, land soared, as the interest rate at which they were discounted fell. This was the start of the great Japanese asset bubble. The rise in asset values allowed domestic demand to replace foreign demand for Japanese output (which had fallen due to the high yen) as the engine of growth, and Japan rapidly grew out of the *endaka fukyo* (high yen) recession.

The BOJ hailed this escape from the deflation forced by the high yen. It became the primary cheerleader of the growing asset bubble. It praised the 'new economy' in which domestic demand, fuelled by the rise in asset prices, led to growth, while giving time to the tradeable sector to adjust to the higher yen. The Japanese government was happy with this outcome, for it allowed it to get its fiscal house in order, without having to run Keynesian fiscal deficits to deal with the endaka fukyo of 1985–6.

But, in the late 1980s, worried by the massive appreciation in land and stock prices, the BOJ sought to prick the bubble by tightening monetary policy. This precipitated another recession, accompanied by another massive yen appreciation—again prompted by growing trade friction with the US. It was only in 1995–6 that the US eased this pressure and allowed the yen to depreciate against the dollar. That immediately led to the end of the first 1990s depression but only temporarily, as subsequently, the usual trade frictions and pressure for yen appreciation remerged, and Japan was plunged into its second endaka fukyo of the 1990s.[7]

After the miracle years, which ended with the oil price shock of the 1970s, the Japanese corporations with access to the high household savings mainly held in Japan Post have not been all that efficient. Detailed work on the Japanese national accounts by Albert Ando[8] finds that the cumulated net savings of Japanese households (at 1990 prices) between 1970 and 1998 was 1,250 trillion yen. The change in their net worth during the same period was 861 trillion yen. Thus, the Japanese household sector suffered a real capital loss of 389 trillion yen! Roughly three-fourths of this huge capital loss is attributable to the loss of market value by Japanese corporations. Over this period, they incurred real capital losses of 405.5 trillion yen in their market value. How did this happen? Working out the rates of return for non-financial and financial corporations for 1996, Ando finds that the returns were just above 2 per cent for the former and 1.6 per cent for the latter. These low returns are due to Japanese corporations having overinvested in plant and equipment using funds retained through a very high rate of depreciation and the large savings channeled through financial institutions. This led to very high capital-output ratios—which continued to rise through the depressed 1990s—and very low rates of return.

Given these pitiful returns, Japanese investors sought higher returns abroad, which made Japan—until the Chinese followed the same mercantilist model—the world's largest creditor nation and the US the largest debtor. But as these foreign capital flows are denominated in dollars, the Japanese have borne the currency risk. With the dollar depreciating against the yen during periods of endaka fukyo, their returns on foreign assets have been virtually wiped out over the 1980s and 1990s. With the returns on their domestic investments having been virtually extinguished by domestic mal-investment, and those on their foreign investments by the appreciating yen, one cannot help but feel sorry for Japanese households.

With the stock market crash of 1 January 1990, the previously much-touted Japanese economic performance, which was supposed to make Japan No. 1 in the world economy of the 1980s, was replaced by economic stagnation with 75 per cent falls in share prices till their trough in March 2003, and 70 per cent falls in property prices till their trough in early 2005, followed by a financial system collapse and deflation.[9] But this crisis had one important political effect. The bureaucracy, which in effect had ruled the country since the Meiji Restoration, was discredited, and the despised politicians came into their own.

With the election of Junichiro Koizumi as the LDP's prime minister, Japan began its economic recovery in 2001. Till the GFC of 2008, Japan saw 'its longest (though not the strongest) period of expansion since 1945'.[10] The crash of 1990 had led to 'three sorts of excesses: excess debt, excess capacity and excess labour'.[11]

Koizumi, in his tenure between 2002 and 2006, dealt with the excess debt by cutting the vast pile of non-performing loans in the banking system by three quarters. Excess capacity due the mal-investments of the 1980s was worked off by attrition over time. By 2005, the restructured (and renamed) MITI reported that capacity utilization rate was back to 1992 levels.[12]

It took longer to absorb excess labour, despite the worsening demographics. But the 1990s saw big changes in the labour market, with the growing substitution of lifetime employment by part-time and temporary labour contracts. Thus, while the part-time and temporary contracts accounted for 18.8 per cent of the labour force in 1990, by 2005 such workers made up 30 per cent of the workforce.[13] But given the excess labour that needed to be absorbed, wages remained flat, and the income inequality index of the gap between the incomes of the bottom 10 per cent and top 10 per cent, which had been below the OECD average, rose. However, this was not due to a rise in top incomes as in the US but because of the stagnation of wages in the lower tier of the two-tier labour market created by the labour reforms of 2001–3.[14]

Emmott argues that since the 1990s, Japan has had 'a stealth revolution, in corporate law, in politics, in its labour markets, in capital markets, in its banking system, the role of the state, the effects of which will become clear only during the next decade.'[15]

There were two legacies of the 1990s that continue to cloud Japan's prospects. The first was the government's response to the deflationary consequences of the crash of 1990. With the 1980s ending with a fiscal surplus, the government undertook a large Keynesian fiscal expansion. This led to a massive rise in public debt. But as the crash was a Hayekian one and required the liquidation of the mal-investments and the bad paper in the banking system, it was not till 2005 that these problems were dealt with. Secondly, the crash had also led to a large monetary contraction. This was not dealt with by a monetary expansion. The BOJ had misdiagnosed the problem. The result was a prolonged price deflation for nearly two decades.

It was not until Shinzo Abe's overwhelming election victory in 2012 that a coherent plan to deal with Japan's post-crash woes was at last devised. This so called 'Abenomics' had three prongs: aggressive monetary easing, flexible fiscal policy, and structural reforms. The first prong has been the most successful. But, as the IMF has warned,[16] without further progress on the other two prongs, deflation risks and prospects of continuing low growth remain.

Russia's Authoritarian Capitalism

I had outlined in Chapter 2 how the Soviet Union's planned economy imploded in 1990–1. After the turmoil of the Yeltsin years, Yegor Gaidar and associated liberals attempted to establish a market economy, but with the accession of Vladimir Putin to the presidency in 2000, a form of authoritarian capitalism was increasingly established. In the 2000s, there was prosperity based on exporting natural resources, which remained hostage—as in the past—to volatile commodity prices. Also, the gradual de facto nationalization of these natural resources does not augur well for their efficient current or future deployment. Moreover, this reliance on foreign exchange windfalls exacerbates the 'Dutch Disease'. The real exchange rate that is entailed discourages non-natural-resource-based exports and creates a boom in non-traded goods (like real estate).[17] Finally, there is the demographic problem facing Russia. Not only is its population declining but also its health status, with an unimaginable fall in male life expectancy. So, even before the most recent turn of events, there were doubts about the sustainability of any Russian economic miracle.

The problem goes back to the two dangers identified by Gaidar, the 'precious bane' of natural resources and post-imperial nostalgia. A classical liberal solution to avoiding the precious bane is to transfer the rents from natural resources directly to the populace, as the US state of Alaska does with its oil revenues, by writing cheques to its tax payers. This avoids the rent-seeking that natural resource rents accruing to the state always generate. It can, as in many African countries, lead to failed states, as the battle to acquire these rents leads to endemic political instability and, often, to civil wars.[18] Moreover, as in the 1970s, rising natural resource rents accruing to the exchequer can be used to feed post-imperial nostalgia, as seems to be happening currently in Russia.

This is harmful to the economy. First, with the de facto nationalization of the enterprises producing these rents, the endemic inefficiencies of state-owned enterprises make the future flows of these rents more unstable. Second, because of the real exchange rate appreciation, many of the human-capital-intensive export industries, on which Russia's long term future increasingly depends, find it difficult to become internationally competitive.

This leads to the second question about the sustainability of the Russian economic strategy relying on natural resource exports for growth. These resources are located in inhospitable places. Russia (unlike China) has always been a labour scarce and land abundant country. With the decline of the Russian population and with most of the natural resources concentrated in Siberia where few Russians want to live, it is difficult to see how effective territorial control over this natural-resource-rich area can be maintained in the future, as it becomes increasingly difficult to find enough Russian 'souls' to fill these Siberian wastes. There is, reportedly, large legal and illegal Chinese migration already into the region. One solution to Russia's eternal dilemma of its divided 'soul' (being both European and Asian) would be a variant on the tsarist 'Alaskan solution': to lease Siberia to the Chinese in return for a share in the rents that the Chinese would extract from the region's natural resources. This would allow Russia to finally escape from its unviable imperial dream, which has entailed authoritarianism, by becoming a natural European state—perhaps even a liberal democracy. But as Yegor Gaidar pointed out at a seminar in Moscow discussing the Russian edition of my book

Reviving the Invisible Hand (2009), no Russian leader would be able to accept any such change of borders. The Chinese may, however, raise the question of the 'unequal treaties' of Aigun and Peking. Through the former, China ceded the north bank of the Amur River to Russia in 1858, and through the latter, in 1860, it gave Russia access to the ice-free waters of the Pacific; the Russian port of Vladivostok was founded in 1860. Thus China, despite its current bonhomie with Russia, remains a serious threat to Russia's territorial integrity.

Russia, nevertheless, needs to facilitate the necessary move from a natural-resource-intensive economy to one that is human-capital intensive. Unlike China, which is still in the 'catch-up' phase of industrialization, with a large supply of agricultural labour still to be absorbed into industry and the associated services, Russia should now be a human-capital-abundant country at the technical frontier. Its future growth depends upon productivity increases, fuelled by new inventions and entrepreneurial talent. It is in this context that the arguments of my book *Reviving the Invisible Hand* are so relevant to Russia. For, as I argued, the dirigiste corporatist model of capitalism—of which Russia's new-found authoritarian capitalism is a variant—is a snare and a delusion. Russia needs to fully adopt the Anglo-Saxon form of capitalism, which requires a legal infrastructure that enforces a transparent and impartial rule of law. This developed in the West from Pope Gregory VII's legal revolution in the eleventh century, which Russia missed with the divorce of Latin and Orthodox Christendom (see Chapter 2).

But, it is equally important that Russian entrepreneurs, inventors, and scientists are given enough private space to carry on the necessary task of 'creative destruction', which lies at the heart of the capitalist process. One of the strongest instrumental arguments for liberal democracy is that through the institutional protections it provides to free speech and enterprise, it promotes this dynamic efficiency of capitalism. But, as the example of the now-extinguished colony of Hong Kong has shown, it is possible to have these economic and civil liberties without political liberty.[19] If Russia's cosmological beliefs predispose it to some form of tsardom, I can only hope that there will soon be a good tsar who implements the economic classical liberalism advocated in that book.[20]

The last time I was in Russia was in April 2012, soon after the flawed re-election of Putin to a third term as President. With temperatures of −5°C, there was no sign of spring. This continuing winter freeze reflected the mood of most of the participants at the annual international academic conference organized by the Higher School of Economics, which I had come to attend. With Putin likely to win the 2018 election setting him to rule Russia for another six years, what are Russia's prospects?

At the conference, many officials downgraded Russian short- to medium-term prospects. But even this was seen as too rosy by Alexei Kudrin, the former finance minister, who argued that the sovereign wealth fund he had set up to channel Russian resource rents was being raided for various populist handouts to counter dissent, and if oil and gas prices fell, Russia would not be able to manage the resulting fiscal and balance of payments crises. There was a consensus that unless Russia weaned itself of its natural resource-led, statist growth model, its prospects looked bleak.

This is underlined by the growing emigration of Russia's skilled youth and increased capital flight (private sector net capital outflows in the first three months of 2012 were $35 billion compared to $20 billion in the first quarter of 2011). The dismal condition of Russian business was underlined in a remarkable address by a brave lawyer, Vladimir Radchenko (the first deputy chairman of the Supreme Court, 1989–2008). He claimed that the Soviet mode of justice still remains. There are three million small- and medium-scale business entrepreneurs in jail for economic crimes. He contrasted this with conditions during the 1920s' New Economic Policy when the share of output from small and medium enterprises (SMEs) in GDP was about the same as today—but when not only were there fewer listed economic crimes but also punishment for them was a fine, not imprisonment. By contrast, today, ordinary profit-making has been criminalized. This lack of a rule of law has led Russian oligarchs to register their companies abroad, fight their legal battles in London, and move their assets and families to the West.

By 2013, growth had slowed down to 1.3 per cent due to a reduction in investment.[21] But worse was to follow with Putin's annexation of Crimea and his undeclared war in Eastern Ukraine in 2014. With the fall in commodity prices, particularly of oil with the US shale gas and oil revolution, and the slowdown in China, the sanctions imposed by the US and the EU made a bad situation even worse. Gazprom, the state-owned gas giant, saw its output drop by 19pc over the year until June 2015, as its European markets dried up with the sanctions. This has seriously eroded Russia's economic base as Gazprom generates a tenth of Russia's GDP and a fifth of its budget revenues. The economy has contracted by 4.9 per cent, real incomes have fallen by 8.4 per cent, and as the central bank has sought to limit the further erosion of its reserves by allowing the rouble to fall, core inflation has risen to 16.7 per cent. Putin's resource-based economic strategy of opening up the Arctic and exploiting its shale reserves has been dented by Russia's lack of the requisite technology and the sanctions, which prevent Western companies from providing this through joint ventures. Thus, as a commentator rightly concluded, 'Russia bet its future on oil, gas and the commodity boom, letting its manufacturing base atrophy … It has now been left high and dry by the commodity slump'.[22]

Notes

1. This section is based in large part on D. Lal, 'The Japanese Slump', in R. Pethig and M. Rauscher (eds), *Challenges to the World Economy* (Berlin: Springer, 2003), pp. 281–90.
2. M.F. Scott, *A New View of Economic Growth* (Oxford: Clarendon Press, 1989).
3. H. Patrick and H. Rosovsky (eds), *Asia's New Giant: How the Japanese Economy Works* (Washington, DC: Brookings Institution, 1976).
4. Bill Emmott, *The Sun Also Sets: Why Japan Will Not Be Number One* (London: Simon and Schuster, 1989).

5. See R. Ponnuru, *The Mystery of Japanese Growth*, Rochester Paper 4 (London: Trade Policy Research Unit, Centre for Policy Studies, 1995); A. Dick, *Industrial Policy and Semiconductors: Missing the Target* (Washington, DC: American Enterprise Institute, 1995); M. Noland and H. Pack, *Industrial Policy in an Era of Globalization: Lessons from Asia* (Washington, DC: Institute of International Economics, 2003); and D. Lal, 'Is the Washington Consensus Dead?', *Cato Journal*, 32, no. 3 (Fall 2012), pp. 493–512.
6. See R. McKinnon and K. Ohno, *Dollar and Yen: Resolving Economic Conflict between the United States and Japan* (Cambridge, MA: MIT Press, 1997), for the role of the high yen in leading to the 1980s' asset bubble and the lost decades of Japan after the financial crash of 1990.
7. The great irony is that an appreciating yen is a completely misguided remedy for curing the structural trade imbalance between the US and Japan. Modern balance of payments theory tells us that in a world of integrated world capital markets and floating exchange rates, trade deficits are the result of the difference between domestic investment and savings. If one country saves less than it invests—as has been true of the US since the 1980s—and the other does the reverse, then a trade deficit in the borrowing and trade surplus in the lending country is as inevitable as night follows day. The Japanese trade surplus was nearly the same size as the deployment of its savings in the US. As long as the US has to rely on Japanese savings to fuel its domestic investment, it will necessarily have a trade deficit with Japan. No appreciation of the yen can prevent that.
8. A. Ando, 'On the Japanese Economy and Japanese National Accounts', NBER Working Paper, No. 8033 (2000).
9. Bill Emmott, *Rivals: How the Power Struggle between China, India, and Japan Will Shape the Next Decade* (London: Penguin Books, 2009), p. 93 and p. 99.
10. Emmott, *Rivals*, p. 94.
11. Emmott, *Rivals*, p. 100.
12. Emmott, *Rivals*, p. 102.
13. Emmott, *Rivals*, p. 103.
14. Emmott, *Rivals*, p. 104.
15. Emmott, *Rivals,* p. 115.
16. IMF, 'Japan: Staff Report for the 2015 Article IV Consultation', *IMF Country Report*, No. 15/197 (Washington, DC: IMF, 2015).

17. See D. Lal, *Reviving the Invisible Hand: The Case for Classical Liberalism in the Twenty-First Century* (Princeton, N.J.: Princeton University Press, 2006), Ch. 4.
18. See D. Lal and H. Myint, *The Political Economy of Poverty, Equity and Growth: A Comparative Study* (Oxford: Clarendon Press, 1996).
19. See Chapter 3.
20. The above three paragraphs are from the Foreword to the Russian edition of my *Reviving the Invisible Hand*, which Gaidar launched at a seminar at the Higher School of Economics in September 2009, just a few weeks before his untimely death. Since then many of my fears about Russia have come true.
21. IMF, 'Russian Federation: Staff Report for the 2014 Article IV Consultation', *IMF Country Report*, No 14/175 (Washington, DC: IMF, 2014).
22. Ambrose Evans-Pritchard, 'Oil and Gas Crunch Pushes Russia Closer to Fiscal Crisis', *The Daily Telegraph* (23 July 2015). Available at http://www.telegraph.co.uk/finance/economics/11759391/Oil-and-gas-crunch-pushes-Russia-closer-to-fiscal-crisis.html (last accessed 8 November 2017).

PART III

A Third World War?

CHAPTER NINE

The American Imperium

The US has become the most powerful imperial power since the ascendancy of Rome. As Robert Kagan has argued in his important book *Dangerous Nation*, the American self-image of being an 'inherently isolationist, passive, and restrained' people is seriously misleading. Colonial America was characterized 'not by isolationism and utopianism, not by cities upon hills and covenants with God, but by aggressive expansionism, acquisitive materialism, and an overarching ideology of civilization that encouraged and justified both'.[1] Like Rome, the American colonists did not look upon themselves as expansionist, but as needing continued expansion to secure the foothold they had established in the New World from threats from indigenous Indian tribes and the competing European empires of England, France, and Spain for control of North America.

But the Anglo-American settlers also felt that they were part of English exceptionalism, which saw its 'manifest destiny' in bringing civilizational benefits to 'barbarous nations'. This belief had grown in England after the Glorious Revolution that its inhabitants 'lived on an oasis of freedom in a global desert of tyranny'. Americans are 'still pursuing at least a version of this early English mission, without the aim of territorial conquest but with the same professed purpose of raising "developing" nations up into conformity with advanced civilization'.[2]

Even before their War of Independence, the American colonists were becoming convinced of their imperial destiny. This was due in part to their great economic success. Kagan says: 'Between 1650 and 1770 their gross national product multiplied twenty-five times, increasing at an annual rate of 3.7 percent, with a per capita increase in wealth that was twice that of Britain's. On the eve of the Revolution, Americans had a higher standard of living than any European country.'[3] This growth was based mainly on local markets, capital, and enterprise.

The American colonists were not against the British Empire. Their major disagreement with the mother country, argues Kagan, was over the terms of the empire. Jefferson's appeal to King George was against one legislature within his realm attempting to subjugate another. Jefferson had a federal view of empire 'akin to what [he] would later imagine as the American "empire of liberty". A century and a half later the British themselves would adopt this idea in the form of the British Commonwealth of Nations'.[4]

The Americans, considering themselves the advance guard of British civilization, looked upon the Enlightenment concepts of 'natural rights' and Locke's 'social compact' as the essence of the British liberties they cherished. But, in breaking from the British crown, they insisted that these rights 'were not merely the product and accretion of centuries of English custom and tradition. They were universal rights, granted by God and enjoyed by all men regardless of nationality, culture, and history'. The Americans were the first to base a nation on natural rights. 'The Declaration of Independence was at once the assertion of this radical principle, a justification for rebellion, and the founding document of American nationhood'.[5]

US foreign policy was founded upon this universalist ideology. It allowed them to form alliances with European powers, which was necessary to secure American independence. 'At America's birth, therefore, foreign policy and national identity were intimately bound together, and they would remain so for the next two centuries'. Unlike other nationalisms, the idea of the American nation was based not on a particular territorial history and its ties of soil and blood, but on a common allegiance to the liberal republican ideology. This has meant that Americans have not only been interested in protecting their national interests as classically defined but 'also believed that their own fate was in some way tied to the cause of liberalism and republicanism both within and beyond their borders'.[6]

The domestic issue of slavery tested the sincerity of this American proclamation of universal human rights. As American expansionism led to several international conflicts—from the Spanish American War in 1898 to the Cold War—'fought under the banner of freedom and natural rights, first for Americans themselves and later on behalf of other peoples in other lands, ... they cast a harsh glare upon the hypocrisies of a nation that proclaimed universal rights yet did not universally honor them'.[7] This tension between the US's national founding principles and its conventional national interest has been a continuing problem for its foreign policy.

But this did not prevent it from engaging in perpetual wars for imperial expansion. For, like Rome, despite their professions to the contrary, Americans are a warlike people. The geopolitical forecaster George Friedman has noted that counting only its major wars—the War of 1812 with the British, the Mexican-American War, World Wars I and II, the Korean War, and the Vietnam War—'the US has been at war for about 10 per cent of its existence'. This does not include minor wars like the Spanish-American War, and Desert Storm. Friedman says:

> During the twentieth century, the United States was at war 15 percent of the time. In the second half of the twentieth century, it was at war 22 percent of the time. And since the beginning of the twenty-first century, in 2001, the United States has been constantly at war. War is central to the American experience, and its frequency is constantly increasing. It is built into American culture and deeply rooted in American geopolitics.[8]

Friedman identifies five geopolitical goals, which have and continue to drive America's grand strategy. The first is the complete domination of North America, which it achieved by successively expanding its territory with the Louisiana Purchase of 1803, the Battle of New Orleans in 1814, and the defeat of the Mexican army by the Texans in the battle of San Jacinto in 1836. This secured a vast, rich country dominated by the US Army that no one could challenge. The second was the Monroe Doctrine, which eliminated any threat to the US from any power in the Western hemisphere. The third, achieved by the end of the nineteenth century, was the complete control by the US Navy of the maritime approaches from both the Atlantic and Pacific, which precluded any invasion of the US. The fourth was achieved after the Second World War. The US not only had the world's largest navy but also controlled all the world's oceans. This allows it to shape the international system, for 'no one goes anywhere on the sea if the US doesn't approve. At the end of the day, maintaining its control of the world's oceans is the single most important goal for the US geopolitically'.[9] The fifth and final goal is to prevent any other nation from challenging US global naval power.

The first US president to enunciate America's role as a world power that would take over the historic role that Britain had played in maintaining global order was Theodore Roosevelt.[10] He was the first US citizen and president to be awarded the Nobel Peace Prize for his role in ending the Russo-Japanese war in 1905 by the Treaty of Portsmouth. In his Nobel speech, he affirmed the essential Hobbesian insight that power not principle was essential in managing international affairs. He argued that 'international society was like a frontier settlement without an effective police force' in which 'an honest man must protect himself; and until other means of securing his safety are devised it is both foolish and wicked to persuade him to surrender his arms while the men who are dangerous to the community retain theirs'.[11] He envisaged the US using its growing power to play the role of a 'global balancer', aka global policeman.

The second US president to be awarded the Nobel Peace Prize was Barrack Obama (even before he had done anything for world peace) for promising to end the US's role as 'globocop'. He has done this by, in effect, making the US retire from its role as a superpower.

These two iconic Nobel Peace Prizes may be taken as marking the rise and (current) fall of the US's commitment to global order. But it was Woodrow Wilson who foreshadowed this denouement of US power. After the Allied victory in the First World War, to prevent a resurgent Germany's first bid for the mastery of Europe, Wilson at Versailles destroyed the Age of Empire and, with the United States retreating into isolationism, left global disorder and economic disintegration to rule for nearly a century during the Age of Nations.[12]

After the Second World War, eschewing Wilsonian idealism in practice if not in its rhetoric, America has, at first surreptitiously and recently more openly, taken over the task of maintaining an imperial pax. Not only its relative economic strength but also its ability to transform it into military power leaves it as the only power capable of maintaining the global pax.

But much more importantly, the Americans also have had the revolution in military affairs, giving them an immense lead in new information-based military technologies, which allow their abundant capital resources to substitute for the increasingly scarce and valuable labour. This new military technology, which minimizes the number of body bags in a war, was shown to stunning effect in the recent military operations in Afghanistan and Iraq.[13] The Americans, today, have both a technological and economic preponderance which is uncontestable for at least the rest of the century. Also, unlike much of the rest of Europe, Russia, Japan, and, in the near future, China, the US is forecast to have not a declining but a rising population—largely through immigration.

Thus, today, there is again an imperial power that has an economic and military predominance unseen since the fall of Rome. The US is indubitably an empire. It is more than a hegemon, as it seeks control over not only foreign but also aspects of domestic policy in other countries. But it is an informal and indirect empire. After its nineteenth-century colonial adventure in the Philippines, it has not sought to acquire territory. Nor is it like the Spanish, and many of the ancient predatory empires, a tribute-seeking empire. It is an empire that has taken over from the British the burden of maintaining a pax to allow free trade and commerce to flourish. This pax brings mutual gains. Given the well-known human tendency to free ride, the US, like Britain in the nineteenth century, has borne much of the costs of providing this global public good, not because of altruism but because the mutual gains from a global liberal economic order benefit America and foster its economic well-being.[14] It has not yet been forced in this promotion of globalization to take direct control permanently over areas that have fallen into the black hole of domestic disorder, as was the case, for instance, with the British takeover of the crumbling Moghul empire in eighteenth-century India.

But, the immediate question is whether this current world hegemon (a term which has been described as 'imperialism with good manners') will be able to maintain this status? An answer depends on the three major correlates of power: population size, relative economic strength, and relative military power. Larger populations can mobilize more warriors and, if they are richer, can translate their relative economic strength into a fighting force to protect their own resource base and/or increase it by seizure from others. Military power, on the other hand, is based on the relative availability of technologically superior weapons and the means to deliver them to serve the foreign policy aims of the contestants.

Economic Strength

A measure of economic strength is provided by relative GDP.[15] Table 9.1(A) provides the data on the GDP of the major economies in 2014. It is clear that despite all the hoopla about China about to overtake the US economically, it is still only half the US size at market prices. If the US and its allies' (formal and informal) GDPs listed in the Table are compared with those of the leaders of the emerging League of Dictators—China and Russia—the economic preponderance of the so called Free World is evident (even without taking into account some of the important members like Australia, South Korea, and Singapore, which are not listed).

Table 9.1 Economic Power in the Twenty-First Century

(A) GDP 2014		
	Billions of Current US$	Percentage of US
1. United States	17,419	100
2. China	10,360	59
3. Japan	4,601	26
4. Germany	3,853	22
5. U.K.	2,942	17
6. France	2,829	16
7. Brazil	2,346	14
8. Italy	2,144	12
9. India	2,067	12
10. Russia	1,861	11
11. Canada	1,787	10
12. Spain	1,404	8
13. Turkey	800	5
(B) GDP Per Capita (Current US$)		
	US$	Percentage of US
1. United States	55,200	100
2. Canada	51,690	94
3. Germany	47,640	86
4. Japan	47,000	85
5. France	43,000	78
6. U.K.	42,690	77
7. Italy	34,280	62
8. Spain	29,940	54
9. Russia	13,210	24
10. Brazil	11,530	21
11. Turkey	10,840	20
12. China	7,380	13
13. India	1,570	3

Source: World Bank, national account data, 2014.

If we look at per capita incomes, the US's lead over China and Russia is enormous. In an economically rational world, instead of using their economic resources to challenge the US militarily, they would follow the example of the previous aspirants for regional or world hegemony—Germany and Japan—by following a trading state strategy to attain economic power, thereby greatly benefitting their populations.

Perhaps China's rapid growth will continue and allow it to overtake the US in the near future. But as we saw in Chapter 7, China's fast growth in the past three decades was based on catch-up and is already slowing. By contrast, the US growth rate, despite the hit from the Great Recession and the predictions of the Cassandras, is recovering and not likely to fall drastically.

Figure 9.1 shows the Conference Board's latest predictions of the growth of GDP in the major countries and regions. Taking their predictions for 2021–5 of an average GDP growth rate of 3.5 per cent p.a. for China and 1.5 per cent p.a. for the US and using the GDP figures for 2014 as the base, it would take twenty-seven years for China to close the GDP gap with the US.

Perhaps the best way to summarize the relative economic strength of the US compared with its competitors is to examine the relative economic strength of Britain in the nineteenth century (in 1870)—see Table 9.2(A). Britain, the predominant power, was faced by competitors 'whose combined [economic] weight was *three times larger* than its own'.[16] By contrast, the US is as big as the next three put together, two of which, Germany and Japan, are its allies. Moreover, as Table 9.2(B) shows, even with the rise of China and India, the US percentage of world GDP has remained fairly stable since 1970. The belief in the US's relative economic decline is not justified. It remains and is likely to remain the predominant economic power for the foreseeable future.

What of military power? Figure 9.2 shows some comparative defence statistics from the International Institute for Strategic Studies' (IISS's) *The Military Balance 2015*. With an annual budget of $581 billion in 2014, it dwarfs most of its competitors, accounting for 36 per cent of the world's military total. This accounted for about 3.37 per cent of US GDP in 2014.[17]

But it is the capability to project its military power globally that makes the US able to maintain its global pax. The central instrument is its navy. As Josef Joffe puts it:

> This is where the United States boasts another superlative no other great power can match: naval tonnage, as a rough-and-ready measure of reach and muscle. At the end of the naughts, the U.S. Navy weighed in with 3.1 million tons.... It exceeds the total

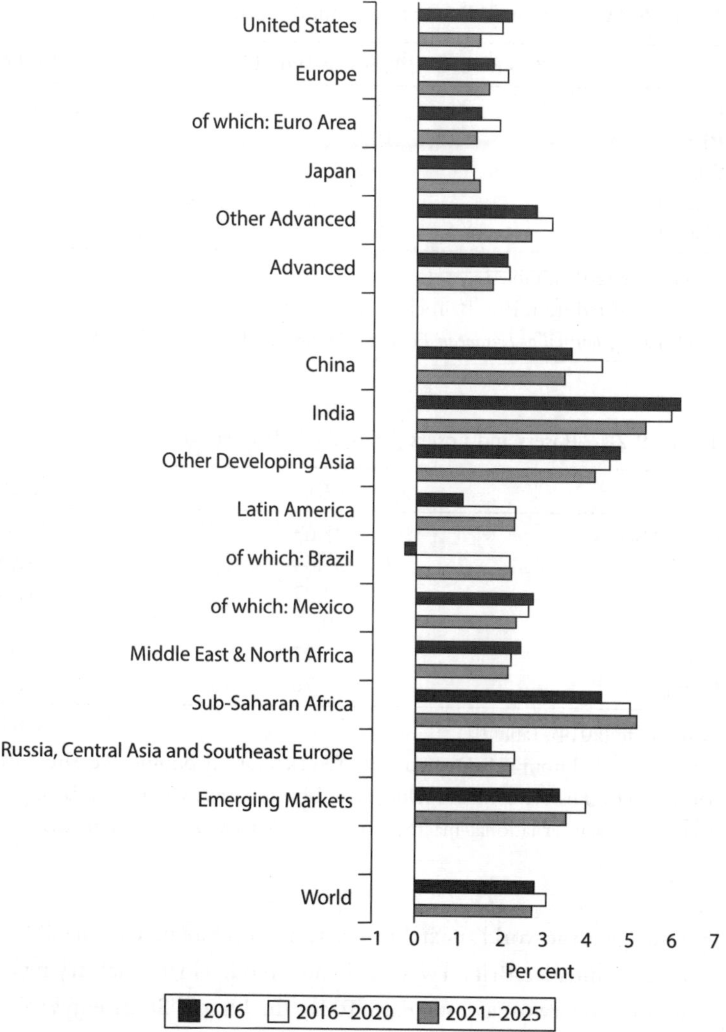

FIGURE 9.1 Growth of GDP, 2016–25

Note: Projections are based on trend growth estimates, which—for the period 2016-2020—are adjusted for remaining output gaps. Europe includes all 28 members of the European Union as well as Switzerland, Norway, and Iceland. Other advanced economies are Australia, Canada, Israel, Hong Kong, South Korea, New Zealand, Singapore, and Taiwan Province of China. Southeast Europe includes Albania, Bosnia and Herzegovina, Macedonia, Serbia and Montenegro, and Turkey.

Source: Conference Board.

Table 9.2a Economic Power in the Nineteenth Century

	GNP 1870 (Billions of 1960 USD)	% of Britain
Russia	22.9	117%
Britain	19.6	100%
France	16.8	86%
Germany	16.6	85%
Habsburg	11.3	58%

Source: Joffe (2014), Table I.
Note: Calculated from Paul Bairoch, 'Europe's Gross National Product, 1800–1975', *Journal of European Economic History*, 5 (1976), pp. 273–340.

Table 9.2b Risers and Losers, 1970–2012: Percentage of World GDP

	1970	2012
United States	27.63	25.37
EU-27	37.64	27.08
Russia	3.27	1.83
Japan	10.07	8.76
India	.97	2.64
China	.76	8.41

Source: Joffe (2014), Table III.
Note: Calculated from U.S. Department of Agriculture, Economic Research Service, 'Real Historical Shares Values'. Available at http://www.ers.usda.gov/data-products/international-macroeconomic-data-set.aspx#.UagMvpymU-w.

> tonnage of the world's next thirteen navies combined. At the height of its dominance, Britain was much more modest in its reach, trying to hold to a two-navy standard. Today, the United States enjoys a *thirteen-navy standard*.... Besides that of the United States, there are only twenty significant navies in the world, that is, with a tonnage (displacement) of 50,000 tons or more. Out of these, eighteen belong to formal allies or friendlies—to nations that will either support the United States in a confrontation or stay out of the fray. That count leaves only China and Russia as worthy opponents.[18]

The major instrument of projecting force is the aircraft carrier. The US has ten, China one, Russia one, India two, France one.[19] All the US carriers are nuclear powered

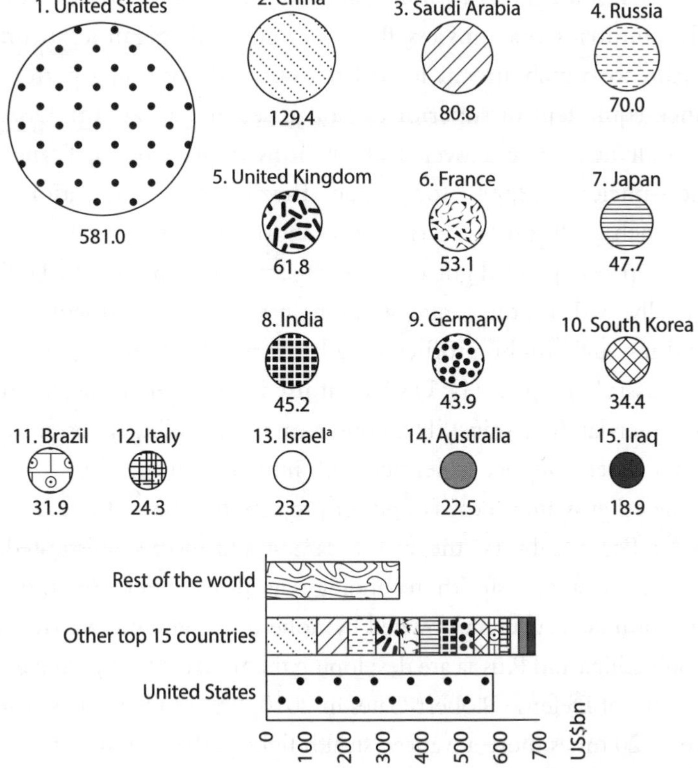

FIGURE 9.2 Top 15 Defence Budgets, 2014, US$ bn
Note: US dollar totals are calculated using average market exchange rates for 2014, derived using IMF data. The relative position of countries will vary not only as a result of actual adjustments in defence spending levels, but also due to exchange-rate fluctuations between domestic currencies and the US dollar. The use of average exchange rates in a small reduces these fluctuations, but the effects of such movements can be significant in a small number of cases.
Source: IISS (2015), p. 21.

and in a class of their own, their displacement exceeding the tonnage of the world's other carriers by factors ranging from two to seven. Three more will go to sea this decade. These behemoths, carrying three times as many planes as China's single carrier, give the United States an 'overwhelming lead in sea-based tactical aviation,' as measured by a seaborne air force that outstrips any other navy's by at least nine hundred aircraft.[20]

Moreover, some aircraft carriers are more equal than others. The only countries that possess fleet carriers with gigantic steam *catapults* to launch aircraft loaded for war and possessing performance equivalent or superior to land-based aircraft are the USA (ten—all nuclear and over 100,000 tons displacement); France (one—nuclear, 42,000 tons); and Brazil (one—conventional, ex-French). All others carry only short take-off aircraft that may (depending on flight deck configuration) also have to land vertically, with all the range, weapons payload, and performance penalties such flight profiles entail: China (1); India (2); Italy (2); Russia (1); Spain (1); USA (9, if used as carriers rather than helicopter-landing ships). Helicopter carriers/landing ships are a further lesser category in service with numerous navies.[21]

The other swifter means of power projection is the air force. The US Air Force 'is by far the world's largest and most sophisticated, given its advanced stealth technology, its drones and 168 fifth-generation tactical aircraft owned by none of its presumptive rivals, though China and Russia are developing them. "By 2929," predicted Secretary of Defense Robert Gates in 2010, "the United States will have.... 20 times more advanced stealth fighters than China."'[22]

The US, today, has a military advantage over its rivals not seen since the Roman empire. Moreover, it has an important advantage over its Roman predecessor. As Joffe says:

> Rome's was an empire of possession; America's is one of bases. The difference between the two is the cost of control. Rome ruled, the United States rents (though the leases are sometimes canceled by landlords whose interests change). Rome conquered, America co-opts.... the American empire has the lightest footprint in history, lighter even than the British one, which could never take a rest from fighting rebellious natives. To lease is cheaper than to own.[23]

America is an indirect empire with an estimated 115 status of force agreements (SOFA)[24] encircling the globe. Britain and France still have few bases. Russia after the collapse of the Soviet Union has about two dozen, but all of them close by in the 'Near Abroad'. Its remaining one in the Middle East in Latakia in Syria is tied to the

Table 9.3 Defence Burdens and Military Expenditure

State	Military Expenditure as % of GDP
Rome (1st–2nd c.)	~45–70%
Habsburg Empire (17th c.)	50–90%
USSR (1981–90)	15.65%
Great Britain (1900)	3.6%
France (end of 17th c.)	~70%

Source: Joffe (2014), Table IX.

fate of Bashar al-Assad in the ongoing Mesopotamian civil war. China has none, but press reports suggest it has acquired one in Gwadar in Pakistan and Djibouti in the Horn of Africa.[25] None of these provide the global reach of the US imperium.

Moreover, compared to past empires (except the British), the costs of maintaining the US pax, as we have seen, is less than 4 per cent of its GDP. As Table 9.3 shows, past empires (except the British) did sink under the military expenditures of maintaining their empires. For the US, it is not the military costs of maintaining its pax but those of the domestic entitlements it has created that could sink its imperium.

There are however fears that the military preponderance that the US had achieved with its 1980s Revolution in Military Affairs (RMA), and most evident in 1991 in the First Gulf War, has dwindled. This is because the IT technologies on which RMA was based have proliferated and become cheaper. 'Colossal computational power, rapid data processing, sophisticated sensors and bandwidth … are all now widely available'.[26] China is seeking to catch up with its stated objective of 'winning a local war in high-tech conditions'. Its aim is to make it too dangerous for US aircraft carriers to operate within the first island chain, and allow it to threaten US bases in Japan and South Korea. This so called 'anti-access/area denial' (A2/AD) strategy is also being developed by Russia, Iran, North Korea, and non-state actors like Hezbollah in Lebanon and ISIS in Mesopotamia. This has led US strategic planners to develop a third offset strategy to maintain its military dominance.[27]

This third offset strategy is based on using the US's advantages in unmanned systems, stealthy aircraft, undersea warfare, and the complex systems engineering required to make everything work together.[28] Much of the research the Pentagon needs is being done by consumer technology companies in Silicon Valley. Artificial intelligence, machine learning, algorithms, big-data processing, 3D printing, compact high-density power systems, and tiny sensors of the kind in smart phones will all be crucial.

To provide the technologies needed for the third offset, the US can rely on a scientific and intellectual infrastructure unmatched by its foes and likely competitors. Of the top twenty universities in the world, seventeen are in the US; of the remainder, two (Oxford and Cambridge) are part of the Anglo world and the third, the University of Tokyo, is part of the Free World. There are no Chinese, Russian, or Indian universities in the top twenty.[29]

In the supply of technology, the US produces 'more science and engineering journal articles than Asia's top ten together, and three times more than China'. In terms of their quality 'in the world's top 1 percent of most-cited articles, the US bests China 49 percent to 4 percent in all fields. It is dramatically more lopsided in subfields like astronomy and biology'.[30]

In terms of patents, according to the OECD ranking of global performance 'the United States leads the pack on "triadic patents", those registered in the United States, the EU, and Japan. The West beats the rest by 85 percent to 15 percent. The BRICs come in at 2 percent. China is listed at the bottom with 1 percent, between Belgium and Austria with their miniscule populations of 11 million and 8 million'.[31]

The myth of China as an emerging technology superpower because of its incredible export growth has been debunked by Michael Beckley.[32] He finds that China is a piggyback economy: 'China's high-technology exports are "not very Chinese, and not very high-tech"—more than 90 per cent are produced by foreign firms and consist of imported components that are merely assembled in China, a practice known as "export processing"'. The foreign share of exports had risen during the naughts, and at their end, it was where it was in the mid-1990s, showing there has been no sign of growing indigenous tech mastery.

The most important reason why the US technological lead will persist is its open door for mobile talent. 'More than three out of every four patents at the top ten patent-producing US universities had at least one foreign-born inventor … Foreign-born inventors played especially large roles in cutting-edge fields that shape the future'. Of the 331 US Nobel Laureates (the largest in the world), one quarter were born abroad. Thus the US, given its openness, has an inexhaustible supply of 'the most mobile capital of all: men and women of ability and ambition. That capital does not wander off to the BRICs'.[33] This will determine relative technological, economic, and military prowess in the twenty-first century and provide the US with the means to maintain its imperium if it is willing.

The US is and is likely to remain the sole superpower for the foreseeable future.

Notes

1. Robert Kagan, *Dangerous Nation: America's Place in the World from Its Earliest Days to the Dawn of the Twentieth Century* (New York: Alfred A. Knopf, 2006), p. 10.
2. Kagan, *Dangerous Nation*, pp. 13–14.
3. Kagan, *Dangerous Nation*, p. 34.
4. Kagan, *Dangerous Nation*, p. 32. It is worth noting that, as I stated in D. Lal, *In Praise of Empires: Globalization and Order* (New York: Palgrave Macmillan, 2004), 'If one reflected on the most important events of the last millennium compared with the first, the ascent of the English-speaking peoples to predominance in the world surely ranked highest' (p. 45). It was Britain's betrayal of the Commonwealth when it joined an EU just as it was beginning to dysfunction in the 1970s that has continued to reverberate in British politics ever since. With Brexit, Britain will be able to find its role in a refurbished Commonwealth including (hopefully) the return of the prodigal son—the US—to lead the association of the English-speaking peoples. For in the words of Andrew Roberts, *A History of*

the English-Speaking Peoples Since 1900 (New York: Harper Perennial, 2008), 'Today they are the last, best hope for Mankind' (p. 647).

5. Kagan, *Dangerous Nation*, p. 41.
6. Kagan, *Dangerous Nation*, p. 42.
7. Kagan, *Dangerous Nation*, p. 44.
8. George Friedman, *The Next 100 Years* (New York: Anchor Books, 2010), pp. 39–40.
9. Friedman, *The Next 100 Years*.
10. As Henry Kissinger, *World Order* (New York: Penguin Press, 2014), notes, Roosevelt pursued an unprecedented foreign policy for the US, based on geopolitical considerations. 'According to it, America as the twentieth century progressed would play a global version of the role that Britain had performed in Europe in the nineteenth century: maintaining peace by guaranteeing equilibrium, hovering offshore of Eurasia, and tilting the balance against any power threatening to dominate a strategic region' (p. 247).
11. Kissinger, *World Order*, p. 248.
12. Wilson, by proclaiming the end of empire and ushering in the Age of Nations, had let the genie of national self-determination out of the bottle, as discussed in Chapter 3.
13. See Max Boot, *War Made New: Technology, Warfare, and the Course of History, 1500 to Today* (New York: Gotham Books, 2006), for details.
14. But recently, President Obama and President Trump have both sought to end this free riding.
15. In Lal, *In Praise of Empires*, I had used the PPP data on relative GDPs to measure this relative strength. But I now believe that GDP at market prices provides a better measure in large part because of the various practical difficulties in deriving believable relative PPP figures. See D. Lal, *Poverty and Progress: Realities and Myths about Global Poverty* (Washington, DC: Cato Institute, 2013; New Delhi: Oxford University Press, 2015), and also because as Josef Joffe, *The Myth of America's Decline: Politics, Economics, and a Half Century of False Prophecies* (New York: Liverlight Publishing, 2014), has argued,

    > Theoretically, PPP is a useful tool, which evens out exchange-rate fluctuations and measures what a dollar actually buys in various countries … In a poor country, labor and land are cheap. Hence a dollar is 'worth more', especially in China, where its buying power is inflated by an artificially low exchange rate … But in the arena of geopolitics and geoeconomics, it is not the low

wage of a migrant worker that counts, or the pittance paid for a haircut or a bowl of rice. It is the price of sophisticated military hardware that China and India buy from Russia, the EU or Israel. High technology, licenses, and oil and other raw materials must also be bought at exchange-rate prices. When the Chinese invest abroad to secure markets, resources, and political allegiance, they must also spend 'real' dollars. So GDP measured in exchange-rate dollars is a more realistic yardstick of national economic power (p. 86).

16. Joffe, *The Myth of America's Decline*, p. 76.
17. IISS, *The Military Balance 2015* (Abingdon: Routledge, 2015), p. 35.
18. Joffe, *The Myth of America's Decline*, p. 94.
19. IISS, *The Military Balance 2015*, p. 24.
20. Joffe, *The Myth of America's Decline*, p. 96, citing Robert O. Work, *The US Navy: Charting a Course for Tomorrow's Fleet* (Washington, DC: Center for Strategic and Budgetary Assessment, 2008), pp. 9–10.
21. I owe this information to MacGregor Knox.
22. Joffe, *The Myth of America's Decline*, p. 96.
23. Joffe, *The Myth of America's Decline*, pp. 99–100.
24. These are classified, but for this estimate, Joffe, *The Myth of America's Decline*, p. 100 cites an op-ed by Secretary of Defense Robert Gates and Secretary of State Condoleezza Rice, 'What We Need Next in Iraq', *Washington Post* (13 February 2008). Available at http://www.washingtonpost.com/wp-dyn/content/article/2008/02/12/AR2008021202001.html (last accessed 9 November 2017).
25. See Andrew Small, *The China–Pakistan Axis: Asia's New Geopolitics* (London: Hurst and Co., 2015), pp. 103–5, on how the economic rationale for Gwadar has been replaced by its use as a potential naval base by Chinese strategists, with the increasing role of the PLA navy in the eastern shores of the Middle East. As part of this strategy, there is a recent report that 'China's navy is seeking a firmer foothold in Africa as the military confirmed it was in talks to open a logistic facility in Djibouti on the Horn of Africa'. See Charles Clover, 'Chinese Seeks Own Navy Facility in Djibouti', *Financial Times* (27 November 2015). Available at https://www.ft.com/content/1c4afbba-94c1-11e5-bd82-c1fb87bef7af (last accessed 9 November 2017).
26. *The Economist*, 'Who's Afraid of America?' (13 June 2015), pp. 62–4.
27. The first offset strategy, to develop technological breakthroughs to offset the advantages of potential foes and reassure friends, was to

counter the Soviet Union's lead in conventional weapons in the 1950s by extending the US's lead in nuclear weapons—the so called 'New Look' strategy. The second offset strategy was developed in the 1970s, once the US realized that the Soviet Union had built an equally large nuclear arsenal. 'Daringly, America responded by investing in a family of untried technologies aimed at destroying enemy forces well behind the front line. Precision-guided missiles, the networked battlefield, reconnaissance satellites, the Global Positioning System (GPS) and radar-beating "stealth" aircraft were among the fruits of the research' (*The Economist*, 'Who's Afraid of America?', p. 62). This was the RMA.

28. *The Economist*, 'Who's Afraid of America?', p. 63. The US is developing 'unmanned combat aircraft that are stealthy enough to penetrate the best air defences and have the range and endurance to pursue mobile targets'. The same technologies could be used in unmanned underwater vehicles, 'to clear mines, hunt enemy submarines in shallow waters, for spying and for resupplying manned submarines, for example, with additional missiles'. To counter the threat to its aircraft carriers, hopes are being placed on two technologies: 'electromagnetic rail guns, which fire projectiles using electricity instead of chemical propellants at 4,500 mph to the edge of space, and so-called directed-energy weapons, most likely powerful lasers. The rail guns are being developed to counter ballistic missile warheads; the lasers could protect against hypersonic cruise missiles. In trials, shots from the lasers cost only a few cents'. To counter the threat against the satellites in its communications networks, 'one option would be to use more robust technologies to transmit data—such as chains of high-altitude, long–endurance drones operating in relays' (p. 64).
29. Joffe, *The Myth of America's Decline*, Table X, p. 178.
30. Joffe, *The Myth of America's Decline*, p. 192.
31. Joffe, *The Myth of America's Decline*, pp. 192–3.
32. Michael Beckley, 'China's Century? Why America's Edge Will Endure', *International Security*, 36, no. 3 (Winter 2011/12), pp. 41–78.
33. Joffe, *The Myth of America's Decline*, p. 205.

CHAPTER TEN

Towards Global Disorder

Recently, the Pope is reported to have declared that we are in the midst of a 'piecemeal World War III'.[1] Given that the US remained the sole superpower after the implosion of the Soviet imperium in1991, how has this come to pass?

The two former Communist imperial behemoths—China and Russia—are again challenging Western hegemony, including its values. The Middle East continues to be in turmoil, with the jihadi ISIS threatening to repeat the feats of the Prophet Muhammad and his successors in creating a new order in the region through a lightning military campaign to conquer Mesopotamia and establish a medieval Salafi Caliphate enforcing sharia law.

The origins of this increasing disorder lie in part in the Great Recession of 2008 in the US, which has tarnished the purportedly free market-based capitalism of the West. An alternative authoritarian capitalism promoted by China and Russia is being claimed as more likely to deliver faster growth, as witnessed by the rising share of these countries in global GDP since the economic crisis of the West. How valid is this analysis and prognosis? I have questioned these economic analyses in Part II and found them wanting.

It is the serious mistakes in maintaining the US's role as the sole superpower under both the younger Bush and Obama that are largely to blame for the growing world disorder. In both Iraq and Afghanistan, the initial military campaigns were resoundingly successful and showed how with its revolution in military affairs, the US is an unmatched military power. But, serious mistakes were made in maintaining and securing the peace. The resultant insurgencies required further expenditure of men and materiel to quell them. This had drastically reduced domestic support in the US for muscular military action.[2]

In Iraq, after the counter insurgency was quelled, much against the dire predictions of the time, relatively free elections were held, and after a hiatus, a multi-ethnic government was formed. But, with Obama's haste in withdrawing all US troops[3] without an agreement (as planned by the Bush administration) to leave a residual force which could have acted as guarantor of a multi-ethnic state, Iraq has again descended into a civil war.[4] With the ongoing one in Syria, this threatens to create a Shia-versus-Sunni war across the Middle East, foretelling another battle of Karbala. Meanwhile, taking advantage of the Syrian Civil War and the military vacuum left in Iraq, the jihadist ISIS has secured vast swathes of territory in northern Syria and large parts of Sunni Iraq to create its Islamic State.

The vacuum left by the US withdrawal is being filled by Russia and Iran, and there is a confusing and confused multi-sided war in Syria between Assad, supported by the Russians and Iran; moderate rebels, allied with the US and some with Turkey; shifting coalitions of non-ISIS jihadist rebels; the Syrian Kurds YPG, allied with the US fighting ISIS; and the Assad regime and Turkey fighting against the YPG and ISIS even though it is a US ally. Meanwhile, millions have been displaced from their homes and are refugees in Lebanon, Jordan, and Turkey. Many of them are seeking safe havens in Europe after Chancellor Merkel opened German borders to Syrian asylum seekers. In Syria, there is in effect a mini–world war.

After the surge in US troops in 2010 in Afghanistan, the Taliban had lost almost all its principal havens in southern Afghanistan; its ability to acquire, transport, and use IEDs had been disrupted; and the International Security Assistance Force (ISAF) was receiving the support of local populations in the fight against the Taliban. In 2011, 'the momentum of the insurgency in the south [had] unquestionably been arrested and probably reversed', wrote Fredrick W. Kagan and Kimberly Kagan,[5] but, Obama made a most heinous mistake in dithering about the Afghan war in his West Point speech, authorizing a troop surge but stating all the troops would be out by 2012.

Though he then backtracked, the lesson US adversaries have learnt was articulated by Hamid Gul, the notorious former head of Pakistan's Inter-Services Intelligence (ISI), who said this 'makes clear that the Taliban are Afghanistan's future, and the Americans are its past'.[6] It is this perception that has given heart to the Pakistan army in its Af-Pak strategy of asymmetric warfare against India and, clandestinely, against the Afghan government. With Obama's commitment to withdraw most US troops by 2016, though then extended to after he left the presidency, Gul's prediction is likely to come true.

For, despite the seemingly difficult hand dealt him by the financial crisis, Obama compounded the US's seeming weakness in fulfilling its superpower role by various missteps, which have led to the impression of the US as a declining superpower. Obama seems to have blinked so often in his time in office that it has worried friends and bolstered US rivals.[7]

The first such 'blink' was unilaterally withdrawing the missile shield aimed at Iran under Russian pressure without getting anything in return and, in the process, letting down the East European countries which were to host the relevant bases. The hope that this 'resetting' of the button would lead to Russian pressure on the Iranians in the nuclear standoff was belied when Putin told then–Secretary of State Hilary Clinton bluntly that Russia would assist Iran in fuelling the Russian-built Bushehr nuclear reactor, which Clinton gamely accepted as being within Iran's rights.

After the Russian invasion of Crimea, Obama belatedly began to confront Putin. The missile shield is rightly being resurrected. Also, despite opposition from the Germans, French, and Italians, Obama reluctantly and in small ways began to face Russia down in Eastern Europe and the Baltics. The US is committing trip-wire forces to NATO, backed up with pre-positioned equipment and airpower, and will be contributing more with the firm support of the Poles and the Baltics.

Nor is Obama's much hyped START II agreement worth much. Under the 2002 Moscow treaty, Bush had already cut the number of US warheads to 2,000—which is not much changed by the new treaty. But, Russia has maintained its right to withdraw from the agreement if the US pursued its missile defence programme, something that Gorbachev sought and was denied in Reagan's abortive attempt to eliminate nuclear weapons. Combined with Obama's promise in his Nuclear Posture Review strategy not to modernize the US nuclear arsenal, the deterrent power of US nuclear arms—which has been the best non-proliferation weapon, as many countries with the ability to develop nuclear weapons have relied on the American nuclear umbrella—will be diminished. Taken together, these two prongs of Obama's nuclear strategy have made an already dangerous world even more dangerous, as more states are likely to develop and rely on their own nuclear weapons. However, under prodding from the much-decried 'military-industrial' complex, Obama reluctantly inaugurated a serious renovation of the US nuclear arsenal and of its delivery systems. These were a response to Russian nuclear sabre rattling and traditional treaty violations and to China's force modernization initiatives.

Then, there was Obama's blinking after he had promised to intervene in the Syrian Civil War if Assad used chemical weapons.[8] The Russians saved his face by persuading Assad to dismantle much of his chemical arsenal but, as recent events have shown, not all. This blink and his failure to enforce an Status of Forces Agreement (SOFA) on Iraq's government has led to the growing multi-faceted sectarian divide in Mesopotamia, as enforcement would have kept a substantial US military presence in Iraq, preventing both the divisive sectarian policies of Maliki and the rise of the new incarnation of al-Qaeda in Iraq in the form of ISIS—which Petraeus's surge had defeated.

But, given the disorder and human misery the rise of ISIS has caused, Obama was reluctantly forced to recommit small numbers of ground troops to Syria and Iraq. His main instrument of warfare in the greater Middle East (including Afghanistan) was the unmanned drone and special force deployments. Their cold-blooded use to kill US enemies, most importantly Osama bin Laden and Anwar al-Awlaki (a US citizen), is significant, but there is a question whether such assassinations are effective in quelling terrorist threats.

Israel pioneered the ruthless dispatch of terrorist leaders one by one. Obama followed them in his drone war against al-Qaeda and then ISIS leaders. But, as David Blair[9] has noted, Ami Ayalon, the head of the Israeli secret service, had observed that 'in 2004, Israel killed two successive leaders of Hamas in a month.... Yet Israel did not make itself safe from terrorism'. Yet the targeted killings of al-Qaeda's leaders do seem to have reduced its effectiveness. The reason of the difference in outcomes is that Hamas is not the brainchild of one man—Osama bin Laden—but formed due to deeper currents within the Israeli–Palestinian conflict. So, unlike al-Qaeda, individuals are not vital to Hamas; those who are killed can be replaced. Whether the targeted drone killings of ISIS's leaders will halt its progress depends upon whether it is more like Hamas or al-Qaeda. We will have to wait and see.

Obama's actions in promoting and, as he hoped, enforcing a nuclear deal with Iran, which he hoped to be an important foreign policy legacy, is being increasingly questioned. It has led to fierce debates in the US about its pros and cons. There are those like the editor of the *National Interest*, Jacob Heilbrunn,[10] who argue that the deal does not go far enough. Heilbrunn favours a grand US strategy in the Middle East in an alliance with Iran. He sees Saudi Arabia as an unreliable and hostile ally. He says, 'Neither country deserves unqualified US allegiance. But reaching an accommodation with Iran would give America a freer hand to play them off against each other, creating a more peaceful balance of power'.

Against this, Henry Kissinger and George Shultz, two of the most distinguished US secretaries of state, have argued[11] that if a balance of power between Iranian and Sunni competition were the US aim as it dissociates itself from Middle East conflicts, 'traditional balance of power theory suggests the need to bolster the weaker side, not the rising or expanding power'. Hence, they argue, as Iran has intensified its efforts to expand and entrench its power in neighbouring states, 'unless political restraint is linked to nuclear restraint, an agreement freeing Iran from sanctions risks empowering Iran's hegemonic efforts'. They rightly conclude, despite Obama's claims, this agreement in effect recognizes Iran as a threshold nuclear state.

Does this matter? In a 1995 paper,[12] I had argued that, even though the benefits in terms of military security provided by nuclear weapons remained inconclusive, and despite the axiomatic abhorrence of nuclear weapons, the fact remains that in spite of their apocalyptic potential, nuclear weapons have not killed anyone since the end of the Second World War. Also, as Lawrence Freedman noted, 'What we do know is that since 1945 Europe has been at peace. This underlies the point that nuclear deterrence maybe a viable policy even if it is not credible ... The Emperor Deterrence may have no clothes, but he is still Emperor'.[13] This is a fact further strengthened by the recent disturbance of the European peace by Putin's annexation of Crimea. This would not have been possible if Ukraine had not given up its nuclear weapons in exchange for the 1994 Budapest Memorandum signed by the US, Britain, and Russia to protect its territorial integrity. This shows the continuing relevance of Hobbes's dictum that 'covenants without the sword, are but words, and no strength to secure a man at all'.

This dictum is also of relevance because of the nuclear arms race that a Shia-Iranian bomb is likely to induce among the major Sunni powers of Saudi Arabia, Turkey, and Egypt. Some have argued that Saudi Arabia already has an implicit lien on Pakistan's Sunni bomb. But with the recent refusal of Pakistan's Parliament to send troops and planes in support of the Saudi-led coalition in Yemen, this must now be in doubt. Others hope that a US nuclear umbrella to the Sunni states can prevent a nuclear arms race in the Middle East. But how credible would such a guarantee be if

Obama has eschewed the use of US military force? As Kissinger and Schultz have rightly argued, 'Previous thinking on nuclear strategy assumed the existence of stable state actors.... How will these doctrines translate into a region where sponsorship of non-state proxies is common, the state structure is under assault, and death on behalf of jihad is a kind of ulfilment?'

When I was a student at Oxford in the early 1960s, a board game called Diplomacy was based on the map of Europe before the First World War. This was replaced by a version with a map based on the Middle East situation in the late 1960s (which was much more benign than it is now). This version provided nuclear as well as conventional arms to the various players. No matter how often we played the game—with different permutations of players and countries, using the rational tactics for a repeated game of chicken, or the tit-for-tat strategy of the prisoner's dilemma, or no strategy at all—within about half an hour, the game usually ended with nuclear bombs having been unleashed on all of the major population centres of the Middle East.

It is for this reason that while having supported the Indian and been relaxed about the Pakistani bomb, I would endorse the US policy of not accepting an Iranian bomb. This means that the sanctions that have brought Iran to the negotiating table should not have been removed until a better deal was negotiated, one which fulfils the goal set out over twenty years by three US presidents (as Kissinger and Schultz note) 'that an Iranian nuclear weapon was contrary to American and global interests—and they were prepared to use force to prevent it.'

But with President Trump's objections and explicit repudiation of Obama's Iranian nuclear deal its future remains clouded. What it has succeeded in promoting is a coalition of Sunni Arab states led by Saudi Arabia seeking to offset the Shia hegemony which they see Iran promoting. President Trump appears to be siding with the Saudi led coalition, which also appears to have the implicit support of Israel. This could lead to another battle of Karbala with the apocalyptic outcomes in the Middle East of the board game we played in Oxford in the 1960s.

Obama's one important and correct initiative was to try and switch the focus of US foreign policy from entanglements in Europe and the Middle East and 'to pivot to Asia'. Though for much of his administration this was largely rhetoric, more recently, as China has trumpeted its 'Chinese Dream' and some of its PLA hawks are arguing for a 'short, sharp war' in the Western Pacific while displaying their shiny new assets, the US Navy and Air Force are developing weapons programmes which promise an effective response to this challenge. The Chinese have obviously forgotten what happened when a paranoid Japan similarly took on what it saw as a weakened and declining power after the Great Depression.

But these belated attempts by Obama to undo the damage to world order that his previous missteps had caused only underline the importance of credible threats of using military force to deter one's enemies. Why has this happened? A perceptive essay by James Traub provides some answers.[14] Obama has a rare gift of speech, which, as he notes in his *Dreams from My Father*, he discovered when as an undergraduate he was asked to give a two-minute speech against the South African apartheid regime at Occidental College in Los Angeles, and all the people playing Frisbee on the lawn stopped to listen. 'I noticed', he writes, 'that people had begun to listen to my opinions. It was a discovery that made me hungry for words. Not words to hide behind but words that could carry a message, support an idea'.[15]

In his first term, Obama gave many foreign policy speeches based on the idealism to 'choose', as he said, 'to work for the world as it *should* be'.[16] Traub says that Obama and his advisors believed that the 'great issues confronting the United States were not the traditional state-to-state questions, but new ones that sought to advance global goods and required global cooperation'. Obama saw himself, as he explained to Traub, with 'a grandmother living in a hut on Lake Victoria and a sister who's half-Indonesian, married to a Chinese–Canadian', as destined to provide the leadership 'needed to enlist the support of citizens as well as leaders'.

He offered a new American narrative to audiences around the world in 2009, including in Moscow where 'Vladimir Putin … must have laughed up his sleeve when he heard Obama say, "The pursuit of power is no longer a zero-sum game"'. But, 'to this day', Traub says, 'his world view is assessed on the single question of when and where he is prepared to use force'.

Increasingly in his second term, this idealist president was mugged by reality. He was, says Traub 'becalmed before a listless and surly public, an openly hostile and increasingly isolationist Congress, and a disintegrating order in the Middle East'. The bright young man, whose face had become sallow, and hair turned to grey, who offered hope and change, increasingly appeared to be broken. 'Obama's trajectory is that of a gifted orator who learned over time that he had put too much store in speech itself.' The world is left with the disorder provoked by his reliance on rhetoric rather than the robust action expected of a superpower.[17]

In a series of fascinating interviews with Jeffrey Goldberg in *The Atlantic*,[18] President Obama has sought to defend his view of America's role in the world and in particular in the Syrian Civil War. As a number of commentators have noted, he displays a surprising arrogance, considering himself, the smartest person in the world, while traducing former presidents, foreign policy advisors, and US allies.

So what was Obama's world view? Goldberg writes, 'He has a tragic realist's understanding of sin, cowardice, and corruption, and a Hobbesian appreciation of how fear shapes human behavior. And yet he consistently, and with apparent sincerity, professes optimism that the world is bending toward justice. He is, in a way, a Hobbesian optimist'. In his optimism, he is echoing the flawed views of Steven Pinker's *The Better Angels of Our Nature*—that the dove has tamed the wolf in human nature, and war may now be defunct. I have questioned this view in Chapter 1.

Obama half realized the US's imperial responsibility for providing the global good of world order. But, says Goldberg, 'He is the rare president who seems at times to resent indispensability, rather than embrace it. "Free riders aggravate me", he told me'. It is his 'mission', Obama explains to Goldberg, 'to spur other countries to take action for themselves, rather than wait for the U.S. to lead'. This led, as he admits, to the Libyan fiasco.

Ultimately, Obama recognizes that it is his Syrian policy by which his presidency will be judged. Goldberg notes that the day when Obama paused to implement his 'red line' against Assad's use of chemical weapons was either 'the day the feckless Barack Obama brought to a premature end America's reign as the world's sole indispensable superpower—or, alternatively, the day the sagacious Barack Obama peered into the Middle Eastern abyss and stepped back from the consuming void'. On the first, his critics are right about the loss of US credibility. As Joe Biden said, 'Big nations do not bluff'. But, the second view is also correct. Though it should be emphasized that given Obama's withdrawal from Iraq, foretelling his desire to rid himself of what he saw as the Middle Eastern albatross, he should have established a 'no-fly zone' in Syria, as the Turks had wanted. This would have grounded Assad's airplanes and the barrel bombs that led to so much civil destruction, but laid down no 'red line' that Obama was unwilling to enforce.

Much worse, the decision not to force Maliki to accept another SFO from 2012 (to replace the earlier one signed by President George W. Bush) meant that the military beachhead—which had been established after General Petraeus's 'surge' had becalmed Iraq's sectarian wars and taken out al-Qaeda in Iraq—was no longer available to stop al-Qaeda's resurgence as ISIS. Realizing the importance of such a military beachhead, President Putin, by contrast, has used his military installations in the port of Tartus to shore up his ally Assad and has left enough military presence behind to maintain Russia's military role in a region that Obama had abdicated.

The great irony, however, as Tamara Cofman Wittes points out, is that avoiding intervention in Syria, which Obama saw as a slippery slope, led to the slipperiest slope of all in Obama's fight against ISIS. For, as Wittes notes, he had to recommit 'American blood and treasure to fighting Islamist extremists on the ground in Iraq, and now in Syria.... An American president who, in May 2013, rejected the notion of a "global war on terror" has now launched one'. At the very end of his presidency, Wittes says, Obama recreated 'the very situation he inherited, decried, and swore to avoid: an escalating war against a vague terrorist enemy, with no geographic boundaries, no clear military or strategic objectives, and no principles or policies that might stop the slide down this slippery slope'.[19]

Meanwhile, Obama's abdication of America's decades-old role as the dominant power in the Middle East to maintain order has led to Russia and Iran filling the vacuum. President Putin has been particularly deft in recognizing that Obama's doctrine provided an opportunity to pursue his own geopolitical ambitions in the Middle East. By co-operating with Obama's global agenda in facilitating the Iran nuclear deal and getting Assad to give up his chemical weapons, and then through a short surgical air operation to buttress his Syrian ally, he has become an essential player in any Syrian settlement. He hopes to use the leverage this provides to weaken the sanctions imposed after his Crimean invasion.

By contrast, Obama is counting on 'the arc of history' to sort out the Middle East. The Obama Doctrine is thus that of a Pontius Pilate washing his hands off his personal responsibility for undermining the American pax.[20]

Unfortunately, Obama seems more and more to resemble a Democratic predecessor, Jimmy Carter. I was in Washington when the Soviets marched into Afghanistan. Carter's prime-time broadcast, which followed, is seared in my memory. There was the ashen-faced president of the US—the defender of the free world—saying he had been assured by the Soviet president that they would not go into Afghanistan!

But, a great virtue of the US political system is that a limp Carter was soon followed by a robust Reagan, who restored the US's superpower status. Given that the US still has all the means to remain a superpower, it would be a serious error for its competitors to believe that there will be no turn in the political wheel, bringing a more assertive administration to power to restore its superpower status. Whether this will happen under President Trump remains to be seen.

Notes

1. See Lisa Pollack, 'A Online Dialogue of First World Problems', *Financial Times* (30 September 2014). Available at https://www.ft.com/content/cc68b72e-3f4c-11e4-984b-00144feabdc0 (last accessed 17 November 2017).
2. In D. Lal, *In Praise of Empires: Globalization and Order* (New York: Palgrave Macmillan, 2004), I had argued the US invasion to topple Saddam Hussein was justified not because of his unsupported and dubious links to al-Qaida, nor his purported continuation of developing weapons of mass destruction, but because of his broken promises to meet the terms of the ceasefire for the First Gulf War over twelve years. 'This was a just war' (pp. 199–200).

   I had also noted the foolish 'dismantling of the only two national institutions which had (however brutally) maintained order in the past—the Iraqi army and the Baath party—without having replacements in the wings' (p. 201). I had also questioned the 'assumption that constructing liberal democracies is possible in the most inhospitable climates' (p. 201), and argued for a loose confederation of Kurdish, Sunni and Shia states. For a US general's analysis of the US's failure in Iraq and Afghanistan, see Daniel P. Bolger, *Why We Lost: A General's Inside Account of the Iraq and Afghanistan Wars* (New York: Houghton Mifflin Harcourt, 2014).

   In Afghanistan, after the brilliant military campaign that dislodged the Taliban, the US attempt to create a democratic, liberal state and a market economy failed. As Jack Fairweather, *The Good War: Why We Couldn't Win the War or the Peace in Afghanistan* (New York: Basic Books, 2014), notes at the end of his exhaustive account of the war, 'the "irresistible illusion" is how Rory Stewart characterized the draw of the Good War. That messianic vision is rooted in the belief that all societies aspire to achieve western-style democracy and that promoting such democracies makes the world more secure and just' (p. 331). He commends grass-roots solutions based on the self-interest of the relevant communities. This requires preventing the Taliban or foreign interests imposing their own hegemonic order. For my own take on the failures in Afghanistan, see D. Lal, 'Endangering the War on Terror by the War on Drugs', *World Economics*, vol. 9, no. 3, July–Sept. 2008, pp. 1–29; reprinted in Lal: *Lost Causes* (London: Biteback Publishing, 2012).

3. However, many are rightly questioning Obama's withdrawal from Iraq, which along with the Syrian Civil War has led to the rise of ISIS. As Tamara Cofman Wittes, who was deputy assistant secretary of state for Near Eastern Affairs from 2009–12, writes, 'after Iraq held elections in 2010, the Obama administration took a hands-off approach to Iraqi domestic politics ... The President and Vice President Biden chose to do very little to constrain Maliki as he began to unravel the tentative political bargains between Sunnis, Shiites and Kurds within federal Iraq'. See Tamara Cofman Wittes, 'The Slipperiest Slope of Them All', *Brookings*, Markaz blog (15 March 2016). Available at https://www.brookings.edu/blog/markaz/2016/03/15/the-slipperiest-slope-of-them-all/ (last accessed 17 November 2017).
4. In a recent interview, the former US Defense Secretary Robert Gates said he 'believes that the outcome [in Iraq] could have been different if the U.S. had kept troops in place. Islamic State wouldn't have spread its influence across the border from Syria. More important than firepower, he says, was having a four-star representative of the U.S. military present who could "bring Sunni and Kurdish and Shia leaders together, make them talk to each other. When that process disappeared, all the external brakes on Maliki disappeared"'.

   On the Arab Spring, 'unbidden, he mentions ... that, along with the entire Obama national-security team, he opposed the president's insistence that Hosni Mubarak of Egypt step down. The White House was also unwise, he adds, to publicly insist that Bashar Assad must go after the Syrian uprising. "I don't think presidents should commit to things they have no idea how to make happen," he says.

   On the Iran nuclear deal, 'his biggest complaint is its missing corollary—the lack of a strong signal that the U.S. remains committed to Iran's geopolitical containment.' The result, he says, is that allies like the Saudis and Israelis now fear the US is deliberately acquiescing in Iran's emergence as the new hegemon in the region. He says the 'real problem with U.S. policy has been the absence of any clear strategy like the one that guided the U.S. in the Cold

War.' See Holman W. Jenkins, Jr., 'The Weekend Interview: The U.S. Has No Global Strategy', *Wall Street Journal* (29 January 2016). Available at https://www.wsj.com/articles/the-u-s-has-no-global-strategy-1454108567 (last accessed 17 November 2017).

5. Fredrick W. Kagan and Kimberly Kagan, *Defining Success in Afghanistan* (Washington, DC: American Enterprise institute, 2011), p. 5.
6. See The Middle East Media Research Institute (MEMRI), 'Former Chief of Pakistani ISI Lt.-Gen. Hamid Gul: I Am an Ideologue of Jihad; as far as al-Qaeda Is Concerned—Come Up With the Evidence for 9/11; You Haven't Even Charged Osama bin Laden; It Is Very Clear That Obama's State of the Union Address Did Not Focus on Terrorism; After Obama's December 1 Speech, It's Clear That the Taliban Are Afghanistan's Future—And the Americans Are Its Past', MEMRI, Special Dispatch No. 2895 (7 April 2010). Available at https://www.memri.org/reports/former-chief-pakistani-isi-lt-gen-hamid-gul-i-am-ideologue-jihad-far-al-qaeda-concerned-%E2%80%93 (last accessed 17 November 2017).
7. See James Mann, *The Obamians: The Struggle inside the White House to Redefine American Power* (New York: Viking Penguin, 2012); and Vali Nasr, *The Dispensable Nation: American Foreign Policy in Retreat* (New York: Doubleday, 2013).
8. In a recent column, the Canadian academic and politician Michael Ignatieff has rightly noted that once Obama had let Assad cross his '"red line"… America was left with a policy in Syria that dare not speak its name'. This is 'to allow Mr Assad and Russian president Vladimir Putin to win by focusing attacks on anti-regime rebels in strongholds such as Aleppo—and then, after a decent interval, to join with them to crush the militants of Isis'. See Michael Ignatieff, 'A Syria Policy That Dares Not Speak Its Name', *Financial Times* (15 February 2016). Available at https://www.ft.com/content/97b863fe-d3ec-11e5-829b-8564e7528e54 (last accessed 17 November 2017).
9. David Blair, 'If You Cut the Head Off a Snake, Will it Grow Another or Simply Die?', *Sunday Telegraph* (4 September 2016).
10. Jacob Heilbrunn, 'Detente Will Force Iran to Compromise with US or Collapse', *Financial Times* (9 April 2015). Available at https://www.ft.com/content/fb43328a-dea3-11e4-b9ec-00144feab7de (last accessed 17 November 2017).

11. Henry Kissinger and George Shultz, 'The Iran Deal and Its Consequences', *Wall Street Journal* (7 April 2015). Available at https://www.wsj.com/articles/the-iran-deal-and-its-consequences-1428447582 (last accessed 17 November 2017).
12. D. Lal, 'Arms and the Man: Costs and Benefits of Nuclear Weapons', in D. Lal, *Unfinished Business: India in the World Economy* (New Delhi: Oxford University Press, 1999 [1995]), pp. 195–210.
13. Lawrence Freedman, *The Evolution of Nuclear Strategy* (London: Macmillan, 1981), p. 399.
14. James Traub, 'When Did Obama Give Up?' *Foreign Policy* (26 February 2015). Available at http://foreignpolicy.com/2015/02/26/when-did-obama-give-up-speeches/ (last accessed 17 November 2017).
15. Barack Obama, *Dreams from My Father: A Story of Race and Inheritance* (New York: Times Books, 1995), p. 105.
16. Traub [2015], emphasis mine.
17. Ironically, as Bruce Thornton noted, Jimmy Carter made news recently for criticizing Barack Obama's foreign policy record. Asked about Obama's 'successes', Carter said they were 'minimal', adding, 'I can't think of many nations in the world where we have a better relationship now than we did when he took over.'

    Thornton then goes on to argue Obama's failures are due to the same bad ideas as Carter's, 'a distrust of American power and influence, a skepticism about America as a force for good in the world, and a preference for diplomatic engagement predicated on a massive failure of imagination in understanding the motives and aims of our adversaries'. See Bruce Thornton, 'Carter and Obama: How To Fail at Foreign Policy', *Frontpage Mag* (6 July 2015). Available at http://www.frontpagemag.com/fpm/259361/carter-and-obama-how-fail-foreign-policy-bruce-thornton (last accessed 17 November 2017).
18. Jeffrey Goldberg, 'The Obama Doctrine', *The Atlantic* (April 2016). Available at https://www.theatlantic.com/magazine/archive/2016/04/the-obama-doctrine/471525/ (last accessed 17 November 2017).
19. Wittes, 'The Slipperiest Slope of Them All'.
20. An apologia for Obama's foreign policy has recently appeared by a senior official who served in the National Security Council, State Department, and the Pentagon, Derek Chollet, *The Long Game: How Obama Defied Washington and Redefined America's Role in the World* (New York: Public Affairs, 2016). He argues that like

Warren Buffet, Obama is playing a long game in a foreign policy debate dominated by day traders. He provides a checklist Obama formulated for this long game for managing American power and making strategic choices. The review of the book in the *Economist* rightly notes, 'But eminently sensible though the checklist appears to be, rather than setting the appropriate conditions for action, it can also be used as way to do too little, too late'. It concluded: 'The president is far from being the feckless wuss portrayed by his critics. But nor is he the master of grand strategy that Mr Chollet makes him out to be. His contempt for the interventionist excesses of his predecessor, his suspicion of arguments to "do more", his arrogant disdain for military advice and his ingrained pessimism about the utility of hard power have had the effect of reducing America's capacity to do good in a bad world.' I agree. See 'Playing It Long', *The Economist* (30 July 2016). Available at https://www.economist.com/news/books-and-arts/21702733-new-book-argues-barack-obamas-grand-strategy-has-made-america-stronger-both-home (last accessed 17 November 2017).

CHAPTER ELEVEN

Flashpoints

The seventy-year peace under the liberal order, recreated and maintained by Pax Americana, is now under threat in Eurasia by three authoritarian and illiberal adversaries: the Islamists in the Middle East and the antagonists in the Sunni-Shia proxy wars, the revanchist Putin in Russia, and China's authoritarian Leninist Communist party (CCP). They are creating regional disorder in the Middle East, Europe, and the Far East. Territorial boundaries, ideological differences, growing nationalism, and a desire to subvert and undermine the global order provided by the US imperium are the major determinants of the militancy of these authoritarian protagonists. With a reluctant superpower no longer willing to be the global policeman, how can the others in the affected regions contain or stem this disorder? I examine each of these regional flashpoints, which are part of the 'piecemeal World War III' feared by the Pope.

Middle East

This is the region encompassing North Africa, Egypt, Israel, Jordan, the old Mesopotamia, Iran, and also what is labelled as Af-Pak. We have seen in Part I how the state system established by the post–World War One settlement in the region is unravelling due to the rise of political Islam under the two rival authoritarian theocratic sectarian powers: the Shia theocracy of Iran and the Wahhabi Sunni theocracy of Saudi Arabia. Both have used their oil wealth to sponsor proxy wars in the region. Both have also sponsored terrorists to further their political aims.

With the relentless march of ISIS through Iraq and Syria, and after its defeat, Syria is left destroyed and fragmented. Its civil war is in a stalemate with various proxies for the outside powers Russia, Iran, the US and Turkey controlling various parts of the country. In Iraq there is a soft partition of the country between the Kurds, the Shias supported by Iran and the Sunni tribesmen who turned against Isis. The main winner in both Iraq and Syria is Iran. It can now envisage a hegemony through proxies, running from Baghdad to Damascus to Beirut restoring it as a great power in Mesopotamia. The other winner in this conflict is Russia. President Putin contributed to ISIS' defeat, prevented Assad from being deposed, and restored Russia as a great power in the Mediterranean. But a political settlement in Syria which would allow him to extricate himself from the Syrian turmoil still seems a long way off.[1] What is certain is that the Sykes–Picot agreement—the basis for the postwar political geography of Mesopotamia—lies in tatters.[2] What are the likely outcomes, and how can the rest of the world deal with the blowback arising from this unravelling?

David Fromkin, in his *A Peace to End All Peace*,[3] identifies the flawed assumption in the Versailles settlement. The modern system of politics invented in Europe, 'characterized by the division of the earth into independent secular states based on national citizenship' could be implanted in the Middle East. What was not recognized (even today) is that 'at least one of these assumptions, the modern belief in secular civil government, is an alien creed in a region most of whose inhabitants for more than a thousand years have avowed faith in a Holy Law that governs all life including government and politics'.[4]

This is confirmed by the latest attempts to establish liberal democracies in West Asia. A detailed study of the electoral outcomes after the Arab Spring by Shadi Hamid[5] (as discussed in Chapter 3) finds that in democratic elections, political Islam has a dominant resonance. So elections lead to *illiberal* democracies, and the supporters of liberal democracy are left with the Hobson's choice of supporting either illiberal democracy or a form of liberal authoritarianism.

Moreover, in an echo of Europe's seventeenth-century Thirty Years' War of religion, the rise of ISIS and the proxy battles between the theocratic regimes of Iran and Saudi Arabia are leading to another battle of Karbala. Meanwhile, a de facto partition of Iraq into a Kurdistan (promised but not implemented in 1921), a Shia Iranian protectorate east and south of Baghdad, and the Sunni Heartland controlled by 'non- ISIS Sunni tribesmen are already in place. Furthermore, the civil war in Syria, despite ISIS' defeat, continues between Assad, ISIS, various other jihadis, and the Syrian Kurds. They have been supported by Russia, the US, and regional powers Turkey, Iran, Saudi Arabia, and the Gulf states into a bewildering mosaic of warring coalitions. With so many contestants, some incident involving the major powers could lead to a wider war. The Syrian Civil War has led to millions of refugees fleeing across the Mediterranean and seeking asylum in the EU. The embedding of terrorists among the refugees is putting the 'open borders' policy of the EU at risk. Along with Brexit (discussed in Chapter 2 and Chapter 5), the survival of the EU as a serious global power must be in question.

Terrorism

The votaries of political Islam, particularly ISIS, the Taliban, and various offshoots of al-Qaeda, have indulged in various acts of terror as a form of guerrilla war, not only in the battlegrounds of West Asia but also in Europe and the US. Though it was the attack on the Twin Towers on 9/11 that signalled this global war by political Islam through terrorism, how serious is it in causing global disorder?

In his *Invisible Armies* (2013), an important book, Max Boot has shown that this is the third wave of terrorism that has struck the West, and it is not the worst.

The first wave was of the anarchists between the 1880s and the 1920s. Their worst attack used a horse-drawn wagon filled with explosives to kill thirty-eight on Wall Street in New York in 1920. Other anarchist bomb attacks include one in Barcelona's opera house, killing twenty-two people in 1893, and eleven attacks in Paris between 1892 and 1894, killing nine people. The anarchists' chief modus operandi was assassination. No terrorist group has murdered so many leaders: the president of France, the prime minister of Spain, the empress of Austria-Hungary, the king of Italy, President William McKinley in the US, and Tsar Alexander II of Russia. This wave died out as anarchist ideology lost its appeal and was succeeded by the Bolsheviks who, instead of bombings, used subversion and military conquest to subserve their cause. This wave led to the creation of Britain's Special Branch to investigate political crimes and of Interpol to link Western police forces.

The second wave was from the 1960s to the 1980s. It was conducted by leftist and nationalist terrorists: the PLO, the Popular Front for the Liberation of Palestine (PFLP), the Red Army faction in West Germany, the Red Brigades in Italy, and the Irish Republican Army (IRA) in Britain. In four years, between 1970 and early 1990, four hundred people were killed in Western Europe, and in five years, 250 were killed. The attacks included the bombing of a Pan Am plane over Lockerbie; attacks on airports in Rome and Vienna; the bombing of the Bologna railway station; and the attack on the 1972 Munich Olympics. There was also the attempt by the IRA to assassinate Mrs Thatcher at the Conservative Party conference in Brighton. This wave ended as the terrorists lost their ideological motivation, partly because the nationalist groups like the PLO and IRA were propitiated by negotiations and territorial compromises, while the leftists imploded with the Soviet Union.

The current third wave of Islamist terrorism has not been as bad as the second terrorist wave and, like it, is likely to end when

Islamist ideology is discredited as 'it fails in Taliban-era Afghanistan or present day Iran or Islamic State'. There is no way to stop these low-tech attacks and, just as with the second wave, 'we will have to tough it out while the ideological extremism of the Islamic world burns itself out'.[6]

The 'war on terror' has not been a success. When it was launched in 2001, John Mueller and I wrote papers on this issue for Richard Rosecrance and Arthur Stein's *No More States?*.[7] The direct costs to the US economy were miniscule ($100 billion—less than 0.8 per cent of GDP). The most serious costs were the increase in the uncertainty associated with doing business and from preventive measures taken as an overreaction to the terrorist threat. Thus, apart from the direct costs of homeland security, there are the costs imposed on travellers in terms of the opportunity costs of the time lost in security searches at airports. These were estimated in 2002 to be $16 and $32 billion annually for the USA. A more recent estimate by John Mueller and Mark Stewart[8] of these indirect costs to US travellers between 2002 and 2011 was $417 billion. The direct costs of extra homeland security were $690 billion. This expenditure would only have been cost effective, they estimate, if it had prevented or deterred four attacks every *day* like the one foiled in Times Square in New York.

Neither are the personal risks that citizens face from terrorism serious. From 1960 until 2001, based on the US State Department data, Mueller estimated that the number of Americans killed by international terrorism (including 9/11) 'is about the same as the number killed over the same period by lightning, or by accident-causing deer, or by severe allergic reaction to peanuts'.[9] While, including both domestic and international terrorism, 'far fewer people were killed by terrorists in the entire world over the [20th century] than died in any number of unnoticed civil wars during the century'.[10]

What of the fears of future terrorist attacks using stolen chemical, biological, and nuclear weapons? Of these, the danger of a 'dirty bomb' using stolen fissile materials is the most pertinent. Biological and chemical weapons are not easy to use by private agents. The damage from a 'dirty bomb' would be localized to the real estate in the area that was made radioactive. The personal danger from the likely 25 per cent increase in radiation over background radiation in the area is miniscule. 'A common recommendation from nuclear scientists and engineers', notes Mueller, 'is that those exposed should calmly walk away'.[11]

The costs of actual and potential terrorism have thus been considerably overblown. Worse, by inducing the unjustified panic that the terrorists seek to create, the war on terror helps foster their aim of creating terror. Even worse, by extending state powers and emasculating civil liberties, it promotes the very illiberal societies and police states the jihadis themselves seek. A terror industry develops with the same rent-seeking purposes as so many other state-sponsored attempts to create risk-free societies.

Terrorism will be always with us; however, our reactions to it can change. For example, even after knowing that driving causes over forty thousand deaths every year in automobile accidents in the US, Americans have not stopped driving. Yet, with the hysteria and panic created by the much smaller number of deaths from terrorism, liberal democracies are willing to devote scarce resources to chasing horrendous phantoms. They would do better to remember the words of an earlier US president: 'the only thing we have to fear is fear itself'.

Other Options

Given the growing failure of the US's war on terror, what can be done to douse or contain these flames from Mesopotamia? President Obama, while abjuring 'boots on the ground', had claimed that he was arming moderate rebel groups in Syria, who, with US air power, would be able to destroy ISIS. He was soon faced by the defection of the main moderate group trained by the US—Division 30—to the al-Qaeda linked Jabhat al-Nusra.[12]

Turkey, which had earlier supported jihadists in Syria to topple Assad, had recently targeted ISIS. But, reversing its peace process with the Kurds has also targeted their Turkish wing, PKK. It seems

Erdoğan is keener on the latter than the former. He is likely to be an unreliable ally against ISIS.

Saudi Arabia and the Gulf states were till recently the main financiers and suppliers of manpower to the Sunni jihadists.[13] They have recently changed their tune as their ISIS Wahhabi fellow travellers have turned their guns on them for not being true to their creed, and announced their intention to march on Mecca and Medina. With the defeat of ISIS and the ascendancy of Crown Prince Muhammad bin Salman (MBS) to virtual complete control of Saudi Arabia, he along with the Crown Prince of the UAE and President Sisi of Egypt have turned against the Muslim Brotherhood and other variants of political Islam. He is also organising a coalition of Sunni Arab states to take on the proxies of Iran in the Middle East. But the military competence of the Saudis after their flagging battle against the Iranian backed Houthi's in Yemen must remain seriously in doubt.

Where does this leave the US as a great power in the Middle East after Obama's abandonment of the region? With President Trump as reluctant as Obama to put US 'boots on the ground' in the Middle East (except Afghanistan), So, how can the US now use military force to maintain its great power role in the Middle East? There is one option: to hire a mercenary army to confront its enemies and those of its allies. As Sean McFate[14] has shown, the US has already used mercenaries called 'contractors' in its military operations; in Iraq, they were half of the military work force and in Afghanistan, 70 per cent. In Liberia, the US State Department hired the private military company DynCorp International to demobilize Charles Taylor's predatory army to create a new army for Liberia. Given the untrustworthiness of the Iraqi army created by the US—whose thirty thousand soldiers fled from Mosul faced by only five hundred ISIS fighters—it seemed recreating it would be a lost cause. But once he replaced the sectarian Nouri al-Maliki as the Iraqi premier, Haider al-Abadi has succeeded in creating a viable army under US tutelage. With the Kurdish peshmerga allied with Syrian rebel troops having defeated ISIS in its capital Raqqa in Syria, the US and its allies seem to have found a viable model for fighting its Islamist enemies—to use local ground troops to do the fighting, with the West providing air cover and other special services.[15]

But, even after ISIS' defeat, it will be necessary to stem the blowback from Mesopotamia. The foreign jihadists recruited from the Muslim diaspora around the world by ISIS could on returning to their homelands undertake terrorist attacks. Also, the failed state of Libya has become a staging post for human traffickers to move large numbers of migrants from the Sahel and North Africa to southern Europe. With ISIS fighters' dispersal in the region, this could also be a route ISIS could take to plant its jihadists in Europe. ISIS-linked but homegrown jihadists have already perpetrated terrorist atrocities in Brussels in Belgium, Paris in France, San Bernardino in California, and in Manchester and London in the UK. They have spread further afield into Southeast Asia, especially Mindanao in the Philippines.

A possible answer to contain this blowback is a cordon sanitaire—a term usually used to control disease epidemics. But the French Prime Minister Clemenceau also used it in March 1919, when he urged the newly independent border states that had seceded from Soviet Russia to form a defensive union and thus quarantine the spread of communism to Western Europe. A similar cordon sanitaire enforced by NATO may now be needed to contain the Islamism spreading from the Middle East. It should begin with Libya, with no one being allowed in or out, but permitting non-military trade. This could, in case the other military options prove infeasible, be extended to cover Syria, Lebanon, non-Kurdish parts of Iraq, Iran, Afghanistan, and Pakistan. For, though a US ally, Pakistan (and Saudi Arabia too till Crown Prince MBS' new dispensation) have been shown over the years to be supporters/financiers of terrorists.[16] Such a cordon would allow the sectarian passions in the region to play out, till like the warriors in the Thirty Years' War, they accept a Peace of Westphalia and join the modern world.

President Trump's recent ban on travel and refugees from some Muslim countries being contested in the US courts can be seen as a first step in creating such a *cordon sanitaire*. Would Russia and China, the other US strategic competitors, object to such a cordon and seek to undermine it? Given that Russia and China are faced with problems of Islamist jihadists in the Caucasus and in Xinjiang, respectively, despite their current fishing in the troubled waters of Syria and Iraq—largely to spite the US—in the long run, as the jihadists spill over into the Caucasus and Xinjiang, they are unlikely to oppose or undermine the cordon.[17]

Russia

In earlier chapters, we have seen how the hope of liberals in Russia and the West that with the end of the Soviet Union, Russia would become a 'normal' country—liberal, democratic, and market-oriented—have been belied by the rise of Vladimir Putin. Edward Lucas, in an important book,[18] shows how this has happened and how Putin has recreated a version of the Soviet state, along with its geopolitical aspirations, while giving up its sclerotic centralized planned economy for authoritarian state capitalism.[19] Russia's actions range from waging war with Georgia to conducting menacing military exercises against Poland and the Baltic states to invading and occupying Eastern Ukraine and incorporating Crimea into Russia, against the specific commitment in the Budapest Accord of 1994. This agreed 'to respect the independence and sovereignty of the existing borders of the Ukraine' in return for its giving up its nuclear weapons.[20] Along with Russia, it was signed by the US, France, and Britain.

Lucas argues that the current confrontation with the West reflects 'a fundamental difference of opinion about the collapse of the Soviet Union'. In the liberated Soviet satellites and the West, the collapse marked 'a triumphant liberation [which] buried the one-party state and the planned economy, and entrenched freedom and the rule of law in their place'. They also believed that a new security order had been settled in Europe, where borders were sacrosanct and disputes over ethnic, linguistic, and minority-rights problems would be settled by peaceful dialogue

But, for many in Russia, the lesson was that 'Communism had indeed failed, but the collapse of the Soviet Union was a humiliating geopolitical setback, whose reversal was only a matter of time'.[21]

It was also believed that the death of communism also meant the end of ideology in Russia. As Boris Yeltsin said a few years after the collapse of the Soviet Union, 'In Russian history during the 20th century, there have been various periods—monarchism, totalitarianism, perestroika, and finally a democratic path of development. Each stage has its own ideology', he continued, but now 'we have none'.[22] In 1996, Yeltsin asked a group to define the 'Russian Idea', but they could not.

A collection of conservative thinkers and politicians calling themselves *Soglasiye vo imya Rossiya* ('Accord in the Name of Russia') also took up the task. They were disturbed by the weakness of the Russian state, which they believed needed to be fixed for Russia to return to its rightful glory. That entailed a return to the Russian tradition of a powerful central government. Putin agreed with their ideals and overall goals, and after he had succeeded in stabilizing the economy, he returned to the question of the Russian idea. He began to argue that Russia was a unique civilization of its own, which could not be made to fit into European or Asian boxes. It had to live by its own uniquely Russian rules and morals. With the help of the Orthodox Church, he began a battle against the liberal (Western) traits that some Russians had begun to adopt. This led to his criminalization of 'homosexual propaganda' and the jailing of the pop group Pussy Riot for hooliganism. These actions were condemned by the West but were popular in Russia.[23]

Putin's conservatism is unlike that in the West, which is based on individualism and a fear of big government. Russian conservatives are advocates of state power for serving the state. They draw on a long tradition of Russian imperial conservatism, embracing Eurasianism. That strain is authoritarian, traditional, anti-American, and anti-European; it values religion and public submission, and, more significantly, it is expansionist.[24]

The ideologue of this contemporary Russian conservatism is Alexander Dugin,[25] who believes with Putin that the collapse of the Soviet Union was the greatest geopolitical catastrophe of the century. Like classical Eurasianists of the 1920s and 1930s,[26] his ideology is 'anti-Western, anti-liberal, totalitarian, ideocratic, and socially traditional. Its nationalism is not Slavic-oriented (although Russians have a special mission to unite and lead) but also applies to other nations of Eurasia. And it labels rationalism as Western and thus promotes a mystical, spiritual, emotional, and messianic world view.'[27]

Dugin and his followers have strongly endorsed Putin's action in Ukraine and asked him to go further and take east and south Ukraine. Russians seemed to agree. Putin's ratings climbed, with 65 per cent of Russians in February 2014 accepting that Crimea and eastern regions of Ukraine are 'essentially Russian territory' and that 'Russia is right to use military force in the defense of the population'.[28]

In line with this neo-Eurasianism, Putin's confrontation with the West over Ukraine has also made him turn east to China[29], to create what has been characterized as a 'League of Dictators'.[30] Both authoritarian regimes feel threatened by Western universal values. They believe that economic growth and stability do not need imported notions of democracy.[31]

The basis of an anti-Western alliance being created by the emerging Russia–China axis is the Shanghai Cooperation Agreement (SCO) between Russia, China, and Central Asia. The core members are the ex-Soviet Central Asian republics of Kazakhstan, Kyrgyzstan, Uzbekistan, and Tajikistan. The SCO is linked to the Collective Security Treaty Organization (CSTO), which, in addition to the previously mentioned Central Asian republics in the SCO, also includes Armenia and Belarus. The CSTO is Russia's answer to NATO. SCO and CSTO create an embryonic security sphere that stretches from the Arctic to the South China Sea and from the Bering Strait to the Polish border. But both China and Russia want to be the leader of this potential alliance. There are also potential rivals in Central Asia, where Kazakhstan and Uzbekistan also want to be the leader. Moreover, China's huge population and shortage of natural resources—apart from coal—are in painful contrast to Russia's demographic collapse and mineral-rich eastern regions. As a result, the two countries may make common cause, but they are not natural allies.[32] The sharp-witted Andrei Piontkovsky calls the notion 'an alliance between a rabbit and a boa constrictor'.[33] It is unlikely to last.

Also, things might no longer be going the neo-Eurasianists way in Russia. As Tony Barber reports:

> Crimea's annexation went down well with millions of Russians, even more so than the August 2008 war with Georgia. In March 2014, some 58 per cent of people questioned in a Levada-Center survey supported annexing parts of neighbouring countries with ethnic Russian minorities. By last March [2015], however, this figure had fallen to 34%. Meanwhile 64 per cent of Russians—up from 56 per cent in 2009—opposed the use of any means, including force, to keep former Soviet republics under Moscow's control.[34]

This reflects the rise of the new middle class. During the Soviet era, the chief losers were what Lucas calls the 'phantom middle class of principled and well-educated people who were deprived of the life they would have enjoyed in capitalist countries'[35], and who despised the nomenklatura—the Soviet ruling caste. During the Gorbachev/Yeltsin years, when talent and adaptability were prized, this class did well. But it was financially ruined in the 1998 financial crisis. But during the subsequent economic boom from 2000, it prospered. For in the Putin era, only dissent is punished and most of the freedoms these 'new Russians' care about—to travel, education, owning property at home or abroad, buying anything they can afford—except political freedoms, are preserved. Hence 'never in Russian history have so many Russians lived so well and so freely. This is a proud boast, and one that even those who dislike Russia's current path must honestly acknowledge'[36]

This middle class (those earning a monthly salary of $900–$1,100) has risen from 16.5 per cent of the Russian population in 2003 to 20 per cent in 2006, and 35 per cent in 2010.[37] They strongly support the status quo and a soft nationalism—'Russia for the ethnic Russians'. The 'most self-consciously modern 'New Russians' are proud of their country and most regard criticism with a mixture of irritation and bewilderment'.[38] They are creating a social force, which so far is politically passive, but which Russia has never had in its history. Its future political behaviour is the biggest question facing the country.[39]

Whether or not Putin is a true believer in the Dugin ideology, there may be a much simpler explanation for Putin's nationalist turn. Andrew Kuchins[40] has argued that Putin—who came to power as a great power balancer, moving at times to the liberal westernizer camp and then to the Russian nationalist camp—has with his annexation of Crimea and support for the hybrid war in Eastern Ukraine firmly moved into the Russian nationalist camp, largely to consolidate his own political position. His high popular ratings during his first presidency were due to Russia's robust economic growth and the resulting rise in Russian living standards. But when he returned to the presidency in 2012, growth stagnated to only 1.3 per cent in 2013, and close to zero when he annexed Crimea. The rouble was losing value, and capital flight was at an all-time high. This was reminiscent of the 1980s, when, despite massive inflows of petrodollars, the economy was stagnant with economic growth close to zero. This, like today, was because of the failure to undertake structural reforms and endemic corruption. Putin is unwilling—like his Soviet predecessors—to undertake the deep structural reforms, which, combined with an anti-corruption campaign, would hurt the vested interests on which his power rests. Without economic growth and prosperity providing the basis of his popularity, he played the nationalist card, on the line of Dugin's ideology. As during most of his tenure in power, Putin's political instincts were right. His popularity ratings immediately jumped about 25 points, putting him into the high 80s, where they have remained as the war in Eastern Ukraine expanded.[41]

This raises the danger that with Western economic sanctions imposed after Putin's Crimean and Ukrainian adventures and the continuing softening of the oil price with the US shale oil and gas revolution, a resumption of Russian economic growth—the past basis for Putin's popularity—is unlikely. This could tempt him to continue his confrontation with the West through hybrid warfare in his near abroad. The Baltic states, with their significant Russian-speaking population, are particularly at risk.[42] But, unlike Ukraine, they are members of NATO, whose Article V commits the US to come to their defence. Would it? Given Obama's reluctance to fight and the number of times he has backtracked on commitments like withdrawing the missile shield promised to the Poles and the Czechs' under Moscow's pressure, Putin may gamble that the response from NATO to a threat in the Baltic, instead of being military, could be a mealy-mouthed one of seeking a diplomatic solution—as has happened in the Syrian imbroglio. This act of appeasement would be 'the end of NATO, with devastating consequences for the continent's future security', while if NATO does confront Russia, 'that could lead to World War Three'.[43]

To avoid this terrible choice, NATO, which had lowered its guard after the implosion of the Soviet Union, needs to again confront and contain Russia as it did in the Cold War. Ultimately, this requires the US to provide the means—once again—to deter a revanchist Russia. To Obama's credit he forced the Europeans at a NATO summit in April 2009 to draw up contingency plans to deal with a Russian invasion, and in 2013, NATO began the Steadfast Jazz exercise 'which involved defending a fictional bit of Europe from an external attack'.[44]

Since then, NATO has developed a Spearhead Force of five thousand land troops designed to deploy in less than forty-eight hours. It has agreed to more than double its Response Force to around thirty thousand troops, and Poland has taken delivery of a US-built Patriot anti-ballistic missile system. Meanwhile, Russia has carried out its own massive military exercises on its western borders, deployed 'ballistic and nuclear capable Iskander missiles in Kaliningrad', and announced a 'Rbs. 20tn upgrade plan on increasing defense capabilities in Crimea, Kaliningrad and the Arctic region'.[45] Moreover, there were (September 2015) reports that the US is planning to replace twenty nuclear weapons at Buchel airbase in western Germany with a more modern variant, and 'the current B61 bombs are to be replaced with B61-12s, a newer version of the weapon which is more accurate and less destructive. The new variants can also be fired as missiles, while the older version had to be dropped from aircraft.'[46] The Russians have threatened counter measures.

Russian propaganda, painting the US as the major threat to Russia, has led to the Levada poll in April [2015] finding 59 per cent of respondents said the US posed a threat to Russia—up from 47 per cent in 2007. Thus 'fear about external threats has replaced economic concerns as the main driver of public sentiment', says Mikhail Dmitriev, an economist and sociologist in Moscow. This has helped Putin maintain popularity ratings at historically high levels 'of more than 80 per cent despite an economic slump—GDP is expected to contract by more than 2 per cent this year [2015].'[47]

However, there may be some hope in its internal politics to prevent Russia and NATO sleepwalking into a Third World War. Forbes has reported that, despite his overwhelming ratings, Kremlinologists are sensing 'a putsch in the air' against Putin. 'The tea leaves say that the Kremlin elite, dubbed by some as Politburo 2.0, is currently deciding whether Putin should go before he makes a bad situation worse'.[48]

The Politburo 2.0 is worried about Putin's next moves in the Ukraine. If he pulls his assets from the pro-Russian rebels, he and the Politburo will be labelled losers. If he launches a new offensive to get a land bridge to Crimea, the West will impose sanctions, ruining the economy and putting the assets of the Politburo at risk. 'Sanctions may include the "nuclear option" of expelling Russia from the SWIFT banking transfer system and bring Russian financial transactions to a standstill. Those who benefited from Putin's kleptocracy would face ruin'. To avoid this, an end of the Putin regime would have to be engineered. 'Putin would have to either resign or cease to exist. Indicators suggest that the process would begin with an assault on Putin's closest associates, which appears underway.'[49]

Whether or not a coup against Putin materializes, and if it does whether his successors will repudiate Russia's anti-Western stance and turn again to the liberal structural reforms needed to resuscitate the Russian economy, remains—in Donald Rumsfeld's phrase—a 'known unknown'. It is in this context that Putin's latest moves in the Syrian Civil War should be seen. By interjecting himself into the conflict on the side of his old ally Bashar al-Assad, he first sends a signal that, unlike the feckless Obama, he will stick by his allies. Second, that with his airbases in Latakia, a NATO enforced no-fly zone, as proposed by Turkey and rejected by Obama, is no longer possible. Third, by fighting ISIS, he hopes to reduce the jihadist threat to the Caucasus.[50] Fourth, he has made Russia an essential player in determining the fate of the past dominions of the Ottoman Empire—an outcome that British imperial policy had always sought to prevent. Finally, and most important, by offering to slow the swarm of migrants fleeing the Syrian Civil War, he offers Europe hope of easing its migration crisis, in exchange for the weakening or removal of the sanctions imposed after his Ukraine adventure. This would reduce the pressures on him from his Politburo 2.0.

Meanwhile, NATO must maintain its firm stance against any further Russian territorial encroachments, particularly in the Baltic States, which remain the flashpoint for a Third World War because of a revanchist Russia.

China

Once China had secured control of the non-Chinese buffer regions of Tibet, Xinjiang, Inner Mongolia, and Manchuria—soon after the CCP had established its control over the Han Heartland—it was a virtual island, enclosed by mountains, jungles, and wastelands. It had secure and easily defensible borders. There are only three points of potential friction. The first is the border in the south-east in Vietnam, which can be easily crossed; as recently as 1979, China fought a short border war with Vietnam, which the Vietnamese won. The second friction point is in eastern Manchuria, touching on Siberia and Korea. Finally, there is a single opening into the rest of Eurasia on the Xinjiang–Kazakhstan border through which the old Silk Road ran, and through which today's China is planning to link all of Eurasia through its new Silk Road.

Then, there is its coast on the Western Pacific. Until the rise of Western sea power, this did not pose any threat, so China had eschewed naval power, except for the brief period under the Ming, when the Chinese developed a powerful navy whose emblematic figure was the Muslim eunuch from Yunnan, Zeng He, who has 'become a poster boy for Beijing's policy of "peaceful rise", an example of China's engagement with the world'.[51]

The Ming navy had been built up primarily to deal with the pirates who raided ships transporting foodgrains from the newly opened area in the Yangtze region by the Song. But when the Grand Canal to Peking was built in 1411, the transport of grain by sea was abolished and the navy abandoned, as it was seen as more a luxury than a necessity.[52] After this 'China didn't possess another naval ship capable of reaching the islands of the South China Sea until given one by the United States 500 years later.'[53] It is the Western Pacific, dominated by the US Navy, which China sees as the major threat to its security.

But this vulnerability is not of invasion. It is economic. China's major economic problem has been that its Heartland, which is also its agricultural region, 'has about one-third of the arable land per person as the rest of the world. This pressure has defined modern Chinese history—both in terms of living with it, and trying to move beyond it'.[54]

Given its secure borders, relatively abundant resources, and a large population, China can, as it has in much of the past, develop without any international intercourse. Once the industrial revolution led to Promethean growth in the West, China's insularity—as it remained an agrarian economy—meant relative poverty. But it allowed centralized control and the maintenance of order and internal unity. Though there was limited trade through the northern Silk Route, which allowed some foreign influences and the creation of some wealth, these could be easily managed.

There have been three periods since the eleventh century when China's 'opening up' has led to accelerated growth. The first was the opening up and creation of a commercial economy by the Song dynasty in the eleventh century, which led to the first Chinese economic miracle. It was, however, based on a form of 'crony capitalism' and was subsequently aborted because of the reassertion of atavistic attitudes to trade and commerce, as well as the failure to bind the state against its predatory rent-seeking instincts. Emblematic of the return to insularity was the dismantling of the Chinese navy by an edict of 1436 by the Ming Emperor.[55]

The second period of growth happened with the opening up of China after the Opium Wars in the nineteenth century and the introduction of industrialism. For the first time, this made the Pacific coast, not Central Asia, the interface with the world. This in turn massively destabilized China.

Trade makes those engaged in it rich. When the foreign powers carved up the Chinese melon in the early twentieth century, the coastal regions involved in trade became relatively wealthy, while the subsistence farmers in the Han interior remained poor. The newly enriched coastal leaders had an interest in intensifying relations with the foreign powers, which made them even wealthier. This increased the regional wealth and income disparity between the coast and the interior. 'In due course, foreigners allied with Chinese coastal merchants and politicians became more powerful in the coastal regions than the central government. The worst geopolitical nightmare of China came true. China fragmented, breaking into regions, some increasingly under the control of foreigners [and their commercial agents]. Beijing lost control over the country.[56]

Mao's threefold aim was to recentralize China, to end the massive inequality between the coastal region and the rest of Han China, and to expel the foreigners. He was reverting to China's classic insular policy and accepted the inevitable result—China became equal but extraordinarily poor. After the fall of the Gang of Four in the 1970s, Deng Xiaoping became the paramount leader and took a gamble. He was worried that without 'opening up' China he could not meet the domestic pressures that were building up for a rise in living standards. Also, the technological gap opened up by Chinese insularity threatened its security. Deng believed that he could avoid the past destabilization of China through his 'Open Door' policy 'by maintaining a strong central government, based on a loyal army and Communist party apparatus. His successors have struggled to maintain that loyalty to the state and not to foreign investors, who can make individuals wealthy. That is the bet that is currently being played out'.[57]

To date, Deng's bet has played out handsomely. Through his Open Door policy, China has become the workshop of the world and the second largest global economy. But, as in the previous periods when China 'opened up', regional disparities have widened; the coastal region has become wealthy, the interior remains poor. This, in part, explains the Bo Xilai affair and its denouement. Bo recognized this disparity and espoused a return to Maoist policies, which proved immensely popular in his relatively backward interior satrapy of Chongqing. Given his connections to the section of the army his father had commanded, he clearly posed a threat of becoming a regional Maoist warlord, shattering China's unity. He and his associates, including those in the army, were purged in traditional Communist fashion.

The second consequence of these regional disparities is that the CCP is now trying to make the interior also a land-based trading hub—distinct from the sea-based coastal hub—as it was in the old imperial days, when the Silk Road provided trading opportunities by land-based trade through Central Asia. This, I conjecture, is the main motivation for the push for linking Eurasia through the Silk Road, besides also providing an alternative route for transporting the natural resources China still needs from the choke points faced by the sea route in the Malacca Straits and Indian Ocean.[58]

While, globalization has greatly benefitted China, for a Leninist party obsessed with centralized control, it also makes China dependent on the outside world. This became apparent with the 2008 GFC. China dealt with the Great Recession in the West and the resulting fall in demand for Chinese manufactured exports. The Chinese instituted a massive debt-fuelled fiscal stimulus to finance infrastructure and housing, much of which was uneconomic. The resulting debt overhang and declining productivity is leading to slower growth (as discussed in Chapter 7. Just like the Japanese 'miracle', the Chinese one, too, seems to be fading).

The hopes raised by the economic road map laid out at the CCP's Third Plenum in 2013 of resuming more sustainable market-based growth seems to be faltering. Policymakers 'find themselves squeezed between the Scylla of the market and the Charybdis of state control'. President Xi Jinping will decide the future of this tussle, and state control will win. For, 'when push comes to shove, state intervention is likely to prevail over what must look like a reckless dabbling with market forces by their technocrats'.[59]

What does the resulting slowdown of growth imply for the future of the CCP[60], its likely future foreign policy, and, therefore, for China?[61] Many Sinologists, who had hitherto applauded the adaptability of the Party to the changing circumstances it faced—particularly after the international outcry over the Tiananmen Square massacre—are now prophesying its end. David Shambaugh, one of the doyens of this group,[62] has recently written an essay in the *Wall Street Journal* titled 'The Coming Chinese Crackup'. He argues that the CCP was traumatized by the demise of its sister party in the Soviet Union, and they came to blame Gorbachev's policies of glasnost and perestroika for its collapse. Xi Jinping, argues Shambaugh, knows China's political system is badly broken and is determined to avoid being another Gorbachev. 'But instead of being the antithesis of Mr. Gorbachev, Mr. Xi may well wind up having the same effect. His despotism is severely stressing China's system and society—and bringing it closer to a breaking point'.[63]

Though it is difficult to say when this will happen, he sees five telltale signs that 'the end game of Chinese Communist rule has now begun'. The first is that the economic elites have arranged to flee if the system begins to crumble. In 2014, 64 per cent of the high-net-worth individuals polled by Shanghai's Hurun Research

Institute 'were either emigrating or planning to do so'. Rich Chinese are sending their children to study abroad in record numbers. Thousands of Chinese women are engaged in birth-tourism to bring home 'infants born as US citizens'. Wealthy Chinese are buying property abroad in record numbers and moving their assets to foreign tax havens. When a country's elites—many of them party members—flee in such large numbers, it is a telling sign of lack of confidence in the regime and the country's future.

Second, Xi has greatly increased political repression, with the Party ordering all its units 'to ferret out any seeming endorsement of the West's "universal values"—including constitutional democracy, civil society, a free press and neoliberal economics'. This is a sign of the leadership's deep insecurity and paranoia and reminiscent of Putinism.

Third, Shambaugh cites recent instances of attending official conferences where regime loyalists were going through the motions of feigned compliance of the latest mantra. 'But', he says, 'it was evident that the propaganda had lost its power, and the emperor had no clothes'.

Fourth, the corruption pervading the Party and the military is extensive, being 'stubbornly rooted in the single-party system, patron-client networks, an economy utterly lacking in transparency, a state controlled media and the absence of the rule of law.' Xi's anti-corruption campaign is a selective purging of Jiang Zemin's allies and political clients. This is highly dangerous as Mr Jiang is still the godfather of Chinese politics and Mr Xi has not 'brought along his own coterie'. Moreover, being a princeling, he is 'widely reviled in Chinese society at large'.

Finally, the ambitious programme for economic reform unveiled at the Third Plenum is stillborn, as it 'challenges powerful, deeply entrenched interest groups—such as state-owned enterprises and local party cadres—and they are plainly blocking its implementation'. This, as we have seen, darkens the prospects for Chinese growth and threatens to break the implicit compact the Party made with its citizens to accept authoritarianism in exchange for continuing prosperity.

But, this fragility of the Party and impending threat to its survival also raises the dire prospect that it will turn, as Putin did after his disputed election in 2011, to play the nationalist card and seize by aggression claimed or disputed territory in its neighbourhood; there are many such flashpoints for Chinese aggression. With forty million 'bare branches' (see Chapter 5), Martin Walker argues, 'understanding the effect of testosterone overload maybe most important for China. A Beijing power struggle between cautious old technocrats and aggressive young nationalists may be decided by mobs of rootless young men, demanding uniforms, rifles and a chance to liberate Taiwan'.[64]

There are many such flashpoints for Chinese aggression to lead to a Third World War. The first is the existing confrontation in the East and South China Seas, where the Chinese claims are disputed by Japan and a whole host of Southeast Asian allies, many of whom have defence treaties with the US.[65] Japan would be threatened by Chinese control of the South China Sea, as it would affect its vital sea lanes to the Indian Ocean. Then, there is the Sino-Indian border, where the territorial dispute could escalate because of Chinese nervousness that the Tibetan exiles sheltered by New Delhi might begin to fight for Tibetan independence.[66] Next, there is Russia, which though currently in an opportunist partnership with China because of their joint opposition to US hegemony is not a natural partner; given the large demographic differences between the two, Chinese encroachment into Siberia could easily sour this newfound friendship. Historically, the Russians have feared a Chinese move into their Pacific maritime provinces; the Chinese have feared a Russian move into Manchuria and beyond. Also, the Russians are wary of growing Chinese influence in Kazakhstan. They may choose to challenge it there, and if they do, and it becomes a serious matter, the secondary pressure point for both sides would be in the Pacific region.

China is now involved in an arms race with the US and Japan in the Western Pacific as it expands its military arsenal of missiles and seeks to create a blue water navy. This is reminiscent of the Kaiser's attempt to challenge Britain's naval power before the First World War. This arms race is also manifesting itself in outer space and in cyberspace and could continue for some time as 'the options for a military tit-for-tat-without-victory look endless—at least as long as economic resources are plentiful'.[67] There's the rub for the Chinese if their economic problems are as serious as argued above. They may also have miscalculated that after the Great Recession the US would no longer have the economic resources for an arms race like the one with the Soviet Union, which finally brought about its demise. From some hawkish statements by the PLA, they seem to be contemplating a 'short, sharp war', much like what the Japanese tried in 1941, which led to their eventual destruction. Nor should they count on the political impediments that have led to a contraction of US military expenditure and the unwillingness of President Obama to commit the US to fight. For after a limp Carter, a robust Reagan raised defence expenditure and began an arms race with the Soviet Union, which brought it down. The same is likely with the current administration of President Donald Trump.

One of Trump's earliest actions was to take a call from the Taiwanese President and to question the 'one China' policy accepted by President Nixon. Though he has backtracked on this to get China's help in rolling back the North Korean nuclear programme, it remains on the table. He has also authorized arm shipments for Taiwan. But it is the belligerent stance of China's ally North Korea that is likely to change the status quo in the north-west of Eurasia. With its recent (July 2017) firing of an intercontinental ballistic missile that could reach Alaska, the North Korean nuclear threat to the US Heartland is imminent. So far China is happy with the status quo, as the US is tied down militarily in the Korean peninsula. But with the deployment of the THAAD anti-missile system in South Korea as a counter to North Korean missiles, China sees it as the start of greater US deployment of anti-ballistic missile systems on the Asian mainland, weakening its nuclear deterrent. With the impending North Korean deployment of nuclear-capable ballistic missiles threatening the US homeland, the US has threatened pre-emptive military action. But with the horrifying collateral damage involved, is this likely? If not, Seoul and Tokyo will have to ask if the US would willingly sacrifice Los Angeles for them? Not likely. They will, as President Trump recommended in his campaign, be forced to develop nuclear deterrents, creating a nuclear balance of terror in East Asia, freezing the status quo. This would thwart the Chinese aim of becoming the Asian hegemon.[68]

Finally, China's assertiveness, and its using of its accumulated economic power to follow the ancient Chinese practice of co-opting their economic competitors into vassals, is leading to a reaction against Chinese hegemony. There is a grand alliance of littoral balancers led by the US forming between Japan, the Philippines, Australia, Vietnam, and India. Though President Duterte of the Philippines recent volte-face to embrace China and denounce the US might be problematic in the short run, it is unlikely to last. Railing against past US imperialism will not give him the license to embrace Chinese imperialism. With some Asian powers like India hesitant to directly join an alliance with the US, they are forming bilateral partnerships with each other and separate bilateral partnerships with the US. This replacement of the old 'hub-and spoke' system of the US alliance system is in many ways stronger and cheaper for the US, as it does not require basing permanent US troops in the alliance countries.[69] It is also reported that the US build-up of military capability in the Western Pacific and South China Sea and a 'wide-ranging Pacific Area Security Treaty Organization of like-minded countries to counter both China and North Korea is potentially in the offing.'[70] It seems that the US may finally be ready to confront the dragon.

China's desire to replace US hegemony in Asia and then in the world remains the most serious flashpoint for war. It cannot succeed given the coalition already emerging against it,[71] but it would end the seventy-year-old peace the world has enjoyed. Not appeasement, as many commentators are recommending for dealing with a rising China, but robust deterrence and containment is needed. For this, it is vital that the US regains its will to fight for the liberal democratic order it has maintained since the Second World War.

Notes

1. See Roula Khalaf, 'Putin Won the Syrian War, But Can He Keep the Peace?', *Financial Times* (20 November 2017).
2. See Abdel Bari Atwani, *The Islamic State: The Digital Caliphate* (London: Saqi, 2015).
3. David Fromkin, *A Peace to End All Peace: The Fall of the Ottoman Empire and the Creation of the Modern Middle East* (New York: Henry Holt, 1989).
4. Fromkin, *A Peace to End All Peace*, p. 564.
5. Shadi Hamid, *Temptations of Power: Islamists and Illiberal Democracies in a New Middle East* (New York: Oxford University Press, 2014).
6. Max Boot, 'The Terrorist Past Had a Message for the Terrorist Present', *Wall Street Journal* (27 July 2016).
7. D. Lal, 'Will Terrorism Defeat Globalization, in R.N. Rosecrane and A.A. Stein (eds), *No More States?* (Lanham, MD: Rowman & Littlefield, 2006), pp. 35–45; and John Mueller, 'Terrorism, Overreaction and Globalization' in R.N. Rosecrance and A.A. Stein (eds), *No More States?* (Lanham, MD: Rowman and Littlefield, 2006), pp. 47–74.
8. John Mueller and Mark G. Stewart, 'Responsible Counterterrorism Policy', *Policy Analysis*, no. 755 (Washington, DC: Cato Institute, September 2014).
9. Mueller, John. 2009. *Overblown: How Politicians and the Terrorism Industry Inflate National Security Threats, and Why We Believe Them.* New York: Free Press.
10. John Mueller, *War and Ideas: Selected Essays* (Abingdon: Routledge, 2011), p. 66.
11. John Mueller, *Atomic Obsession: Nuclear Alarmism from Hiroshima to Al-Qaeda* (New York: Oxford University Press, 2010), p. 195.
12. Nabih Bulos, 'US-Trained Syria Rebels Do a Deal with al-Qaeda-Linked Group', *Daily Telegraph* (16 August 2015). Available at http://www.telegraph.co.uk/news/worldnews/middleeast/syria/11806496/US-trained-Syria-rebels-do-a-deal-with-al-Qaeda-linked-group.html (last accessed 19 November 2017).

13. See Patrick Cockburn, *The Rise of Islamic State: ISIS and the New Sunni Revolution* (London:Verso, 2015).
14. Sean McFate, *The Modern Mercenary: Private Armies and What They Mean for World Order* (New York: Oxford University Press, 2014), Fig. 3.1.
15. See Con Coughlin, 'At Last, a Working Model for Military Intervention, *The Daily Telegraph* (5 July 2017).
16. For Saudi Arabia, see Stephen Schwartz, *The Two Faces of Islam: The House of Sa'ud from Tradition to Terror* (New York: Doubleday, 2002); for Pakistan, see Ahmed Rashid, *Pakistan on the Brink: The Future of America, Pakistan, and Afghanistan* (New York: Viking, 2012), and Carlotta Gall, *The Wrong Enemy: America in Afghanistan, 2001–2014* (London: Penguin Books, 2014).
17. MacGregor Knox has pointed out to me that such a cordon will 'require a *genuine* mass casualty attack in Western Europe' to motivate feeble Western European states and the EU 'to override four generations of international law and silence the bleating of the Left, the NGOs, the UN and the world's innumerable do-gooders'. He also suggests that a Chinese style 'Great Firewall' in reverse—to cut the Arab world or selected areas thereof from the Internet and the global banking system—might also be worth considering.
18. Edward Lucas, *The New Cold War: Putin's Russia and the Threat to the West* (London: Bloomsbury, 2014).
19. MacGregor Knox has pointed out to me that 'authoritarian state capitalism' sounds more orderly than the realities of Putin's system, which is better described as a KGB/FSB-Mafia conglomerate.
20. I pointed this out in a letter to the *Financial Times* (16 October 2014), commenting on a letter from the Russian ambassador to the UK in which he argued that there was a lack of understanding in the area of strategic forces as a part of a formal post–Cold War agreement. More recently, in response to a leader in the *Financial Times* (19 August 2015) on why Europe's leaders must not lose focus on Ukraine, Alexander Novikov of the Russian embassy, responding in a letter (24 August 2015), invoked the diplomatic principle *pacta sunt servanda* or 'treaties must be implemented'. R.V. Arnaudo rightly responded to this in a letter (29 August): 'Now, that's enough to make a cat laugh. What about implementing the 1994 Budapest Accord.'

21. Lucas, *The New Cold War*, p. x.
22. Anton Barbashin and Hannah Thoburn, 'Putin's Brain: Alexander Dugin and the Philosophy behind Putin's Invasion of Crimea', *Foreign Affairs* (31 March 2014). Available at https://www.foreignaffairs.com/articles/russia-fsu/2014-03-31/putins-brain (last accessed 19 November 2017).
23. Barbashin and Thoburn, 'Putin's Brain'.
24. Barbashin and Thoburn, 'Putin's Brain'.
25. He achieved fame in 1991 with a pamphlet called 'The War of the Continents', in which he described a geopolitical struggle between land powers and sea powers. Dugin's geopolitical views seem plagiarized from Halford Mackinder (see Part II). This is confirmed by the current [2015] Russian ambassador's article in the *Telegraph*—see Alexander Yakovenko, 'The West Is Mean to Russia, but Let's Be Friends', *Financial Times* (22 June 2015). Available at http://www.telegraph.co.uk/news/worldnews/europe/russia/11690039/The-West-is-mean-to-Russia-but-lets-be-friends.html (last accessed 19 November 2017). In which he writes, 'If we accept the so-called Heartland theory of that great 19th century strategist Sir Halford Mackinder that, in a continuous struggle between land and sea power, Russia is in the right place geographically and geopolitically—she occupies the global Heartland. What else need we aspire to?'
26. MacGregor Knox has pointed out to me that this goes back much further than the 1920s White Russian exiles. The architects of the Russo-Japanese war believed in a specifically Asian destiny for Russia. And hatred of and ressentiment against the West, along with an absurd mixture of inferiority and superiority complexes resembling those of the Islamic world and Chinese Empire, has been the core of 'Russianness' from the beginning. Worse still, Russian statecraft, such as it is, derives first of all from the Mongol conquerors whose patronage the prince of Moscow slavishly sought and won.
27. Barbashin and Thoburn, 'Putin's Brain'. The authors also note that after a failed political career, Dugin was made a professor of Moscow State University in 2008. Dugin's form of neo-Eurasianism is 'proving to be a strong contender for the role of Russia's chief ideology. Whether he can control it as he has controlled so many others is a question that may determine his longevity'.

28. Barbashin and Thoburn, 'Putin's Brain'.
29. For analyses of this turn, see Dmitri Trenin, 'Greater Asia: A China-Russia Entente?', *The Globalist* (16 June 2015). Available at https://www.theglobalist.com/from-greater-europe-to-greater-asia-toward-a-sino-russian-entente/ (last accessed 19 November 2017); and Kathrin Hille, 'Outcry in Russia over China Land Lease Agreement', *Financial Times* (25 June 2015). Available at https://www.ft.com/content/700a9450-1b26-11e5-8201-cbdb03d71480 (last accessed 19 November 2017).
30. See the rather alarmist book by Douglas E. Schoen and Melik Kaylan, *The Russia-China Axis: The New Cold War and America's Crisis of Leadership* (New York: Encounter Books, 2014).
31. Lucas, *The New Cold War*, p. 264.
32. This was highlighted by a recent report in the *FT* that, 'plans to hand a stretch of remote Siberian territory have triggered a storm of protest in Russia, underlining how a relationship hailed by the leaders of both countries is being undermined by deep-rooted distrust' (Hille, 'Outcry in Russia over China Land Lease Agreement'.)
33. Lucas, *The New Cold War*, pp. 265–7.
34. Tony Barber, 'Russia Can Break Out of Putin's Thrall', *Financial Times* (24 August 2015). Available at https://www.ft.com/content/3325f082-469d-11e5-b3b2-1672f710807b (last accessed 19 November 2017).
35. Lucas, *The New Cold War*, p. 50.
36. Lucas, *The New Cold War*, p. 54.
37. Lucas, *The New Cold War*, p. 56.
38. Lucas, *The New Cold War*, p. 57.
39. Lucas, *The New Cold War*, p. 56.
40. Andrew Kuchins, 'Policy Brief: Putin Goes Nationalist', *Rising Powers Initiative*, Sigur Center for Asian Studies, George Washington University, Washington D.C. (April 2015). Available at http://www.risingpowersinitiative.org/policy-brief-putin-goes-nationalist/ (last accessed 19 November 2017).
41. Kuchins, 'Policy Brief'.
42. Putin has also attempted to divide the European coalition arrayed against him. He had hoped for a special relationship with Angela Merkel. 'But', writes Edward Lucas, 'Mrs. Merkel loathes Mr. Putin … On their first meeting, he took care to bring his Labrador, in the

knowledge that the German chancellor has a childhood terror of dogs. The animal sniffed Mrs. Merkel's legs. She did not respond to this typical piece of KGB psychological pressure. But she and her advisers have never forgotten the insult' (Lucas, *The New Cold War*, p. xxiii). Trust in Putin has plummeted in Germany from three quarters in 2003, to less than a third in 2013. 'After the initial crisis in Ukraine, 62% of Germans said they were in favour of increasing political pressure on Russia (though only a minority supported economic sanctions)' (Lucas, *The New Cold War*, p. xxiv).

43. Lucas, *The New Cold War*, p. xxx.
44. Lucas, *The New Cold War*, p. xxviii.
45. Henry Foy, Kathrin Hille, and Richard Milne, 'Russia: Border Tensions', *Financial Times* (9 June 2015). Available at https://www.ft.com/content/2cf60498-0e14-11e5-8ce9-00144feabdc0 (last accessed 19 November 2017).
46. Roland Oliphant, Justin Huggler, Raf Sanchez, 'Russia Threatens US with Nuclear Arms "Counter-Measures"', *The Daily Telegraph* (23 September 2015). Available at http://www.telegraph.co.uk/news/worldnews/europe/russia/11886639/Russia-threatens-US-with-nuclear-arms-counter-measures.html (last accessed 19 November 2017).
47. Foy, Hille, and Milne, 'Russia'.
48. Paul Roderick Gregory, 'Is a Slow Putsch against Putin Under Way?', *Forbes* (20 August 2015). Available at https://www.forbes.com/sites/paulroderickgregory/2015/08/20/is-a-slow-putsch-against-putin-under-way/#6f3d3e405b66 (last accessed 19 November 2017).
49. Gregory, 'Is a Slow Putsch against Putin Under Way?'.
50. David Gardner reports that Walid Jumblatt, the Lebanese Druze leader who has links with Russia going back to the Soviets, has said 'Russia's "objectives are military co-ordination with the Syrian regime and to search [out] and kill Chechen leaders" of ISIS. "Putin's obsession is his own Sunnis; he has tens of millions of Sunnis" and the beginnings of an ISIS presence in the northern Caucasus'. See David Gardner, 'Putin Keeps World Guessing on Motives for Military Build-Up in Syria', *Financial Times* (28 September 2015). Available at https://www.ft.com/content/a44e865c-65f1-11e5-a57f-21b88f7d973f (last accessed 19 November 2017).

51. Bill Hayton, *The South China Sea: The Struggle for Power in Asia* (New Haven: Yale University Press, 2014), p. 24. Hayton also cites the work of the Australian historian Geoff Wade, 'The Zeng He Voyages: A Reassesment', *ARI Working Paper*, No. 31 (October 2004), an expert on the Ming dynasty, who has systematically destroyed this rosy official view, as well as the views of Gavin Menzies (*1421: The Year China Discovered America [New York: William Murrow, 2003]*), that Chinese eunuch admirals circumnavigated the world. Unlike the official propaganda that Zeng He was the '"outstanding envoy of peace and friendship"', Wade argues that the 'voyages were not peace missions but clear shows of force.' The overall purpose was 'to control trade routes and to give the usurping emperor [the third Ming emperor whom Zeng He had helped to win a succession battle for the throne] legitimacy at home through the enforced paying of homage to him by foreign rulers' (p. 25).
52. See Mark Elvin, *The Pattern of the Chinese Past* (Stanford: Stanford University Press, 1973), p. 220.
53. Hayton, *The South China Sea*, p. 26.
54. Stratfor, 'The Geopolitics of China: A Great Power Enclosed', *Stratfor Worldview*, 25 March 2012. Available at https://worldview.stratfor.com/article/geopolitics-china-great-power-enclosed (last accessed 19 November 2017).
55. See D. Lal, *Unintended Consequences: The Impact of Factor Endowments, Culture, and Politics on Long-Run Economic Performance* (Cambridge, MA: MIT Press, 1998), Ch. 3; and W.H. McNeill, *The Pursuit of Power: Technology, Armed Force, and Society since A.D. 1000* (Chicago: University of Chicago Press, 1982), Ch. 2.
56. Stratfor, 'The Geopolitics of China'.
57. Stratfor, 'The Geopolitics of China'.
58. This is confirmed by Andrew Small, *The China-Pakistan Axis: Asia's New Geopolitics* (London: Hurst and Co., 2015), who notes that one of China's leading foreign policy intellectuals Wang Jisi contended 'that Beijing's internal efforts to rebalance between coastal and interior regions need an international dimension to underpin them, drawing on China's traditional historical, economic and political focus on the interior rather than the maritime realm. On the economic front, the "westward" economy, running down the old Silk Road, now has the highest growth rate and the highest

growth potential. On the security front, he argues that the separatist, terrorist and extremist threat is best negated through a strategy to stabilize not only China's western periphery but also the countries surrounding it' (p. 163). As he notes, 'When the new leadership in Beijing took office in November 2012, it soon demonstrated that it bought important elements of the underlying case that Wang Jisi had been making' (p. 164).

59. David Pilling, 'China's Push-Me-Pull-You Policies Leave the World Reeling', *Financial Times* (27 August 2015). Available at https://www.ft.com/content/d79abecc-4a58-11e5-9b5d-89a026fda5c9 (last accessed 19 November 2017).
60. The best book on the nature and evolution of the CCP is by the *Financial Times*'s former bureau chief in China, Richard McGregor, *The Party: The Secret World of China's Communist Rulers* (New York: Harper Perennial, 2012).
61. A recent book by Kerry Brown, *CEO, CHINA: The Rise of Xi Jinping* (London: I. B. Taurus, 2016), argues that the CCP is like the Catholic Church and Xi Jinping is like Pope Francis attempting to cleanse it of its defects while maintaining the thread of continuity of its millennial history. This is unconvincing, and also unlike the Catholic Church, which has a potent 'good' it can sell—salvation, Xi Jinping's 'Chinese Dream' is unlikely to have the same mass appeal to save the CCP. The post-2012 CCP regime is better described as a Maoist-nationalist imperialist aspirant.
62. He published an earlier book entitled *China's Communist Party: Atrophy and Adaptation* (Oakland, CA: University of California Press, 2008).
63. David Shambaugh, 'The Coming Chinese Crackup', *Wall Street Journal* (6 March 2015). Available at https://www.wsj.com/articles/the-coming-chinese-crack-up-1425659198 (last accessed 19 November 2017). For a fuller explication of his arguments, see David Shambaugh, *China's Future* (Cambridge: Polity Press, 2016). The same point was made by the Harvard Sinologist Roderick MacFarquhar at a Mont Pelerin Society conference in Hong Kong in 2014.
64. Martin Walker, 'The Geopolitics of Sexual Frustration', *Foreign Policy* (20 October 2009). Available at http://foreignpolicy.com/2009/10/20/the-geopolitics-of-sexual-frustration/ (last accessed 19 November 2017).

65. See Hayton, *The South China Sea*. He provides a detailed history of these disputed islands and rocks, which shows how China's historical claims to its 'nine dashed line' covering most of the South China Sea are murky.
66. It should be remembered that China's most formidable foe during the Tang Dynasty was the Tibetan empire, which threatened its trade on the Silk Road in the early seventh and mid-ninth centuries. China rightly fears that after the Dalai Lama dies, the Tibetan exiles in India, dissatisfied with the Dalai Lama's moderate position, may adopt a militant stance towards China. It is also concerned 'that China's strategic competitors, such as the US and India, could recruit these Tibetan groups to rouse their brethren across the border into militancy in an effort to destabilize China. This worry is not baseless: the CIA trained Tibetan exiles as insurgents to do exactly that during the Cold War'. See Stratfor, 'Tibet: An Ancient Threat to Modern China', *Stratfor Worldview* (16 July 2015). Available at https://worldview.stratfor.com/article/tibet-ancient-threat-modern-china (last accessed 19 November 2017).
67. Jonathan Holslag, *China's Coming War with Asia* (Cambridge: Polity Press, 2015), p. 160. This book also provides an account of the military measures taken by the US and its allies and China in this arms race. On the recent Chinese parade showcasing its anti-carrier missile, see Stratfor, 'China Flaunts Its Missile Arsenal', *Stratfor Worldview* (5 September 2015). Available at https://worldview.stratfor.com/article/china-flaunts-its-missile-arsenal (last accessed 19 November 2017).
68. See D. Lal, 'In the Shadow of the Dragon', *Business Standard* (30 May 2017). Available at http://www.business-standard.com/article/opinion/in-the-shadow-of-the-dragon-117053001980_1.html (last accessed 19 November 2017).
69. See Stratfor, 'In the Pacific, New Military Agreements for a New Alliance Structure', *Stratfor Worldview* (9 June 2015). Available at https://www.stratfor.com/geopolitical-diary/pacific-new-military-agreements-new-alliance-structure (last accessed 19 November 2017).
70. See Lal, 'In the Shadow of the Dragon'.
71. As Philip Bowring, 'China's Delusions of Regional Hegemony', *Financial Times* (10 August 2015), has noted:

    China's two closest allies are Pakistan and North Korea … It is a poor foundation for Asian leadership. The reality is that China is very far from being a natural leader for Asia. Japan is hostile, South Korea is wary, Southeast Asia mostly nervous if not hostile, and India now as concerned with building sea power to counter China's developing presence west of the Strait of Malacca as with its Pakistan border.... Among those who want to balance Chinese claims to leadership of Asia are long time US allies such as Japan, Australia and South Korea, but also countries such as Vietnam, India, Indonesia and the Philippines, which were once either enemies of America or neutral towards it. Now totaling 1.8 billion people, these last four economies are likely to grow faster than China over the next two decades. All perceive China as potentially expansive at their expense.... Other Asian states are not out to confront it, but they fear its delusions. They will want to quash any ambition Beijing might harbour of resurrecting an imaginary history of 'tributary states.' Likewise, they repudiate invented historical claims to the South China Sea.

CHAPTER TWELVE

India Amid Global Disorder

With the growing world disorder caused by the seeming desire of the world's superpower (the US) to retire under President Obama and its status still unclear under the new President Trump, India is—as in the children's game 'the piggy in the middle'—caught in-between two of the flashpoints for a Third World War discussed in the last chapter: the turmoil in the Islamic world and the hegemonic ambition of China. In my current period of retirement, as I now spend part of the year in New Delhi, for me this danger is of more than academic concern.

As we saw in Chapter 2, the system of protectorates reminiscent of the Roman empire constructed by Lord Curzon to protect the British Indian empire was breached to the West, with the ending of the Raj, by the partition of India, and to the north by the 1952 Chinese annexation of Tibet. China is also seeking to encroach on one of the three protectorates created by Curzon in the north-east in Nepal. Of the two others, Sikkim is absorbed into the Indian Union, and Bhutan, while still independent, is part of Curzon's northern frontier system still protecting India, though being wooed by China.

Meanwhile, while India has strengthened its maritime frontiers, it is being challenged by China's 'string of pearls' maritime strategy.

With China's strategic alliance with Pakistan—which has included providing it with the means to become a nuclear state, the development of the Pakistani port of Gwadar in the Arabian Sea as a deep-water port and potential naval base, and linking it with the Karakoram Highway to western China—India would seem to be militarily encircled by the Chinese dragon. The continuing asymmetric war by Pakistan over Kashmir, and China's continuing border dispute with India—particularly its claim to the northeastern Indian state of Arunachal Pradesh, which the Chinese claim as South Tibet—could provide flashpoints for war with these nuclear neighbours of India.[1]

Pakistan

Though the threat from Pakistan creates a great deal of popular agitation in India, it is the Chinese threat which is more potent. As an article on a Chinese strategic issues website is recently reported to have said: 'There cannot be two suns in the sky. China and India cannot really deal with each other harmoniously'.[2]

The military threat from Pakistan is greatly exaggerated. India's economy is eight times Pakistan's. Its military budget is seven times that of Pakistan. Pakistan's post–financial crash per capita growth rate is about 1 per cent compared to 5.7 per cent per annum for India. Pakistan's investment rate of 11 per cent of GDP is one third of India's.[3] It is inconceivable that Pakistan can close the military and economic gap with India. It has sought to close its inferiority in conventional arms by building a larger nuclear arsenal including short-range tactical weapons. But as numerous war games show-going back to the days when NATO hoped to counter the conventional superiority of Russia through deploying tactical nuclear weapons during the Cold War- the use of tactical nuclear weapons can lead to rapid escalation to full-scale nuclear war. This would turn Pakistan—and parts of India—into a nuclear wasteland.[4] Moreover, if Pakistan envisages a scenario in which an Indian armoured thrust through the Punjab border would be countered by using tactical nuclear weapons, it will in effect be firing these weapons on its own soil, in its densely populated Pakistani Punjab, with devastating consequences for its own population. Hence this threat is not credible.[5] Pakistan has also used asymmetric warfare (terrorism) against India, but jihadists are now turning against the Pakistani army itself, adding to the impression that Pakistan is a failing state. Pakistan's 'elusive quest for parity' with India is bound to fail. A rational state would accept this, come to terms with India—accepting the territorial status quo as envisaged in the abortive Manmohan Singh–Musharraf talks—and join the subcontinental free trade area on offer. This would provide immense gains from trade to Pakistan. But the Pakistan Army, which still controls foreign policy in the democratic civilian regime, has demurred.[6]

The Pakistani military has lost every war in which it has fought. Given the current disparity in its military and economic strength with India, it is—as far as India is concerned—a paper tiger. If this is the case, it makes no sense for much of the Indian forces to be deployed on its Western frontier rather than on its northern borders to deal with the more potent threat from China. In an important book, the Indian national security strategist Bharat Karnad[7] has argued that given this asymmetry and to assuage the fears of the Pakistani army, India should unilaterally withdraw part of its current forces from the Pakistan border and reassign them to deal with the growing threat from China.

Pakistan's deployment of terrorists for asymmetric warfare has also failed. Ironically, the jihadis created by Pakistan are now increasingly turning against their sponsors—as witnessed in their attack on the secondary school for the children of military personnel in Peshawar.[8, 9]

There is some hope that the imbalance of military power having pushed Pakistan into dire economic straits, as it has expanded its India-centric infrastructure for war, will at some stage persuade the Pakistani army that instead of becoming a vassal of the Chinese, it would be in its and its country's interest to end the frozen Indo-Pak conflict, and revive the strategic unity of the subcontinent destroyed by partition.[10] As I have argued elsewhere,[11] the only final solution to the Kashmir dispute is to accept the Line of Control (LOC) as the international border. This would allow trade between the two countries, with Pakistan accepting the Most Favoured Nation principle, leading to a free trade agreement with immense economic benefits to the two countries. This sort of agreement has been mooted many times and nearly came to pass with the quasi agreement between President Musharraf and Prime Minister Manmohan Singh in 2007.[12]

China

If this could be achieved, the Indian foreign policy initiatives begun under Manmohan Singh and strengthened under Narendra Modi would fructify. These include countering Chinese moves to alienate its neighbours and taking the implicit battle with China to China's own periphery through an increased naval presence under India's 'Look East' policy. This would counter China's aim of strategically and economically encircling India. India still has various options to resist China as the Asian, and with the purported American decline, the global, hegemon. Having woken up, it will hopefully not end up as the proverbial cooked frog in a South Asian pot heated slowly by the Chinese.[13]

China's attempts to entice some of India's neighbours have already come unstuck, as its aim of converting them first into economic and then strategic vassals have become evident (see Chapter 2). But some missteps by the Modi government have given China a new opening. Myanmar's military dictator cancelled various economic projects with China while moving towards a democratic polity. But India's foolish chest-thumping after a routine operation against anti-Indian militants, which had been quietly accepted by the Myanmar government in the past, has left the government fuming, providing another new opening to China. In Sri Lanka, the change in government has loosened China's links but not eliminated its need for Chinese investments. Bangladesh has been enticed away from the Chinese embrace by a long-pending border agreement signed by the Modi government. But, the blockade of Nepal after a revolt by the Nepalese Mahadesis on the Indo-Nepal border against their perceived disenfranchisement in the new Constitution has led the Nepalese government to seek fuel supplies from China.[14] The Maldives remains in turmoil after India's serious error 'in not supporting President Nasheed when he was under threat of being deposed'.[15] His successor has been looking to China to build its infrastructure. Hopefully, more skilful diplomacy will be able to keep these neighbours out of China's clutches.

If this can be done and if Pakistan ends its enmity with India, it may be possible to revive an idea suggested by President Ayub Khan of a subcontinental security pact. This security pact, says Karnad, was to be concluded by neighbouring states as a defence against Chinese aggression.[16] This did not come to pass. But Karnad argues that India now has to attempt to create an Indian 'Monroe Doctrine' by defining its security perimeter 'in the quadrant bounded by the East African littoral, the Caspian Sea, Central Asian Republics, the South East Nations and Antarctica'.[17]

As India, given its economic weakness relative to China, does not have the means to do this by itself, it will have to form—as it is beginning to do—alliances against Chinese aggressiveness. Central to these is the US. The US's hope that China's economic rise, which it helped to promote, would lead it to act as a responsible trading state, which would help to maintain the US-led international global order, has been belied. China, through mercantilist policies (to which the US turned a blind eye), has become an economic and military power that seeks to challenge US hegemony. With its rise, it is throwing its weight around. The more the West offers inducements to buy or pay the price for its good behaviour,[18] the more China instead 'seeks to create an extended Chinese Monroe Doctrine'.[19] To Obama's credit, he recognized this danger and sought to 'pivot' US foreign assets—including military—to Asia. This US pivot to Asia is rightly seen by the Chinese as a way to contain their aggressive rise.

But, as George W. Bush—and later Obama as well—saw clearly, this pivot to balance China cannot be done without India.

However, given the reluctance Obama showed in exercising US military power against threats to international order by Russia and the jihadists in the Middle East, how far can Asian states threatened by an aggressive China rely on the US to provide security in the face of a crisis with China? For, India (particularly its Nehruvian elite)—without the US treaty obligations that provide some sense of security (though diminished under the limp Obama) to South Korea, Japan, and the Philippines—has had cause to distrust the US. This distrust is borne from the US's actions during the Indo-Pak war that created Bangladesh,[20] the sanctions it imposed after India's first and second nuclear test, and what is seen as its attempts to balance India through providing military aid to Pakistan.[21] But from President Trump's recent statements on Af-Pak and the Indo-Pacific, the US attitude to both Pakistan and China is changing and is more in line with Indian interests.

Given its past disappointments with US actions against its interests, India is thus reluctant to enter into a formal alliance with the US.[22] US policymakers now recognize this. A recent Council on Foreign Relations Task Force[23] has proposed an alternative model of partnership

> borrowed from the business world, that of a joint venture.... Just as joint ventures in business bring together parties to advance a shared objective without subordinating their many other interests, so should India and the US pursue their shared ambitions without assuming that each will—or even should—see eye to eye with the other on every matter. Reframing ties in this way will better explain how convergence on the need for open sea lanes, for example, may not presume agreement on climate change, and how convergence on the Asia-Pacific may not presuppose like-mindedness on the Middle East.[24]

The problem that worries India and other countries in the Indo-Pacific is that the US strategy to deal with a rising and increasingly aggressive China is based on the premise that China can be co-opted into the liberal order, which would avoid 'threats levied against its principal guardian, the United States'.[25] The Obama administration had continued this 'cooperate-but-hedge' policy of its predecessors, but with much greater emphasis on co-operating than hedging. This is based on the erroneous 'benign diagnosis of China's strategic objectives in Asia', without understanding and digesting the reality that China's grand strategy in Asia today is to undermine US vital national interests and it has had some success.[26]

Given this US ambivalence towards China, India and the other Asian countries threatened by China have begun to form strategic partnerships among themselves. India had been cool in cementing these potential ties because of a fear of provoking China when it is relatively weak. But the new Modi government has been much more proactive in promoting strategic ties with Japan and ASEAN, shifting its 'Look East' policy to 'Act East', and being willing to offend China by signing a joint statement (after Modi's US visit) with President Obama (reaffirmed on Modi's meeting with President Trump), which asserted India's interest in seeing freedom of navigation being maintained with the current status quo in the Western Pacific, particularly the South China Sea.

What India is hopefully beginning to do is to assert its naval presence in the Indian Ocean and West Pacific by strengthening its maritime partnerships with the navies of Japan, Australia, Singapore, and Vietnam, and lately with Australia.[27] This would allow it and its partners to control the naval choke points of the Straits of Hormuz and Malacca. These were crucial during the British Raj to convert the Indian Ocean into an Indian lake, preventing any maritime threat to India. By providing armaments, particularly to Vietnam, the Modi government has shown a greater willingness to play an active role in regional security.

To counter China's string of pearls strategy, Karnad delineates a layered littoral/oceanic defence. The outermost perimeter in the east would depend on Japan and Taiwan, which can take care of themselves. The second defensive tier consists of Vietnam and the Philippines 'that requires a proactive policy to keep the ramparts strong. The innermost tier consists of Thailand and Singapore backed by India's Andaman Command'. Karnad argues for strengthening the second tier states 'with nuclear missiles and other strategic impact weapons as the BrahMos supersonic anti-ship cruise missile, and training crews for submarines, surface combatants, and fighter pilots, which would deny the Chinese navy unobstructed freedom in the South China Sea and, in crises, bottle up China's powerful South Sea Fleet in its China base on Hainan Island'. Making use of the docking rights and bases already offered by Vietnam and the Philippines, Indian naval flotillas frequently traversing the South China Sea 'putting in at Nha Trang, Da Nang, and Subic Bay, and the US Navy's carriers constantly plying the Asian waters, it would maintain the status of the South China Sea as an internationally navigable waterway, not sovereign Chinese territory, and reassure the local states'.[28]

In the western Indian Ocean, after procrastinating over the long-standing offer from Mauritius to anchor an Indian military presence in the two-island set of the Agalegas nearest to the Indian mainland, PM Modi finally signed an accord in March 2015 for developing defence infrastructure 'permitting Indian military use of the Agalegas'.[29] Building these islands as military bases 'would enable Indian forces to sandwich any hostile Chinese naval actions out of Sri Lanka, assuming Colombo can survive being treated as a belligerent by India'.[30]

The Indian Navy runs surveillance from Gan, a former British base in the Maldives. There is an Indian electronic intelligence post on the northern coast of Mozambique, with similar facilities in the Seychelles, Mauritius, and the Maldives to 'monitor the south-western Indian Ocean, with overlapping and extended 24/7 real-time surveillance'. However, India has not taken up the

> berthing-basing option ashore in Mozambique on the African littoral. Mozambique being 'keen to have a major Indian naval shore installation',[31] India has also not taken up the Philippines' offer 'of the former US naval port at Subic Bay and Clark air force base for onshore use and military positioning.... New Delhi has not responded formally, but Indian naval ships in the South China Sea have taken to routinely pulling into Manila and Subic Bay on impromptu port calls and 'goodwill visits'.[32]

This reluctance to establish foreign military bases is based partly on the economic cost, given India's still relatively weak economy; partly on the desire to free ride on the robust US naval presence in the Indo-Pacific, including its major base in Diego Garcia; and partly because most of the friendly states seeking security assurances from India 'have gained from China's economic largesse and trade concessions which they cannot do without.' So while not denying anything 'by way of physical access or whatever else is needed in military terms,.... they expect India to be sensitive and discreet, and not disclose the details of the ongoing and underway strategic co-operation programs and projects, just so they can preserve the facade of equidistance and the beneficial economic relationship with China'.[33] But what is undoubtedly being built up is 'an elastic *cordon sanitaire* around seaward China that may bend but will not break'.[34] India, therefore, seems to be on the way of dealing with its maritime vulnerabilities.[35]

What about the northern threat from the Chinese PLA ensconced on the Tibetan plateau? Karnad argues, based on interviews with India's past and current military brass, that if the PLA intrudes to take Tawang or intrudes inside Arunachal Pradesh to take Indian territory, there are plans for an 'escalatory counter-strategy of offensive air actions', targeting 'the fragile high altitude desert ecology of Tibet'. The first response will be making 2,000 km deep strikes into Tibet targeting the Qinghai–Lhasa railway, which is built on permafrost, which will cave in. While 'Su-30 bombing sorties with 20–30 gravity bombs will be ordered to destroy the permafrost along the LOC so that the entire Chinese line and border infrastructure collapses and isolates the aggressor PLA units. The IAF has a slate of graded responses to provide fire-breaks for possible termination of conflict'.[36]

In this escalatory ladder of conventional warfare, India would, apart from attacking the vulnerable permafrost and logistics infrastructure on its northern border, also have the upper hand because of China's massive domestic infrastructure that offers 'attractive targets to air-launched ordinance'. The most potent of these would be an attack on the Three Gorges Dam, which would cause havoc because of heavy flooding downstream. A Chinese government official assessment in 1987 simply assumed that war would not threaten the dam. More objective Chinese analysts, however, believe the dam would be struck, and the consequences of its destruction 'for the military, and for the entire nation would be disastrous'.[37] That is why it appears that 'Taipei has this dam in its crosshairs. Taipei is convinced that posing a credible threat to this dam will "deter Chinese coercion"[38] (Wertz). New Delhi maybe thinking along similar lines'.[39]

The triad of India's nuclear deterrent hopefully precludes the danger of a Chinese escalation to the nuclear level. In this context, one of India's strengths is its formidable missile power, developed indigenously after the Western ban on technology transfer following India's first nuclear test in the early 1970s.[40]

Tibet

Finally, there is India's Tibet card. Despite the series of errors that have led to India recognizing Chinese sovereignty over Tibet, there is a diplomatic loophole it has left for itself. 'It may have accepted Chinese "sovereignty" but only over an "autonomous" Tibet, and in so far as Tibetan autonomy is a sham India is free to reconsider its attitude to occupied Tibet'.[41] As the Dalai Lama has also demanded an autonomous Tibet and not independence for the last sixty years, this would also have great resonance among his many supporters in the West, including Hollywood actors like Richard Gere. India should organize a public campaign for 'a verifiably autonomous Tibet'.[42]

Given the rising ethnic dissent in Tibet (and Xinjiang), India can, secondly, revive the option last exercised in the late 1950s when it joined the US in training Khampa warriors in guerrilla warfare and launching operations inside Tibet.[43] Establishment 22, located in Dehradun in the Himalayan foothills, is operational as the centre for training the Special Frontier Force (SFF), manned by Tibetan exiles and officered by the Indian Army.[44]

There has clearly been a rethink by the Indian government of India's Tibet policy. To counter China's claim on the north-eastern

Indian state of Arunachal Pradesh, Indian foreign ministers (S.M. Krishna in 2007 and Sushma Swaraj in 2014) had announced that 'India will not recognize "One China" if Beijing doesn't align its policy and pronouncements to include Arunachal Pradesh in the "One India" concept'.[45] At his investiture ceremony, Narendra Modi formally invited Lobsang Sangay, the elected prime minister of the Tibetan Government in Exile to whom the Dalai Lama has handed over his political role.

But the Modi government has been reluctant to play the Tibet card because of the infrastructure investment dangled by President Xi on his first meeting with Modi in 2014. But, in line with the Chinese strategy of enticing its enemies with economic deals, less than $3 billion of the $100 billion promised by Xi to improve Indian infrastructure has been released, as China seeks to influence policy rather than improve its infrastructure by releasing these funds in dribs and drabs.[46]

The other inducements to preclude India from playing the Tibet card are the periodic Chinese statements of resolving the border dispute. But this is also a false hope. As Shyam Saran, the former Indian foreign secretary and the Indian interlocutor on these border talks, notes, 'In the series of talks between the Special Representatives of the two prime ministers, now in their 11th year, little progress has been recorded on settling the border issue', and that 'any prospect of changing the status quo at the border is dependent upon our ability to make any attempt to change it costly and risky to the other side'.[47]

It is clearly time to play the Tibet card and argue for an autonomous Tibet, which will restore the buffer on India's northern frontier that Lord Curzon, the best geopolitician who sought to ensure Indian security, had so assiduously tried to create, and which Nehru and subsequent Indian governments so foolishly allowed to be annexed by China. Even though it is unlikely that China would at present agree to this, keeping the Tibet issue alive and denouncing the bloody repression of non-Han minorities generally would be in the interests of India, the US, and many of China's neighbours.

Indigenous Defence Industry

India has also lagged China in developing an indigenous defence industry. Instead, it has relied on imports for its conventional weaponry, making it the largest arms importer in the world. But this import dependency—particularly for spare parts—makes India reliant on foreign sources for supplies in the case of a prolonged military conflict. This is particularly ironic as Nehru had envisaged 'a versatile, advanced and flourishing defense industrial sector'[48] and laid its foundations by entrusting Homi Bhabha with developing the nuclear, space, and missile programmes, which have proved more than their worth. But these programmes were based on 'mission-mode research, development, and production. No expense or effort was spared nor were any systematic hurdles tolerated by the Indian government'.[49]

By contrast, no such urgency, technological challenge, or sense of purpose informed projects to develop conventional military armaments. Instead imports, which offered those involved in their purchase corrupt pay-offs, were preferred. Among the seminal projects initiated in the late 1950s that did not reach fruition, 'the most remarkable was one that built a supersonic fighter aircraft in record time. If it had been properly followed up, India would have had a world-class Indian aviation and aerospace industry'.[50]

Another missed opportunity to establish a first rate indigenous defence industry was lost with the demise of the Soviet Union, when unable to afford the salaries of Russia's nuclear and missile scientists and the skilled designers and production engineers of conventional armaments from the Russian defence industry, a desperate Boris Yeltsin offered them to India. The Narasimha Rao government rejected the offer 'because the emoluments sought for the Russian personnel (which were a pittance—involving at that time, free boarding and lodging and a monthly stipend of $200 for each of the imported personnel) surpassed the pay-scale of top civil servants'![51] India's loss was China's gain 'as Beijing grabbed the Russians, which may explain the surge in the last decade in the quality and variety of weapons programs under development by the Chinese defence companies'.[52]

These Indian own goals have meant that now India finds itself on the back foot not only in its relative economic performance compared with China but also in conventional military hardware. The new Modi government has realized the lacunae and is now trying to build up the domestic defence industry by opening it up to private industry, allowing foreign investment, and imposing the indigenization of imported foreign technology. But given the time it takes for these defence projects to fructify, China will continue to have an edge in the supply of conventional military hardware.

Meanwhile, India will have to continue participating and strengthening the implicit cordon sanitaire around China with its friends and allies, while going full speed ahead with the economic reforms required to put it on a double- digit GDP growth path for the next two decades—using the means this will provide to create a technologically advanced and efficient domestic defence industry to produce conventional weapons, while continually upgrading its strategic weapons to deter any attacks on its frontiers. But the threat from a paranoid and increasingly insecure political regime in China will continue to present a danger of war with China, particularly if the CCP, with no obvious means of legitimizing its authoritarian one-party rule, falters in its implicit compact of providing rising living standards to its populace with an inevitably slowing economy. The CCP might, then, be tempted to play the nationalist card by using its forty million 'bare branches'[53] (see Chapter 5) to rampage through its neighbourhood. It is to be hoped the CCP will be deterred by the cordon sanitaire its neighbours are constructing to counter its aggressiveness and will revert to the trading state strategy it followed in its spectacular economic rise, which has served it and its people so brilliantly. But this seems unlikely.

Notes

1. In an important book, Andrew Small, *The China-Pakistan Axis: Asia's New Geopolitics* (London: Hurst and Co., 2015), shows the changing nature of the China–Pakistan axis. It was forged after the 1959 flight

of the Dalai Lama to India and the subsequent 1962 Indo-China border war. But China refused to enter the 1965 and 1971 Indo-Pak wars on the side of Pakistan. 'The nuclearization of the subcontinent fundamentally changed China's handling of subsequent Indo-Pakistani confrontations, and Zulfiqar Ali Bhutto's successors were to receive an even cooler reception when they flew to Beijing during periods of conflict to solicit Chinese support' (p. 25).

2. John Elliott, 'China Aims to Block India's Place in the Sun', *Financial Times* (13 August 2009). Available at http://www.ft.com/cms/s/0/26b241ba-8809-11de-82e4-00144feabdc0,dwp_uuid=a6dfcf08-9c79-11da-8762-0000779e2340.html (last accessed 20 November 2017). Also published in *Riding the Elephant* blog. Available at https://ridingtheelephant.wordpress.com/2009/08/13/china-aims-to-block-india%E2%80%99s-place-in-the-sun (last accessed 20 November 2017). The article also said, 'India's national unity is weak and that China could exploit this by supporting separatist forces, such as those active in India's north-eastern state of Assam, and split the country into 20 or 30 sovereign states.' Elliott, who was the *Financial Times*'s first South Asian correspondent (1983–8), comments that it 'almost certainly reflects Beijing thinking, even though the founder of the website has claimed the anonymous writer has no known government links'.
3. T.N. Ninan, *The Turn of the Tortoise: The Challenge and Promise of India's Future* (New Delhi: Allen Lane, Penguin, 2015), p. 266.
4. Praveen Swami summarizes the results of these war games. In 1955, Exercise Carte Blanche showed that when NATO used 'its new tactical nuclear weapons to beat back Soviet armour driving towards the heart of Europe. In less than a week, the answers were in: 1.7 million dead, 3.5 million injured, large parts of Europe levelled by 335 nuclear bombs. The mock-Soviets won, despite NATO's use of tactical nuclear weapons. That is, if the desolation could be called victory.' Similarly, 'in 1972, the Soviet general staff completed the last of a series of exercises simulating a European nuclear war. The numbers were stark: eight million dead, 85 per cent of Soviet industrial capacity wiped out, the army degraded by a factor of 1,000; the European part of the country reduced to an uninhabitable wasteland. The two Cold War adversaries came to the conclusion, in the 1980s, that a war in Europe was unwinnable—and focused on enhancing their conventional defensive means instead'. See Praveen Swami,

'Pakistan's Nuclear Weapons May Not Deter Indian Retaliation, but Destruction Mutual', *Indian Express* (28 October 2015). Available at http://indianexpress.com/article/opinion/columns/pakistans-nuclear-weapons-may-not-deter-indian-retaliation-but-destruction-mutual/ (last accessed 20 November 2017).

5. Bharat Karnad, *Why India Is Not a Great Power (Yet)* (New Delhi: Oxford University Press, 2015), also argues against the perceived threat from Pakistan's recent proclaimed intention of using tactical nuclear weapons to counter an Indian conventional attack. He argues that the original Indian plan to advance into Pakistan from the semi-desert area on its south-west border has been changed. The new strategy is 'for the independent battle groups to rush headlong towards a few Pakistani cities in the "strategic corridor" running north to south near the Indian border and to quickly close in on these industrial and population centres'. The Indian Army marching lock stop with any Pakistani attempts to withdraw deeper into their own territory presents Pakistani nuclear planners with a dilemma. 'Initiating first use of nuclear weapons in these circumstances immediately outside their own cities may take out bits of Indian armor without appreciably slowing down the concentration of armored/mechanized units operating in sealed, hatch down mode (T-72 and T-90 tanks in the Indian inventory being operable in an irradiated environment) around Pakistani cities. The thermal flash, kinetic death blows, and radiation from the Pakistani nuclear device use will severely impact the unprotected Pakistani military units and population in the surrounded cities as much as they will do the Indian forces'. If the Pakistani nuclear strategists then target sites within India, 'the hostilities will spiral into a total war, which Pakistan cannot survive, because of an adverse "exchange ratio" (the ratio of destruction suffered to destruction imposed on the adversary)' (pp. 352–3). Evidently this strategy 'has been extensively gamed by the Indian military and Strategic forces', p. 399.
6. However, in an important book, C. Christine Fair, *Fighting to the End: The Pakistan Army's Way of War* (New York: Oxford University Press, 2014), has argued that this is unlikely given the ideology of the Pakistan Army, which has effectively ruled Pakistan since its creation. The basis of this ideology is the 'two-nation' theory, which views Muslims as a 'nation' distinct from and in opposition to Hindus. 'It defines the threat from India in ideational and civilizational as well

as military terms. For the army, acquiescing to India is tantamount to accepting that the two-nation theory is illegitimate or defunct, thus undermining the founding logic of Pakistan itself. No military, political, or diplomatic defeat Pakistan has yet suffered has been adequate to persuade the army to revise its anti-status quo position' (p. 278). To pursue these objectives 'the tools will likely remain its alliances with the United States and China as well as the asymmetric warfare under Pakistan's ever expanding nuclear umbrella' (p. 281).

These alliances for the Pakistanis are however also a means of rent-seeking, particularly in its relations with the US (p. 199). By contrast, Pakistan has been unable to convince China that it 'owes' Pakistan anything. 'In recent years, Pakistan's military and civilian officials have busily obscured China's repeated failures to act as the all-weather friend'. They cannot contemplate 'the possibility that China will not strongly support Pakistan in a future Indo-Pakistani conflict [as they have not since 1965]' (p. 200). She argues that it is time for the US to call the Pakistan military's bluff (p. 282). Also see Hussain Haqqani, *Magnificent Delusions: Pakistan, the United States, and an Epic History of Misunderstanding* (New York: Public Affairs, 2013); Anatol Lieven, *Pakistan: A Hard Country* (London: Penguin, 2012); Ahmed Rashid, *Pakistan on the Brink: The Future of America, Pakistan, and Afghanistan* (New York: Viking, 2012); Ian Talbot, *Pakistan: A New History* (London: Hurst and Company, 2012); and S.P. Cohen, *The Pakistan Army* (Karachi: Oxford University Press, 1998), *The Idea of Pakistan* (Washington, DC: Brookings Institution, 2004), and *The Future of Pakistan* (Washington, DC: Brookings Institution, 2011).

7. Karnad, *Why India Is Not a Great Power (Yet)*, argues that Indo-Pak wars have been gentlemanly wars because of the shared socio-cultural fabric and the history of the two militaries as part of the same colonial force. The convention has developed of 'prosecuting conventional conflicts of limited duration, scale, and with the utmost restraint'. This has also facilitated a nuclear *modus vivendi* (p. 166).
8. In this contest, Small, *The China-Pakistan Axis*, provides a fascinating account of another dimension of the China–Pakistan axis concerning terrorism. One of the major concerns of the Chinese is to counter the threat from Islamic Uighur militants to its control of the restive Chinese region of Xinjiang, which borders Pakistan's northern frontiers. With Pakistan's use of Islamist militants to fight it proxy wars in India and Afghanistan, when these turned on the

Chinese in June 2007 in the so called Lal Masjid (Red Mosque) encounter (see pp. ix–xvi), the Pakistani military's storming of the mosque 'led to the irrevocable altering of the relationship between Pakistan's military and the its militants' (p. x), but it has led to militants from Baluchistan to Federally Administered Tribal Areas (FATA) targeting Chinese interests and workers so that 'Pakistan was on its way to becoming the single most dangerous overseas location for Chinese workers' (p. xv). This has also 'threatened to derail the two side's plans to add a serious economic dimension to a partnership that has been almost entirely about security' (p. 4). But obsessed with the Uighur issue the Chinese 'have started to raise the broader concerns about the creeping "Islamisation" of the Pakistani army. It is one thing for China to provide comprehensive military assistance to an avowedly India-centric army, but quite another if elements in that army have goals that extend beyond the logic of balancing and deterrence towards the demand of *jihad*' (p. 91). The Uighur issue also led the Chinese to have 'tea with the Taliban' to deal with the threat posed to its security by the instability in Afghanistan. After the US withdrawal from Afghanistan was mooted the Chinese came to care more 'about stability in Afghanistan than Pakistan did, and was less hung up on India's role in the country which many on the Chinese side saw as potentially helpful if it took the form of investment and support for political stability'. The worst nightmare for China is 'civil war, a buoyant insurgency that could destabilize Pakistan too, proxy wars taking off between New Delhi and Islamabad and an environment in which terrorist groups hostile to China might flourish' (p. 162). This brings the Chinese role closer to being a regional stabilizer in the Af-Pak region, closer to the US and Indian aims, and that is why I have not emphasized any threats to Indian security from the Af-Pak region in the text.

9. Christine Fair, *Fighting to the End*, explains the utility of one of the major terrorist organizations, Lashkar-e-Taiba (LeT), which was responsible for the terrorist attack in Mumbai, India. Unlike other Deobandi groups, which have increasingly launched terrorist attacks inside Pakistan, the LeT is committed to the integrity of the Pakistani state. Since 2002, it has also expanded into providing social services (p. 238). But it has continued to conduct Pakistan's 'irregular warfare as enabled by Pakistan's expanding nuclear umbrella' (p. 259). Thus, 'LeT should be seen as serving two functions simultaneously:

prosecuting Pakistan's external policies while also undermining Deobandi groups that advocate attacking within Pakistan'. It aligns with the strategic goals of the Pakistan Army: to preserve and protect not just the state but also the state's ideology (p. 260).

10. See Khaled Ahmed, 'When Reality Outruns Strategy', *Indian Express* (3 March 2014). Available at http://indianexpress.com/article/opinion/columns/when-reality-outruns-strategy/ (last accessed 20 November 2017).
11. D. Lal, 'The Status Quo in Kashmir?', in Richard Rosecrance and Arthur Stein: *No More States* (Lanham, MD: Rowan and Littlefield, 2006), pp. 145–59.
12. See Sanjay Baru, *The Accidental Prime Minister: The Making and Unmaking of Manmohan Singh* (New Delhi: Viking-Penguin, 2014), Ch. 10.
13. John W. Garver, 'The Diplomacy of Rising China in South Asia', *Orbis*, 56, no. 3 (Summer 2012), pp. 391–411, describes the Chinese strategy vis-à-vis India as follows: 'A Chinese fable tells of how a frog in a pot of lukewarm water feels quite comfortable and safe. He does not notice as the water temperature slowly rises until, at last, the frog dies and is thoroughly cooked. This homily, *wen shui zhu qingwa* in Chinese, describes fairly well China's strategy for growing its influence in South Asia in the face of a deeply suspicious India: move forward slowly and carefully, rouse minimal suspicion and don't cause an attempt at escape by the intended victim' (p. 391).
14. See Shyam Saran, 'Put Neighbourhood Policy Back on Track', *Business Standard* (10 November 2015). Available at http://www.business-standard.com/article/opinion/shyam-saran-put-neighbourhood-policy-back-on-track-115111001450_1.html (last accessed 20 November 2017). The article outlines the nature of the Nepal crisis and India's failure to take pre-emptive action to prevent it.
15. Saran, 'Put Neighbourhood Policy Back on Track'. The latest threat to Indian interest is Maldives government's hasty signing of a free trade agreement (FTA) with China.
16. Karnad, *Why India Is Not a Great Power (Yet)*, p. 139.
17. Karnad, *Why India Is Not a Great Power (Yet)*, p. 20.
18. Karnad, *Why India Is Not a Great Power (Yet)*, p. 98.
19. Karnad, *Why India Is Not a Great Power (Yet)*, p. 99.
20. See Gary J. Bass, *The Blood Telegram: India's Secret War in East Pakistan* (New Delhi: Random House India, 2013).

21. See Carlotta Gall, *The Wrong Enemy: American in Afghanistan, 2001–2014* (London: Penguin Books, 2014).
22. Charles R. Kaye, Joseph S. Nye, Jr., and Alyssa Ayres, 'A New Indo-US Partnership Model', *Indian Express* (11 November 2015). Available at http://indianexpress.com/article/opinion/columns/a-new-indo-us-partnership-model/ (last accessed 20 November 2017). The authors note that

    'Americans are accustomed to specific terms when thinking about allies and partners. Washington sees alliance relationships as the closest forms of partnership—a relationship of mutual support and obligation. But Washington also expects its allies and closest partners to endorse, or at least not reject outright, American policy positions. In India, on the other hand, a strong sense of policy independence creates a different assumption for Delhi's relationships, one focused on maximizing independence and limiting obligations. For this reason, even though India and the US have much stronger convergence of views than they used to on many global developments, it still comes as a surprise for many in Washington when Indian officials appear to embrace positions that Americans see as impossible to understand, such as during Russia's invasion of Ukraine, which India carefully refrained from criticizing'.

23. Alyssa Ayres, Charles R. Kaye, Joseph S. Nye, Jr., and Christopher M. Tuttle, 'Working with a Rising India: A Joint Venture for the New Century, Council on Foreign Relations', Independent Task force Report No. 73 (New York: Council on Foreign Relations, 2015).
24. Kaye, Nye Jr, and Ayres, 'A New Indo-US Partnership Model'.
25. Robert D. Blackwill and Ashley J. Tellis, 'Revising U.S. Grand Strategy toward China, Council on Foreign Relations', Council Special Report No. 72 (New York: Council on Foreign Relations, 2015), p. 16. They argue that Washington needs a new grand strategy toward China that centres on balancing the rise of Chinese power rather than continuing to assist its ascendancy. This must derive from clear recognition that preserving US primacy in the global system ought to remain the central objective of US grand strategy in the twenty-first century. This requires 'recreating a technology-control regime involving U.S. allies that prevents China from acquiring military and strategic capabilities enabling it to inflict "high-leverage

strategic harm" on the U.S. and its partners; concertedly building up the power-political capacities of U.S. friends and allies on China's periphery; and improving the capability of U.S. military forces to effectively project power along the Asian rimlands despite any Chinese opposition—all while continuing to work with China in the diverse ways that befit its importance to U.S. national interests' (pp. 4–5).

26. Blackwill and Tellis, 'Revising U.S. Grand Strategy toward China', pp. 38–9.
27. Darshana M. Baruah, 'South China Sea: Time for India to Mark Its Presence', *RSIS Commentary*, no. 225, (Singapore: S. Rajaratnam School of International Studies, 17 November 2014).
28. Karnad, *Why India Is Not a Great Power (Yet)*, pp. 254–5. He also notes that a Vietnamese military delegation in late June 2011 'offered the port Nha Trang on the South China Sea with line-of-sight on Hainan Island for the Indian Navy's exclusive use—the only foreign navy so favoured—besides agreeing to accord docking rights to Indian naval ships in Cam Ranh Bay, 60 miles down the coast'. Because of India's reluctance to establish foreign bases, though using both Nha Trang and Cam Ranh Bay as docking stations, it has 'stationed its naval personnel in Cam Ranh Bay to man a signals intercept/electronic intelligence station monitoring Chinese naval activity and communications traffic ex-Hainan Island, which hosts both the South China Fleet headquarters and the PLA's Cyber Command' (p. 256).
29. Karnad, *Why India Is Not a Great Power (Yet)*, p. 257.
30. Karnad, *Why India Is Not a Great Power (Yet)*, p. 256.
31. Karnad, *Why India Is Not a Great Power (Yet)*, p. 267.
32. Karnad, *Why India Is Not a Great Power (Yet)*, p. 266.
33. Karnad, *Why India Is Not a Great Power (Yet)*, p. 265.
34. Karnad, *Why India Is Not a Great Power (Yet)*, p. 264.
35. Also see C. Raja Mohan, *Samudra Manthan: Sino-Indian Rivalry in the Indo-Pacific* (New Delhi: Oxford University Press, 2013).
36. Mohan, *Samudra Manthan*, p. 330.
37. D. Qing, *The River Dragon Has Come!: The Three Gorges Dam and the Fate of China's Yangtze River and Its People* (New York: M.E. Sharp, 1998), pp. 171–2, 175.
38. R.R. Wertz, 'Special Report: Three Gorges Dam' (2011). Available at http://www.ibiblio.org/chinesehistory/contents/07spe/specrep01.html (last accessed 20 November 2017).

39. Karnad, *Why India Is Not a Great Power (Yet)*, p. 333.
40. For details see, Karnad, *Why India Is Not a Great Power (Yet)*, pp. 373–93. He argues that despite 'the unbridgeable gap in strategic forces that China has opened up with India, it is suicidal for New Delhi to expect that the threat from a small force of small-yield weapons would be either deter or be dissuasive' (p. 385). He argues for India developing megaton thermonuclear weapons to make its nuclear deterrence of China more persuasive. He also argues for a credible nuclear deterrent against possible nuclear threats from its medium-range nuclear missiles based in Tibet, Chengdu, and Xinjiang. In the face of a rapid Chinese conventional attack in Arunachal Pradesh, which the Indian forces cannot tackle, any Indian desire to threaten nuclear escalation in these circumstances would not be credible given its limited nuclear arsenal. He says:

    The only credible nuclear deterrent in the circumstances are atomic demolition munitions (ADMs) placed just behind the prepared defensive line along the ingress routes of the PLA in the mountains, a line beyond which Chinese intrusion is deemed unacceptable. It may be a very long border but there are surprisingly few valleys providing easy routes for the PLA to intrude in strength across the Himalayan watershed and these are restricted to the western and eastern ends of the disputed border. The public announcement of placement of ADMs without disclosing their locations would transform the onus and risk of breaching the LAC and tripping the nuclear wire to China….The possibility of whole mountainsides coming down and burying its forces, and of units that escape being either destroyed in detail or, taken prisoners of war, affording India political and negotiating leverage, is not a prospect Beijing will take lightly'. (pp. 391–2).

41. Karnad, *Why India Is Not a Great Power (Yet)*, p. 112.
42. Karnad, *Why India Is Not a Great Power (Yet)*, p. 112.
43. See K. Conboy and J. Morrison, *The CIA's Secret War in Tibet* (Lawrence, KS: University of Kansas Press, 2002).
44. Karnad, *Why India Is Not a Great Power (Yet)*, p. 110.
45. P.D. Samanta, 'One China? What about One India Policy: Sushma Swaraj to Wang Yi', *Indian Express* (12 June 2014). Available at http://indianexpress.com/article/india/india-others/one-china-what-about-one-india-policy-sushma-to-wang/ (last accessed 20 November 2017).

46. Karnad, *Why India Is Not a Great Power (Yet)*, p. 112.
47. S. Saran, 'India–China Border Dispute—Coping with Asymmetry', *Business Standard* (14 April 2014). Available at http://www.business-standard.com/article/opinion/shyam-saran-india-china-border-dispute-coping-with-asymmetry-114041300669_1.html (last accessed 20 November 2017). Also see his account of China's changing position on the border in S. Saran, '1962—The View from Beijing', *Business Standard* (14 April 2014). Available at http://www.business-standard.com/article/opinion/shyam-saran-1962-the-view-from-beijing-114040701205_1.html (last accessed 20 November 2017).
48. Karnad, *Why India Is Not a Great Power (Yet)*, p. 422.
49. Karnad, *Why India Is Not a Great Power (Yet)*, p. 421.
50. Karnad, *Why India Is Not a Great Power (Yet)*, p. 422. India, like the US and Russia, raided the German military complex at the end of the Second World War for talent. The US and Russia did this to develop missiles; India did it for aviation. 'In 1957, Nehru hired Dr. Kurt Tank, the legendary designer of Focke-Wulf Fw 190 fighter and other planes for the wartime Nazi Luftwaffe, to design and develop a Mach 1-plus capable multi-role jet plane at HAL, Bangalore. Four years later, the first prototype of the Marut HF-24 fighter bomber rolled out for a test flight, the first such warplane produced outside the US and Europe' (p. 422). But the stages required to make it operational were stymied by Nehru's decision to make it a 'non-aligned aircraft' in association with Egypt, which never fructified. Then, a proposal by Hawker-Siddley to equip the HF-24 with a powerful jet engine was vetoed by Krishna Menon. Despite this, in 1967, when Tank returned to Germany, 'the West German government evinced interest in manufacturing the HF-24 under license in Germany and for further joint development of the aircraft. Berlin no doubt planned to build and equip the plane with a more powerful engine and thus restart a full-fledged combat aircraft industry. But Nehru died in 1964 and there was no one in the Indian government with the strategic foresight to approve such a collaborative venture' (p. 423). Much worse, the IAF then sabotaged the Kurt Tank-trained team of HAL designers working on a Mk-II version of the Marut, and saw to it that there was an end to the design and development capacity created by Kurt Tank at HAL, so that there was no indigenous capacity to produce 'warplanes that it feared it would be

compelled to fly' (p. 423). It was after a fifteen-year break 'and the loss of the Tank-trained generation of gifted aircraft designers, that such a capability was revived with the Tejas Light Combat Aircraft program'. But, with these aircraft now in production, the IAF is still dragging its feet on their deployment because of 'the services and military's antagonism generally to locally produced military goods' (p. 424).

51. Karnad, *Why India Is not a Great Power (Yet)*, rightly notes that the 'result would have been a leap in the quality of Indian-made armaments of all types, in the transmission of esoteric technology development skills, and the diffusion of these skills and capabilities to the Indian industry at large' (p. 429).
52. Karnad, *Why India Is Not a Great Power (Yet)*, p. 429.
53. Brahma Chellaney, *Asian Juggernaut: The Rise of India, China, and Japan* (New York: Harper Business, 2010), provides this estimate of 'marriageable men in mainland China [who] may have to do without wives', (p. 31). Also see Martin Walker, 'The Geopolitics of Sexual Frustration', *Foreign Policy* (20 October 2009). Available at http://foreignpolicy.com/2009/10/20/the-geopolitics-of-sexual-frustration/ (last accessed 19 November 2017). Walker argues that 'understanding the effect of the testosterone overload maybe most important in China. A Beijing power struggle between cautious old technocrats and aggressive young nationalists may be decided by mobs of rootless young men, demanding uniforms, rifles and a chance to liberate Taiwan'.

Conclusion

The centenary of the start of the First World War has been marked by a flurry of books[1] that examine the causes and consequences of this catastrophe, which ended the first LIEO. It saw the beginning of the end of the British pax, which had maintained global order for nearly a century. It has also led to speculations about whether, following the Global Financial Crisis (GFC) and the ensuing economic weakness of the successor imperial power (the US), another Great War could occur with rising powers challenging the American pax. As in 1914, and at the beginning of the Second World War that followed, there are various flashpoints we have identified, where there are current crises caused by rising or revanchist powers, which in different ways challenge the current global hegemon and could lead to war.

E.H. Carr in his flawed classic—*The Twenty Years' Crisis*,[2] which advocated realism versus idealism in international relations—had 'eschewed any single-factor structural explanation as to why wars occur or systems break down'. He identified 'three critical factors that have to be present to make any potential crisis dangerous and threatening: the existence of powerful and resentful states situated outside of the international order; a profound and sustained disruption of the global economy; and finally, the unwillingness or inability by any single power or "hegemon" to underwrite the international order.'[3]

Great Recession and Disruption of Global Economy

I have argued at length that though there was a fear of Carr's second critical factor during the GFC, sensible monetary policy on the part of the US Federal Reserve (though belated) did not allow it to turn into a 1930s Great Depression. The international global economy did not disintegrate as it did in the interwar years, despite some continuing policy errors relating to departures from classical liberalism. The most important of these errors, which partly caused the Great Recession, were the entitlements of Wall Street created by the ending of Glass-Steagall and the creation of universal banks. In these, risk-taking investment bankers who had in the past operated under unlimited liability in partnerships, where their necessary gambles were undertaken with their own 'skin in the game', could now form limited liability public companies. Given these were covered by deposit insurance, this meant that they could offload part of the costs of any failed bets onto the general public.[4] This has rightly caused public uproar and led to the rise of populist movements—which are also questioning the virtues of Anglo-American capitalism, the source of the untold global prosperity in this second period of globalization under the US pax. But, with the global economy slowly on the mend, despite the Jeremiahs, and the faults in the alternative authoritarian state capitalist models of China and Russia becoming apparent, I am much more confident both about the resilience and continued acceptance of Anglo-American capitalism.

Resentful States

However, as I have argued in this book, Carr's first condition for making war—'the existence of powerful and resentful states'—likely is currently met. We have two states, China and Russia, one a rising the other a revanchist great power, which are unwilling to accept the US-led international order. Then there are the ideological Islamist fundamentalist states of Iran and Saudi Arabia, which with their proxies are battling to impose their sectarian versions of Islam on their co-religionists, followed by a battle with the 'crusaders' to establish an Islamist international order.

Russia and Middle East

The threat to international order posed by three of the resentful states—Russia, Iran and Saudi Arabia—can, I have argued, be readily contained. Consistent and robust economic sanctions and the strengthening of NATO's military deterrence against Putin's past and any future aggression can readily deal with a Russia that is demographically and economically constrained.

The ongoing sectarian battle between the Sunni-led proxies of Saudi Arabia and the Shia-led proxies of Iran—with Turkey an interested bystander and potential arbiter and hegemon of the region—does not threaten international order. The rest of the world has no dogs in this fight, particularly after President Obama's failure to sign an SFO agreement with the Iraqis means that the military beachhead it had established in Mesopotamia no longer exists to allow it to be the arbiter of the region. The same will apply to the Af-Pak region once Western troops leave, as they are scheduled to do. This may be a pity for the inhabitants of these regions. But, having failed to establish any form of sustainable liberal order, it is now best to let the contestants fight it out, as in the religious Thirty Years' War in Europe, until mutual exhaustion leads to some form of Treaty of Westphalia and, hopefully, a Muslim Enlightenment.

Meanwhile, to thwart any blowback from Islamist militants seeking to establish their worldwide dominion through terrorism[5] and proselytizing Wahhabism among the Muslims settled in the West, I have argued for a 'cordon sanitaire' over much of the Middle East and Af-Pak. This will mean an end to the deal signed by Franklin Roosevelt and Ibn Saud on the USS *Quincy*. But with the fracking and oil sands revolutions in North America, the economic dangers of any resulting oil embargo from Middle Eastern oil producers have greatly diminished. The ending of this agreement would also allow the ending of the spread of intolerant

Wahhabism through the madrasas Saudi oil money has financed around the world.

China

This leaves China as the most potent of the resentful and powerful states seeking to change the US-led international order. I have argued that this is the greatest threat, which could lead to another world war. *The Next Great War?*[6]—a useful book by international theorists associated with the Belfer Center at Harvard—provides various perspectives on the risk of a US–China conflict by analogy with the causes of the First World War.

Various authors have suggested the similarities of prospective clashes between China and the treaty allies of the US in the Western Pacific, and those in Europe before World War I. Thus, Margaret MacMillan, a recent historian of that war, notes, 'it is tempting—and sobering—to compare today's relationship between China and the US, with that between Germany and England a century ago'.[7] While the other recent historian of the Great War—Christopher Clark—writes, 'I must say I was struck by the … insight … that our world is getting more like 1914, not less like it'.[8] Kevin Rudd, the former prime minister of Australia, explicitly states that the Western Pacific 'increasingly resembles a twenty-first century maritime redux of the Balkans a century ago—a tinder box on water'.[9]

International relations theorists are increasingly exercised by what has been called the Thucydidean trap. As Coker[10] explains, the actual trap Thucydides saw in the Peloponnesian War between Athens and Sparta was more complex than many theorists have assumed. 'Thucydides argued that neither Athens nor Sparta wanted to go to war against each other. But their respective allies persuaded them that war was inevitable, which led both powers to seize a decisive early advantage. They made this decision because they listened to their clients'.[11] Is this likely today?

China's only allies are its two client states: the rogue states of Pakistan and North Korea. But the Chinese, as we have seen, have not succumbed to Pakistan's pleas to get involved in the wars it has fought with India since 1965. This is unlikely to change. Nor is China likely to let an unpredictable North Korea lead it into a war with the US. The real danger, as Henry Kissinger has argued, 'is of an accident, incident or simply miscalculation on the Korean Peninsula, and Kissinger is particularly critical of the fact that the United States and China do not appear to have a plan to deal with that situation should it arise'.[12]

For the US, too, none of its regional allies would want to embroil their patron in a war. Moreover, as the US has increasingly shifted its 'hub-and-spoke' mode of its regional alliances to relying much more on bilateral alliances between and among its allies, the danger of it being dragged into an unwanted war by its allies in China's littoral also seems low.

This leaves Taiwan. The Chinese are determined to complete the unification of their country by absorbing Taiwan. The US is not committed by treaty but a Congressional commitment 'to take appropriate action in the event of a Chinese attack'. But, for the Chinese, this may no longer be necessary. With the growing inter-state economic relations, 'a Taiwanese defence minister has even stated that China stands to gain more from "buying" Taiwan than it does from attacking it'. However, Taiwan remains a flashpoint, not least because 'Taiwan is now a vital part of the US Navy's plans for the maritime containment of the Chinese mainland along the first island chain'.[13] It is like a giant US aircraft carrier just off the Chinese coast.

The role of the military in domestic politics and its control by civil authorities may be crucial if any of these flashpoints are to lead to war. Though, many believe that a rogue military scenario[14] is unlikely in China, as it clearly is for the US, there are signs that the undisputed civil control over the Chinese military may be breaking down. The reluctant intervention by the military in Tiananmen Square may be a sign of the shifting civil–military balance in China. The Bo Xilai affair, when he sought the help of the 14th Group Army commanded by his father in the past, also alarmed the CCP leadership. We have seen their growing paranoia and lack of trust between them and the various security agencies in Chapter 2. Also, as Coker notes, President Xi has 'rehabilitated a group of ultra-hawkish generals and military advisers, some of whom are outspoken in their belief in an "inevitable" showdown with the United States'. More serious are the signs that the PLA has increasingly been acting unilaterally.[15] 'The Central Military Commission seems to hold itself unaccountable to all but the most senior party leaders, and possibly only to the party general secretary, who is also its chairman'. More worrying is that while the civilian leadership is unsure of America's decline, the military seems convinced 'that China will overtake the United States by 2025, and thereafter be in a better position to assume global leadership'.[16]

There are many, particularly of the realist school, who suggest given these dangers of conflict between the US and China, America should appease China.[17] This is like the argument that the arch realist E.H. Carr made in his book about dealing with a rising Germany. But though agreeing with much of his realist stance, Hans Morgenthau and Hedley Bull—realists both—castigated Carr for

> lacking any objective perspective of his own from which to make an ethical judgment about the world, and was always compelled to 'surrender' to what Morgenthau called 'the immanence of power'. It was no accident that Carr had been in favour of appeasement, for it flowed logically from what Bull defined as his 'relativist and instrumentalist conception of morals' in which it was impossible to distinguish good from evil, right and wrong.[18]

But, would other countries (particularly the US) tolerate Chinese hegemony? Lee Kuan Yew correctly described what it would imply. 'At the core of their mindset is their world before colonization and the exploitation and humiliation that brought. In Chinese, China means "Middle Kingdom"—recalling a world in which they were dominant in the region, other states related to them as supplicants to a superior, and vassals came to Beijing bearing tribute'.[19] Even Lee's small Singapore is not willing to be so treated and is a robust member of the de facto alliance against any Chinese hegemony developing in Asia.

In fact, as we saw in Chapter 2, the Chinese never developed the political habits of interstate interaction among states, which presumed a formal equality as in the states system in Europe. Their view of interstate relations has been and (as Lee emphasized) is still based on the formal inequality of states, with the Chinese emperor at the centre, receiving deference through tribute paid by lesser nations. Western international relations theorists—who assume that the Chinese are similar actors to other participants in the European-type state system and advocate appeasement of a rising power—will only confirm China's belief in its superior cunning and its belief that the US can be easily manipulated to allow it to attain the Asian (and then global) hegemony it seeks.

There are signs that China's economic diplomacy (in line with its way of dealing with 'barbarians' outlined in Chapter 2), by entangling other states in an economic web before turning them into vassals, is also coming apart in their interactions with other Asian (Myanmar) and African (Zambia) states. But it is their territorial disputes with India and the littoral states of the Western Pacific that continue to be serious flashpoints for war. The Chinese are following their ancient policy based on Sun Tzu of deliberately provoking crises in territorial disputes with neighbours, forcing bilateral negotiations, and settling the dispute in their favour because of their predominant military and economic power. Thus, they have refused to accept the jurisdiction of the International Court at The Hague to settle the territorial dispute in the South China Sea with the Philippines, which had taken them to court and won its case that there is no basis for China's claim to own the whole of the South and East China Seas.

This makes it imperative that the Chinese mindset about interstate relations is changed, if necessary through force. Despite signs of the weakening of the Chinese economy, relying on this weakness to temper aggressive Chinese territorial moves would be imprudent. For, as the CCP's only aim is its own survival as the ruler of China, any economic domestic disorder flowing from a stalling economy is likely to induce it to play the nationalist card.

It is only by assembling the requisite coalition of states with overwhelming military and economic power to explicitly counter this Chinese aggressiveness that the crises China has and will continue to provoke can be countered without war.[20] The explicit containment of China must be the policy to avoid war in the Indo-Pacific. This might convert China to a normal member of the international society of states and might allow it to develop as a trading state, with much benefit to its still relatively impoverished population. But this seems unlikely without at least ano ther Cold War.

Hegemon Maintaining Global Order

For this containment of China, the US is vital. This is the third of Carr's critical factors for preventing crises from turning into war—'the unwillingness or inability by any single power or "hegemon" to underwrite international order'. As I have argued at length, the view of the US as a weakened economic and military giant after the GFC is invalid. It has all the means to remain the world's sole superpower. It has the ability (as it is tentatively beginning to do) to create an overwhelming coalition of states to oppose China's bid to attain Asian and, thereafter, global hegemony. Its problem in fulfilling this superpower role has been the unwillingness of its previous president tc use force, even when the 'red lines' he laid down have been crossed. Fortunately, his term has come to an end and his successor (and particularly his military advisers) is already proving to be more robust in accepting and fulfilling the US's superpower role as the enforcer of global order, most importantly in the Indo-Pacific.

The Chinese are hoping that just as Britain in effect transferred its superpower role to the United States, the latter should [and will]—with China's rise—do the same.[21] But this is not going to happen because of the differences in their world views. As Christopher Coker notes:

> The British and Americans not only spoke in similar terms. Of possibly equal importance was the fact that they were both heirs to a liberal tradition that emphasized reason and an empirically verifiable view of life. In short, Britain's appeasement of the United States was normative. It had little to do with the balance of power and everything to do with intrinsic beliefs.[22]

From a US perspective, the analogy of Britain's loss of leadership in the international system provides little by way of comfort to China, given the absence of a similar kind of cultural affinity between it and the United States. 'The United States is unlikely to surrender its position willingly', says Coker.[23] Nor is it likely, as the Chinese hope, to share its hegemony in a G2[24] world.

But there is another candidate for this transfer, if the need arises. India is a major and, now, willing partner of the US. In the economic race between the Chinese hare and the Indian tortoise, India, because of the hold of the failed Nehruvian economic policies, has been steadily outpaced by China. But with the repudiation of the Nehru–Gandhi dynasty at the 2014 election and the partial dismantling of the remaining constraints on Indian growth, it may no longer be too optimistic to hope that India may achieve its potential GDP growth rate of 10–11 per cent p.a. over the next two decades. If this happens, then as China's economy slows to a 3.5 per cent p.a. growth rate, India can by 2027–8 catch up and surpass the Chinese hare.[25]

Meanwhile, even though India is threatened by the rogue state of Pakistan on its west, and Pakistan's 'all weather' ally China to the north, it is now beginning to strengthen its defences, not least by at last beginning to produce its conventional weapons indigenously, as it already has with its armoury of missiles. The strategic partnerships with the US, Japan, and Australia are growing. Its growing naval strength and 'Act East' policy is now beginning to challenge China in the Indo-Pacific. But, as in all things, given its noisy democracy, India will only hasten slowly. It will remain at the centre of the flashpoints for war in Af-Pak and the Indo-Pacific region. But, if it can complete its economic and military modernization in the next two decades, it could eventually be a candidate for taking over the burden of maintaining global order when and if the US is no longer able or willing to do so.[26] Meanwhile, the US remains the only hope of preventing another Great War, if the inevitable crises precipitated by its rivals and competitors are not to lead to another conflagration in Eurasia.[27]

Notes

1. See Margaret MacMillan, *The War that Ended Peace: The Road to 1914* (Profile Books, 2013); Christopher Clark, *The Sleepwalkers: How Europe Went to War in 1914* (London: Penguin Books, 2013). Also see Niall Ferguson, *The Pity of War: Explaining World War I* (London: Penguin, 1998).
2. E.H. Carr, *The Twenty Years' Crisis, 1919–1939: An Introduction the Study of International Relations* (Basingstoke: Palgrave, 2001 [1981]). The book is flawed because of Carr's diatribe against laissez-faire economics and advocacy of Soviet-style central planning.
3. Michael Cox, introduction to Carr, *The Twenty Years' Crisis*, p. lvi.
4. See my UCLA colleague Axel Leijonhufvud's excellent article on the causes and consequences of the Great Recession. He emphasizes the role of the ending of unlimited liability of investment bankers and the risky behaviour it provoked as one major cause of the financial crisis, and also how the subsequent US official response to the crisis, which allowed the banks to earn interest on their reserves with the Fed as part of the quantitative easing (QE) programmes, has continued to provide explicit subsidies to bankers at tax payers' expense. Even without reinstating Glass–Steagall, the change in the law, which had prevented investment bankers from incorporating into limited liability companies, should be re-examined and if possible reinstated. Leijonhufvud also shows how the crisis was a Hayekian crisis and that ignoring the changes in the money supply in the conduct of monetary policy has been a grave error. The income distribution effects of the great recession and the policies adopted to counter it have led to continuing large gains for Wall Street bankers, which have fuelled continuing political discontent. Axel Leijonhufvud, 'Monetary Muddles', *Cato Journal*, 35, no. 2 (2015), pp. 179–92.

5. As I have argued in D. Lal, 'Will Terrorism Defeat Globalization', in Richard N. Rosecrance and Arthur A. Stein (eds), *No More States?: Globalization, National Self-Determination, and Terrorism* (Lanham, MD: Rowman and Littlefield, 2006), Ch. 3. Reprinted in D. Lal, *Lost Causes: The Retreat from Classical Liberalism* (London: Biteback Publishing, 2012), Ch. 6. And also in Ch. 11, I argue terrorism poses a small threat to the liberal international economic order, and its economic costs are even smaller.
6. Richard N. Rosecrance and Steven E. Miller (eds), *The Next Great War?: The Roots of World War I and the Risks of U.S.–China Conflict* (Cambridge, MA: MIT Press, 2015).
7. M. MacMillan, 'The Rhyme of History: Lessons of the Great War', *The Brookings Essay* (Washington, DC: Brookings Institution, 14 December 2013).
8. Cited in Arthur A. Stein, 'Respites or Resolutions? Recurring Crises and the Origins of War', in Rosecrance and Miller (eds), *The Next Great War?*, Ch. 2.
9. K. Rudd, 'Lessons from Europe 1914 for Asia 2014: Reflections on the Centenary of the Outbreak of World War I', in Rosecrance and Miller (eds), *The Next Great War?*, Ch. 13.
10. Christopher Coker, *The Improbable War: China, the United States and the Logic of Great Power Conflict* (New York: Oxford University Press, 2015).
11. Coker, *The Improbable War*, p. 109.
12. Coker, *The Improbable War*, p. 114.
13. Coker, *The Improbable War*, p. 115.
14. The one case of an undisputed rogue military is China's ally and 'all weather friend' Pakistan. Stephen Van Evra, 'European Militaries and the Origins of World War I', in Rosecrance and Miller (eds), *The Next Great War?*, Ch. 11, states that the First World War was caused when militaries of Europe went rogue. Though he argues that the Chinese military is firmly under civilian CCP control, this is increasingly doubtful. But he is right in seeing parallels between Pakistan and Wilhelmine Germany. He concludes that 'Pakistan's rogue military is turning Pakistan toward becoming a rogue state' (p. 172–4).
15. 'One example was the EP-3 spy plane crisis in which an American plane was forced down without the Chinese foreign ministry being

informed. Another was the test launch of an anti-satellite weapon in January 2007. A third was the test flight of the J-20 stealth fighter in January 2011 during the visit of the US defense secretary, Robert Gates, to China. It is rumored that even the president was unaware of the flight in advance' (Coker, *The Improbable War*, p. 135). Then there was the incursion by the PLA across the Indo-Tibetan border on the very day President Xi was making his inaugural visit to meet the Indian PM in his hometown of Ahmadabad after Modi's resounding election victory in 2014.

16. Coker, *The Improbable War*, p. 135.
17. The main proponent is the Australian defence academic Hugh White, *The China Choice: Why We Should Share Power* (Oxford: Oxford University Press, 2013). Also see Henry Kissinger, *On China* (New York: Penguin, 2011); and Zbigniew Brzezinski, *Strategic Vision: America and the Crisis of Global Power* (New York: Basic Books, 2012).
18. Michael Cox, Preface in Carr, *The Twenty Years Crisis*, p. xiii.
19. Cited in Graham Allison, 'The Thucydides Trap', in Rosecrance and Miller (eds), *The Next Great War?*, p. 76.
20. How would a US-Sino war play out? Coker, *The Improbable War*, Ch. 4, provides a useful summary of current strategic thinking on the issue. One important point is that China is a land power the US a sea power. The Chinese now control the Asia-Pacific mainland, apart from Russia—a declining power—and South Korea, which is a treaty ally of the US. China is seeking to extend its strategic depth inland. China's recent New Silk Road initiative seems an application of Mackinder's view that Eurasia was inaccessible to sea power, but lay open to railways, which would extend state power. This Mackinder strategy offers the chance to outflank the United States through Central and north-west Asia in terms of overland access to the Persian Gulf and the Indian Ocean. That China is able to play the Eurasia card shows the fecklessness of Obama in voluntarily surrendering the land-based military beachheads it had established in Iraq and Afghanistan, whereby it could have countered this Chinese move. However, given the instability in Central and north-west Asia and the threat of Islamic jihadists in the region, it remains a gamble for China. Hence it is also challenging the US in the Pacific with the

aim, as many PLA generals have stated, of pushing the US Navy back to Guam and Hawaii.

In this sea battle a strategy of 'Offshore Control, a classic blockade strategy' has been proposed by T.X. Hammes, 'Sorry, AirSea Battle Is No Strategy', *The National Interest* (7 August 2013). Available at http://nationalinterest.org/commentary/sorry-airsea-battle-no-strategy-8846 (last accessed 21 November 2017). Coker says this strategy 'would involve a combination of ground, naval and air, and rented platforms which would allow the US Navy and its allies to intercept and divert the super tankers and post-PANAMAX container ships that are essential to China's economy. A maritime exclusion zone would be policed inside the first island chain. The US Navy could intercept and subject inspected ships to seizure and sale' (Coker, *The Improbable War*, p. 153).

The two other forms of warfare discussed by Coker are cyber warfare and warfare in outer space. It is well known that 'China probably has the most effective and certainly the most robust cyber-espionage system in the world' (p. 159). Though, unlike other forms of warfare, it is difficult to pin attribution in a cyber-attack, the US is now involving Silicon Valley firms in devising ways to attribute attacks and methods to combat them.

There is an emerging arms race between the Chinese and the Americans in militarizing outer space despite the Outer Space Treaty, which prohibits the armament of space. The use of space is crucial to the network-centric warfare of the Revolution in Military Affairs, which was seen in action in the Second Gulf War. But given the US lead in its space assets compared with China's, Geoffrey Forden, a former US weapons inspector, in a comprehensive scenario of a possible US–China space war concludes that '[T]he United States may be the country most dependent on space for its military activities. But it is also the least vulnerable, because of the tremendous redundancy of its space assets'. See Geoffrey Forden, 'How China Loses the Coming Space War (Pt. 2)', *Wired* (1 October 2008). Available at https://www.wired.com/2008/01/inside-the-ch-1/ (last accessed 21 November 2017).

A more radical solution to the problem of the militarization of space is provided by Everett Dolman. The low-earth orbit is important for intelligence satellites, and unmanned aerial vehicles.

Dolman suggests that 'the US should withdraw from the space treaty, put weapons in space and seize control of low-earth orbit. Through the use of space-based laser or other kinetic energy weapons the US would then seek to prevent other states from putting weapons in space with the aim of guaranteeing the free commercial use of space just as the Royal Navy guaranteed free navigation at sea by eliminating piracy' (p. 157). Dolman consequently argues that 'the US should use its military power to guarantee a safe space environment (including protection from space debris)'. Everett Dolman, *Pure Strategy: Power and Principle in the Space and Information Age* (London: Frank Cass, 2005), p. 169.

21. Coker, *The Improbable* War, notes, 'Liu Ming, a PLA colonel and professor at the National Defence University, claims that it is possible that the United States could follow Britain's example and simply vacate the role of world leader to China' (p. 90). They are perhaps being influenced, suggests Coker, by a counterfactual history of the obscure territorial dispute between Venezuela and the British colony of Guyana by Andrew Roberts (2003). In his counterfactual history Roberts 'captures the realization among British policy-makers that their country could not win a protracted war. War in 1895, at best would have concluded with Britain conceding the province of Quebec. The British were realists. The war with Venezuela should have happened but it did not. The British never really contemplated a war with the United States in the period that followed' (Coker, *The Improbable* War, p. 92).
22. Coker, *The Improbable War*, p. 95–6.
23. Coker, *The Improbable War*, p. 97.
24. This refers to the constant refrain of President Xi that China and America should work together to maintain global order in particular the global economic system But China's authoritarian capitalism will not allow this as is apparent from the President Trump's refusal to accord 'market economy' status at the WTO.
25. This assumes China's GDP in 2012 was three times India's, and India, from 2016, grows at over 7 per cent per annum, faster than China's expected growth rate of 3.5 per cent per annum.
26. Ashley Tellis, *India as a New Global Power: An Action Agenda for the United States* (Washington, DC: Carnegie Endowment for International Peace, 2005), has argued that after the Indo-US

nuclear deal and India's subsequent informal strategic alliance with the US, there should be a grander strategy to prevent China's rise as the Asian hegemon: a baton-passing across the Anglosphere from the United States to India, as from the UK to the US in the early twentieth century. India was to be not only a short-term ally but also a like-minded successor, which the US would 'help become a major world power in the twenty first century' (p. 25).

27. With the election of Donald Trump to the US presidency, a few weeks ago as I write, there have been numerous comments about his likely foreign policy. The one I find most cogent is by Edward Luttwak, 'Enough Hysterics, Donald Trump's Foreign Policy Isn't Reckless or Radical', *Foreign Policy* (17 November 2016). Available at http://foreignpolicy.com/2016/11/17/enough-hysterics-donald-trumps-foreign-policy-isnt-reckless-or-radical/ (last accessed 21 November 2017). He argues that Trump's disengagement from Afghanistan and Iraq, and a deal with Russia over Ukraine 'would release more military resources for the containment of China'. Unlike Obama, who resisted US 'freedom of navigation patrols' in the South China Sea, he is unlikely 'to stop Pacific Command from doing its job of "keeping the sea lanes open"—the polite expression for denying territorial claims over coral reefs, rocks and shoals'. His views on radical Islam and its Wahhabi sponsor Saudi Arabia mean he is likely to act tough, as with any breaches by Iran of the agreed nuclear deal. On trade, he is likely to concentrate on using existing anti-dumping law to deal with import surges like Chinese steel, rather than abrogate any existing trade treaties which would require Congressional approval, which he is unlikely to get. TPP however will be dead. All in all, Luttwak sees Trump acing like Reagan, who refused to endorse the establishment consensus on détente in the Cold War, which did not lead to a nuclear war but the end of the Soviet Union. The 'League of Dictators' can thus probably expect a more robust response from the US than they did from the limp Obama.

For alternative views, which see Trump as an isolationist Jacksonian president, see Max Boot, 'Trump's "America First" Is the Twilight of American Exceptionalism', *Foreign Policy* (22 November, 2016). Available at http://foreignpolicy.com/2016/11/22/trumps-america-first-is-the-twilight-of-american-exceptionalism-obama/

(last accessed 21 November 2017). Also see Robert Kagan, 'Trump Marks the End of America as World's "Indispensable Nation"', *Financial Times* (19 November 2016). Available at https://www.ft.com/content/782381b6-ad91-11e6-ba7d-76378e4fef24 (last accessed 21 November 2017).

Appendix: The Rise and Fall of Empires—A Model[1]

The maintenance of international order raises the same issues that arise in maintaining domestic order. So, we must begin by explaining how a state arises with a monopoly of coercive power within its borders. The state has to be given a monopoly of violence to maintain the peace as 'covenants without the sword, are but words, and of no strength to secure a man at all'.[2] From the historical record, the state as an institution arose with the development of sedentary civilizations. Before that, the stateless tribal societies studied by anthropologists in Africa are likely to have been the norm. Though warfare to 'take others' resources was endemic in these societies, it is with settled agriculture that organized means of protecting one's own or taking others resources arose. The resulting monopoly of violence of the state could have arisen as the result of a Mafia-type protection racket, whereby some roving bandits decided that instead of making periodic raids, they could make higher returns from settling down and exploiting the villagers. Alternatively, it could have arisen because of the communal needs for the organization of peasant villages—as social contract theorists have claimed. Economic historians have not been able to resolve which of these routes—the predatory or contractual—gave rise to the state in the agrarian civilizations of Eurasia.

Nevertheless, there is some evidence from the earliest states established in the river valleys of the Tigris and Euphrates in

Mesopotamia, the Nile Valley in Egypt, and the Indus Valley in India that in these earliest Eurasian civilizations, the state arose as a communal form of organization—a contractual origin. But, because of the encroachments of the nomads who besieged these civilizations from the northern steppes and the southern deserts, they were transformed by predatory intruders—roving bandits who turned into stationary bandits. We also need to provide a framework to explain the rise and fall of these empires.

Domestic Order and the Predatory State[3]

Once sedentary agriculture came to be practiced in the ancient river valleys of Eurasia, we can expect that groups with a comparative advantage in 'taking' (roving bandits) decided that their take could be increased if they settled down (that is, became stationary bandits) and provided the basic public goods of law and order. These public goods financed by part of the tax takings would have led to the enforcement of property rights, which would raise the productivity of the economy and thence the tax revenue. But, the state will be inherently prone to predation because of its monopoly of violence within its territory. The aim of this predatory state (like of the Mafia gang controlling a neighbourhood) would be to maximize its net revenues—its net takings.[4]

Once established, the major threat to the predatory state lies in its being overthrown by rival predators (gangsters) who wish to take over its takings. The incumbent Mafia leader (predator), however, has a number of important advantages against external and internal rivals seeking to overthrow him and take over his territory. The first advantage is that he will already have invested in the infrastructure of 'coercion'—in the form of fortifications, armaments, roads, courtrooms, bureaus, etc.—some of which the rival will have to invest in to challenge the incumbent. The incumbent will, thus, already have some sunk costs in his established system of coercion, which the challenger will have to incur anew. Both will, of course, have to incur similar costs in running the state, in terms of expenditures on the police, the bureaucracy, the army, judges, etc. So it is the sunk, fixed costs that provide a major barrier to entry for an external rival challenging the current predator controlling the state.

For internal rivals trying to organize a coup, the military technology and the physical size of the 'naturally' defensible territory will be vital. Ceteris paribus, a physically smaller territory would be easier to take over than a larger one, while the changing technology of warfare, which makes large scale an advantage in the violence industry, would tend to favour the incumbent. Thus, the cannon revolution in the fifteenth century allowed the development of larger centralizing states by eliminating local competitors hiding in their newly vulnerable castles.

For external rivals, 'amalgamation' costs and geography will be important in making a successful challenge. For in both these respects, the incumbent may also have an important advantage. Thus, the incumbent may have been able to instil 'loyalty' among the populace under his control for ethnic, 'nationalist', or ideological reasons. Given the resulting ethnic, linguistic, and religious differences between the external rival and the people in the incumbent's territory, the indigenous predator can count on a form of loyalty that the external rival cannot. This would require any challenger to spend extra resources to pacify and amalgamate a hostile population. Quite often, external rivals have minimized these amalgamation costs by adopting the 'culture' of the people they are taking over. The barbarians who destroyed the Roman empire and the successive nomads from the steppes who have attacked China have followed this path of cultural assimilation with their newly acquired subjects.

Finally, given the existing military technology, the geography of the territory controlled by the incumbent may provide natural barriers to the entry of an external rival. The system of ancient Greek city states was preserved because of its geography. But, with Athens' development of sea power, the geographical barrier could be overcome. Later, in medieval Europe, as communications and military technology improved, larger nation states could be created within natural geographical boundaries: the sea protecting

England; the Pyrenees, the Alps, and the northern marches providing the natural defences of Spain, France, the Netherlands, and Italy. These raised the entry costs for external predators.

It is these barriers to the entry to challengers that allow the incumbent predator to extract revenue from his subjects. The higher the barriers, the greater the 'rent' he can extract from his monopoly in coercion. But, if he raises his takings beyond the 'natural' level allowed by these 'sunk costs' and 'barriers to entry', a challenger would be able to displace him by providing his subjects the same protection for lower takings.

But, human beings are mortal. It would be rational for an individual predatory ruler to raise his takings from his prey in the later part of his life, even if this threatens his state with internal coups or foreign invasions. This is where the 'selfish gene' enters. If the individual predator cares about his genes embodied in his progeny, he will wish to create a dynasty where his natural monopoly in coercion with its takings is passed on to his kin. This dynastic motive will then prevent him from acting myopically and allowing his profitable natural monopoly to become contestable by raising his takings above the long-run sustainable level. But, as the level of this sustainable rent and the accompanying tax burden is necessarily uncertain, it is as likely that, ceteris paribus, cycles of fiscal predation and thence the rise and fall of dynasties could emerge, as happened in India.

International Anarchy and Imperial Hegemony

If there are no natural geographical barriers preventing an easy conquest, competing predatory states will arise, each trying to extend its territory. For, the revenue ('rents') available will rise as more territory with its inhabitants is conquered and incorporated into a particular state. But, the extension of territory will also increase the costs of maintaining and running the state. So, given the relative costs and the revenues (benefits) that can be extracted by an extension of its territory, there will be a natural limit to the geographical size of the state, where the marginal costs of acquiring new territory is equal to the marginal increase in revenue (rents) it provides.

With these natural limits to the size of the state governed not only by geography but also by the state of communications, transport, and military technology, as well as the productive capacity of the economy, a number of competing states in a particular region could arise This occurred in ancient times in the vast alluvial Indo-Gangetic plain in northern India—as the costs of any single state conquering all the others were too high—or in the ancient system of city state's in Greece, protected from each other by their geography. They would then comprise an anarchical international society of states.[5]

This anarchical equilibrium would, however, breakdown if one of the competing states obtains an improvement in its military technology or in the productivity of its economy, which it can turn into a decisive military advantage, allowing it to overcome its rivals and establish its hegemony or empire. But, as with the domestic predatory state, the imperial state would also face rising fiscal costs of expansion.

These rising costs would to some extent be mitigated by another important source of takings (revenue), which historically has arisen with empire, long-distance trade. Till the nineteenth century transport revolution based on the steam engine, long-distance trade was expensive and consisted mainly of high-value and non-bulky goods, which were most often not produced in the receiving areas. This long-distance trade was even more precarious than sedentary agriculture, as it was more susceptible to the depredations of roving bandits. Providing protection to such high-value trade would offer even higher 'rents' (above those available from protecting agriculture) once the stationary bandit had established his 'protection' regime. Thus a symbiosis developed between long-distance trade and empires: empires facilitated trade, and taxing trade provided the means to extend the empire.

Slaves were another important form of takings from warfare and a motive for the extension of empires. All the Eurasian civilizations faced the common problem of providing an adequate supply of labour to work the land, which was abundant. Slaves provided an important addition to the domestic supply of labour. Maintaining a continuous and numerous supply of slaves depended upon warfare. Slavery has been ubiquitous through human history.[6] One of the motives behind Rome's continual wars to extend its territory was to augment the supply of the slaves on whom its agriculture depended, while the Islamic empires, with their dependence on mamlukes to protect and run their empires, were also dependent on a steady supply of slave labour.

Notes

1. D. Lal, *The Hindu Equilibrium: India c. 1500 B.C.–2000 A.D.*, Abridged and Revised Edition (Oxford and New York: Oxford University Press, 2005 [1988]), Ch. 13.2. The tax-cum-public goods equilibrium, which can be derived from the model (but not discussed below), also allows a classification of what I have termed autonomous states (as opposed to factional ones) into predatory, Platonic guardian, and bureaucrat-maximizing states—see D. Lal and H. Myint, *The Political Economy of Poverty, Equity and Growth: A Comparative Study* (Oxford: Clarendon Press, 1996), pp. 264–7. These differ in the objectives they seek to subserve. The predatory state is only concerned with maximizing its net revenue; the Platonic guardian state with maximizing social welfare; the bureaucrat-maximizing state with the number of bureaucrats. It can be shown that the Platonic guardian state provides the optimal level of public goods with the lowest tax rate. The bureaucrat and predatory states' tax rates are determined by the entries to barriers to rivals as shown in note 3, but they differ in the level of public goods provided, with the bureaucrat-maximizing state providing more than the predatory state, and perhaps even over-providing them beyond the optimal level. See Lal and Myint, *The Political Economy of Poverty, Equity and Growth*.
2. T. Hobbes, *Leviathan* (Cambridge: Cambridge University Press, 1996 [1651]), p. 223.
3. See Lal, *The Hindu Equilibrium* for details. A brief outline of the model may be helpful. The best way to look at the state is as a two-good multi-product natural monopoly, providing 'protection' and

'justice'. But this monopoly is 'contestable', and the height of the barriers to entry to either internal or external rivals will determine the maximum 'rent' it can extract from its prey. The height of these barriers determines the relative differences in costs of the incumbent (TCi) controller of this natural monopoly—the state—and those of new entrants (TCe) who wish to replace it. These costs will consist partly of the variable costs of running the state and the fixed costs in the form of the infrastructure of coercion. The variable costs of running the state can be expected to be the same for the incumbent as well as any rival seeking to challenge him. But, the incumbent will have an advantage over any potential rival in so far as part of the fixed costs for him will be sunk costs. If the total costs for any new entrant are K, and the sunk costs for the incumbent, inclusive of the geographic and cultural 'barriers to entry', are a fraction (s) of these, its total cost curve will lie below the new entrants by this fraction sK. Moreover, as the fixed costs of weaponry, fortifications, buildings, etc., are lumpy, the average of this fixed cost component will initially decline with respect to the territory controlled. But as the territory to be controlled expands, the average costs of both maintaining or contesting the natural monopoly are likely to rise. This gives us the shape of the total cost curves of the incumbent and new entrant seeking to contest him for the natural monopoly—the state.

Until the state reaches a certain territorial size, the average costs of maintaining/contesting the state are declining, as the fixed cost component is spread over a larger area. But after this critical level, the average costs begin to rise as the rising variable costs of running the larger state and any incremental fixed costs increase total costs.

As long as the territory to be controlled lies in the decreasing average cost part of the total cost curve, the incumbent can find a tax rate that allows him to extract the full 'monopoly' rents from his prey determined by the barriers to entry of sK. So, ceteris paribus, there will be a disincentive for him to extend his territorial control beyond the decreasing average cost portion of his total cost curve.

Moreover, depending on the shape of the fixed cost curve in controlling a given territory, there may be no tax rate that will prevent entry, and political instability in the territory will be the norm. While, if the territory is large enough and the fixed costs required to establish a state under one sovereign over the whole region are prohibitive, there may be a number of competing states in an otherwise homogenous region. Even if all their cost curves are identical, there may also not be a stable equilibrium in the *number* of states in the territory.

4. The designation 'predatory' is to show the similarity between the relationships between sovereign and subjects, as in the predator–prey models of the natural world. R.M. Goodwin, 'A Growth Cycle', in C.H. Feinstein (ed.), *Socialism, Capitalism, and Economic Growth* (Cambridge: Cambridge University Press, 1967), speaks of how there is a symbiosis in the interests of the predator and the prey, but the predator is not interested in the welfare of the prey except to see them become fatter and tastier before his meal!
5. Hirshleifer sets out a simple model to explain why anarchy need not be chaotic and also the factors that lead it to breakdown into hegemony. Consider two groups who are rational, self-interested, and only concerned with maximizing their own income. There are two ways of obtaining income: by making or taking. So there are two 'technologies' to produce income: a technology of production and another of appropriating through conflict (war). Each group starts off with given resources. It can use these resources in both the technology of production and of war. Each group will choose a preferred balance between productive and conflictual effort in equilibrium. The social outcome will depend upon the interactions between these separate optimizing decisions and, thereby, the levels of production, war, and the distribution of the total product between the two claimants.

   The basic structure of the model is as follows: Assume there are two contenders (I = 1,2) who divide their available resources (Ri) between production (Ei) and fighting (Fi). Assuming that the aggregate resource base (R = R1 + R2) is constant, and is hence not effected by fighting, and that the unit costs of transforming resources into productive or fighting effort are a, and b respectively:

   $$Ri = aiEi + biFi.$$

   The income that each contender gets is determined by a production function (the same for both):

   $$Yi = (eiRi)\ \hat{}h \text{ (where } ei = Ei/Ri).$$

But as Ri depends in part upon how much of the aggregate resources (R) can be obtained by fighting, this will depend upon the relative success in fighting (pi), which in turn depends upon the technology of fighting. This technology and, hence, the relative success ratio in fighting (p1/p2) will depend upon relative fighting effort (Fi/F2) and the decisiveness of the fighting outcome (m): p1/p2 = (F1/F2)^m.

From these, the equilibrium success ratio in the steady state can be derived as:

$$p1/p2 = (f1/f2)^{\wedge}\,(m/1\text{-}m),\ \text{where } fi = Fi/Ri.$$

This simple anarchical system will be dynamically stable if (i) m < 1, and (ii) Yi > y (subsistence income). See J. Hirshleifer, 'Anarchy and its Breakdown', *Journal of Political Economy*, 103, no. 1 (1995), pp. 26–52. Reprinted in his *The Dark Side of the Force—Economic Foundations of Conflict Theory* (Cambridge: Cambridge University Press, 2001), Ch. 6.

There would be an anarchical social equilibrium—a spontaneous order in the sense of Friedrich Hayek, *Law, Legislation and Liberty* (Chicago: Chicago University Press, 1973). There could be total peace or some equilibrium fighting in this anarchic social equilibrium. The most crucial parameter in the model is the one relating to the decisiveness of conflict. This 'decisiveness' (m) factor amplifies the ratio of military inputs (fighting efforts) into the ratio of consequences (division of the loot or power). If this differs between the contestants and is sufficiently high for one of them, even with a small force superiority the anarchical society will collapse into hegemony. For when the country with the higher decisiveness parameter will increase its fighting effort, the other will try and match this with initially increasing its fighting effort (but proportionately less than the country with the improvement in decisiveness), but will eventually give up the unequal struggle and concentrate more of its efforts and resources to producing income instead.

Moreover, if, ceteris paribus, the aggregate of resources is fixed and the number of contestants rises, then each will have a higher fighting intensity and lower income—as each will have a smaller share of the fixed aggregate resources and more of these will be diverted to fighting. If, with an unchanged decisiveness factor, one agent has a rise in its productivity coefficient in transforming resources into income and/or fighting, it improves its edge against its competitors. But, if the improvement is only in the income transforming coefficient, then apart from the increase in the income of the more productive economy, there is no other change in the anarchical equilibrium. But, if the improvement is in the technology of fighting, so that the coefficient of transforming resources into fighting falls, then the country with the fighting improvement sees both its fighting intensity and income rise, while the others will also raise their fighting intensities (but by less than that in the country with the military advance) and have lower incomes. Furthermore, when the decisiveness of conflict is not sufficiently high, it can pay the smaller and weaker contestant to fight harder—to increase its fighting intensity—by investing more in conflict than productive activity. This leads to what Hirshleifer calls 'the paradox of power', whereby poorer or weaker contenders gain at the expense of their richer or stronger rivals. This does not mean that the weaker side defeats the stronger in an absolute sense. Rather, the weaker side does relatively better as it is willing to commit more of its resources to the battle. It does not lose as heavily as might be expected from counting up the resources available.

As Hirshleifer pointed out to me in a private communication, the model does not explain asymmetrical warfare, like guerrilla warfare, where the dominant and the insurgent are fighting in very different ways. Similarly, this applies to a sea power fighting a land power. Then, decisiveness one way may differ from decisiveness the other way. One side might be fighting in such a way that it can't gain much, but can't lose much either (low m). While for the other side, the opposite holds (high m). In the Napoleonic Wars, Britain's island geography meant she could never be successfully invaded, so for her it was a relatively low-m war, which she could fight for a long time. Whereas Napoleon's continental opponents were forced to fight symmetrical wars against him, and most often rapidly went down to defeat. Napoleon's defeat in Russia was due to asymmetrical warfare. The Russians were fighting in a low-m way—when defeated they could withdraw into the interior. It was, however, a high-m contest for Napoleon, who had to win big, if he was to survive.

6. See M.I. Finley, 'Slavery', in D.L. Sills (ed.), *International Encyclopedia of the Social Sciences*, Vol. 14 (New York: Macmillan, 1968); and E. Domar, 'The Causes of Slavery or Serfdom: A Hypothesis', *Journal of Economic History*, 30, No. 1 (March 1970), pp. 18–32. That this was an 'efficient' institution particularly in the production of crops subject to increasing returns to scale had been shown by F.W. Fogel and S. Engerman, *Time on the Cross* (New York: Little Brown, 1974) and F.W. Fogel, *Without Consent or Contract: The Rise and Fall of American Slavery* (New York: Norton, 1989). For the common problems faced by Eurasian civilizations in tying scarce labour down to abundant land, see D. Lal, *Unintended Consequences: The Impact of Factor Endowments, Culture, and Politics on Long-Run Economic Performance* (Cambridge, MA: MIT Press, 1998). There is, however, one historical puzzle that Stan Engerman has pointed out to me in personal correspondence. Quincy Wright has estimated that after about 1300 CE, northern Europeans did not enslave other northern Europeans, yet in the next six centuries they fought numerous wars that killed and wounded more people than were involved in the transatlantic slave trade. I would argue (see Lal, *Hindu Equilibrium*) that as slavery requires either a state that can enforce slave contracts or else an obvious way to differentiate slaves—like the pigmentation of their skins—medieval Europe could not tie labour down to scarce land through slavery, and instead adopted a much looser form of control through serfdom.

Bibliography

2013. 'China's Fiddled Figures'. *Wall Street Journal.*

Acemoglu, Daron and James A. Robinson. 2015. 'The Rise and Decline of General Laws of Capitalism'. *Journal of Economic Perspectives* 29(1): 3–28.

Acemoglu, Daron, Simon Johnson, and James A. Robinson. 2002. 'Reversal of Fortune: Geography and Institutions in the Making of the Modern World Income Distribution'. *Quarterly Journal of Economics* 117(4): 1231–94.

Acharya, S. 2015. 'How Fast Is India Growing?'. *Business Standard.* Available at http://www.business-standard.com/article/opinion/shankar-acharya-how-fast-is-india-growing-115040801305_1.html (last accessed 13 November 2017).

Acheson, D. 1996. 'Ethics in International Relations Today', in D.L. Larson, *The Puritan Ethic in United States Foreign Policy*, pp. 134–5. Princeton, NJ: Van Norstrand.

Acton, Lord. 1985 [1862]. *Essays on Freedom and Power.* Boston: Beacon Press.

Ahmed, Akbar. 2013. *The Thistle and the Drone: How America's War on Terror Became a Global War on Tribal Islam*. Washington, DC: Brookings.

Ahmed, Khaled. 2014. 'When Reality Outruns Strategy'. *Indian Express.* Available at http://indianexpress.com/article/opinion/columns/when-reality-outruns-strategy/ (last accessed 20 November 2017).

Aiyar, Pallavi. 2008. *Smoke and Mirrors: An Experience of China.* New Delhi: Fourth Estate.

Aiyar, S.S. 2016. 'Recycling Government Assets: A Revolutionary Solution for Infrastructure', *Times of India.*

Alesina, A. and S. Ardagna. 2009. 'Large Changes in Fiscal Policy: Taxes Versus Spending', NBER Working Paper, No. 15438, National Bureau of Economic Research, Cambridge, MA.

Allison, Graham. 2015. 'The Thucydides Trap', in Rosecrance and Miller (eds), *The Next Great War*, pp. 73–80. Cambride, MA: MIT Press.

Almqvist, K. and A. Linklater (ed.). 2010. *On the Idea of America*. Stockholm: Axel and Margaret Ax:son Johnson Foundation.

Anderson, B. 1991. *Imagined Communities: Reflections on the Origin and Spread of Nationalism*. London: Verso.

Ando, A. 2000. 'On the Japanese Economy and Japanese National Accounts'. NBER Working Paper, No. 8033, National Bureau of Economic Research, Cambridge, MA.

Ansar, Atif, Bent Flyvbjerg, Alexander Budzier, and Daniel Lunn. 2016. 'Does Infrastructure Investment Lead to Economic Growth or Economic Fragility? Evidence from China'. *Oxford Review of Economic Policy* 32(3): 360–90, 377.

Aron, Raymond. 1966. *Peace and War: A Theory of International Relations*. London: Weidenfeld and Nicolson.

Atwani, Abdel Bari. 2015. *The Islamic State: The Digital Caliphate*. London: Saqi.

Authers, J. 2010. *The Fearful Rise of Markets: Global Bubbles, Synchronized Meltdowns, and How to Prevent Them in the Future*. Upper Saddle River, NJ: FT Press.

Ayres, Alyssa, Charles R. Kaye, Joseph S. Nye, Jr., and Christopher M. Tuttle. 2015. 'Working with a Rising India: A Joint Venture for the New Century, Council on Foreign Relations'. Independent Task force Report No. 73. New York: Council on Foreign Relations.

Bader, Jeffrey A. 2012. *Obama and China's Rise*. Washington, DC: Brookings Institution.

Bairoch, Paul. 1976. 'Europe's Gross National Product, 1800–1975', *Journal of European Economic History*, 5: 273–340.

Bank of England. 2009. 'Quantitative Easing', *Quarterly Bulletin*, 2009 Q2: 90–100.

Barbashin, Anton and Hannah Thoburn. 2014. 'Putin's Brain: Alexander Dugin and the Philosophy behind Putin's Invasion of Crimea'. *Foreign Affairs*. Available at https://www.foreignaffairs.com/articles/russia-fsu/2014-03-31/putins-brain (last accessed 19 November 2017).

Barber, Tony. 2015. 'Russia Can Break Out of Putin's Thrall'. *Financial Times*. Available at https://www.ft.com/content/3325f082-469d-11e5-b3b2-1672f710807b (last accessed 19 November 2017).

Barro, Robert and Josef Ursua. 2009. 'Stock Market Crashes and Depressions', NBER Working Paper, No. 14760, National Bureau of Economic Research, Cambridge, MA.

Baru, Sanjaya. 2014. *The Accidental Prime Minister: The Making and Unmaking of Manmohan Singh*. New Delhi:Viking-Penguin.

Baruah, Darshana M. 2014. 'South China Sea: Time for India to Mark Its Presence', *RSIS Commentary*, No. 225. Singapore: S. Rajaratnam School of International Studies.

Bass, Gary J. 2013. *The Blood Telegram: India's Secret War in East Pakistan*. New Delhi: Random House India.

Beckley, Michael. 2011/12. 'China's Century? Why America's Edge Will Endure', *International Security* 36(3) (Winter): 41–78.

Benston, G.J. 2000. *The Separation of Investment and Commercial Banking*. London: Macmillan.

Berlin, Isaiah. 1978. *Russian Thinkers*. London: Penguin Books.

Berlin, Isaiah. 1979 [1972]. *Against the Current*. London: Pimlico.

Bernanke, B.S. 2010. 'Monetary Policy and the Housing Bubble', speech delivered at the annual meeting of the American Economic Association, Atlanta, Georgia on 3 January 2010. Available online at https://www.federalreserve.gov/newsevents/speech/bernanke20100103a.htm (last accessed 29 January 2018).

Bernanke, B.S. 2015. 'The Taylor Rule: A Benchmark for Monetary Policy?' Available online at http://brookings.edu/blogs/ben-bernanke/posts/2015/04/28-taylor-rule-monetary-policy?cid=00900015020089101US00 (last accessed 30 January 2018).

Bernanke, B.S. and M. Getler. 1995. 'Inside the Black Box: The Credit Channel of Monetary Policy Transmission'. *Journal of Economic Perspectives* 9(4): 27–48.

Bhalla, S.S. 2007. *Second among Equals: The Middle-Class Kingdoms of India and China*. Washington, DC: Peterson Institute for International Economics.

Bhalla, S.S. 2013. 'The Great Growth-Dole Tradeoff', *The Indian Express*, 20 July.

Bhalla, S.S. 2014. 'Billionaires and Crony Socialism'. *Indian Express*. Available at http://indianexpress.com/article/opinion/columns/billionaires-and-crony-socialism (last accessed 13 November 2017).

Bhalla, S.S. 2015. 'No Proof Required: New GDP Is for Real'. *Indian Express*. Available at http://indianexpress.com/article/opinion/

columns/no-proof-required-new-gdp-is-for-real (last accessed 13 November 2017).

Bix, Herbert P. 2001. *Hirohito and the Making of Modern Japan*. New York: Harper Collins Perennial.

Blackwill, Robert D. and Ashley J. Tellis. 2015. 'Revising U.S. Grand Strategy toward China, Council on Foreign Relations', Council Special Report No. 72. New York: Council on Foreign Relations.

Blair, David. 2016. 'If You Cut the Head Off a Snake, Will It Grow Another Or Simply Die?', *Sunday Telegraph*, London, 4 September.

Blanchard, O.J. and S. Fischer (eds). 1990. *NBER Macroeconomics Annual 1990*. Cambridge, MA: MIT Press.

Blume, Lawrence E. and Steven N. Durlauf. 2015. 'Capital in the Twenty-First Century: A Review Essay', *Journal of Political Economy* 123(4): 749–77.

Blyth, M. 2013. *Austerity: The History of a Dangerous Idea*. New York: Oxford University Press.

Bolger, Daniel P. 2014. *Why We Lost: A General's Inside Account of the Iraq and Afghanistan Wars*. New York: Houghton Mifflin Harcourt.

Boot, Max. 2006. *War Made New: Technology, Warfare, and the Course of History, 1500 to Today*. New York: Gotham Books.

Boot, Max. 2013. *Invisible Armies*. New York: W.W. Norton.

Boot, Max. 2016a. 'The Terrorist Past Had a Message for the Terrorist Present', *Wall Street Journal*, Washington, DC, 27 July.

Boot, Max. 2016b. 'Trump's "America First" Is the Twilight of American Exceptionalism'. *Foreign Policy*. Available at http://foreignpolicy.com/2016/11/22/trumps-america-first-is-the-twilight-of-american-exceptionalism-obama/ (last accessed 21 November 2017).

Boserup, E. 1965. *The Conditions of Agricultural Growth: The Economics of Agrarian Change under Population Pressure*. London: Allen & Unwin.

Bosworth, B., S.M. Collins, and A. Virmani. 2006. 'Sources of Growth in the Indian Economy', in S. Bery, B. Bosworth, and A. Panagariya (eds), *India Policy Forum 2006–07*, vol. 3. Washington, DC: Brookings Institute; New Delhi: NCAER; and New Delhi: Sage Publications.

Bowering, Gerhard, ed. 2013. *The Princeton Encyclopedia of Islamic Political Thought*. Princeton, NJ: Princeton University Press.

Bowring, Philip. 2015. 'China's Delusions of Regional Hegemony', *Financial Times*. Available at https://www.ft.com/content/b8b90350-3f46-11e5-b98b-87c7270955cf (last accessed 22 February 2018).

Brewer, J. 1990. *The Sinews of Power: War, Money and the English State, 1688–1783*. Cambridge, MA: Harvard University Press.

Bridges, J. and R. Thomas. 2012. 'The Impact of QE on the UK Economy—Some Supportive Monetarist Arithmetic', Bank of England Working Paper No. 442, London.

Brinton, C. 1938. *The Anatomy of Revolution*. New York: Vintage.

Brown, Kerry. 2016. *CEO, CHINA: The Rise of Xi Jinping*. London: I.B. Taurus.

Brunner, K. and A. Meltzer. 1968. 'Liquidity Traps for Money, Bank Credit and Interest Rates', *Journal of Political Economy*, 76 (January-February): 1–37.

Brunner, K. and A. Meltzer. 1971. 'The Uses of Money: Money in the Theory of an Exchange Economy', *American Economic Review*, 61 (December): 784–805.

Brzezinski, Zbigniew. 1997. *The Grand Chessboard*. New York: Basic Books.

Brzezinski, Zbigniew. 2012. *Strategic Vision: America and the Crisis of Global Power.* New York: Basic Books.

Bull, H. 1995. *The Anarchical Society*. New York: Columbia University Press.

Bulos, Nabih. 2015. 'US-Trained Syria Rebels Do a Deal with al-Qaeda-Linked Group', *Daily Telegraph*. Available at http://www.telegraph.co.uk/news/worldnews/middleeast/syria/11806496/US-trained-Syria-rebels-do-a-deal-with-al-Qaeda-linked-group.html (last accessed 19 November 2017).

Business Standard. 2013. 'America Still Remains the Promised Land for Most Migrants, Says Survey', *Business Standard*. Available at http://www.business-standard.com/article/economy-policy/america-still-remains-the-promised-land-for-most-migrants-says-survey-113032200582_1.html (last accessed 7 November 2017).

Cagan, P. 2008. 'Monetarism', *The New Palgrave Dictionary of Economics*, 2nd edition. New York: Palgrave Macmillan.

Cain, P.J. and A.J. Hopkins. 2002. *British Imperialism 1688–2000*, Second Edition. Harlow: Longman.

Calomiris, C.W. 2000. *US Bank Deregulation in Historical Perspective*. Cambridge: Cambridge University Press.

Carr, E.H. 2001 [1981]. *The Twenty Years' Crisis, 1919–1939: An Introduction the Study of International Relations*. Basingstoke: Palgrave.

Castaneda, J.G. 1995. *The Mexican Shock*. New York: New Press.

Central Statistics Office. 2015. 'No Room for Doubt on New GDP Numbers'. *Economic and Political Weekly*, 50(6).

Chagnon, N. 1968. *Yanomamo: The Fierce People.* New York: Simon and Schuster.

Chellaney, Brahma. 2010. *Asian Juggernaut: The Rise of India, China, and Japan.* New York: Harper Business.

Chellaney, Brahma. 2011. *Water: Asia's New Battleground.* Washington, DC: Georgetown University Press.

Chen Wang and Chen Long. 2012. 'Debunking Misconceptions on China?', *Institute for New Economic Thinking.* www.ineteconomics.org/blog/china-seminar.

Chenery, H., M.S. Ahluwalia, C.L.G. Bell, J.H. Duloy, and R. Jolly. 1974. *Redistribution with Growth.* New York: Oxford University Press.

Chetty, R., N. Hendren, P. Kline, E. Saez, and N. Turner. 2014. 'Is the United States Still a Land of Opportunity? Recent Trends in Intergenerational Mobility', *American Economic Review*, 104(5): 141–7.

Cheung, Steven. 1969. *The Theory of Share Tenancy.* Chicago: Chicago University Press.

Cheung, Steven. 2008. *The Economic System of China.* Hong Kong: Arcadia Press.

Chollet, Derek. 2016. *The Long Game: How Obama Defied Washington and Redefined America's Role in the World.* New York: Public Affairs.

Choyleva, D. 2015. 'Do Not Bank on China Debt Swap to Work Monetary Magic', *Financial Times*, 29 June.

Clark, Christopher. 2013. *The Sleepwalkers: How Europe Went to War in 1914.* London: Penguin Books.

Clover, Charles. 2015. 'Chinese Seeks Own Navy Facility in Djibouti'. *Financial Times*. Available at https://www.ft.com/content/1c4afbba-94c1-11e5-bd82-c1fb87bef7af (last accessed 9 November 2017).

Coase, Ronald and N. Wang. 2012. *How China Became Capitalist.* New York: Palgrave-Macmillan.

Cockburn, Patrick. 2015. *The Rise of Islamic State: ISIS and the New Sunni Revolution.* London: Verso.

Cohen, S.P. 1998. *The Pakistan Army.* Karachi: Oxford University Press.

Cohen, S.P. 2004. *The Idea of Pakistan.* Washington, DC: Brookings Institution.

Cohen, S.P. 2011. *The Future of Pakistan.* Washington, DC: Brookings Institution.

Cohn, B. 1987. *An Anthropologist among the Historians*. New Delhi: Oxford University Press.

Coker, Christopher. 2015. *The Improbable War: China, the United States and the Logic of Great Power Conflict*. New York: Oxford University Press.

Colley, L. 1992. *Britons: Forging the Nation 1707–1837*, Revised Edition. New Haven, CT: Yale University Press.

Congdon, Tim. 2005. *Money and Asset Prices in Boom and Bust*. London: Institute of Economic Affairs.

Congdon, Tim. 2009. *Central Banking in a Free Society*. London: Institute of Economic Affairs.

Congdon, Tim. 2010. 'Monetary Policy at the Zero Bound', *World Economics*, 11(1): 11–45.

Congdon, Tim. 2015. 'In Praise of Expansionary Fiscal Contraction', *Economic Affairs*, 35(1): 21–34.

Cooper, R. 2007. 'Living with Global Imbalances', Brookings Papers on Economic Activity, 2: 91–107.

Corden, W.M. 2007. 'Those Current Account Imbalances: A Sceptical View', *The World Economy*, 30.

Coughlin, Con. 2017. 'At Last, a Working Model for Military Intervention'. *The Daily Telegraph*.

Cowen, Tyler. 2011. *The Great Stagnation*. New York: Dutton.

Crone, Patricia. 1980. *Slaves on Horses: The Evolution of the Islamic Polity*. Cambridge: Cambridge University Press.

Crone, Patricia and Martin Hinds. 1986. *God's Caliph: Religious Authority in the First Centuries of Islam*. Cambridge: Cambridge University Press.

Crone, Patricia and Michael Cook. 1977. *Hagarism: The Making of the Islamic World*. Cambridge: Cambridge University Press.

Crossley, Pamela. 2010. *The Wobbling Pivot: China since 1800*. W. Sussex: Wiley-Blackwell, Chichester.

Curzon, George N. 1907. *Frontiers*. Oxford: Clarendon Press. Facsimile Edition, Elibron Classics.

Darwin, John. 2007. *After Tamerlane: The Global History of Empire*. London: Penguin.

Davis, Bob and Richard Silk. 2013. 'China's Producers Struggle to Absorb Free Fall in Prices'. *Wall Street Journal*. Available at https://www.wsj.com/articles/SB10001424127887324059704578472412943132102 (last accessed 22 February 2018).

Deaton, Angus and Ron Miller. 1995. 'International Commodity Prices, Macroeconomic Performance, and Politics in Sub-Saharan Africa', *Princeton Essays in International Finance*, 79.

Deaton, Angus. 2009. 'Instruments of Development: Randomization in the Tropics, and the Search for the Elusive Keys to Economic Development', NBER Working Paper, No. 1469, National Bureau of Economic Research, Cambridge, MA.

Deaton, Angus. 2012. *The Great Escape*. Princeton, N.J.: Princeton University Press.

Deerr, Noel. 1949. *The History of Sugar.* London: Chapman and Hall.

Dick, A. 1995. *Industrial Policy and Semiconductors: Missing the Target*. Washington, DC: American Enterprise Institute.

Dolman, Everett. 2005. *Pure Strategy: Power and Principle in the Space and Information Age*. London: Frank Cass.

Dolman, Everett. 2012. 'New Frontiers, Old Realities', *Strategic Studies Quarterly*, 6(1): 78–80.

Domar, E. 1970. 'The Causes of Slavery or Serfdom: A Hypothesis', *Journal of Economic History* 30(1): 18–32.

Doyle, M. 1986. *Empires*. Ithaca: Cornell University Press.

Doyle, M. 1997. *Ways of War and Peace: Realism, Liberalism, and Socialism*. New York: W.W. Norton.

Dumont, L. 1970. *Homo Hierarchicus: The Caste System and Its Implications.* London: Weidenfeld and Nicholson.

Eakin, Hugh. 2015. 'Shifting Sands in Saudi', *The Spectator*.

Ebrahimi, Helia. 2012. 'Gentle Giant Paul Volcker Has Too Little Time Left to Fix the World', *The Daily Telegraph*, 23 September.

Eichengreen, Barry. 2015. *Hall of Mirrors: The Great Depression, the Great Recession, and the Uses—and Misuses—of History.* New York: Oxford University Press.

Elliott, John. 2009. 'China Aims to Block India's Place in the Sun'. *Financial Times*. Available at http://www.ft.com/cms/s/0/26b241ba-8809-11de-82e4-00144feabdc0,dwp_uuid=a6dfcf08-9c79-11da-8762-0000779e2340.html (last accessed 20 November 2017).

Elvin, Mark. 1973. *The Pattern of the Chinese Past*. Stanford: Stanford University Press.

Emmott, Bill. 1989. *The Sun Also Sets: Why Japan Will Not Be Number One.* London: Simon and Schuster.

Emmott, Bill. 2009. *Rivals: How the Power Struggle between China, India and Japan Will Shape the Next Decade*. London: Penguin Books.

Engerman, Stanley. 1983. 'Contract Labor, Sugar, and Technology in the 19th Century', *Journal of Economic History*, 43.

Engerman, Stanley and Ken Sokoloff. 1994. 'Factor Endowments, Institutions and Differential Paths of Growth among the New World Economies: A View from Economic Historians of the United States', NBER Working Paper, Historical Paper No. 66, National Bureau of Economic Research, Cambridge, MA.

Erlich, A. 1967. *The Soviet Industrialization Debate, 1924–1928*. Cambridge, MA: Harvard University Press.

Erumban, Abdul Azeez and Klaas de Vries. 2014. 'Projecting Global Economic Growth', Economics Program Working Paper Series, EPWP#14-03, The Conference Board, New York.

Evans, Richard. 1993. *Deng Xiaoping and the Making of Modern China*. London: Hamish Hamilton.

Evans-Pritchard, Ambrose. 2015. 'Oil and Gas Crunch Pushes Russia Closer to Fiscal Crisis'. *The Daily Telegraph*. Available at http://www.telegraph.co.uk/finance/economics/11759391/Oil-and-gas-crunch-pushes-Russia-closer-to-fiscal-crisis.html (last accessed 8 November 2017).

Evra, Stephen Van. 2015. 'European Militaries and the Origins of World War I', in Richard N. Rosecrance and Steven E. Miller (eds), *The Next Great War?: The Roots of World War I and the Risks of U.S.–China Conflict*, pp. 149–177. Cambridge, MA: MIT Press.

Fair, C. Christine. 2014. *Fighting to the End: The Pakistan Army's Way of War.* New York: Oxford University Fair Press.

Fairbank, J.K. and M. Goodman. 2006. *China: A New History*, pp. 40–1. Cambridge, MA: Harvard University Press.

Fairweather, Jack. 2014. *The Good War: Why We Couldn't Win the War or the Peace in Afghanistan*. New York: Basic Books.

Faitelson, Yakov. 2013. 'A Jewish Majority in the Land of Israel: The Resilient Jewish State', *The Middle East Quarterly*, Fall 2013.

Ferguson, Niall. 1998. *The Pity of War: Explaining World War I.* London: Penguin.

Fernando-Armesto, F. 1995. *Millennium: A History of the Last Thousand Years*. New York: Scribner.

Findlay, Ronald and Kevin O'Rourke. 2007. *Power and Plenty: Trade, War, and the World Economy in the Second Millennium*. Princeton N.J.: Princeton University Press.

Finer, S. 1997. *The History of Government from the Earliest Times*, vols 1 and 2. Oxford: Oxford University Press.

Finer, S. 1999. *The History of Government from the Earliest Times*, vol. 3. Oxford: Oxford University Press.

Finley, M.I. 1968. 'Slavery', in D.L. Sills (ed.), *International Encyclopedia of the Social Sciences*, Vol. 14. New York: Macmillan.

Fisher, Irving. 1933. 'The Debt-Deflation Theory of Great Depressions', *Econometrica*, 1(4): 337–57.

Fogel, F.W. and S. Engerman. 1974. *Time on the Cross.* New York: Little Brown.

Fogel, Robert. 1989. *Without Consent or Contract.* New York: Norton.

Fong, Mei. 2016. *One Child: The Story of China's Most Radical Experiment.* Boston: Houghton Mifflin Harcourt.

Forden, Geoffrey. 2008. 'How China Loses the Coming Space War (Pt. 2)', *Wired*. Available at https://www.wired.com/2008/01/inside-the-ch-1/ (last accessed 21 November 2017).

Foy, Henry, Kathrin Hille, and Richard Milne. 2015. 'Russia: Border Tensions', *Financial Times*, 9 June 2015. Available at https://www.ft.com/content/2cf60498-0e14-11e5-8ce9-00144feabdc0 (last accessed 19 November 2017).

Frank, Gunder. 1998. *Reorient: Global Economy in the Asian Age.* Berkeley: University of California Press.

Freedman, Lawrence. 1981. *The Evolution of Nuclear Strategy*. London: Macmillan.

Friedberg, Aaron L. 2011. *A Contest for Supremacy: China, America and the Struggle for Mastery in Asia.* New York: W.W. Norton.

Friedman, B.M. 1990. 'Targets and Instruments of Monetary Policy', in B.M. Friedman and F.H. Hahn (eds), *Handbook of Monetary Economics, Vol. 2.* Amsterdam: North Holland.

Friedman, B.M. 2008. 'Money Supply', in *The New Palgrave Dictionary of Economics*, 2e, pp. 745–1. New York: Palgrave Macmillan.

Friedman, George. 2010. *The Next 100 Years*. New York: Anchor Books.

Friedman, George. 2015a. 'A Net Assessment of Europe'. Geopolitical Weekly, *Stratfor Worldview.* Available at https://worldview.stratfor.com/weekly/net-assessment-europe (last accessed 2 October 2017).

Friedman, George. 2015b. 'A Net Assessment of East Asia'. Geopolitical Weekly, *Stratfor Worldview.* Available at https://worldview.stratfor.com/article/net-assessment-east-asia (last accessed on 2 October 2017).

Friedman, Milton. 1970. 'The Counter-Revolution in Monetary Theory', Inaugural Wincott Memorial Lecture, Occasional Paper 33. London: Institute of Economic Affair.

Fromkin, David. 1989. *A Peace to End All Peace: The Fall of the Ottoman Empire and the Creation of the Modern Middle East*. New York: Henry Holt.

Gaddis, John Lewis. 2004. *Surprise, Security and the American Experience*. Cambridge, MA: Harvard University Press.

Gaidar, Yegor. n.d. 'Public Expectations and Trust towards the Government: Post-Revolution Stabilization and Its Discontents'. Available at www.iet.ru/files/persona/gaidar/un_en.htm (last accessed 2 October 2017).

Gaidar, Yegor. 2007. *Collapse of an Empire: Lessons for Modern Russia*. Washington, DC: Brookings.

Gaidar, Yegor. 2012. *Russia: A Long View*. Cambridge, MA: MIT Press.

Gall, Carlotta. 2014. *The Wrong Enemy: America in Afghanistan, 2001–2014*. London: Penguin Books.

Ganesh, Janan. 2014. 'UKIP Has Exposed the Conflict in the Tory Soul', *Financial Times*.

Gardner, David. 2014. 'Look Beyond Saudi Arabia for Sunni Leadership', *Financial Times*.

Gardner, David. 2015. 'Putin Keeps World Guessing on Motives for Military Build-Up in Syria', *Financial Times*. Available at https://www.ft.com/content/a44e865c-65f1-11e5-a57f-21b88f7d973f (last accessed 19 November 2017).

Garnaut, John. 2012. 'Rotting from Within', foreignpolicy.org. Available at http://foreignpolicy.com/2012/04/16/rotting-from-within/ (last accessed 30 January 2018).

Garver, John W. 2012. 'The Diplomacy of Rising China in South Asia', *Orbis* 56(3): 391–411.

Gates, Robert and Condoleezza Rice. 2008. 'What We Need Next in Iraq', *Washington Post*. Available at http://www.washingtonpost.com/wp-dyn/content/article/2008/02/12/AR2008021202001.html (last accessed 9 November 2017).

Gellner, Ernest. 1981. *Muslim Society*. Cambridge: Cambridge University Press.

Gellner, Ernest. 1983. *Nations and Nationalism*, Second Edition. Ithaca: Cornell University Press.

Giavazzi, F. and M. Pagano. 1990. 'Can Severe Fiscal Contractions Be Expansionary? Tales of Two Small European Countries', in O.J. Blanchard and S. Fischer (eds), *NBER Macroeconomics Annual 1990.* Cambridge, MA: MIT Press.

Gilmour, David. 1994. *Curzon: Imperial Statesman.* New York: Farrar, Strauss and Giroux.

Gluck, C. 1985. *Japan's Modern Myths: Ideology in the Late Meiji Period.* Princeton, NJ: Princeton University Press.

Gokarn, S. 2014. 'Bang for the Buck', *Business Standard.* Available at http://www.business-standard.com/article/opinion/subir-gokarn-bang-for-the-buck-114032300691_1.html (last accessed 13 November 2017).

Goldberg, Jeffrey. 2016. 'The Obama Doctrine'. *The Atlantic.* Available at https://www.theatlantic.com/magazine/archive/2016/04/the-obama-doctrine/471525/ (last accessed 17 November 2017).

Goldstone, Jack (ed). 2003. *Revolutions: Theoretical, Comparative, and Historical Studies*, Third Edition. Belmont CA: Thomson Wadsworth.

Goodwin, R.M. 1967. 'A Growth Cycle', in C.H. Feinstein (ed.), *Socialism, Capitalism, and Economic Growth.* Cambridge: Cambridge University Press.

Gopal, S. 1975, 1979, 1984. *Jawaharlal Nehru*, vol. 1–3. New Delhi: Oxford University Press.

Gordon, Robert. 2012. 'Is US Economic Growth Over? Faltering Innovation Confronts the Six Headwinds', NBER Working Paper, No. 18315, National Bureau of Economic Research, Cambridge, MA.

Goujon, Reva. 2016. 'The Global Order after the Brexit', *Stratfor Worldview.* Available at https://www.stratfor.com/weekly/global-order-after-brexit?newer=1477472433&topics=284, accessed on 2 Oct 2017.

Gourevitch, P.A. 1993. 'Democracy and Economic Policy: Elective Affinities and Circumstantial Conjectures', *World Development*, 21(8): 1271–80.

Government of India. 2006–16. *Economic Survey 2006–16.* New Delhi: Ministry of Finance.

Grabell, Michael. 2012. *Money Well Spent? The Truth behind the Trillion-Dollar Stimulus, the Biggest Economic Recovery Plan in History.* New York: Public Affairs.

Gregory, Paul Roderick. 2015. 'Is a Slow Putsch against Putin Under Way?', *Forbes*. Available at https://www.forbes.com/sites/paulroderickgregory/2015/08/20/is-a-slow-putsch-against-putin-under-way/#6f3d3e405b66 (last accessed 19 November 2017).

Gregory, Paul Roderick. 2016. 'Do Alternative Estimates Show China Entering a Period of Stagnation?', *Forbes*, 15 August.

Gruber, James. 2013. 'Why a China Crash May Be Imminent', *Forbes*. Available at https://www.forbes.com/sites/jamesgruber/2013/02/23/a-china-crash-may-be-imminent/#40d89eb42f7e (last accessed 13 November 2017).

Guha, K. 2009. 'White House Hit in Skirmishes Over Spending', *Financial Times*, Washington, DC, 9 July.

Gulati, A. 2009. 'Emerging Trends in Indian Agriculture: What Can We Learn from These?', *Agricultural Economics Research Review*, 22 (July–December): 171–84.

Gulati, A. 2010. 'Accelerating Agriculture Growth', in S. Acharya and R. Mohan (eds), *India's Economic Performance*. New Delhi: Oxford University Press.

Gulati, A. 2012. 'Reforming Agriculture', *Seminar* 629.

Gulati, A. 2015. 'Economic Survey 2015: Growth in Agriculture Remains a Worry', *Economic Times*. Available at https://economictimes.indiatimes.com/news/economy/agriculture/economic-survey-2015-growth-in-agriculture-remains-a-worry-says-ashok-gulati/articleshow/46402798.cms (last accessed 13 November 2017).

Gwartney, J. and R. Lawson. 2003. *Economic Freedom of the World: 2003 Annual Report*. Vancouver: Fraser Institute.

Haas, Mark L. 2007. 'A Geriatric Peace? The Future of U.S. Power in a World of Aging Populations', *International Security*, 32(1): 112–47.

Haberler, Gottfried. 1986. 'Reflections on Hayek's Business Cycle Theory', *Cato Journal*, 6(2): 422.

Haldane, A.G. 2011. 'Control Rights (And Wrongs)', Wincott Annual Memorial Lecture, London, 24 October 2011. Available online at https://www.bis.org/review/r111026a.pdf (last accessed 20 February 2018).

Haldane, A.G. 2012. 'The Dog and the Frisbee', paper for Federal Reserve Bank of Kansas City's 36th economic policy symposium, 'The Changing Policy Landscape' Jackson Hole, Wyoming. Available at https://www.bankofengland.co.uk/-/media/boe/files/

news/2012/august/the-dog-and-the-frisbee-paper-by-andy-haldane.pdf (accessed 5 February 2018).

Hallpike, C. 1986. *The Principles of Social Evolution.* Oxford: Clarendon Press.

Halper, Lezlee Brown and Stefan Halper. 2014. *Tibet: An Unfinished Story.* Gurgaon: Hachette India; London: C. Hurst & Co.

Hamid, Shadi. 2014. *Temptations of Power: Islamists and Illiberal Democracies in a New Middle East.* New York: Oxford University Press.

Hammes, T.X. 2013. 'Sorry, AirSea Battle Is No Strategy', *The National Interest.* Available at http://nationalinterest.org/commentary/sorry-airsea-battle-no-strategy-8846 (last accessed 21 November 2017).

Hanke, Steve H. and Stephen J.K Walters. 1997. 'Economic Freedom, Prosperity, and Equality: A Survey', *Cato Journal*, 17(2): 117–46.

Hansen, Bent. 1991. *The Political Economy of Poverty, Equity, and Growth: Egypt and Turkey.* New York: Oxford University Press.

Haqqani, Hussain. 2013. *Magnificent Delusions: Pakistan, the United States, and an Epic History of Misunderstanding.* New York: Public Affairs.

Harberger, Arnold. 1998. 'A Vision of the Growth Process', *American Economic Review*, 88(1): 1–32.

Harding, Luke. 2016. *A Very Expensive Poison: The Definitive Story of the Murder of Litvinenko and Russia's War with the West.* London: Guardian Faber.

Hayek, Friedrich. 1944/2007. *The Road to Serfdom.* Chicago: University of Chicago Press.

Hayek, Friedrich. 1960. *The Constitution of Liberty*, p. 86. London: Routledge and Kegan Paul.

Hayek, Friedrich. 1973. *Law, Legislation and Liberty.* Chicago: Chicago University Press.

Hayton, Bill. 2014. *The South China Sea: The Struggle for Power in Asia.* New Haven, CT: Yale University Press.

Heckscher, E. 1955. *Mercantilism.* London: Allen and Unwin.

Heilbrunn, Jacob. 2015. 'Detente Will Force Iran to Compromise with US or Collapse', *Financial Times.* Available at https://www.ft.com/content/fb43328a-dea3-11e4-b9ec-00144feab7de (last accessed 17 November 2017).

Herman, A. 2001. *How the Scots Invented the Modern World.* New York: Three Rivers Press.

Hetzel, Robert. 2012. *The Great Recession: Market Failure or Policy Failure?* New York: Cambridge University Press.

Hille, Kathrin. 2015a. 'Echoes of Great Game as Putin Looks to China', *Financial Times*, 6 July.

Hille, Kathrin. 2015b. 'Outcry in Russia over China Land Lease Agreement', *Financial Times*. Available at https://www.ft.com/content/700a9450-1b26-11e5-8201-cbdb03d71480 (last accessed 19 November 2017).

Hiro, Dilip. 2010. *Inside Central Asia*. New Delhi: Harper Collins.

Hirshleifer, J. 1995. 'Anarchy and Its Breakdown', *Journal of Political Economy*, 103: 26–52.

Hirshleifer, J. 2001. *The Dark Side of the Force: Economic Foundations of Conflict Theory*. Cambridge: Cambridge University Press.

Hobbes, T. 1996 [1651]. *Leviathan*. Cambridge: Cambridge University Press.

Hobson, J.A. 1948 [1902]. *Imperialism: A Study*, Revised Edition. London: Allen and Unwin.

Hodges, P. and D.B. van Scheltinga. 2015. 'China's Collapsing Stock Market Underlines Need for New Normal Reforms', *Financial Times*, 27 July.

Hoffman, V. J. 1995. 'Muslim Fundamentalists: Psychosocial Profiles', in Martin E. Marty and R. Appleby (eds), *Fundamentalisms Comprehended*, p. 206. Chicago: University of Chicago Press.

Holland, Tom. 2012. *In the Shadow of the Sword*. London: Little, Brown.

Holslag, Jonathan. 2015. *China's Coming War with Asia*. Cambridge: Polity Press.

Hosking, Geoffrey. 2009. 'Power and People in Russia', In K. Almqvist and A. Linklater (eds), *On Russia*, p. 79. Stockholm: Axel and Margaret Ax:son Johnson Foundation.

Houlder, Vanessa. 2014. 'Taxing Time Ahead As Offshore Rules Come Under More Scrutiny', *Financial Times*, 13 June. Available at https://www.ft.com/content/2b4c7be8-f233-11e3-ac7a-00144feabdc0 (last accessed 19 February 2018).

Hourani, Albert. 1991. *A History of the Arab Peoples*. Cambridge, MA: Harvard University Press.

Howard-Johnston, James. 2010. *Witnesses to a World Crisis: Historians and Histories of the Middle East in the Seventh Century*. Oxford: Oxford University Press.

Huang, Yasheng. 2008. *Capitalism with Chinese Characteristics: Entrepreneurship and the State*. Cambridge: Cambridge University Press.

Huang, Yasheng. 2011. 'Rethinking the Beijing Consensus', *Asia Policy*, 11: 1–26.

Hudson, Valerie and Andrea den Boer. 2005. *Bare Branches: The Security Implications of Asia's Surplus Male Population*. Cambridge, MA: MIT Press.

Hume, D. 1740. *A Treatise of Human Nature*. Oxford: Oxford University Press.

Hume, D. 1750. *An Enquiry Concerning the Principles of Morals*. Oxford: Oxford University Press.

Hume, D. 1757, 1993 [1779]. *Dialogues* and *Natural History of Religion*, Oxford World's Classics. Oxford: Oxford University Press.

Hume, D. 1989 [1777]. *Essays, Moral, Political, and Literary*. Indianapolis: Liberty Classics.

Ignatieff, Michael. 2016. 'A Syria Policy That Dares Not Speak Its Name', *Financial Times*. Available at https://www.ft.com/content/97b863fe-d3ec-11e5-829b-8564e7528e54 (last accessed 17 November 2017).

International Institute for Strategic Studies (IISS). 2015. *The Military Balance 2015*. Abingdon: Routledge.

International Monetary Fund (IMF). 2013. *Reassesing the Role and Modalities of Fiscal Policy in Advanced Economies*. Washington, DC: IMF.

International Monetary Fund (IMF). 2014. 'Russian Federation: Staff Report for the 2014 Article IV Consultation', *IMF Country Report*, No. 14/175. Washington, DC: IMF.

International Monetary Fund (IMF). 2015. 'Japan: Staff Report for the 2015 Article IV Consultation', *IMF Country Report*, No. 15/197. Washington, DC: IMF.

Jasay, Anthony de. 1985. *The State*. Indianapolis: Liberty Fund.

Jenkins, Holman W., Jr. 2016. 'The Weekend Interview: The U.S. Has No Global Strategy', *Wall Street Journal*. Available at https://www.wsj.com/articles/the-u-s-has-no-global-strategy-1454108567 (last accessed 17 November 2017).

Jenkins, R. 1999. *Democratic Politics and Economic Reform in India*. Cambridge: Cambridge University Press.

Jenner, W.J.F. 1992. *The Tyranny of History: The Roots of China's Crisis*. London: Allen Lane.

Joffe, Josef. 2014. *The Myth of America's Decline: Politics, Economics, and a Half Century of False Prophecies*. New York: Liverlight Publishing.

Judt, T. 2011. *A Grand Illusion? An Essay on Europe*. 23–4. New York: New York University Press.

Kagan, Fredrick W. and Kimberly Kagan. 2011. *Defining Success in Afghanistan*. Washington, DC: American Enterprise Institute.

Kagan, Robert. 2006. *Dangerous Nation: America's Place in the World from Its Earliest Days to the Dawn of the Twentieth Century*. New York: Alfred A. Knopf.

Kagan, Robert. 2016. 'Trump Marks the End of America as World's "Indispensable Nation"', *Financial Times*. Available at https://www.ft.com/content/782381b6-ad91-11e6-ba7d-76378e4fef24 (last accessed 21 November 2017).

Kaldor, Nicholas. 1955. 'Alternative Theories of Distribution', *Review of Economic Studies* 23(2): 83–100.

Kaplan, Robert D. 2012. *The Revenge of Geography: What the Map Tells Us About Coming Conflicts and the Battle Against Fate*. New York: Random House.

Kaplan, Robert D. 2014. *Asia's Cauldron: The South China Sea and the End of a Stable Pacific*. New York: Random House.

Kapur, Devesh. 2014. 'Western Anti-Capitalists Take Too Much for Granted', *Financial Times*, 23 July.

Karnad, Bharat. 2015. *Why India Is Not a Great Power (Yet)*. New Delhi: Oxford University Press.

Kaye, Charles R., Joseph S. Nye, Jr., and Alyssa Ayres. 2015. 'A New Indo-US Partnership Model', *Indian Express*. Available at http://indianexpress.com/article/opinion/columns/a-new-indo-us-partnership-model/ (last accessed 20 November 2017).

Kazmin, Amy. 2014. 'India Struggles to Build Up Infrastructure Dream', *Financial Times*. Available at https://www.ft.com/content/a4152f94-1627-11e4-93ec-00144feabdc0 (last accessed 13 November 2017).

Kedourie, E. 1993 [1960]. *Nationalism*. Oxford: Blackwells.

Kennedy, Paul. 1989. *The Rise and Fall of the Great Powers.* London: Fontana Press.

Kepel, G. 2002. 'The Jihad in Search of a Cause', *Financial Times*.

Keynes, John Maynard. 1924. *A Tract on Monetary Reform*. New York: Harcourt Bruce.

Khalaf, Roula. 2017. 'Putin Won the Syrian War, But Can He Keep the Peace?', *Financial Times*, 28 November.

Khaldun, Ibn. 1967 [1379]. *The Muqaddimah: An Introduction to History.* Princeton, NJ: Princeton University Press.

Kiernan, Ben. 2008. *The Pol Pot Regime: Race, Power, and Genocide in Cambodia under the Khmer Rouge, 1975–79*, Third Edition. New Haven, CT: Yale University Press.

Kirkby, Jasper et.al. 2011. 'Role of Sulphuric Acid, Ammonia and Galactic Cosmic Rays in Atmospheric Aerosol Nucleation', *Nature*, 476(7361): 429–33.

Kissinger, Henry and George Shultz. 2015. 'The Iran Deal and Its Consequences', *Wall Street Journal*. Available at https://www.wsj.com/articles/the-iran-deal-and-its-consequences-1428447582 (last accessed 17 November 2017).

Kissinger, Henry. 2011. *On China*. New York: Penguin.

Kissinger. Henry. 2014. *World Order.* New York: Penguin Press.

Knight, Amy. 2016. 'Getting Away with Murder', *Times Literary Supplement*, 3 August.

Kolawski, L. and S. Hampsire (eds). 1974. *The Socialist Idea: A Reappraisal.* London: Weidenfeld and Nicholson.

Kotkin, J. 2010. *The Next Hundred Million: America in 2050.* New York: Penguin Books.

Krusell, Per and Anthony A. Smith Jr. 2015. 'Is Piketty's "Second Law of Capitalism" Fundamental?', *Journal of Political Economy*, 123(4): 725–48.

Kuchins, Andrew. 2015. 'Policy Brief: Putin Goes Nationalist', *Rising Powers Initiative*, Sigur Center for Asian Studies, George Washington University, Washington D.C. Available at http://www.risingpowersinitiative.org/policy-brief-putin-goes-nationalist/ (last accessed 19 November 2017).

Kupperman, Karen Ordahl. 1993. *Providence Island, 1630–1641: The Other Puritan Colony.* Cambridge: Cambridge University Press.

Kynge, James. 2007. *China Shakes the World*. New York: Mariner Books.

Laeven, Luc and Fabian Valencia. 2010. 'Resolution of Banking Crises: The Good, the Bad, and the Ugly', IMF Working Paper, No. WP/10/146.

Lal, D. 1976. 'Distribution and Development', *World Development*, 4(9): 725–38.

Lal, D. 1985. 'Nationalism, Socialism and Planning: Influential Ideas in the South', *World Development* 13(6): 749–59.

Lal, D. 1986. 'Review of John E. Roemer, *A General Theory of Exploitation and Class*, Harvard, 1982', *Journal of Economic Behavior and Organization*, 7: 101–14.

Lal, D. 1989. 'The Limits of International Cooperation', 20th Annual Wincott Lecture, Occasional Paper 83(190). London: Institute of Economic Affairs.

Lal, D. 1990. 'The Fable of the Three Envelopes: The Analytics and Political Economy of the Reform of Chinese State Owned Enterprises', *European Economic Review*, 34: 1213–31.

Lal, D. 1993 [1985]. 'Nationalism, Socialism and Planning: Influential Ideas in the South', *World Development*, 13(6): 749–59.

Lal, D. 1993. *The Repressed Economy.* Aldershot: Edward Elgar.

Lal, D. 1995. 'India and China: Contrasts in Economic Liberalization?', *World Development*, 23(9): 1475–94.

Lal, D. 1998. *Unintended Consequences: The Impact of Factor Endowments, Culture, and Politics on Long-Run Economic Performance.* Cambridge, MA: MIT Press.

Lal, D. 1999 [1995]. 'Arms and the Man: Costs and Benefits of Nuclear Weapons', in D. Lal, *Unfinished Business: India in the World Economy*, pp. 195–210. New Delhi: Oxford University Press.

Lal, D. 1999a. 'EMU and Globalization', Policy Series No. 17, *Politeia*, London, reprinted as Ch. 4 in D. Lal. 2012. *Lost Causes: The Retreat from Classical Liberalism*. London: Biteback Publishing.

Lal, D. 1999b. *Unfinished Business: India in the World Economy*. New Delhi: Oxford University Press.

Lal, D. 2003a. 'Is Democracy Necessary for Development?', in S. Ramaswamy and J.W. Casson (eds), *Development and Democracy*. Lebanon, NH: University Press of New England.

Lal, D. 2003b. 'The Japanese Slump', in R. Pethig and M. Rauscher (eds), *Challenges to the World Economy*, pp. 281–90. Berlin: Springer.

Lal, D. 2004. *In Praise of Empires*. New York: Palgrave Macmillan.

Lal, D. 2005 [1988]. *The Hindu Equilibrium: India c. 1500 B.C.–2000 A.D.*, Abridged and Revised Edition. Oxford and New York: Oxford University Press.

Lal, D. 2006a. 'A Proposal to Privatize Chinese Enterprises and End Financial Repression', *Cato Journal* 26(2) Spring–Summer: 275–86.

Lal, D. 2006b. *Reviving the Invisible Hand: The Case for Classical Liberalism in the Twenty-First Century*. Princeton, NJ: Princeton University Press.

Lal, D. 2006c. 'The Status Quo in Kashmir?', in R.N. Rosecrance and A.A. Stein (eds), *No More States? Globalization, National Self-Determination, and Terrorism*, pp. 145–59. Lanham, MD: Rowan and Littlefield.

Lal, D. 2006d. 'Will Terrorism Defeat Globalization', in R.N. Rosecrance and A.A. Stein (eds), *No More States? Globalization, National Self-Determination, and Terrorism*, pp. 35–45. Lanham, MD: Rowman & Littlefield.

Lal, D. 2008a. 'An Indian Economic Miracle?', *Cato Journal*, 28(1): 11–34.

Lal, D. 2008b. 'Endangering the War on Terror by the War on Drugs', *World Economics*, 9(3): 1–29.

Lal, D. 2010. 'The Great Crash of 2008: Causes and Consequences', *Cato Journal*, 30(2): 265–77.

Lal, D. 2011. 'India's Post-Liberalization Blues', *World Economics*, 12(4).

Lal, D. 2012a. 'Is the Washington Consensus Dead?', *Cato Journal* 32(3): 493–512.

Lal, D. 2012b. *Lost Causes: The Retreat from Classical Liberalism*. London: Biteback Publishing.

Lal, D. 2012c. 'The Tsar in Winter', *Business Standard*, 21 April.

Lal, D. 2013a. 'A Demographic Time Bomb', *Business Standard*. Available at http://www.business-standard.com/article/opinion/a-demographic-time-bomb-113031500651_1.html (last accessed 13 November 2017).

Lal, D. 2013b. *Poverty and Progress: Realities and Myths about Global Poverty*. New Delhi: Oxford University Press.

Lal, D. 2014. 'The Future of Palestine', *Business Standard*. Available at http://www.business-standard.com/article/opinion/deepak-lal-the-future-of-palestine-114121901411_1.html (last accessed on 2 October 2017).

Lal, D. 2016a. 'Geopolitics of Oil and the Dollar', *Business Standard*. Available at http://www.business-standard.com/article/opinion/deepak-lal-geopolitics-of-oil-and-the-dollar-116083001415_1.html (last accessed 23 February 2018).

Lal, D. 2016b. 'The Indian Economy: From Growth to Stagflation to Liberal Reform', *World Economics*, 17(1): 63–104.

Lal, D. 2016c. 'The Migrant Crisis and "Europe"', *Business Standard*. Available at http://www.business-standard.com/article/opinion/deepak-lal-the-migrant-crisis-and-europe-116012701152_1.html (last accessed 23 February 2018).

Lal, D. 2017. 'In the Shadow of the Dragon', *Business Standard*. Available at http://www.business-standard.com/article/opinion/in-the-shadow-of-the-dragon-117053001980_1.html (last accessed 19 November 2017).

Lal, D. and H. Myint. 1996. *The Political Economy of Poverty, Equity and Growth: A Comparative Study*. Oxford: Clarendon Press.

Lal, D. and I. Natarajan. 2001. 'The Virtuous Circle: Savings, Distribution and Growth Interactions in India', in D. Lal and R.H. Snape (eds),

Trade, Development and Political Economy, pp. 213–28. Basingstoke: Palgrave.

Lawson, Nigel. 2016. 'Thanks to Brexit We Can Finish the Thatcher Revolution', *Financial Times*. Available at https://www.ft.com/content/6cb84f70-6b7c-11e6-a0b1-d87a9fea034f (last accessed 23 February 2018).

Leijonhufvud, Axel. 2009. 'Wicksell, Hayek, Keynes, Friedman: Whom Should We Follow?', paper presented at the Special Meeting of the MPS on 'The End of Globalizing Capitalism? Classical Liberal Responses to the Global Financial Crisis', New York City (5–7 March).

Leijonhufvud, Axel. 2015. 'Monetary Muddles', *Cato Journal*, 35(2): 179–92.

Lenin, Vladimir Ilyich. 1916/1939. *Imperialism: The Highest Stage of Capitalism*. Russian edition: 1916; English edition: London: Lawrence and Wishart, 1939.

Lewis, B. 1992. 'Muslims, Christians, and Jews: The Dream of Coexistence', *New York Review of Books* 39(6).

Lewis, Leo. 2015. 'Tokyo Steps Up Warnings over Beijing's Maritime Ambitions', *Financial Times*, 21 July.

Lewis, P. 1962. *Quiet Crisis in India: Economic Development and American Policy*. Washington, DC: Brookings Institution.

Lieven, Anatol. 2012. *Pakistan: A Hard Country*. London: Penguin.

Lin, Justin. 2012. *Demystifying the Chinese Economy*. Cambridge: Cambridge University Press.

Lindberg, Tod. 2014. 'Making Sense of the "International Community"', Working Paper, International Institutions and Global Governance Program, Council on Foreign Relations, New York.

Lindert, Peter H. and Peter J. Morton. 1989. 'How Sovereign Debt Has Worked', in J. Sachs (ed.), *Developing Country Debt and Economic Performance*, pp. 39–106. Chicago: University of Chicago Press.

Lipset, S.M. 1959. *Political Man: The Social Bases of Politics*. London: Heinemann.

Liska, G. 1967. *Imperial America: The International Politics of Primacy*. Baltimore, MD: Johns Hopkins Press.

Little, I.M.D. 1982. *Economic Development: Theory, Policy, and International Relations*. New York: Basic Books.

Lucas, Edward. 2014. *The New Cold War: Putin's Russia and the Threat to the West*. London: Bloomsbury.

Luttwak, E. 2012. *The Rise of China vs. the Logic of Strategy*. Cambridge, MA: Belknap Press, Harvard University.

Luttwak, E. 2016. 'Enough Hysterics, Donald Trump's Foreign Policy Isn't Reckless or Radical', *Foreign Policy*. Available at http://foreignpolicy.com/2016/11/17/enough-hysterics-donald-trumps-foreign-policy-isnt-reckless-or-radical/ (last accessed 21 November 2017).

Macdonald, J. 2006. *A Sovereign Nation Deep in Debt: The Financial Roots of Democracy.* New York: Farrar, Strauss and Giroux.

Machiavelli, Niccolò. 1950 [1513]. *The Prince*. New York: Modern Library.

Mackenzie, Kate. 2013. 'China Is Having a Credit-Fuelled Non-Recovery', *Financial Times*. Available at https://ftalphaville.ft.com/2013/04/15/1459132/china-is-having-a-credit-fuelled-non-recovery (last accessed 13 November 2017).

MacMillan, Margaret. 2013a. 'The Rhyme of History: Lessons of the Great War', *The Brookings Essay.* Washington, DC: Brookings Institution.

MacMillan, Margaret. 2013b. *The War that Ended Peace: The Road to 1914*. London: Profile Books.

Maddison, Angus. 2001. *The World Economy: A Millennial Perspective*. Paris: OECD.

Maddison, Angus. 2004. *Historical Statistics for the World Economy, 1–2003 AD*. Paris: OECD.

Maddison, Angus. 2007a. *Chinese Economic Performance in the Long Run*. Paris: OECD.

Maddison, Angus. 2007b. *Contours of the World Economy, 1–2030 AD: Essays in Macro-Economic History*. Oxford: Oxford University Press.

Mahan, A.T. 1900. *The Problem of Asia: And Its Effect upon International Policies.* London: Sampson Low, Marston.

Mahan, A.T. 1987 [1894]. *The Influence of Sea Power upon History 1660–1783*. New York: Dover Publications.

Maisonneuve, Phillip Bagnoli, Guillaume Bousquet, and Francesca Spinelli. 2012. 'Long-Term Growth Scenarios', *OECD Economics Department Working Paper*, No. 1000, Paris.

Mankiw, N. Gregory. 2015. 'Yes, r>g. So What?', *American Economic Review*, 105(5): 43–7.

Mann, James. 2012. *The Obamians: The Struggle Inside the White House to Redefine American Power.* New York: Viking Penguin.

Mansfield, E.D. and J. Snyder. 1995. 'Democratization and War', *Foreign Affairs*, 74(3): 79–97.

Mansfield, Edwin. 1968. *The Economics of Technical Change*. London: Longmans.

Marshall, Tim. 2015. *Prisoners of Geography*. London: Elliot and Thompson.

Marty, Martin E. and R. Scott Appleby, eds. 1993. *Fundamentalisms and the State: Remaking Polities, Economies, and Militance*. Chicago: University of Chicago Press.

Masao, Maruyama. 1964. 'Japanese Thought', *Journal of Social and Political Ideas in Japan*, 44.

McClelland, J.S. 1996. *A History of Western Political Thought*. London: Routledge.

McFate, Sean. 2014. *The Modern Mercenary: Private Armies and What They Mean for World Order*. New York: Oxford University Press.

McGregor, Richard. 2012. *The Party: The Secret World of China's Communist Rulers*. New York: Harper Perennial.

McKinnon, R. and K. Ohno. 1997. *Dollar and Yen: Resolving Economic Conflict between the United States and Japan*. Cambridge, MA: MIT Press.

McNeill, W.H. 1963. *The Rise of the West*. Chicago: Chicago University Press.

McNeill, W.H. 1979a. *A World History*, Third Edition. New York: Oxford University Press.

McNeill, W.H. 1979b. *The Pursuit of Power*. Chicago: University of Chicago Press.

Mead, Walter Russell. 2008. *God and Gold*. New York: Vintage.

Mearsheimer, John J. 2001. *The Tragedy of Great Power Politics*. New York: W.W. Norton.

Meltzer, A.H. 1995. 'Monetary, Credit (and Other) Transmission Processes: A Monetarist Perspective', *Journal of Economic Perspectives*, 9(4): 49–72.

Meltzer, A.H. 2003–9. *A History of the Federal Reserve*, 3 vols. Chicago: University of Chicago Press.

Menzies, Gavin. 2003. *1421: The Year China Discovered America*. New York: William Murrow.

Mill, J.S. 1910. *Representative Government*. London: Everyman Library.

Minogue, Kenneth. 1995. *Politics: A Very Short Introduction*. Oxford: Oxford University Press.

Mitter, Rana. 2014. *China's War with Japan, 1937–1945*. London: Penguin Books.

Mohan, C. Raja. 2013. *Samudra Manthan: Sino-Indian Rivalry in the Indo-Pacific*. New Delhi: Oxford University Press.

Moore, Charles. 2016a. 'David Cameron's Beloved Single Market is a Ploy Designed to Subjugate British Rights', *The Telegraph*. Available at www.telegraph.co.uk/news/2016/06/10/david-cameron-is-offering-voters-a-false-choice-in-the-eu-refere (last accessed on 28 September 2017).

Moore, Charles. 2016b. 'The "Single Market"–Two Little Words That Mean Something Very Different'. *Daily Telegraph*.

Morishima, M. 1982. *Why Has Japan 'Succeeded'?* Cambridge: Cambridge University Press.

Morse, R.M. 1964. 'The Heritage of Latin America', in L. Hartz (ed.), *The Founding of New Societies: Studies in the History of the United States, Latin America, South Africa, Canada, and Australia*. New York: Harcourt, Brace and World.

Mudelsee, M. 2001. 'The Phase Relations among Atmospheric CO2 Content, Temperature and Global Ice Volume Over the Past 420ka', *Quaternary Science Reviews*, 20(4): 583–9.

Mueller, John. 2006. 'Terrorism, Overreaction and Globalization', in R.N. Rosecrance and A.A. Stein (eds), *No More States? Globalization, National Self-Determination, and Terrorism*. Lanham, MD: Rowman and Littlefield.

Mueller, John. 2009. *Overblown: How Politicians and the Terrorism Industry Inflate National Security Threats, and Why We Believe Them*. New York: Free Press.

Mueller, John. 2010. *Atomic Obsession: Nuclear Alarmism from Hiroshima to Al-Qaeda*. New York: Oxford University Press.

Mueller, John. 2011. *War and Ideas: Selected Essays*. Abingdon: Routledge.

Mueller, John and Mark Stewart. 2008. *Chasing Ghosts: The Policing of Terrorism*. New York: Oxford University Press.

Mueller, John and Mark Stewart. 2014. 'Responsible Counterterrorism Policy', *Policy Analysis*, No. 755. Washington, DC: Cato Institute.

Murphy, K. 2015. 'Explaining Inequality', Becker Friedman Institute. Available at https://bfi.uchicago.edu/feature-story/explaining-inequality (last accessed 23 February 2018).

Murray, Charles. 1984. *Losing Ground: American Social Policy, 1950–1980*. New York: Basic Books.

Murray, Charles. 2012a. *Coming Apart: The State of White America, 1960–2010*. New York: Crown Forum.

Murray, Charles. 2012b. 'The New American Divide'. The Saturday Essay. *Wall Street Journal*, 21 January.

Murray, Charles. 2012c. 'Why Economics Can't Explain our National Divide'. *Wall Street Journal*, 16 March.

Nasr, Vali. 2007. *The Shia Revival: How Conflicts within Islam Will Shape the Future.* New York: W.W. Norton.

Nasr, Vali. 2013. *The Dispensable Nation: American Foreign Policy in Retreat.* New York: Doubleday.

Ninan, T.N. 2015. *The Turn of the Tortoise: The Challenge and Promise of India's Future.* New Delhi: Allen Lane, Penguin.

Nitze, William A. 2017. 'Putin's Failure as a Grand Strategist', *The Globalist.* Available at www.theglobalist.com/putins-failure-as-a-grand-strategist (last accessed on 28 September 2017).

Noland, M. and H. Pack. 2003. *Industrial Policy in an Era of Globalization: Lessons from Asia.* Washington, DC: Institute of International Economics.

Nye Jr., Joseph S. 2015. *Is the American Century Over?* Cambridge: Polity Press.

Oakeshott, Michael. 1991. *On Human Conduct.* New York: Oxford University Press.

Oakeshott, Michael. 1993. *Morality and Politics in Modern Europe.* New Haven, CT: Yale University Press.

Obama, Barack. 1995. *Dreams from My Father: A Story of Race and Inheritance.* New York: Times Books.

Obstfield, M. 2012. 'Does the Current Account Still Matter?', *American Economic Review*, 102(3).

Oliphant, Roland, Justin Huggler, and Raf Sanchez. 2015. 'Russia Threatens US with Nuclear Arms "Counter-Measures"', *The Daily Telegraph.* Available at http://www.telegraph.co.uk/news/worldnews/europe/russia/11886639/Russia-threatens-US-with-nuclear-arms-counter-measures.html (last accessed 19 November 2017).

Orphanides, A. 2008. *Taylor Rules: The New Palgrave Dictionary of Economics.* New York: Palgrave Macmillan.

Pamuk, Orhan. 2006. *Istanbul: Memories and the City.* New York: Vintage.

Panikkar, K.M. 1959. *Geographical Factors in Indian History.* Bombay: Bhartiya Vidya Bhavan.

Patrick, H. and H. Rosovsky (eds). 1976. *Asia's New Giant: How the Japanese Economy Works.* Washington, DC: Brookings Institution.

Paz, Octavio. 1988. *Sor Juana.* Cambridge, MA: Harvard University Press.

Pettis, Michael. 2011. 'The Last Chinese Banking Crisis Actually WAS Painful, and the Next Will Be Worse', Op-Ed, *Business* Insider. Available at http://www.businessinsider.com/china-non-performing-loans-2011-1 (last accessed 13 November 2017).

Pettis, Michael. 2013. 'Hello 2013: Chinese Banking and Economic Reform', Beyondbrics blog, *Financial Times*. Available at http://blogs.ft.com/beyond-brics/2013/01/08/hello-2013-michael-pettis-chinese-banking-in-2013/ (last accessed 23 February 2018).

Piketty, Thomas. 2014. *Capital in the Twenty-First Century*. Cambridge, MA: Belknap Press.

Piketty, Thomas and Emmanuel Saez. 2003. 'Income Inequality in the United States, 1913–1998', *Quarterly Journal of Economics*, 118(1): 1–39.

Pilling, David. 2015. 'China's Push-Me-Pull-You Policies Leave the World Reeling', *Financial Times*. Available at https://www.ft.com/content/d79abecc-4a58-11e5-9b5d-89a026fda5c9 (last accessed 19 November 2017).

Pinker, Steven. 2011. *The Better Angels of Our Nature*. London: Penguin Books.

Plamenatz, J. 1960. *On Alien Rule and Self-Government*. London: Longmans.

Plamenatz, J. 1973. 'Two Types of Nationalism', in E. Kamenka (ed.), *Nationalism: The Nature and Evolution of an Idea*. London: Arnold.

Pollack, Lisa. 2014. 'A Online Dialogue of First World Problems', *Financial Times*. Available at https://www.ft.com/content/cc68b72e-3f4c-11e4-984b-00144feabdc0 (last accessed 17 November 2017).

Ponnuru, R. 1995. 'The Mystery of Japanese Growth', Rochester Paper 4. London: Trade Policy Research Unit, Centre for Policy Studies.

Poole, W. 1970. 'Optimal Choice of Monetary Policy Instruments in a Simple Stochastic Macro Model', *Quarterly Journal of Economics*, 84: 197–216.

Przeworski, Adam and Fernando Limongi. 1997. 'Political Rights and Economic Growth', *Journal of Economic Perspectives*, 7(3): 51–69.

Purcell, John and Jeffrey Kaufman. 1993. *The Risks of Sovereign Lending: Lessons from History*. New York: Salmon Brothers.

Pyle, Kenneth B. 2007. *Japan Rising: The Resurgence of Japanese Power and Purpose*. New York: Public Affairs.

Qing, D. 1998. *The River Dragon Has Come!: The Three Gorges Dam and the Fate of China's Yangtze River and Its People*. New York: M.E. Sharp.

Rahman, F. 1979. *Islam*. Chicago: University of Chicago Press.

Rajan, R.G. 2010. *Fault Lines: How Hidden Fractures Still Threaten the World Economy.* Princeton, NJ: Princeton University Press.

Rajan, R.G. and L. Zingales. 2004. *Saving Capitalism from the Capitalists: Unleashing the Power of Financial Markets to Create Wealth and Spread Opportunity*. New York: Crown Business.

Ramo, J.C. 2004. *The Beijing Consensus*. London: Foreign Policy Center.

Rashid, Ahmed. 2012. *Pakistan on the Brink: The Future of America, Pakistan, and Afghanistan*. New York: Viking.

Reinhart, C.M. 2012. 'A Series of Unfortunate Events: Common Sequencing Patterns in Financial Crises', NBER Working Paper, No. 17941, National Bureau of Economic Research, Cambridge, MA.

Reinhart, C.M. and K.S. Rogoff. 2008. 'This Time Is Different: A Panoramic View of Eight Centuries of Financial Crises', NBER Working Paper, No. 13882, National Bureau of Economic Research, Cambridge, MA.

Reinhart, C.M. and K.S. Rogoff. 2009. *This Time Is Different: Eight Centuries of Financial Folly.* Princeton, NJ: Princeton University Press.

Reinhart, C.M., K.S. Rogoff, and M. Savastano. 2003. 'Debt Intolerance', NBER Working Paper, No. 9908, National Bureau of Economic Research, Cambridge, MA.

Rickards, J. 2016. 'R.I.P. the Petrodollar: March 1975—Sept. 4, 2016', *Jim Rickards' Strategic Intelligence.* Available at https://agorafinancial.com/2016/07/25/r-i-p-petrodollar-march-1975-sept-4-2016/ (last accessed 23 February 2018).

Ridley, Matt. 2011. 'The Shale Gas Shock', GWPF Report 2. London: Global Warming Policy Foundation.

Riedel, Bruce. 2015. *JFK's Forgotten Crisis: Tibet, the CIA, and the Sino-Indian War.* Washington, DC: Brookings Institution.

Roberts, Andrew. 2003. 'The Whale against the Wolf: The Anglo-American War of 1896', in Robert Cowley (ed.), *What Ifs? Of American History: Eminent Historians Imagine What Might Have Been*, pp. 163–78. London: Macmillan.

Roberts, Andrew. 2008. *A History of the English-Speaking Peoples since 1900.* New York: Harper Perennial.

Rodinson, Maxime. 1973. *Muhammad.* London: Pelican Books.

Rosecrance, Richard. 1986. *The Rise of the Trading State: Commerce and Conquest in the Modern World.* New York: Basic Books.

Rosecrance, Richard N. and Steven E. Miller (eds). 2015. *The Next Great War?: The Roots of World War I and the Risks of U.S.–China Conflict.* Cambridge, MA: MIT Press.

Rothman, Andy. 2012. 'Misunderstanding China: Popular Western Illusions Debunked', Special Report, CLSA Asia-Pacific Markets.

Rudd, K. 2015. 'Lessons from Europe 1914 for Asia 2014: Reflections on the Centenary of the Outbreak of World War I', in Richard N. Rosecrance and Steven E. Miller (eds), *The Next Great War?: The Roots of World War I and the Risks of U.S.–China Conflict*, pp. 193–210. Cambridge, MA: MIT Press.

Ruthven, M. 2002. *A Fury for God: The Islamist Attack on America.* London: Granta Books.

Ryckman, Pierre. 1978. *Chinese Shadows.* London: Penguin Books.

Saavala, Minna. 2012. *Middle-Class Moralities: Everyday Struggle over Belonging and Prestige in India.* New Delhi: Orient Blackswan.

Salvaterra, Neanda. 2016. 'Oil at $50 tests Shale-Band Theory', *Wall Street Journal*, 213, August. Available at https://www.wsj.com/articles/oil-at-50-tests-shale-band-theory-1471951749 (last accessed 23 February 2018).

Samanta, P.D. 2014. 'One China? What about One India Policy: Sushma Swaraj to Wang Yi', *Indian Express.* Available at http://indianexpress.com/article/india/india-others/one-china-what-about-one-india-policy-sushma-to-wang/ (last accessed 20 November 2017).

Sanderson, H. and M. Forsythe. 2013. *China's Superbank: Debt Oil and Influence—How China Development Bank Is Rewriting the Rules of Finance.* Singapore: John Wiley & Sons.

Saran, Shyam. 2014a. '1962—The View from Beijing'. *Business Standard.* Available at http://www.business-standard.com/article/opinion/shyam-saran-1962-the-view-from-beijing-114040701205_1.html (last accessed 20 November 2017).

Saran, Shyam. 2014b. 'India–China Border Dispute—Coping with Asymmetry', *Business Standard.* Available at http://www.business-standard.com/article/opinion/shyam-saran-india-china-border-dispute-coping-with-asymmetry-114041300669_1.html (last accessed 20 November 2017).

Saran, Shyam. 2015. 'Put Neighbourhood Policy Back on Track', *Business Standard.* Available at http://www.business-standard.com/article/opinion/shyam-saran-put-neighbourhood-policy-back-on-track-115111001450_1.html (last accessed 20 November 2017).

Schmookler, J. 1966. *Invention and Economic Growth.* Cambridge, MA: Harvard University Press.

Schoen, Douglas E. and Melik Kaylan. 2014. *The Russia-China Axis: The New Cold War and America's Crisis of Leadership.* New York: Encounter Books.

Schumpeter, J.A. 1955. *Imperialism and Social Classes: Two Essays by Joseph Schumpeter.* Auburn: Ludwig von Mises Institute.

Schwartz, Stephen. 2002. *The Two Faces of Islam: The House of Sa'ud from Tradition to Terror.* New York: Doubleday.

Scott, M.F. 1989. *A New View of Economic Growth.* Oxford: Clarendon Press.

Shambaugh, David. 2008. *China's Communist Party: Atrophy and Adaptation.* Oakland, CA: University of California Press.

Shambaugh, David. 2015. 'The Coming Chinese Crackup', *Wall Street Journal.* Available at https://www.wsj.com/articles/the-coming-chinese-crack-up-1425659198 (last accessed 19 November 2017).

Shambaugh, David. 2016. *China's Future.* Cambridge: Polity Press.

Sharma, Shankar. 2012. Review of Walter and Howie. *Red Capitalism, Business Standard.*

Shaviv, Nir and Jan Vezier. 2003. 'Clestial Driver of Phanerozic Climate?', *Geological Society of America Today*, 13(7): 4–10.

Sheen, Seongho. 2013. 'Northeast Asia's Aging Population and Regional Security: "Demographic Peace?"' *Asian Survey* 53(2): 292–318.

Shourie, A. 2006. *Falling over Backwards: An Essay on Reservations and Judicial Populism.* New Delhi: ASA Publications.

Simms, Brendan. 2013. *Europe: The Struggle for Supremacy 1453 to the Present.* London: Allen Lane.

Small, Andrew. 2015. *The China–Pakistan Axis: Asia's New Geopolitics.* London: Hurst and Co.

Solow, Barbara l. 1991. 'Slavery and Colonization', in Barbara L. Solow (ed.), *Slavery and the Rise of the Atlantic Economies*, pp. 21–42. Cambridge: Cambridge University Press.

Spykman, Nicholas J. 2007 [1942]. *America's Strategy in World Politics: The United States and the Balance of Power.* New Jersey: Transactions Publishers, New Brunswick.

Srinivas, M.N. 1996. *Village, Caste, Gender and Method: Essays in Indian Social Anthropology.* New Delhi: Oxford University Press.

Stein, Arthur A. 2015. 'Respites or Resolutions? Recurring Crises and the Origins of War', in Richard N. Rosecrance and Steven E. Miller (eds), *The Next Great War?: The Roots of World War I and the Risks of U.S.–China Conflict*, pp. 13–24. Cambridge, MA: MIT Press.

Stratfor. 2010. 'The Geopolitics of Turkey: Searching for More', *Stratfor Worldview.* Available at https://worldview.stratfor.com/article/geopolitics-turkey-searching-more, accessed on 2 October 2017.

Stratfor. 2011a. 'The Geopolitics of Israel: Biblical and Modern' *Stratfor Worldview.* Available at https://worldview.stratfor.com/article/geopolitics-israel-biblical-and-modern (last accessed 23 February 2018).

Stratfor. 2011b. 'The Geopolitics of the Palestinians', *Stratfor Worldview.* Available at https://worldview.stratfor.com/article/geopolitics-palestinians-0 (last accessed 2 October 2017).

Stratfor. 2012a. 'The Driving Forces behind Japan's Remilitarization', *Stratfor Worldview.* Available at https://worldview.stratfor.com/article/driving-forces-behind-japans-remilitarization (last accessed 2 October 2017).

Stratfor. 2012b. 'The Geopolitics of China: A Great Power Enclosed'. *Stratfor Worldview.* Available at https://worldview.stratfor.com/article/geopolitics-china-great-power-enclosed (last accessed 19 November 2017).

Stratfor. 2012c. 'The Geopolitics of Japan: An Island Power Adrift', *Stratfor Worldview.* Available at https://worldview.stratfor.com/article/geopolitics-japan-island-power-adrift (last accessed on 2 October 2017).

Stratfor. 2015a. 'China Flaunts Its Missile Arsenal'. *Stratfor Worldview.* Available at https://worldview.stratfor.com/article/china-flaunts-its-missile-arsenal (last accessed 19 November 2017).

Stratfor. 2015b. 'In the Pacific, New Military Agreements for a New Alliance Structure'. *Stratfor Worldview.* Available at https://www.stratfor.com/geopolitical-diary/pacific-new-military-agreements-new-alliance-structure (last accessed 19 November 2017).

Stratfor. 2015c. 'Tibet: An Ancient Threat to Modern China'. *Stratfor Worldview.* Available at https://worldview.stratfor.com/article/tibet-ancient-threat-modern-china (last accessed 19 November 2017).

Suter, Christian. 1992. *Debt Cycles in the World Economy: Foreign Loans, Financial Crises and Debt Settlements, 1820–1990.* Boulder, CO: Westview.

Svensmark, H. 2007. 'Cosmoclimatology', *Astronomy and Geography,* 48(1): 1.18–1.24.

Svensmark, H. and N. Calder. 2007. *The Chilling Stars: A New Theory of Climate Change.* London: Icon Books.

Swami, Praveen. 2015. 'Pakistan's Nuclear Weapons May Not Deter Indian Retaliation, but Destruction Mutual', *Indian Express.* Available at http://indianexpress.com/article/opinion/columns/pakistans-nuclear-weapons-may-not-deter-indian-retaliation-but-destruction-mutual/ (last accessed 20 November 2017).

Talbot, Ian. 2012. *Pakistan: A New History.* London: Hurst and Company.

Tanzi, V. and L. Schuknecht. 2000. *Public Spending in the Twentieth Century.* Cambridge: Cambridge University Press.

Tao, Jingzhou. 2016. 'China Turns Away From the Market', *Financial Times*, 31 August.

Taylor, A.J.P. 2001 [1945]. *The Course of German History.* London: Routledge Classics.

Taylor, C. 1974. 'Socialism and Weltanschung', in L. Kolakowski and S. Hampshire (eds), *The Socialist Idea: A Reappraisal.* London: Weidenfeld and Nicholson.

Taylor, J.B. (ed.) 1999. *Monetary Policy Rules.* Chicago: Chicago University Press.

Taylor, J.B. 2007. 'Housing and Monetary Policy', NBER Working Paper No. 13682, National Bureau of Economic Research, Cambridge, MA.

Taylor, J.B. 2009. *Getting Off Track: How Government Actions and Interventions Caused, Prolonged, and Worsened the Financial Crisis.* Stanford, CA: Hoover Institution Press.

Taylor, J.B. 2015. 'Taylor on Bernanke: Monetary Rules Work Better Than "Constrained Discretion"', *Wall Street Journal*, 2 May.

Tellis, Ashley. 2005. *India as a New Global Power: An Action Agenda for the United States.* Washington, DC: Carnegie Endowment for International Peace.

Tett, Gillian. 2009. *Fools Gold.* London: Little Brown.

The Economist. 2014. 'Taming the West', *The Economist*, 21 June.

The Economist. 2015. 'Who's Afraid of America?', *The Economist*, 13 June.

The Economist. 2016. 'Playing It Long'. *The Economist.* Available at https://www.economist.com/news/books-and-arts/21702733-new-book-argues-barack-obamas-grand-strategy-has-made-america-stronger-both-home (last accessed 17 November 2017).

The Economist. 2017. 'All the Crown Prince's Men: Saudi Arabia's Unprecedented Shake-Up', *The Economist*, 5 November.

The Economist. 2017. 'Enter Tsar Vladimir', *The Economist*, 26 October.

The Middle East Media Research Institute (MEMRI). 2010. 'Former Chief of Pakistani ISI Lt.-Gen. Hamid Gul: I Am an Ideologue of Jihad; as far as al-Qaeda Is Concerned—Come Up With the Evidence for 9/11; You Haven't Even Charged Osama bin Laden; It Is Very Clear That Obama's State of the Union Address Did Not Focus on Terrorism; After Obama's December 1 Speech, It's Clear That the Taliban Are Afghanistan's Future—And the Americans Are Its Past', MEMRI, Special Dispatch No. 2895. Available at https://www.memri.org/reports/former-chief-pakistani-isi-lt-gen-hamid-gul-i-am-ideologue-jihad-far-al-qaeda-concerned-%E2%80%93 (last accessed 17 November 2017).

Thomas, R. 1997. 'The Demand for M4: A Sectoral Analysis. Part 1–The Personal Sector'. Bank of England Working Paper, No. 61.

Thornton, Bruce. 2015. 'Carter and Obama: How To Fail at Foreign Policy', *Frontpage Mag*. Available at http://www.frontpagemag.com/fpm/259361/carter-and-obama-how-fail-foreign-policy-bruce-thornton (last accessed 17 November 2017).

Tilly, Charles. 1990. *Coercion, Capital and European States AD 992–1992*. New York: Wiley-Blackwell.

Tilly, Charles. 1992. *Coercion, Capital and European States, AD 992–1992*, revised edition. New York: Wiley-Blackwell.

Tocqueville, A. De. 1990. *Democracy in America*. New York: Vintage Books.

Tooley, James. 2013. *The Beautiful Tree: A Personal Journey into How the World's Poorest People Are Educating Themselves*. Washington, DC: Cato Institute.

Toynbee, A.J. 1995. *A Study of History*, Abridged Edition. New York: Barnes and Noble Books.

Traub, James. 2015. 'When did Obama Give Up?', *Foreign Policy*. Available at http://foreignpolicy.com/2015/02/26/when-did-obama-give-up-speeches/ (last accessed 17 November 2017).

Trenin, D.V. 2007. *Getting Russia Right*. Washington, DC: Carnegie Endowment.

Trenin, Dmitri. 2015. 'Greater Asia: A China-Russia Entente?', *The Globalist*. Available at https://www.theglobalist.com/from-greater-europe-to-greater-asia-toward-a-sino-russian-entente/ (last accessed 19 November 2017).

Tucker, Robert. 1975. 'Oil: The Issue of an American Intervention', *Commentary*, 1 January. Available at https://www.commentarymagazine.com/articles/oil-the-issue-of-american-intervention (last accessed 30 October 2017).

US Energy Information Administration (EIA). 2011. *World Shale Gas Resources*. Washington, DC: EIA.

US National Intelligence Council (NIC). 2012. *Global Trends 2030: Alternative Worlds.* Washington, DC: US NIC. Available online at https://www.dni.gov/files/documents/GlobalTrends_2030.pdf (last accessed 30 October 2017).

Vaidyanathan, A. 2006. 'Agrarian Crisis: Nature, Causes, and Remedies', *The Hindu*, 8 November.

ValueWalk. 2013. 'China Addicted to Debt, Now at 205% of GDP: CLSA'. *ValueWalk*. Available at http://www.valuewalk.com/2013/05/china-addicted-to-debt/ (last accessed 13 November 2017).

Veizer, Jan. 2005. 'Celestial Climate Driver', *Geoscience Canada*, 32(1): 13–30.

Veliz, Claudio. 1994. *The New World of the Gothic Fox.* Berkeley: University of California Press.

Vinacke, Harold, 1950. *A History of the Far East in Modern Times.* London: Allen and Unwin.

Viner, Jacob. 1948. 'Power Versus Plenty as Objectives of Foreign Policy in the Seventeenth and Eighteenth Centuries', *World Politics*, 1(1): 1–29.

Wade, Geoff. 2004. 'The Zeng He Voyages: A Reassesment', Asia Research Institute Working Paper, No. 31, Singapore.

Walker, Martin. 2009. 'The Geopolitics of Sexual Frustration', *Foreign Policy*. Available at http://foreignpolicy.com/2009/10/20/the-geo-politics-of-sexual-frustration/ (last accessed 19 November 2017).

Wallerstein, Immanuel. 1980. *The Modern World System*, 3 vols. New York: Academic Press.

Wallison, Peter J. 2010. 'The Dodd-Frank Act: Creative Destruction, Destroyed', *Financial Services Outlook*, American Enterprise Institute. Available online at http://www.aei.org/publication/the-dodd-frank-act-creative-destruction-destroyed/ (last accessed 20 February 2018).

Walter, C.E. and F.J.T. Howie. 2011. *Red Capitalism: The Fragile Financial Foundation of China's Extraordinary Rise.* Singapore: John Wiley & Sons.

Walters, Alan A. 1971. 'Money in Boom and Slump: An Empirical Inquiry into British Experience since the 1880s', Hobart Paper 44, Third Edition. London: Institute of Economic Affairs.

Wansbrough, John. 1978. *The Sectarian Milieu: Content and Composition of Islamic Salvation History.* Oxford: Oxford University Press.

Weil, David N. 2015. 'Capital and Wealth in the Twenty-First Century', *American Economic Review*, 105(5): 34–7.

Wertz, R.R. 2011. 'Special Report: Three Gorges Dam'. Available at http://www.ibiblio.org/chinesehistory/contents/07spe/specrep01.html (last accessed 20 November 2017).

White, Hugh. 2013. *The China Choice: Why We Should Share Power.* Oxford: Oxford University Press, 2013.

Whyte, Martin King. 2013. 'China Needs Justice, Not Equality: How to Calm the Middle Kingdom', *Foreign Affairs*. Available at https://www.foreignaffairs.com/articles/china/2013-05-05/china-needs-justice-not-equality (last accessed 13 November 2017).

Wicksell, K. 1898/1936. *Interest and Prices*. London: Macmillan.

Wikipedia. 2018. 'Gülen Movement'. Available online at https://en.wikipedia.org/wiki/G%C3%BClen_movement (accessed 1 February 2018).

Winship, S. 2013. 'Overstating the Costs of Inequality'. *National Affairs*, 15 (Spring).

Witsoe, J. 2006. *India's Second Green Revolution? The Socio-Political Implications of Corporate-Led Agricultural Growth*. Philadelphia: Centre for Advanced Studies of India, University of Pennsylvania.

Wittes, Tamara Cofman. 2016. 'The Slipperiest Slope of Them All', Markaz blog, 15 March, Brookings Institution. Available at https://www.brookings.edu/blog/markaz/2016/03/15/the-slipperiest-slope-of-them-all/ (last accessed 17 November 2017).

Wolf, M. 2014. 'How the Financial Crisis Changed the World', *Economic Affairs*, 34(3): 286–303.

Wolf, M. 2015. 'China Risks an Economic Discontinuity', *Financial Times,* 2 September.

Wolferen, Karel van. 1989. *The Enigma of Japanese Power.* London: Macmillan, 1989.

Work, Robert O. 2008. *The US Navy: Charting a Course for Tomorrow's Fleet.* Washington, DC: Center for Strategic and Budgetary Assessment.

World Bank. 2012. *China 2030: Building a Modern, Harmonious and Creative High-Income Society.* Washington, DC: The World Bank.

Wu, Harry. 2014. 'China's Growth and Productivity Performance Revisited—Accounting for China's Sources of Growth with a New Data Set', Conference Board, EPWP, No. 14–01. Available at https://www.conference-board.org/pdf_free/workingpapers/EPWP1401.pdf (last accessed 13 November 2017).

Wynia, G. 1990 [1984]. *The Politics of Latin American Development*, Second Edition. Cambridge: Cambridge University Press.

Yakovenko, Alexander. 2015. 'The West Is Mean to Russia, But Let's Be Friends', *The Telegraph*. Available at http://www.telegraph.co.uk/news/worldnews/europe/russia/11690039/The-West-is-mean-to-Russia-but-lets-be-friends.html (last accessed 19 November 2017).

Yellen, Janet. 2014. 'Perspectives on Inequality and Opportunity from the Survey on Consumer Finances', speech delivered at the Conference on Economic Opportunity and Inequality, Federal Reserve Bank of Boston, Boston. Available at https://www.federalreserve.gov/newsevents/speech/yellen20141017a.htm (last accessed 7 November 2017).

Yergin, Daniel. 2011. *The Quest: Energy, Security, and the Remaking of the Modern World*. New York: Allen Lane.

Zakaria, Fareed. 1999. *From Wealth to Power: The Unusual Origins of America's World Role.* Princeton, NJ: Princeton University Press.

Zakaria, Fareed. 2000. *The Post-American World and the Rise of the Rest.* London: Penguin.

Zakaria, Fareed. 2003 [1997]. *The Future of Freedom: Illiberal Democracies at Home and Abroad*, Revised Edition. New York: W.W. Norton.

Zingales, L. 2012. *A Capitalism for the People: Recapturing the Lost Genius of American Prosperity*. New York: Basic Books.

Index

C

D

E

H

I

J

K

L

M

N

O

P

Q

R

S

T

U

V

W

X

Y

Z

About the Author

Deepak Lal is the James S. Coleman Professor Emeritus of International Development Studies at the University of California at Los Angeles, professor emeritus of political economy at University College London, and a senior fellow at the Cato Institute. He was a member of the Indian Foreign Service (1963–6) and has served as a consultant to the Indian Planning Commission, the World Bank, the Organization for Economic Cooperation and Development, various UN agencies, South Korea, and Sri Lanka.

From 1984 to 1987, he was research administrator at the World Bank. He is the author of a number of books, including *The Poverty of Development Economics*; *The Hindu Equilibrium*; *Against Dirigisme*; *The Political Economy of Poverty, Equity and Growth*; *Unintended Consequences: The Impact of Factor Endowments, Culture, and Politics on Long-Run Economic Performance*; and *Reviving the Invisible Hand: The Case for Classical Liberalism in the 21st Century*.